SIXTEENTH EDITION

# DATABASE PROCESSING
## FUNDAMENTALS, DESIGN, AND IMPLEMENTATION

David M. Kroenke

David J. Auer
Western Washington University

Scott L. Vandenberg
Siena College

Content Management: Stephanie Kiel
Content Production: Rudrani Mukherjee
Product Management: Marcus Scherer
Product Marketing: Wayne Stevens
Rights and Permissions: Jenell Forschler
Please contact https://support.pearson.com/getsupport/s/ with any queries on this content

Cover Image: *tide pool* by Donna Auer

---

**Library of Congress Cataloging-in-Publication Data**
Names: Kroenke, David M., 1946- author. | Auer, David J, author. | Vandenberg, Scott L, author.
Title: Database processing : fundamentals, design, and implementation / David M Kroenke, David J Auer, Western Washington University, Scott L Vandenberg, Siena College.
Description: Sixteenth edition. | Hoboken, NJ : Pearson Education, [2022] | Includes bibliographical references and index. | Summary: "The 16th edition of Database Processing: Fundamentals, Design, and Implementation refines the organization and content of this classic textbook to reflect a new teaching and professional workplace environment. Students and other readers of this book will benefit from new content and features in this edition"-- Provided by publisher.
Identifiers: LCCN 2020042625 | ISBN 9780136930174
Subjects: LCSH: Database management.
Classification: LCC QA76.9.D3 K7365 2021 | DDC 005.74--dc23
LC record available at https://lccn.loc.gov/2020042625

1 2020

ISBN 10:    0-13-693017-4
ISBN 13: 978-0-13-693017-4

# Contents

ntents

## PART 2 ■ Database Design                          151

### Chapter 3: The Relational Model and Normalization   152

### Chapter 4: Database Design Using Normalization   197

### Chapter 5: Data Modeling with the Entity-Relationship Model   218

**Appendices**

# Foreword to the 40th Anniversary Edition

**Authors' Note:** The "Foreword to the 40th Anniversary Edition" was originally written for inclusion in the 15th edition of *Database Processing*. We believe the topics covered here (including the history of the development of database systems, the story of the book itself, and the "lessons learned" during those processes) are important enough that we have retained it in this subsequent edition of the book.

## David Kroenke

The publisher has asked me to write a short history of this text for this, the 40th anniversary edition. The details of each edition and how they changed are instructive, but this text and the discipline of database processing grew up together, and the story of how that happened might be more helpful to students who will work in disciplines, such as Big Data, that are emerging today.

## We Didn't Know What We Were Doing

Database processing technology originated in the period 1970 to 1975, though not necessarily by that name. At the time, the U.S. government used the term *data bank*. Others used *data base* as well as *database*. I liked the latter and used it when I began work on this text in 1975.

In 1971, I was an officer in the U.S. Air Force, assigned to a Pentagon team that was building and using a simulation of World War III. It was the height of the Cold War, and the Department of Defense wanted a means to assess the efficacy of current and proposed weapons systems.

By a stroke of good luck, I was assigned to work on the data manager portion of that simulation. (The term *Database Management System [DBMS]* was not yet in use.) The logical data model of that data manager was similar to that of the set-based system that Bachmann had developed at General Electric (then a mainframe manufacturer) and that later became the CODASYL DBTG standard.[1]

Our simulation was slow and long-running; a typical run would take 10 to 12 hours. We were constrained more by input and output of data than by CPU time, and I developed low-level, re-entrant, assembly language routines for getting and putting data to and from main memory on parallel channels.

In addition to our project and Bachmann's, IBM was developing a manufacturing-oriented data manager in concert with North American Aviation. That project eventually became IBM's product IMS.[2] Another government project of that era resulted in the data manager named Total.

---

[1] CODASYL, the Committee on Data Systems Languages, was the committee, chaired by Grace Hopper (see *https://en.wikipedia.org/wiki/Grace_Hopper*), that developed the COBOL language standard. DBTG, the database task group, was a subcommittee tasked with developing a data modeling standard. The DBTG model was popular for a short while but was replaced by the relational model by the 1980s.

[2] IBM IMS is still a functional DBMS product—see *www.ibm.com/it-infrastructure/z/ims*.

In retrospect, I'd say the one thing we had in common was that none of us knew what we were doing. We didn't have any data models, best practices, or design principles. We didn't even know how to program. This was long before GoTo-less programming, which led to structured programming and eventually to object-oriented programming. We did know that life was easier if we developed some sort of a logic chart before we began, but that was about it. We'd pick up our coding pads (everything was done via punched cards) and start to work.

There were no debugging tools. When a job would fail, we'd receive a hexadecimal printout of the CPU registers and the contents of main memory. (The printout would be 12 to 18 inches thick.) There were no hexadecimal calculators, so we'd manually add and subtract hexadecimal numbers to navigate our way around the printout, sticking rulers in the listing as place markers. Stiff, wooden rulers were the best.

Again, though, we were just trying to solve a problem. We didn't have any idea that the technology we were developing would become an important part of the emerging world. Imagine Amazon or your college without database processing. But all of that was in the future. We were just trying to get the "darn thing" to run and somehow solve the particular problem that we'd been assigned.

For example, an important function of those early systems was to manage relationships. In our simulation, we had bombers and tankers and opposing radar sites and opposing air-to-air missiles. We needed to keep track of which of those was assigned or related to which. We just wrote programs to do that. A decade or two later someone discovered in surprise, "Hey, there's as much information in the relationships as there is in the data."

We made stuff up as we went along. The first edition of this text included no definition of *database*. When a reviewer pointed that out, I made one up for the second edition. "A self-describing collection of integrated records." Completely fabricated, but it's worked now for 35 years, so it must have been serviceable.

Situations like that were common in those early projects. We made stuff up that would help us solve our problem. Progress was slow, mistakes were frequent, failures were common. Millions of dollars and labor hours were wasted. But gradually, over time, database technology emerged.

## Origin of This Text

In 1973 I completed my military commitment and following John Denver's song "Rocky Mountain High" moved my family from Washington, D.C., to Colorado State University. The business school hired me as an instructor while I attended graduate school in statistics and engineering across the street. To my delight, I was assigned to teach a course titled File Management, the predecessor of today's Database Processing course (see Figure FM-1).

As does any young instructor, I wanted to teach what I knew, and that was the rudiments of database processing. So, I began to formulate a database course, and by the spring of 1975, I was looking for a textbook. I asked the book reps if they had such a book, and none did. The sales rep for SRA, however, asked, "No, but we're looking for one. Why don't you write it?" My department chair, Bob Rademacher, encouraged me to do so, and on June 29, 1975, I signed the contract.

The draft and all the diagrams were written in number 2 pencil on the back of old coding sheets, as shown in Figure FM-2. The text would go to a typist, who'd do the best she could to decipher my writing. I'd proof the typing, and she'd produce another typed manuscript (long before word processing—pages had to be retyped to remove errors). Those pages would then go to a copy editor, and I would redo them again and send them back to the typist for a round or two. Eventually, the final typed manuscript would go to a compositor, who would produce long gray sheets (called galleys) of text to be proofed. After that, the text would be glued (I'm not kidding) to makeup pages, integrating the art that had been following a similar pathway, and then those pages would be photographed and sent to a printer.

The final draft of the first edition was completed in January 1976, and the text was published in January 1977. We were proud that it only took a year.

**FIGURE FM-1**

David Kroenke Loses
Control of Students Excited
by Database Technology

**FIGURE FM-2**

How Textbooks Were Written

## Contents of the First Edition

*Database Processing* was the first such textbook aimed at the information systems market. C. J. Date had produced *Database Systems* prior to this text, but his book was aimed at computer science students.[3] No one knew what should be in an information systems database book. I made it up, we sent drafts to reviewers, and they approved it. (They didn't know either.)

The first edition (see Figure FM-3) had chapters on file management and data structures. It also had chapters on hierarchical, network, and relational data models. By the way, E. F. Codd, the creator of the relational data model, was relatively unknown at that point, and he was happy to review the relational chapter. The text also featured a description of the features and functions of five DBMS products: ADABAS, System 2000, Total, IDMS, and IMS. (To my knowledge, only IMS is still in use today.) It wrapped up with a chapter on database administration.

When writing that last chapter, I thought it would be a good idea to talk with an auditor to learn what auditors looked for when auditing database systems. Accordingly, I drove to Denver and met with one of the top auditors at one of the then-Big-Eight firms. I didn't learn much, just some high-level hyperbole about using commonly accepted auditing standards. The next day, the phone rang in my office and an executive in New York City invited me out

**FIGURE FM-3**

Cover of the First Edition of
Database Processing

---

[3]C. J. Date's book *An Introduction to Database Systems* is currently in its eighth edition.

**FIGURE FM-4**

Hot Marketing Handout
1977—Note Text Price

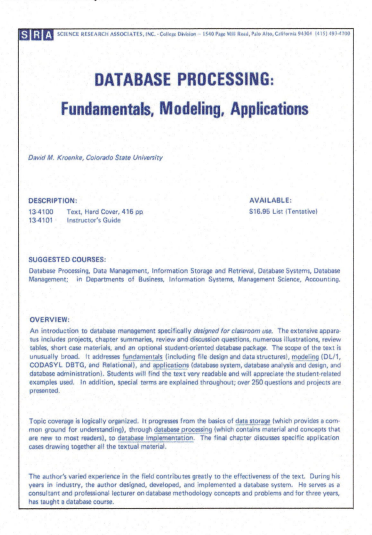

to that firm for a job interview for a position to develop and teach database auditing standards to their staff. None of us knew what we were doing!

I had no idea of how incredibly fortunate I was to stumble into a discipline that would become one of the most important in the information systems field, to have experience and knowledge to put into a text, to have a supportive department, and, finally, to have what was at that time a superb publisher with an outstanding sales and marketing team (see Figure FM-4). Because it was all I had known, I thought it was normal. Ah, youth.

## Lessons Learned

At age 71, I'm not quite consigned to watching the daytime weather channel but have reached the stage when people start listing lessons learned. I'll try to keep it brief. Here are my five lessons learned, developed as both a database technology bystander and participant.

### Don't Confuse Luck with Exceptional Ability

According to an independent study at the time, the second edition of this text had 91 percent of the market. It was the first, and it had a great publisher with a superb sales force. That success was due, truly, to lucky timing and good fortune. At that point I should have doubled down and made sure that the 91 percent were satisfied while sending Thanksgiving turkeys to the 9 percent not in the fold.

Instead, what did I do? Ignored the book and joined Microrim to help develop the R:Base products.[4] Five years later when I returned to the book, numerous competitors had emerged, and the book had lost half of its market. I'd thought I could jump back in and regain that early success, but the market had a hard lesson for me.

I mention this because I've seen it elsewhere as well. Microsoft was built and managed by superior business professionals like Bill Gates, Steve Ballmer, Jon Shirley, Steve Okey, and, in the database domain, David Kaplan. Between 1985 and 2000, hundreds of employees joined the firm and were issued stock options. They were largely competent professionals, but no different from the same level of professionals one would have found at 3M, Procter and Gamble, Boeing, and so on. The difference was that during that interval, their Microsoft stock split seven times.

Many of those competent professionals understood that they had been very, very lucky to get on the Microsoft bus when they did. They took their stock proceeds and reinvested in index funds or something else safe and have been enjoying life on the golf course with their families ever since. However, some of the just-competent professionals confused their good luck with exceptional personal ability and founded their own companies or started venture capital firms. Most lost their money. They were good, but they weren't of the same caliber as Gates et al.

Joseph Conrad said it: "It is the mark of an inexperienced man not to believe in luck."

## Marketing Trumps Technology

If you have a chance to invest in an average technology with superb marketing or superb technology with average marketing, take the former. Marketing is far more important than technology.

IBM's IMS uses a hierarchical data model. Representing many-to-many relationships with hierarchies is a pain. With IMS the database developer is forced to write all sorts of design and coding machinations that should have been done by the DBMS or avoided by using a different DBMS. In the early days, I watched an IBM technical sales representative present those machinations as a skill that every good database developer must already have. "Surely you know how to do the XYZ?" (I don't remember the name they'd given that dance). Because none of us in the audience knew any better, we all assumed that we were deficient if we didn't know how to do the XYZ. The deficiency was in the product, not us, but we were duped by good marketing.

Developed by Wayne Ratcliff, Ashton-Tate's dBase[5] was the most successful relational microcomputer DBMS product until Microsoft entered the picture with Microsoft Access. In fact, dBase was neither a DBMS nor relational—it was a file management system. However, Ashton-Tate's marketing convinced Osborne to place a free copy of dBase on every one of its Osborne II computers. The Osborne II was the micro or personal computer (PC) of choice for a new cadre of application developers, and they wrote millions of lines of dBase code. They used what they had and thought it was fine. When better products came along, there was no way that any small developer was going to rewrite existing code or learn new products. The new graphical user interface in Microsoft Windows, the Microsoft Office package, and cheap Microsoft Access pricing was the only force strong enough to push Ashton-Tate off its leading position.

Salsa, a product that I helped Wall Data develop, implemented the semantic object model[6] and was selected as the runner-up to Netscape Navigator for product of the year in 1996. (The other runner-up was Internet Explorer.) Salsa failed—not because of the technology but because of the marketing. We tried to sell it as an end-user product, and it was a developer product. It was as if we'd invented Gore-Tex and we were out trying to sell it to people standing in the rain. We should have sold it to the clothing manufacturers. Marketing 101. I still have nightmares about the superior technology that washed down that drain.

---

[4]For more information on R:Base, see the Wikipedia article R:Base at *https://en.wikipedia.org/wiki/R:Base* (accessed October 2020). Now called RBASE, this is still a functional DBMS product—see *www.rbase.com* (accessed October 2020).

[5]dBase is still a functional DBMS product—see *www.dbase.com* (accessed October 2020).

[6]The **semantic object model** is a data modeling methodology created by David M. Kroenke that is similar to the E-R model discussed in Chapters 5 and 6. We have included it in Database Processing through the fifteenth edition, but have dropped a discussion of it from this edition because it is not widely used.

## Christensen's Model Informs

I don't know anyone who made substantial money in mainframes that did well in the micro-computer industry. Accustomed to the features and power of mainframes, we viewed micro-computers as toys. We termed the TRS-80 micro the Trash-80. I bought an early Apple, and it crashed on me, and I thought to myself, "This will never amount to anything."

This phenomenon is addressed by Clayton Christensen is his disruptive innovation model.[7] His thesis is that when a disruptive technology comes along, companies that have success in the disrupted technology are unable to capitalize on the opportunities of the new technology. Kodak could not adapt to digital photography; Swiss watch makers could not adapt to digital watches. Textbook publishers could not adapt to book rentals and used books sales by Amazon. Microsoft lost its way when it achieved its goal of "A computer on every desk and in every home." It struggled to adapt to the Internet.

Don't look for the market leaders in Big Data or robotics to come from existing, large vendors. They will come from smaller companies that can position themselves to thrive in the new environment. If you haven't learned Christensen's model, you should.

## Good-Enough Fashion Will Do

For the most part, the relational model supplanted all the other data models. Because of Codd's insights on the use of functional dependencies for relational design, it provided sound design principles. Also, fixed-length records (as, in practice, they were at first) fit nicely with existing file management capabilities. It worked. Thousands of papers were written on the topic.

However, today's technology readily supports the storage and searching of multiple fields in un-normalized documents. In 1980, technology constraints required designers to take a document like a sales order and break it up into its pieces: Invoice, Salesperson, Customer, Line-item, Product. They would then store those pieces and then put them all back together with Structured Query Language (SQL) when someone wanted the original sales order. That makes no sense today. It's like driving your car into a parking garage and having staff pull off your front tires and put them in the pile of front tires, your steering wheel into a pile of steering wheels, and so on, and then, when you come back, put it all back together. Even though it's unnecessary, it's happening right now in zillions of data centers.

So why is the relational model still in use? Because it's good enough and still in fashion.

Fashion is important. Consider normalization theory. Codd's first paper addressed normalization through third normal form. However, in later papers, he and others showed that this wasn't enough. Relations in third normal form still had anomalies, which led to fourth and fifth and then Boyce-Codd (BCNF) Normal Forms. Despite this, one still hears people talk about third normal form as the be-all, end-all of relational design. Third normal form is good enough and still in fashion. It was as if progress stopped at third normal form (not in this text, though, where all of these forms are taught).

I suspect that someday soon, the whole relational mess will no longer be good enough and we'll move to XML or JSON or some other form of document storage (as we discuss in Chapter 13 and Appendix H). I've been saying that for 10 years, though, and it hasn't happened yet.

Another example of good enough and fashion is the entity-relationship (E-R) model. The E-R model is nothing more than a thin cover over the relational model. Entities are essentially logical relations, and relationships are a slim version of foreign keys. E-R operates at too low a level of abstraction. Other models like the semantic object model and other object-oriented models are better. None succeeded. The E-R model was in fashion and good enough.

---

[7] Christensen, Clayton M. *The Innovator's Dilemma: When New Technologies Cause Great Firms to Fail* (Reprint edition) (Brighton, MA: Harvard Business Review Press, 2016).

## When It's Over, It's Over

By the turn of the century, I'd been writing and revising this text for 25 years. Although I was exceedingly grateful to the thousands of professors and students who had used this book over those years, I also knew I was done. Partly, I said to myself, because it had settled down, the early crazy days were long gone, and partly because 25 years is a long time to work on a textbook.

To my great good fortune, I found David Auer, who agreed to take over the revisions of this text. I am most grateful to David for his hard work and for his fidelity to the underlying goals and philosophy of this text. The rest of this story is his.

## David Auer

I was introduced to David Kroenke while working on the Instructor's Manual for the ninth edition of *Database Processing*. Because we were both living and teaching in western Washington State, we could get together for meals and discussions. This led to my working on the companion textbook, *Database Concepts*, being a technical reader for the 10th edition of *Database Processing*, and then being asked to become a coauthor for the 11th edition of *Database Processing*.

I am very fortunate to be able to work with David on these projects. If you have read his portion of this foreword, you will have gotten a brief glimpse into the mind of a very creative and articulate person. He was also in the right place at the right time to be part of the creation of the computer-driven world that we live in and work in today. He has made many important contributions over his career, and the book you are reading is certainly one of them—the first textbook on database systems for management information systems classes and still one of the leading textbooks in the field!

David constantly revised and expanded *Database Processing* as new topics became relevant. My main contributions to the 11th and following editions were making MySQL a DBMS discussed on the same level as Microsoft SQL Server and Oracle Database; formalizing the treatment of Web database applications; and introducing new current topics such as non-relational databases, Big Data, and cloud computing. I have also revised and updated our treatment of Structured Query Language while maintaining the practical and "immediately usable on your own computer" presentation that has always been a hallmark of this book.

The main challenge now is to keep the book current with the changing technology and techniques in our app-driven, Internet, and cloud computing world of today, where databases are used ubiquitously to support applications such as Facebook, Twitter, and Instagram. To this end, we have brought two new coauthors on board for this edition: Scott Vandenberg and Robert Yoder, who are researching and teaching these topics.

Although this 15th edition of *Database Processing* marks the 40th anniversary of the book, we look forward to providing you with many more years of current, accurate, and usable knowledge about the world of databases and how they are used.

# Preface

The 16th edition of *Database Processing: Fundamentals, Design, and Implementation* refines the organization and content of this classic textbook to reflect a new teaching and professional workplace environment. Students and other readers of this book will benefit from new content and features in this edition.

## New to This Edition

Content and features new to the 16th edition of *Database Processing: Fundamentals, Design, and Implementation* include the following:

- The book has been reorganized to reintegrate material previously pushed into the appendices. Chapter 12 has been split into two chapters. Chapter 12 now covers only data warehouse and business intelligence systems and integrates material previously covered in Appendix J ("Business Intelligence Systems"). This brings important topics such as data mining into the main text, and expands the coverage of reporting systems (including RFM reporting), and includes specific, extended examples of Market Basket Analysis and Decision Trees. Chapter 13 covers Big Data, NoSQL (non-relational DBMSs), and cloud computing, which integrates material previously found in Appendix K ("Big Data"). This includes coverage of the CAP theorem, more detailed and specific examples of data using all four varieties of NoSQL DBMS (key-value, graph, document, and column), and an extensive hands-on introduction to creating both relational and document data using the Microsoft Azure cloud platform. In addition, a new online Chapter 10D is dedicated to the non-relational ArangoDB DBMS, which was previously covered in Appendix L ("JSON and Document Databases"). By creating Chapter 10D, we are acknowledging the importance of non-relational DBMSs in today's mobile and app-driven world and getting them the prominence they deserve. This new chapter, in addition to introducing ArangoDB, can stand alone as an introduction to document database concepts, design, and querying: it goes beyond just describing a DBMS and necessarily includes introductory content similar to the relational content in the rest of book so that the specifics of ArangoDB can be put into context.
- Chapter 9 now includes a brief section on physical database design (expanded on in Appendix F) as well as specific examples of GRANT and REVOKE commands.
- The book has been updated to reflect the use of Microsoft SQL Server 2019, the current version of Microsoft SQL Server. Microsoft has made SQL Server Developer Edition (a one-user version of SQL Server Enterprise Edition) available for download at no cost, and therefore we use this Developer Edition instead of the Express Edition as the basis for our work with SQL Server in the book. Although most of the topics covered are backward compatible with Microsoft SQL Server 2016 and earlier versions, all material in the book now uses SQL Server 2019 in conjunction with Microsoft Office 2019 exclusively.
- Oracle's Oracle Database is now updated to use Oracle Database 18c Express Edition (Oracle Database XE) as the preferred Oracle Database product for use on personal computers (whether in the classroom or at home) and as our standard version of Oracle Database in this book. All important Oracle Database techniques can

now be covered using Oracle Database XE with the Oracle SQL Developer GUI, and Oracle recommends Oracle Database XE for instructional purposes. Specific examples of Oracle Database backup and recovery have been added. All of our discussion and examples will also apply to the current version of Oracle Database Enterprise Edition, Oracle Database 19c, if your class is using it.

- Online Chapter 10C, "Managing Databases with MySQL," has been streamlined and updated to MySQL 8.0.
- Microsoft Windows 10 is the sole operating system generally discussed and illustrated in the text. We are not using Microsoft Windows Server 2019 for any of our systems, which means that everything in the book is compatible with and can be replicated on computers running the Microsoft Windows 10 OS.
- We have updated online Appendix G, "Getting Started with Web Servers, PHP, and the NetBeans IDE" to cover current versions of the software. We are now using the NetBeans IDE instead of the Eclipse PDT IDE. This provides a better development environment with a much simpler set of product installations because the Java JDK and NetBeans are installed in one combined installation. This new material provides a simplified (but still detailed) introduction to the installation and use of the Microsoft IIS Web server, PHP, the Java JDK, and the NetBeans in Appendix G. All of these tools are then used for Web database-application development as discussed in Chapter 11.

> **BY THE WAY**  With the 16th edition of Database Processing, we say a fond farewell to our coverage of the semantic object model (SOM). David Kroenke is the creator of the semantic object model, and we have included a discussion of it since he created it. Unfortunately, as David himself writes in the "Foreword to the 40th Anniversary Edition," "marketing trumps technology," and the SOM never caught on in the industry. The extended E-R model became and remains the standard database modeling methodology. Farewell, old friend!

## Fundamentals, Design, and Implementation

With today's technology, it is impossible to utilize a DBMS successfully without first learning fundamental concepts. After years of developing databases with business users, we have developed what we believe to be a set of essential database concepts. These are augmented by the concepts necessitated by the increasing use of the Internet, the World Wide Web, and commonly available analysis tools. Thus, the organization and topic selection of the 16th edition are designed to:

- Present an early introduction to SQL queries.
- Use a "spiral approach" to database design.
- Use a consistent, generic Information Engineering (IE) Crow's Foot E-R diagram notation for data modeling and database design.
- Provide a detailed discussion of specific normal forms within a discussion of normalization that focuses on pragmatic normalization techniques.
- Use current DBMS technology: Microsoft Access 2019, Microsoft SQL Server 2019, Oracle Database Express Edition 18c, MySQL 8.0, and ArangoDB 3.7.
- Create Web database applications based on widely used Web development technology.
- Provide an introduction to business intelligence (BI) systems.

- Discuss the dimensional database concepts used in database designs for data warehouses and online analytical processing (OLAP).
- Discuss the emerging and important topics of server virtualization, cloud computing, Big Data, and the NoSQL (Not only SQL) movement.

These changes have been made because it has become obvious that the basic structure of the earlier editions (up to and including the 9th edition–the 10th edition introduced many of the changes we used in the 11th through 15th editions and retain in the 16th edition) was designed for a teaching environment that no longer exists. The structural changes to the book were made for several reasons:

- Unlike the early years of database processing, today's students have ready access to data modeling and DBMS products.
- Today's students are too impatient to start a class with lengthy conceptual discussions on data modeling and database design. They want to do something, see a result, and obtain feedback.
- In the current economy, students need to reassure themselves that they are learning marketable skills.

## Early Introduction of SQL DML

Given these changes in the classroom environment, this book provides an early introduction to SQL data manipulation language (DML) SELECT statements. The discussion of SQL data definition language (DDL) and additional DML statements occurs in Chapters 7 and 8. By encountering SQL SELECT statements in Chapter 2, students learn early in the class how to query data and obtain results, seeing firsthand some of the ways that database technology will be useful to them.

The text assumes that students will work through the SQL statements and examples with a DBMS product. This is practical today because nearly every student has access to Microsoft Access. Therefore, Chapters 1 and 2 and Appendix A ("Getting Started with Microsoft Access 2019") are written to support an early introduction of Microsoft Access 2019 and the use of Microsoft Access 2019 for SQL queries. (Microsoft Access 2019 QBE query techniques are also covered.)

If a non-Microsoft Access-based approach is desired, versions of Microsoft SQL Server 2019, Oracle Database, and MySQL 8.0 are readily available for use. Free versions of the three major enterprise DBMS products covered in this book (SQL Server 2019 Developer Edition; Oracle Database Express Edition 18c [Oracle Database XE], and MySQL 8.0 Community Edition) are available for download. Thus, students can actively use a DBMS product by the end of the first week of class.

> **BY THE WAY** The presentation and discussion of SQL are spread over four chapters so students can learn about this important topic in small bites. SQL SELECT statements are taught in Chapter 2. SQL data definition language (DDL) and SQL data manipulation language (DML) statements are presented in Chapter 7. Correlated subqueries and EXISTS/NOT EXISTS statements are described in Chapter 8, and SQL transaction control language (TCL) and SQL data control language (DCL) are discussed in Chapter 9. Each topic appears in the context of accomplishing practical tasks. Correlated subqueries, for example, are used to verify functional dependency assumptions, a necessary task for database redesign.
>
> This box illustrates another feature used in this book: BY THE WAY boxes are used to separate comments from the text discussion. Sometimes they present ancillary material; other times they reinforce important concepts.

## A Spiral Approach to the Database Design Process

Today, databases arise from three sources: (1) from the need to integrate existing data from spreadsheets, data files, and database extracts; (2) from the need to develop new information systems projects; and (3) from the need to redesign an existing database to adapt to changing requirements. We believe that the fact that these three sources exist presents instructors with a significant pedagogical opportunity. Rather than teach database design just once from data models, why not teach database design three times, once for each of these sources? In practice, this idea has turned out to be even more successful than expected.

### Database Design Iteration 1: Databases from Existing Data

Considering the design of databases from existing data, if someone were to email us a set of tables and say, "Create a database from them," how would we proceed? We would examine the tables in light of normalization criteria and then determine whether the new database was for a production system that allows new data to be inserted for each new transaction or for a business intelligence (BI) data warehouse that allow users to only query data for use in reports and data analysis. Depending on the answer, we would normalize the data, pulling them apart (for the production transaction processing system), or denormalize the data, joining them together (for the BI system data warehouse). All of this is important for students to know and understand.

Therefore, the first iteration of database design gives instructors a rich opportunity to teach normalization not as a set of theoretical concepts but rather as a useful toolkit for making design decisions for databases created from existing data. Additionally, the construction of databases from existing data is an increasingly common task that is often assigned to junior staff members. Learning how to apply normalization to the design of databases from existing data not only provides an interesting way of teaching normalization, it is also common and useful!

We prefer to teach and use a pragmatic approach to normalization and present this approach in Chapter 3. However, we are aware that many instructors like to teach normalization in the context of a step-by-step normal form presentation (1NF, 2NF, 3NF, then BCNF), and Chapter 3 now includes additional material to provide more support for this approach as well.

In today's workplace, large organizations are increasingly licensing standardized software from vendors such as SAP, Oracle, and Siebel. Such software already has a database design component. But with every organization running the same software, many are learning that they can gain a competitive advantage only if they make better use of the data in those predesigned databases. Hence, students who know how to extract data and create read-only databases for reporting and data mining have obtained marketable skills in the world of ERP and other packaged software solutions.

### Database Design Iteration 2: Data Modeling and Database Design

The second source of databases is from new systems development. Although not as common as in the past, many databases are still created from scratch. Thus, students still need to learn data modeling, and they still need to learn how to transform data models into database designs that are then implemented in a DBMS product.

#### *The IE Crow's Foot Model as a Design Standard*

This edition uses a generic, standard IE Crow's Foot notation. Your students should have no trouble understanding the symbols and using the data modeling or database design tool of your choice.

IDEF1X (which was used as the preferred E-R diagram notation in the ninth edition of this text) is explained in Appendix C, "E-R Diagrams and the IDEF1X and UML Standards," in case your students will graduate into an environment where it is used or if you prefer to use it in your classes. UML is also explained in this appendix in case you prefer to use UML in your classes.

> **BY THE WAY** The choice of a data modeling tool is somewhat problematic. Of the two most readily available tools, Microsoft Visio 2019 has been rewritten as a very rudimentary database design tool, whereas Oracle's MySQL Workbench is a database design tool, not a data modeling tool. MySQL Workbench cannot produce an N:M relationship as such (as a data model requires) but has to immediately break it into two 1:N relationships (as database design does). Therefore, the intersection table must be constructed and modeled. This confounds data modeling with database design in just the way that we are attempting to teach students to avoid.
>
> To be fair to Microsoft Visio 2019, it is true that data models with N:M relationships can be drawn using the standard Microsoft Visio 2019 drawing tools. Unfortunately, Microsoft has chosen to remove many of the best database design tools that were in Microsoft Visio 2010, and Microsoft Visio 2019 lacks the tools that made it a favorite of Microsoft Access and Microsoft SQL Server users. For a full discussion of these tools, see Appendix D, "Getting Started with Microsoft Visio 2019," and Appendix E, "Getting Started with the MySQL Workbench Data Modeling Tools."
>
> Good data modeling tools are available, but they tend to be more complex and expensive. Two examples are Visible Systems' Visible Analyst and erwin Inc.'s erwin Data Modeler. Visible Analyst is available in a student edition (at a modest price), and a free trial period is available for erwin Data Modeler. ER-Assistant is a free and simple program that uses the same notation as in this book.

### Database Design from E-R Data Models

As we discuss in Chapter 6, designing a database from data models consists of three tasks: representing entities and attributes with tables and columns; representing maximum cardinality by creating and placing foreign keys; and representing minimum cardinality via constraints, triggers, and application logic.

The first two tasks are straightforward. However, designs for minimum cardinality are more difficult. Required parents are easily enforced using NOT NULL foreign keys and referential integrity constraints. Required children are more problematic. In this book, however, we simplify the discussion of this topic by limiting the use of referential integrity actions and by supplementing those actions with design documentation. See the discussion around Figure 6-29.

Although the design for required children is complicated, it is important for students to learn. It also provides a reason for students to learn about triggers as well. In any case, the discussion of these topics is much simpler than it was in prior editions because of the use of the IE Crow's Foot model and ancillary design documentation.

### Database Implementation from Database Designs

Of course, to complete the process, a database design must be implemented in a DBMS product. This is discussed in Chapter 7, where we introduce SQL DDL for creating tables and SQL DML for populating the tables with data.

### Database Design Iteration 3: Database Redesign

Database redesign, the third iteration of database design, is both common and difficult. As stated in Chapter 8, information systems cause organizational change. New information systems give users new behaviors, and as users behave in new ways, they require changes in their information systems.

Database redesign is, by nature, complex. Depending on your students, you may wish to skip it, and you can do so without loss of continuity. Database redesign is presented after the discussion of SQL DDL and DML in Chapter 7 because it requires the use of advanced SQL. It also provides a practical reason to teach correlated subqueries and EXISTS/NOT EXISTS statements.

## David M. Kroenke

### Work Experience

David M. Kroenke has more than 50 years of experience in the computer industry. He began as a computer programmer for the U.S. Air Force, working both in Los Angeles and at the Pentagon, where he developed one of the world's first DBMS products while part of a team that created a computer simulation of World War III. That simulation served a key role for strategic weapons studies during a 10-year period of the Cold War.

From 1973 to 1978, Kroenke taught in the College of Business at Colorado State University. In 1977 he published the first edition of *Database Processing*, a significant and successful textbook that, more than 40 years later, you now are reading in its 16th edition. In 1978, he left Colorado State and joined Boeing Computer Services, where he managed the team that designed database management components of the IPAD project. After that, he joined with Steve Mitchell to form Mitchell Publishing and worked as an editor and author, developing texts, videos, and other educational products and seminars. Mitchell Publishing was acquired by Random House in 1986. During those years, he also worked as an independent consultant, primarily as a database disaster repairman helping companies recover from failed database projects.

In 1982, Kroenke was one of the founding directors of the Microrim Corporation. From 1984 to 1987, he served as the Vice President of Product Marketing and Development and managed the team that created and marketed the DBMS product RBASE 5000 as well as other related products.

For the next five years, Kroenke worked independently while he developed a new data modeling language called the *semantic object model*. He licensed this technology to the Wall Data Corporation in 1992 and then served as the Chief Technologist for Wall Data's Salsa line of products. He was awarded three software patents on this technology.

After 1998, Kroenke has continued consulting and writing. His current interests concern the practical applications of data mining techniques on large organizational databases. An avid sailor, he wrote *Know Your Boat: The Guide to Everything That Makes Your Boat Work*, which was published by McGraw-Hill in 2002. Now retired, Kroenke recently wrote *An Old Man and a Three Legged Dog*, a story of his travels with his dog Brie, which he published in 2020 and which is available at Amazon.com.

### Consulting

Kroenke has consulted with numerous organizations during his career. In 1978, he worked for Fred Brooks, consulting with IBM on a project that became the DBMS product DB2. In 1989, he consulted for the Microsoft Corporation on a project that became Microsoft Access. In the 1990s, he worked with Computer Sciences Corporation and with General Research Corporation for the development of technology and products that were used to model all of the U.S. Army's logistical data as part of the CALS project. Additionally, he has consulted for Boeing Computer Services, the U.S. Air Force Academy, Logicon Corporation, and other smaller organizations.

## Publications

- *Database Processing*, Pearson Prentice Hall, 16 editions, 1977-present (coauthor with David Auer, 11th, 12th, 13th, and 14th editions; coauthor with David Auer, Scott Vandenberg, and Robert Yoder 15th edition; coauthor with David Auer and Scott Vandenberg 16th edition)
- *Database Concepts*, Pearson Prentice Hall, nine editions, 2004-present (coauthor with David Auer, third, fourth, fifth, sixth, and seventh editions; coauthor with David Auer, Scott Vandenberg, and Robert Yoder eighth and ninth editions)
- *Using MIS*, Pearson Prentice Hall, 11 editions, 2006-present (coauthor with Randall J. Boyle, eighth, ninth, 10th, and 11th edition)
- *Experiencing MIS*, Pearson Prentice Hall, nine editions, 2007-present (coauthor with Randall J. Boyle, sixth, seventh, eighth, and ninth editions)
- *MIS Essentials*, Pearson Prentice Hall, four editions, 2009-present
- *Processes, Systems, and Information: An Introduction to MIS*, Pearson Prentice Hall, two editions, 2013-present (coauthor with Earl McKinney)
- *An Old Man and a Three Legged Dog*, 2020 (Self-published at Amazon.com)
- *Essentials of Processes, Systems, and Information*, Pearson Prentice Hall, 2013 (coauthor with Earl McKinney)
- *Know Your Boat: The Guide to Everything That Makes Your Boat Work*, McGraw-Hill, 2002
- *Management Information Systems*, Mitchell Publishing/Random House, three editions, 1987-1992
- *Business Computer Systems*, Mitchell Publishing/Random House, five editions, 1981-1990
- *Managing Information for Microcomputers*, Microrim Corporation, 1984 (coauthor with Donald Nilson)
- *Database Processing for Microcomputers*, Science Research Associates, 1985 (coauthor with Donald Nilson)
- *Database: A Professional's Primer*, Science Research Associates, 1978

## Teaching

Kroenke taught in the College of Business at Colorado State University from 1973 to 1978. He also has taught part time in the Software Engineering program at Seattle University. From 1990 to 1991, he served as the Hanson Professor of Management Science at the University of Washington. Most recently, he taught at the University of Washington from 2002 to 2008. During his career, he has been a frequent speaker at conferences and seminars for computer educators. In 1991, the International Association of Information Systems named him Computer Educator of the Year.

## Education

B.S., Economics, U.S. Air Force Academy, 1968
M.S., Quantitative Business Analysis, University of Southern California, 1971
Ph.D., Engineering, Colorado State University, 1977

## Personal

Kroenke lives on Whidbey Island in Washington State and has two grown children and three grandchildren. He enjoys skiing, sailing, and building small boats.

# David J. Auer

## Work Experience

David J. Auer has more than 30 years of experience teaching college-level business and information systems courses and for over 20 years has worked professionally in the field of information technology. He served as a commissioned officer in the U.S. Air Force, with assignments to NORAD and the Alaskan Air Command in air defense operations. He later taught both business administration and music classes at Whatcom Community College and business courses for the Chapman College Residence Education Center at Whidbey Island Naval Air Station. He was a founder of the Puget Sound Guitar Workshop (now in its 41st year of operations). He worked as a psychotherapist and organizational development consultant for the Whatcom Counseling and Psychiatric Clinic's Employee Assistance Program and provided training for the Washington State Department of Social and Health Services. He taught for Western Washington University's College of Business and Economics from 1981 to June 2015 and served as the college's Director of Information Systems and Technology Services from 1994 to 2014. Now a Senior Instructor Emeritus at Western Washington University, he continues his writing projects.

## Publications

- *Database Processing*, Pearson Prentice Hall, six editions, 2009-present (coauthor with David Kroenke; 15th edition coauthor with David Kroenke, Scott Vandenberg, and Robert Yoder; 16th edition coauthor with David Kroenke and Scott Vandenberg)
- *Database Concepts*, Pearson Prentice Hall, seven editions, 2007-present (coauthor with David Kroenke; eighth and ninth edition coauthor with David Kroenke, Scott Vandenberg, and Robert Yoder)
- *Network Administrator: NetWare 4.1*, Course Technology, 1997 (coauthor with Ted Simpson and Mark Ciampa)
- *New Perspectives on Corel Quattro Pro 7.0 for Windows 95*, Course Technology, 1997 (coauthor with June Jamrich Parsons, Dan Oja, and John Leschke)
- *New Perspectives on Microsoft Excel 7 for Windows 95–Comprehensive*, Course Technology, 1996 (coauthor with June Jamrich Parsons and Dan Oja)
- *New Perspectives on Microsoft Office Professional for Windows 95–Intermediate*, Course Technology, 1996 (coauthor with June Jamrich Parsons, Dan Oja, Beverly Zimmerman, Scott Zimmerman, and Joseph Adamski)
- *Microsoft Excel 5 for Windows–New Perspectives Comprehensive*, Course Technology, 1995 (coauthor with June Jamrich Parsons and Dan Oja)
- *Introductory Quattro Pro 6.0 for Windows*, Course Technology, 1995 (coauthor with June Jamrich Parsons and Dan Oja)
- *Introductory Quattro Pro 5.0 for Windows*, Course Technology, 1994 (coauthor with June Jamrich Parsons and Dan Oja)
- *The Student's Companion for Use with Practical Business Statistics*, Irwin, two editions 1991 and 1993

## Teaching

Auer taught in the College of Business and Economics at Western Washington University from 1981 to June 2015. From 1975 to 1981, he taught part time for community colleges, and from 1981 to 1984, he taught part time for the Chapman College Residence Education Center System. During his career, he has taught a wide range of courses in Quantitative Methods, Production and Operations Management, Statistics, Finance, and Management Information Systems. In MIS, he has taught Principles of Management Information Systems, Business Database Development, Computer Hardware and Operating Systems, Telecommunications, Network Administration, and Fundamentals of Web Site Development.

## Education

B.A., English Literature, University of Washington, 1969
B.S., Mathematics and Economics, Western Washington University, 1978
M.A., Economics, Western Washington University, 1980
M.S., Counseling Psychology, Western Washington University, 1991

## Personal

Auer is married, recently moved to Whidbey Island, Washington, and has two grown children and four grandchildren. He is active in his community. Previously he has been president of his neighborhood association in Bellingham, Washington, and served on the City of Bellingham Planning and Development Commission. Now the owner of an Australian Shepard, he is on the board of directors of the organization that supports off-leash dog parks on Whidbey Island, and is also Treasurer of his community association. He enjoys music, playing acoustic and electric guitar, five-string banjo, and a bit of mandolin.

# Scott L. Vandenberg

## Work Experience

Scott L. Vandenberg has over 28 years' experience teaching computer science to college students in computer science and business. Before completing his PhD, he worked for brief periods at Standard Oil Research, Procter & Gamble headquarters, and IBM Research. He taught for two years at the University of Massachusetts-Amherst before joining the faculty at Siena College in 1993. His main teaching interests are in the areas of database management systems and introductory computer science, with research, consulting, and publications focused on those areas as well. Some of his earlier scholarly work included development of data models, query languages, and algebras for object-oriented databases and databases involving sequential and tree-structured data. More recent research has involved applying database technology to help solve data science problems in the areas of biology and epidemiology. He has also published several papers relating to introductory computer science curricula and was a co-principal investigator on a multiyear NSF grant to develop methods to broaden participation and increase retention in computer science. Vandenberg has published over 20 papers related to his scholarly activity.

## Publications

- *Database Concepts*, Pearson Prentice Hall, eighth and ninth editions, 2017 and 2019 (coauthor with David Kroenke, David Auer, and Robert Yoder)
- *Database Processing*, Pearson Prentice Hall, 15th edition, 2018 (coauthor with David Kroenke, David Auer, and Robert Yoder)

## Teaching

Vandenberg has been on the computer science faculty at Siena College since 1993, where he regularly teaches three different database courses at several levels to both computer science majors and business majors. Prior to arriving at Siena, he taught undergraduate and graduate courses in database systems at the University of Massachusetts-Amherst. Since arriving at Siena, he also has taught graduate and undergraduate database courses at the University of Washington in Seattle. He has developed five different database courses over this time. His other teaching experience includes introductory computer science, introductory programming, data structures, management information systems, and three years teaching Siena's interdisciplinary freshman writing course.

## Education

B.A., Computer Science and Mathematics, Cornell University, 1986
M.S., Computer Science, University of Wisconsin-Madison, 1987
Ph.D., Computer Science, University of Wisconsin-Madison, 1993

## Personal

Vandenberg is married; lives in Averill Park, New York; and has two children. When not playing with databases, he enjoys playing ice hockey and studying medieval history.

# PART 1

# Getting Started

The two chapters in Part 1 provide an introduction to database processing. In Chapter 1, we discuss the importance of databases to support Internet Web applications and smartphone and other mobile apps. We then consider the characteristics of databases and describe important database applications. Chapter 1 discusses the various database components, provides a survey of the knowledge you need to learn from this text, and summarizes the history of database processing.

You will start working with a database in Chapter 2 and use that database to learn how to use Structured Query Language (SQL), a database-processing language, to query database data. You will learn how to query both single and multiple tables. Together, these two chapters will give you a sense of what databases are and how they are processed.

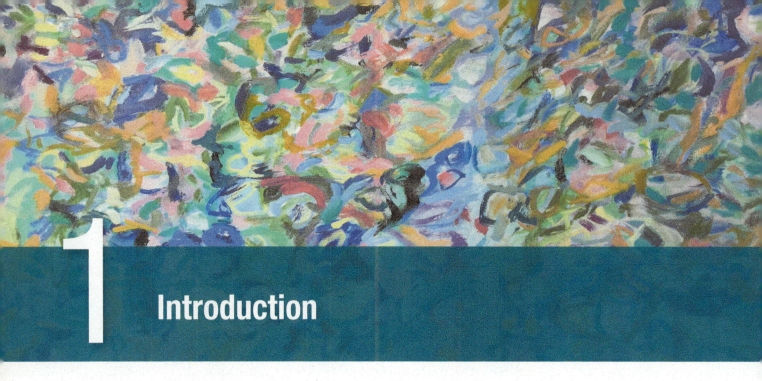

# 1 Introduction

## Chapter Objectives

- To understand the importance of databases in Internet Web applications and smartphone apps
- To understand the nature and characteristics of databases
- To survey some important and interesting database applications
- To gain a general understanding of tables and relationships
- To describe the components of a Microsoft Access database system and explain the functions they perform
- To describe the components of an enterprise-class database system and explain the functions they perform
- To define the term *database management system* (DBMS) and describe the functions of a DBMS

- To define the term *database* and describe what is contained within the database
- To define the term *metadata* and provide examples of metadata
- To define and understand database design from existing data
- To define and understand database design as new systems development
- To define and understand database redesign of an existing database
- To understand the history and development of database processing

**This chapter discusses** the importance of databases in the Internet world and then introduces database processing concepts. We will first consider the nature and characteristics of databases and then survey a number of important and interesting database applications. Next, we will describe the components of a database system and then, in general terms, describe how databases are designed. After that, we will survey the knowledge that you need to work with databases as an application developer or as a database administrator. Finally, we conclude this introduction with a brief history of database processing.

To really understand databases and database technology, you will need to actively use some database product. Fortunately, in today's computer environment, easily obtainable versions of most major database products are available, and we will make use of them. However, this chapter assumes a minimal knowledge of database use. It assumes that you have used a basic database product such as

Microsoft Access to enter data into a form, to produce a report, and possibly to execute a query. If you have not done these things, you should obtain a copy of Microsoft Access 2019 and work through the tutorial in Appendix A.

## The Importance of Databases in the Internet and Mobile App World

Let's stop for a moment and consider the incredible information technology available for our use today.

The **personal computer (PC)** became widely available with the introduction of the **Apple II** in 1977 and the **IBM Personal Computer (IBM PC)** in 1981. PCs were networked into **local area networks (LANs)** using the **Ethernet networking technology**, which was developed at the **Xerox Palo Alto Research Center (Xerox PARC)**[1] in the early 1970s and adopted as a national standard in 1983.

The **Internet**–the global computer network of networks–was created as the Department of Defense **Advanced Research Projects Agency Network (ARPANET)** in 1969 and then grew and was used to connect all the LANs (and other types of networks). The Internet became widely known and used when the **World Wide Web**[2] (also referred to as **the Web** and **WWW**) became easily accessible in 1993. Everyone got a computer software application called a **Web browser** and starting *browsing* to **Web sites**. Online retail Web sites such as Amazon.com (online since 1995) and "brick-and-mortar" stores with an online presence such as Best Buy appeared, and people started extensively *shopping online.*

In the early 2000s, **Web 2.0**[3] Web sites started to appear–Web sites that allowed users to add content to Web sites that had previously held static content. Web applications such as Facebook, Wikipedia, and Twitter appeared and flourished.

In a parallel development, the **mobile phone** or **cell phone** was demonstrated and developed for commercial use in the 1970s. After decades of mobile phone and cell phone network infrastructure development, the **smartphone** appeared. Apple brought out the **iPhone** in 2007. Google created the **Android operating system**, and the first Android-based smartphone entered the market in 2008. Twelve years later, in 2020 (as this is being written) smartphones and **tablet computers (tablets)** are widely used, and thousands of application programs known as **apps** are widely available and in daily use. Most Web applications now have corresponding smartphone and tablet apps (you can "tweet" from either your computer or your smartphone)!

The latest development is the **Internet of Things (IoT)**,[4] where devices such as smart speakers, smart home devices (smoke detectors and thermostats), and even appliances such as refrigerators connect to the Internet and are network accessible. In particular, smart speakers such as the Amazon Echo series, Apple HomePod, the Google Home series, and Harmon Kardon INVOKE enable users to interact by voice with network-accessible apps via virtual assistants such as Amazon Alexa, Apple's Siri, Google Assistant, and Microsoft Cortana.

---

[1] The mouse and the multi-window graphical user interface commonly used in computer operating systems today were also developed at Xerox PARC. From there, they were adapted and popularized by Apple and Microsoft. For more information, see the Wikipedia article **PARC (company)** (accessed April 2020) at *https://en.wikipedia.org/wiki/PARC_(company).*

[2] The World Wide Web and the first Web browser were created by Tim Berners-Lee in 1989 and 1990, respectively. For more information, see the Wikipedia articles **World Wide Web** (accessed April 2020) at *https://en.wikipedia.org/wiki/World_Wide_Web* and **World Wide Web Consortium** (accessed April 2020) at *https://en.wikipedia.org/wiki/World_Wide_Web_Consortium.* Also see the World Wide Web Consortium (W3C) Web site (accessed April 2020) at *https://www.w3.org/Consortium/.*

[3] The term *Web 2.0* was originated by Darcy DiNucci in 1999 and introduced to the world at large in 2004 by publisher Tim O'Reilly. See the Wikipedia article **Web 2.0** (accessed April 2020) at *https://en.wikipedia.org/wiki/Web_2.0.*

[4] For more information, see the Wikipedia article **Internet of Things** (accessed April 2020) at *https://en.wikipedia.org/wiki/Internet_of_things.* The article states that there were 8.4 billion network-capable IoT devices in 2017, with an expected 30 billion IoT devices by 2020!

What many people do not understand is that in today's Web application, smartphone app, and IoT environment, most of what they do depends upon databases.

We can define **data** as recorded facts and numbers. We can initially define a *database* (we will give a better definition later in this chapter) as the structure used to hold or store that data. We process that data to provide *information* (which we also define in more detail later in this chapter) for use in the Web applications and smartphone apps.

Do you have a Facebook account? If so, all your posts, your comments, your "likes," and other data you provide to Facebook (such as photos) are stored in a *database*. When your friend posts an item, it is initially stored in the *database* and then displayed to you.

Do you have a Twitter account? If so, all your tweets are stored in a *database*. When your friend tweets something, it is initially stored in the *database* and then displayed to you.

Do you shop at **Amazon.com**? If so, how do you find what you are looking for? You enter some words in a Search text window on the Amazon home Web page (if you are using a Web browser) and click the Go button. Amazon's computers then search Amazon's *databases* and return a formatted report on screen of the items that matched what you searched for.

The search process is illustrated in Figure 1-1, where we search the Pearson Higher Education Web page for books authored by *David Kroenke*. Figure 1-1(a) shows the upper portion of the Pearson Higher Education Web page, with a Search text box and button in the upper right corner of the Web page. As shown in Figure 1-1(b), we enter the author name *Kroenke* in the text box and then click the **Search button**. The Pearson catalog database is searched, and the Web application returns a *Search Results Higher Education* page containing a listing of books authored by David Kroenke (with our companion book, *Database Concepts*, the second book listed) as shown in Figure 1-1(c).

**FIGURE 1-1**

Searching a Database in a Web Browser

(a) The Pearson Higher Education Web Site Home Page

(b) Entering Author Name *Kroenke* as the Search Keyword

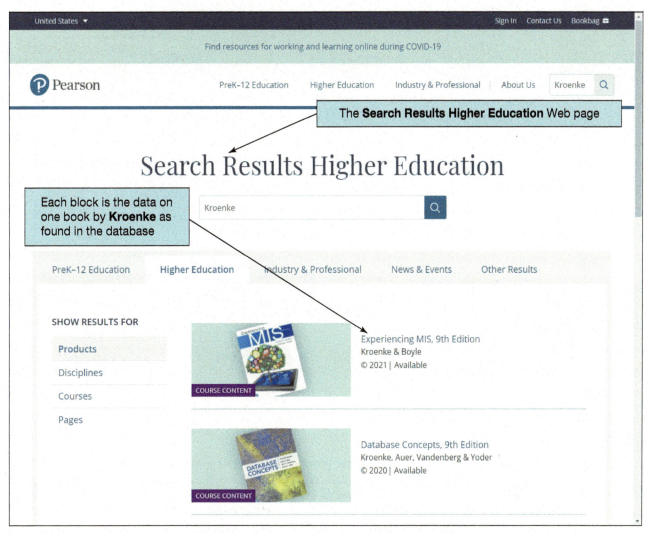

The **Search Results Higher Education** Web page

Each block is the data on one book by **Kroenke** as found in the database

**FIGURE 1-1**
Continued

(c) Books by Author *Kroenke* Found in the Database

**BY THE WAY** It is much more effective to see this process than to just read about it. Take a minute, open a Web browser, and go to Amazon.com (or any other online retailer, such as Best Buy, Crutchfield, or REI). Search for something you are interested in and watch the database search results be displayed for you. You just used a *database*.

**BY THE WAY** Even if you are simply shopping in a local grocery store (or a coffee shop or pizzeria), you are interacting with databases. Businesses use **point of sale (POS) systems** to record every purchase in a database, to monitor inventory, and, if you have a sales promotion card from the store (the one you use to get those special prices for "card holders only"), to keep track of everything you buy for marketing purposes. All the data POS systems gather is stored in, of course, a *database*.

The use of databases by Web applications and smartphone apps is illustrated in Figure 1-2. In this figure, people have computers (desktop or notebook) and smartphones, which are examples of **devices** used by people, who are referred to as **users**. On these devices are **client** applications (Web browsers, apps) used by people to obtain **services** such as searching, browsing, online purchasing, and tweeting over the Internet or cell phone

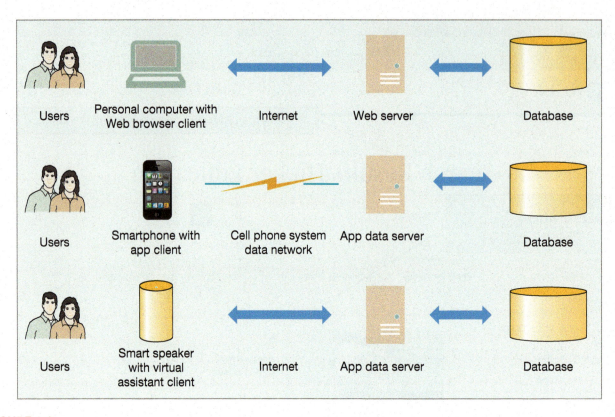

**FIGURE 1-2**

The Internet and Mobile
Device World

networks. These services are provided by **server** computers, and these are the computers that hold the databases containing the data needed by the client applications.

This structure is known as **client-server architecture**, and it supports most of the Web applications in use today. The simple fact is that without databases, we could not have the ubiquitous Web applications and apps that are currently used by so many people.

## The Characteristics of Relational Databases

The purpose of a database is to help people keep track of things. Databases are created and controlled by software applications called database management systems (DBMSs). We can basically sort all DBMSs and the databases they manage into two categories: **relational databases** and **non-relational databases**. Historically, the first databases were non-relational databases, but when the relational database was introduced, it quickly became the most commonly used type of database, and it remains so today. We will discuss the relational database model in depth in Chapter 3, so for now we just need to understand a few basic facts about how a relational database helps people track things of interest to them.

You should, however, be aware that Web and mobile apps such as search tools (for example, Google, Bing and DuckDuckGo), Web 2.0 social networks (for example, Facebook and Twitter), and scientific data collection tools generate enormous datasets, which are currently referred to as **Big Data**. Big Data datasets are often stored in new types of non-relational databases, and so the non-relational database is making a resurgence. We will discuss this after we complete our introduction of relational databases.

To understand how a relational database works, we start with the fact that a relational database stores data in tables. A **table** has rows and columns, like those in a spreadsheet. A database usually has multiple tables, and each table contains data about a different type of thing. For example, Figure 1-3 shows a database with two tables: the STUDENT table holds data about students, and the CLASS table holds data about classes.

The STUDENT table

This row stores the data for Sam Cooke

The CLASS table

This column stores the ClassName for each class

**FIGURE 1-3**

The STUDENT and CLASS Tables

Each **row** of a table has data about a particular occurrence, or **instance** of the thing of interest. For example, each row of the STUDENT table has data about one of four students: Cooke, Lau, Harris, and Greene. Similarly, each row of the CLASS table has data about a particular class. Because each row *records* the data for a specific instance, rows are also known as **records**. Each **column** of a table stores a characteristic common to all rows. For example, the first column of STUDENT stores StudentNumber, the second column stores LastName, and so forth. Columns are also known as **fields**.

> **BY THE WAY**   A table and a *spreadsheet* (also known as a *worksheet*) are very similar in that you can think of both as having rows, columns, and cells. The details that define a table as something different from a spreadsheet are discussed in Chapter 3. For now, the main differences you will see are that tables have column names instead of identifying letters (for example, *Name* instead of *A*) and that the rows are not necessarily numbered.
>
> Although, in theory, you could switch the rows and columns by putting instances in the columns and characteristics in the rows, this is never done. Every database in this text and 99.999999 percent of all databases throughout the world store instances in rows and characteristics in columns.

## A Note on Naming Conventions

In this text, table names appear in capital letters. This convention will help you to distinguish table names in explanations. However, you are not required to set table names in capital letters. Microsoft Access and similar programs will allow you to write a table name as STUDENT, student, Student, or stuDent or in some other way.

Additionally, in this text column names begin with a capital letter. Again, this is just a convention. You could write the column name Term as term, teRm, or TERM or in any other way. To ease readability, we will sometimes create compound column names in which the first letter of each element of the compound word is capitalized. Thus, in Figure 1-3 the STUDENT table has columns StudentNumber, LastName, FirstName, and EmailAddress. Again, this capitalization is just a convenient convention. However, following these or other consistent conventions will make interpretation of database structures easier. For example, you will always know that STUDENT is the name of a table and that Student is the name of a column of a table.

### A Database Has Data and Relationships

Figure 1-3 illustrates how relational database tables are structured to store data, but a relational database is not complete unless it also shows the relationships among the rows of data. To see why this is important, examine Figure 1-4. In this figure, the database contains all of the basic data shown in Figure 1-3 together with a GRADE table. Unfortunately, the relationships among the data are missing. In this format, the GRADE data are useless. It is like the joke about the sports commentator who announced: "Now for tonight's baseball scores: 2-3, 7-2, 1-0, and 4-5." The scores are useless without knowing the teams that earned them. Thus, a database contains both data and the relationships among the data.

Figure 1-5 shows the complete database that contains not only the data about students, classes, and grades but also the relationships among the rows in those tables. For example, StudentNumber 1, who is Sam Cooke, earned a Grade of 3.7 in ClassNumber 10, which is Chem101. He also earned a Grade of 3.5 in ClassNumber 40, which is Acct101.

Figure 1-5 illustrates an important characteristic of database processing. Each row in a table is uniquely identified by a **primary key**, and the values of these keys are used to create the relationships between the tables. For example, in the STUDENT table StudentNumber serves as the primary key. Each value of StudentNumber is unique and identifies a particular student. Thus, StudentNumber 1 identifies Sam Cooke. Similarly, ClassNumber in the CLASS table identifies each class. If the numbers used in primary key columns such as StudentNumber and ClassNumber are automatically generated and assigned in the database itself, then the key is also called a **surrogate key**.

**FIGURE 1-4**

The STUDENT, CLASS, and GRADE Tables

**FIGURE 1-5**

The Key Database Characteristic: Related Tables

Figure 1-6 shows a Microsoft Access 2019 view of the tables and relationships shown in Figure 1-5. In Figure 1-6, primary keys in each table are marked with key symbols, and connecting lines representing the relationships are drawn from the foreign keys (in GRADE) to the corresponding primary keys (in STUDENT and CLASS). The symbols on the relationship line (the number 1 and the infinity symbol) mean that, for example, one student in STUDENT can be linked to many grades in GRADE.

By comparing Figures 1-4, 1-5, and 1-6, we can see how the primary keys of STUDENT and CLASS were added to the GRADE table to provide GRADE with a primary key of (StudentNumber, ClassNumber) to uniquely identify each row. When more than one column in a table must be combined to form the primary key, we call this a **composite key**. More important, in GRADE StudentNumber and ClassNumber each now serves as a

**FIGURE 1-6**

Microsoft Access 2019 View of Tables and Relationships

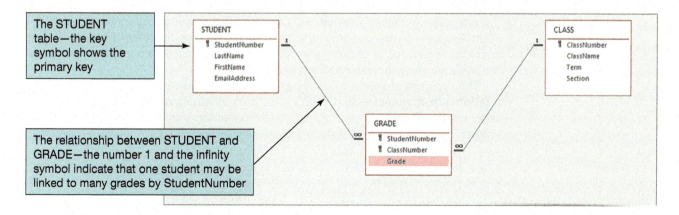

**foreign key**. A foreign key provides the link between two tables. By adding a foreign key, we create a **relationship** between the two tables.

### Databases Create Information

In order to make decisions, we need information upon which to base those decisions. Because we have already defined *data* as recorded facts and numbers, we can now define[5] **information** as:

- Knowledge derived from data
- Data presented in a meaningful context
- Data processed by summing, ordering, averaging, grouping, comparing, or other similar operations

Databases record facts and figures, so they record data. They do so, however, in a way that enables them to produce information. The data in Figure 1-5 can be manipulated to produce a student's GPA, the average GPA for a class, the average number of students in a class, and so forth. In Chapter 2, you will be introduced to a language called Structured Query Language (SQL) that you can use to produce information from database data.

To summarize, relational databases store data in tables, and they represent the relationships among the rows of those tables. They do so in a way that facilitates the production of information. We will discuss the relational database model in depth in Part 2 of this book.

## Database Examples

Today, database technology is part of almost every information system. This fact is not surprising when we consider that every information system needs to store data and the relationships among those data. Still, the vast array of applications that use this technology is staggering. Consider, for example, the applications listed in Figure 1-7.

### Single-User Database Applications

In Figure 1-7, the first application is used by a single salesperson to keep track of the customers she has called and the contacts that she has had with them. Most salespeople do not build their own contact manager applications; instead, they license products such as GoldMine or Act!

### Multiuser Database Applications

The next applications in Figure 1-7 are those that involve more than one user. The patient-scheduling application, for example, may have 15 to 50 users. These users will be appointment clerks, office administrators, nurses, dentists, doctors, and so forth. A database like this one may have as many as 100,000 rows of data in perhaps 5 or 10 different tables.

When more than one user employs a database application, there is always the chance that one user's work may interfere with another's. Two appointment clerks, for example, might assign the same appointment to two different patients. Special concurrency-control mechanisms are used to coordinate activity against the database to prevent such conflicts. You will learn about these mechanisms in Chapter 9.

The third row of Figure 1-7 shows an even larger database application. A **customer relationship management (CRM)** system is an information system that manages customer contacts from initial solicitation through acceptance, purchase, continuing purchase, support, and so forth. CRM systems are used by salespeople, sales managers, customer

---

[5]These definitions are from David M. Kroenke's books *Using MIS*, 11th ed. (Upper Saddle River, NJ: Prentice-Hall, 2020) and *Experiencing MIS*, 8th ed. (Upper Saddle River, NJ: Prentice-Hall, 2019). See these books for a full discussion of these definitions as well as a discussion of a fourth definition, "a difference that makes a difference."

| Application | Example Users | Number of Users | Typical Size | Remarks |
|---|---|---|---|---|
| Sales contact manager | Salesperson | 1 | 2,000 rows | Products such as GoldMine and Act! are database-centric. |
| Patient appointment (doctor, dentist) | Medical office | 15 to 50 | 100,000 rows | Vertical market software vendors incorporate databases into their software products. |
| Customer relationship management (CRM) | Sales, marketing, or customer service departments | 500 | 10 million rows | Major vendors such as Microsoft and Oracle PeopleSoft Enterprise build applications around the database. |
| Enterprise resource planning (ERP) | An entire organization | 5,000 | 10 million+ rows | SAP uses a database as a central repository for ERP data. |
| E-commerce site | Internet users | Possibly millions | 1 billion+ rows | Drugstore.com has a database that grows at the rate of 20 million rows per day! |
| Digital dashboard | Senior managers | 500 | 100,000 rows | Displays extractions, summaries, and consolidations of operational database data. |
| Data mining | Business analysts | 25 | 100,000 to millions+ | Data are extracted, reformatted, cleaned, and filtered for use by statistical data mining tools. |

**FIGURE 1-7**

Example Database Applications

service and support staff, and other personnel. A CRM database in a larger company might have 500 users and 10 million or more rows in perhaps 50 or more tables. According to Microsoft, in 2004 Verizon had an SQL Server customer database that contained more than 15 terabytes of data. If those data were published in books, a bookshelf 450 miles long would be required to hold them.

An **enterprise resource planning (ERP)** is an information system that touches every department in a manufacturing company. It includes sales, inventory, production planning, purchasing, and other business functions. SAP is the leading vendor of ERP applications, and a key element of its product is a database that integrates data from these various business functions. An ERP system may have 5,000 or more users and perhaps 100 million rows in several hundred tables.

### E-Commerce Database Applications

E-commerce is another important database application. Databases are a key component of e-commerce order entry, billing, shipping, and customer support. Surprisingly, however, the largest databases at an e-commerce site are not order-processing databases. The largest databases are those that track customer browser behavior. Most of the prominent e-commerce companies, such as Amazon.com and Drugstore.com, keep track of the Web pages and the Web page components that they send to their customers. They also track customer clicks, additions to shopping carts, order purchases, abandoned shopping carts, and so forth.

**E-commerce** companies use Web activity databases to determine which items on a Web page are popular and successful and which are not. They also can conduct experiments to determine if a purple background generates more orders than a blue one, and so forth. Such Web usage databases are huge. For example, Drugstore.com adds 20 million rows to its Web log database each day!

### Reporting and Data Mining Database Applications

Two other example applications in Figure 1-7 are digital dashboards and data mining applications. These applications use the data generated by order processing and other operational systems to produce information to help manage the enterprise. Such applications do not generate new data but instead summarize existing data to provide insights to management. **Digital dashboards** and other reporting systems assess past and current performance. **Data mining** applications predict future performance. We will consider such applications in Chapter 12. The bottom line is that database technology is used in almost every information system and involves databases ranging in size from a few thousand rows to many millions of rows.

> **BY THE WAY**  Do not assume that just because a database is small that its structure is simple. For example, consider parts distribution for a company that sells $1 million in parts per year and parts distribution for a company that sells $100 million in parts per year. Despite the difference in sales, the companies have similar databases. Both have the same kinds of data, about the same number of tables of data, and the same level of complexity in data relationships. Only the amount of data varies from one to the other. Thus, although a database for a small business may be small, it is not necessarily simple.

## The Components of a Database System

As shown in Figure 1-8, a **database system** is typically defined to consist of four components: users, the database application, the database management system (DBMS), and the database. However, given the importance of **Structured Query Language (SQL)**, an internationally recognized standard language that is understood by all commercial relational DBMS products, in database processing and the fact that database applications typically send SQL statements to the DBMS for processing, we can refine our illustration of a database system to appear as shown in Figure 1-9.

Starting from the right of Figure 1-9, the **database** is a collection of related tables and other structures. The **database management system (DBMS)** is a computer program

**FIGURE 1-8**

The Components of a Database System

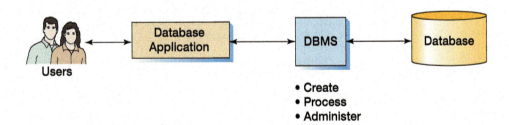

**FIGURE 1-9**

The Components of a Database System with SQL

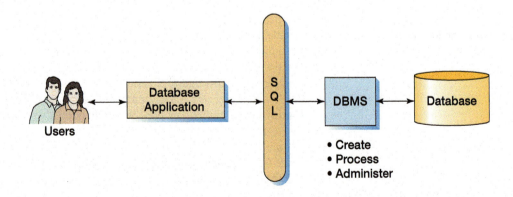

used to create, process, and administer the database. The DBMS receives requests encoded in SQL and translates those requests into actions on the database. The DBMS is a large, complicated program that is licensed from a software vendor; companies almost never write their own DBMS programs.

A **database application** is a set of one or more computer programs that serves as an intermediary between the user and the DBMS. Application programs read or modify database data by sending SQL statements to the DBMS. Application programs also present data to users in the format of forms and reports. Application programs can be acquired from software vendors, and they are also frequently written in-house. The knowledge you gain from this text will help you write database applications.

**Users**, the final component of a database system, employ a database application to keep track of things. They use forms to read, enter, and query data, and they produce reports to convey information.

## Database Applications and SQL

Figure 1-9 shows that users interact directly with database applications. Figure 1-10 lists the basic functions of database applications.

First, an application program creates and processes forms. Figure 1-11 shows a typical form for entering and processing student enrollment data for the Student-Class-Grade database shown in Figures 1-5 and 1-6. Notice that this form hides the structure of the underlying tables from the user. By comparing the tables and data in Figure 1-5 to the form in Figure 1-11, we can see that data from the CLASS table appears at the top of the form, and data from the STUDENT table is presented in a tabular section labeled Class Enrollment Data.

The goal of this form, like that for all data entry forms, is to present the data in a format that is useful for the users, regardless of the underlying table structure. Behind the form, the application processes the database in accordance with the users' actions. The application generates an SQL statement to insert, update, or delete data for any of the tables that underlie this form.

The second function of application programs is to process user queries. The application program first generates a query request and sends it to the DBMS. Results are then formatted and returned to the user. Applications use SQL statements and pass them to the DBMS for processing. To give you a taste of SQL, here is a sample SQL statement for processing the STUDENT table in Figure 1-5:

```
SELECT    LastName, FirstName, EmailAddress
FROM      STUDENT
WHERE     StudentNumber > 2;
```

This SQL statement is a query statement, which asks the DBMS to obtain specific data from a database. In this case, the query asks for the last name, first name, and email address of all students with a StudentNumber greater than 2. The results of this SQL statement are shown (as displayed in Microsoft Access 2019) in Figure 1-12 and will include the LastName, FirstName, and EmailAddress for students Harris and Greene.

**FIGURE 1-10**

Basic Functions of
Application Programs

| Basic Functions of Application Programs |
| --- |
| Create and process forms |
| Process user queries |
| Create and process reports |
| Execute application logic |
| Control the application itself |

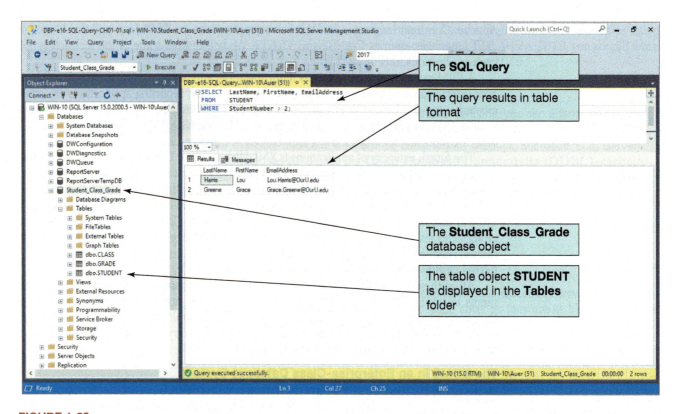

**FIGURE 1-20**

**Microsoft SQL Server 2019**

## Oracle Database

The current version of the **Oracle Database Enterprise Edition** DBMS is **Oracle Database 19c**, with **Oracle Database 20c** currently in preview mode. Oracle Database Enterprise Edition is complex and available only for use with purchased user licenses. Fortunately, Oracle also makes a freely downloadable and more user-friendly version of Oracle Database called **Oracle Database 18c Express Edition**, commonly referred to as **Oracle Database XE**. The current version of Oracle Database XE has all the features we discuss in this book, and we will use this version for our work with Oracle Database. Figure 1-21 shows the same SQL query used to produce the query results in Figure 1-12 and the associated query results when the SQL is executed in the Oracle Database XE using **Oracle SQL Developer** as the user client interface.

Oracle Database XE is a great learning tool, and it can also be used for smaller production databases. For a complete discussion of Oracle Database, Oracle Database XE, and Oracle SQL Developer, see online Chapter 10B, "Managing Databases with Oracle Database."

Note that in Figure 1-21 we are again using exactly the same SQL statement we used previously, but now you can see how it is entered into a text editor window in Oracle SQL Developer and how to click a button to run the SQL statement against the Student_Class_Grade Database (note that specific naming conventions exist for each DBMS) tables (the STUDENT, CLASS, and GRADE table objects). You can also see how the query results, which match those shown in Figure 1-12 but are sorted in a different order, are displayed in a separate Query Result window.

## MySQL 8.0

Figure 1-22 shows the same SQL query used to produce the query results in Figure 1-12 and the associated query results when the SQL is executed in Oracle's **MySQL Community Server 8.0** DBMS. We are displaying the query and results in the user client interface to MySQL 8.0, which is **MySQL Workbench**.

MySQL Community Server 8.0 edition can be downloaded for free; is a standard, full-strength edition of MySQL; and may be used in production environments. However, if you want the full product support package, you have to purchase **MySQL Enterprise Edition 8.0** from Oracle. MySQL is a popular product and is widely used for Web database applications. This version is a great learning tool, and more information can be found in online Chapter 10C, "Managing Databases with MySQL 8.0."

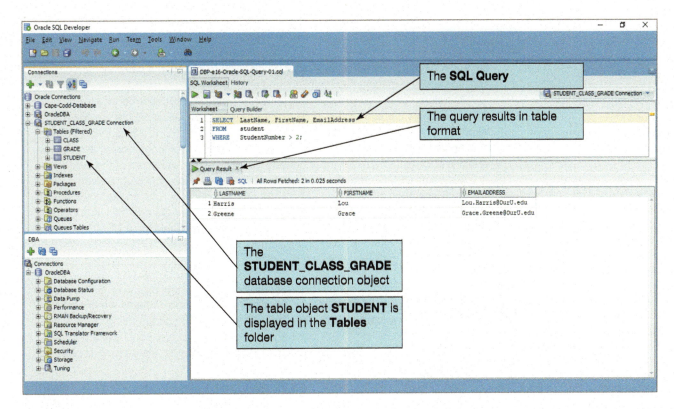

**FIGURE 1-21**

**Oracle Database XE**

Note that in Figure 1-22 we are again using exactly the same SQL statement we used previously, but now you can see how it is entered into a text editor window in the MySQL Workbench and which button to click to run the SQL query against the student_class_grade _database (note that MySQL uses all lowercase letters in object names) tables. You can also see how the query results, which match those shown in Figure 1-12 but are sorted in a different order, are displayed in a separate Results window.

**FIGURE 1-22**

**MySQL 8.0**

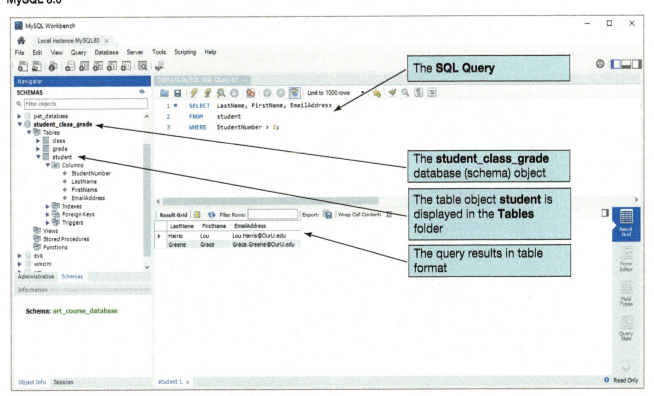

> **BY THE WAY** DBMS products, whether on a personal computer or a server, do not simply run by themselves. Like all other applications, they require that the computer have an **operating system (OS)** installed to handle the basic system operations (writing and reading files, printing, and so on).
>
> Therefore, when you are selecting a DBMS product, you must be aware of which OS will support the use of that product. Today, the main OS products are **Microsoft Windows** (for desktop and notebook computers), **Microsoft Windows Server** (for servers), **Apple macOS** for Mac (previously Macintosh) desktops and notebooks, and various versions of **Linux** (notable for the shareware development environment of the product).
>
> Microsoft DBMS products (Microsoft Access and Microsoft SQL Server) run on Microsoft operating systems, and Microsoft SQL Server now runs on the Linux OS as well. Oracle Database products will run on both the Windows OS and the Linux OS, but not on Apple macOS. MySQL is the only one of these three relational DBMS products that runs on *all* of the three operating systems.

> **BY THE WAY** This book is designed for *learning by doing*, which means we expect that you will have a DBMS available for your use. If you are using this book as a textbook for a class, in today's class environment you will probably have a computer lab available to you where you can use the DBMS product your instructor has selected for class use.
>
> However, there is no reason why you can't install a copy of a DBMS (and supporting management utilities) on you own person computer. While some of the work in Chapters 1 and 2 (and even some of the SQL work in Chapter 7) can be done with Microsoft Access 2019, you should really be using an enterprise-class product to appreciate how these DBMSs work. Each of the three relational enterprise-class DBMS products we have just introduced has a free and downloadable version available. We have three online chapters available specifically intended to help you download, install, and use Microsoft SQL Server 2019 (see online Chapter 10A, "Managing Databases with Microsoft SQL Server 2019"), Oracle Database XE (see online Chapter 10B, "Managing Databases with Oracle Database"), and/or MySQL 8.0 (see online Chapter 10C, "Managing Databases with MySQL 8.0").
>
> We will start using a DBMS (we will use Microsoft SQL Server 2019 to create the examples in this book) in Chapter 2, where we will start discussing using Structured Query Language (SQL) to run queries against a database to obtain answers to questions about the data. We recommend that you install your preferred DBMS on your personal computer now so that you are ready to follow along with us as we work through Chapter 2.

## Database Design

**Database design (as a process)** is the creation of the proper structure of database tables, the proper relationships between tables, appropriate data constraints, and other structural components of the database. Correct database design is both important and difficult. Consequently, the world is full of poorly designed databases. Such databases do not perform well. They may require application developers to write overly complex and contrived SQL to get wanted data, they may be difficult to adapt to new and changing requirements, or they may fail in some other way.

Because database design is both important and difficult, we will devote most of the first half of this text to the topic. As shown in Figure 1-23, there are three types of database design:

- Database design from existing data
- Database design for new systems development
- Database redesign of an existing database

**FIGURE 1-23**

Three Types of Database
Design

| Types of Database Design Process |
| --- |
| • From existing data (Chapters 3 and 4) |
| Analyze spreadsheets and other data tables |
| Extract data from other databases |
| Design using normalization principles |
| • New systems development (Chapters 5 and 6) |
| Create data model from application requirements |
| Transform data model into database design |
| • Database redesign (Chapter 8) |
| Migrate databases to newer databases |
| Integrate two or more databases |
| Reverse-engineer and design new databases using normalization principles and data model transformation |

Note: Chapter 7 discusses database implementation using SQL. You need that
knowledge before you can understand database redesign.

## Database Design from Existing Data

The first type of database design involves databases that are constructed from existing data, as shown in Figure 1-24. In some cases, a development team is given a set of spreadsheets or a set of text files with tables of data. The team is required to design a database and import the data from those spreadsheets and tables into a new database.

Alternatively, databases can be created from extracts of other databases. This alternative is especially common in business intelligence (BI) systems, which include reporting and data mining applications. For example, data from an operational database, such as a CRM or ERP database, may be copied into a new database that will be used only for studies and analysis. As you will learn in Chapter 12, such databases are used in facilities

**FIGURE 1-24**

Databases Originating from
Existing Data

| EmpNum | EmpName | DeptNum | DeptName |
|--------|---------|---------|----------|
| 100 | Jones | 10 | Accounting |
| 150 | Lau | 20 | Marketing |
| 200 | McCauley | 10 | Accounting |
| 300 | Griffin | 10 | Accounting |

(a) One-Table Design

OR?

| DeptNum | DeptName |
|---------|----------|
| 10 | Accounting |
| 20 | Marketing |

| EmpNum | EmpName | DeptNum |
|--------|---------|---------|
| 100 | Jones | 10 |
| 150 | Lau | 20 |
| 200 | McCauley | 10 |
| 300 | Griffin | 10 |

(b) Two-Table Design

**FIGURE 1-25**

Data Import: One or Two Tables?

called **data warehouses** and **data marts**. The data warehouse and data mart databases store data specifically organized for research and reporting purposes, and these data often are exported to other analytical tools, such as SAS's *Enterprise Miner*, IBM's *SPSS Modeler*, or TIBCO's *Spotfire*.

When creating a database from existing data, database developers must determine the appropriate structure for the new database. A common issue is how the multiple files or tables in the new database should be related. However, even the import of a single table can pose design questions. Figure 1-25 shows two different ways of importing a simple table of employees and their departments. Should this data be stored as one table or two?

Decisions such as this are not arbitrary. Database professionals use a set of principles, collectively called **normalization**, or **normal forms**, to guide and assess database designs. You will learn those principles and their role in database design in Chapter 3.

## Database Design for New Systems Development

A second way that databases are designed is for the development of new information systems. As shown in Figure 1-26, requirements for a new system, such as desired data entry forms and reports, user requirements statements, use cases (scenarios of users interacting with an information system to obtain a desired result), and other requirements, are analyzed to create the database design.

In all but the simplest system development projects, the step from user requirements to database design is too big. Accordingly, the development team proceeds in two steps. First, the team creates a **data model** from the requirements statements and then transforms that data model into a database design. You can think of a data model as a blueprint that is used as a design aid on the way to a **database design (as a product)**, which is the basis for constructing the actual database in a DBMS product.

Note that we have just given a second meaning to the term *database design*—previously we used it to mean the *process of designing a database*, and now we are using it to mean *the annotated diagram that is the result of that process*. The term is used both ways, so be careful that you understand how it is being used in a particular context! In Chapter 5, you will learn about the most popular data modeling technique: **entity-relationship (ER) data modeling**. You also will see how to use the entity-relationship model to represent a variety of common form and report patterns. Then, in Chapter 6, you will learn how to transform entity-relationship data models into database designs.

**FIGURE 1-26**

Databases Originating from
New Systems Development

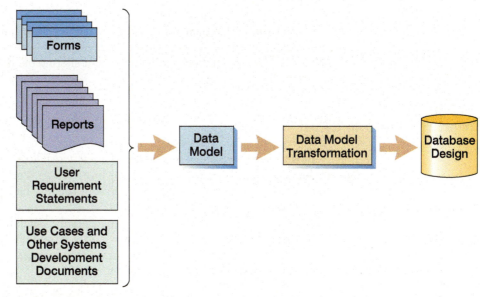

Systems Requirements

## Database Redesign

Database redesign also requires that databases are designed. As shown in Figure 1-27, there are two common types of database redesign.

In the first, a database is adapted to new or changing requirements. This process sometimes is called **database migration**. In the migration process, tables may be created, modified, or removed; relationships may be altered; data constraints may be changed; and so forth.

The second type of database redesign involves the integration of two or more databases. This type of redesign is common when adapting or removing legacy systems. It is also common for enterprise application integration, when two or more previously separate information systems are adapted to work with each other.

Database redesign is complicated. There is no getting around that fact. If this is your first exposure to database design, your instructor may skip this topic. If this is the case, after you have gained more experience you should reread this material. In spite of its difficulty, database redesign is important.

**FIGURE 1-27**

Databases Originating from
Database Redesign

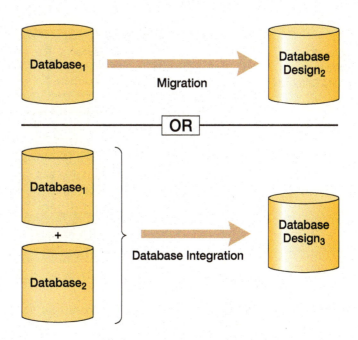

To understand database redesign, you need to know SQL statements for defining database structures and more advanced SQL statements for querying and updating a database. Consequently, we will not address database redesign until Chapter 8, after we present SQL statements and techniques for creating and altering the tables that make up a database in Chapter 7.

## What You Need to Learn

In your career, you may work with database technology either as a user or as a database administrator. As a user, you may be a **knowledge worker** who prepares reports, mines data, and does other types of data analysis, or you may be a **programmer** who writes applications that process the database. Alternatively, you might be a **database administrator (DBA)** who designs, constructs, and manages the database itself. Users are primarily concerned with constructing SQL statements to store and retrieve the data they want. Database administrators are primarily concerned with the management of the database. The domains for each of these roles are shown in Figure 1-28.

> **BY THE WAY**   The most exciting and interesting jobs in technology are always those on the leading edge. If you live in the United States and are concerned about outsourcing, a study by the Rand Corporation[8] indicates that the most secure jobs in the United States involve the adaptation of new technology to solve business problems in innovative ways. Working with databases will help you learn problem-solving skills, and 5 of the top 10 jobs recently listed on the CNNMoney Web site use database knowledge and related skills (see *http://money.cnn.com/pf/best-jobs/*).

Both users and database administrators need all of the knowledge in this text. However, the emphasis on each topic differs for the two groups. Figure 1-29 shows our opinion as to the relative importance of each topic to each group. Discuss this table with your instructor. He or she may have knowledge about your local job market that affects the relative importance of these topics.

**FIGURE 1-28**

Working Domains of Knowledge Workers, Programmers, and Database Administrators

[8]Lynn A. Karoly and Constantijn W. A. Panis, *The 21st Century at Work* (Santa Monica, CA: The Rand Corporation, 2004).

| Topic | Chapter | Importance to Database Administrator | Importance to Knowledge Worker and Programmer |
|---|---|:---:|:---:|
| Basic SQL | Chapter 2 | 1 | 2 |
| The relational database model | Chapter 3 | 2 | 2 |
| Design via normalization | Chapter 4 | 2 | 1 |
| Data models | Chapter 5 | 2 | 1 |
| Data model transformation | Chapter 6 | 2 | 1 |
| SQL DDL and constraint enforcement | Chapter 7 | 3 | 1 |
| Database redesign | Chapter 8 | 3 | 1 |
| Database administration | Chapter 9 | 3 | 1 |
| SQL Server, Oracle Database, MySQL, and ArangoDB specifics | Chapters 10, 10A, 10B, 10C, and 10D | 3 | 1 |
| Database application technology | Chapters 11, 12, 13 | 1 | 3 |

1 = Very important; 2 = Important; 3 = Less important          Warning: Opinions vary, ask your instructor for his or hers.

**FIGURE 1-29**

Priorities of What You Need
to Know

## A Brief History of Database Processing

Database processing emerged around 1970 and has been continuously evolving and changing since then. This continual change has made it a fascinating and thoroughly enjoyable field in which to work. Figure 1-30 summarizes the major eras of database processing.

> **BY THE WAY**   For additional history of database processing, the computer industry itself, and the development of this book, see the Forward to the 40th Anniversary Edition at the beginning of this book. Although it was originally written for the previous edition (the 15th edition) of this book, we have retained it in this new edition.

### The Early Years

Prior to 1970, all data were stored in separate files, most of which were kept on reels of magnetic tape. Magnetic disks and drums (magnetic cylinders that are now obsolete) were exceedingly expensive and had a very small storage capacity. Even the now obsolete 1.44-megabyte floppy disk had more capacity than many disks of that era. Memory was expensive as well. In 1969, we were processing payroll on a computer that had just 32,000 *bytes* of memory, whereas the computer on which this history is being written has 16 *gigabytes* of memory.

Integrated processing was an important but very difficult problem. An insurance company, for example, wanted to relate customer account data to customer claim data. Accounts were stored on one magnetic tape, and claims were stored on another. To process claims, the data on the two tapes had to be integrated somehow.

The need for data integration drove the development of the first database technology. By 1973, several commercial DBMS products had emerged and were in use by the mid-1970s.

The first edition of this text, copyrighted 1977, featured the DBMS products ADABAS, System2000, Total, IDMS, and IMS. Of those five, ADABAS, IDMS, and IMS are still in use, and none of them has substantial market share today.

Those early DBMS products varied in the way that they structured data relationships. One method, called **Data Language/I (DL/I)**, used hierarchies or trees (see Appendix G) to represent relationships. IMS, which was developed and licensed by IBM, was based on this model. IMS had success at many organizations, particularly among large manufacturers, and is still in limited use today.

Another technique for structuring data relationships used data structures called *networks*. The CODASYL Committee (the group that developed the programming language COBOL) sponsored a subcommittee called the Database Task Group (DBTG). This sub-committee developed a standard data model that came to bear its name: the **CODASYL DBTG** model. It was an unnecessarily complicated model (everyone's favorite idea made it into the committee's design), but several successful DBMS products were developed using it.

**FIGURE 1-30**

Database History

| Era | Years | Important Products | Remarks |
|---|---|---|---|
| Predatabase | Before 1970 | File managers | All data were stored in separate files. Data integration was very difficult. File storage space was expensive and limited. |
| Early database | 1970–1980 | ADABAS, System2000, Total, IDMS, IMS | First products to provide related tables. CODASYL DBTG and hierarchical data models (DL/I) were prevalent. |
| Emergence of relational model | 1978–1985 | DB2, Oracle Database, Ingres | Early relational DBMS products had substantial inertia to overcome. In time, the advantages weighed out. |
| Microcomputer DBMS products | 1982–1992+ | dBase-II, R:base, Paradox, Microsoft Access | Amazing! A database on a micro. All micro DBMS products were eliminated by Microsoft Access in the early 1990s. |
| Object-oriented DBMS | 1985–2000 | Oracle ODBMS, Gemstone, O2, Versant | Never caught on. Required relational database to be converted. Too much work for perceived benefit. |
| Data Warehouses | 1998–present | Red Brick Warehouse, Prism Warehouse Manager, others built with existing relational DBMS products | Created to allow data analysis and the use of business intelligence (BI) systems as discussed in Chapter 12. |
| Web databases | 1995–present | IIS, Apache, PHP, ASP.NET, and Java | Stateless characteristic of HTTP was a problem at first. Early applications were simple one-stage transactions. Later, more complex logic developed. |
| Open source DBMS products | 1995–present | MySQL, PostgresQL, and other products | Open source DBMS products provide much of the functionality and features of commercial DBMS products at reduced cost. |

**FIGURE 1-30**

Continued

| XML and Web services | 1998–present | XML, SOAP, WSDL, UDDI, and other standards | XML provides tremendous benefits to Web-based database applications. Very important today. May replace relational databases during your career. See Chapter 11 and Appendix H. |
|---|---|---|---|
| Big Data, the NoSQL movement, and cloud computing | 2009–present | Hadoop, Cassandra, Hbase, CouchDB, ArangoDB, MongoDB, JSON, Microsoft Azure, Amazon Web Services (AWS), Google Cloud, and other products | Web applications such as Facebook and Twitter use Big Data technologies. The NoSQL movement is geared toward processing large datasets using NoSQL data models, which replace relational databases with nonrelational data structures such as XML and JSON and which may supplant relational databases during your career. Many companies now rely on cloud computing services to host their servers, applications, and data. See Chapters 12 and 13. |

The most successful was IDMS, and its vendor, the Cullinane Corporation, was the first software company to be listed on the New York Stock Exchange. To the best of our knowledge, no IDMS database is in use today.

## The Emergence and Dominance of the Relational Model

In 1970, a then little-known IBM engineer named Edgar Frank Codd (better known as just E. F. Codd) published a paper in the *Communications of the ACM*[9] in which he applied the concepts of a branch of mathematics called relational algebra to the problem of "shared data banks," as databases were then known. The results of this work are now the **relational model** for databases, and all relational database DBMS products are built on this model.

Codd's work was at first viewed as too theoretical for practical implementation. Practitioners argued that it was too slow and required so much storage that it would never be useful in the commercial world. However, the relational model and relational database DBMS products became adopted as the best way to create and manage databases.

The 1977 edition of this text featured a chapter on the relational model (which Codd himself reviewed). Many years later, Wayne Ratliff, the creator of the *dBase* series of products for personal computers, stated that he had the idea for *dBase* while reading that very chapter.[10]

The relational model, relational algebra, and, later, SQL made sense. They were not needlessly complicated; rather, they seemed to boil down the data integration problem to a few essential ideas. Over time, Codd convinced IBM management to develop relational model DBMS products. The result was IBM's DB2 and its variants, which are still very popular today.

Meanwhile, other companies were considering the relational model as well, and by 1980 several more relational DBMS products had been released. The most prominent and

---

[9]E. F. Codd, "A Relational Model of Data for Large Shared Databanks," *Communications of the ACM*, June 1970, pp. 377-387. A downloadable copy of this paper in PDF format is available at *https://dl.acm.org/doi/10.1145/362384.362685* (accessed October 2020).

[10]C. Wayne Ratliff, "dStory: How I Really Developed dBASE," *Data Based Advisor*, March 1991, p. 94. For more information of Wayne Ratliff, dBase II, and also his work with FoxPro (now Microsoft Visual FoxPro), see the Wikipedia article *Wayne Ratliff* at *http://en.wikipedia.org/wiki/Wayne_Ratliff* (accessed October 2020). For the history of dBase, see the Wikipedia article *dBase* at *http://en.wikipedia.org/wiki/DBASE* (accessed October 2020).

important of those was Oracle Corporation's Oracle Database (the product was originally just named *Oracle* but was renamed *Oracle Database* after Oracle Corporation acquired other products and needed to distinguish its DBMS product from the others). Oracle Database achieved success for many reasons, one of which was that it would run on just about any computer and just about any operating system. (Some users complained, "Yes, and equally badly on all of them." Another, when asked "Should we sell it to Communist Russia?" responded, "Only as long as they have to take the documentation with it.")

However, in addition to being able to run on many different types of machines, Oracle Database had, and continues to have, an elegant and efficient internal design. You will learn aspects of that design in the concurrency-control section in Chapter 10B. That excellent design, together with hard-driving and successful sales and marketing, has pushed Oracle Database to the top of the DBMS market.

Meanwhile, Gordon Moore and others were hard at work at Intel. By the early 1980s, personal computers were prevalent, and DBMS products were developed for them. Developers of microcomputer DBMS products saw the advantages of the relational model and developed their products around it. dBase was the most successful of the early products, but another product, R:base, was the first to implement true relational algebra and other operations on the PC. Later, another relational DBMS product named Paradox was developed for personal computers. Eventually, Paradox was acquired by Borland.

Alas, it all came to an end when Microsoft entered the picture. Microsoft released Microsoft Access in 1991 and priced it at $99. No other PC DBMS vendor could survive at that price point. Microsoft Access killed R:base and Paradox, and then Microsoft bought a dBase "work-alike" product called FoxPro and used it to eliminate dBase. Microsoft's product, renamed Microsoft Visual FoxPro, has now itself been discontinued.

Thus, Microsoft Access is the only major survivor of that bloodbath of PC DBMS products. Today, the main challenge to Microsoft Access actually comes from the Apache Software Foundation and the open source software development community, who have taken over development of OpenOffice.org, a downloadable suite of free software products that includes the personal database OpenOffice.org Base and its sister product LibreOffice. LibreOffice is a related development of OpenOffice that was started when Oracle Corporation acquired Sun Microsystems in early 2013.

## Post-Relational Developments

In the mid-1980s, **object-oriented programming (OOP)** emerged, and its advantages over traditional structured programming were quickly recognized. By 1990, some vendors had developed **object-oriented DBMS (OODBMS or ODBMS)** products. These products were designed to make it easy to store the data encapsulated in OOP objects. Several special-purpose OODBMS products were developed, and Oracle added OOP constructs to Oracle to enable the creation of a hybrid called an **object-relational DBMS**.

OODBMS never caught on, and today that category of DBMS products is fading away. There were two reasons for their lack of acceptance. First, using an OODBMS required that the relational data be converted from relational format to object-oriented format. By the time OODBMS emerged, billions upon billions of bytes of data were stored in relational format in organizational databases. No company was willing to undergo the expensive travail of converting those databases to be able to use the new OODBMS.

Second, object-oriented databases had no substantial advantage over relational databases for most commercial database processing. As you will see in the next chapter, SQL is not object oriented. But it works, and thousands of developers have created programs that use it. Without a demonstrable advantage over relational databases, only a few organizations were willing to take on the task of converting its data to OODBMS format.

When you buy a product or service, whether in a store or online, your purchase becomes a business **transaction**. The transaction data needs to be recorded in the company's accounts, and by the late 1980s, database applications for **online transaction processing (OLTP)** systems were well understood and in wide use. It became clear, however, that **data analysis** of this stored data should *not* be done on the production database—we do not want any chance of breaking the production database while we are doing our analysis of company data! Therefore, we create another place to store the data for data analysis, and this is called a **data warehouse**. The first formal presentation of the idea of, and indeed the use of the term, data warehouse was in a 1988 article by IBM researchers B. A. Devlin and P. T. Murphy.[11]

We use the data warehouse for such work as **online analytical processing (OLAP)**. OLAP is an example of a **business intelligence (BI) system**. BI systems are tools used to analyze and report on company data. Data warehouses and BI systems are introduced in Chapter 2 with an extended discussion in Chapter 12.

Meanwhile, the Internet took off. By the mid-1990s, it was clear that the Internet was one of the most important phenomena in history. It changed forever the ways that customers and businesses relate to each other. Early Web sites were nothing more than online brochures, but within a few years dynamic Web sites that involved querying and processing databases began to appear.

However, one substantial problem existed. **Hypertext Transport Protocol (HTTP)**, the technology used to connect to Web pages over the Internet, is a stateless protocol. This means that a Web server receives a request from a user, processes the request, and then forgets about the user and the request. Many database interactions are multistage. A customer views products, adds one or more to a shopping cart, views more products, adds more to the shopping cart, and eventually checks out. A stateless protocol cannot be used for such applications.

Over time, capabilities emerged to overcome this problem. Web application developers learned to add SQL statements to their Web applications, and soon thousands of databases were being processed over the Web. As we discussed earlier in this chapter, today's Internet and mobile device world relies on the user having (1) a Web browser or (2) a mobile app to access an application powered by data in a database. Figure 1-2 illustrated this environment.

The Web browser user interface is now commonly used on PCs. When an application with a Web user interface, such as the Web application that lets you shop at amazon.com, is dependent on a database to store the data needed by the application, we call this a Web database application. Figure 1-31 illustrates a **Web database application** for the Wedgewood Pacific (WP) company, which manufactures and sells consumer drones.[12] (We will create the database for WP in the end-of-chapter exercises.) Applications and Web pages use an **application programming interface (API)** in a programming language such as PHP or JavaScript to connect to a DBMS. This allows them to send SQL commands to the DBMS and receive results back. You will learn more about such processing in Chapter 11.

An interesting phenomenon was the emergence of open source DBMS products. Open source products generally make the source code widely available so that a group of programmers not bound to a single company can contribute to the program. Further, some forms of these products are usually offered as free downloads, although other editions, usually with advanced features, or product support must be purchased from the company that owns the product.

A good example of this is the MySQL DBMS. MySQL was originally released in 1995 by the Swedish company MySQL AB. In February 2008, Sun Microsystems bought MySQL AB, and in January 2013 Oracle Corporation completed its acquisition of Sun Microsystems. This means that Oracle Corporation now owns two major DBMS products: Oracle Database and Oracle MySQL. At present, MySQL continues to be available via the free MySQL Community Server edition can be downloaded from the MySQL Web site. MySQL has

---

[11] The article was B. A. Devlin and P. T. Murphy, "An Architecture for a Business and Information System," *IBM Systems Journal* (Volume 27, Issue 1, 1988). The article is available at *https://www.semanticscholar.org/paper/An-Architecture-for-a-Business-and-Information-Devlin-Murphy/c22ce1eeafb01f0682e194a2a22349aa141b78f6* (accessed September 2020).

[12] The technical term is **unmanned aerial vehicle (UAV)**. See the Wikipedia article **Unmanned aerial vehicle** (accessed April 2020) at *https://en.wikipedia.org/wiki/Unmanned_aerial_vehicle*.

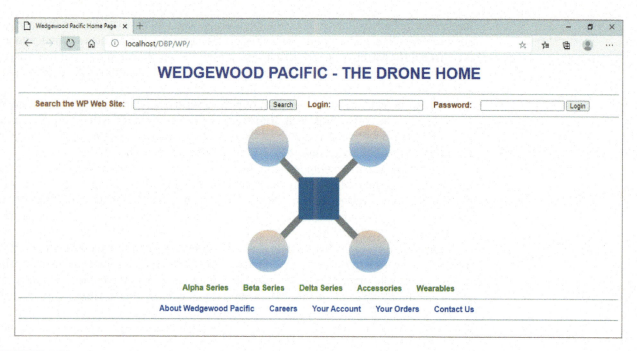

**FIGURE 1-31**

**The Wedgewood Pacific Web Page**

proven to be especially popular with Web site developers who need to run Web page queries against an SQL DBMS on a Web server running the Linux operating system.[13] We will work with MySQL in online Chapter 10C.

MySQL is not the only open source DBMS product–there are many others available, with PostgreSQL begin one of the most widely used. One interesting outcome of the emergence of open source DBMS products is that companies that typically sell proprietary (closed source) DBMS products now offer free versions of their products. For example, Microsoft now offers both SQL Server 2019 Developer and Express editions as free downloads, and Oracle Corporation makes its Oracle Database Express Edition 18c (Oracle Database XE) available for free. Although neither of the Express editions is as complete or as powerful (for example, in terms of maximum data storage allowed) as some other versions the companies sell, they are useful for projects that require a small database. They are also ideal for students learning to use databases. Microsoft SQL Server 2019 Developer edition, on the other hand, is identical to the full featured Enterprise edition but is limited to only one user. Again, this is a great learning platform.

In the late 1990s, **eXtensible Markup Language (XML)** was defined to overcome the problems that occur when HTML is used to exchange business documents. The design of the XML family of standards not only solved the problems of HTML, it also meant that XML documents were superior for exchanging views of database data. In 2002, Bill Gates said that "XML is the lingua-franca of the Internet Age." As you will learn in Chapter 11 and Appendix H, "XML," however, two key problems that are not fully resolved are (1) getting data from a database and putting it into an XML document and (2) taking data from an XML document and putting it into a database. In fact, this is where future application programmers can enter the picture.

XML database processing was given a further boost with the definition of XML Web service standards such as SOAP (originally an acronym, it is now itself just used as the name of

---

[13]Not all users of MySQL and contributors to the MySQL code were happy with Oracle's acquisition of MySQL. They took the last open source iteration of the MySQL code and forked it (which means they took an alternate development path [i.e., "fork in the road"]) into the open source **MariaDB DBMS**, which maintains a lot of compatibility and interoperability with MySQL. See the Wikipedia article **MariaDB** (accessed April 2020) at *https://en.wikipedia.org/wiki/MariaDB* and the MariaDB Web site at *https://mariadb.com/* (accessed October 2020). Interestingly enough, both products are apparently named after Finnish developer Monty Widenius's two daughters, My and Maria (see *https://mariadb.com/kb/en/why-is-the-software-called-mariadb/*) (accessed October 2020).

the standard), WSDL (Web Services Description Language), UDDI (Universal Description, Discovery, and Integration), and others. Using Web services, it is possible to expose nuggets of database processing to other programs that use the Internet infrastructure. This means, for example, that in a supply chain management application a vendor can expose portions of its inventory application to its suppliers. Further, it can do so in a standardized way.

The last row in Figure 1-30 brings us up to the present. Following the development of XML, the **NoSQL ("Not only SQL") movement** and **Big Data** have emerged in recent years, particularly following a 2009 conference organized around work on open source **distributed databases** (discussed in Chapter 12). The NoSQL movement should really be called a *NoRelational* movement because the work is really on databases that do not follow the relational model introduced in this chapter and discussed in Chapter 3. The Big Data movement is based on the need for information systems to handle increasingly large sets of data and, together with NoSQL (non-relational) databases, is the basis for such applications as Facebook and Twitter. Thus, Big Data has been responsible for the reappearance of non-relational DBMS products. These large datasets will usually be processed on server clusters that can handle the storage and parallel processing requirements for Big Data. One popular non-relational data model[14] is the **document database** model, which bases its data structuring on either XML or, more recently, **JavaScript Object Notation (JSON)**. (As of April 2020, the most popular non-relational database is **MongoDB**, which is a document database DBMS that ranks fifth in popularity.)[15] More document DBMSs support or use JSON than XML, but both standards remain important.

The need for non-relational databases arose out of the development of Web 2.0 applications that allowed users to create and store data that would be subsequently displayed on a Web page. These applications required a database with different capabilities (specifically the ability to quickly create and store massive amounts of data), and non-relational databases were created to handle this data. For example, both Facebook and Twitter use the Apache Software Foundation's Cassandra database. In this book, we will use **ArangoDB DBMS** from the German company triAGENS GmgH. Figure 1-32 shows a query in **ArangoDB query language (AQL)**, which is ArangoDB's equivalent of SQL, to obtain the same results we got with the SQL query we used in Figures 1-18, 1-20, 1-21, and 1-22. Note that although the same data is returned, it is structured and formatted very differently using JSON output. Also be aware of some column names generated by ArangoDB but not found in our relational databases—_key, _id, and _rev.

---

**BY THE WAY**   While relational databases still are the most popular databases and continue to play a big role in the DBMS market, the companies that make them have definitely felt the effects of the presence of the new non-relational DBMSs and have adjusted their relational products. These adjustments have included facilitating data transfer between relational and non-relational databases and even incorporating non-relational components into primarily relational DBMS systems. For example, Microsoft SQL Server 2019 supports non-relational *graph* databases, and MySQL supports non-relational *document* data.

---

Until recently, companies bought their computer and networking hardware (server computers, routers, switches, and so on) and kept them in-house on the business premises. Currently, however, many companies are opting to use hardware owned and operated by another company. This can result in lower business costs for companies because they do not incur the costs of buying, housing, and maintaining computer hardware and the software that runs on the hardware. So, for example, a company may decide to use a product such

---

[14] The different types of non-relational data models will be discussed in Chapter 13.

[15] The DBMS popularity rankings are from the Web site DB-Engines at *https://db-engines.com/en/ranking* (accessed April 2020). Of the top 10 DBMS products, seven are relational, and three are non-relational.

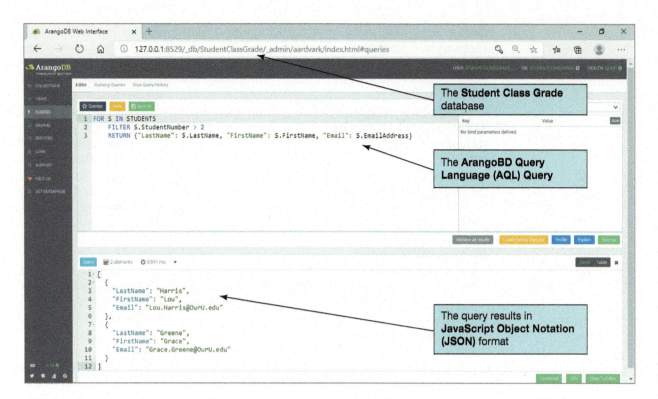

**FIGURE 1-32**

ArangoDB Non-Relational DBMS

as **Microsoft Office 365 Business** or **Microsoft Azure** as the platform to host their email services or Web server. In this case, we say that the company's computing resources are **"in the cloud"** and that the company is using **cloud computing**. Figure 1-33 shows the Microsoft Azure cloud services dashboard page. Note that we are hosting various resources here—including a Microsoft Azure SQL (the Azure version of SQL Server) database named WP and also a Microsoft Azure Cosmos DB account (Cosmos DB is a non-relational DBMS). The list of options in the left-hand column gives a good idea of the services available in cloud computing.

Basically, if you actually know where your company's servers are, you are not using cloud computing. If the servers are off-site somewhere and you only know they are at somebody else's **data center** (a facility that houses many servers and their associated infrastructure), you are using cloud computing. Many companies besides Microsoft offer cloud computing services. For example, Amazon offers **Amazon Web Services (AWS)**, and Google offers the **Google Cloud** platform.

We will discuss the NoSQL movement and Big Data, together with the associated topics of distributed databases, **virtualization**, cloud computing, Big Data, non-relational databases, and a more detailed treatment of document databases and JSON, in Chapters 12 and 13. Appendix H, "XML", will discuss XML in detail.

> **BY THE WAY**   Today, there are as many opportunities for innovation as there were for Wayne Ratliff in 1977. Perhaps you can read Chapter 13, "Big Data, NoSQL, and the Cloud," and Appendix H, "XML," and join the NoSQL, Big Data, and cloud computing movements to help develop alternatives to relational database technology. Just as in 1977, no product has a lock on the future. Opportunity awaits you!

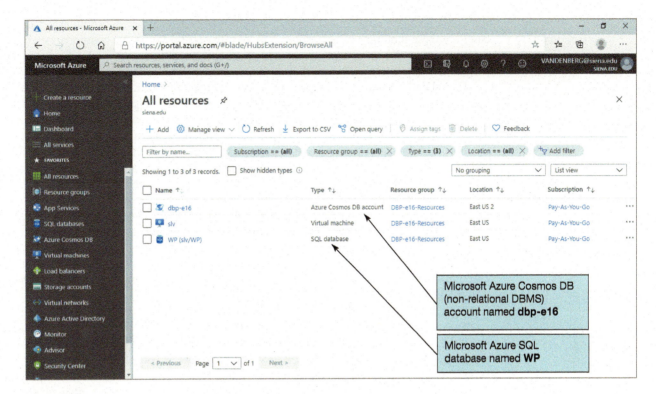

**FIGURE 1-33**

Microsoft Azure Cloud Services

# Summary

Today's Internet and mobile app world depends upon databases. Personal computers use Web clients to browse, shop, and communicate online. Smartphones and other app interfaces such as smart speakers (part of the Internet of Things (IoT) use apps over cell phone data networks to do the same. All these applications rely on databases.

The purpose of a database is to help people keep track of things. Databases are controlled by database management systems (DBMSs). We can sort DBMSs into two categories: relational and non-relational. We described relational databases here and will deal with non-relational databases in Chapter 13. Relational databases store data in tables in which each table has data about a different type of thing. Instances of the thing are stored in the rows of tables, and the characteristics of those instances are stored in columns. In this text, table names are written in all capital letters; column names are written in initial capital letters. Databases store data and the relationships among the data. Databases are structured so that information can be created from the stored data.

Figure 1-7 lists many important examples of database applications. Databases can be processed by a single user or by many users. Those that support many users require special concurrency-control mechanisms to ensure that one user's work does not conflict with a second user's work.

Some databases involve just a few users and thousands of rows of data in a few tables. At the other end of the spectrum, some large databases, such as those that support ERP applications, support thousands of users and include many millions of rows in several hundred different tables.

Some database applications support e-commerce activities. Some of the largest databases are those that track users' responses to Web pages and Web page components. These databases are used to analyze customers' responses to different Web-based marketing programs.

Digital dashboards, data mining applications, and other reporting applications use database data that is generated by transaction processing systems to help manage the enterprise. Digital dashboards and reporting systems assess past and current performance. Data mining applications predict future performance. The basic components of a database system are the database, the database management system (DBMS), one or more database applications, and users. Because Structured Query Language (SQL) is an internationally recognized language for processing databases, it can be considered a fifth component of a database system.

The functions of database applications are to create and process forms, to process user queries, and to create and process reports. Application programs also execute specific application logic and control the application. Users provide data and data changes and read data in forms, queries, and reports.

A DBMS is a large, complicated program used to create, process, and administer a database. DBMS products are almost always licensed from software vendors. Specific functions of a DBMS are summarized in Figure 1-14.

A database is a self-describing collection of integrated tables. A relational database is a self-describing collection of related tables. Tables are integrated because they store data about the relationships among rows of data. Tables are related by storing linking values of a common column. A database is self-describing because it contains a description of its contents within itself, which is known as metadata. Most DBMS products carry metadata in the form of tables. As shown in Figure 1-16, databases also contain indexes, triggers, stored procedures, security features, and backup and recovery data.

Microsoft Access is a personal database product and contains not just a DBMS but rather an application generator plus a DBMS. The application generator consists of application components that create and process forms, reports, and queries. The default Microsoft Access DBMS product is called the Access Data Engine (ADE), which is not licensed as a separate product.

Enterprise-class database systems do not combine applications and the DBMS as Microsoft Access does. Instead, applications are programs separate from each other and from the DBMS. Figure 1-18 shows four categories of database applications: client-server applications, Web applications, reporting applications, and XML Web services applications.

As of April 2020, the three most popular enterprise-class relational DBMS products are Oracle Database, MySQL, and Microsoft SQL Server. Microsoft Access ranks 10th, even though it is just a personal DBMS product. Free downloadable versions of Oracle Database, MySQL, and Microsoft SQL Server are available, and we recommend that you install one of these on you own computer for your own use with this book. Instructions are available in online Chapters 10A (Microsoft SQL Server), 10B (Oracle Database), and 10C (MySQL).

Database design is both difficult and important. Most of the first half of this text concerns database design. New databases arise in three ways: from existing data, from new systems development, and from database redesign. Normalization is used to guide the design of databases from existing data. Data models are used to create a blueprint from system requirements. The blueprint is later transformed into a database design. Most data models are created using the entity-relationship model. Database redesign occurs when an existing database is adapted to support new or changed requirements or when two or more databases are integrated.

With regard to database processing, you can have one of two roles: user or database administrator. You may be a *user* of a database/DBMS as a knowledge worker or as an application programmer. Alternatively, you might be a *database administrator* who designs, constructs, and manages the database itself. The domains of each role are shown in Figure 1-25, and the priorities as to what you need to know for each role are shown in Figure 1-26.

The history of database processing is summarized in Figure 1-27. In the early years, prior to 1970, database processing did not exist, and all data were stored in separate files. The need for integrated processing drove the development of early DBMS products.

The CODASYL DBTG and DL/I data models were prevalent. Of the DBMS products used at that time, only ADABAS and IMS are still in use.

The relational model rose to prominence in the 1980s. At first, the relational model was judged to be impractical, but over time relational products such as DB2 and Oracle Database achieved success. During this time, DBMS products were developed for personal computers as well. dBase, R:base, and Paradox were all PC DBMS products that were eventually consumed by the success of Microsoft Access.

Object-oriented DBMS products were developed in the mid-1980s but never achieved commercial success. The concepts of a data warehouse and online analytical processing (OLAP) were introduced in the late 1980s. More recently, Web-based databases have been developed to support e-commerce. Open source DBMS products are readily available, forcing commercial DBMS vendors to offer limited-capacity free versions of their enterprise products. Features and functions, such as XML and XML Web services, have been implemented to overcome the stateless nature of HTTP. The NoSQL movement, non-relational databases (such as document databases using JSON or XML), Big Data, virtualization, and cloud computing are at the leading edge of current database processing.

# Key Terms

Access Database Engine (ADE)
Advanced Research Projects Agency Network (ARPANET)
Amazon Web Services (AWS)
Amazon.com
Android operating system
app
Apple II
Apple macOS
application programming interface (API)
ArangoDB DBMS
ArangoDB query language (AQL)
Big Data
business intelligence (BI) system
cell phone
client
client-server architecture
cloud computing
CODASYL DBTG
column
composite key
concurrency
customer relationship management (CRM)
data
data analysis
data center
Data Language/I (DL/I)
data mart
data model
data mining
data warehouse

database
database administrator (DBA)
database application
database design (as a process)
database design (as a product)
database management system (DBMS)
database migration
database system
device
digital dashboard
distributed database
document database
enterprise resource planning (ERP)
enterprise-class database system
entity-relationship (ER) data modeling
Ethernet networking technology
eXtensible Markup Language (XML)
e-commerce
Hypertext Transfer Protocol (HTTP)
field
foreign key
Google Cloud
IBM Personal Computer (IBM PC)
"in the cloud"
index
information
instance
integrated table
Internet
Internet of Things (IoT)
iPhone
JavaScript Object Notation (JSON)
Joint Engine Technology (JET)

knowledge worker
Linux
local area network (LAN)
MariaDB DBMS
metadata
Microsoft Azure
Microsoft Office 365 Business
Microsoft Windows
Microsoft Windows Server
Microsoft SQL Server 2019
Microsoft SQL Server 2019 Developer Edition
Microsoft SQL Server 2019 Express Edition
Microsoft SQL Server Management Studio
mobile phone
MongoDB
MySQL Community Server 8.0
MySQL Enterprise Edition 8.0
MySQL Workbench
non-relational database
NoSQL ("not only SQL") movement
normal forms
normalization
object-oriented DBMS (OODBMS or ODBMS)
object-oriented programming (OOP)
object-relational DBMS
Office Access Connectivity Engine (ACE)
online analytical processing (OLAP)
online transaction processing (OLTP)

Open Database Connectivity (ODBC)
operating system (OS)
Oracle Database 18c Express Edition
Oracle Database 19c
Oracle Database 20c
Oracle Database Enterprise Edition
Oracle Database SQL Developer
Oracle Database XE
personal computer (PC)
personal database system
point of sale (POS) system
primary key
programmer
record

referential integrity constraints
relational database
relational model
relationship
row
Search button
self-describing
server
service
smartphone
Structured Query Language (SQL)
surrogate key
table
tablet computer (tablet)

transaction
unmanned aerial vehicle (UAV)
user
view
virtualization
Web (the)
Web 2.0
Web browser
Web database application
Web site
World Wide Web
WWW
Xerox Palo Alto Research Center
   (Xerox PARC)

# Review Questions

**1.1**  Describe the historic development of Internet, smartphone, and mobile app technology from the early days of personal computers (PCs) to today's Internet Web application and smartphone app-based information systems environment.

**1.2**  Why do today's Internet Web applications and mobile apps need databases?

**1.3**  Read the description of the search process on the Pearson Web site. Using your own computer, find another retailer Web site (other than any of those discussed or mentioned in this chapter), and search for something of interest to you. Write up a description (with screen shots if possible) of your search.

**1.4**  What is the purpose of a database?

**1.5**  What are the two categories of databases? Which is the most commonly used type of database?

**1.6**  Give an example of two related tables other than the example used in this book. Use the STUDENT and GRADE tables in Figure 1-5 as an example pattern for your tables. Name the tables and columns using the conventions in this book.

**1.7**  For the tables you created in Review Question 1.6, what are the primary keys of each table? Do you think that any of these primary keys could be *surrogate keys*? Are any of these primary keys *composite keys*?

**1.8**  Explain how the two tables you provided in Review Question 1.6 are related. Which table contains the foreign key, and what is the foreign key?

**1.9**  Show your two tables from Review Question 1.6 without the columns that represent the relationships. Explain how the value of your two tables is diminished without the relationships.

**1.10**  Define the terms *data* and *information*. Explain how the two terms differ.

**1.11**  Give an example of information that could be determined using the two tables you provided in your answer to Review Question 1.6.

**1.12**  Give examples of a single-user database application and a multiuser database application other than the ones shown in Figure 1-7.

**1.13**  What problem can occur when a database is processed by more than one user?

**1.14** Give an example of a database application that has hundreds of users and a very large and complicated database. Use an example other than one in Figure 1-7.

**1.15** What is the purpose of the largest databases at e-commerce companies such as Amazon.com?

**1.16** How do the e-commerce companies use the databases discussed in Review Question 1.15?

**1.17** How do digital dashboard and data mining applications differ from transaction processing applications?

**1.18** Explain why a small database is not necessarily simpler than a large one.

**1.19** Explain the components in Figure 1-9.

**1.20** What are the functions of application programs?

**1.21** What is Structured Query Language (SQL), and why is it important?

**1.22** What does DBMS stand for?

**1.23** What are the functions of the DBMS?

**1.24** Define the term *database*.

**1.25** Why is a database considered to be self-describing?

**1.26** What is metadata? How does this term pertain to a database?

**1.27** What advantage is there in storing metadata in tables?

**1.28** List the components of a database other than user tables and metadata.

**1.29** Is Microsoft Access a DBMS? Why or why not?

**1.30** Describe the components shown in Figure 1-17.

**1.31** What is the function of the application generator in Microsoft Access?

**1.32** What is the name of the DBMS engine within Microsoft Access? Why do we rarely hear about that engine?

**1.33** Why does Microsoft Access hide important database technology?

**1.34** Why would someone choose to replace the native Microsoft Access DBMS engine with SQL Server?

**1.35** Name the components of an enterprise-class database system.

**1.36** Name and describe the four categories of database applications that would use an enterprise-class database system.

**1.37** How do database applications read and write database data?

**1.38** Name the three most popular enterprise-class DBMS products as described in this chapter. Where does Microsoft Access rank? Given that Microsoft Access is not an enterprise-class DBMS product, what accounts for this ranking?

**1.39** List several consequences of a poorly designed database.

**1.40** Explain two ways that a database can be designed from existing data.

**1.41** Describe the general process of designing a database for a new information system.

**1.42** Explain two ways that databases can be redesigned.

**1.43** What does the term *database migration* mean?

**1.44** Summarize the various ways that you might work with database technology.

**1.45**  What job functions does a knowledge worker perform?

**1.46**  What job functions does a database administrator perform?

**1.47**  Explain the meaning of the domains in Figure 1-28.

**1.48**  What need drove the development of the first database technology?

**1.49**  What are Data Language/I and CODASYL DBTG?

**1.50**  Who was E. F. Codd?

**1.51**  What were the early objections to the relational model?

**1.52**  Name two early relational DBMS products.

**1.53**  What are some of the reasons for the success of Oracle Database?

**1.54**  Name three early personal computer DBMS products.

**1.55**  What happened to the products in your answer to Review Question 1.54?

**1.56**  What was the purpose of OODBMS products? State two reasons that OODBMS products were not successful.

**1.57**  What is a data warehouse? Why are data warehouses needed? What are online transaction processing (OLTP) and online analytical processing (OLAP), and what are the differences between them?

**1.58**  What characteristic of HTTP was a problem for database processing applications?

**1.59**  What is an open source DBMS product?

**1.60**  What has been the response of companies that sell proprietary DBMS products to the open source DBMS products? Include two examples in your answer.

**1.61**  What is XML? What comment did Bill Gates make regarding XML?

**1.62**  What is the NoSQL *movement*? Name two applications that rely on NoSQL databases.

**1.63**  What is a document database?

**1.64**  What is JSON?

**1.65**  What is cloud computing? Name three of the major vendors of cloud platforms.

## Exercises

To perform the following projects, you will need a computer that has Microsoft Access installed. If you have no experience working with Microsoft Access, read Appendix A before you proceed.

For this set of project questions, we will create a Microsoft Access database for Wedgewood Pacific (WP). Founded in 1987 in Seattle, Washington, the company manufactures and sells consumer drone aircraft. This is an innovative and rapidly developing market. In October 2020, the Federal Aviation Administration (FAA) said that over 1,700,000 drones had been registered under the new FAA drone registration rules.[16] Of these, only about 500,000 were commercial drones, and the rest were drones for recreational use! The FAA also reported that over 198,000 remote pilots had been certified.

---

[16] See *https://www.faa.gov/uas/resources/by_the_numbers/* (accessed October 2020).

WP currently produces three drone models: the Alpha III, the Bravo III, and the Delta IV. These products are created by WP's Research and Development group and produced at WP's production facilities. WP manufactures some of the parts used in the drones, but also purchases some parts from other suppliers.

The company is located in two buildings. One building houses the Administration, Legal, Finance, Accounting, Human Resources, and Sales and Marketing departments, and the second houses the Information Systems, Research and Development, and Production departments. The company database contains data about employees, departments, projects, assets (such as finished goods inventory, parts inventory, and computer equipment), and other aspects of company operations.

In the following project questions, we will start by creating the WP.accdb database with the following two tables:

**DEPARTMENT (DepartmentName, BudgetCode, OfficeNumber, DepartmentPhone)**

**EMPLOYEE (EmployeeNumber, FirstName, LastName, *Department*, Position, *Supervisor*, OfficePhone, EmailAddress)**

Where

**Department in EMPLOYEE must exist in DepartmentName in DEPARTMENT**

**Supervisor in EMPLOYEE must exist in EmployeeNumber in EMPLOYEE**

Note that the second referential integrity constraint shows two columns in the EMPLOYEE table. This indicates that this is a recursive relationship. Recursive relationships are discussed in Chapters 2, 5, and 6.

**1.66** Create a Microsoft Access database named WP.accdb.

**1.67** Figure 1-34 shows the column characteristics for the WP database DEPARTMENT table. Using the column characteristics, create the DEPARTMENT table in the WP.accdb database.

**1.68** Figure 1-35 shows the data for the WP database DEPARTMENT table. Using Datasheet view, enter the data shown in Figure 1-35 into your DEPARTMENT table.

**1.69** Figure 1-36 shows the column characteristics for the WP database EMPLOYEE table. Using the column characteristics, create the EMPLOYEE table in the WP.accdb database.

**1.70** Create the relationship and referential integrity constraint between DEPARTMENT and EMPLOYEE. Enable enforcing of referential integrity and cascading of data updates, but do *not* enable cascading of data from deleted records.

■ **NOTE:**   We will *not* create the recursive relationship and referential integrity constraint between Supervisor and EmployeeNumber in EMPLOYEE at this time. We will do this in the Chapter 2 Wedgewood Pacific Exercises after we have discussed queries on recursive relationships.

**FIGURE 1-34**

Database Column Characteristics for the WPC Database DEPARTMENT Table

| Column Name | Type | Key | Required | Remarks |
|---|---|---|---|---|
| DepartmentName | Short Text (35) | Primary Key | Yes | |
| BudgetCode | Short Text (30) | No | Yes | |
| OfficeNumber | Short Text (15) | No | Yes | |
| DepartmentPhone | Short Text (12) | No | Yes | |

| DepartmentName | BudgetCode | OfficeNumber | DepartmentPhone |
|---|---|---|---|
| Administration | BC-100-10 | BLDG01-210 | 360-285-8100 |
| Legal | BC-200-10 | BLDG01-220 | 360-285-8200 |
| Human Resources | BC-300-10 | BLDG01-230 | 360-285-8300 |
| Finance | BC-400-10 | BLDG01-110 | 360-285-8400 |
| Accounting | BC-500-10 | BLDG01-120 | 360-285-8405 |
| Sales and Marketing | BC-600-10 | BLDG01-250 | 360-285-8500 |
| InfoSystems | BC-700-10 | BLDG02-210 | 360-285-8600 |
| Research and Development | BC-800-10 | BLDG02-250 | 360-285-8700 |
| Production | BC-900-10 | BLDG02-110 | 360-285-8800 |

| Column Name | Type | Key | Required | Remarks |
|---|---|---|---|---|
| EmployeeNumber | AutoNumber | Primary Key | Yes | Surrogate Key |
| FirstName | Short Text (25) | No | Yes | |
| LastName | Short Text (25) | No | Yes | |
| Department | Short Text (35) | No | Yes | |
| Position | Short Text (35) | No | No | |
| Supervisor | Number | No | No | Long Integer |
| OfficePhone | Short Text (12) | No | No | |
| EmailAddress | Short Text (100) | No | Yes | |

**1.71** Figure 1-37 shows the data for the WP database EMPLOYEE table. Using Datasheet view, enter the first three rows of the data shown in Figure 1-37 into your EMPLOYEE table.

**1.72** Using the Microsoft Access form wizard, create a data input form for the EMPLOYEE table and name it WP Employee Data Form. Make any adjustments necessary to the form so that all data display properly. Use this form to enter the rest of the data in the EMPLOYEE table shown in Figure 1-37 into your EMPLOYEE table.

**1.73** Using the Microsoft Access report wizard, create a report named Wedgewood Pacific Employee Report that presents the data contained in your EMPLOYEE table sorted first by employee last name and then by employee first name. Make any adjustments necessary to the report so that all headings and data display properly. Print a copy of this report.

**1.74** Using the Microsoft Access form wizard, create a form that has all the data from both tables. When asked how you want to view your data, select *by DEPARTMENT*.

| Employee Number | FirstName | LastName | Department | Position | Super-visor | OfficePhone | EmailAddress |
|---|---|---|---|---|---|---|---|
| 1 | Mary | Jacobs | Administration | CEO | | 360-285-8110 | Mary.Jacobs@WP.com |
| 2 | Rosalie | Jackson | Administration | Admin Assistant | 1 | 360-285-8120 | Rosalie.Jackson@WP.com |
| 3 | Richard | Bandalone | Legal | Attorney | 1 | 360-285-8210 | Richard.Bandalone@WP.com |
| 4 | George | Smith | Human Resources | HR3 | 1 | 360-285-8310 | George.Smith@WP.com |
| 5 | Alan | Adams | Human Resources | HR1 | 4 | 360-285-8320 | Alan.Adams@WP.com |
| 6 | Ken | Evans | Finance | CFO | 1 | 360-285-8410 | Ken.Evans@WP.com |
| 7 | Mary | Abernathy | Finance | FA3 | 6 | 360-285-8420 | Mary.Abernathy@WP.com |
| 8 | Tom | Caruthers | Accounting | FA2 | 6 | 360-285-8430 | Tom.Caruthers@WP.com |
| 9 | Heather | Jones | Accounting | FA2 | 6 | 360-285-8440 | Heather.Jones@WP.com |
| 10 | Ken | Numoto | Sales and Marketing | SM3 | 1 | 360-285-8510 | Ken.Numoto@WP.com |
| 11 | Linda | Granger | Sales and Marketing | SM2 | 10 | 360-285-8520 | Linda.Granger@WP.com |
| 12 | James | Nestor | InfoSystems | CIO | 1 | 360-285-8610 | James.Nestor@WP.com |
| 13 | Rick | Brown | InfoSystems | IS2 | 12 | | Rick.Brown@WP.com |
| 14 | Mike | Nguyen | Research and Development | CTO | 1 | 360-285-8710 | Mike.Nguyen@WP.com |
| 15 | Jason | Sleeman | Research and Development | RD3 | 14 | 360-285-8720 | Jason.Sleeman@WP.com |
| 16 | Mary | Smith | Production | OPS3 | 1 | 360-285-8810 | Mary.Smith@WP.com |
| 17 | Tom | Jackson | Production | OPS2 | 16 | 360-285-8820 | Tom.Jackson@WP.com |
| 18 | George | Jones | Production | OPS2 | 17 | 360-285-8830 | George.Jones@WP.com |
| 19 | Julia | Hayakawa | Production | OPS1 | 17 | | Julia.Hayakawa@WP.com |
| 20 | Sam | Stewart | Production | OPS1 | 17 | | Sam.Stewart@WP.com |

**FIGURE 1-37**

WP Database EMPLOYEE Data

Choose the default options for other questions that the wizard asks. Open your form and page through your departments.

1.75 Using the Microsoft Access report wizard, create a report that has all the data from both tables. When asked how you want to view your data, select *by DEPARTMENT*. For the data contained in your EMPLOYEE table in the report, specify that it will be sorted first by employee last name and then by employee first name. Make any adjustments necessary to the report so that all headings and data display properly. Print a copy of this report.

1.76 Explain to the level of detail in this chapter what is going on within Microsoft Access in Project Questions 1.72, 1.73, 1.74, and 1.75. What subcomponent created the form and report? Where is the data stored? What role do you think SQL is playing?

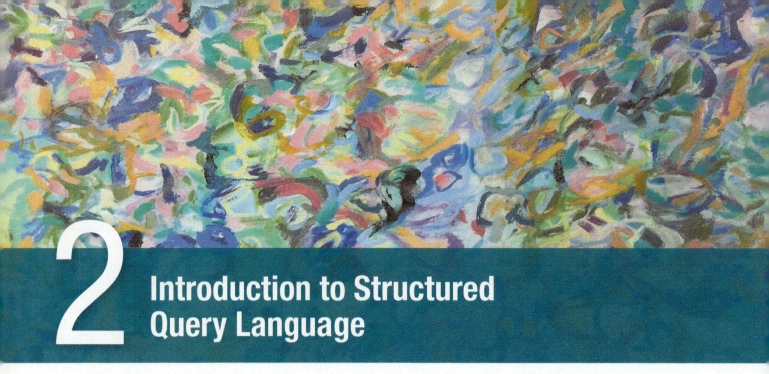

# 2 Introduction to Structured Query Language

## Chapter Objectives

- To understand the use of extracted datasets in business intelligence (BI) systems
- To understand the use of ad-hoc queries in business intelligence (BI) systems
- To understand the history and significance of Structured Query Language (SQL)
- To understand the SQL SELECT/FROM/WHERE framework as the basis for database queries
- To create SQL queries to retrieve data from a single table
- To create SQL queries that use the SQL SELECT, FROM, WHERE, ORDER BY, GROUP BY, and HAVING clauses
- To create SQL queries that use the SQL DISTINCT, TOP, and TOP PERCENT keywords
- To create SQL queries that use the SQL comparison operators, including BETWEEN, LIKE, IN, and IS NULL

- To create SQL queries that use the SQL logical operators, including AND, OR, and NOT
- To create SQL queries that use the SQL built-in aggregate functions of SUM, COUNT, MIN, MAX, and AVG with and without the SQL GROUP BY clause
- To create SQL queries that retrieve data from a single table while restricting the data based upon data in another table (subquery)
- To create SQL queries that retrieve data from multiple tables using the SQL join and JOIN ON operations
- To create SQL queries on recursive relationships
- To create SQL queries that retrieve data from multiple tables using the SQL OUTER JOIN operation
- To create SQL queries that retrieve data from multiple tables using SQL set operators UNION, INTERSECT, and EXCEPT

**In today's business** environment, users typically use data stored in databases to produce information that can help them make business decisions. In Chapter 12 and Appendix J, "Business Intelligence Systems," we will take an in-depth look at **business intelligence (BI) systems**, which are information systems used to support management decisions by producing information for assessment, analysis, planning, and control. In this chapter, we will see how BI systems users use **ad-hoc queries**, which are essentially questions that can be answered using database data. For example, in English an ad-hoc query might be "How many customers in Portland, Oregon, bought our green baseball cap?" These queries are called *ad-hoc* because they are created by the user as needed rather than programmed into an application.

This approach to database querying has become important enough that some companies produce dedicated applications to help users who are not familiar with database structures create ad-hoc queries. One example is Open Text's Open Text Business Intelligence product (formerly known as *LiveLink ECM BI Query*), which uses a user-friendly **graphical user interface (GUI)** to simplify the creation of ad-hoc queries. Personal databases such as Microsoft Access also have ad-hoc query tools available. Microsoft Access uses a GUI style called **query by example (QBE)** to simplify ad-hoc queries.

However, **Structured Query Language (SQL)**—the universal query language of relational DBMS products—is always behind the user-friendly GUIs. In this chapter, we will introduce SQL by learning how to write and run SQL queries. We will then return to SQL in Chapter 7 to learn how to use it for other purposes, such as how to create and add data to the databases themselves.

## Cape Codd Outdoor Sports

For our work in this chapter, we will use data from Cape Codd Outdoor Sports. (Although based on a real outdoor retail equipment vendor, Cape Codd Outdoor Sports is a fictitious company.) The Cape Codd Outdoor Sports Web site is shown in Figure 2-1. Cape Codd Outdoor Sports, or just Cape Codd for short, sells recreational outdoor equipment in 15 retail stores across the United States and Canada. It also sells merchandise over the Internet from a Web storefront application and via mail order based on annual catalogs that are sent to all recorded customers in early January of each year. All retail sales are recorded in a sales database managed by the Oracle Database 19c DBMS, as shown in Figure 2-2. This type of sales system is commonly known as an **online transaction processing (OLTP)** system and is used to record all sales transactions of the company (whether in a store, on the Web, or from mail order or phone order sales). OLTP systems are the backbone of businesses as they operate today.

**FIGURE 2-1**

**The Cape Codd Retail Sales Web Site Home Page**

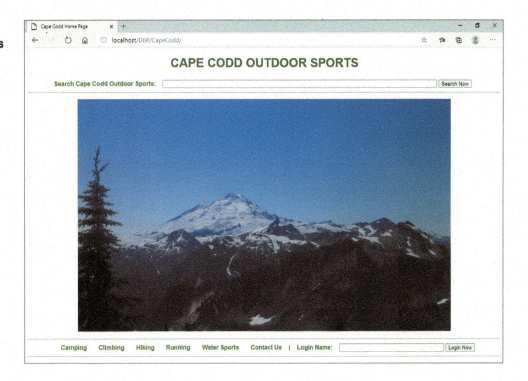

FIGURE 2-2

The Cape Codd Retail Sales
Data Extraction Process

## Business Intelligence Systems and Data Warehouses

You will notice in Figure 2-3 that BI systems typically store their associated data in a **data warehouse**, which is a database system that has data, programs, and personnel that specialize in the preparation of data for BI processing. Data warehouses will be discussed in detail in Chapter 12, so for now we will simply note that data warehouses vary in scale and scope. They can be as simple as a sole employee processing a data extract on a part-time basis or as complex as a department with dozens of employees maintaining libraries of data and programs.

Figure 2-3 shows the components of a typical company-wide data warehouse. Data are read from operational databases (the databases that store the company's current day-to-day transaction data), from other internal data, or from external data sources by the **Extract, Transform, and Load (ETL) system**. The ETL system then cleans and prepares the data for BI processing. This can be a complex process, but the data is then stored in the **data warehouse DBMS** for use by BI users who access the data by using various BI tools.

**FIGURE 2-3**

Components of a Data
Warehouse

As described in Chapter 1, the DBMS used for the data warehouse stores both databases and the metadata for those databases.

> **BY THE WAY**   A small, specialized data warehouse is referred to as a **data mart**. Data marts and their relationship to data warehouses are discussed in Chapter 12. Note that the DBMS used for the data warehouse may or may not be the same DBMS product used for the operational databases. For example, operational databases may be stored in an Oracle Database 19c DBMS, whereas the data warehouse uses a Microsoft SQL Server 2019 DBMS.

### The Cape Codd Outdoor Sports Extracted Retail Sales Data Database

Cape Codd's marketing department wants to perform an analysis of (1) in-store sales and (2) catalog content. Accordingly, marketing analysts ask the IT department to extract retail sales data from the operational database. The extracted data will be stored in a database named *Cape_Codd* in the data warehouse DBMS. This is the database name in SQL Server 2019–other DBMSs may use a variant of that name depending upon their naming conventions. (For example, MySQL does not use uppercase characters in database names, and thus the name would be *cape_codd*.) The Cape_Codd database will be a **relational database**, as described in Chapter 1. (Relational databases will be discussed in more depth in Chapter 3.) Each table in the database will have a **primary key** consisting of one or more columns that will uniquely identify each row (or **record**) in the table. Some tables will also have one or more **foreign keys**, which are used to create **relationships** between tables to logically link the tables together.

To perform the in-store sales marketing study, the marketing analysts do not need all of the order data. They want just the RETAIL_ORDER, ORDER_ITEM, SKU_DATA, and BUYER tables and columns shown in Figure 2-4. Looking at this figure, it is easy to see that some columns that would be needed in an operational sales OLTP database are *not* included in the extracted data. For example, the RETAIL_ORDER table does *not* have CustomerLastName, CustomerFirstName, and OrderDay columns. Similarly, not all catalog data is needed, but the market analysts do need similar data from different years to be able to compare the catalog content from year to year, so the CATALOG_SKU_2020 and CATALOG_SKU_2021 tables shown in Figure 2-4 are needed. The data types for the columns in these tables are shown in Figure 2-5.

**FIGURE 2-4**

Cape Codd Extracted Retail Sales Data Database Tables and Relationships

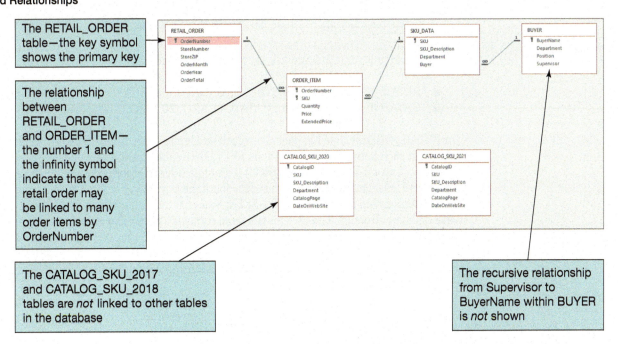

| Table | Column | Data Type |
|---|---|---|
| RETAIL_ORDER | OrderNumber | Integer |
| | StoreNumber | Integer |
| | StoreZIP | Character (9) |
| | OrderMonth | Character (12) |
| | OrderYear | Integer |
| | OrderTotal | Currency |
| ORDER_ITEM | OrderNumber | Integer |
| | SKU | Integer |
| | Quantity | Integer |
| | Price | Currency |
| | ExtendedPrice | Currency |
| SKU_DATA | SKU | Integer |
| | SKU_Description | Character (35) |
| | Department | Character (30) |
| | Buyer | Character (35) |
| BUYER | BuyerName | Character (35) |
| | Department | Character (30) |
| | Position | Character (10) |
| | Supervisor | Character (35) |
| CATALOG_SKU_20## | CatalogID | Integer |
| | SKU | Integer |
| | SKU_Description | Character (35) |
| | Department | Character (30) |
| | CatalogPage | Integer |
| | DateOnWebSite | Date |

As shown in Figures 2-4 and 2-5, six tables are needed:

- RETAIL_ORDER, ORDER_ITEM, SKU_DATA, and BUYER for retail sales analysis
- CATALOG_SKU_2020 and CATALOG_SKU_2021 for catalog content analysis

The RETAIL_ORDER table has data about each retail sales order, the ORDER_ITEM table has data about each item in an order, and the SKU_DATA table has data about each *stock-keeping unit (SKU)*. A **stock-keeping unit (SKU)** is a unique identifier for each particular item that Cape Codd sells. The BUYER table has data about the buyers in the Purchasing Department who are responsible for purchasing the SKUs. Note that these four tables are linked in a relational database structure. The BUYER table also contains a **recursive relationship**, which is a relationship between columns in the same table. Here, the Supervisor column (as a foreign key) is linked to the BuyerName column (the primary key in the table). The relationships are shown in Figure 2-4 (except for the recursive relationship within the BUYER table[1]), and the

---

[1]This figure shows the relationships as they appear in the Microsoft Access 2019 Relationships window. Unfortunately, Microsoft Access 2019 cannot properly display recursive relationships. We will discuss how Microsoft Access displays recursive relationships later in this chapter.

primary keys and foreign keys are clearly visible in Figure 2-6 (which *does* show the recursive relationship within the BUYER table). CATALOG_SKU_2020 and CATALOG_SKU_2021 have data about the content in the annual printed catalog and the items available for sale on the Cape Codd Web site. Because some items are added to the Web site after the catalog is printed, an item on the Web site may not be in the corresponding catalog. Note that these two tables are free standing, meaning that although they do have primary keys, they are not linked to any other tables via foreign keys. The data stored in the tables is shown in Figure 2-6.

> **BY THE WAY**    The dataset shown is a small dataset we are using to illustrate the concepts explained in this chapter. A "real-world" data extract would produce a much larger dataset, but our dataset is big enough for our purposes while also keeping the database easily manageable.

**FIGURE 2-6**

Sample Data in the Cape Codd Extracted Retail Sales Database

(a) The Linked RETAIL_ORDER, ORDER_ITEM, SKU_DATA, and BUYER Tables

CATALOG_SKU_2020

CATALOG_SKU_2021

**(b) The Non-Linked CATALOG_SKU_2020 and CATALOG_SKU_2021 Tables**

FIGURE 2-6
Continued

### The RETAIL_ORDER Table

As shown in Figures 2-4, 2-5, and 2-6, the RETAIL_ORDER table has columns for Order-Number, StoreNumber, StoreZIP (the ZIP code of the store selling the order), OrderMonth, OrderYear, and OrderTotal. We can write this information in the following format, with OrderNumber underlined to show that it is the primary key of the RETAIL_ORDER table:

**RETAIL_ORDER (OrderNumber, StoreNumber, StoreZIP, OrderMonth, OrderYear, OrderTotal)**

Sample data for RETAIL_ORDER are shown in Figure 2-6. This extract includes only data for retail store sales—operational data for other types of sales (and returns and other sales-related transactions) are not copied during the extraction process. Further, the data extraction process selects only a few columns of the operational data—the point-of-sale (POS) and other sales applications process far more data than that shown here. The operational database also stores the data in a different format. For example, the order data in the Oracle Database 19c operational database contain a column named OrderDate that stores the data in the date format MM/DD/YYYY (e.g., 10/22/2020 for October 22, 2020). The extraction program used to populate the database of retail sales extracted data converts OrderDate into two separate values of OrderMonth and OrderYear. This is done because this is the data format that marketing wants. Such filtering and data transformation are typical of a data extraction process.

### The ORDER_ITEM Table

As shown in Figures 2-4, 2-5, and 2-6, the ORDER_ITEM table has columns for OrderNumber, SKU, Quantity, Price, and ExtendedPrice (which equals Quantity × Price). We can write this information in the following format, with both OrderNumber and SKU underlined to show that together they are the **composite primary key** of the ORDER_ITEM table and with them also italicized to show that they are also foreign keys:

**ORDER_ITEM (*OrderNumber*, *SKU*, Quantity, Price, ExtendedPrice)**

Thus, the ORDER_ITEM table stores an extract of the items purchased in each order. There is one row in the table for each item in an order, and this item is identified by its SKU. To understand this table, think about a sales receipt you get from a retail store. That receipt has data for one order. It includes basic order data such as the date and order total, and it has one line for each item you purchase. The rows in the ORDER_ITEM table correspond to the lines on such an order receipt.

The OrderNumber column in ORDER_ITEM relates each row in ORDER_ITEM to the corresponding OrderNumber in the RETAIL_ORDER table. SKU identifies the actual item purchased by its SKU number. Further, the SKU column in ORDER_ITEM relates each row in ORDER_ITEM to its corresponding SKU in the SKU_DATA table (discussed in the next section). Quantity is the number of items of that SKU purchased in that order. Price is the price of each item, and ExtendedPrice is equal to Quantity × Price.

ORDER_ITEM data are shown in the bottom part of Figure 2-6. The first row relates to order 1000 and to SKU 201000. For SKU 201000, one item was purchased for $300.00, and the ExtendedPrice was $300.00. The second row shows the second item in order 1000. There, 1 of item 202000 was purchased for $50.00, and the ExtendedPrice is 1 × $50.00, or $50.00. This table structure of an ORDER table related to an ORDER_ITEM table is typical for a sales system with many items in one order. We will discuss it in detail in Chapters 5 and 6, where we will create a data model of a complete order and then design the database for that data model.

> **BY THE WAY**   You would expect the total of ExtendedPrice for all rows for a given order to equal OrderTotal in the RETAIL_ORDER table. *It does not*. For order 1000, for example, the sum of ExtendedPrice in the relevant rows of ORDER_ITEM is $300.00 + $130.00 = $430.00. However, the OrderTotal for order 1000 is $445.00. The difference occurs because OrderTotal includes tax, shipping, and other charges that do not appear in the data extract.

### The SKU_DATA Table

As shown in Figures 2-4, 2-5, and 2-6, the SKU_DATA table has columns SKU, SKU_Description, Department, and Buyer. We can write this information in the following format, with SKU underlined to show that it is the primary key of the SKU_DATA table:

*SKU_DATA (SKU, SKU_Description, Department, Buyer)*

SKU is an integer value that identifies a particular product sold by Cape Codd. For example, SKU 100100 identifies a yellow, standard-size SCUBA tank, whereas SKU 100200 identifies the magenta version of the same tank. SKU_Description contains a brief text description of each item. Department and Buyer identify the department and individual who is responsible for purchasing the product. As with the other tables, these columns are a subset of the SKU data stored in the operational database. The Buyer column in SKU_DATA (*italicized because it is a foreign key*) relates each row in SKU_DATA to the corresponding BuyerName in the BUYER table.

### The BUYER Table

As shown in Figures 2-4, 2-5, and 2-6, the BUYER table has columns BuyerName, Department, Position, and Supervisor. We can write this information in the following format, with BuyerName underlined to show that it is the primary key of the BUYER table, and Supervisor in italics because it is a foreign key in a recursive relationship to BuyerName with the BUYER table itself:

*BUYER (BuyerName, Department, Position, Supervisor)*

Buyer name is the combined first and last names of the buyer. Department is the Cape Codd organizational unit the buyer works in, which is Purchasing for all buyers. Note that this column uses different data values than the Department column in SKU_DATA, which uses product department values (i.e., Water Sports, etc.). This illustrates an important point: *column names that are the same in different tables may actually contain very different types of data.* It would be better to use different names, but that is not always done!

> **BY THE WAY**  The set of possible data values for a column is referred to as a **domain**. If two columns share the same set of data values, we say that their data comes from the same domain. In the case where two columns do *not* share the same set of values, such as with SKU_DATA.Department and BUYER.Department, we say that their data comes from different domains.

The Position column records the buyer's rank within the Purchasing department, and Supervisor records who the buyer reports to. Note that as Manager of Purchasing, Mary Smith has no supervisor, and thus there is *no* Supervisor data for her. A missing data value like this is called a **null value**. We will discuss null values in detail in Chapter 4, but for now understand that we treat a null value just like any other data value, and we can search for null values in a table using the same techniques we will use to search for any other data value.

As with the other tables, these columns are a subset of the data stored in the operational database, and, in fact, the data in BUYER is actually a subset of the data in a table named EMPLOYEE, which contains data on all Cape Codd employees, not just those in the Purchasing department. The Supervisor column in BUYER relates each row in BUYER to another row in BUYER that contains the Supervisor's name as BuyerName. Thus, data in one row in BUYER can refer to another row that is also in BUYER, forming a recursive relationship. We will define and discuss recursive relationships later in this chapter and also in Chapters 3, 5, and 6.

### The CATALOG_SKU_20## Tables

As shown in Figures 2-4, 2-5, and 2-6, all the CATALOG_SKU_20## tables have the same columns, consisting of CatalogID, SKU, SKU_Description, Department, CatalogPage, and DateOnWebSite. We can write this information in the following format, with CatalogID underlined to show that it is the primary key of each CATALOG_SKU_20## table:

CATALOG_SKU_20## (<u>CatalogID</u>, SKU, SKU_Description, Department, CatalogPage, DateOnWebSite)

CatalogID is an integer value that identifies a particular catalog item in the tables. SKU, SKU_Description, and Department have the same meaning as in the SKU_DATA table. CatalogPage is an integer that shows on which page in the printed catalog the item appeared, and DateOnWebSite shows the first date that the item could be seen on the Cape Codd Web site. As with the other tables, these columns are a subset of the CATALOG_SKU_20## data stored in the operational database. Also note that although we could use the SKU column as a foreign key to link to the SKU_DATA table, we are *not* creating the link at this time—the CATALOG_SKU_20## tables are not linked to any other table.

Note that in the CATALOG_SKU_2020 table, the row with CatalogID 2017003 has *no value* for CatalogPage. Similarly, note that in the CATALOG_SKU_2021 table, in the row with CatalogID 2018007, there is again *no value* for CatalogPage. These are additional examples of *null values.*

### The Complete Cape Codd Data Extract Schema

A database **schema** is a complete logical view of the database, containing all the tables, all the columns in each table, the primary key of each table (indicated by underlining the column names of the primary key columns), and the foreign keys that link the tables together (indicated by italicizing the column names of the foreign key columns). The schema for the Cape_Codd sales data extract database therefore is:

**RETAIL_ORDER (OrderNumber, StoreNumber, StoreZIP, OrderMonth, OrderYear, OrderTotal)**

**ORDER_ITEM (*OrderNumber*, *SKU*, Quantity, Price, ExtendedPrice)**

**SKU_DATA (SKU, SKU_Description, Department, *Buyer*)**

**BUYER (BuyerName, Department, Position, *Supervisor*)**

**CATALOG_SKU_2020 (CatalogID, SKU, SKU_Description, Department, CatalogPage, DateOnWebSite)**

**CATALOG_SKU_2021 (CatalogID, SKU, SKU_Description, Department, CatalogPage, DateOnWebSite)**

Note how the composite primary key for ORDER_ITEM also contains the foreign keys linking this table to RETAIL_ORDER and SKU_DATA.

> **BY THE WAY**   In the Review Questions at the end of this chapter, we will extend this schema to include three additional tables: WAREHOUSE, INVENTORY, and CATALOG_SKU_2019. Some of the figures in this chapter include these three tables in the Cape Codd database, but they are not used in our discussion of SQL in the chapter text.

### Data Extracts Are Common

Before we continue, realize that the data extraction process described here is not just an academic exercise. To the contrary, such extraction processes are realistic, common, and important BI system operations. Right now, hundreds of businesses worldwide are using their BI systems to create extract databases just like the one created by Cape Codd.

In the next sections of this chapter, you will learn how to write SQL statements to process the extracted data via an ad-hoc **SQL query**, which is how SQL is used to "ask questions" about the data in the database. This knowledge is exceedingly valuable and practical. Again, right now, as you read this paragraph, hundreds of people are writing SQL to create information from extracted data. The SQL you will learn in this chapter will be an essential asset to you as a knowledge worker, application programmer, or database administrator. Invest the time to learn SQL—it will pay great dividends later in your career.

## SQL Background

SQL was developed by the IBM Corporation in the late 1970s. It was endorsed as a national standard by the **American National Standards Institute (ANSI)** in 1986 and by the **International Organization for Standardization (ISO)** (and no, that's not a typo—the acronym is *ISO*, not *IOS!*) in 1987. Subsequent versions of SQL were adopted in 1989 and 1992. The 1992 version is sometimes referred to as SQL-92 and sometimes as ANSI-92 SQL. In 1999, SQL:1999 (also referred to as SQL3), which incorporated some object-oriented concepts, was released. This was followed by the release of SQL:2003 in 2003; SQL:2006 in 2006; SQL:2008 in 2008; SQL:2011 in 2011; and, most recently, SQL:2016 in 2016. Each of these added new features or extended existing SQL features, the most important of which for us are the SQL standardization of the INSTEAD OF trigger (SQL triggers are discussed in Chapter 7) in SQL:2008, the support for **Extensible Markup Language (XML)** (XML is discussed in Chapter 11 and Appendix H, "XML") added in SQL:2009, and the support for **JavaScript Object Notation (JSON)** (JSON is discussed in Chapter 13) added in SQL:2016. Our discussions in this chapter and in Chapter 7 mostly focus on common language features that have been in SQL since SQL-92 but do include some features from SQL:2003 and SQL:2008.

> **BY THE WAY** Although there is an SQL *standard*, that does not mean that SQL is *standardized* across DBMS products! Indeed, each DBMS implements SQL in its own peculiar way, and you will have to learn the idiosyncrasies of the SQL dialect your DBMS uses.
>
> In this book, we are using Microsoft's SQL Server 2019 SQL syntax, with some limited discussion of the different SQL dialects. The Oracle Database SQL syntax is used in Chapter 10B, and the MySQL 8.0 SQL syntax is used in Chapter 10C.

SQL is not a complete programming language, like Java or C#. Instead, it is called a **data sublanguage** because it has only those statements needed for creating and processing database data and metadata. You can use SQL statements in many different ways. You can submit them directly to the DBMS for processing. You can embed SQL statements into client/server application programs. You can embed them into Web pages, and you can use them in reporting and data extraction programs. You also can execute SQL statements directly from Visual Studio.NET and other development tools.

SQL statements are commonly divided into categories, five of which are of interest to us here:

- **Data definition language (DDL)** statements, which are used for creating tables, relationships, and other database structures.
- **Data manipulation language (DML)** statements, which are used for inserting, querying, modifying, and deleting data.
- **SQL/Persistent Stored Modules (SQL/PSM)** statements, which extend SQL by adding procedural programming capabilities, such as variables and flow-of-control statements, that provide some programmability within the SQL framework.
- **Transaction control language (TCL)** statements, which are used to mark transaction boundaries and control transaction behavior.
- **Data control language (DCL)** statements, which are used to grant database permissions (or to revoke those permissions) to users and groups so that the users or groups can perform various operations on the data in the database.

This chapter considers only DML statements for querying data. The remaining DML statements for inserting, modifying, and deleting data are discussed in Chapter 7, where we will also discuss SQL DDL statements. SQL/PSM is introduced in Chapter 7, and the specific variations of it used with each DBMS are discussed in detail in Chapter 10A for SQL Server 2019, Chapter 10B for Oracle Database 19c and Oracle Database XE, and Chapter 10C for MySQL 8.0. TCL and DCL statements are covered in Chapter 9.

> **BY THE WAY** Some authors treat SQL queries as a separate part of SQL rather than as a part of SQL DML. We note that the SQL/Framework section of the SQL specification includes queries as part of the "SQL-data statements" class of statements along with the rest of the SQL DML statements and treat them as SQL DML statements.

> **BY THE WAY** The four actions listed for SQL DML are sometimes referred to as **CRUD**: create, read, update, and delete. We do *not* use this term in this book, but now you know what it means.

SQL is ubiquitous, and SQL programming is a critical skill. Today, nearly all DBMS products process SQL, with the only exceptions being some of the emerging NoSQL and Big Data movement products. Enterprise-class DBMSs such as Microsoft SQL Server 2019, Oracle

Database , and Oracle MySQL 8.0 require that you know SQL. With these products, all data manipulation is expressed using SQL.

As explained in Chapter 1, if you have used Microsoft Access, you have used SQL, even if you didn't know it. Every time you process a form, create a report, or run a query, Microsoft Access generates SQL and sends that SQL to Microsoft Access's internal ACE DBMS engine. To do more than elementary database processing, you need to uncover the SQL hidden by Microsoft Access. Further, once you know SQL, you will find it easier to write a query statement in SQL rather than fight with the graphical forms, buttons, and other paraphernalia that you must use to create queries with the Microsoft Access query-by-example-style GUI.

## The SQL SELECT/FROM/WHERE Framework

This section introduces the fundamental statement framework for SQL query statements. After we discuss this basic structure, you will learn how to submit SQL statements to Microsoft Access, SQL Server, Oracle Database, and MySQL. If you choose, you can then follow along with the text and process the SQL statements as they are explained in the rest of this chapter. The basic form of SQL queries uses the **SQL SELECT/FROM/WHERE framework**. In this framework:

- The **SQL SELECT clause** specifies which *columns* are to be listed in the query results.
- The **SQL FROM clause** specifies which *tables* are to be used in the query.
- The **SQL WHERE clause** specifies which *rows* are to be listed in the query results.

Let's work through some examples so that this framework makes sense to you.

### Reading Specified Columns from a Single Table

We begin very simply. Suppose we want to obtain the values that are in the SKU_DATA table. To do this, we write an SQL SELECT statement that contains all the column names in the table. An SQL statement to read that data is the following:

```
SELECT    SKU, SKU_Description, Department, Buyer
FROM      SKU_DATA;
```

Using the data in Figure 2-6, when the DBMS processes this statement, the result will be:

|    | SKU    | SKU_Description                  | Department   | Buyer        |
|----|--------|----------------------------------|--------------|--------------|
| 1  | 100100 | Std. Scuba Tank, Yellow          | Water Sports | Pete Hansen  |
| 2  | 100200 | Std. Scuba Tank, Magenta         | Water Sports | Pete Hansen  |
| 3  | 100300 | Std. Scuba Tank, Light Blue      | Water Sports | Pete Hansen  |
| 4  | 100400 | Std. Scuba Tank, Dark Blue       | Water Sports | Pete Hansen  |
| 5  | 100500 | Std. Scuba Tank, Light Green     | Water Sports | Pete Hansen  |
| 6  | 100600 | Std. Scuba Tank, Dark Green      | Water Sports | Pete Hansen  |
| 7  | 101100 | Dive Mask, Small Clear           | Water Sports | Nancy Meyers |
| 8  | 101200 | Dive Mask, Med Clear             | Water Sports | Nancy Meyers |
| 9  | 201000 | Half-dome Tent                   | Camping      | Cindy Lo     |
| 10 | 202000 | Half-dome Tent Vestibule         | Camping      | Cindy Lo     |
| 11 | 203000 | Half-dome Tent Vestibule - Wide  | Camping      | Cindy Lo     |
| 12 | 301000 | Light Fly Climbing Harness       | Climbing     | Jerry Martin |
| 13 | 302000 | Locking Carabiner, Oval          | Climbing     | Jerry Martin |

When SQL statements are executed, the statements transform tables. SQL statements start with a table, process that table in some way, and then place the results in another table structure. Even if the result of the processing is just a single number, that number is considered to be a table with one row and one column. As you will learn at the end of this chapter, some SQL statements process multiple tables. Regardless of the number of input tables, though, the result of every SQL statement is a single table.

Notice that SQL statements terminate with a semicolon (;) character. The semicolon is required by the SQL standard. Although some DBMS products will allow you to omit the semicolon, some will not, so develop the habit of terminating SQL statements with a semicolon.

SQL statements can also include an **SQL comment**, which is a block of text that is used to document the SQL statement but is not executed as part of the SQL statement. SQL comments are enclosed in the symbols **/\* and \*/**, and any text between these symbols is ignored when the SQL statement is executed. For example, here is the previous SQL query with an SQL comment added to document the query by including a query name:

```
/* *** SQL-Query-CH02-01 *** */
SELECT    SKU, SKU_Description, Department, Buyer
FROM      SKU_DATA;
```

Because the SQL comment is ignored when the SQL statement is executed, the output from this query is identical to the SQL query output shown earlier. We will use similar comments to label the SQL statements in this chapter as an easy way to reference a specific SQL statement in the text.

SQL provides a shorthand notation for querying all of the columns of a table. The shorthand is to use an **SQL asterisk (\*) wildcard character** to indicate that we want all the columns to be displayed:

```
/* *** SQL-Query-CH02-02 *** */
SELECT    *
FROM      SKU_DATA;
```

The result will again be a table with all rows and all four of the columns in SKU_DATA:

|  | SKU | SKU_Description | Department | Buyer |
|---|---|---|---|---|
| 1 | 100100 | Std. Scuba Tank, Yellow | Water Sports | Pete Hansen |
| 2 | 100200 | Std. Scuba Tank, Magenta | Water Sports | Pete Hansen |
| 3 | 100300 | Std. Scuba Tank, Light Blue | Water Sports | Pete Hansen |
| 4 | 100400 | Std. Scuba Tank, Dark Blue | Water Sports | Pete Hansen |
| 5 | 100500 | Std. Scuba Tank, Light Green | Water Sports | Pete Hansen |
| 6 | 100600 | Std. Scuba Tank, Dark Green | Water Sports | Pete Hansen |
| 7 | 101100 | Dive Mask, Small Clear | Water Sports | Nancy Meyers |
| 8 | 101200 | Dive Mask, Med Clear | Water Sports | Nancy Meyers |
| 9 | 201000 | Half-dome Tent | Camping | Cindy Lo |
| 10 | 202000 | Half-dome Tent Vestibule | Camping | Cindy Lo |
| 11 | 203000 | Half-dome Tent Vestibule - ... | Camping | Cindy Lo |
| 12 | 301000 | Light Fly Climbing Harness | Climbing | Jerry Martin |
| 13 | 302000 | Locking Carabiner, Oval | Climbing | Jerry Martin |

**BY THE WAY**   In the SQL SELECT statement, the SELECT clause and the FROM clause are the only *required* clauses in the statement. We will have a complete query by simply telling SQL which columns should be read from which table. In the rest of this chapter, we will discuss other clauses, such as the WHERE clause, that can be used as part of an SQL SELECT statement. All of these other clauses, however, are *optional*.

## Specifying Column Order in SQL Queries from a Single Table

Suppose we want to obtain just the values of the Department and Buyer columns of the SKU_DATA table. In this case, we specify only the column names of the Department and Buyer columns, and an SQL SELECT statement to read that data is the following:

```
/* *** SQL-Query-CH02-03 *** */
SELECT    Department, Buyer
FROM      SKU_DATA;
```

Using the data in Figure 2-6, when the DBMS processes this statement, the result will be:

| | Department | Buyer |
|---|---|---|
| 1 | Water Sports | Pete Hansen |
| 2 | Water Sports | Pete Hansen |
| 3 | Water Sports | Pete Hansen |
| 4 | Water Sports | Pete Hansen |
| 5 | Water Sports | Pete Hansen |
| 6 | Water Sports | Pete Hansen |
| 7 | Water Sports | Nancy Meyers |
| 8 | Water Sports | Nancy Meyers |
| 9 | Camping | Cindy Lo |
| 10 | Camping | Cindy Lo |
| 11 | Camping | Cindy Lo |
| 12 | Climbing | Jerry Martin |
| 13 | Climbing | Jerry Martin |

The order of the column names in the SELECT phrase determines the order of the columns in the results table. Thus, if we switch Buyer and Department in the SELECT phrase, they will be switched in the output table as well. Hence, the SQL statement:

```
/* *** SQL-Query-CH02-04 *** */
SELECT    Buyer, Department
FROM      SKU_DATA;
```

produces the following result table:

| | Buyer | Department |
|---|---|---|
| 1 | Pete Hansen | Water Sports |
| 2 | Pete Hansen | Water Sports |
| 3 | Pete Hansen | Water Sports |
| 4 | Pete Hansen | Water Sports |
| 5 | Pete Hansen | Water Sports |
| 6 | Pete Hansen | Water Sports |
| 7 | Nancy Meyers | Water Sports |
| 8 | Nancy Meyers | Water Sports |
| 9 | Cindy Lo | Camping |
| 10 | Cindy Lo | Camping |
| 11 | Cindy Lo | Camping |
| 12 | Jerry Martin | Climbing |
| 13 | Jerry Martin | Climbing |

# Submitting SQL Statements to the DBMS

Before continuing the explanation of SQL, it will be useful for you to learn how to submit SQL statements to specific DBMS products. That way, you can work along with the text by keying and running SQL statements as you read the discussion. The particular means by which you submit SQL statements depends on the DBMS. Here we will describe the process for Microsoft Access 2019, Microsoft SQL Server 2019, Oracle Database, and MySQL 8.0.

> **BY THE WAY**   You can learn SQL without running the queries in a DBMS, so if for some reason you do not have Microsoft Access, SQL Server, Oracle Database, or MySQL readily available, do not despair. You can learn SQL without them. It is just that SQL statements are easier to understand and remember if you can run the SQL while you read. However, given that there are free downloadable versions of Microsoft SQL Server 2019 Developer and Express editions, Oracle Database XE, and MySQL 8.0 Server Community Edition, you can have an installed DBMS to run these SQL examples even if you have not purchased Microsoft Access 2019. See Chapters 10A, 10B, and 10C for specific instructions for creating databases using each of these products. The SQL scripts needed to create the Cape Codd Outdoor Sports database used in this chapter are available at *www.pearsonhighered.com/kroenke*.

## Using SQL in Microsoft Access 2019

Before you can execute SQL statements, you need a computer that has Microsoft Access installed, and you need a Microsoft Access database that contains the tables and sample data in Figure 2-6. Microsoft Access is part of many versions of the Microsoft Office suite, so it should not be too difficult to find a computer that has it.

Because Microsoft Access is commonly used in classes that use this book as a textbook, we will look at how to use SQL in Microsoft Access in some detail. Before we proceed, however, we need to discuss a specific peculiarity of Microsoft Access: the limitations of the default version of SQL used in Microsoft Access.

### Does Not Work with Microsoft Access ANSI-89 SQL

As mentioned previously, our discussion of SQL is based on SQL features present in SQL standards since the ANSI SQL-92 standard (which Microsoft refers to as ANSI-92 SQL). Unfortunately, Microsoft Access 2019 still defaults to the earlier SQL-89 version—Microsoft calls it ANSI-89 SQL or Microsoft Jet SQL (after the Microsoft Jet DBMS engine, since replaced by the ACE DBMS engine, used by Microsoft Access). ANSI-89 SQL differs significantly from SQL-92; therefore, some features of the SQL-92 language will not work in Microsoft Access.

Microsoft Access 2019 (and the earlier Microsoft Access 2003, 2007, 2010, 2013 and 2016 versions) does contain a setting that allows you to use SQL-92 instead of the default ANSI-89 SQL. Microsoft included this option to allow Microsoft Access tools such as forms and reports to be used in application development for Microsoft SQL Server, which supports newer SQL standards. To set the option in Microsoft Access 2019, click the **File** command tab and then click the **Options** command to open the Access Options dialog box. In the Access Options dialog box, click the **Object Designers** button to display the Access Options Object Designers page, as shown in Figure 2-7.

As shown in Figure 2-7, the **SQL Server Compatible Syntax (ANSI 92)** options control which version of SQL is used in a Microsoft Access 2019 database. If you check the **This database** check box, you will use SQL-92 syntax in the current database. Or you can check the **Default for new databases** check box to make SQL-92 syntax the default for all new databases you create. When you click the **OK** button to save the changed SQL syntax option, the SQL syntax information dialog box shown in Figure 2-8 will be displayed. Read the information, and then click the **OK** button to close the dialog box.

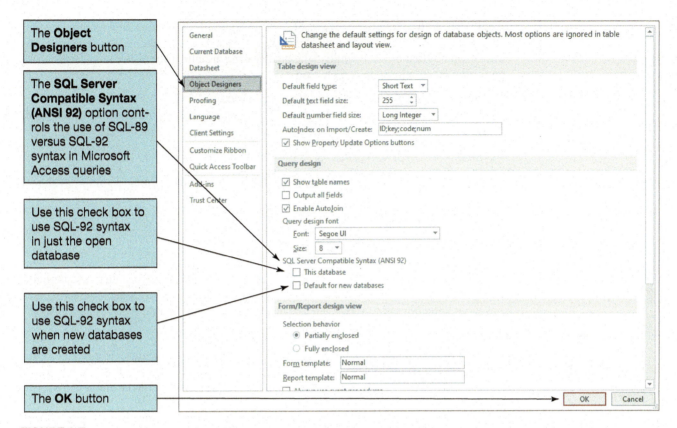

The **Object Designers** button

The **SQL Server Compatible Syntax (ANSI 92)** option controls the use of SQL-89 versus SQL-92 syntax in Microsoft Access queries

Use this check box to use SQL-92 syntax in just the open database

Use this check box to use SQL-92 syntax when new databases are created

The **OK** button

**FIGURE 2-7**

The Microsoft Access 2019 Options Object Designers Page

Unfortunately, very few Microsoft Access users or organizations using Microsoft Access are likely to set the Microsoft Access SQL version to the SQL-92 option, and in this chapter, we assume that Microsoft Access is running in the default ANSI-89 SQL mode. One advantage of doing so is that it will help you understand the limitations of Microsoft Access ANSI-89 SQL and how to cope with them.

In the discussion that follows, we use "Does Not Work with Microsoft Access ANSI-89 SQL" boxes to identify SQL commands and SQL clauses that do not work in Microsoft Access ANSI-89 SQL. We also identify any workarounds that are available. Remember that the one permanent workaround is to choose to use the SQL-92 syntax option in the databases you create!

Nonetheless, two versions of the Microsoft Access 2019 Cape Codd Outdoor Sports database are available at *www.pearsonhighered.com/kroenke* for your use with this chapter. The Microsoft Access database file named *Cape-Codd.accdb* is set to use Microsoft Access ANSI-89, whereas the Microsoft Access database file named *Cape-Codd-SQL-92.accdb* is set to use Microsoft Access SQL-92. Choose the one you want to use (or use them both and compare the results!). Note that these files contain three additional tables (INVENTORY, WAREHOUSE, and CATALOG_SKU_2019) that we will not use in this chapter but that you will need for the Review Questions at the end of the chapter.

**FIGURE 2-8**

The Microsoft Access 2019 SQL Syntax Information Dialog Box

Alternatively, of course, you can create your own Microsoft Access database and then add the tables and data in Figures 2-4, 2-5, and 2-6, as described in Appendix A. If you create your own database, look at the Review Questions at the end of this chapter and create the WAREHOUSE, INVENTORY, and CATALOG_SKU_2019 tables shown there in addition to the RETAIL_ORDER, ORDER_ITEM, SKU_DATA, and BUYER tables shown in the chapter discussion. This will ensure that what you see on your monitor matches the screenshots in this chapter. Whether you download the database file or build it yourself, you will need to do one or the other before you can proceed.

### Processing SQL Statements in Microsoft Access 2019

To process an SQL statement in Microsoft Access 2019, first open the database in Microsoft Access as described in Appendix A and then create a new tabbed Query window.

#### Opening a Microsoft Access Query Window in Design View

1. Click the **Create** command tab to display the Create command groups, as shown in Figure 2-9.
2. Click the **Query Design** button.
3. The Query1 tabbed document window is displayed in Design view, along with the Show Table dialog box, as shown in Figure 2-10.
4. Click the **Close** button on the Show Table dialog box. The Query1 document window now looks as shown in Figure 2-11, with the Query Tools contextual command tab and the Design command tab displayed. This window is used for creating and editing Microsoft Access queries in Design view and is used with Microsoft Access QBE (Query By Example).

Note that in Figure 2-11 the Select button is selected in the Query Type group on the Design tab. You can tell this is so because active or selected buttons are always shown highlighted in gray on the Ribbon. This indicates that we are creating a query that is the equivalent of an SQL SELECT statement.

Also note that in Figure 2-11 the View gallery is available in the Results group of the Design tab. We can use this gallery to switch between Design view and SQL view. However, we can also just use the displayed SQL View button to switch to SQL view. The SQL View button is being displayed because Microsoft Access considers that to be the view you would most likely choose in the gallery if you used it. Microsoft Access always presents a "most likely needed" view choice as a button above the View gallery.

**FIGURE 2-9**

The Create Command Tab

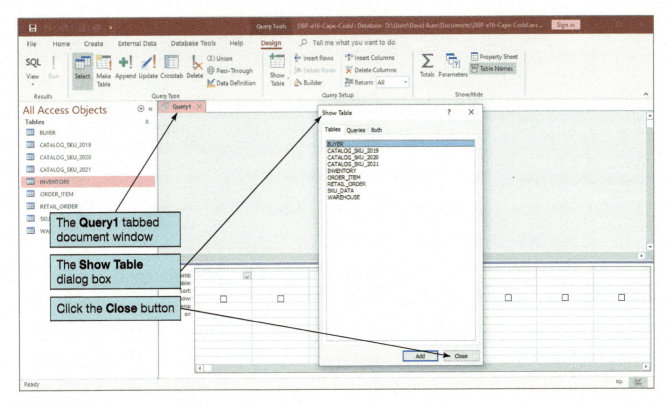

**FIGURE 2-10**

The Show Table Dialog Box

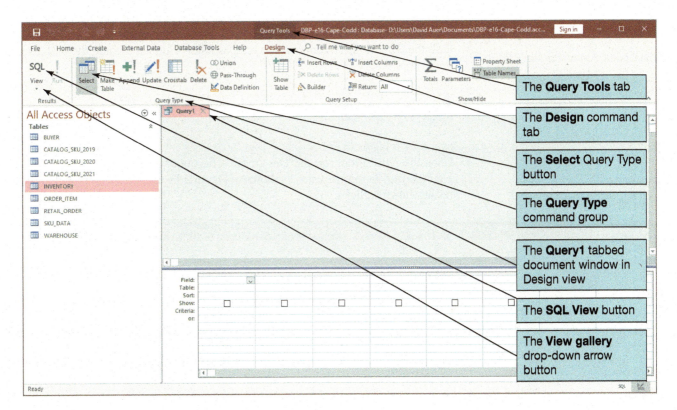

**FIGURE 2-11**

The Query Tools Contextual
Command Tab

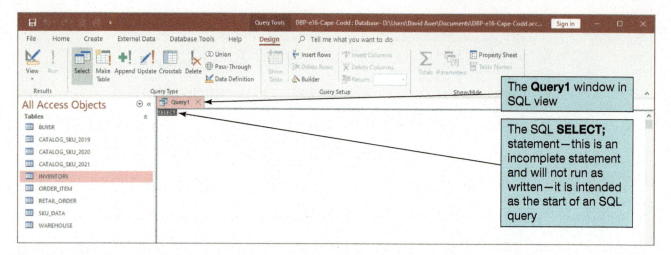

**FIGURE 2-12**

**The Query1 Window in SQL View**

For our example SQL query in Microsoft Access, we will use SQL-Query-CH02-01, the first SQL query earlier in our discussion:

```
/* *** SQL-Query-CH02-01 *** */
SELECT     SKU, SKU_Description, Department, Buyer
FROM       SKU_DATA;
```

***Opening a Microsoft Access SQL Query Window and Running a Microsoft Access SQL Query***

1. Click the **SQL View** button in the Results group on the Design tab. The Query1 window switches to the SQL view, as shown in Figure 2-12. Note the basic SQL command **SELECT**; that's shown in the window. This is an incomplete command, and running it will not produce any results.

2. Edit the SQL SELECT command to read as follows (do *not* include the SQL comment line):

```
SELECT     SKU, SKU_Description, Department, Buyer
FROM       SKU_DATA;
```

as shown in Figure 2-13.

3. Click the **Run** button on the Design tab. The query results appear, as shown in Figure 2-14. Compare the results shown in Figure 2-14 to the SQL-Query-CH02-01 results shown earlier.

**FIGURE 2-13**

**The SQL Query**

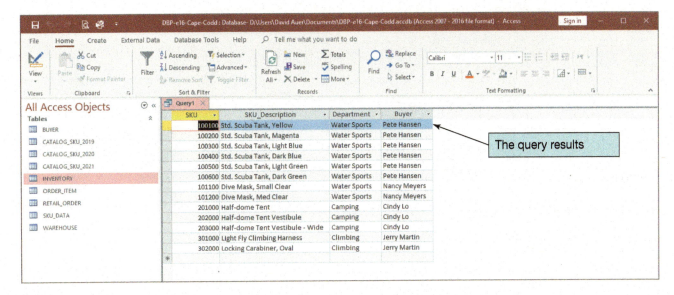

**FIGURE 2-14**

**The SQL Query Results**

Because Microsoft Access is a personal database and includes an application generator, we can save Microsoft Access queries for future use. Enterprise-level DBMS products generally do not allow us to save queries (although they do allow us to save SQL Views within the database and SQL query scripts as separate files–we will discuss these methods later).

***Saving a Microsoft Access SQL Query***

1. To save the query, click the **Save** button on the Quick Access Toolbar. The Save As dialog box appears, as shown in Figure 2-15.
2. Type in the query name **SQL-Query-CH02-01** and then click the **OK** button. The query is saved, and the window is renamed with the query name. As shown in Figure 2-16, the query document window is now named SQL-Query-CH02-01, and a newly created SQL-Query-CH02-01 query object appears in a Queries section of the Navigation Pane.

**FIGURE 2-15**

**The Save As Dialog Box**

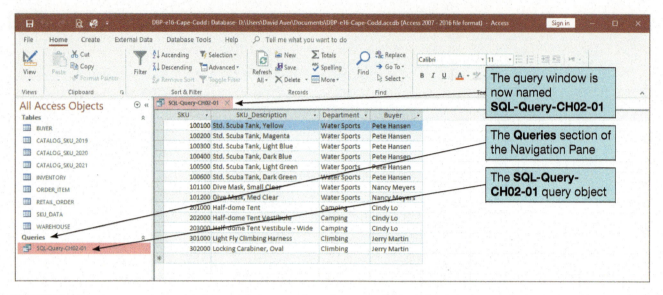

**FIGURE 2-16**

The Named and Saved
Query

3. Close the SQL-Query-CH02-01 window by clicking the document window's **Close** button.

4. If Microsoft Access displays a dialog box asking whether you want to save changes to the design of the query SQL-Query-CH02-01, click the **Yes** button.

At this point, you should work through each of the other three queries in the preceding discussion of the SQL SELECT/FROM/WHERE framework. Save each query as SQL-Query-CH02-##, where ## is a sequential number from 02 to 04 that corresponds to the SQL query label shown in the SQL comment line of each query.

## Using SQL in Microsoft SQL Server 2019

Before you can use SQL statements with Microsoft SQL Server, you need access to a computer that has SQL Server installed and that has a database with the tables and data shown in Figures 2-4, 2-5, and 2-6. Your instructor may have installed SQL Server in your computer lab and entered the data for you. If so, follow his or her instructions for accessing that database.

Otherwise, you will need to obtain a copy of SQL Server 2019 and install it on your computer. At this time, read the material in Chapter 10A about obtaining and installing SQL Server 2019.

After you have SQL Server 2019 installed, you will need to read the discussion for using SQL Server in Chapter 10A that explains how to create the Cape_Codd database (note the use of the underscore in the database name) and how to run the SQL Server scripts for creating and populating the Cape_Codd database tables. The SQL Server 2019 scripts for the Cape_Codd database are available on our Web site at *www.pearsonhighered.com/kroenke*.

SQL Server 2019 uses the Microsoft SQL Server Management Studio as the GUI tool for managing the SQL Server DBMS and the databases controlled by the DBMS. The Microsoft SQL Server Management Studio, which we will also refer to as just the SQL Server Management Studio, is installed as part of the SQL Server 2019 installation process and is discussed in Chapter 10A. Figure 2-17 shows the execution of SQL-Query-CH02-01 (note that the SQL comment is *not* included in the SQL statement as run—also note that the SQL comment *could* have been included in the SQL code if we had chosen to include it):

```
/* *** SQL-Query-CH02-01 *** */

SELECT    SKU, SKU_Description, Department, Buyer
FROM      SKU_DATA;
```

### Running an SQL Query in SQL Server Management Studio

1. Click the **New Query** button to display a new tabbed query window.

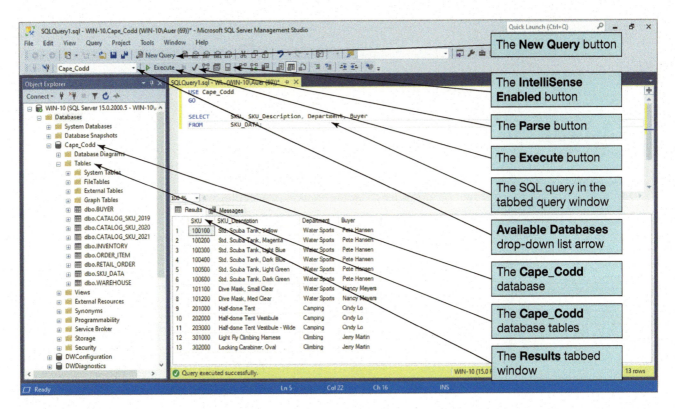

**FIGURE 2-17**

Running an SQL Query in
SQL Server Management
Studio

2. If the Cape Codd database is not displayed in the Available Database box, select it in the Available Databases drop-down list.
3. Click the **Intellisense Enabled** button to *disable* Intellisense.
4. Type the SQL SELECT command (*without* the SQL comment line shown earlier):

```
SELECT     SKU, SKU_Description, Department, Buyer
FROM       SKU_DATA;
```

The SQL query window now appears as shown in Figure 2-17.

5. At this point you can check the SQL command syntax before actually running the command by clicking the **Parse** button. A Results window will be displayed in the same location shown in Figure 2-17, but with the message "Command(s) completed successfully" if the SQL command syntax is correct or with an error message if there is a problem with the syntax.
6. Click the **Execute** button to run the query. The results are displayed in a results window, as shown in Figure 2-17.

Note that in Figure 2-17 the *Cape_Codd* database object in the Object Browser in the left side window of the SQL Server Management Studio has been expanded to show the tables in the Cape_Codd database. Many of the functions of the SQL Server Management Studio are associated with the objects in the Object Browser and are often accessed by right-clicking the object to display a shortcut menu.

> **BY THE WAY**    We are using Microsoft SQL Server 2019 running in Windows 10. When we give specific sequences of steps to follow in the text or figures in this book, we use the command terminology used by SQL Server 2019 and associated utility programs in Microsoft Windows 10. If you are running a workstation operating system such as Microsoft Windows 7, Microsoft Windows 8.1, Microsoft Server 2016, or Linux, the terminology may vary somewhat.

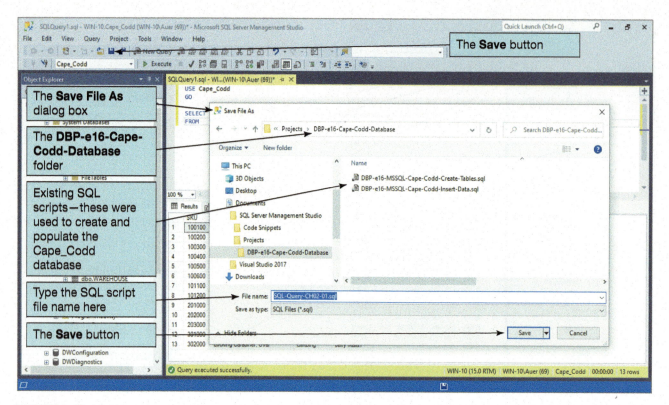

**FIGURE 2-18**

Saving an SQL Query as an SQL Script in SQL Server Management Studio

SQL Server 2019 is an enterprise-class DBMS product and, as is typical of such products, does not store queries within the DBMS. (It does store SQL Views, which can be considered a type of query, and we will discuss SQL Views in Chapter 7.) However, you can save queries as SQL script files. An **SQL script file** is a separately stored plain-text file, and it usually uses a file name extension of *.sql*. An SQL script can be opened and run as an SQL command (or set of commands). Often used to create and populate databases, scripts can also be used to store a query or set of queries. Figure 2-18 shows the SQL query being saved as an SQL script.

Note that in Figure 2-18 the SQL scripts are shown in a folder named *DBP-e16-Cape-Codd-Database*, as described in Chapter 10A. We recommend that you create a folder for each database in the Projects folder. We have created the folder named *DBP-e16-Cape-Codd-Database* to store the script files associated with the Cape_Codd database.

### Saving an SQL Server Query as an SQL Script in SQL Server Management Studio

1. Click the **Save** button. The Save File As dialog box appears, as shown in Figure 2-18.
2. Browse to the *\Documents\SQL Server Management Studio\Projects\DBP-e16-Cape-Codd-Database* folder.
3. Note that there are already two SQL script names displayed in the dialog box. These are the SQL scripts that were used to create and populate the Cape_Codd database tables.
4. In the File Name text box, type the SQL script file name *SQL-Query-CH02-01*.
5. Click the **Save** button.

To rerun the saved query, you would click the **Open File** button shown in Figure 2-18 to open the Open File dialog box, open the SQL script containing the query, and then click the **Execute** button.

At this point, you should work through each of the other three queries in the preceding discussion of the SQL SELECT/FROM/WHERE framework. Save each query as SQL-Query-CH02-##, where ## is a sequential number from 02 to 04 that corresponds to the SQL query label shown in the SQL comment line of each query. You can then continue working through the rest of the example SQL statements as you read the chapter.

## Using SQL in Oracle Database

Before you can enter SQL statements into Oracle Database, you need access to a computer that has Oracle Database installed and that has a database with the tables and data shown in Figures 2-4, 2-5, and 2-6. Your instructor may have installed Oracle Database 18c, Oracle Database 19c or Oracle Database XE on a computer in the lab and entered the data for you. If so, follow his or her instructions for accessing that database.

Otherwise, you will need to obtain a copy of Oracle Database XE and install it on your computer. At this time, read the material in Chapter 10B about obtaining and installing Oracle Database XE.

After you have installed Oracle Database XE, you will need to read the introductory discussion for Oracle Database in Chapter 10B that explains how to create the Cape Codd database. Note that database names are a bit complex in Oracle Database, and we explain this in Chapter 10B—here we use the generic name *Cape Codd* or *Cape Codd database*. Oracle Database scripts for creating and populating the Cape Codd database tables are available on our Web site at *www.pearsonhighered.com/kroenke*.

Although Oracle users have been dedicated to the Oracle SQL*Plus command-line tool, professionals are moving to the new Oracle SQL Developer GUI tool. This application is installed as part of the Oracle Database 19c installation, but if you are using Oracle Database XE, you will need to download and install SQL Developer separately, as discussed in Chapter 10B. We will use it as our standard GUI tool for managing the databases created by the Oracle Database DBMS.

Figure 2-19 shows the execution of SQL-Query-CH02-01 (note that the SQL comment is *not* included in the SQL statement as run—also note that the SQL comment *could* have been included in the SQL code if we had chosen to include it):

```
/* *** SQL-Query-CH02-01 *** */

SELECT    SKU, SKU_Description, Department, Buyer

FROM      SKU_DATA;
```

### Running an SQL Query in Oracle SQL Developer

**FIGURE 2-19**

Running an SQL Query in Oracle SQL Developer

1. Open the **Cape-Codd-Database** connection in SQL Developer. A tabbed SQL Worksheet will be displayed.

2. In the tabbed SQL Worksheet, type the SQL SELECT command (*without* the SQL comment line shown earlier):

```
SELECT    SKU, SKU_Description, Department, Buyer
FROM      SKU_DATA;
```

as shown in Figure 2-19.

3. Click the **Execute** button to run the query. The results are displayed in a results window, as shown in Figure 2-19.

Note that in Figure 2-19, the *Cape-Codd-Database* object in the left-side Connection object browser of Oracle SQL Developer has been expanded to show the tables in the Cape Codd database. Many of the functions of SQL Developer are associated with the objects in the Connections object browser and are often accessed by right-clicking the object to display a shortcut menu.

---

**BY THE WAY**   We are using Oracle Database XE running in Microsoft Windows 10. When we give specific sequences of steps to follow in the text or figures in this book, we use the command terminology used by Oracle Database and associated utility programs in Microsoft Windows 10. If you are running a workstation operating system such as Microsoft Windows 7, Microsoft Windows 8.1, Microsoft Server 2019, or Linux, the terminology may vary somewhat.

---

Oracle Database is an enterprise-class DBMS product and, as is typical of such products, does not store queries within the DBMS. (It does store SQL Views, which can be considered a type of query, and we will discuss SQL Views later in this chapter.) However, you can save queries as SQL script files. An **SQL script file** is a separately stored plain-text file, and it usually has a file name extension of *.sql*. An SQL script can be opened and run as an SQL command (or set of commands). Often used to create and populate databases, scripts can also be used to store a query or set of queries. Figure 2-20 shows the SQL query being saved as an SQL script.

Note that in Figure 2-20 the SQL scripts are shown in a folder named *Users\{UserName}\ Documents\SQL Developer\DBP-e16-Cape-Codd-Database* as described in Chapter 10B.

We recommend that you create a folder in your Documents folder named *SQL Developer* and then create a subfolder for each database in the SQL Developer folder. We have created a folder named *DBP-e16-Cape-Codd-Database* to store the script files associated with the Cape Codd database.

### Saving an SQL Script in Oracle SQL Developer

1. Click the **Save** button. The Save dialog box appears, as shown in Figure 2-20.
2. Click the **Documents** button on the Save dialog box to move to the Documents folder, and then browse to the DBP-e16-Cape-Codd-Database folder.
3. Note that there are already two SQL script names displayed in the dialog box. These are the SQL scripts that were used to create and populate the Cape Codd database tables, and they are available on our Web site at *www.pearsonhighered.com/kroenke*.
4. In the File Name text box, type the SQL script file name *SQL-Query-CH02-01.sql*.
5. Click the **Save** button.

To rerun the saved query, you would click the SQL Developer **Open File** button to open the Open File dialog box, browse to the query file, open the query file, and then click the **Execute** button.

At this point, you should work through each of the other three queries in the preceding discussion of the SQL SELECT/FROM/WHERE framework. Save each query as SQLQuery-CH02-##, where ## is a sequential number from 02 to 04 that corresponds to the SQL

**FIGURE 2-20**

Saving an Oracle SQL Query
as an SQL Script in Oracle
SQL Developer

query label shown in the SQL comment line of each query. You can then continue working
through the rest of the example SQL statements as you read the chapter.

### Using SQL in Oracle MySQL 8.0

Before you can use SQL statements with Oracle MySQL 8.0, you need access to a computer that has MySQL installed and that has a database with the tables and data shown in
Figures 2-4, 2-5, and 2-6. Your instructor may have installed MySQL 8.0 in your computer
lab and entered the data for you. If so, follow his or her instructions for accessing that
database.

Otherwise, you will need to obtain a copy of MySQL Community Server 8.0 and install
it on your computer. At this time, read the material in Chapter 10C about obtaining and
installing MySQL Community Server 8.0.

After you have MySQL Community Sever 8.0 installed, you will need to read the discussion for MySQL Community Server 8.0 in Chapter 10C that explains how to create
the cape_codd database (note the use of all lowercase characters and an underscore in the
database name) and to run the MySQL scripts for creating and populating the cape_codd
database tables. The MySQL 8.0 SQL scripts for the cape_codd database are available on our
Web site at *www.pearsonhighered.com/kroenke*.

MySQL uses the MySQL Workbench as the GUI tool for managing the MySQL 8.0
DBMS and the databases controlled by the DBMS. This tool can be installed along with the
MySQL DBMS using the MySQL Installer, and this is discussed in Chapter 10C. SQL statements are created and run in the MySQL Workbench, and Figure 2-21 shows the execution
of SQL-Query-CH02-01 (note that the SQL comment is *not* included in the SQL statement
as run—also note that the SQL comment *could* have been included in the SQL code if we had
chosen to include it):

```
/* *** SQL-Query-CH02-01 *** */

SELECT    SKU, SKU_Description, Department, Buyer

FROM      SKU_DATA;
```

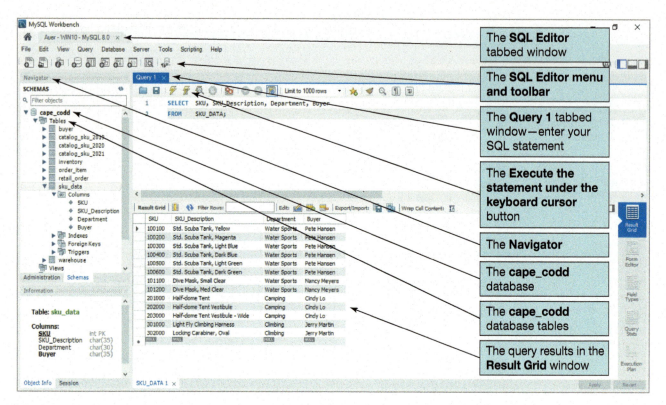

**FIGURE 2-21**

Running an SQL Query in the MySQL Workbench

*Running an SQL Query in the MySQL Workbench*

1. To make the cape_codd database the default schema (active database), right-click the cape_codd schema (database) object to display the shortcut menu and then click the **Set as Default Schema** command.
2. In the Query 1 tabbed window in the SQL Editor tabbed window, type the SQL SELECT command (*without* the SQL comment line shown earlier):

```
SELECT    SKU, SKU_Description, Department, Buyer
FROM      SKU_DATA;
```

The SQL query window now appears as shown in Figure 2-21.
3. Click the **Execute the statement under the keyboard cursor** button to run the query. The results are displayed in a tabbed Result Grid window, as shown in Figure 2-21.

Note that in Figure 2-21 the *cape_codd* database object in the Navigator in the left-side window of the MySQL Workbench has been expanded to show the tables in the cape_codd database. Many of the functions of the MySQL Workbench are associated with the objects in the Navigator and are often accessed by right-clicking the object to display a shortcut menu.

---

**BY THE WAY**   We are using MySQL 8.0 Community Server running in Windows 10. When we give specific sequences of steps to follow in the text or figures in this book, we use the command terminology used for MySQL 8.0 and associated utility programs in Microsoft Windows 10. If you are running a workstation operating system such as Microsoft Windows 7, Microsoft Windows 8.1, Microsoft Server 2016, or Linux, the terminology may vary somewhat.

MySQL 8.0 is an enterprise-class DBMS product and, as is typical of such products, does not store queries within the DBMS. (It does store SQL Views, which can be considered a type of query, and we will discuss SQL Views later in this chapter.) However, you can save MySQL queries as SQL script files. An **SQL script file** is a separately stored plain-text file, and it usually uses a file name extension of *.sql*. An SQL script file can be opened and run as an SQL command. Figure 2-22 shows the SQL query being saved as an SQL script file.

Note that in Figure 2-22 the query will be saved in a folder named *My Documents\ MySQL Workbench\Schemas\DBP-e16-Cape-Codd-Database* as described in Chapter 10C. By default, MySQL Workbench stores files in the user's Documents folder. We recommend that you create a subfolder for each MySQL database. We have created the folder named *DBP-e16-Cape-Codd-Database* to store the script files associated with the cape_codd database.

### Saving a MySQL Query in MySQL Workbench

1. Click the **Save the script to a file** button. The Save SQL Script dialog appears, as shown in Figure 2-22.
2. Browse to the *Documents\MySQL Workbench\Schemas\DBP-e16-Cape-Codd-Database* folder.
3. In the File name text box, type the SQL query file name *SQL-Query-CH02-01*.
4. Click the **Save** button.

To rerun the saved query, you would click the **File | Open SQL Script** menu command to open the Open SQL Script dialog box, then select and open the SQL query *.sql files, and, finally, click the **Execute the statement under the keyboard cursor** button.

At this point, you should work through each of the other three queries in the preceding discussion of the SQL SELECT/FROM/WHERE framework. Save each query as SQLQuery-CH02-##, where ## is a sequential number from 02 to 04 that corresponds to the SQL query label shown in the SQL comment line of each query. You can then continue working through the rest of the example SQL statements as you read the chapter.

**FIGURE 2-22**

Saving a MySQL Query as an SQL Script in the MySQL Workbench

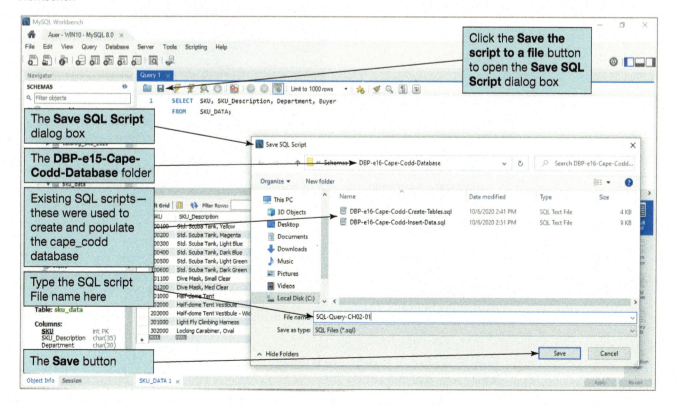

## SQL Enhancements for Querying a Single Table

Now that we know how to run SQL queries in the DBMS product that we are using, we can return to our discussion of SQL syntax itself. We started our discussion of SQL queries with SQL statements for processing a single table, and now we will add SQL features to those queries. As we proceed, you will begin to see how powerful SQL can be for querying databases and for creating information from existing data.

> **BY THE WAY**   The SQL results shown in this chapter were generated using Microsoft SQL Server 2019. Query results from other DBMS products will be similar but may vary a bit.

### Reading Specified Rows from a Single Table

Now that we know how to designate which *columns* will be included in the results of an SQL query, we need to discuss how to control which *rows* are included in the results.

Notice that in the results to SQL-Query-CH02-04 some rows are duplicated. The data in the first and second rows, for example, are identical. We can eliminate duplicates by using the **SQL DISTINCT keyword** as follows:

```
/* *** SQL-Query-CH02-05 *** */
SELECT     DISTINCT Buyer, Department
FROM       SKU_DATA;
```

The result of this statement, where all of the duplicate rows have been removed, is:

|   | Buyer | Department |
|---|-------|------------|
| 1 | Cindy Lo | Camping |
| 2 | Jerry Martin | Climbing |
| 3 | Nancy Meyers | Water Sports |
| 4 | Pete Hansen | Water Sports |

> **BY THE WAY**   The reason that SQL does not automatically eliminate duplicate rows is that it can be very time consuming to do so. To determine if any rows are duplicates, every row must be compared with every other row. If there are 100,000 rows in a table, checking that many rows will take a long time. Hence, by default duplicates are not removed. However, it is always possible to force their removal using the DISTINCT keyword.

We can also control how many rows are displayed by using the **SQL TOP {NumberOfRows} function** (SQL Server only, though Oracle Database and MySQL use a LIMIT clause to achieve the same effect). For example, if we want to see only the rows one through five from SQL-Query-CH02-04, we write:

```
/* *** SQL-Query-CH02-06 *** */
SELECT     TOP 5 Buyer, Department
FROM       SKU_DATA;
```

The result of this statement displays only the first five of the eight rows in the results for SQL-Query-CH02-04. Note that because we are *not* using the DISTINCT keyword, we get some identical duplicated rows in the result:

|   | Buyer | Department |
|---|---|---|
| 1 | Pete Hansen | Water Sports |
| 2 | Pete Hansen | Water Sports |
| 3 | Pete Hansen | Water Sports |
| 4 | Pete Hansen | Water Sports |
| 5 | Pete Hansen | Water Sports |

The SQL TOP function can also be used to display a percentage of the resulting rows by using the **SQL TOP {Percentage} PERCENT function** (SQL Server only, though Oracle Database uses a LIMIT clause to achieve the same effect). For example, if we want to see 75 percent of the data from SQL-Query-CH02-04, we write:

```
/* *** SQL-Query-CH02-07 *** */
SELECT    TOP 75 PERCENT Buyer, Department
FROM      SKU_DATA;
```

The result of this statement displays only the first ten of the 13 rows in the results for SQL-Query-CH02-04. Note that, again, because we are *not* using the DISTINCT keyword, we get some identical duplicated rows in the result:

|   | Buyer | Department |
|---|---|---|
| 1 | Pete Hansen | Water Sports |
| 2 | Pete Hansen | Water Sports |
| 3 | Pete Hansen | Water Sports |
| 4 | Pete Hansen | Water Sports |
| 5 | Pete Hansen | Water Sports |
| 6 | Pete Hansen | Water Sports |
| 7 | Nancy Meyers | Water Sports |
| 8 | Nancy Meyers | Water Sports |
| 9 | Cindy Lo | Camping |
| 10 | Cindy Lo | Camping |

The DISTINCT, TOP {NumberOfRows} and TOP {Percentage} PERCENT functions provide some help in controlling which rows are displayed in a result, but the real power for controlling rows in the output to the SQL SELECT statement is in the WHERE clause. Suppose we want all of the *columns* of the SKU_DATA table, but we want only the *rows* for the Water Sports department. We can obtain that result by using the SQL WHERE clause as follows:

```
/* *** SQL-Query-CH02-08 *** */
SELECT    *
FROM      SKU_DATA
WHERE     Department = 'Water Sports';
```

The result of this statement will be:

| | SKU | SKU_Description | Department | Buyer |
|---|---|---|---|---|
| 1 | 100100 | Std. Scuba Tank, Yellow | Water Sports | Pete Hansen |
| 2 | 100200 | Std. Scuba Tank, Magenta | Water Sports | Pete Hansen |
| 3 | 100300 | Std. Scuba Tank, Light Blue | Water Sports | Pete Hansen |
| 4 | 100400 | Std. Scuba Tank, Dark Blue | Water Sports | Pete Hansen |
| 5 | 100500 | Std. Scuba Tank, Light Green | Water Sports | Pete Hansen |
| 6 | 100600 | Std. Scuba Tank, Dark Green | Water Sports | Pete Hansen |
| 7 | 101100 | Dive Mask, Small Clear | Water Sports | Nancy Meyers |
| 8 | 101200 | Dive Mask, Med Clear | Water Sports | Nancy Meyers |

> **BY THE WAY**    SQL is very fussy about single quotes. It wants the plain, nondirectional quotes found in basic text editors. The fancy directional quotes produced by many word processors will produce errors, so if you copy and paste a query from certain word processing programs, you may get a syntax error. For example, the data value 'Water Sports' is correctly stated, but 'Water Sports' is not. Do you see the difference?

The equal sign (=) that appears in the WHERE clause of SQL-Query-CH02-08 is an **SQL comparison operator**. A list of common SQL comparison operators is shown in Figure 2-23.

In an SQL WHERE clause, if the column contains text or date data, the comparison values must be enclosed in single quotation marks ('{text or date data}'). For example, in the CATALOG_SKU_2020 table, only the SKUs that were available on the Cape Codd Web site

**FIGURE 2-23**

SQL Comparison Operators

| SQL Comparison Operators | |
|---|---|
| **Operator** | **Meaning** |
| = | Is equal to |
| <> | Is NOT Equal to |
| < | Is less than |
| > | Is greater than |
| <= | Is less than OR equal to |
| >= | Is greater than OR equal to |
| IN | Is equal to one of a set of values |
| NOT IN | Is NOT equal to one of a set of values |
| BETWEEN | Is within a range of numbers (includes the end points) |
| NOT BETWEEN | Is NOT within a range of numbers (includes the end points) |
| LIKE | Matches a sequence of characters |
| NOT LIKE | Does NOT match a sequence of characters |
| IS NULL | Is equal to NULL |
| IS NOT NULL | Is NOT equal to NULL |

on January 1, 2020 actually appeared in the printed catalog. To see these items, we use the following query:

```
/* *** SQL-Query-CH02-09 *** */

SELECT      *
FROM        CATALOG_SKU_2020
WHERE       DateOnWebSite = '01-JAN-2020';
```

The result of this statement will be:

|   | CatalogID | SKU | SKU_Description | Department | CatalogPage | DateOnWebSite |
|---|-----------|-----|----------------|------------|-------------|---------------|
| 1 | 20200001 | 100100 | Std. Scuba Tank, Yellow | Water Sports | 23 | 2020-01-01 |
| 2 | 20200002 | 100300 | Std. Scuba Tank, Light Blue | Water Sports | 23 | 2020-01-01 |
| 3 | 20200004 | 101100 | Dive Mask, Small Clear | Water Sports | 26 | 2020-01-01 |
| 4 | 20200005 | 101200 | Dive Mask, Med Clear | Water Sports | 26 | 2020-01-01 |
| 5 | 20200006 | 201000 | Half-dome Tent | Camping | 46 | 2020-01-01 |
| 6 | 20200007 | 202000 | Half-dome Tent Vestibule | Camping | 46 | 2020-01-01 |
| 7 | 20200008 | 301000 | Light Fly Climbing Harness | Climbing | 77 | 2020-01-01 |
| 8 | 20200009 | 302000 | Locking Carabiner, Oval | Climbing | 79 | 2020-01-01 |

**BY THE WAY**  When using a date in the WHERE clause, you can usually enclose it in single quotes just as you would a character string as shown in SQL-Query-CH02-09. However, when using Microsoft Access 2019, you *must* enclose dates within the # symbol. For example:

```
/* *** SQL-Query-CH02-09-Access *** */

SELECT      *
FROM        CATALOG_SKU_2020
WHERE       DateOnWebSite = #01/01/2020#;
```

Oracle Database and MySQL 8.0 can also have idiosyncrasies when using date data in SQL statements, and this is discussed in Chapters 10B and 10C, respectively. SQL-Query-CH02-09 will work as written in Oracle Database, but in MySQL the date constant will need to be written as '2020-01-01'.

If the column contains numeric data, however, the comparison values need not be in quotes. Thus, to find all of the SKU rows with a value greater than 200,000, we would use the SQL statement (note that no comma is included in the numeric value code):

```
/* *** SQL-Query-CH02-10 *** */

SELECT      *
FROM        SKU_DATA
WHERE       SKU > 200000;
```

The result is:

|   | SKU | SKU_Description | Department | Buyer |
|---|-----|----------------|------------|-------|
| 1 | 201000 | Half-dome Tent | Camping | Cindy Lo |
| 2 | 202000 | Half-dome Tent Vestibule | Camping | Cindy Lo |
| 3 | 203000 | Half-dome Tent Vestibule - Wide | Camping | Cindy Lo |
| 4 | 301000 | Light Fly Climbing Harness | Climbing | Jerry Martin |
| 5 | 302000 | Locking Carabiner, Oval | Climbing | Jerry Martin |

## Reading Specified Columns and Rows from a Single Table

So far, we have generally selected certain columns and *all* rows, or we have selected *all* columns and certain rows (the exceptions being our discussion of the DISTINCT, TOP {NumberOfRows}, and TOP {Percentage} PERCENT functions). However, we can combine these operations to select certain columns and certain rows by naming the columns we want and then using the SQL WHERE clause. For example, to obtain the SKU_Description and Department of all products in the Climbing department, we use the SQL query:

```
/* *** SQL-Query-CH02-11 *** */
SELECT    SKU_Description, Department
FROM      SKU_DATA
WHERE     Department = 'Climbing';
```

The result is:

| | SKU_Description | Department |
|---|---|---|
| 1 | Light Fly Climbing Harness | Climbing |
| 2 | Locking Carabiner, Oval | Climbing |

SQL does not require that the column used in the WHERE clause also appear in the SELECT clause column list. Thus, we can specify:

```
/* *** SQL-Query-CH02-12 *** */
SELECT    SKU_Description, Buyer
FROM      SKU_DATA
WHERE     Department = 'Climbing';
```

where the qualifying column, Department, does not appear in the SELECT clause column list. The result is:

| | SKU_Description | Buyer |
|---|---|---|
| 1 | Light Fly Climbing Harness | Jerry Martin |
| 2 | Locking Carabiner, Oval | Jerry Martin |

> **BY THE WAY**  Standard practice is to write SQL statements with the SELECT, FROM, and WHERE clauses on separate lines. This practice is just a coding convention, however, and SQL parsers do not require it. You could write the code for SQL-Query-CH02-12 all altogether as:
>
> ```
> SELECT SKU_Description, Buyer FROM SKU_DATA WHERE
> Department = 'Climbing';
> ```
>
> All DBMS products would process the statement written in this fashion. However, the standard multiline coding convention makes SQL easier to read, and we encourage you to write your SQL code according to it.

## Sorting the SQL Query Results

The order of the rows produced by an SQL statement is arbitrary and determined by programs in the bowels of each DBMS. If you want the DBMS to display the rows in a particular order, you can add the **SQL ORDER BY clause** to the SELECT/FROM/WHERE framework. For example, to sort the rows in the ORDER_ITEM table by OrderNumber in ascending order (the default sorting order), you use the SQL statement:

```
/* *** SQL-Query-CH02-13 *** */

SELECT       *
FROM         ORDER_ITEM
ORDER BY     OrderNumber;
```

SQL-Query-CH02-13 will generate the following results:

|   | OrderNumber | SKU | Quantity | Price | ExtendedPrice |
|---|---|---|---|---|---|
| 1 | 1000 | 201000 | 1 | 300.00 | 300.00 |
| 2 | 1000 | 202000 | 1 | 130.00 | 130.00 |
| 3 | 2000 | 101100 | 4 | 50.00 | 200.00 |
| 4 | 2000 | 101200 | 2 | 50.00 | 100.00 |
| 5 | 3000 | 101200 | 1 | 50.00 | 50.00 |
| 6 | 3000 | 101100 | 2 | 50.00 | 100.00 |
| 7 | 3000 | 100200 | 1 | 300.00 | 300.00 |

We can sort by two columns by adding a second column name. For example, to sort first by OrderNumber and then by Price within OrderNumber, we use the following SQL query:

```
/* *** SQL-Query-CH02-14 *** */

SELECT       *
FROM         ORDER_ITEM
ORDER BY     OrderNumber, Price;
```

The result for this query is:

|   | OrderNumber | SKU | Quantity | Price | ExtendedPrice |
|---|---|---|---|---|---|
| 1 | 1000 | 202000 | 1 | 130.00 | 130.00 |
| 2 | 1000 | 201000 | 1 | 300.00 | 300.00 |
| 3 | 2000 | 101100 | 4 | 50.00 | 200.00 |
| 4 | 2000 | 101200 | 2 | 50.00 | 100.00 |
| 5 | 3000 | 101200 | 1 | 50.00 | 50.00 |
| 6 | 3000 | 101100 | 2 | 50.00 | 100.00 |
| 7 | 3000 | 100200 | 1 | 300.00 | 300.00 |

If we want to sort the data by Price and then by OrderNumber, we would simply reverse the order of those columns in the ORDER BY clause as follows:

```
/* *** SQL-Query-CH02-15 *** */

SELECT       *
FROM         ORDER_ITEM
ORDER BY     Price, OrderNumber;
```

This SQL query has the following results:

| | OrderNumber | SKU | Quantity | Price | ExtendedPrice |
|---|---|---|---|---|---|
| 1 | 2000 | 101100 | 4 | 50.00 | 200.00 |
| 2 | 2000 | 101200 | 2 | 50.00 | 100.00 |
| 3 | 3000 | 101200 | 1 | 50.00 | 50.00 |
| 4 | 3000 | 101100 | 2 | 50.00 | 100.00 |
| 5 | 1000 | 202000 | 1 | 130.00 | 130.00 |
| 6 | 1000 | 201000 | 1 | 300.00 | 300.00 |
| 7 | 3000 | 100200 | 1 | 300.00 | 300.00 |

---

**BY THE WAY**　Note to Microsoft Access users: Unlike the SQL Server output shown here, Microsoft Access displays dollar signs in the output of currency data.

---

By default, rows are sorted in *ascending* order. To sort in *descending order*, add the **SQL DESC keyword** after the column name. Thus, to sort first by Price in descending order and then by OrderNumber in ascending order, we use the SQL query:

```
/* *** SQL-Query-CH02-16 *** */
SELECT        *
FROM          ORDER_ITEM
ORDER BY      Price DESC, OrderNumber ASC;
```

The result is:

| | OrderNumber | SKU | Quantity | Price | ExtendedPrice |
|---|---|---|---|---|---|
| 1 | 1000 | 201000 | 1 | 300.00 | 300.00 |
| 2 | 3000 | 100200 | 1 | 300.00 | 300.00 |
| 3 | 1000 | 202000 | 1 | 130.00 | 130.00 |
| 4 | 2000 | 101100 | 4 | 50.00 | 200.00 |
| 5 | 2000 | 101200 | 2 | 50.00 | 100.00 |
| 6 | 3000 | 101200 | 1 | 50.00 | 50.00 |
| 7 | 3000 | 101100 | 2 | 50.00 | 100.00 |

Because the default order is ascending, it is not necessary to specify ASC in the last SQL statement. Thus, the following SQL statement is equivalent to the previous SQL query:

```
/* *** SQL-Query-CH02-17 *** */
SELECT        *
FROM          ORDER_ITEM
ORDER BY      Price DESC, OrderNumber;
```

This query produces the same results:

| | OrderNumber | SKU | Quantity | Price | ExtendedPrice |
|---|---|---|---|---|---|
| 1 | 1000 | 201000 | 1 | 300.00 | 300.00 |
| 2 | 3000 | 100200 | 1 | 300.00 | 300.00 |
| 3 | 1000 | 202000 | 1 | 130.00 | 130.00 |
| 4 | 2000 | 101100 | 4 | 50.00 | 200.00 |
| 5 | 2000 | 101200 | 2 | 50.00 | 100.00 |
| 6 | 3000 | 101200 | 1 | 50.00 | 50.00 |
| 7 | 3000 | 101100 | 2 | 50.00 | 100.00 |

## SQL WHERE Clause Options

SQL includes a number of SQL WHERE clause options that greatly expand SQL's power and utility. In this section, we consider five options: compound clauses, sets of values, ranges, wildcards, and NULL values.

### Compound SQL WHERE Clauses Using Logical Operators

SQL WHERE clauses can include multiple conditions by using the **SQL logical operators**, which include the AND, OR, and NOT operators and which are summarized in Figure 2-24.

The **SQL AND operator** requires that each row in the results meets *both* of the conditions specified in the WHERE clause. For example, to find all of the rows in SKU_DATA that have *both* a Department named Water Sports and a Buyer named Nancy Meyers, we can use the SQL AND operator in our query code:

```
/* *** SQL-Query-CH02-18 *** */
SELECT      *
FROM        SKU_DATA
WHERE       Department='Water Sports'
    AND     Buyer='Nancy Meyers';
```

The results of this query are:

|   | SKU | SKU_Description | Department | Buyer |
|---|-----|----------------|------------|-------|
| 1 | 101100 | Dive Mask, Small Clear | Water Sports | Nancy Meyers |
| 2 | 101200 | Dive Mask, Med Clear | Water Sports | Nancy Meyers |

The **SQL OR operator** requires that each row in the results meets *one or the other or both* of the conditions specified in the WHERE clause. Thus, to find all of the rows of SKU_DATA for either the Camping *or* Climbing departments, we can use the SQL OR operator in the SQL query:

```
/* *** SQL-Query-CH02-19 *** */
SELECT      *
FROM        SKU_DATA
WHERE       Department='Camping'
    OR      Department='Climbing';
```

This SQL query gives us the following results:

|   | SKU | SKU_Description | Department | Buyer |
|---|-----|----------------|------------|-------|
| 1 | 201000 | Half-dome Tent | Camping | Cindy Lo |
| 2 | 202000 | Half-dome Tent Vestibule | Camping | Cindy Lo |
| 3 | 203000 | Half-dome Tent Vestibule - Wide | Camping | Cindy Lo |
| 4 | 301000 | Light Fly Climbing Harness | Climbing | Jerry Martin |
| 5 | 302000 | Locking Carabiner, Oval | Climbing | Jerry Martin |

**FIGURE 2-24**

SQL Logical Operators

| SQL Logical Operators | |
|---|---|
| **Operator** | **Meaning** |
| AND | Both conditions are TRUE |
| OR | One or the other or both of the conditions are TRUE |
| NOT | Negates the associated condition |

The **SQL NOT operator** negates or reverses a condition. For example, to find all of the rows in SKU_DATA that have a Department named Water Sports but *not* a Buyer named Nancy Meyers, we can use the SQL NOT operator in our query code:

```
/* *** SQL-Query-CH02-20 *** */
SELECT        *
FROM          SKU_DATA
WHERE         Department='Water Sports'
    AND NOT   Buyer='Nancy Meyers';
```

The results of this query are:

| | SKU | SKU_Description | Department | Buyer |
|---|---|---|---|---|
| 1 | 100100 | Std. Scuba Tank, Yellow | Water Sports | Pete Hansen |
| 2 | 100200 | Std. Scuba Tank, Magenta | Water Sports | Pete Hansen |
| 3 | 100300 | Std. Scuba Tank, Light Blue | Water Sports | Pete Hansen |
| 4 | 100400 | Std. Scuba Tank, Dark Blue | Water Sports | Pete Hansen |
| 5 | 100500 | Std. Scuba Tank, Light Green | Water Sports | Pete Hansen |
| 6 | 100600 | Std. Scuba Tank, Dark Green | Water Sports | Pete Hansen |

Three or more AND and OR conditions can be combined, but in such cases it is often easiest to use SQL IN and NOT IN comparison operators.

### SQL WHERE Clauses Using Sets of Values

When we want to include a set of values in the SQL WHERE clause, we use the **SQL IN operator** or the **SQL NOT IN operator** (Figure 2-23). For example, suppose we want to obtain all of the rows in SKU_DATA for the set of buyers Nancy Meyers, Cindy Lo, and Jerry Martin. We could construct a WHERE clause with two OR conditions, but an easier way to do this is to use the SQL IN operator, which specifies the set of values to be used in the SQL query:

```
/* *** SQL-Query-CH02-21 *** */
SELECT    *
FROM      SKU_DATA
WHERE     Buyer IN ('Nancy Meyers', 'Cindy Lo', 'Jerry Martin');
```

In this format, the set of values is enclosed in parentheses. A row is selected if Buyer is equal to any one of the values provided. The result is:

| | SKU | SKU_Description | Department | Buyer |
|---|---|---|---|---|
| 1 | 101100 | Dive Mask, Small Clear | Water Sports | Nancy Meyers |
| 2 | 101200 | Dive Mask, Med Clear | Water Sports | Nancy Meyers |
| 3 | 201000 | Half-dome Tent | Camping | Cindy Lo |
| 4 | 202000 | Half-dome Tent Vestibule | Camping | Cindy Lo |
| 5 | 203000 | Half-dome Tent Vestibule - Wide | Camping | Cindy Lo |
| 6 | 301000 | Light Fly Climbing Harness | Climbing | Jerry Martin |
| 7 | 302000 | Locking Carabiner, Oval | Climbing | Jerry Martin |

Similarly, if we want to find rows of SKU_DATA for which the buyer is someone *other* than Nancy Meyers, Cindy Lo, or Jerry Martin, we would use the SQL NOT IN operator, which specifies the set of values to be *excluded* from the SQL query:

```
/* *** SQL-Query-CH02-22 *** */
SELECT    *
FROM      SKU_DATA
WHERE     Buyer NOT IN ('Nancy Meyers', 'Cindy Lo', 'Jerry Martin');
```

The result is:

|   | SKU | SKU_Description | Department | Buyer |
|---|-----|----------------|------------|-------|
| 1 | 100100 | Std. Scuba Tank, Yellow | Water Sports | Pete Hansen |
| 2 | 100200 | Std. Scuba Tank, Magenta | Water Sports | Pete Hansen |
| 3 | 100300 | Std. Scuba Tank, Light Blue | Water Sports | Pete Hansen |
| 4 | 100400 | Std. Scuba Tank, Dark Blue | Water Sports | Pete Hansen |
| 5 | 100500 | Std. Scuba Tank, Light Green | Water Sports | Pete Hansen |
| 6 | 100600 | Std. Scuba Tank, Dark Green | Water Sports | Pete Hansen |

Observe an important difference between the IN and NOT IN operators:

- A row qualifies for an IN condition if the column is *equal* to *any* of the values in the parentheses.
- A row qualifies for a NOT IN condition if it is *not equal* to *all* of the items in the parentheses.

### SQL WHERE Clauses Using Ranges of Values

When we want to include or exclude a range of numerical values in the SQL WHERE clause, we use the **SQL BETWEEN operator** or the **SQL NOT BETWEEN operator** (Figure 2-23).

For example, suppose that we want to find all the rows in the ORDER_ITEM table where ExtendedPrice ranges from $100.00 to $200.00, including the end points of the range, $100.00 and $200.00. We could use the SQL query:

```
/* *** SQL-Query-CH02-23 *** */
SELECT     *
FROM       ORDER_ITEM
WHERE      ExtendedPrice >= 100
   AND     ExtendedPrice <= 200
ORDER BY   ExtendedPrice;
```

The SQL query produces the results sorted in order of ascending ExtendedPrice so that we can easily see the smallest and largest values:

|   | OrderNumber | SKU | Quantity | Price | ExtendedPrice |
|---|-------------|-----|----------|-------|---------------|
| 1 | 3000 | 101100 | 2 | 50.00 | 100.00 |
| 2 | 2000 | 101200 | 2 | 50.00 | 100.00 |
| 3 | 1000 | 202000 | 1 | 130.00 | 130.00 |
| 4 | 2000 | 101100 | 4 | 50.00 | 200.00 |

However, rather than specifying the range of values by using a compound SQL WHERE clause, we can accomplish the same results by using the SQL BETWEEN operator. Note how the SQL BETWEEN operator is used to create a simple, one-line WHERE clause in this SQL query:

```
/* *** SQL-Query-CH02-24 *** */
SELECT      *
FROM        ORDER_ITEM
WHERE       ExtendedPrice BETWEEN 100 AND 200
ORDER BY    ExtendedPrice;
```

The results of SQL-Query-CH02-24 are identical to those from SQL-Query-CH02-23 shown earlier, and note again that the specified end values of the range are included in the SQL query results:

| | OrderNumber | SKU | Quantity | Price | ExtendedPrice |
|---|---|---|---|---|---|
| 1 | 3000 | 101100 | 2 | 50.00 | 100.00 |
| 2 | 2000 | 101200 | 2 | 50.00 | 100.00 |
| 3 | 1000 | 202000 | 1 | 130.00 | 130.00 |
| 4 | 2000 | 101100 | 4 | 50.00 | 200.00 |

On the other hand, if we want to find all the rows in the ORDER_ITEM table *excluding* the ExtendedPrice range from $100.00 to $200.00, we can use the SQL NOT BETWEEN operator. In this case, the SQL query is:

```
/* *** SQL-Query-CH02-25 *** */
SELECT      *
FROM        ORDER_ITEM
WHERE       ExtendedPrice NOT BETWEEN 100 AND 200
ORDER BY    ExtendedPrice;
```

This gives us the following results (again sorted from lowest to highest ExtendedPrice):

| | OrderNumber | SKU | Quantity | Price | ExtendedPrice |
|---|---|---|---|---|---|
| 1 | 3000 | 101200 | 1 | 50.00 | 50.00 |
| 2 | 1000 | 201000 | 1 | 300.00 | 300.00 |
| 3 | 3000 | 100200 | 1 | 300.00 | 300.00 |

### SQL WHERE Clauses That Use Character String Patterns

There are times when we want to uses the SQL WHERE clause to find matching sets or patterns of *character strings*. **Character strings** include the data that we store in a CHAR or VARCHAR data type column (CHAR columns use a fixed number of bytes to store the data, whereas VARCHAR columns adjust the number of bytes used to fit the actual length of the data—see Chapter 6 for a full discussion of data types) and are composed of letters, numbers, and special characters. For example, the name *Smith* is a character string, as are *360-567-9876* and *Joe#34@elsewhere.com*. To find rows with values that match or do not match specific character string patterns, we use the **SQL LIKE operator** and the **SQL NOT LIKE operator** (Figure 2-23).

To help specify character string patterns, we use two SQL wildcard characters:

- The **SQL underscore (_) wildcard character**, which represents a single, unspecified character in a specific position in the character string.
- The **SQL percent sign (%) wildcard character**, which represents any sequence of contiguous, unspecified characters (including spaces) in a specific position in the character string.

For example, suppose we want to find the rows in the SKU_DATA table for all buyers whose first name begins with *Pete*. To find such rows, we use the SQL LIKE operator with the SQL percent sign (%) wildcard character, as shown in the SQL-Query-CH02-26 query:

```
/* *** SQL-Query-CH02-26 *** */

SELECT    *

FROM      SKU_DATA

WHERE     Buyer LIKE 'Pete%';
```

When used as an SQL wildcard character, the percent symbol (%) stands for any sequence of characters. When used with the SQL LIKE operator, the character string 'Pete%' means any sequence of characters that starts with the letters *Pete*. The result of this SQL query is:

| | SKU | SKU_Description | Department | Buyer |
|---|---|---|---|---|
| 1 | 100100 | Std. Scuba Tank, Yellow | Water Sports | Pete Hansen |
| 2 | 100200 | Std. Scuba Tank, Magenta | Water Sports | Pete Hansen |
| 3 | 100300 | Std. Scuba Tank, Light Blue | Water Sports | Pete Hansen |
| 4 | 100400 | Std. Scuba Tank, Dark Blue | Water Sports | Pete Hansen |
| 5 | 100500 | Std. Scuba Tank, Light Green | Water Sports | Pete Hansen |
| 6 | 100600 | Std. Scuba Tank, Dark Green | Water Sports | Pete Hansen |

> **Does Not Work with Microsoft Access ANSI-89 SQL**
>
> Microsoft Access ANSI-89 SQL uses wildcards, but not the SQL-92 standard wildcards. Microsoft Access uses the **Microsoft Access asterisk (*) wildcard character** instead of a percent sign to represent multiple characters.
>
> **Solution:** Use the Microsoft Access asterisk (*) wildcard in place of the SQL-92 percent sign (%) wildcard in Microsoft Access ANSI-89 SQL statements. Thus, the preceding SQL query would be written as follows for Microsoft Access:
>
> ```
> /* *** SQL-Query-CH02-26-Access *** */
>
> SELECT    *
>
> FROM      SKU_DATA
>
> WHERE     Buyer LIKE 'Pete*';
> ```

Next, suppose we want to find the rows in SKU_DATA for which the SKU_Description includes the word *Tent* somewhere in the description. Because the word *Tent* could be at the front, at the end, or in the middle, we need to place a wildcard on both ends of the SQL LIKE phrase as follows:

```
/* *** SQL-Query-CH02-27 *** */

SELECT    *

FROM      SKU_DATA

WHERE     SKU_Description LIKE '%Tent%';
```

This query will find rows in which the word *Tent* occurs in any place in the SKU_Description. The result is:

| | SKU | SKU_Description | Department | Buyer |
|---|---|---|---|---|
| 1 | 201000 | Half-dome Tent | Camping | Cindy Lo |
| 2 | 202000 | Half-dome Tent Vestibule | Camping | Cindy Lo |
| 3 | 203000 | Half-dome Tent Vestibule - Wide | Camping | Cindy Lo |

Sometimes we need to search for a particular value in a particular location in the column. For example, assume SKU values are coded such that a 2 in the third position from the right has some particular significance; maybe it means that the product is a variation of another product. For whatever reason, assume that we need to find all SKUs that have a 2 in the third column from the right. Suppose we try the following SQL query:

```
/* *** SQL-Query-CH02-28 *** */

SELECT      *

FROM        SKU_DATA

WHERE       SKU LIKE '%2%';
```

The result of this query is:

| | SKU | SKU_Description | Department | Buyer |
|---|---|---|---|---|
| 1 | 100200 | Std. Scuba Tank, Magenta | Water Sports | Pete Hansen |
| 2 | 101200 | Dive Mask, Med Clear | Water Sports | Nancy Meyers |
| 3 | 201000 | Half-dome Tent | Camping | Cindy Lo |
| 4 | 202000 | Half-dome Tent Vestibule | Camping | Cindy Lo |
| 5 | 203000 | Half-dome Tent Vestibule - Wide | Camping | Cindy Lo |
| 6 | 302000 | Locking Carabiner, Oval | Climbing | Jerry Martin |

This is *not* what we wanted. We mistakenly retrieved all rows that had a 2 in *any* position in the value of SKU. To find the products we want, we cannot use the SQL wildcard character %. Instead, we must use the SQL underscore (_) wildcard character, which represents a single, unspecified character in a specific position. The following SQL statement will find all SKU_DATA rows with a value of 2 in the third position from the right:

```
/* *** SQL-Query-CH02-29 *** */

SELECT      *

FROM        SKU_DATA

WHERE       SKU LIKE '%2__';
```

Observe that there are *two* underscores in this SQL query—one for the first position on the right and another for the second position on the right. This query gives us the result that we want:

| | SKU | SKU_Description | Department | Buyer |
|---|---|---|---|---|
| 1 | 100200 | Std. Scuba Tank, Magenta | Water Sports | Pete Hansen |
| 2 | 101200 | Dive Mask, Med Clear | Water Sports | Nancy Meyers |

> **BY THE WAY**  Although our example in SQL-Query-CH02-29 is correct, it does oversimplify this type of wildcard search a bit. In SQL-Query-CH02-29, SKU is an *INTEGER* valued column (with the values automatically converted by the DBMS to character strings during the query).
>
> If SKU had been a VARCHAR column, the same query would work. But if SKU had been a CHAR column, the query may not have worked because there could be extra spaces to the right of the characters used as padding to completely fill the CHAR length. For example, if we store the value "four" in a CHAR(8) column named *Number*, the DBMS will actually store "four____" ("four" plus four spaces). To deal with these extra spaces, we use the RTRIM function to remove the trailing blanks before the comparison is performed:
>
> ```
> WHERE    RTRIM(Number) LIKE 'four';
> ```

**Does Not Work with Microsoft Access ANSI-89 SQL**

Microsoft Access ANSI-89 SQL uses wildcards, but not the SQL-92 standard wildcards. Microsoft Access uses the **Microsoft Access question mark (?) wildcard character** instead of an underscore (_) to represent a single character.

Solution: Use the Microsoft Access question mark (?) wildcard in place of the SQL-92 underscore (_) wildcard in Microsoft Access ANSI-89 SQL statements. Thus, the preceding SQL query would be written as follows for Microsoft Access:

```
/* *** SQL-Query-CH02-29-Access *** */

SELECT      *

FROM        SKU_DATA

WHERE       SKU LIKE '*2??';
```

Furthermore, Microsoft Access can sometimes be fussy about stored trailing spaces in a text field. You may have problems with a WHERE clause like this:

```
WHERE       SKU LIKE '10?200';
```

Solution: Use the right trim function RTRIM to eliminate trailing spaces:

```
WHERE       RTRIM(SKU) LIKE '10?200';
```

---

**BY THE WAY**    The SQL wildcard percent sign (%) and underscore (_) characters are specified in the SQL-92 standard. They are accepted by all DBMS products *except Microsoft Access*. So why does Microsoft Access use the asterisk (*) character instead of the percent sign (%) and the question mark (?) instead of the underscore? These differences exist because Microsoft Access is, as we noted earlier, using the SQL-89 standard (which Microsoft calls ANSI-89 SQL). In that standard, the asterisk (*) and the question mark (?) are the correct wildcard characters. Switch a Microsoft Access database to SQL-92 (which Microsoft calls ANSI-92 SQL) in the Access Options dialog box, and the percent sign (%) and underscore (_) characters will work.[2]

### SQL WHERE Clauses That Use NULL Values

As we discussed earlier in this chapter, a missing data value is called a *null value*. In relational databases, null values are indicated with the special marker **NULL** (written as shown in uppercase letters). When we want to include or exclude rows that contain NULL values, we use the **SQL IS NULL operator** or the **SQL IS NOT NULL operator** (Figure 2-23). Note that in this situation the **SQL IS keyword** is equivalent to an *is equal to* comparison operator. However, the *is equal to* comparison operator is *never* used with NULL values, and the IS NULL and IS NOT NULL operators are *never* used with values other than NULL.

For example, suppose that we want to find all the SKUs in the CATALOG_SKU_2020 table that were *not* included in the printed catalog. Because SKUs that were not in the catalog have a CatalogPage value of NULL, we can use the IS NULL operator to find them. Thus, we can use the following SQL query:

```
/* *** SQL-Query-CH02-30 *** */

SELECT      *

FROM        CATALOG_SKU_2020

WHERE       CatalogPage IS NULL;
```

---

[2]Note that additional wildcard characters can be used in Microsoft Access character string patterns. For more information on both ANSI-89 and ANSI-92 versions of Microsoft Access wildcard characters, see *https://support.microsoft.com/en-us/office/access-wildcard-character-reference-af00c501-7972-40ee-8889-e18abaad12d1?ui=en-us&rs=en-us&ad=us* (accessed October 2020).

This query gives us the result that we want:

| | CatalogID | SKU | SKU_Description | Department | CatalogPage | DateOnWebSite |
|---|---|---|---|---|---|---|
| 1 | 20200003 | 100400 | Std. Scuba Tank, Dark Blue | Water Sports | NULL | 2020-08-01 |

Similarly, if we want to find all the SKUs in the CATALOG_SKU_2020 table that *were*, we can use the IS NOT NULL operator to find them. This gives us the following SQL query:

```
/* *** SQL-Query-CH02-31 *** */
SELECT       *
FROM         CATALOG_SKU_2020
WHERE        CatalogPage IS NOT NULL;
```

This query gives us the following results:

| | CatalogID | SKU | SKU_Description | Department | CatalogPage | DateOnWebSite |
|---|---|---|---|---|---|---|
| 1 | 20200001 | 100100 | Std. Scuba Tank, Yellow | Water Sports | 23 | 2020-01-01 |
| 2 | 20200002 | 100300 | Std. Scuba Tank, Light Blue | Water Sports | 23 | 2020-01-01 |
| 3 | 20200004 | 101100 | Dive Mask, Small Clear | Water Sports | 26 | 2020-01-01 |
| 4 | 20200005 | 101200 | Dive Mask, Med Clear | Water Sports | 26 | 2020-01-01 |
| 5 | 20200006 | 201000 | Half-dome Tent | Camping | 46 | 2020-01-01 |
| 6 | 20200007 | 202000 | Half-dome Tent Vestibule | Camping | 46 | 2020-01-01 |
| 7 | 20200008 | 301000 | Light Fly Climbing Harness | Climbing | 77 | 2020-01-01 |
| 8 | 20200009 | 302000 | Locking Carabiner, Oval | Climbing | 79 | 2020-01-01 |

## Performing Calculations in SQL Queries

It is possible to perform certain types of calculations in SQL query statements. One group of calculations involves the use of SQL built-in functions. Another group involves simple arithmetic operations on the columns in the SELECT statement. We will consider each in turn.

### Using SQL Built-in Aggregate Functions

There are five standard **SQL built-in aggregate functions** for performing arithmetic on table columns: **SUM**, **AVG**, **MIN**, **MAX**, and **COUNT**. These are summarized in Figure 2-25. Some DBMS products extend these standard built-in functions by providing additional functions. Here we will focus only on the five standard SQL built-in aggregate functions.

**FIGURE 2-25**

SQL Built-In Aggregate Functions

| SQL Built-in Aggregate Functions | |
|---|---|
| **Function** | **Meaning** |
| COUNT(*) | Count the number of rows in the table |
| COUNT ({Name}) | Count the number of rows in the table where column {Name} IS NOT NULL |
| SUM | Calculate the sum of all values (numeric columns only) |
| AVG | Calculate the average of all values (numeric columns only) |
| MIN | Calculate the minimum value of all values |
| MAX | Calculate the maximum value of all values |

Suppose we want to know the sum of OrderTotal for all of the orders in RETAIL_ORDER. We can obtain that sum by using the SQL built-in SUM function:

```
/* *** SQL-Query-CH02-32 *** */
SELECT     SUM(OrderTotal)
FROM       RETAIL_ORDER;
```

The result will be:

Recall that the result of an SQL statement is always a table. In this case, the table has one cell (the intersection of one row and one column that contains the sum of OrderTotal). But because the OrderTotal sum is not a column in a table, the DBMS has no column name to provide. The preceding result was produced by Microsoft SQL Server 2019, and it names the column '(No column name)'. Other DBMS products take other, equivalent actions.

This result is ugly. We would prefer to have a meaningful column name, and SQL allows us to assign one using the **SQL AS keyword**. We can use the AS keyword in the query as follows:

```
/* *** SQL-Query-CH02-33 *** */
SELECT     SUM(OrderTotal) AS OrderSum
FROM       RETAIL_ORDER;
```

The result of this modified query will be:

This result has a much more meaningful column label. The name *OrderSum* is arbitrary—we are free to pick any name that we think would be meaningful to the user of the result. We could pick *OrderTotal_Total*, *OrderTotalSum*, or any other label that we think would be useful.

The utility of the built-in functions increases when you use them with an SQL WHERE clause. For example, we can write the following SQL query:

```
/* *** SQL-Query-CH02-34 *** */
SELECT     SUM(ExtendedPrice) AS Order3000Sum
FROM       ORDER_ITEM
WHERE      OrderNumber=3000;
```

The result of this query is:

The SQL built-in functions can be mixed and matched in a single statement. For example, we can create the following SQL statement:

```
/* *** SQL-Query-CH02-35 *** */
SELECT     SUM(ExtendedPrice) AS OrderItemSum,
           AVG(ExtendedPrice) AS OrderItemAvg,
           MIN(ExtendedPrice) AS OrderItemMin,
           MAX(ExtendedPrice) AS OrderItemMax
FROM       ORDER_ITEM;
```

The result of this query is:

| | OrderItemSum | OrderItemAvg | OrderItemMin | OrderItemMax |
|---|---|---|---|---|
| 1 | 1180.00 | 168.571428 | 50.00 | 300.00 |

The SQL built-in COUNT function sounds similar to the SUM function, but it produces very different results. The COUNT function *counts* the number of rows, whereas the SUM function *adds* the values in a column. For example, we can use the SQL built-in COUNT function to determine how many rows are in the ORDER_ITEM table:

```
/* *** SQL-Query-CH02-36 *** */
SELECT       COUNT(*) AS NumberOfRows
FROM         ORDER_ITEM;
```

The result of this query is:

| | NumberOfRows |
|---|---|
| 1 | 7 |

This result indicates that there are seven rows in the ORDER_ITEM table. Notice that we need to provide an asterisk (*) after the COUNT function when we want to count rows. COUNT is the only built-in function whose parameter can be the asterisk (as used in SQL-Query-CH02-36) or a column name (as used in SQL-Query-CH02-37 that follows). When used with a column name, it counts the number of rows that contain valid data—that is, data other than the NULL value.

The COUNT, MIN, and MAX functions can be used on any type of data, but the SUM and AVG functions can only be used with numeric data. Also note that the SQL DISTINCT keyword can be used with any of the SQL aggregate functions (except in Microsoft Access), but it is most commonly used with the COUNT function.

The COUNT function can produce some surprising results. For example, suppose you want to count the number of departments in the SKU_DATA table. First, we use the following query:

```
/* *** SQL-Query-CH02-37 *** */
SELECT       COUNT(Department) AS DeptCount
FROM         SKU_DATA;
```

The result of SQL-Query-CH02-37 is:

| | DeptCount |
|---|---|
| 1 | 13 |

However, this is the number of rows in the SKU_DATA table, *not* the number of unique values of Department, as shown in Figure 2-6. If we want to count the unique values of Department, we need to use the SQL DISTINCT keyword as follows:

```
/* *** SQL-Query-CH02-38 *** */
SELECT       COUNT(DISTINCT Department) AS DeptCount
FROM         SKU_DATA;
```

The result of SQL-Query-CH02-38 is correct:

| | DeptCount |
|---|---|
| 1 | 3 |

> ### Does Not Work with Microsoft Access ANSI-89 SQL
>
> Microsoft Access does not support the DISTINCT keyword as part of the COUNT expression, so although the SQL command with COUNT(Department) will work, the SQL command with COUNT(DISTINCT Department) will fail.
>
> **Solution:** Use an SQL subquery structure (discussed later in this chapter) with the DISTINCT keyword in the subquery itself. This SQL query works:
>
> ```
> /* *** SQL-Query-CH02-38-Access *** */
> SELECT    COUNT(*) AS DeptCount
> FROM      (SELECT DISTINCT Department
>            FROM SKU_DATA) AS DEPT;
> ```
>
> Note that this query is a bit different from the other SQL queries using subqueries we show in this text because this subquery is in the FROM clause instead of (as you'll see) the WHERE clause. Basically, this subquery builds a new temporary table named DEPT containing only distinct Department values, and the query counts the number of those values.

When using the COUNT function with a column name, the result is the number of rows that have valid data other that the NULL value. Thus, if we count the number of rows with page numbers in the CATALOG_SKU_2020 table, we should get eight rows as a result instead of nine because one SKU did not appear in the catalog. We can do this with the following SQL query:

```
/* *** SQL-Query-CH02-39 *** */
SELECT     COUNT(CatalogPage) AS Catalog2020NumberOfSKU
FROM       CATALOG_SKU_2020;
```

SQL-Query-CH02-39 gives us the expected result:

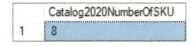

You should be aware of two limitations to SQL built-in functions. First, except for grouping (defined later), you *cannot* combine table column names with an SQL built-in function. For example, what happens if we run the following SQL query?

```
/* *** SQL-Query-CH02-40 *** */
SELECT     Department, COUNT(*)
FROM       SKU_DATA;
```

The result in SQL Server 2019 is:

```
Messages
  Msg 8120, Level 16, State 1, Line 278
  Column 'SKU_DATA.Department' is invalid in the select list
  because it is not contained in either an aggregate function or the GROUP BY clause.

  Completion time: 2020-07-06T14:47:07.3319406-07:00
```

This is the specific SQL Server 2019 error message. However, you will receive an equivalent message from Microsoft Access 2019 or Oracle Database. MySQL 8.0, unfortunately, will process this query and give a meaningless result: an arbitrary department name paired with the number of departments.

The second problem with the SQL built-in aggregate functions that you should understand is that you cannot use them in an SQL WHERE clause. This is because the SQL WHERE clause operates on *rows* (choosing which rows will be displayed), whereas the aggregate functions operate on *columns* (each function calculates a single value based on all the attribute values stored in a column). Thus, you cannot use the following SQL statement:

```
/* *** SQL-Query-CH02-41 *** */

SELECT       *

FROM         RETAIL_ORDER

WHERE        OrderTotal > AVG(OrderTotal);
```

An attempt to use such a statement will also result in an error statement from the DBMS:

```
Messages
  Msg 147, Level 15, State 1, Line 285
  An aggregate may not appear in the WHERE clause unless it is in a subquery
  contained in a HAVING clause or a select list, and the column being aggregated is an outer reference.

  Completion time: 2020-07-06T14:50:57.6364576-07:00
```

Again, this is the specific SQL Server 2019 error message, but other DBMS products will give you an equivalent error message. The desired result of this query can be computed using an SQL subquery (discussed later in this chapter). The desired result can also be obtained using a sequence of SQL views, which will be discussed in Chapter 7.

## SQL Expressions in SQL SELECT Statements

It is possible to do basic arithmetic in SQL statements. For example, suppose we want to compute the values of extended price, perhaps because we want to verify the accuracy of the data in the ORDER_ITEM table. To compute the extended price, we can use the SQL expression *Quantity * Price* in the SQL query:

```
/* *** SQL-Query-CH02-42 *** */

SELECT       OrderNumber, SKU, (Quantity * Price) AS EP

FROM         ORDER_ITEM

ORDER BY     OrderNumber, SKU;
```

The result is:

| | OrderNumber | SKU | EP |
|---|---|---|---|
| 1 | 1000 | 201000 | 300.00 |
| 2 | 1000 | 202000 | 130.00 |
| 3 | 2000 | 101100 | 200.00 |
| 4 | 2000 | 101200 | 100.00 |
| 5 | 3000 | 100200 | 300.00 |
| 6 | 3000 | 101100 | 100.00 |
| 7 | 3000 | 101200 | 50.00 |

An **SQL expression** is basically a formula or set of values that determines the exact results of an SQL query. We can think of an SQL expression as anything that follows an actual or implied *is equal to* (=) comparison operator (or any other comparison operator, such as greater than [>], less than [<], and so on) or that follows certain SQL comparison operator keywords, such as LIKE and BETWEEN. Thus, the SELECT clause in the preceding query includes the implied *is equal to* (=) sign as EP = Quantity * Price. For another example, in the following WHERE clause:

```
WHERE    Buyer IN ('Nancy Meyers', 'Cindy Lo', 'Jerry Martin');
```

the SQL expression consists of the enclosed set of three text values following the IN keyword.

Now that we know how to use an SQL expression to calculate the value of extended price, we can compare this computed value to the value of ExtendedPrice that is already stored in ORDER_ITEM by using the following SQL query:

```
/* *** SQL-Query-CH02-43 *** */
SELECT    OrderNumber, SKU,
          (Quantity * Price) AS EP, ExtendedPrice
FROM      ORDER_ITEM
ORDER BY  OrderNumber, SKU;
```

The result of this statement now allows us to visually compare the two values to ensure that the stored data are correct:

|   | OrderNumber | SKU | EP | ExtendedPrice |
|---|---|---|---|---|
| 1 | 1000 | 201000 | 300.00 | 300.00 |
| 2 | 1000 | 202000 | 130.00 | 130.00 |
| 3 | 2000 | 101100 | 200.00 | 200.00 |
| 4 | 2000 | 101200 | 100.00 | 100.00 |
| 5 | 3000 | 100200 | 300.00 | 300.00 |
| 6 | 3000 | 101100 | 100.00 | 100.00 |
| 7 | 3000 | 101200 | 50.00 | 50.00 |

**BY THE WAY**   The parentheses shown enclosing the expression *Quantity * Price* are not required and do not affect the calculation, but they are useful to help us see the expression in the SQL query syntax.

Expressions can also be used in the SQL WHERE clause (but they may *not* include SQL built-in aggregate functions—see SQL-Query-CH02-41 earlier). For example, if we want to test whether (Quantity * Price) is equal to ExtendedPrice and then display the OrderNumber and SKU only when (Quantity * Price) is *not* equal to ExtendedPrice, we use the following SQL query:

```
/* *** SQL-Query-CH02-44 *** */
SELECT    OrderNumber, SKU
FROM      ORDER_ITEM
WHERE     (Quantity * Price) <> ExtendedPrice
ORDER BY  OrderNumber, SKU;
```

The result of this statement is the **empty set** that contains no values. In terms of SQL-Query-CH02-44, this means that there are *no* rows where (Quantity * Price) is *not* equal to ExtendedPrice, which means that all the values are correct.

| OrderNumber | SKU |
|---|---|

Another use for SQL expressions in SQL statements is to perform character string manipulation. Suppose we want to combine (using the *concatenation* operator, which is the plus sign [+] in SQL Server 2019) the Buyer and Department columns into a single column named Sponsor. To do this, we can use the following SQL statement:

```
/* *** SQL-Query-CH02-45 *** */
SELECT     SKU, SKU_Description,
           (Buyer+' in '+Department) AS Sponsor
FROM       SKU_DATA
ORDER BY   SKU;
```

The result will include a column named Sponsor that contains the combined text values:

> **BY THE WAY**  The concatenation operator, like many SQL syntax elements, varies from one DBMS product to another. Oracle Database uses a double vertical bar (||) as the concatenation operator, and SQL-Query-CH02-45 is written for Oracle Database as:
>
> ```
> /* *** SQL-Query-CH02-45-Oracle-Database *** */
> SELECT     SKU, SKU_Description,
>            (Buyer||' in '||Department) AS Sponsor
> FROM       SKU_DATA
> ORDER BY   SKU;
> ```
>
> MySQL uses the concatenation string function CONCAT() as the concatenation operator with the elements to be concatenated separated by commas with the parentheses, and SQL-Query-CH02-45 is written for MySQL as:
>
> ```
> /* *** SQL-Query-CH02-45-MySQL *** */
> SELECT     SKU, SKU_Description,
>            CONCAT(Buyer,' in ',Department) AS Sponsor
> FROM       SKU_DATA
> ORDER BY   SKU;
> ```

| | SKU | SKU_Description | Sponsor | |
|---|---|---|---|---|
| 1 | 100100 | Std. Scuba Tank, Yellow | Pete Hansen | in Water Sports |
| 2 | 100200 | Std. Scuba Tank, Magenta | Pete Hansen | in Water Sports |
| 3 | 100300 | Std. Scuba Tank, Light Blue | Pete Hansen | in Water Sports |
| 4 | 100400 | Std. Scuba Tank, Dark Blue | Pete Hansen | in Water Sports |
| 5 | 100500 | Std. Scuba Tank, Light Green | Pete Hansen | in Water Sports |
| 6 | 100600 | Std. Scuba Tank, Dark Green | Pete Hansen | in Water Sports |
| 7 | 101100 | Dive Mask, Small Clear | Nancy Meyers | in Water Sports |
| 8 | 101200 | Dive Mask, Med Clear | Nancy Meyers | in Water Sports |
| 9 | 201000 | Half-dome Tent | Cindy Lo | in Camping |
| 10 | 202000 | Half-dome Tent Vestibule | Cindy Lo | in Camping |
| 11 | 203000 | Half-dome Tent Vestibule - Wide | Cindy Lo | in Camping |
| 12 | 301000 | Light Fly Climbing Harness | Jerry Martin | in Climbing |
| 13 | 302000 | Locking Carabiner, Oval | Jerry Martin | in Climbing |

The result of SQL-Query-CH02-45 is ugly because of the extra spaces in each row. We can eliminate these extra spaces by using more advanced functions. The syntax and use of such functions vary from one DBMS to another, however, and a discussion of the features of each product will take us away from the point of this discussion. To learn more, search on *string functions* in the documentation for your specific DBMS product. Just to illustrate the possibilities, however, here is an SQL Server 2019 statement using the RTRIM function (which also works in Microsoft Access, Oracle Database, and MySQL) that strips the tailing blanks off the right-hand side of Buyer and Department:

```
/* *** SQL-Query-CH02-46 *** */
SELECT      SKU, SKU_Description,
            RTRIM(Buyer)+' in '+RTRIM(Department) AS Sponsor
FROM        SKU_DATA
ORDER BY    SKU;
```

The result of this query is much more visually pleasing:

| | SKU | SKU_Description | Sponsor |
|---|---|---|---|
| 1 | 100100 | Std. Scuba Tank, Yellow | Pete Hansen in Water Sports |
| 2 | 100200 | Std. Scuba Tank, Magenta | Pete Hansen in Water Sports |
| 3 | 100300 | Std. Scuba Tank, Light Blue | Pete Hansen in Water Sports |
| 4 | 100400 | Std. Scuba Tank, Dark Blue | Pete Hansen in Water Sports |
| 5 | 100500 | Std. Scuba Tank, Light Green | Pete Hansen in Water Sports |
| 6 | 100600 | Std. Scuba Tank, Dark Green | Pete Hansen in Water Sports |
| 7 | 101100 | Dive Mask, Small Clear | Nancy Meyers in Water Sports |
| 8 | 101200 | Dive Mask, Med Clear | Nancy Meyers in Water Sports |
| 9 | 201000 | Half-dome Tent | Cindy Lo in Camping |
| 10 | 202000 | Half-dome Tent Vestibule | Cindy Lo in Camping |
| 11 | 203000 | Half-dome Tent Vestibule - ... | Cindy Lo in Camping |
| 12 | 301000 | Light Fly Climbing Harness | Jerry Martin in Climbing |
| 13 | 302000 | Locking Carabiner, Oval | Jerry Martin in Climbing |

## Grouping Rows in SQL SELECT Statements

In SQL queries, rows can be grouped together according to common values using the **SQL GROUP BY clause**. This is a powerful feature, but it can be difficult to understand.

To illustrate how grouping works, imagine that you are on the Cape Codd sales analysis team, and your boss asks you the question: "How many products from each department were there in the printed Cape Codd 2020 catalog?"

By simply looking at the data in the CATALOG_SKU_2020 table shown in Figure 2-26, you can easily see that the rows fall into three *groups* based on the values of Department. These groups are Water Sports (rows 1–5), Camping (rows 6–7), and Climbing (rows 8–9). A quick count of the rows in each group shows that Water Sports has five rows, Camping has two rows, and Climbing has two rows. Checking the values of CatalogPage, you can see that only the value for row 3 is NULL, which means that all SKUs except SKU 100400 appeared in the 2020 catalog. Therefore, Water Sports had four items in the Cape Codd 2020 catalog, Camping had two items, and Climbing had two items.

If you need to prepare a report for your boss, you could put this information into a spreadsheet, as shown in Figure 2-27. This spreadsheet clearly shows the data *grouped by Department*, with the corresponding (in alphabetical order) Camping, Climbing, and Water Sports groups.

| | CatalogID | SKU | SKU_Description | Department | CatalogPage | DateOnWebSite |
|---|---|---|---|---|---|---|
| 1 | 20200001 | 100100 | Std. Scuba Tank, Yellow | Water Sports | 23 | 2020-01-01 |
| 2 | 20200002 | 100300 | Std. Scuba Tank, Light Blue | Water Sports | 23 | 2020-01-01 |
| 3 | 20200003 | 100400 | Std. Scuba Tank, Dark Blue | Water Sports | NULL | 2020-08-01 |
| 4 | 20200004 | 101100 | Dive Mask, Small Clear | Water Sports | 26 | 2020-01-01 |
| 5 | 20200005 | 101200 | Dive Mask, Med Clear | Water Sports | 26 | 2020-01-01 |
| 6 | 20200006 | 201000 | Half-dome Tent | Camping | 46 | 2020-01-01 |
| 7 | 20200007 | 202000 | Half-dome Tent Vestibule | Camping | 46 | 2020-01-01 |
| 8 | 20200008 | 301000 | Light Fly Climbing Harness | Climbing | 77 | 2020-01-01 |
| 9 | 20200009 | 302000 | Locking Carabiner, Oval | Climbing | 79 | 2020-01-01 |

This group of rows is for the **Water Sports** department

This SKU did not appear in the catalog

This group of rows is for the **Camping** department

This group of rows is for the **Climbing** department

**FIGURE 2-26**

Department Groups in the CATALOG_SKU_2020 Table

To create the grouped data output shown in Figure 2-27 in an SQL query, we use the SQL GROUP BY clause in an SQL SELECT statement. This is shown in SQL-Query-CH02-47:

```
/* *** SQL-Query-CH02-47 *** */
SELECT      Department, COUNT(SKU) AS NumberOfCatalogItems
FROM        CATALOG_SKU_2020
GROUP BY    Department;
```

The result for this query is:

| | Department | NumberOfCatalogItems |
|---|---|---|
| 1 | Camping | 2 |
| 2 | Climbing | 2 |
| 3 | Water Sports | 5 |

The results for SQL-Query-CH02-47 display the correct grouping by Department, but there is an error in the NumberOfCatalogItems for the Water Sports department. This is because SKU 100400 is included in the count but did not appear in the catalog. To fix this problem, we revise the SQL query by adding a WHERE clause to include only the rows for SKUs that have a CatalogPage number value:

```
/* *** SQL-Query-CH02-48 *** */
SELECT      Department, COUNT(SKU) AS NumberOfCatalogItems
FROM        CATALOG_SKU_2020
WHERE       CatalogPage IS NOT NULL
GROUP BY    Department;
```

**FIGURE 2-27**

Grouping Data into Department Groups

Data is now grouped by **Department**

This is the **Camping** group

This is the **Climbing** group

This is the **Water Sports** group

This change gives us the correct results:

| | Department | NumberOfCatalogItems |
|---|---|---|
| 1 | Camping | 2 |
| 2 | Climbing | 2 |
| 3 | Water Sports | 4 |

Now imagine that your boss asks you the question: "How many products from each department were there in the printed Cape Codd 2020 catalog where the department had three or more listed products?" We can easily answer this question: only the Water Sports department had three or more catalog items. Water Sports had four catalog items, and Camping and Climbing only had two each. To get the correct answer from the grouped data output in an SQL query we use the **SQL HAVING clause** in an SQL SELECT statement. Noting that 3 *or more* is mathematically equivalent to *more than 2*, we can write the needed SQL HAVING clause for the SQL query. This is shown in SQL-Query-CH02-49 (note that we use *COUNT(SKU)* in the HAVING clause, *not* the alias *NumberOfCatalogItems*):

```
/* *** SQL-Query-CH02-49 *** */
SELECT      Department, COUNT(SKU) AS NumberOfCatalogItems
FROM        CATALOG_SKU_2020
WHERE       CatalogPage IS NOT NULL
GROUP BY    Department
HAVING      COUNT(SKU) > 2;
```

The result for this query is exactly the result we wanted:

| | Department | NumberOfCatalogItems |
|---|---|---|
| 1 | Water Sports | 4 |

Note that SQL built-in aggregate functions *can* be used in the SQL HAVING clause because they are working on the *set of column values in each group*. Earlier we noted that those functions *cannot* be used in the WHERE clause because the WHERE clause is applied to each *single row*. It is easy to get confused between the SQL WHERE clause and the SQL HAVING clause. The best way to understand the difference is to remember that:

- The SQL WHERE clause specifies which *rows* will be used to determine the groups.
- The SQL HAVING clause specifies which *groups* will be used in the final result.

Nonetheless, be aware that there is a potential ambiguity in statements that include both WHERE and HAVING clauses. The results vary depending on whether the WHERE condition is applied before or after the HAVING. To eliminate this ambiguity, the WHERE clause is *always* applied *before* the HAVING clause.

We can include more than one column in a GROUP BY expression. For example, imagine that your boss asks you the question: "How many SKUs is each buyer in each department responsible for?" To answer this question, we will have to group first by Department and then by Buyer. Therefore, we use the following SQL statement:

```
/* *** SQL-Query-CH02-50 *** */
SELECT      Department, Buyer,
            COUNT(SKU) AS Dept_Buyer_SKU_Count
FROM        SKU_DATA
GROUP BY    Department, Buyer;
```

This groups rows according to the value of Department first, then according to Buyer, and then counts the number of rows for each combination of Department and Buyer. The result is:

| | Department | Buyer | Dept_Buyer_SKU_Count |
|---|---|---|---|
| 1 | Camping | Cindy Lo | 3 |
| 2 | Climbing | Jerry Martin | 2 |
| 3 | Water Sports | Nancy Meyers | 2 |
| 4 | Water Sports | Pete Hansen | 6 |

When using the GROUP BY clause, *any and all* column names in the SELECT clause that are *not* used by or associated with an SQL built-in function *must* appear in the GROUP BY clause. In SQL-Query-CH02-51, the column name SKU is not used in the GROUP BY clause, and therefore the query produces an error:

```
/* *** SQL-Query-CH02-51 *** */
SELECT      Department, SKU,
            COUNT(SKU) AS Dept_SKU_Count
FROM        SKU_DATA
GROUP BY    Department;
```

The resulting error message is:

```
Messages
  Msg 8120, Level 16, State 1, Line 367
  Column 'SKU_DATA.SKU' is invalid in the select list
  because it is not contained in either an aggregate function or the GROUP BY clause.
```

This is the specific SQL Server 2019 error message, but other DBMS products will give you an equivalent error message. Statements like this one are invalid because there are many values of SKU for each Department group. The DBMS has no place to put those multiple values in the result. If you do not understand the problem, try to process this statement by hand. It cannot be done. MySQL 8.0, unfortunately, will process this query and return a result in which an arbitrary SKU value is chosen to be in the result.

Of course, the SQL ORDER BY clause can also be used with SQL queries using the SQL GROUP BY clauses, as shown in the following query:

```
/* *** SQL-Query-CH02-52 *** */
SELECT      Department, COUNT(SKU) AS Dept_SKU_Count
FROM        SKU_DATA
WHERE       SKU <> 302000
GROUP BY    Department
HAVING      COUNT(SKU) > 1
ORDER BY    Dept_SKU_Count;
```

The result is:

| | Department | Dept_SKU_Count |
|---|---|---|
| 1 | Camping | 3 |
| 2 | Water Sports | 8 |

Notice that one of the rows of the Climbing department has been removed from the count because it did not meet the WHERE clause condition and that the Climbing department itself is removed from the final results because it did not meet the HAVING clause requirement. Without the ORDER BY clause, the rows would be presented in arbitrary order of Department.

With it, the order is as shown. In general, to be safe, always place the WHERE clause before the GROUP BY clause. Some DBMS products do not require that placement, but others do.

**Does Not Work with Microsoft Access ANSI-89 SQL**

Microsoft Access does not properly recognize the alias Dept_SKU_Count in the ORDER BY clause and creates a parameter query that requests an input value of as yet nonexistent Dept_SKU_Count! However, it doesn't matter whether you enter parameter values or not—click the **OK** button and the query will run. The results will be basically correct, but they will not be sorted correctly.

**Solution:** Use the Microsoft Access QBE GUI to modify the query structure. The correct QBE structure is shown in Figure 2-28. The resulting Microsoft Access ANSI-89 SQL is:

```
/* *** SQL-Query-CH02-52-Access-A *** */
SELECT      SKU_DATA.Department, COUNT(SKU) AS Dept_SKU_Count
FROM        SKU_DATA
WHERE       (((SKU_DATA.SKU)<>302000))
GROUP BY    SKU_DATA.Department
HAVING      COUNT(SKU) > 1
ORDER BY    COUNT(SKU);
```

which can be edited down to:

```
/* *** SQL-Query-CH02-52-Access-B *** */
SELECT      Department, COUNT(SKU) AS Dept_SKU_Count
FROM        SKU_DATA
WHERE       SKU <> 302000
GROUP BY    Department
HAVING      COUNT(SKU) > 1
ORDER BY    COUNT(SKU);
```

**FIGURE 2-28**

Editing the SQL Query in the Microsoft Access 2019 QBE GUI Interface

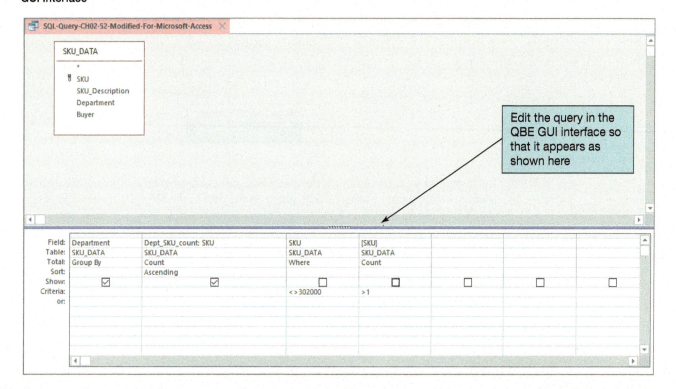

## Querying Two or More Tables with SQL

So far in this chapter we've worked with only one table. Now we will conclude by describing SQL statements for querying two or more tables.

Imagine that your boss asks you the question: "What is the total revenue generated by SKUs managed by the Water Sports department?" We can compute the total revenue as the sum of ExtendedPrice, but we have a problem. ExtendedPrice is stored in the ORDER_ITEM table, and Department is stored in the SKU_DATA table. We need to process data in two tables, and all of the SQL presented so far operates on a single table at a time.

SQL provides two different techniques for querying data from multiple tables:

- The SQL subquery
- The SQL join

As you will learn, although both work with multiple tables, they are used for slightly different purposes.

### Querying Multiple Tables with Subqueries

We will begin our discussion of multiple table queries with the *SQL subquery*. To understand how a subquery works, let's return to the problem of how we can obtain the sum of ExtendedPrice for items managed by the Water Sports department. Looking at the ORDER_ITEM table data structure in Figure 2-4, we can see that if we somehow knew the SKU values for the Water Sports items, we could use them in a WHERE clause with the IN keyword.

Looking at the SKU_DATA table data in Figure 2-6, we can determine that the SKU values for items in Water Sports are 100100, 100200, 100300, 100400, 100500, 100600, 101100, and 101200. Knowing those values, we can obtain the sum of their ExtendedPrice with the following SQL query:

```
/* *** SQL-Query-CH02-53 *** */
SELECT      SUM(ExtendedPrice) AS WaterSportsRevenue
FROM        ORDER_ITEM
WHERE       SKU IN (100100, 100200, 100300, 100400, 100500, 100600,
            101100, 101200);
```

The result is:

|   | WaterSportsRevenue |
|---|---|
| 1 | 750.00 |

But in general, we do *not* know the necessary SKU values ahead of time. However, we do have a way to obtain them by using an SQL query on the data in the SKU_DATA table. To obtain the SKU values for the Water Sports department, we use the following SQL statement:

```
/* *** SQL-Query-CH02-54 *** */
SELECT      SKU
FROM        SKU_DATA
WHERE       Department = 'Water Sports';
```

The result of this SQL statement is the set of SKU numbers that we need:

|   | SKU |
|---|-----|
| 1 | 100100 |
| 2 | 100200 |
| 3 | 100300 |
| 4 | 100400 |
| 5 | 100500 |
| 6 | 100600 |
| 7 | 101100 |
| 8 | 101200 |

Now we need to combine the last two SQL statements to obtain the result we want. We replace the list of values in the WHERE clause of the first SQL query with the second SQL statement as follows:

```
/* *** SQL-Query-CH02-55 *** */
SELECT     SUM(ExtendedPrice) AS WaterSportsRevenue
FROM       ORDER_ITEM
WHERE      SKU IN
           (SELECT    SKU
            FROM      SKU_DATA
            WHERE     Department = 'Water Sports');
```

The result of the query is the same result we obtained before when we knew which specific values of SKU to use:

|   | WaterSportsRevenue |
|---|--------------------|
| 1 | 750.00 |

In SQL-Query-CH02-55, the second SELECT statement, the one enclosed in parentheses, is called an **SQL subquery**. An SQL subquery is an SQL query statement used to determine a set of values that are provided (or returned) to the SQL query (often referred to as the **top level query**) that used (or called) the subquery. A subquery is often described as a *nested query* or a *query within a query*.

It is important to note that SQL queries using subqueries still function like a single table query in the sense that only the columns of the top level query can be displayed in the query results. For example, in SQL-Query-CH02-55, because the Department column is only in the SKU_DATA table (the table used in the subquery itself), the values of the Department column *cannot* be displayed in the final results.

We can use multiple subqueries to process three or even more tables. For example, suppose we want to know the names of the buyers who manage any product purchased in January 2018. First, note that Buyer data is stored in the SKU_DATA table and OrderMonth and OrderYear data are stored in the RETAIL_ORDER table.

Now, we can use an SQL query with two subqueries to obtain the desired data as follows:

```
/* *** SQL-Query-CH02-56 *** */
SELECT      DISTINCT Buyer, Department
FROM        SKU_DATA
WHERE       SKU IN
            (SELECT    SKU
             FROM      ORDER_ITEM
             WHERE     OrderNumber       IN
                       (SELECT          OrderNumber
                        FROM            RETAIL_ORDER
                        WHERE           OrderMonth = 'January'
                          AND           OrderYear = 2021));
```

The result of this statement is:

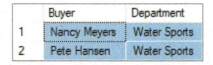

To understand this statement, work from the bottom up. The bottom SELECT statement obtains the list of OrderNumbers of orders sold in January 2018. The middle SELECT statement obtains the SKU values for items sold in orders in January 2018. Finally, the top-level SELECT query obtains Buyer and Department for all of the SKUs found in the middle SELECT statement.

Any parts of the SQL language that you learned earlier in this chapter can be applied to a table generated by a subquery, regardless of how complicated the SQL looks. For example, in SQL-Query-CH02-56 we apply the DISTINCT keyword on the results to eliminate duplicate rows. We can also apply the GROUP BY and ORDER BY clauses, as well as aggregates, to SQL-Query-CH02-56 as follows to form SQL-Query-CH02-57:

```
/* *** SQL-Query-CH02-57 *** */
SELECT      Buyer, Department, COUNT(SKU) AS Number_Of_SKU_Sold
FROM        SKU_DATA
WHERE       SKU IN
            (SELECT    SKU
             FROM      ORDER_ITEM
             WHERE     OrderNumber  IN
                       (SELECT          OrderNumber
                        FROM            RETAIL_ORDER
                        WHERE           OrderMonth = 'January'
                          AND           OrderYear = 2021))
GROUP BY    Buyer, Department
ORDER BY    Number_Of_SKU_Sold;
```

---

**Does Not Work with Microsoft Access ANSI-89 SQL**

This query fails in Microsoft Access ANSI-89 SQL for the same reason previously described on page 99.

**Solution:** See the solution described in the "Does Not Work with Microsoft Access ANSI-89 SQL" box on page 99. The correct Microsoft Access ANSI-89 SQL statement for this query is:

```
/* *** SQL-Query-CH02-57-Access *** */
SELECT     Buyer, Department, COUNT(*) AS Number_Of_SKU_Sold
FROM       SKU_DATA
WHERE      SKU IN
           (SELECT   SKU
            FROM      ORDER_ITEM
            WHERE     OrderNumber   IN
                      (SELECT       OrderNumber
                       FROM         RETAIL_ORDER
                       WHERE        OrderMonth = 'January'
                          AND       OrderYear = 2021))
GROUP BY   Buyer, Department
ORDER BY   COUNT(*) ASC;
```

---

The result is:

| | Buyer | Department | Number_Of_SKU_Sold |
|---|---|---|---|
| 1 | Pete Hansen | Water Sports | 1 |
| 2 | Nancy Meyers | Water Sports | 2 |

## Querying Multiple Tables with Joins

Subqueries are very powerful, but as noted, they do have a serious limitation: the selected data can come only from the top-level table. Therefore, we cannot use a subquery to display data obtained from more than one table. To do so, we must use an SQL **join** instead.

In an **SQL join operation**, the **SQL JOIN operator** is used to combine two or more tables by concatenating (sticking together) the rows of one table with the rows of another table. If the JOIN operator is actually used as part of the SQL statement syntax, we refer to the join operation as an **explicit join**. If the JOIN operator itself does not appear in the SQL statement, we refer to the join operation as an **implicit join**.

Consider how we might combine the data in the RETAIL_ORDER and ORDER_ITEM tables. We can concatenate the rows of one table with the rows of the second table with the following SQL statement, where we simply list the names of the tables we want to combine:

```
/* *** SQL-Query-CH02-58 *** */
SELECT      *
FROM        RETAIL_ORDER, ORDER_ITEM;
```

This is known as a **CROSS JOIN**, and the result is what is mathematically known as the **Cartesian product** of the rows in the tables, which means that this statement will just stick every row of one table together with every row of the second table. For the data in Figure 2-6, the result is:

| | OrderNumber | StoreNumber | StoreZIP | OrderMonth | OrderYear | OrderTotal | OrderNumber | SKU | Quantity | Price | ExtendedPrice |
|---|---|---|---|---|---|---|---|---|---|---|---|
| 1 | 1000 | 10 | 98110 | December | 2020 | 445.00 | 3000 | 100200 | 1 | 300.00 | 300.00 |
| 2 | 1000 | 10 | 98110 | December | 2020 | 445.00 | 2000 | 101100 | 4 | 50.00 | 200.00 |
| 3 | 1000 | 10 | 98110 | December | 2020 | 445.00 | 3000 | 101100 | 2 | 50.00 | 100.00 |
| 4 | 1000 | 10 | 98110 | December | 2020 | 445.00 | 2000 | 101200 | 2 | 50.00 | 100.00 |
| 5 | 1000 | 10 | 98110 | December | 2020 | 445.00 | 3000 | 101200 | 1 | 50.00 | 50.00 |
| 6 | 1000 | 10 | 98110 | December | 2020 | 445.00 | 1000 | 201000 | 1 | 300.00 | 300.00 |
| 7 | 1000 | 10 | 98110 | December | 2020 | 445.00 | 1000 | 202000 | 1 | 130.00 | 130.00 |
| 8 | 2000 | 20 | 02335 | December | 2020 | 310.00 | 3000 | 100200 | 1 | 300.00 | 300.00 |
| 9 | 2000 | 20 | 02335 | December | 2020 | 310.00 | 2000 | 101100 | 4 | 50.00 | 200.00 |
| 10 | 2000 | 20 | 02335 | December | 2020 | 310.00 | 3000 | 101100 | 2 | 50.00 | 100.00 |
| 11 | 2000 | 20 | 02335 | December | 2020 | 310.00 | 2000 | 101200 | 2 | 50.00 | 100.00 |
| 12 | 2000 | 20 | 02335 | December | 2020 | 310.00 | 3000 | 101200 | 1 | 50.00 | 50.00 |
| 13 | 2000 | 20 | 02335 | December | 2020 | 310.00 | 1000 | 201000 | 1 | 300.00 | 300.00 |
| 14 | 2000 | 20 | 02335 | December | 2020 | 310.00 | 1000 | 202000 | 1 | 130.00 | 130.00 |
| 15 | 3000 | 10 | 98110 | January | 2021 | 480.00 | 3000 | 100200 | 1 | 300.00 | 300.00 |
| 16 | 3000 | 10 | 98110 | January | 2021 | 480.00 | 2000 | 101100 | 4 | 50.00 | 200.00 |
| 17 | 3000 | 10 | 98110 | January | 2021 | 480.00 | 3000 | 101100 | 2 | 50.00 | 100.00 |
| 18 | 3000 | 10 | 98110 | January | 2021 | 480.00 | 2000 | 101200 | 2 | 50.00 | 100.00 |
| 19 | 3000 | 10 | 98110 | January | 2021 | 480.00 | 3000 | 101200 | 1 | 50.00 | 50.00 |
| 20 | 3000 | 10 | 98110 | January | 2021 | 480.00 | 1000 | 201000 | 1 | 300.00 | 300.00 |
| 21 | 3000 | 10 | 98110 | January | 2021 | 480.00 | 1000 | 202000 | 1 | 130.00 | 130.00 |

Because there are 3 rows of retail orders and 7 rows of order items, there are 3 times 7, or 21, rows in this table. Notice that the retail order with OrderNumber 1000 has been combined with all seven of the rows in ORDER_ITEM, the retail order with OrderNumber 2000 has been combined with all seven of the same rows, and, finally, the retail order with OrderNumber 3000 has again been combined with all seven rows.

This is illogical—what we really need to do is to select only those rows for which the OrderNumber of RETAIL_ORDER (primary key) matches the OrderNumber in ORDER_ITEM (foreign key). This is known as an **inner join**, and this is easy to do—we simply add an SQL WHERE clause to the query requiring that the values in the two columns are equal to each other as follows:

```
/* *** SQL-Query-CH02-59 *** */
SELECT     *
FROM       RETAIL_ORDER, ORDER_ITEM
WHERE      RETAIL_ORDER.OrderNumber = ORDER_ITEM.OrderNumber;
```

The result is:

| | OrderNumber | StoreNumber | StoreZIP | OrderMonth | OrderYear | OrderTotal | OrderNumber | SKU | Quantity | Price | ExtendedPrice |
|---|---|---|---|---|---|---|---|---|---|---|---|
| 1 | 3000 | 10 | 98110 | January | 2021 | 480.00 | 3000 | 100200 | 1 | 300.00 | 300.00 |
| 2 | 2000 | 20 | 02335 | December | 2020 | 310.00 | 2000 | 101100 | 4 | 50.00 | 200.00 |
| 3 | 3000 | 10 | 98110 | January | 2021 | 480.00 | 3000 | 101100 | 2 | 50.00 | 100.00 |
| 4 | 2000 | 20 | 02335 | December | 2020 | 310.00 | 2000 | 101200 | 2 | 50.00 | 100.00 |
| 5 | 3000 | 10 | 98110 | January | 2021 | 480.00 | 3000 | 101200 | 1 | 50.00 | 50.00 |
| 6 | 1000 | 10 | 98110 | December | 2020 | 445.00 | 1000 | 201000 | 1 | 300.00 | 300.00 |
| 7 | 1000 | 10 | 98110 | December | 2020 | 445.00 | 1000 | 202000 | 1 | 130.00 | 130.00 |

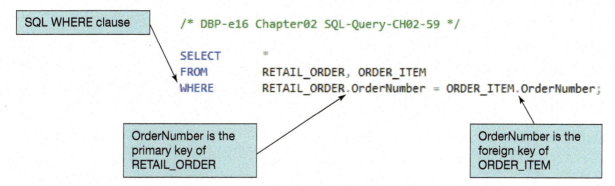

**FIGURE 2-29**

**Using Primary Key and Foreign Key Values in the SQL WHERE Clause in an SQL Join**

The use of the matching primary and foreign keys in the SQL WHERE clause is shown in Figure 2-29. Although this query is technically correct, it will be easier to interpret the results if we sort the results using an ORDER BY clause:

```
/* *** SQL-Query-CH02-60 *** */

SELECT      *
FROM        RETAIL_ORDER, ORDER_ITEM
WHERE       RETAIL_ORDER.OrderNumber = ORDER_ITEM.OrderNumber
ORDER BY    RETAIL_ORDER.OrderNumber, ORDER_ITEM.SKU;
```

The result is:

|   | OrderNumber | StoreNumber | StoreZIP | OrderMonth | OrderYear | OrderTotal | OrderNumber | SKU | Quantity | Price | ExtendedPrice |
|---|---|---|---|---|---|---|---|---|---|---|---|
| 1 | 1000 | 10 | 98110 | December | 2020 | 445.00 | 1000 | 201000 | 1 | 300.00 | 300.00 |
| 2 | 1000 | 10 | 98110 | December | 2020 | 445.00 | 1000 | 202000 | 1 | 130.00 | 130.00 |
| 3 | 2000 | 20 | 02335 | December | 2020 | 310.00 | 2000 | 101100 | 4 | 50.00 | 200.00 |
| 4 | 2000 | 20 | 02335 | December | 2020 | 310.00 | 2000 | 101200 | 2 | 50.00 | 100.00 |
| 5 | 3000 | 10 | 98110 | January | 2021 | 480.00 | 3000 | 100200 | 1 | 300.00 | 300.00 |
| 6 | 3000 | 10 | 98110 | January | 2021 | 480.00 | 3000 | 101100 | 2 | 50.00 | 100.00 |
| 7 | 3000 | 10 | 98110 | January | 2021 | 480.00 | 3000 | 101200 | 1 | 50.00 | 50.00 |

Looking at the statement syntax in SQLQuery-CH02-60, note that the SQL JOIN keyword is not used anywhere in the SQL statement—therefore, this is an *implicit* inner join.

If you compare this result with the data in Figure 2-6, you will see that only the appropriate order items are associated with each retail order. You also can tell that this has been done by noticing that in each row, the value of OrderNumber from RETAIL_ORDER (the first column) equals the value of OrderNumber from ORDER_ITEM (the seventh column). This was not true for our first result.

You can think of the join operation working as follows. Start with the first row in RETAIL_ORDER. Using the value of OrderNumber in this first row (1000 for the data in Figure 2-6), examine the rows in ORDER_ITEM. When you find a row in ORDER_ITEM where OrderNumber is also equal to 1000, join all the columns of the first row of RETAIL_ORDER with the columns from the row you just found in ORDER_ITEM.

For the data in Figure 2-6, the first row of ORDER_ITEM has OrderNumber equal to 1000, so you join the first row of RETAIL_ORDER with the columns from the first row in ORDER_ITEM to form the first row of the join. The result is:

|   | OrderNumber | StoreNumber | StoreZIP | OrderMonth | OrderYear | OrderTotal | OrderNumber | SKU | Quantity | Price | ExtendedPrice |
|---|---|---|---|---|---|---|---|---|---|---|---|
| 1 | 1000 | 10 | 98110 | December | 2020 | 445.00 | 1000 | 201000 | 1 | 300.00 | 300.00 |

Now, still using the OrderNumber value of 1000, look for a second row in ORDER_ITEM that has OrderNumber equal to 1000. For our data, the second row of ORDER_ITEM has such a value. So, join the first row of RETAIL_ORDER to the second row of ORDER_ITEM to obtain the second row of the join as follows:

| | OrderNumber | StoreNumber | StoreZIP | OrderMonth | OrderYear | OrderTotal | OrderNumber | SKU | Quantity | Price | ExtendedPrice |
|---|---|---|---|---|---|---|---|---|---|---|---|
| 1 | 1000 | 10 | 98110 | December | 2020 | 445.00 | 1000 | 201000 | 1 | 300.00 | 300.00 |
| 2 | 1000 | 10 | 98110 | December | 2020 | 445.00 | 1000 | 202000 | 1 | 130.00 | 130.00 |

Continue in this way, looking for matches for the OrderNumber value of 1000. At this point, no more OrderNumber values of 1000 appear in the sample data, so now you move to the second row of RETAIL_ORDER, obtain the new value of OrderNumber (2000), and begin searching for matches for it in the rows of ORDER_ITEM. In this case, the third row has such a match, so you combine those rows with the previous result to obtain the new result:

| | OrderNumber | StoreNumber | StoreZIP | OrderMonth | OrderYear | OrderTotal | OrderNumber | SKU | Quantity | Price | ExtendedPrice |
|---|---|---|---|---|---|---|---|---|---|---|---|
| 1 | 1000 | 10 | 98110 | December | 2020 | 445.00 | 1000 | 201000 | 1 | 300.00 | 300.00 |
| 2 | 1000 | 10 | 98110 | December | 2020 | 445.00 | 1000 | 202000 | 1 | 130.00 | 130.00 |
| 3 | 2000 | 20 | 02335 | December | 2020 | 310.00 | 2000 | 101100 | 4 | 50.00 | 200.00 |

You continue until all rows of RETAIL_ORDER have been examined. The final result is:

| | OrderNumber | StoreNumber | StoreZIP | OrderMonth | OrderYear | OrderTotal | OrderNumber | SKU | Quantity | Price | ExtendedPrice |
|---|---|---|---|---|---|---|---|---|---|---|---|
| 1 | 1000 | 10 | 98110 | December | 2020 | 445.00 | 1000 | 201000 | 1 | 300.00 | 300.00 |
| 2 | 1000 | 10 | 98110 | December | 2020 | 445.00 | 1000 | 202000 | 1 | 130.00 | 130.00 |
| 3 | 2000 | 20 | 02335 | December | 2020 | 310.00 | 2000 | 101100 | 4 | 50.00 | 200.00 |
| 4 | 2000 | 20 | 02335 | December | 2020 | 310.00 | 2000 | 101200 | 2 | 50.00 | 100.00 |
| 5 | 3000 | 10 | 98110 | January | 2021 | 480.00 | 3000 | 100200 | 1 | 300.00 | 300.00 |
| 6 | 3000 | 10 | 98110 | January | 2021 | 480.00 | 3000 | 101100 | 2 | 50.00 | 100.00 |
| 7 | 3000 | 10 | 98110 | January | 2021 | 480.00 | 3000 | 101200 | 1 | 50.00 | 50.00 |

Actually, that is the theoretical result. But remember that row order in an SQL query can be arbitrary, as is shown in the results to SQL-Query-CH02-59. To ensure that you get the previous result, you need to add an ORDER BY clause to the query, as shown in SQL-Query-CH02-60.

You may have noticed that we introduced a new variation in SQL statement syntax in the previous two queries, where the terms RETAIL_ORDER.OrderNumber, ORDER_ITEM.OrderNumber, and ORDER_ITEM.SKU were used. The new syntax is simply **TableName.ColumnName**, and it is used to specify exactly which table each column is linked to. RETAIL_ORDER.OrderNumber simply means the OrderNumber from the RETAIL_ORDER table. Similarly, ORDER_ITEM.OrderNumber refers to the OrderNumber in the ORDER_ITEM table, and ORDER_ITEM.SKU refers to the SKU column in the ORDER_ITEM table. You can always qualify a column name with the name of its table like this. We have not done so previously because we were working with only one table, but the SQL statements shown previously would have worked just as well with syntax like SKU_DATA.Buyer rather than just Buyer or ORDER_ITEM.Price instead of Price.

The process of creating a result table by combining data from two tables via an SQL join operation is called **joining two tables**. When the tables are joined using an inner join with an *is equal to* condition (like the one on OrderNumber), this join is called an **equijoin**. When people say *join*, 99.99999 percent of the time they mean an *equijoin*.

We can use a join to obtain data from two or more tables. For example, using the data in Figure 2-6, suppose we want to show the name of the Buyer and the ExtendedPrice of the sales of all SKU items managed by that Buyer. The following SQL query will obtain that result:

```
/* *** SQL-Query-CH02-61 *** */

SELECT      Buyer, SKU_DATA.SKU, SKU_Description,

            OrderNumber, ExtendedPrice

FROM        SKU_DATA, ORDER_ITEM

WHERE       SKU_DATA.SKU = ORDER_ITEM.SKU;
```

The result is:

| | Buyer | SKU | SKU_Description | OrderNumber | ExtendedPrice |
|---|---|---|---|---|---|
| 1 | Pete Hansen | 100200 | Std. Scuba Tank, Magenta | 3000 | 300.00 |
| 2 | Nancy Meyers | 101100 | Dive Mask, Small Clear | 2000 | 200.00 |
| 3 | Nancy Meyers | 101100 | Dive Mask, Small Clear | 3000 | 100.00 |
| 4 | Nancy Meyers | 101200 | Dive Mask, Med Clear | 2000 | 100.00 |
| 5 | Nancy Meyers | 101200 | Dive Mask, Med Clear | 3000 | 50.00 |
| 6 | Cindy Lo | 201000 | Half-dome Tent | 1000 | 300.00 |
| 7 | Cindy Lo | 202000 | Half-dome Tent Vestibule | 1000 | 130.00 |

Again, the result of every SQL statement is just a single table, so we can apply any of the SQL syntax you learned for a single table to this result. For example, we can use the GROUP BY and ORDER BY clauses to obtain the total revenue from each SKU managed by each buyer, as shown in the following SQL query:

```
/* *** SQL-Query-CH02-62 *** */
SELECT      Buyer, SKU_DATA.SKU, SKU_Description,
            SUM(ExtendedPrice) AS BuyerSKURevenue
FROM        SKU_DATA, ORDER_ITEM
WHERE       SKU_DATA.SKU = ORDER_ITEM.SKU
GROUP BY    Buyer, SKU_DATA.SKU, SKU_Description
ORDER BY    BuyerSKURevenue DESC;
```

The result is:

| | Buyer | SKU | SKU_Description | BuyerSKURevenue |
|---|---|---|---|---|
| 1 | Pete Hansen | 100200 | Std. Scuba Tank, Magenta | 300.00 |
| 2 | Nancy Meyers | 101100 | Dive Mask, Small Clear | 300.00 |
| 3 | Cindy Lo | 201000 | Half-dome Tent | 300.00 |
| 4 | Nancy Meyers | 101200 | Dive Mask, Med Clear | 150.00 |
| 5 | Cindy Lo | 202000 | Half-dome Tent Vestibule | 130.00 |

**Does Not Work with Microsoft Access ANSI-89 SQL**

This query fails in Microsoft Access ANSI-89 SQL for the same reason previously described on page 99.

Solution: See the solution described in the "Does Not Work with Microsoft Access ANSI-89 SQL" box on page 99. The correct Microsoft Access ANSI-89 SQL statement for this query is:

```
/* *** SQL-Query-CH02-62-Access *** */
SELECT      Buyer, SKU_DATA.SKU, SKU_Description,
            SUM(ExtendedPrice) AS BuyerSKURevenue
FROM        SKU_DATA, ORDER_ITEM
WHERE       SKU_DATA.SKU = ORDER_ITEM.SKU
GROUP BY    Buyer, SKU_DATA.SKU, SKU_Description
ORDER BY    Sum(ExtendedPrice) DESC;
```

You may have noticed that in SQL-Query-CH02-62 the GROUP BY clause used groupings on Buyer, SKU, and SKU_Description. Given the matching values of SKU and SKU Description, this may seem unnecessary. In fact, however, as mentioned earlier, SQL syntax requires that *any* column name entered in the SELECT clause that is not used in an aggregate function *must* also be entered in the GROUP BY clause. To demonstrate this, we will run SQL-Query-CH02-62 without SKU_Description in the GROUP BY clause as SQL-Query-CH02-63:

```
/* *** SQL-Query-CH02-63 *** */
SELECT      Buyer, SKU_DATA.SKU, SKU_Description,
            SUM(ExtendedPrice) AS BuyerSKURevenue
FROM        SKU_DATA, ORDER_ITEM
WHERE       SKU_DATA.SKU = ORDER_ITEM.SKU
GROUP BY    Buyer, SKU_DATA.SKU
ORDER BY    BuyerSKURevenue DESC;
```

The result is an error message (this one is for SQL Server 2019):

```
Messages
  Msg 8120, Level 16, State 1, Line 469
  Column 'SKU_DATA.SKU_Description' is invalid in the select list
  because it is not contained in either an aggregate function or the GROUP BY clause.

  Completion time: 2020-07-06T15:42:17.2220469-07:00
```

Microsoft Access 2019 and Oracle Database will give similar error messages. In this particular case, MySQL 8.0 will execute the query give us the result we want because every SKU has only one SKU_Description. However, as in SQL-Query-CH02-51, MySQL 8.0 will often return nonsense from such queries: In SQL-Query-CH02-51, a department has many SKUs, so MySQL 8.0 arbitrarily chooses one.

We can extend this implicit join syntax to join three or more tables. For example, suppose we want to obtain the Buyer, SKU, SKU_Description, OrderNumber, OrderMonth, and ExtendedPrice for all purchases of items managed by each buyer. To retrieve that data, we need to join three tables together, as shown in this SQL query:

```
/* *** SQL-Query-CH02-64 *** */
SELECT      Buyer, SKU_DATA.SKU, SKU_Description,
            RETAIL_ORDER.OrderNumber, OrderMonth, ExtendedPrice
FROM        SKU_DATA, ORDER_ITEM, RETAIL_ORDER
WHERE       SKU_DATA.SKU = ORDER_ITEM.SKU
AND         ORDER_ITEM.OrderNumber=RETAIL_ORDER.OrderNumber;
```

The result is:

|   | Buyer | SKU | SKU_Description | OrderNumber | OrderMonth | ExtendedPrice |
|---|-------|-----|-----------------|-------------|------------|---------------|
| 1 | Pete Hansen | 100200 | Std. Scuba Tank, Magenta | 3000 | January | 300.00 |
| 2 | Nancy Meyers | 101100 | Dive Mask, Small Clear | 2000 | December | 200.00 |
| 3 | Nancy Meyers | 101100 | Dive Mask, Small Clear | 3000 | January | 100.00 |
| 4 | Nancy Meyers | 101200 | Dive Mask, Med Clear | 2000 | December | 100.00 |
| 5 | Nancy Meyers | 101200 | Dive Mask, Med Clear | 3000 | January | 50.00 |
| 6 | Cindy Lo | 201000 | Half-dome Tent | 1000 | December | 300.00 |
| 7 | Cindy Lo | 202000 | Half-dome Tent Vestibule | 1000 | December | 130.00 |

### Comparing Subqueries and Joins

Subqueries and joins both process multiple tables, but they differ slightly. As mentioned earlier, a subquery can be used only to retrieve data from the top table, whereas a join can be used to obtain data from any number of tables. Thus, a join can do everything a subquery can do and more. So why learn subqueries? For one, if you just need data from a single table, you might use a subquery because it is easier to write and understand. This is especially true when processing multiple tables.

In Chapter 8, however, you will learn about a type of subquery called a **correlated subquery**. A correlated subquery can do work that is not possible with joins. Thus, it is important for you to learn about both joins and subqueries, even though right now it appears that joins are uniformly superior. If you're curious, ambitious, and courageous, jump ahead and read the discussion of correlated subqueries in Chapter 8.

### The SQL JOIN ON Syntax

So far, we have learned to code SQL joins using implicit join syntax. However, there is another way to code join statements. In this second case, we create explicit joins using the **SQL JOIN ON syntax**. This SQL JOIN syntax is referred to as an *SQL INNER JOIN* as opposed to an *SQL OUTER JOIN*, which is discussed later in this chapter, and most SQL dialects allow, but do not require, the **SQL INNER keyword** to be used in the SQL statement. The following query, where we have deliberately omitted the INNER keyword, is the equivalent of SQL-Query-CH02-60:

```
/* *** SQL-Query-CH02-65 *** */

SELECT      *
FROM        RETAIL_ORDER JOIN ORDER_ITEM
       ON   RETAIL_ORDER.OrderNumber = ORDER_ITEM.OrderNumber
ORDER BY    RETAIL_ORDER.OrderNumber, ORDER_ITEM.SKU;
```

The result is:

| | OrderNumber | StoreNumber | StoreZIP | OrderMonth | OrderYear | OrderTotal | OrderNumber | SKU | Quantity | Price | ExtendedPrice |
|---|---|---|---|---|---|---|---|---|---|---|---|
| 1 | 1000 | 10 | 98110 | December | 2020 | 445.00 | 1000 | 201000 | 1 | 300.00 | 300.00 |
| 2 | 1000 | 10 | 98110 | December | 2020 | 445.00 | 1000 | 202000 | 1 | 130.00 | 130.00 |
| 3 | 2000 | 20 | 02335 | December | 2020 | 310.00 | 2000 | 101100 | 4 | 50.00 | 200.00 |
| 4 | 2000 | 20 | 02335 | December | 2020 | 310.00 | 2000 | 101200 | 2 | 50.00 | 100.00 |
| 5 | 3000 | 10 | 98110 | January | 2021 | 480.00 | 3000 | 100200 | 1 | 300.00 | 300.00 |
| 6 | 3000 | 10 | 98110 | January | 2021 | 480.00 | 3000 | 101100 | 2 | 50.00 | 100.00 |
| 7 | 3000 | 10 | 98110 | January | 2021 | 480.00 | 3000 | 101200 | 1 | 50.00 | 50.00 |

Although these two join syntaxes are functionally equivalent, the implicit join syntax is early SQL standard syntax and is considered to have been replaced by the explicit SQL JOIN ON join syntax as of the 1992 SQL-92 standard. Most people think that the SQL JOIN ON syntax is easier to understand than the first. Note that when using the SQL JOIN ON syntax:

- The **SQL JOIN keyword** is placed between the table names in the SQL FROM clause, where it replaces the comma that previously separated the two table names.
- The **SQL ON keyword** now leads into an **SQL ON clause**, which includes the statement of matching key values that was previously in an SQL WHERE clause.
- The SQL WHERE clause is no longer used as part of the join, which makes it easier to read the actual restrictions on the rows in the query in the WHERE clause itself.

Note that the JOIN ON syntax still requires a statement of primary key to foreign key equivalence, as shown in Figure 2-30. Also note that the SQL ON clause does *not* replace the SQL WHERE clause, which can still be used to determine which rows will be displayed. For

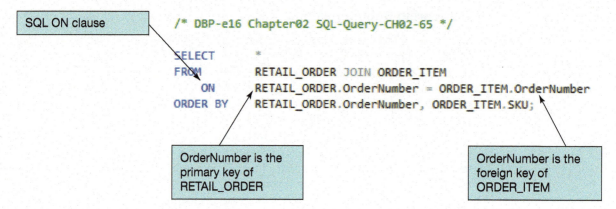

FIGURE 2-30

Using Primary Key and
Foreign Key Values in the
SQL ON Clause in an SQL
Join

example, we can use the SQL WHERE clause to limit the records shown to those for the
OrderYear of 2020:

```
/* *** SQL-Query-CH02-66 *** */

SELECT      *

FROM        RETAIL_ORDER JOIN ORDER_ITEM

        ON  RETAIL_ORDER.OrderNumber = ORDER_ITEM.OrderNumber

WHERE       OrderYear = 2020

ORDER BY    RETAIL_ORDER.OrderNumber, ORDER_ITEM.SKU;
```

The result is:

| | OrderNumber | StoreNumber | StoreZIP | OrderMonth | OrderYear | OrderTotal | OrderNumber | SKU | Quantity | Price | ExtendedPrice |
|---|---|---|---|---|---|---|---|---|---|---|---|
| 1 | 1000 | 10 | 98110 | December | 2020 | 445.00 | 1000 | 201000 | 1 | 300.00 | 300.00 |
| 2 | 1000 | 10 | 98110 | December | 2020 | 445.00 | 1000 | 202000 | 1 | 130.00 | 130.00 |
| 3 | 2000 | 20 | 02335 | December | 2020 | 310.00 | 2000 | 101100 | 4 | 50.00 | 200.00 |
| 4 | 2000 | 20 | 02335 | December | 2020 | 310.00 | 2000 | 101200 | 2 | 50.00 | 100.00 |

### Does Not Work with Microsoft Access ANSI-89 SQL

This query fails in Microsoft Access ANSI-89 SQL because Microsoft Access does require the use of the
SQL keyword INNER.

**Solution:** Add the SQL keyword INNER into the state-
ment. The correct Microsoft Access ANSI-89 SQL statement for this query is:

```
/* *** SQL-Query-CH02-66-Access *** */

SELECT      *

FROM        RETAIL_ORDER INNER JOIN ORDER_ITEM

        ON  RETAIL_ORDER.OrderNumber = ORDER_ITEM.OrderNumber

WHERE       OrderYear = 2020

ORDER BY    RETAIL_ORDER.OrderNumber, ORDER_ITEM.SKU;
```

This same correction will be needed for all other INNER JOIN statements in the rest of
this chapter.

You can use the SQL JOIN ON syntax as an alternative format for joins of three or more tables as well. If, for example, you want to obtain a list of the order data, order line data, and SKU data, you can use the following SQL statement:

```
/* *** SQL-Query-CH02-67 *** */
SELECT      RETAIL_ORDER.OrderNumber, StoreNumber, OrderYear,
            ORDER_ITEM.SKU, SKU_Description, Department
FROM        RETAIL_ORDER JOIN ORDER_ITEM
        ON  RETAIL_ORDER.OrderNumber = ORDER_ITEM.OrderNumber
            JOIN        SKU_DATA
                ON   ORDER_ITEM.SKU=SKU_DATA.SKU
WHERE       OrderYear = 2020
ORDER BY  RETAIL_ORDER.OrderNumber, ORDER_ITEM.SKU;
```

The result is:

|   | OrderNumber | StoreNumber | OrderYear | SKU | SKU_Description | Department |
|---|---|---|---|---|---|---|
| 1 | 1000 | 10 | 2020 | 201000 | Half-dome Tent | Camping |
| 2 | 1000 | 10 | 2020 | 202000 | Half-dome Tent Vestibule | Camping |
| 3 | 2000 | 20 | 2020 | 101100 | Dive Mask, Small Clear | Water Sports |
| 4 | 2000 | 20 | 2020 | 101200 | Dive Mask, Med Clear | Water Sports |

You can make that statement even simpler by using the SQL AS keyword to create a **table alias** for one or more tables in an SQL query as well as for naming output columns:

```
/* *** SQL-Query-CH02-68 *** */
SELECT      RO.OrderNumber, StoreNumber, OrderYear,
            OI.SKU, SKU_Description, Department
FROM        RETAIL_ORDER AS RO JOIN ORDER_ITEM AS OI
        ON  RO.OrderNumber = OI.OrderNumber
            JOIN        SKU_DATA AS SD
                ON   OI.SKU = SD.SKU
WHERE       OrderYear = 2020
ORDER BY  RO.OrderNumber, OI.SKU;
```

The result again is:

|   | OrderNumber | StoreNumber | OrderYear | SKU | SKU_Description | Department |
|---|---|---|---|---|---|---|
| 1 | 1000 | 10 | 2020 | 201000 | Half-dome Tent | Camping |
| 2 | 1000 | 10 | 2020 | 202000 | Half-dome Tent Vestibule | Camping |
| 3 | 2000 | 20 | 2020 | 101100 | Dive Mask, Small Clear | Water Sports |
| 4 | 2000 | 20 | 2020 | 101200 | Dive Mask, Med Clear | Water Sports |

> **BY THE WAY**    Oracle Database and MySQL create aliases in a similar manner, but Oracle Database does not allow use of the SQL AS keyword. In Oracle Database, the table name is just followed immediately by the alias to be used. This is shown in SQL-Query-CH02-68-Oracle:
>
> ```
> /* *** SQL-Query-CH02-68-Oracle *** */
> SELECT      RO.OrderNumber, StoreNumber, OrderYear,
>             OI.SKU, SKU_Description, Department
> FROM        RETAIL_ORDER RO JOIN ORDER_ITEM OI
>      ON     RO.OrderNumber = OI.OrderNumber
>             JOIN      SKU_DATA SD
>                  ON   OI.SKU = SD.SKU
> WHERE       OrderYear = 2020
> ORDER BY    RO.OrderNumber, OI.SKU;
> ```

One final note on SQL joins: although so far we have created SQL joins by using matching primary key and foreign key values, SQL joins are not restricted to these matches. In fact, any matching columns in two tables can be the basis for joins regardless of whether the columns are key columns or not. For example, imagine that your boss asks you the question: "Who are the buyers responsible for products in the Cape Codd 2020 catalog?"

In this case, the data on products in the 2020 catalog is in the CATALOG_SKU_2020 table, and the data on buyers is in the SKU_DATA table. A quick glance at Figure 2-4 shows that these two tables are not linked by a primary key to foreign key relationship–in fact, CATALOG_SKU_2020 is a freestanding table and not linked to any other table in the database.

Nonetheless, we can get the results we want with the following SQL query:

```
/* *** SQL-Query-CH02-69 *** */
SELECT     CatalogID, CS2020.SKU, CS2020.SKU_description, Buyer
FROM       CATALOG_SKU_2020 AS CS2020 JOIN SKU_DATA AS SD
     ON    CS2020.SKU = SD.SKU
WHERE      CatalogPage IS NOT NULL
ORDER BY   CatalogID;
```

This query uses an explicit join on SKU, even though SKU is not a key in the CATALOG_SKU_2020 table. The results are exactly what we need to answer the question:

|   | CatalogID | SKU | SKU_description | Buyer |
|---|-----------|-----|-----------------|-------|
| 1 | 20200001 | 100100 | Std. Scuba Tank, Yellow | Pete Hansen |
| 2 | 20200002 | 100300 | Std. Scuba Tank, Light Blue | Pete Hansen |
| 3 | 20200004 | 101100 | Dive Mask, Small Clear | Nancy Meyers |
| 4 | 20200005 | 101200 | Dive Mask, Med Clear | Nancy Meyers |
| 5 | 20200006 | 201000 | Half-dome Tent | Cindy Lo |
| 6 | 20200007 | 202000 | Half-dome Tent Vestibule | Cindy Lo |
| 7 | 20200008 | 301000 | Light Fly Climbing Harness | Jerry Martin |
| 8 | 20200009 | 302000 | Locking Carabiner, Oval | Jerry Martin |

## SQL Queries on Recursive Relationships

The term **recursive** means that something recurs or repeats. In computer programming languages, a **recursive procedure** is a block of code that calls itself. In database structures, a *recursive relationship* is a relationship between two columns in the same table.

In the Cape Codd Outdoor Sports data extract, the BUYER table has a recursive relationship: the Supervisor column holds value of the BuyerName column as data and serves as a foreign key referencing BuyerName as the associated primary key. We can see this relationship clearly in the BUYER table data, here sorted to list buyers by their Position from highest (Manager) to lowest (Buyer 1):

```
/* *** SQL-Query-CH02-70 *** */

SELECT    BuyerName, Department, Position, Supervisor
FROM      BUYER
ORDER BY  Position DESC;
```

The results of SQL-Query-CH02-70 are:

|   | BuyerName | Department | Position | Supervisor |
|---|-----------|------------|----------|------------|
| 1 | Mary Smith | Purchasing | Manager | NULL |
| 2 | Pete Hansen | Purchasing | Buyer 3 | Mary Smith |
| 3 | Cindy Lo | Purchasing | Buyer 2 | Mary Smith |
| 4 | Jerry Martin | Purchasing | Buyer 1 | Cindy Lo |
| 5 | Nancy Meyers | Purchasing | Buyer 1 | Pete Hansen |

Note that as Manager, Mary Smith does not have a Supervisor and thus has a NULL value in that column. Thus, an SQL query on a recursive relationship is technically a single table query because both columns are in the same table. Unfortunately, however, SQL query statements only allow foreign key to primary key matching between two different tables!

The solution is to use table aliases to create two aliased versions of the same single table. Thus, we have SQL-Query-CH02-71 that lists each BuyerName and that person's Supervisor:

```
/* *** SQL-Query-CH02-71 *** */

SELECT      S.BuyerName AS SupervisorName,
            S.Position AS SupervisorPosition,
            B.BuyerName, B.Position
FROM        BUYER S JOIN BUYER B
      ON    S.BuyerName = B.Supervisor
ORDER BY    S.BuyerName;
```

The result is:

|   | SupervisorName | SupervisiorPosition | BuyerName | Position |
|---|----------------|---------------------|-----------|----------|
| 1 | Cindy Lo | Buyer 2 | Jerry Martin | Buyer 1 |
| 2 | Mary Smith | Manager | Cindy Lo | Buyer 2 |
| 3 | Mary Smith | Manager | Pete Hansen | Buyer 3 |
| 4 | Pete Hansen | Buyer 3 | Nancy Meyers | Buyer 1 |

As we would expect, this query fails in Microsoft Access ANSI-89 SQL because Microsoft Access does require the use of the SQL keyword INNER.

**Solution:** Add the SQL keyword INNER into the statement. The correct Microsoft Access ANSI-89 SQL statement for this query is:

```
/* *** SQL-Query-CH02-71-ACCESS *** */
SELECT      S.BuyerName AS SupervisorName,
            S.Position AS SupervisorPosition,
            B.BuyerName, B.Position
FROM        BUYER S INNER JOIN BUYER B
       ON   S.BuyerName = B.Supervisor
ORDER BY    S.BuyerName;
```

In Figure 2-4, we intentionally left out the recursive relationship within the BUYER relationship. We did this because the only way Microsoft Access can illustrate recursive relationships created in Microsoft Access is to actually show a second, aliased version of the BUYER table, as shown in Figure 2-31.

## Outer Joins

The SQL joins we have used so far have been inner joins, where only rows that have matching values in the joined tables are displayed in the results. Suppose that we would like to see how product sales at Cape Codd Outdoor Sports are related to the buyers—are the buyers acquiring products that sell? We can start with SQL-Query-CH02-72:

```
/* *** SQL-Query-CH02-72 *** */
SELECT      OI.OrderNumber, Quantity,
            SD.SKU, SKU_Description, Department, Buyer
FROM        ORDER_ITEM AS OI JOIN SKU_DATA AS SD
       ON   OI.SKU = SD.SKU
ORDER BY    OI.OrderNumber, SD.SKU;
```

**FIGURE 2-31**

A Recursive Relationship in Microsoft Access 2019

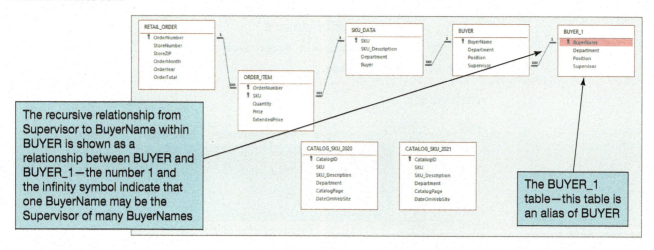

The recursive relationship from Supervisor to BuyerName within BUYER is shown as a relationship between BUYER and BUYER_1—the number 1 and the infinity symbol indicate that one BuyerName may be the Supervisor of many BuyerNames

The BUYER_1 table—this table is an alias of BUYER

This produces the following result set:

| | OrderNumber | Quantity | SKU | SKU_Description | Department | Buyer |
|---|---|---|---|---|---|---|
| 1 | 1000 | 1 | 201000 | Half-dome Tent | Camping | Cindy Lo |
| 2 | 1000 | 1 | 202000 | Half-dome Tent Vestibule | Camping | Cindy Lo |
| 3 | 2000 | 4 | 101100 | Dive Mask, Small Clear | Water Sports | Nancy Meyers |
| 4 | 2000 | 2 | 101200 | Dive Mask, Med Clear | Water Sports | Nancy Meyers |
| 5 | 3000 | 1 | 100200 | Std. Scuba Tank, Magenta | Water Sports | Pete Hansen |
| 6 | 3000 | 2 | 101100 | Dive Mask, Small Clear | Water Sports | Nancy Meyers |
| 7 | 3000 | 1 | 101200 | Dive Mask, Med Clear | Water Sports | Nancy Meyers |

This result is correct, but it shows the names of only five of the 13 SKU items in the SKU_DATA table. What happened to the other SKU items and their associated buyers? Look closely at the data in Figure 2-6, and you will see that the SKU items and their buyers that do not appear in the results. For example, SKU 100100 with buyer Pete Hansen is an SKU item that has *never been sold* as part of a retail order. Therefore, the primary key values of these SKU items do not match any foreign key value in the ORDER_ITEM table, and because they have no match, they do not appear in the result of this join statement. What can we do about this case when we are creating an SQL query in which we want to see what does and does not sell?

Consider the STUDENT and LOCKER tables in Figure 2-32(a), where we have drawn the two tables to highlight the relationships between the rows in each table. The STUDENT table shows the student number (StudentPK), the name of the student (StudentName), and the student's locker number (LockerFK) for students at a university. The LOCKER table shows the LockerPK (locker number) and LockerType (full size or half size) of lockers at the recreation center on campus. If we run a standard join using SQL JOIN ON syntax between these two tables as shown in SQL-Query-CH02-73, we get a table of students who have lockers assigned to them together with their assigned locker. This result is shown in Figure 2-32(b).

```
/* *** EXAMPLE CODE - DO NOT RUN *** *//* *** SQL-Query-CH02-73 *** */
SELECT     StudentPK, StudentName, LockerFK, LockerPK, LockerType
FROM       STUDENT JOIN LOCKER
     ON    STUDENT.LockerFK = LOCKER.LockerPK
ORDER BY   StudentPK;
```

The type of SQL join is known as an **SQL inner join**, and we can also run the query using the **SQL INNER JOIN phrase**. This is shown in SQL-Query-CH02-74, which produces exactly the same result shown in Figure 2-32(b).

```
/* *** EXAMPLE CODE - DO NOT RUN *** */
/* *** SQL-Query-CH02-74 *** */
SELECT     StudentPK, StudentName, LockerFK, LockerPK, LockerType
FROM       STUDENT INNER JOIN LOCKER
     ON    STUDENT.LockerFK = LOCKER.LockerPK
ORDER BY   StudentPK;
```

Now suppose we want to show all the rows already in the join, but also want to show any rows (students) in the STUDENT table that are not included in the inner join. This means

**STUDENT**                                                                 **LOCKER**

| StudentPK | StudentName | LockerFK |
|-----------|-------------|----------|
| 1 | Adams | NULL |
| 2 | Buchanan | NULL |
| 3 | Carter | 10 |
| 4 | Ford | 20 |
| 5 | Hoover | 30 |
| 6 | Kennedy | 40 |
| 7 | Roosevelt | 50 |
| 8 | Truman | 60 |

| LockerPK | LockerType |
|----------|------------|
| 10 | Full |
| 20 | Full |
| 30 | Half |
| 40 | Full |
| 50 | Full |
| 60 | Half |
| 70 | Full |
| 80 | Full |
| 90 | Half |

**(a)** The STUDENT and LOCKER Tables Aligned to Show Row Relationships

Only the rows where LockerFK=LockerPK are shown—note that some StudentPK and some LockerPK values are not in the results

| StudentPK | StudentName | LockerFK | LockerPK | LockerType |
|-----------|-------------|----------|----------|------------|
| 3 | Carter | 10 | 10 | Full |
| 4 | Ford | 20 | 20 | Full |
| 5 | Hoover | 30 | 30 | Half |
| 6 | Kennedy | 40 | 40 | Full |
| 7 | Roosevelt | 50 | 50 | Full |
| 8 | Truman | 60 | 60 | Half |

**(b)** INNER JOIN of the STUDENT and LOCKER Tables

All rows from STUDENT are shown, even where there is no matching LockerFK=LockerPK value

| StudentPK | StudentName | LockerFK | LockerPK | LockerType |
|-----------|-------------|----------|----------|------------|
| 1 | Adams | NULL | NULL | NULL |
| 2 | Buchanan | NULL | NULL | NULL |
| 3 | Carter | 10 | 10 | Full |
| 4 | Ford | 20 | 20 | Full |
| 5 | Hoover | 30 | 30 | Half |
| 6 | Kennedy | 40 | 40 | Full |
| 7 | Roosevelt | 50 | 50 | Full |
| 8 | Truman | 60 | 60 | Half |

**(c)** LEFT OUTER JOIN of the STUDENT and LOCKER Tables

All rows from LOCKER are shown, even where there is no matching LockerFK=LockerPK value

| StudentPK | StudentName | LockerFK | LockerPK | LockerType |
|-----------|-------------|----------|----------|------------|
| 3 | Carter | 10 | 10 | Full |
| 4 | Ford | 20 | 20 | Full |
| 5 | Hoover | 30 | 30 | Half |
| 6 | Kennedy | 40 | 40 | Full |
| 7 | Roosevelt | 50 | 50 | Full |
| 8 | Truman | 60 | 60 | Half |
| NULL | NULL | NULL | 70 | Full |
| NULL | NULL | NULL | 80 | Full |
| NULL | NULL | NULL | 90 | Half |

**FIGURE 2-32**

Types of Joins

**(d)** RIGHT OUTER JOIN of the STUDENT and LOCKER Tables

that we want to see *all students*, including those who have *not been assigned a locker*. This is called an **outer join**. To do this, we use the **SQL outer join**, which is designed for this very purpose. And because the table we want is listed first in the query and is thus on the left side of the table listing, we specifically use an **SQL left outer join**, which uses the **SQL LEFT OUTER JOIN syntax**. This is shown in SQL-Query-CH02-75, which produces the results shown in Figure 2-32(c).

```
/* *** EXAMPLE CODE - DO NOT RUN *** */
/* *** SQL-Query-CH02-75 *** */
SELECT     StudentPK, StudentName, LockerFK, LockerPK, LockerType
FROM       STUDENT LEFT OUTER JOIN LOCKER
     ON    STUDENT.LockerFK = LOCKER.LockerPK
ORDER BY   StudentPK;
```

In the results shown in Figure 2-32(c), note that all the rows from the STUDENT table are now included and that rows that have no match in the LOCKER table are shown with NULL values. Looking at the output, we can see that the students Adams and Buchanan have no linked rows in the LOCKER table. This means that Adams and Buchanan have not been assigned a locker in the recreation center.

If we want to show all the rows already in the join, but now also any rows in the LOCKER table that are not included in the inner join, we specifically use an **SQL right outer join**, which uses the **SQL RIGHT OUTER JOIN syntax** because the table we want is listed second in the query and is thus on the right side of the table listing. This means that we want to see *all lockers*, including those that have *not been assigned to a student*. This is shown in SQL-Query-CH02-76, which produces the results shown in Figure 2-32(d).

```
/* *** EXAMPLE CODE - DO NOT RUN *** */
/* *** SQL-Query-CH02-76 *** */
SELECT     StudentPK, StudentName, LockerFK, LockerPK, LockerType
FROM       STUDENT RIGHT OUTER JOIN LOCKER
     ON    STUDENT.LockerFK = LOCKER.LockerPK
ORDER BY   LockerPK;
```

In the results shown in Figure 2-32(d), note that all the rows from the LOCKER table are now included and that rows that have no match in the STUDENT table are shown with NULL values. Looking at the output, we can see that the lockers numbered 70, 80, and 90 have no linked rows in the STUDENT table. This means that these lockers are currently unassigned to a student and available for use.

In terms of our question about SKUs and buyers, this means that we can use an SQL OUTER JOIN and specifically an SQL RIGHT OUTER JOIN to obtain the desired results:

```
/* *** SQL-Query-CH02-77 *** */
SELECT     OI.OrderNumber, Quantity,
           SD.SKU, SKU_Description, Department, Buyer
FROM       ORDER_ITEM AS OI RIGHT OUTER JOIN SKU_DATA AS SD
     ON    OI.SKU = SD.SKU
ORDER BY   OI.OrderNumber, SD.SKU;
```

This produces the following results, which clearly show the SKUs and their associated buyers that have not been part of a retail order (in particular, note that we haven't sold any of the 300000 range SKUs, which are climbing equipment—perhaps management should look into that):

|    | OrderNumber | Quantity | SKU | SKU_Description | Department | Buyer |
|----|-------------|----------|-----|----------------|------------|-------|
| 1  | NULL | NULL | 100100 | Std. Scuba Tank, Yellow | Water Sports | Pete Hansen |
| 2  | NULL | NULL | 100300 | Std. Scuba Tank, Light Blue | Water Sports | Pete Hansen |
| 3  | NULL | NULL | 100400 | Std. Scuba Tank, Dark Blue | Water Sports | Pete Hansen |
| 4  | NULL | NULL | 100500 | Std. Scuba Tank, Light Green | Water Sports | Pete Hansen |
| 5  | NULL | NULL | 100600 | Std. Scuba Tank, Dark Green | Water Sports | Pete Hansen |
| 6  | NULL | NULL | 203000 | Half-dome Tent Vestibule - Wide | Camping | Cindy Lo |
| 7  | NULL | NULL | 301000 | Light Fly Climbing Harness | Climbing | Jerry Martin |
| 8  | NULL | NULL | 302000 | Locking Carabiner, Oval | Climbing | Jerry Martin |
| 9  | 1000 | 1 | 201000 | Half-dome Tent | Camping | Cindy Lo |
| 10 | 1000 | 1 | 202000 | Half-dome Tent Vestibule | Camping | Cindy Lo |
| 11 | 2000 | 4 | 101100 | Dive Mask, Small Clear | Water Sports | Nancy Meyers |
| 12 | 2000 | 2 | 101200 | Dive Mask, Med Clear | Water Sports | Nancy Meyers |
| 13 | 3000 | 1 | 100200 | Std. Scuba Tank, Magenta | Water Sports | Pete Hansen |
| 14 | 3000 | 2 | 101100 | Dive Mask, Small Clear | Water Sports | Nancy Meyers |
| 15 | 3000 | 1 | 101200 | Dive Mask, Med Clear | Water Sports | Nancy Meyers |

**BY THE WAY**    It is easy to forget that inner joins will drop nonmatching rows. Some years ago, one of the authors had a very large organization as a consulting client. The client had a budgetary-planning application that included a long sequence of complicated SQL statements. One of the joins in that sequence was an inner join that should have been an outer join. As a result, some 3,000 employees dropped out of the budgetary calculations. The mistake was discovered only months later when the actual salary expense exceeded the budget salary expense by a large margin. The mistake was an embarrassment all the way to the board of directors.

## Using SQL Set Operators

Mathematicians use the term **set theory** to describe mathematical operations on sets, where a **set** is defined as a group of distinct items. A relational database table meets the definition of a set, so it is little wonder that SQL includes a group of **set operators** for use with SQL queries.

**Venn diagrams set** are the standard method of visualizing sets and their relationships. As shown in Figure 2-33:

- A set is represented by a labeled circle, as shown in Figure 2-33(a).
- A **subset** is a portion of a set that is contained entirely within the set, as shown in Figure 2-33(b).
- The **union** of two sets is shown in Figure 2-33(c) and represents the two sets together to get a set that contains all values in both sets. This is equivalent to an OR logical operation (A OR B).
- The **intersection** of two sets is shown in Figure 2-33(d), and represents the area common to both sets. This is equivalent to an AND logical operation (A AND B).
- The **complement** of set B in set A is shown in Figure 2-33(e), and represents everything in set A that is not in set B. This is equivalent to a logical operation using A AND (NOT B). It is also equivalent to the set difference (A − B).

**FIGURE 2-33**

Venn Diagrams

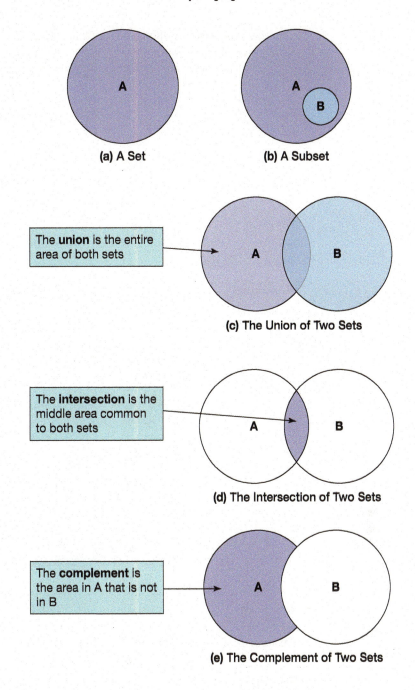

(a) A Set                                    (b) A Subset

The **union** is the entire area of both sets

(c) The Union of Two Sets

The **intersection** is the middle area common to both sets

(d) The Intersection of Two Sets

The **complement** is the area in A that is not in B

(e) The Complement of Two Sets

SQL provides **SQL set operators** for each of these set operations, and these are shown in Figure 2-34. Note that in order to use SQL set operators, the number of table columns involved in the operations *must* be the same in each SELECT component, and corresponding

**FIGURE 2-34**

SQL Set Operators

| SQL Set Operators | |
|---|---|
| **Operator** | **Meaning** |
| UNION | The result is all the row values in one or both tables |
| INTERSECT | The result is all the row values common to both tables |
| EXCEPT | The result is all the row values in the first table but not the second |

columns *must* have the same or compatible (e.g., CHAR and VARCHAR, as discussed in Chapter 6) data types!

To illustrate SQL set operations, imagine that your boss asks you the question: "What products were available for sale (by either catalog or Web site) in 2020 or 2021?" Looking at Figure 2-6(b), we can see that to answer this question we must combine all the data in the CATALOG_SKU_2020 and CATALOG_SKU_2021 tables. We do this using the **SQL UNION operator**, as shown in SQL-Query-CH02-78:

```
/* *** SQL-Query-CH02-78 *** */
SELECT     SKU, SKU_Description, Department
FROM       CATALOG_SKU_2020
UNION
SELECT     SKU, SKU_Description, Department
FROM       CATALOG_SKU_2021;
```

This produces the following results, which clearly show all the SKUs available for sale in one or both years:

|    | SKU | SKU_Description | Department |
|----|-----|----------------|------------|
| 1 | 100100 | Std. Scuba Tank, Yellow | Water Sports |
| 2 | 100200 | Std. Scuba Tank, Magenta | Water Sports |
| 3 | 100300 | Std. Scuba Tank, Light Blue | Water Sports |
| 4 | 100400 | Std. Scuba Tank, Dark Blue | Water Sports |
| 5 | 101100 | Dive Mask, Small Clear | Water Sports |
| 6 | 101200 | Dive Mask, Med Clear | Water Sports |
| 7 | 201000 | Half-dome Tent | Camping |
| 8 | 202000 | Half-dome Tent Vestibule | Camping |
| 9 | 203000 | Half-dome Tent Vestibule - Wide | Camping |
| 10 | 301000 | Light Fly Climbing Harness | Climbing |
| 11 | 302000 | Locking Carabiner, Oval | Climbing |

Now imagine that your boss asks you the question: "What products were available for sale (by either catalog or Web site) in *both* 2020 and 2021?" Looking at the Venn diagrams in Figure 2-33 and table data in Figure 2-6(b), we can see that to answer to this question, we must find the data in the CATALOG_SKU_2020 and CATALOG_SKU_2021 tables

**BY THE WAY**   If we compare the output of SQL-Query-CH02-78 to the data in the CATALOG-SKU_2020 and CATALOG_SKU_2021, we will note that there are no duplicate rows in the query output. For example, SKU 201000, the Half-Dome Tent, is in each table, but only appears once in the query output. If, for some reason, we wanted the duplicated rows to be displayed in the query output as well, we would simply add the **SQL ALL keyword** to the query:

```
/* *** SQL-Query-CH02-78-ALL *** */
SELECT     SKU, SKU_Description, Department
FROM       CATALOG_SKU_2020
UNION ALL
SELECT     SKU, SKU_Description, Department
FROM       CATALOG_SKU_2021;
```

that appears in *both* tables. We do this using the **SQL INTERSECT operator** (note that neither Microsoft Access 2019 nor MySQL 8.0 support this operator), as shown in SQL-Query-CH02-79:

```
/* *** SQL-Query-CH02-79 *** */
SELECT      SKU, SKU_Description, Department
FROM        CATALOG_SKU_2020
INTERSECT
SELECT      SKU, SKU_Description, Department
FROM        CATALOG_SKU_2021;
```

This produces the following results, which clearly show all the SKUs available for sale in both years:

|   | SKU | SKU_Description | Department |
|---|-----|----------------|------------|
| 1 | 100100 | Std. Scuba Tank, Yellow | Water Sports |
| 2 | 101100 | Dive Mask, Small Clear | Water Sports |
| 3 | 101200 | Dive Mask, Med Clear | Water Sports |
| 4 | 201000 | Half-dome Tent | Camping |
| 5 | 202000 | Half-dome Tent Vestibule | Camping |
| 6 | 301000 | Light Fly Climbing Harness | Climbing |
| 7 | 302000 | Locking Carabiner, Oval | Climbing |

Finally, imagine that your boss asks you the question: "What products were available for sale (by either catalog or Web site) in 2020 but *not* in 2021?" Looking at the Venn diagrams in Figure 2-33 and table data in Figure 2-6(b), we can see that to answer this question, we must find the data in the CATALOG_SKU_2020 table that did *not* also appear in the CATALOG_SKU_2021 table. We do this using the **SQL EXCEPT operator** (note that Oracle Database calls this the **SQL MINUS operator**, and that neither Microsoft Access 2019 nor MySQL 8.0 support this operation) as shown in SQL-Query-CH02-80:

```
/* *** SQL-Query-CH02-80 *** */
SELECT      SKU, SKU_Description, Department
FROM        CATALOG_SKU_2020
EXCEPT
SELECT      SKU, SKU_Description, Department
FROM        CATALOG_SKU_2021;
```

This produces the following results, which clearly show the SKUs that were available for sale in only the 2020 catalog:

|   | SKU | SKU_Description | Department |
|---|-----|----------------|------------|
| 1 | 100300 | Std. Scuba Tank, Light Blue | Water Sports |
| 2 | 100400 | Std. Scuba Tank, Dark Blue | Water Sports |

This completes our discussion of SQL query statements. We have covered the needed SQL syntax to allow you to write ad-hoc SQL queries on one or more tables, displaying only the specific row, column, or calculated values that you want to see. In Chapter 7, we will return to SQL to discuss SQL DDL, some other parts of SQL DML, and SQL/PSM. In Chapter 8, we will also return to SQL to discuss correlated subqueries.

# Summary

Wow! That was a full chapter!

Structured Query Language (SQL) was developed by IBM and has been endorsed by the ANSI SQL-92 and following standards. SQL is a data sublanguage that can be embedded into full programming languages or submitted directly to the DBMS. Knowing SQL is critical for knowledge workers, application programmers, and database administrators.

All DBMS products process SQL. Microsoft Access hides SQL, but SQL Server, Oracle Database, and MySQL require that you use it.

We are primarily interested in five categories of SQL statements: DML, DDL, SQL/PSM statements, TCL, and DCL. DML statements include statements for querying data and for inserting, updating, and deleting data. This chapter addresses only DML query statements. Additional DML statements, DDL, and SQL/PSM are discussed in Chapter 7. TCL and DCL are discussed in Chapter 9.

The examples in this chapter are based on six tables extracted from the operational database at Cape Codd Outdoor Sports. Such database extracts are common and important. Sample data for the six tables is shown in Figures 2-6(a) and 2-6(b).

The basic structure of an SQL query statement is SELECT/FROM/WHERE. The columns to be selected are listed after SELECT, the table(s) to process is (are) listed after FROM, and any restrictions on data values are listed after WHERE. In a WHERE clause, character and date data values must be enclosed in single quotes. Numeric data need not be enclosed in quotes. You can submit SQL statements directly to Microsoft Access, SQL Server, Oracle Database, and MySQL, as described in this chapter.

This chapter explained the use of the following SQL clauses: SELECT, FROM, WHERE, ORDER BY, GROUP BY, and HAVING. By default, the WHERE clause is applied before the HAVING clause. This chapter explained the use of the following SQL keywords: DISTINCT, TOP, and TOP PERCENT. We discussed SQL comparison operators, including the SQL keywords IN, NOT IN, BETWEEN, NOT BETWEEN, LIKE, NOT LIKE, IS NULL, and IS NOT NULL. We used the SQL wildcard characters % (* for Microsoft Access) and _ (? for Microsoft Access). We learned the SQL logical operators AND, OR, and NOT. We used the SQL built-in aggregate functions COUNT, SUM, AVG, MIN, and MAX. We discussed the SQL alias operator AS and the SQL set operators UNION, UNION ALL, INTERSECT, and EXCEPT. You should know how to mix and match these features to obtain the results you want.

You can query multiple tables using subqueries and joins. Subqueries are nested queries that commonly use the SQL comparison operators IN and NOT IN. An SQL SELECT expression is placed inside parentheses. Using a subquery, you can display data from the top table only. An implicit join is created by specifying multiple table names in the FROM clause. An SQL WHERE clause is used to obtain an equijoin. In most cases, equijoins are the most sensible option. Joins can display data from multiple tables. In Chapter 8, you will learn another type of subquery that can perform work that is not possible with joins.

Queries on recursive relationships are queries on a single table but use table aliases to structure the SQL statement as a query between two different tables.

Since the SQL-92 standard, the explicit SQL JOIN ON syntax has been considered the proper syntax for SQL joins. Rows that have no match in the join condition are dropped from the join results when using a regular, or INNER, join. To keep such rows, use a LEFT OUTER or RIGHT OUTER join rather than an INNER join.

# Key Terms

/* and */

ad-hoc queries

American National Standards Institute (ANSI)

AVG

business intelligence (BI) systems

Cartesian product

character strings

complement

composite primary key

correlated subquery

COUNT

CROSS JOIN

CRUD

data control language (DCL)

data definition language (DDL)

data manipulation language (DML)

data mart

data sublanguage

data warehouse

data warehouse DBMS

domain

empty set

equijoin

explicit join

Extensible Markup Language (XML)

Extract, Transform, and Load (ETL) system

foreign key

graphical user interface (GUI)

implicit join

inner join

International Organization for Standardization (ISO)

intersection

JavaScript Object Notation (JSON)

join

joining two tables

MAX

Microsoft Access asterisk (*) wildcard character

Microsoft Access question mark (?) wildcard character

MIN

NULL

null value

online transaction processing (OLTP)

outer join

primary key

query by example (QBE)

relational database

record

recursive

recursive procedure

recursive relationship

relationship

schema

set

set operators

set theory

SQL ALL keyword

SQL AND operator

SQL AS keyword

SQL asterisk (*) wildcard character

SQL BETWEEN operator

SQL built-in aggregate functions

SQL comment

SQL comparison operator

SQL DESC keyword

SQL DISTINCT keyword

SQL EXCEPT operator

SQL expression

SQL FROM clause

SQL GROUP BY clause

SQL HAVING clause

SQL IN operator

SQL INNER keyword

SQL inner join

SQL INNER JOIN phrase

SQL INTERSECT operator

SQL IS keyword

SQL IS NOT NULL operator

SQL IS NULL operator

SQL JOIN keyword

SQL join operation

SQL JOIN ON syntax

SQL JOIN operator

SQL LEFT OUTER JOIN syntax

SQL left outer join

SQL LIKE operator

SQL logical operators

SQL MINUS operator

SQL NOT BETWEEN operator

SQL NOT IN operator

SQL NOT LIKE operator

SQL NOT operator

SQL ON clause

SQL ON keyword

SQL OR operator

SQL ORDER BY clause

SQL outer join

SQL percent sign (%) wildcard character

SQL/Persistent Stored Modules (SQL/PSM)

SQL query

SQL RIGHT OUTER JOIN syntax

SQL right outer join

SQL script file

SQL SELECT clause

SQL SELECT/FROM/WHERE framework

SQL Server Compatible Syntax (ANSI 92)

SQL set operators

SQL subquery

SQL TOP {NumberOfRows} function

SQL TOP {Percentage} PERCENT function

SQL underscore (_) wildcard character

SQL UNION operator

SQL WHERE clause

stock-keeping unit (SKU)

Structured Query Language (SQL)

subset

SUM

table alias

TableName.ColumnName

top level query

transaction control language (TCL)

union

Venn diagram

# Review Questions

**2.1** What is an online transaction processing (OLTP) system? What is a business intelligence (BI) system? What is a data warehouse?

**2.2** What is an ad-hoc query?

**2.3** What does SQL stand for, and what is SQL?

**2.4** What does SKU stand for? What is an SKU?

**2.5** Summarize how data were altered and filtered in creating the Cape Codd data extraction.

**2.6** Explain in general terms the relationships among the RETAIL_ORDER, ORDER_ITEM, SKU_DATA, and BUYER tables. What is the relationship of these tables to the CATALOG_SKU_2020 and CATALOG_SKU_2021 tables?

**2.7** Summarize the background of SQL.

**2.8** What is SQL-92? How does it relate to the SQL statements in this chapter?

**2.9** What features have been added to SQL in versions subsequent to SQL-92?

**2.10** Why is SQL described as a data sublanguage?

**2.11** What does DML stand for? What are DML statements?

**2.12** What does DDL stand for? What are DDL statements?

**2.13** What is the SQL SELECT/FROM/WHERE framework?

**2.14** Explain how Microsoft Access uses SQL.

**2.15** Explain how enterprise-class DBMS products use SQL.

The Cape Codd Outdoor Sports sale extraction database has been modified to include three additional tables: the INVENTORY table, the WAREHOUSE table, and the CATALOG_SKU_2019 table. The table schemas for these tables, together with the RETAIL_ORDER, ORDER_ITEM, SKU_DATA, BUYER, CATALOG_SKU_2020, and CATALOG_SKU_2021 tables, are as follows:

RETAIL_ORDER (**OrderNumber**, **StoreNumber**, **StoreZIP**, **OrderMonth**, **OrderYear**, **OrderTotal**)

ORDER_ITEM (*OrderNumber*, **SKU**, **Quantity**, **Price**, **ExtendedPrice**)

SKU_DATA (**SKU**, **SKU_Description**, **Department**, *Buyer*)

BUYER (**BuyerName**, **Department**, **Position**, *Supervisor*)

WAREHOUSE (**WarehouseID**, **WarehouseCity**, **WarehouseState**, **Manager**, **SquareFeet**)

INVENTORY (*WarehouseID*, **SKU**, **SKU_Description**, **QuantityOnHand**, **QuantityOnOrder**)

CATALOG_SKU_2019 (**CatalogID**, **SKU**, **SKU_Description**, **CatalogPage**, **DateOnWebSite**)

CATALOG_SKU_2020 (**CatalogID**, **SKU**, **SKU_Description**, **CatalogPage**, **DateOnWebSite**)

CATALOG_SKU_2021 (**CatalogID**, **SKU**, **SKU_Description**, **CatalogPage**, **DateOnWebSite**)

The nine tables in the revised Cape Codd database schema are shown in Figure 2-35. The column characteristics for the WAREHOUSE table are shown in Figure 2-36, the

**FIGURE 2-35**

**The Cape Codd Database with the WAREHOUSE, INVENTORY and CATALOG_SKU_2019 Tables**

column characteristics for the INVENTORY table are shown in Figure 2-37, and the column characteristics for the CATALOG_SKU_2019 table are shown in Figure 2-38. The data for the WAREHOUSE table are shown in Figure 2-39, the data for the INVENTORY table are shown in Figure 2-40, and the data for the CATALOG_SKU_2019 table is shown in Figure 2-41.

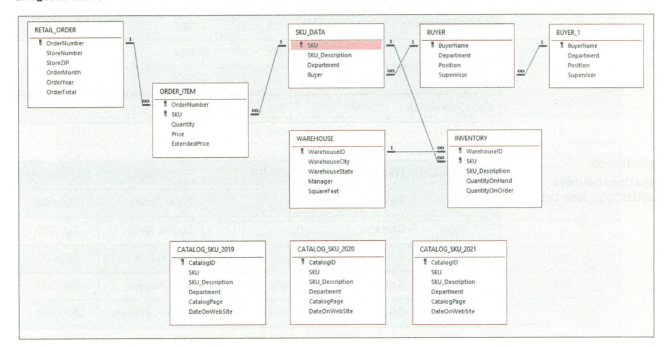

**FIGURE 2-36**

Column Characteristics for the Cape Codd Database WAREHOUSE Table

**WAREHOUSE**

| Column Name | Type | Key | Required | Remarks |
|---|---|---|---|---|
| WarehouseID | Integer | Primary Key | Yes | Surrogate Key |
| WarehouseCity | Character (30) | No | Yes | |
| WarehouseState | Character (2) | No | Yes | |
| Manager | Character (35) | No | No | |
| SquareFeet | Integer | No | No | |

**FIGURE 2-37**

Column Characteristics for the Cape Codd Database INVENTORY Table

**INVENTORY**

| Column Name | Type | Key | Required | Remarks |
|---|---|---|---|---|
| WarehouseID | Integer | Primary Key, Foreign Key | Yes | REF: WAREHOUSE |
| SKU | Integer | Primary Key, Foreign Key | Yes | REF: SKU_DATA |
| SKU_Description | Character (35) | No | Yes | |
| QuantityOnHand | Integer | No | No | |
| QuantityOnOrder | Integer | No | No | |

**2.46**  Write an SQL statement to show the SKU, SKU_Description, and WarehouseID for all items stored in a warehouse managed by 'Lucille Smith'. Use a join, but do not use JOIN ON syntax.

**2.47**  Write an SQL statement to show the SKU, SKU_Description, and WarehouseID for all items stored in a warehouse managed by 'Lucille Smith'. Use a join using JOIN ON syntax.

**2.48**  Write an SQL statement to show the WarehouseID and average QuantityOnHand of all items stored in a warehouse managed by 'Lucille Smith'. Use a subquery.

**2.49**  Write an SQL statement to show the WarehouseID and average QuantityOnHand of all items stored in a warehouse managed by 'Lucille Smith'. Use a join, but do not use JOIN ON syntax.

**2.50**  Write an SQL statement to show the WarehouseID and average QuantityOnHand of all items stored in a warehouse managed by 'Lucille Smith'. Use a join using JOIN ON syntax.

**2.51**  Write an SQL statement to show the WarehouseID, WarehouseCity, WarehouseState, Manager, SKU, SKU_Description, and QuantityOnHand of all items stored in a warehouse managed by 'Lucille Smith'. Use a join using JOIN ON syntax.

**2.52**  Write an SQL statement to display the WarehouseID, the sum of QuantityOnOrder, and the sum of QuantityOnHand, grouped by WarehouseID and QuantityOnOrder. Name the sum of QuantityOnOrder as TotalItemsOnOrder and the sum of Quantity OnHand as TotalItemsOnHand. Use only the INVENTORY table in your SQL statement.

**2.53**  Explain why you cannot use a subquery in your answer to Review Question 2.52.

**2.54**  Explain how subqueries and joins differ.

**2.55**  Write an SQL statement to join WAREHOUSE and INVENTORY and include all rows of WAREHOUSE in your answer, regardless of whether they have any INVENTORY. Include all columns of both tables, but do not repeat the join column.

**Use *both* the CATALOG_SKU_2019 and CATALOG_SKU_2020 tables to answer Review Questions 2.56 through 2.60 (for Microsoft Access 2019 and MySQL 8.0, 2.56 and 2.57 only):**

**2.56**  Write an SQL statement to display the SKU, SKU_Description, and Department of all SKUs that appear in *either* the Cape Codd 2019 catalog (either in the printed catalog or on the Web site) *or* the Cape Codd 2020 catalog (either in the printed catalog or on the Web site) *or* both.

**2.57**  Write an SQL statement to display the SKU, SKU_Description, and Department of all SKUs that appear in *either* the Cape Codd 2019 catalog (only in the printed catalog itself) *or* the Cape Codd 2020 catalog (only in the printed catalog itself) *or* both.

**2.58**  Write an SQL statement to display the SKU, SKU_Description, and Department of all SKUs that appear in *both* the Cape Codd 2019 catalog (either in the printed catalog or on the Web site) *and* the Cape Codd 2020 catalog (either in the printed catalog or on the Web site).

**2.59**  Write an SQL statement to display the SKU, SKU_Description, and Department of all SKUs that appear in *both* the Cape Codd 2019 catalog (only in the printed catalog itself) *and* the Cape Codd 2020 catalog (only in the printed catalog itself).

**2.60**  Write an SQL statement to display the SKU, SKU_Description, and Department of all SKUs that appear in *only* the Cape Codd 2019 catalog (either in the printed catalog or on the Web site) *and not* in the Cape Codd 2020 catalog (either in the printed catalog or on the Web site).

# Exercises

For this set of project questions, we will extend the Microsoft Access 2019 database for Wedgewood Pacific (WP) that we created in Chapter 1. Founded in 1987 in Seattle, Washington, this company manufactures and sells consumer drone aircraft. This is an innovative and rapidly developing market. In October 2020, the Federal Aviation Administration (FAA) said that over 1,700,000 drones had been registered under the new FAA drone registration rules.[3] Of these, only about 500,000 were commercial drones, and the rest were drones for recreational use! The FAA also reported that over 198,000 remote pilots had been certified.

WP currently produces three drone models: the Alpha III, the Bravo III, and the Delta IV. These products are created by WP's Research and Development group and produced at WP's production facilities. WP manufactures some of the parts used in the drones but also purchases some parts from other suppliers.

The company is located in two buildings. One building houses the Administration, Legal, Finance, Accounting, Human Resources, and Sales and Marketing departments, and the second houses the Information Systems, Research and Development, and Production departments. The company database contains data about employees; departments; projects; assets, such as finished goods inventory, parts inventory, and computer equipment; and other aspects of company operations.

In the following project questions, we have already created the WP.accdb database with the following two tables (see Chapter 1 Project Questions):

**DEPARTMENT (DepartmentName, BudgetCode, OfficeNumber, DepartmentPhone)**

**EMPLOYEE (EmployeeNumber, FirstName, LastName, *Department*, Position, *Supervisor*, OfficePhone, EmailAddress)**

Now we will add in the following two tables:

**PROJECT (ProjectID, ProjectName, *Department*, MaxHours, StartDate, EndDate)**

**ASSIGNMENT (*ProjectID*, *EmployeeNumber*, HoursWorked)**

Where

**Department in EMPLOYEE must exist in DepartmentName in DEPARTMENT**

**Supervisor in EMPLOYEE must exist in EmployeeNumber in EMPLOYEE**

**Department in PROJECT must exist in DepartmentName in DEPARTMENT**

**EmployeeNumber in ASSIGNMENT must exist in EmployeeNumber in EMPLOYEE**

**ProjectID in ASSIGNMENT must exist in ProjectID in PROJECT**

The four tables in the revised WP database schema are shown in Figure 2-42 without the recursive relationship in the EMPLOYEE table (which we will add in the following exercise questions). The column characteristics for the PROJECT table are shown in Figure 2-43, and the column characteristics for the ASSIGNMENT table are shown in Figure 2-45. Data for the PROJECT table are shown in Figure 2-44, and the data for the ASSIGNMENT table are shown in Figure 2-46.

---

[3]See *https://www.faa.gov/uas/resources/by_the_numbers/* (accessed October 2020).

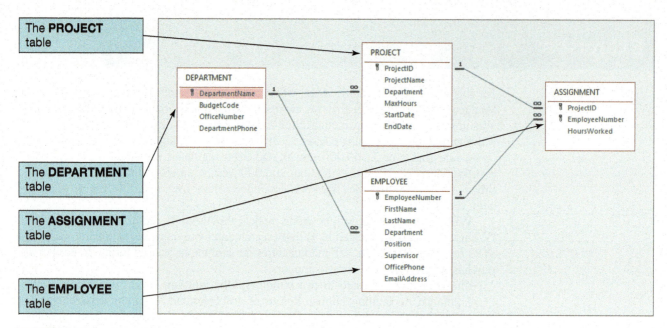

**FIGURE 2-42**

The WP Database with the
PROJECT and ASSIGNMENT
Tables

**2.61** Figure 2-43 shows the column characteristics for the WP PROJECT table. Using the column characteristics, create the PROJECT table in the WP.accdb database.

**2.62** Create the relationship and referential integrity constraint between PROJECT and DEPARTMENT. In the Edit Relationship dialog box, enable enforcing of referential integrity and cascading of data updates, but do *not* enable cascading of data from deleted records. *Note:* We will define cascading actions in Chapter 6.

**2.63** Figure 2-44 shows the data for the WP PROJECT table. Using the Datasheet view, enter the data shown in Figure 2-44 into your PROJECT table.

**2.64** Figure 2-45 shows the column characteristics for the WP ASSIGNMENT table. Using the column characteristics, create the ASSIGNMENT table in the WP.accdb database.

**2.65** Create the relationship and referential integrity constraint between ASSIGNMENT and EMPLOYEE. In the Edit Relationship dialog box, enable enforcing of referential integrity, but do *not* enable either cascading updates or the cascading of data from deleted records.

**2.66** Create the relationship and referential integrity constraint between ASSIGNMENT and PROJECT. In the Edit Relationship dialog box, enable enforcing of referential integrity and cascading of deletes, but do *not* enable cascading updates.

**FIGURE 2-43**

Column Characteristics for
the WP Database PROJECT
Table

**PROJECT**

| Column Name | Type | Key | Required | Remarks |
|---|---|---|---|---|
| ProjectID | Integer | Primary Key | Yes | Surrogate Key |
| ProjectName | Character (50) | No | Yes | |
| Department | Character (35) | Foreign Key | Yes | REF: DEPARTMENT |
| MaxHours | Number (8,2) | No | Yes | |
| StartDate | Date | No | No | |
| EndDate | Date | No | No | |

| ProjectID | ProjectName | Department | MaxHours | StartDate | EndDate |
|---|---|---|---|---|---|
| 1000 | 2021 Q3 Production Plan | Production | 100.00 | 05/10/21 | 06/15/21 |
| 1100 | 2021 Q3 Marketing Plan | Sales and Marketing | 135.00 | 05/10/21 | 06/15/21 |
| 1200 | 2021 Q3 Portfolio Analysis | Finance | 120.00 | 07/05/21 | 07/25/21 |
| 1300 | 2021 Q3 Tax Preparation | Accounting | 145.00 | 08/10/21 | 10/15/21 |
| 1400 | 2021 Q4 Production Plan | Production | 100.00 | 08/10/21 | 09/15/21 |
| 1500 | 2021 Q4 Marketing Plan | Sales and Marketing | 135.00 | 08/10/21 | 09/15/21 |
| 1600 | 2021 Q4 Portfolio Analysis | Finance | 140.00 | 10/05/21 | |

**FIGURE 2-44**

Sample Data for the WP Database PROJECT Table

**2.67** Figure 2-46 shows the data for the WP ASSIGNMENT table. Using the Datasheet view, enter the data shown in Figure 2-46 into your ASSIGNMENT table.

**2.68** In Exercise 2.63, the table data was entered after referential integrity constraints were created in Exercise 2.62. In Exercise 2.67, the table data was entered after referential integrity constraints were created in Exercises 2.65 and 2.66. Why was the data entered after the referential integrity constraints were created instead of before the constraints were created?

**2.69** Using Figure 2-31 for reference, create the recursive relationship and referential integrity constraint between Supervisor and BuyerName in BUYER. In the Edit Relationship dialog box, enable enforcing of referential integrity and cascading of data updates, but do *not* enable cascading of data from deleted records. *HINT:* to create a recursive relationship, add another copy of the BUYER table to the relationships window by right-clicking in that window and selecting Show Table.

**2.70** Using Microsoft Access SQL, create and run queries to answer the following questions. Save each query using the query name format SQL-Query-02-##, where the ## sign is replaced by the letter designator of the question. For example, the first query will be saved as SQL-Query-02-A.

**A.** What projects are in the PROJECT table? Show all information for each project.

**B.** What are the ProjectID, ProjectName, StartDate, and EndDate values of projects in the PROJECT table?

**C.** What projects in the PROJECT table started before August 1, 2018? Show all the information for each project.

**D.** What projects in the PROJECT table have not been completed? Show all the information for each project.

**FIGURE 2-45**

Column Characteristics for the WP Database ASSIGNMENT Table

**ASSIGNMENT**

| Column Name | Type | Key | Required | Remarks |
|---|---|---|---|---|
| ProjectID | Integer | Primary Key, Foreign Key | Yes | REF: PROJECT |
| EmployeeNumber | Integer | Primary Key, Foreign Key | Yes | REF: EMPLOYEE |
| HoursWorked | Number (6,2) | No | No | |

**FIGURE 2-46**

Sample Data for the WP
Database ASSIGNMENT
Table

| ProjectID | EmployeeNumber | HoursWorked |
|-----------|----------------|-------------|
| 1000 | 1 | 30.00 |
| 1000 | 6 | 50.00 |
| 1000 | 10 | 50.00 |
| 1000 | 16 | 75.00 |
| 1000 | 17 | 75.00 |
| 1100 | 1 | 30.00 |
| 1100 | 6 | 75.00 |
| 1100 | 10 | 55.00 |
| 1100 | 11 | 55.00 |
| 1200 | 3 | 20.00 |
| 1200 | 6 | 40.00 |
| 1200 | 7 | 45.00 |
| 1200 | 8 | 45.00 |
| 1300 | 3 | 25.00 |
| 1300 | 6 | 40.00 |
| 1300 | 8 | 50.00 |
| 1300 | 9 | 50.00 |
| 1400 | 1 | 30.00 |
| 1400 | 6 | 50.00 |
| 1400 | 10 | 50.00 |
| 1400 | 16 | 75.00 |
| 1400 | 17 | 75.00 |
| 1500 | 1 | 30.00 |
| 1500 | 6 | 75.00 |
| 1500 | 10 | 55.00 |
| 1500 | 11 | 55.00 |
| 1600 | 3 | 20.00 |
| 1600 | 6 | 40.00 |
| 1600 | 7 | 45.00 |
| 1600 | 8 | 45.00 |

**E.** Who are the employees assigned to each project? Show ProjectID, Employee-Number, LastName, FirstName, and OfficePhone.

**F.** Who are the employees assigned to each project? Show ProjectID, ProjectName, and Department. Show EmployeeNumber, LastName, FirstName, and OfficePhone.

**G.** Who are the employees assigned to each project? Show ProjectID, ProjectName, Department, and DepartmentPhone, Show EmployeeNumber, LastName, First-Name, and OfficePhone. Sort by ProjectID in ascending order.

**H.** Who are the employees assigned to projects run by the marketing department? Show ProjectID, ProjectName, Department, and DepartmentPhone. Show EmployeeNumber, LastName, FirstName, and OfficePhone. Sort by ProjectID in ascending order.

**I.** How many projects are being run by the Marketing department? Be sure to assign an appropriate column name to the computed results.

**J.** What is the total MaxHours of projects being run by the Marketing department? Be sure to assign an appropriate column name to the computed results.

**K.** What is the average MaxHours of projects being run by the Marketing department? Be sure to assign an appropriate column name to the computed results.

**L.** How many projects are being run by each department? Be sure to display each DepartmentName and to assign an appropriate column name to the computed results.

**M.** Who supervises each employee at Wedgewood Pacific? Include the names of employees with no supervisor in the results of the query.

**N.** Write an SQL statement to join EMPLOYEE, ASSIGNMENT, and PROJECT using the JOIN ON syntax. Run this statement.

**O.** Write an SQL statement to join EMPLOYEE and ASSIGNMENT and include all rows of EMPLOYEE in your answer, regardless of whether they have an ASSIGNMENT. Run this statement.

**2.71** Using Microsoft Access QBE, create and run new queries to answer the questions in Exercise 2.70. Save each query using the query name format QBE-Query-02-##, where the ## sign is replaced by the letter designator of the question. For example, the first query will be saved as QBE-Query-02-A. *HINT:* In questions G and H, the default approach of accepting all joins will not work, and you may have to delete some joins from the initial QBE query.

# Case Questions

## Marcia's Dry Cleaning Case Questions

Marcia Wilson owns and operates Marcia's Dry Cleaning, which is an upscale dry cleaner in a well-to-do suburban neighborhood. Marcia makes her business stand out from the competition by providing superior customer service. She wants to keep track of each of her customers and their orders. Ultimately, she wants to notify them that their clothes are ready via email. To provide this service, she has developed an initial database with several tables. Three of those tables are as follows:

CUSTOMER (**CustomerID**, FirstName, LastName, Phone, EmailAddress, *ReferredBy*)

INVOICE (**InvoiceNumber**, *CustomerID*, DateIn, DateOut, TotalAmount)

INVOICE_ITEM (*InvoiceNumber*, **ItemNumber**, Item, Quantity, UnitPrice)

Where

ReferredBy in CUSTOMER must exist in CustomerID in CUSTOMER

CustomerID in INVOICE must exist in CustomerID in CUSTOMER

InvoiceNumber in INVOICE_IITEM must exist in InvoiceNumber in INVOICE

In this database schema, the primary keys are underlined and the foreign keys are shown in italics. Note that CUSTOMER contains a recursive relationship between ReferredBy and CustomerID, where ReferredBy contains the CustomerID value of the existing customer who referred the new customer to Marcia's Dry Cleaning. The database that Marcia has created is named MDC, and the three tables in the MDC database schema are shown in Figure 2-47.

The column characteristics for the tables are shown in Figures 2-48, 2-49, and 2-50. The relationship between CUSTOMER and INVOICE should enforce referential integrity, but not cascade updates or deletions, whereas the relationship between INVOICE and INVOICE_ITEM should enforce referential integrity and cascade both updates and deletions. The data for these tables are shown in Figures 2-51, 2-52, and 2-53.

You will need to create and set up a database named MDC_CH02 for use with these case questions. A Microsoft Access 2019 database named MDC_CH02.accdb and SQL scripts for creating the MDC_CH02 database in Microsoft SQL Server, Oracle Database, and MySQL are available on our Web site at *www.pearsonhighered.com/kroenke*.

**FIGURE 2-47**

The MDC Database

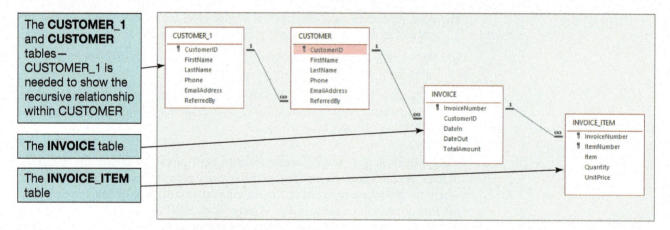

The **CUSTOMER_1** and **CUSTOMER** tables— CUSTOMER_1 is needed to show the recursive relationship within CUSTOMER

The **INVOICE** table

The **INVOICE_ITEM** table

**FIGURE 2-48**

Column Characteristics for the MDC Database CUSTOMER Table

**CUSTOMER**

| Column Name | Type | Key | Required | Remarks |
|---|---|---|---|---|
| CustomerID | Integer | Primary Key | Yes | Surrogate Key |
| FirstName | Character (25) | No | Yes | |
| LastName | Character (25) | No | Yes | |
| Phone | Character (12) | No | No | |
| EmailAddress | Character (100) | No | No | Use Varchar |
| ReferredBy | Integer | Foreign Key | No | REF: CustomerID |

**FIGURE 2-49**

Column Characteristics for the MDC Database INVOICE Table

**INVOICE**

| Column Name | Type | Key | Required | Remarks |
|---|---|---|---|---|
| InvoiceNumber | Integer | Primary Key | Yes | Surrogate Key |
| CustomerID | Integer | Foreign Key | Yes | REF: CUSTOMER |
| DateIn | Date | No | Yes | |
| DateOut | Date | No | No | |
| TotalAmount | Number (8,2) | No | No | |

**FIGURE 2-50**

Column Characteristics
for the MDC Database
INVOICE_ITEM Table

**INVOICE_ITEM**

| Column Name | Type | Key | Required | Remarks |
|---|---|---|---|---|
| InvoiceNumber | Integer | Primary Key, Foreign Key | Yes | REF: INVOICE |
| ItemNumber | Integer | Primary Key | Yes | Sequential number, but *not* a surrogate key |
| Item | Character (50) | No | Yes | |
| Quantity | Integer | No | Yes | |
| UnitPrice | Number (8,2) | No | Yes | |

If you are using the Microsoft Access 2019 MDC_CH02.accdb database, simply copy it to an appropriate location in your Documents folder. Otherwise, you will need to use the discussion and instructions necessary for setting up the MDC_CH02 database in the DBMS product you are using:

**FIGURE 2-51**

Sample Data for the MDC
Database CUSTOMER Table

- For Microsoft SQL Server 2019, see online Chapter 10A.
- For Oracle Database, see online Chapter 10B.
- For MySQL 8.0 Community Server, see online Chapter 10C.

| CustomerID | FirstName | LastName | Phone | EmailAddress | RefferedBy |
|---|---|---|---|---|---|
| 1 | Nikki | Kaccaton | 723-543-1233 | Nikki.Kaccaton@somewhere.com | |
| 2 | Brenda | Catnazaro | 723-543-2344 | Brenda.Catnazaro@somewhere.com | 1 |
| 3 | Bruce | LeCat | 723-543-3455 | Bruce.LeCat@somewhere.com | 2 |
| 4 | Betsy | Miller | 723-654-3211 | Betsy.Miller@somewhere.com | 3 |
| 5 | George | Miller | 723-654-4322 | George.Miller@somewhere.com | 4 |
| 6 | Kathy | Miller | 723-514-9877 | Kathy.Miller@somewhere.com | 2 |
| 7 | Betsy | Miller | 723-514-8766 | Betsy.Miller@elsewhere.com | 1 |

**FIGURE 2-52**

Sample Data for the MDC
Database INVOICE Table

| InvoiceNumber | CustomerNumber | DateIn | DateOut | TotalAmount |
|---|---|---|---|---|
| 2021001 | 1 | 04-Oct-21 | 06-Oct-21 | $158.50 |
| 2021002 | 2 | 04-Oct-21 | 06-Oct-21 | $25.00 |
| 2021003 | 1 | 06-Oct-21 | 08-Oct-21 | $49.00 |
| 2021004 | 4 | 06-Oct-21 | 08-Oct-21 | $17.50 |
| 2021005 | 6 | 07-Oct-21 | 11-Oct-21 | $12.00 |
| 2021006 | 3 | 11-Oct-21 | 13-Oct-21 | $152.50 |
| 2021007 | 3 | 11-Oct-21 | 13-Oct-21 | $7.00 |
| 2021008 | 7 | 12-Oct-21 | 14-Oct-21 | $140.50 |
| 2021009 | 5 | 12-Oct-21 | 14-Oct-21 | $27.00 |

**FIGURE 2-53**

Sample Data for the MDC
Database INVOICE_ITEM
Table

| InvoiceNumber | ItemNumber | Item | Quantity | UnitPrice |
|---|---|---|---|---|
| 2021001 | 1 | Blouse | 2 | $3.50 |
| 2021001 | 2 | Dress Shirt | 5 | $2.50 |
| 2021001 | 3 | Formal Gown | 2 | $10.00 |
| 2021001 | 4 | Slacks-Mens | 10 | $5.00 |
| 2021001 | 5 | Slacks-Womens | 10 | $6.00 |
| 2021001 | 6 | Suit-Mens | 1 | $9.00 |
| 2021002 | 1 | Dress Shirt | 10 | $2.50 |
| 2021003 | 1 | Slacks-Mens | 5 | $5.00 |
| 2021003 | 2 | Slacks-Womens | 4 | $6.00 |
| 2021004 | 1 | Dress Shirt | 7 | $2.50 |
| 2021005 | 1 | Blouse | 2 | $3.50 |
| 2021005 | 2 | Dress Shirt | 2 | $2.50 |
| 2021006 | 1 | Blouse | 5 | $3.50 |
| 2021006 | 2 | Dress Shirt | 10 | $2.50 |
| 2021006 | 3 | Slacks-Mens | 10 | $5.00 |
| 2021006 | 4 | Slacks-Womens | 10 | $6.00 |
| 2021007 | 1 | Blouse | 2 | $3.50 |
| 2021008 | 1 | Blouse | 3 | $3.50 |
| 2021008 | 2 | Dress Shirt | 12 | $2.50 |
| 2021008 | 3 | Slacks-Mens | 8 | $5.00 |
| 2021008 | 4 | Slacks-Womens | 10 | $6.00 |
| 2021009 | 1 | Suit-Mens | 3 | $9.00 |

Once you have set up your MDC_CH02 database, create an SQL script named *MDC-CH02-CQsql*, and use it to record and store SQL statements that answer each of the following questions (if the question requires a written answer, use an SQL comment to record your answer):

**A.** Show all data in each of the tables.

**B.** List the LastName, FirstName, and Phone of all customers.

**C.** List the LastName, FirstName, and Phone for all customers with a FirstName of 'Nikki'.

**D.** List the LastName, FirstName, Phone, DateIn, and DateOut of all orders in excess of $100.00.

**E.** List the LastName, FirstName, and Phone of all customers whose first name starts with 'B'.

**F.** List the LastName, FirstName, and Phone of all customers whose last name includes the characters 'cat'.

**G.** List the LastName, FirstName, and Phone for all customers whose second and third digits (from the left) of their phone number are 23. For example, any phone number with an area code of "723" would meet the criteria.

**H.** Determine the maximum and minimum TotalAmount.

**I.** Determine the average TotalAmount.

**J.** Count the number of customers.

**K.** Group customers by LastName and then by FirstName.

**L.** Count the number of customers having each combination of LastName and FirstName.

**M.** Show the LastName, FirstName, and Phone of all customers who have had an order with TotalAmount greater than $100.00. Use a subquery. Present the results sorted by LastName in ascending order and then FirstName in descending order.

**N.** Show the LastName, FirstName, and Phone of all customers who have had an order with TotalAmount greater than $100.00. Use a join, but do not use JOIN ON syntax. Present results sorted by LastName in ascending order and then FirstName in descending order.

**O.** Show the LastName, FirstName, and Phone of all customers who have had an order with TotalAmount greater than $100.00. Use a join using JOIN ON syntax. Present results sorted by LastName in ascending order and then FirstName in descending order.

**P.** Show the LastName, FirstName, and Phone of all customers who have had an order with an Item named 'Dress Shirt'. Use a subquery. Present results sorted by LastName in ascending order and then FirstName in descending order.

**Q.** Show the LastName, FirstName, and Phone of all customers who have had an order with an Item named 'Dress Shirt'. Use a join, but do not use JOIN ON syntax. Present results sorted by LastName in ascending order and then FirstName in descending order.

**R.** Show the LastName, FirstName, and Phone of all customers who have had an order with an Item named 'Dress Shirt'. Use a join using JOIN ON syntax. Present results sorted by LastName in ascending order and then FirstName in descending order.

**S.** Who referred each customer to Marcia's Dry Cleaning? Show columns named CustomerLastName, CustomerFirstName, ReferredByLastName, and ReferredBy-FirstName. Include the names of customers who were not referred by any other customer in the results of the query.

**T.** Show the LastName, FirstName, and Phone of all customers who have had an order with an Item named 'Dress Shirt'. Use a combination of a join using JOIN ON syntax and a subquery. Present results sorted by LastName in ascending order and then FirstName in descending order.

**U.** Show the LastName, FirstName, Phone, and TotalAmount of all customer orders that included an Item named 'Dress Shirt'. Also show the LastName, FirstName, and Phone of *all other customers*. Present results sorted by TotalAmount in ascending order, then LastName in ascending order, and then FirstName in descending order. *HINT:* In Microsoft Access 2019, you will either need to use a UNION statement or a sequence of two queries to solve this because Microsoft Access disallows nesting an INNER join inside a LEFT OUTER or RIGHT OUTER join. The other DBMS products can complete this question with one query (not a UNION statement).

# The Queen Anne Curiosity Shop Project Questions

The Queen Anne Curiosity Shop is an upscale home furnishings store in a well-to-do urban neighborhood. It sells both antiques and current-production household items that complement or are useful with the antiques. For example, the store sells antique dining room tables and new tablecloths. The antiques are purchased from both individuals and wholesalers, and the new items are purchased from distributors. The store's customers include individuals, owners of bed-and-breakfast operations, and local interior designers who work with both individuals and small businesses. The antiques are unique, though some multiple items, such as dining room chairs, may be available as a set (sets are never broken). The new items are not unique, and an item may be reordered if it is out of stock. New items are also available in various sizes and colors (for example, a particular style of tablecloth may be available in several sizes and in a variety of colors).

**Assume that the Queen Anne Curiosity Shop designs a database with the following tables:**

**CUSTOMER** (<u>CustomerID</u>, LastName, FirstName, EmailAddress, EncryptedPassword, Address, City, State, ZIP, Phone, *ReferredBy*)

**ITEM** (<u>ItemID</u>, ItemDescription, CompanyName, PurchaseDate, ItemCost, ItemPrice)

**SALE** (<u>*SaleID*</u>, *CustomerID*, SaleDate, SubTotal, Tax, Total)

**SALE_ITEM** (<u>*SaleID*</u>, <u>SaleItemID</u>, *ItemID*, ItemPrice)

**The referential integrity constraints are:**

**ReferredBy in CUSTOMER must exist in CustomerID in CUSTOMER**

**CustomerID in SALE must exist in CustomerID in CUSTOMER**

**SaleID in SALE_ITEM must exist in SaleID in SALE**

**ItemID in SALE_ITEM must exist in ItemID in ITEM**

**Assume that CustomerID of CUSTOMER, ItemID of ITEM, SaleID of SALE, and SaleItemID of SALE_ITEM are all surrogate keys with values as follows:**

| | | |
|---|---|---|
| **CustomerID** | **Start at 1** | **Increment by 1** |
| **ItemID** | **Start at 1** | **Increment by 1** |
| **SaleID** | **Start at 1** | **Increment by 1** |

The database that the Queen Anne Curiosity Shop has created is named QACS, and the four tables in the QACS database schema are shown in Figure 2-54. Note that CUSTOMER contains a recursive relationship between ReferredBy and CustomerID, where ReferredBy contains the CustomerID value of the existing customer who referred the new customer to the Queen Anne Curiosity Shop.

The column characteristics for the tables are shown in Figures 2-55, 2-56, 2-57, and 2-58. The relationships CUSTOMER-to-SALE and ITEM-to-SALE_ITEM should enforce referential integrity, but not cascade updates or deletions, whereas the relationship between SALE and SALE_ITEM should enforce referential integrity and cascade both updates and deletions. The data for these tables are shown in Figures 2-59, 2-60, 2-61, and 2-62.

You will need to create and set up a database named QACS_CH02 for use with the Queen Anne Curiosity Shop project questions. A Microsoft Access 2019 database named QACS_CH02.accdb and SQL scripts for creating the QACS_CH02 database in Microsoft SQL Server, Oracle Database, and MySQL are available on our Web site at *www.pearsonhighered.com/kroenke*.

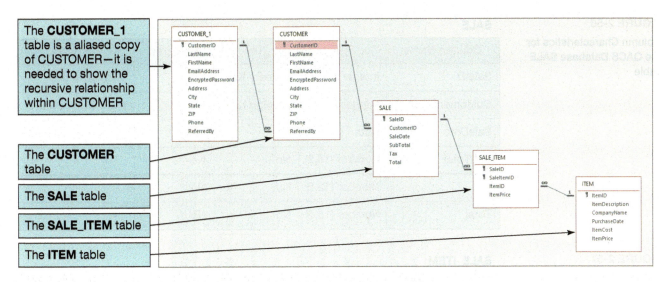

**FIGURE 2-54**

**The QACS Database**

If you are using the Microsoft Access 2019 QACS_CH02.accdb database, simply copy it to an appropriate location in your Documents folder. Otherwise, you will need to use the discussion and instructions necessary for setting up the QACS_CH02 database in the DBMS product you are using:

- For Microsoft SQL Server 2019, see online Chapter 10A.
- For Oracle Database, see online Chapter 10B.
- For MySQL 8.0 Community Server, see online Chapter 10C.

Once you have set up your QACS_CH02 database, create an SQL script named *QACS-CH02-PQsql*, and use it to record and store SQL statements that answer each of the following questions (if the question requires a written answer, use an SQL comment to record your answer):

**A.** Show all data in each of the tables.

**B.** List the LastName, FirstName, and Phone of all customers.

**FIGURE 2-55**

**Column Characteristics for the QACS Database CUSTOMER Table**

**CUSTOMER**

| Column Name | Type | Key | Required | Remarks |
|---|---|---|---|---|
| CustomerID | Integer | Primary Key | Yes | Surrogate Key |
| LastName | Character (25) | No | Yes | |
| FirstName | Character (25) | No | Yes | |
| EmailAddress | Character (100) | No | No | Use Varchar |
| EncryptedPassword | Character(50) | No | No | Use Varchar |
| Address | Character (35) | No | No | |
| City | Character (35) | No | No | |
| State | Character (2) | No | No | |
| ZIP | Character (10) | No | No | |
| Phone | Character (12) | No | Yes | |
| ReferredBy | Integer | Foreign Key | No | REF: CustomerID |

**FIGURE 2-64**

Column Characteristics for the MI Database ITEM Table

**ITEM**

| Column Name | Type | Key | Required | Remarks |
|---|---|---|---|---|
| ItemID | Integer | Primary Key | Yes | Surrogate Key |
| Description | Character (255) | No | Yes | Use Varchar |
| PurchaseDate | Date | No | Yes | |
| Store | Character (50) | No | Yes | |
| City | Character (35) | No | Yes | |
| Quantity | Integer | No | Yes | |
| LocalCurrencyAmount | Number (18,2) | No | Yes | |
| ExchangeRate | Number (12,6) | No | Yes | |

**FIGURE 2-65**

Column Characteristics for the MI Database SHIPMENT Table

**SHIPMENT**

| Column Name | Type | Key | Required | Remarks |
|---|---|---|---|---|
| ShipmentID | Integer | Primary Key | Yes | Surrogate Key |
| ShipperName | Character (35) | No | Yes | |
| ShipperInvoiceNumber | Integer | No | Yes | |
| DepartureDate | Date | No | No | |
| ArrivalDate | Date | No | No | |
| InsuredValue | Number (12,2) | No | No | |

**FIGURE 2-66**

Column Characteristics for the MI Database SHIPMENT_ITEM Table

**SHIPMENT_ITEM**

| Column Name | Type | Key | Required | Remarks |
|---|---|---|---|---|
| ShipmentID | Integer | Primary Key, Foreign Key | Yes | REF: SHIPMENT |
| ShipmentItemID | Integer | Primary Key | Yes | Sequential number, but *not* a surrogate key |
| ItemID | Integer | Foreign Key | Yes | REF: ITEM |
| Value | Number (12,2) | No | Yes | |

discussion and instructions necessary for setting up the MI_CH02 database in the DBMS product you are using:

- For Microsoft SQL Server 2019, see online Chapter 10A.
- For Oracle Database, see online Chapter 10B.
- For MySQL 8.0 Community Server, see online Chapter 10C.

| ItemID | Description | PurchaseDate | Store | City | Quantity | LocalCurrencyAmount | ExchangeRate |
|--------|-------------|--------------|-------|------|----------|---------------------|--------------|
| 1 | QE Dining Set | 07-Apr-21 | Eastern Treasures | Manila | 2 | 403405 | 0.01774 |
| 2 | Willow Serving Dishes | 15-Jul-21 | Jade Antiques | Singapore | 75 | 102 | 0.5903 |
| 3 | Large Bureau | 17-Jul-21 | Eastern Sales | Singapore | 8 | 2000 | 0.5903 |
| 4 | Brass Lamps | 20-Jul-21 | Jade Antiques | Singapore | 40 | 50 | 0.5903 |

**FIGURE 2-67**

Sample Data for the MI Database ITEM Table

Once you have set up your MI_CH02 database, create an SQL script named *MI-CH02-PQ.sql*, and use it to record and store SQL statements that answer each of the following questions (if the question requires a written answer, use an SQL comment to record your answer):

**A.** Show all data in each of the tables.

**B.** List the ShipmentID, ShipperName, and ShipperInvoiceNumber of all shipments.

**C.** List the ShipmentID, ShipperName, and ShipperInvoiceNumber for all shipments that have an insured value greater than $10,000.00.

**D.** List the ShipmentID, ShipperName, and ShipperInvoiceNumber of all shippers whose name starts with 'AB'.

**E.** List the ShipmentID, ShipperName, ShipperInvoiceNumber, and ArrivalDate of all shipments that departed in December. *HINT:* For the DBMS you are using, research how to extract a month or day from a date value so it can be compared to a number.

**F.** List the ShipmentID, ShipperName, ShipperInvoiceNumber, and ArrivalDate of all shipments that departed on the tenth day of any month. *HINT:* For the DBMS you are using, research how to extract a month or day from a date value so it can be compared to a number.

**FIGURE 2-68**

Sample Data for the MI Database SHIPMENT Table

| ShipmentID | ShipperName | ShipperInvoiceNumber | DepartureDate | ArrivalDate | InsuredValue |
|------------|-------------|----------------------|---------------|-------------|--------------|
| 1 | ABC Trans-Oceanic | 2017651 | 10-Dec-20 | 15-Mar-21 | $15,000.00 |
| 2 | ABC Trans-Oceanic | 2018012 | 10-Jan-21 | 20-Mar-21 | $12,000.00 |
| 3 | Worldwide | 49100300 | 05-May-21 | 17-Jun-21 | $20,000.00 |
| 4 | International | 399400 | 02-Jun-21 | 17-Jul-21 | $17,500.00 |
| 5 | Worldwide | 84899440 | 10-Jul-21 | 28-Jul-21 | $25,000.00 |
| 6 | International | 488955 | 05-Aug-21 | 11-Sep-21 | $18,000.00 |

**FIGURE 2-69**

Sample Data for the MI Database SHIPMENT_ITEM Table

| ShipmentID | ShipmentItemID | ItemID | Value |
|------------|----------------|--------|-------|
| 3 | 1 | 1 | $15,000.00 |
| 4 | 1 | 4 | $1,200.00 |
| 4 | 2 | 3 | $9,500.00 |
| 4 | 3 | 2 | $4,500.00 |

**G.** Determine the maximum and minimum InsuredValue.

**H.** Determine the average InsuredValue.

**I.** Count the number of shipments.

**J.** Show ItemID, Description, Store, and a calculated column named USCurrencyAmount that is equal to LocalCurrencyAmount multiplied by the ExchangeRate for all rows of ITEM.

**K.** Group item purchases by City and Store.

**L.** Count the number of purchases having each combination of City and Store.

**M.** Show the ShipperName, ShipmentID, and DepartureDate of all shipments that have an item with a value of $1,000.00 or more. Use a subquery. Present results sorted by ShipperName in ascending order and then DepartureDate in descending order.

**N.** Show the ShipperName, ShipmentID, and DepartureDate of all shipments that have an item with a value of $1,000.00 or more. Use a join. Present results sorted by ShipperName in ascending order and then DepartureDate in descending order.

**O.** Show the ShipperName, ShipmentID, and DepartureDate of the shipments for items that were purchased in Singapore. Use a subquery. Present results sorted by ShipperName in ascending order and then DepartureDate in descending order.

**P.** Show the ShipperName, ShipmentID, and DepartureDate of all shipments that have an item that was purchased in Singapore. Use a join, but do not use JOIN ON syntax. Present results sorted by ShipperName in ascending order and then DepartureDate in descending order.

**Q.** Show the ShipperName, ShipmentID, and DepartureDate of all shipments that have an item that was purchased in Singapore. Use a join using JOIN ON syntax. Present results sorted by ShipperName in ascending order and then DepartureDate in descending order.

**R.** Show the ShipperName, ShipmentID, the DepartureDate of the shipment, and Value for items that were purchased in Singapore. Use a combination of a join and a subquery. Present results sorted by ShipperName in ascending order and then DepartureDate in descending order.

**S.** Show the ShipperName, ShipmentID, the DepartureDate of the shipment, and Value for items that were purchased in Singapore. Also show the ShipperName, ShipmentID, and DepartureDate for all other shipments. Present results sorted by Value in ascending order, then ShipperName in ascending order, and then DepartureDate in descending order. *HINT:* In Microsoft Access 2019 you will either need to use a UNION statement or a sequence of two queries to solve this because Microsoft Access disallows nesting an INNER join inside a LEFT or RIGHT join. The other DBMS products can do it with one query (not a UNION statement).

# Database Design

The four chapters in Part 2 discuss database design principles and techniques. Chapters 3 and 4 describe the design of databases that arise from existing data sources, such as spreadsheets, text files, and database extracts. We begin in Chapter 3 by defining the relational model and discussing normalization, a process that transforms relations with modification problems. Then, in Chapter 4, we use normalization principles to guide the design of databases from existing data.

Chapters 5 and 6 examine the design of databases that arise from the development of new information systems. Chapter 5 describes the entity-relationship data model, a tool used to create plans for constructing database designs. As you will learn, such data models are developed by analyzing forms, reports, and other information systems requirements. Chapter 6 concludes this part by describing techniques for transforming entity-relationship data models into database designs.

# 3

# The Relational Model and Normalization

## Chapter Objectives

- To understand basic relational terminology
- To understand the characteristics of relations
- To understand alternative terminology used in describing the relational model
- To be able to identify functional dependencies, determinants, and dependent attributes
- To identify primary, candidate, and composite keys

- To be able to identify possible insertion, deletion, and update anomalies in a relation
- To be able to place a relation into BCNF normal form
- To understand the special importance of domain/key normal form
- To be able to identify multivalued dependencies
- To be able to place a relation in fourth normal form

**As we discussed** in Chapter 1, databases arise from three sources: from existing data, from the development of new information systems, and from the redesign of existing databases. In this chapter and the next, we consider the design of databases from existing data, such as data from spreadsheets or extracts of existing databases.

The premise of Chapters 3 and 4 is that you have received one or more tables of data from some source that are to be stored in a new database. The question is: Should this data be stored as is, or should it be transformed in some way before it is stored? For example, consider the two tables as shown in Figure 3-1(a). These are the SKU_DATA and ORDER_ITEM tables extracted from the Cape Codd Outdoor Sports database as used in the database in Chapter 2.

You can design the new database to store this data as two separate tables, or you can join the tables together and design the database with just one table, as shown in table SKU_ITEM_DATA Figure 3-1(b). Each alternative has advantages and disadvantages. When you make the decision to use one design, you obtain certain advantages at the expense of certain costs. The purpose of this chapter is to help you understand those advantages and costs.

Such questions do not seem difficult, and you may be wondering why we need two chapters to answer them. In truth, even a single table can have surprising complexity. Consider, for example, the table in Figure 3-2, which shows sample data

**FIGURE 3-1**

How Many Tables?

**ORDER_ITEM**

| | OrderNumber | SKU | Quantity | Price | ExtendedPrice |
|---|---|---|---|---|---|
| 1 | 1000 | 201000 | 1 | 300.00 | 300.00 |
| 2 | 1000 | 202000 | 1 | 130.00 | 130.00 |
| 3 | 2000 | 101100 | 4 | 50.00 | 200.00 |
| 4 | 2000 | 101200 | 2 | 50.00 | 100.00 |
| 5 | 3000 | 100200 | 1 | 300.00 | 300.00 |
| 6 | 3000 | 101100 | 2 | 50.00 | 100.00 |
| 7 | 3000 | 101200 | 1 | 50.00 | 50.00 |

**SKU_DATA**

| | SKU | SKU_Description | Department | Buyer |
|---|---|---|---|---|
| 1 | 100100 | Std. Scuba Tank, Yellow | Water Sports | Pete Hansen |
| 2 | 100200 | Std. Scuba Tank, Magenta | Water Sports | Pete Hansen |
| 3 | 100300 | Std. Scuba Tank, Light Blue | Water Sports | Pete Hansen |
| 4 | 100400 | Std. Scuba Tank, Dark Blue | Water Sports | Pete Hansen |
| 5 | 100500 | Std. Scuba Tank, Light Green | Water Sports | Pete Hansen |
| 6 | 100600 | Std. Scuba Tank, Dark Green | Water Sports | Pete Hansen |
| 7 | 101100 | Dive Mask, Small Clear | Water Sports | Nancy Meyers |
| 8 | 101200 | Dive Mask, Med Clear | Water Sports | Nancy Meyers |
| 9 | 201000 | Half-dome Tent | Camping | Cindy Lo |
| 10 | 202000 | Half-dome Tent Vestibule | Camping | Cindy Lo |
| 11 | 203000 | Half-dome Tent Vestibule - Wide | Camping | Cindy Lo |
| 12 | 301000 | Light Fly Climbing Harness | Climbing | Jerry Martin |
| 13 | 302000 | Locking Carabiner, Oval | Climbing | Jerry Martin |

(a) Data Stored in Two Tables

**SKU_ITEM_DATA**

| | OrderNumber | SKU | Quantity | Price | SKU_Description | Department | Buyer |
|---|---|---|---|---|---|---|---|
| 1 | 1000 | 201000 | 1 | 300.00 | Half-dome Tent | Camping | Cindy Lo |
| 2 | 1000 | 202000 | 1 | 130.00 | Half-dome Tent Vestibule | Camping | Cindy Lo |
| 3 | 2000 | 101100 | 4 | 50.00 | Dive Mask, Small Clear | Water Sports | Nancy Meyers |
| 4 | 2000 | 101200 | 2 | 50.00 | Dive Mask, Med Clear | Water Sports | Nancy Meyers |
| 5 | 3000 | 100200 | 1 | 300.00 | Std. Scuba Tank, Magenta | Water Sports | Pete Hansen |
| 6 | 3000 | 101100 | 2 | 50.00 | Dive Mask, Small Clear | Water Sports | Nancy Meyers |
| 7 | 3000 | 101200 | 1 | 50.00 | Dive Mask, Med Clear | Water Sports | Nancy Meyers |

(b) Data Stored in One Table

**FIGURE 3-2**

PRODUCT_BUYER—A Very
Strange Table

**PRODUCT_BUYER**

| | BuyerName | SKU_Managed | CollegeMajor |
|---|---|---|---|
| 1 | Pete Hansen | 100100 | Business Administration |
| 2 | Pete Hansen | 100200 | Business Administration |
| 3 | Pete Hansen | 100300 | Business Administration |
| 4 | Pete Hansen | 100400 | Business Administration |
| 5 | Pete Hansen | 100500 | Business Administration |
| 6 | Pete Hansen | 100600 | Business Administration |
| 7 | Nancy Meyers | 101100 | Art |
| 8 | Nancy Meyers | 101100 | Info Systems |
| 9 | Nancy Meyers | 101200 | Art |
| 10 | Nancy Meyers | 101200 | Info Systems |
| 11 | Cindy Lo | 201000 | History |
| 12 | Cindy Lo | 202000 | History |
| 13 | Jenny Martin | 301000 | Business Administration |
| 14 | Jenny Martin | 301000 | English Literature |
| 15 | Jenny Martin | 302000 | Business Administration |
| 16 | Jenny Martin | 302000 | English Literature |

extracted from a corporate database. This simple table has three columns: the buyer's name, the **SKU (stock keeping unit)** of the products that the buyer purchases, and the names of the buyer's college major(s). Buyers manage more than one SKU, and they can have multiple college majors.

To understand why this is an odd table, suppose that Nancy Meyers is assigned a new SKU, say 101300. What addition should we make to this table? Clearly, we need to add a row for the new SKU, but if we add just one row, say the row ('Nancy Meyers', 101300, 'Art'), it will appear that she manages product 101300 as an Art major but not as an Info Systems major. To avoid such an illogical state, we need to add two rows: ('Nancy Meyers', 101300, 'Art') and ('Nancy Meyers', 101300, 'Info Systems').

This is a strange requirement. Why should we have to add two rows of data simply to record the fact that a new SKU has been assigned to a buyer? Further, if we assign the product to Pete Hansen instead, we would only have to add one row, but if we assigned the product to a buyer who had four majors, we would have to add four new rows.

The more one thinks about the table in Figure 3-2, the stranger it becomes. What changes should we make if SKU 101100 is assigned to Pete Hansen? What changes should we make if SKU 100100 is assigned to Nancy Meyers? What should we do if all the SKU values in Figure 3-2 are deleted? Later in this chapter, you will learn that these problems arise because this table has a problem called a *multivalued dependency.* Even better, you will learn how to remove that problem.

Tables can have many different patterns; some patterns are susceptible to serious problems and other patterns are not. Before we can address this question, however, you need to learn some basic terms.

## Relational Model Terminology

Figure 3-3 lists the most important terms used by the relational model. By the time you finish Chapters 3 and 4, you should be able to define each of these terms and explain how each pertains to the design of relational databases. Use this list of terms as a check on your comprehension.

### Relations

So far, we have used the terms *table* and *relation* interchangeably. In fact, a relation is a special case of a table. This means that all relations are tables, but not all tables are relations. Codd defined the characteristics of a relation in his 1970 paper that laid the foundation for the relational model.[1] Those characteristics are summarized in Figure 3-4.

| BY THE WAY | In Figure 3-4 and in this discussion, we use the term **entity** to mean some identifiable thing. A customer, a salesperson, an order, a part, and a lease are all examples of what we mean by an entity. When we introduce the entity-relationship model in Chapter 5, we will make the definition of entity more precise. For now, just think of an entity as some identifiable thing that users want to track. |

---

[1] E. F. Codd, "A Relational Model of Data for Large Shared Data Banks," *Communications of the ACM,* June 1970, pp. 377-387. A downloadable copy of this paper in PDF format is available at *http://dl.acm.org/citation.cfm?id=362685* (accessed October 2020).

**FIGURE 3-3**

Important Relational Model
Terms

| Important Relational Terms |
|---|
| Relation |
| Functional dependency |
| Determinant |
| Candidate key |
| Composite key |
| Primary key |
| Surrogate key |
| Foreign key |
| Referential integrity constraint |
| Normal form |
| Multivalued dependency |

## Characteristics of Relations

A **relation** has a specific definition, as shown in Figure 3-4, and for a table to be a relation, the criteria of this definition must be met. First, the rows of the table must store data about an entity, and the columns of the table must store data about the characteristics of those entities. Next, the names of the columns are unique; no two columns in the same relation may have the same name.

Further, in a relation, all of the values in a column are of the same kind. If, for example, the second column of the first row of a relation has FirstName, then the second column of every row in the relation has FirstName. This is an important requirement that is known as the **domain integrity constraint**, where the term **domain** means a grouping of data that meets a specific type definition. For example, FirstName would have a domain of names such as *Albert, Bruce, Cathy, David, Edith,* and so forth, and all values of FirstName *must* come from the names in that domain. The EMPLOYEE table shown in Figure 3-5 meets these criteria and is a relation.

**FIGURE 3-4**

Characteristics of Relations

| Characteristics of Relations |
|---|
| Rows contain data about an entity. |
| Columns contain data about attributes of the entities. |
| All entries in a column are of the same kind. |
| Each column has a unique name. |
| Cells of the table hold a single value. |
| The order of the columns is unimportant. |
| The order of the rows is unimportant. |
| No two rows may be identical. |

| EmployeeNumber | FirstName | LastName | Department | EmailAddress | Phone |
|---|---|---|---|---|---|
| 100 | Jerry | Johnson | Accounting | JJ@somewhere.com | 518-834-1101 |
| 200 | Mary | Abernathy | Finance | MA@somewhere.com | 518-834-2101 |
| 300 | Liz | Smathers | Finance | LS@somewhere.com | 518-834-2102 |
| 400 | Tom | Caruthers | Accounting | TC@somewhere.com | 518-834-1102 |
| 500 | Tom | Jackson | Production | TJ@somewhere.com | 518-834-4101 |
| 600 | Eleanore | Caldera | Legal | EC@somewhere.com | 518-834-3101 |
| 700 | Richard | Bandalone | Legal | RB@somewhere.com | 518-834-3102 |

**FIGURE 3-5**

Sample EMPLOYEE Relation

**BY THE WAY**   Columns in different relations may have the same name. In Chapter 2, for example, two relations had a column named SKU. When there is risk of confusion, we precede the column name with the relation name followed by a period. Thus, the name of the SKU column in the SKU_DATA relation is SKU_DATA.SKU, and column C1 of relation R1 is named R1.C1. Because relation names are unique within a database and because column names are unique within a relation, the combination of relation name and column name uniquely identifies every column in the database.

Each cell of a relation has only a single value or item; multiple entries are not allowed. The table in Figure 3-6 is *not* a relation because the Phone values of employees Caruthers and Bandalone store multiple phone numbers.

In a relation, the order of the rows and the order of the columns are immaterial. No information can be carried by the ordering of rows or columns. The table in Figure 3-7 is not a relation because the entries for employees Caruthers and Caldera require a particular row arrangement. If the rows in this table were rearranged, we would not know which employee has the indicated Fax and Home numbers.

Finally, according to the last characteristic in Figure 3-4, for a table to be a relation, no two rows can be identical. As you learned in Chapter 2, some SQL statements do produce tables with duplicate rows. In such cases, you can use the DISTINCT keyword to force uniqueness. Such row duplication occurs only as a result of SQL manipulation. Tables that you design to be stored in the database should never contain duplicate rows.

**FIGURE 3-6**

Non-relational Table— Multiple Entries per Cell

| EmployeeNumber | FirstName | LastName | Department | EmailAddress | Phone |
|---|---|---|---|---|---|
| 100 | Jerry | Johnson | Accounting | JJ@somewhere.com | 518-834-1101 |
| 200 | Mary | Abernathy | Finance | MA@somewhere.com | 518-834-2101 |
| 300 | Liz | Smathers | Finance | LS@somewhere.com | 518-834-2102 |
| 400 | Tom | Caruthers | Accounting | TC@somewhere.com | 518-834-1102, 518-834-1191, 518-834-1192 |
| 500 | Tom | Jackson | Production | TJ@somewhere.com | 518-834-4101 |
| 600 | Eleanore | Caldera | Legal | EC@somewhere.com | 518-834-3101 |
| 700 | Richard | Bandalone | Legal | RB@somewhere.com | 518-834-3102, 518-834-3191 |

| EmployeeNumber | FirstName | LastName | Department | EmailAddress | Phone |
|---|---|---|---|---|---|
| 100 | Jerry | Johnson | Accounting | JJ@somewhere.com | 518-834-1101 |
| 200 | Mary | Abernathy | Finance | MA@somewhere.com | 518-834-2101 |
| 300 | Liz | Smathers | Finance | LS@somewhere.com | 518-834-2102 |
| 400 | Tom | Caruthers | Accounting | TC@somewhere.com | 518-834-1102 |
| | | | | Fax: | 518-834-9911 |
| | | | | Home: | 518-723-8795 |
| 500 | Tom | Jackson | Production | TJ@somewhere.com | 518-834-4101 |
| 600 | Eleanore | Caldera | Legal | EC@somewhere.com | 518-834-3101 |
| | | | | Fax: | 518-834-9912 |
| | | | | Home: | 518-723-7654 |
| 700 | Richard | Bandalone | Legal | RB@somewhere.com | 518-834-3102 |

**FIGURE 3-7**

Non-relational Table—
Order of Rows Matters
and Kind of Column
Entries Differs in Email

> **BY THE WAY**  Do not fall into a common trap. Even though every cell of a relation must have a single value, this does not mean that all values must have the same length. The table in Figure 3-8 is a relation even though the length of the Comment column varies from row to row. It is a relation because, even though the comments have different lengths, there is only *one* comment per cell.

**FIGURE 3-8**

Relation with Variable-
Length Column Values

| EmployeeNumber | FirstName | LastName | Department | EmailAddress | Phone | Comments |
|---|---|---|---|---|---|---|
| 100 | Jerry | Johnson | Accounting | JJ@somewhere.com | 518-834-1101 | Joined the Accounting Department in March after completing his MBA. Will take the CPA exam this fall. |
| 200 | Mary | Abernathy | Finance | MA@somewhere.com | 518-834-2101 | |
| 300 | Liz | Smathers | Finance | LS@somewhere.com | 518-834-2102 | |
| 400 | Tom | Caruthers | Accounting | TC@somewhere.com | 518-834-1102 | |
| 500 | Tom | Jackson | Production | TJ@somewhere.com | 518-834-4101 | |
| 600 | Eleanore | Caldera | Legal | EC@somewhere.com | 518-834-3101 | |
| 700 | Richard | Bandalone | Legal | RB@somewhere.com | 518-834-3102 | Is a full-time consultant to Legal on a retainer basis. |

FIGURE 3-9

Three Sets of Equivalent
Terms

| Table | Column | Row |
|-------|--------|-----|
| Relation | Attribute | Tuple |
| File | Field | Record |

## Alternative Terminology

As defined by Codd, the columns of a relation are called **attributes**, and the rows of a relation are called **tuples** (rhymes with "couples"). Most practitioners, however, do not use these academic-sounding terms and instead use the terms *column* and *row*. Also, even though a table is not necessarily a relation, most practitioners mean *relation* when they say *table*. Thus, in most conversations the terms *relation* and *table* are synonymous. In fact, for the rest of this book *table* and *relation* will be used synonymously.

Additionally, a third set of terminology can be used. Some practitioners use the terms *file, field*, and *record* for the terms *table, column*, and *row*, respectively. These terms arose from traditional data processing and are common in connection with legacy systems. Sometimes people mix and match these terms. You might hear someone say, for example, that a relation has a certain column and contains 47 records. These three sets of terms are summarized in Figure 3-9.

## To Key or Not to Key—That Is the Question!

Again, as defined by Codd, the rows of a relation must be unique (no two rows may be identical), but there is no requirement for a designated *primary key* in the relation. You will recall that in Chapter 1, we described a *primary key* as a column (or columns) with a set of values that uniquely identify each row.

However, the requirement that no two rows be identical *implies* that a primary key *can* be defined for the relation. Further, in the "real world" of databases, every relation (or table as they are more often referred to in daily use) *does* have a defined primary key.

To understand how to designate or assign a primary key for a relation, we need to learn about the different types of keys used in relational databases, and this means we need to learn about functional dependencies, which are the foundation upon which keys are built. We will then discuss specifically how to assign primary keys in relations.

## Functional Dependencies

Functional dependencies are the heart of the database design process, and it is vital for you to understand them. We will first explain the concept in general terms and then examine two examples. We will then be able to define exactly what a *functional dependency* is.

We begin with a short excursion into the world of algebra. Suppose you are buying boxes of cookies and someone tells you that each box costs $5.00. With this fact, you can compute the cost of several boxes with the following formula:

$$\text{CookieCost} = \text{NumberOfBoxes} \times \$5$$

A more general way to express the relationship between CookieCost and NumberOfBoxes is to say that CookieCost *depends on* NumberOfBoxes. Such a statement tells us the character of the relationship between CookieCost and NumberOfBoxes, even though it doesn't give us the formula. More formally, we can say that CookieCost is **functionally dependent** on NumberOfBoxes. Such a statement can be written as:

**NumberOfBoxes → CookieCost**

This expression can be read as "NumberOfBoxes *determines* CookieCost." The variable on the left, here NumberOfBoxes, is called the **determinant**.

Using another formula, we can compute the extended price of a part order by multiplying the quantity of the item by its unit price, or:

$$\text{ExtendedPrice} = \text{Quantity} \times \text{UnitPrice}$$

In this case, we say that ExtendedPrice is functionally dependent on Quantity and Unit-Price, or:

**(Quantity, UnitPrice) → ExtendedPrice**

Here the determinant is the composite (Quantity, UnitPrice).

### Functional Dependencies That Are Not Equations

In general, a **functional dependency** exists when the value of one or more attributes determines the value of another attribute. Many functional dependencies exist that do not involve equations.

Consider an example. Suppose you know that a sack contains red, blue, or yellow objects. Further, suppose you know that the red objects weigh 5 pounds, the blue objects weigh 5 pounds, and the yellow objects weigh 7 pounds. If a friend looks into the sack, sees an object, and tells you the color of the object, you can tell her the weight of the object. We can formalize this as:

**ObjectColor → Weight**

Thus, we can say that Weight is functionally dependent on ObjectColor and that ObjectColor determines Weight. The relationship here does not involve an equation, but the functional dependency holds. Given a value for ObjectColor, you can determine the object's weight.

If we also know that the red objects are balls, the blue objects are cubes, and the yellow objects are cubes, we can also say:

**ObjectColor → Shape**

Thus, ObjectColor determines Shape. We can put these two together to state:

**ObjectColor → (Weight, Shape)**

Thus, ObjectColor determines Weight and Shape.

Another way to represent these facts is to put them into a table:

| ObjectColor | Weight | Shape |
|-------------|--------|-------|
| Red         | 5      | Ball  |
| Blue        | 5      | Cube  |
| Yellow      | 7      | Cube  |

This table meets all of the conditions listed in Figure 3-4, and therefore it is a relation. You may be thinking that we performed a trick or sleight of hand to arrive at this relation, but in truth, the only reason for having relations is *to store instances of functional dependencies*. If there were a formula by which we could take ObjectColor and somehow compute Weight and Shape, then we would not need the table. We would just make the computation. Similarly, if there were a formula by which we could take EmployeeNumber and compute EmployeeName and HireDate, then we would not need an EMPLOYEE relation. However, because there is no such formula, we must store the combinations of EmployeeNumber, EmployeeName, and HireDate in the rows of a relation.

---

**BY THE WAY**    Perhaps the easiest way to understand functional dependencies is:
> *If I tell you one specific fact, can you respond with a unique associated fact?*

Using the earlier table, if I tell you that the ObjectColor is Red, can you uniquely tell me the associated Shape? *Yes*, you can, and it is Ball. Therefore, ObjectColor *determines* Shape, and a functional dependency exists with ObjectColor as the determinant.

Now, if I tell you that that the Shape is Cube, can you tell me the uniquely associated ObjectColor? *No*, you cannot because it could be either Blue or Yellow. Therefore, Shape *does not determine* ObjectColor, and ObjectColor is *not* functionally dependent on Shape.

---

## Composite Functional Dependencies

The determinant of a functional dependency can consist of more than one attribute. For example, a grade in a class is determined by both the student and the class, or:

$$(\text{StudentNumber, ClassNumber}) \rightarrow \text{Grade}$$

In this case, the determinant is called a **composite determinant**.

Notice that both the student and the class are needed to determine the grade. In general, if $(A, B) \rightarrow C$, then neither A nor B will determine C by itself. However, if $A \rightarrow (B, C)$, then it is true that $A \rightarrow B$ and $A \rightarrow C$. (This is known as the **decomposition rule**.) Work through examples of your own for both of these cases so that you understand why this is true. Also note that if $A \rightarrow B$ and $A \rightarrow C$, then it is true that $A \rightarrow (B, C)$. (This is known as the **union rule**.)

## Finding Functional Dependencies

To fix the idea of functional dependency in your mind, consider what functional dependencies exist in the SKU_DATA and ORDER_ITEM tables in Figure 3-1.

### Functional Dependencies in the SKU_DATA Table

To find functional dependencies in a table, we must ask "Does any column determine the value of another column?" For example, consider the values of the SKU_DATA table in Figure 3-1:

|    | SKU    | SKU_Description                  | Department   | Buyer        |
|----|--------|----------------------------------|--------------|--------------|
| 1  | 100100 | Std. Scuba Tank, Yellow          | Water Sports | Pete Hansen  |
| 2  | 100200 | Std. Scuba Tank, Magenta         | Water Sports | Pete Hansen  |
| 3  | 100300 | Std. Scuba Tank, Light Blue      | Water Sports | Pete Hansen  |
| 4  | 100400 | Std. Scuba Tank, Dark Blue       | Water Sports | Pete Hansen  |
| 5  | 100500 | Std. Scuba Tank, Light Green     | Water Sports | Pete Hansen  |
| 6  | 100600 | Std. Scuba Tank, Dark Green      | Water Sports | Pete Hansen  |
| 7  | 101100 | Dive Mask, Small Clear           | Water Sports | Nancy Meyers |
| 8  | 101200 | Dive Mask, Med Clear             | Water Sports | Nancy Meyers |
| 9  | 201000 | Half-dome Tent                   | Camping      | Cindy Lo     |
| 10 | 202000 | Half-dome Tent Vestibule         | Camping      | Cindy Lo     |
| 11 | 203000 | Half-dome Tent Vestibule - Wide  | Camping      | Cindy Lo     |
| 12 | 301000 | Light Fly Climbing Harness       | Climbing     | Jerry Martin |
| 13 | 302000 | Locking Carabiner, Oval          | Climbing     | Jerry Martin |

Consider the last two columns. If we know the value of Department, can we determine a unique value of Buyer? No, we cannot because a Department may have more than one Buyer. In these sample data, 'Water Sports' is associated with Pete Hansen and Nancy Meyers. Therefore, Department does not functionally determine Buyer.

What about the reverse? Does Buyer determine Department? In every row, for a given value of Buyer, do we find the same value of Department? Every time Jerry Martin appears, for example, is he paired with the same department? The answer is yes. Further, every time Cindy Lo appears, she is paired with the same department. The same is true for the other buyers. Therefore, assuming that these data are representative, Buyer does determine Department, and we can write:

**Buyer → Department**

Does Buyer determine any other column? If we know the value of Buyer, do we know the value of SKU? No, we do not because a given buyer has many SKUs assigned to him or her. Does Buyer determine SKU_Description? No, because a given value of Buyer occurs with many values of SKU_Description.

> **BY THE WAY**   As stated, for the Buyer → Department functional dependency, a Buyer is paired with one and only one value of Department. Notice that a buyer can appear more than once in the table, but, if so, that buyer is always paired with the same department. This is true for all functional dependencies. If A → B, then each value of A will be paired with one and only one value of B. A particular value of A may appear more than once in the relation, but, if so, it is always paired with the same value of B. Note, too, that the reverse is not necessarily true. If A → B, then a value of B may be paired with many values of A.

What about the other columns? It turns out that if we know the value of SKU, we also know the values of all of the other columns. In other words:

**SKU → SKU_Description**

because a given value of SKU will have just one value of SKU_Description. Next,

**SKU → Department**

because a given value of SKU will have just one value of Department. And, finally,

**SKU → Buyer**

because a given value of SKU will have just one value of Buyer.
We can combine these three statements as:

**SKU → (SKU_Description, Department, Buyer)**

For the same reasons, SKU_Description determines all of the other columns, and we can write:

**SKU_Description → (SKU, Department, Buyer)**

In summary, the functional dependencies in the SKU_DATA table are:

**SKU → (SKU_Description, Department, Buyer)**
**SKU_Description → (SKU, Department, Buyer)**
**Buyer → Department**

## Functional Dependencies in the ORDER_ITEM Table

Now consider the ORDER_ITEM table in Figure 3-1. For convenience, here is a copy of the data in that table:

| | OrderNumber | SKU | Quantity | Price | ExtendedPrice |
|---|---|---|---|---|---|
| 1 | 1000 | 201000 | 1 | 300.00 | 300.00 |
| 2 | 1000 | 202000 | 1 | 130.00 | 130.00 |
| 3 | 2000 | 101100 | 4 | 50.00 | 200.00 |
| 4 | 2000 | 101200 | 2 | 50.00 | 100.00 |
| 5 | 3000 | 100200 | 1 | 300.00 | 300.00 |
| 6 | 3000 | 101100 | 2 | 50.00 | 100.00 |
| 7 | 3000 | 101200 | 1 | 50.00 | 50.00 |

What are the functional dependencies in this table? Start on the left. Does OrderNumber determine another column? It does not determine SKU because several SKUs are associated with a given order. For the same reasons, it does not determine Quantity, Price, or ExtendedPrice.

What about SKU? SKU does not determine OrderNumber because several OrderNumbers are associated with a given SKU. It does not determine Quantity or ExtendedPrice for the same reason.

What about SKU and Price? From this data, it does appear that:

**SKU → Price**

but that might not be true in general. In fact, we know that prices can change after an order has been processed. Further, an order might have special pricing due to a sale or promotion. To keep an accurate record of what the customer actually paid, we need to associate a particular SKU price with a particular order. Thus:

**(OrderNumber, SKU) → Price**

Considering the other columns, Quantity, Price, and ExtendedPrice do not determine anything else. You can decide this by looking at the sample data. You can reinforce this conclusion by thinking about the nature of sales. Would a Quantity of 2 ever determine an OrderNumber or an SKU? This makes no sense. At the grocery store, if I tell you I bought two of something, you have no reason to conclude that my OrderNumber was 1010022203466 or that I bought carrots. Quantity does not determine OrderNumber or SKU.

Similarly, if I tell you that the price of an item was $3.99, there is no logical way to conclude what my OrderNumber was or that I bought a jar of green olives. Thus, Price does not determine OrderNumber or SKU. Similar comments pertain to ExtendedPrice. It turns out that no single column is a determinant in the ORDER_ITEM table.

What about pairs of columns? We already know that:

**(OrderNumber, SKU) → Price**

Examining the data, (OrderNumber, SKU) determines the other two columns as well. Thus:

> **(OrderNumber, SKU) → (Quantity, Price, ExtendedPrice)**

This functional dependency makes sense. It means that given a particular order and a particular item on that order, there is only one quantity, one price, and one extended price.

Notice, too, that because the value of ExtendedPrice is computed from the formula ExtendedPrice = (Quantity * Price) we have:

> **(Quantity, Price) → ExtendedPrice**

In summary, the functional dependencies in ORDER_ITEM are:

> **(OrderNumber, SKU) → (Quantity, Price, ExtendedPrice)**
> **(Quantity, Price) → ExtendedPrice**

No single skill is more important for designing databases than the ability to identify functional dependencies. Make sure you understand the material in this section. Work through Exercises 3.58 and 3.59, the Regional Labs case questions, and the Queen Anne Curiosity Shop and Morgan Importing project questions at the end of the chapter. Ask your instructor for help if necessary. You *must* understand functional dependencies and be able to work with them.

### When Are Determinant Values Unique?

In the previous section, you may have noticed an irregularity. Sometimes the determinants of a functional dependency are unique in a relation, and sometimes they are not. Consider the SKU_DATA relation, with determinants SKU, SKU_Description, and Buyer. In SKU_DATA, the values of both SKU and SKU_Description are unique in the table. For example, the SKU value 100100 appears just once. Similarly, the SKU_Description value 'Half-dome Tent' occurs just once. From this, it is tempting to conclude that values of determinants are always unique in a relation. However, this is *not* true.

For example, Buyer is a determinant, but it is not unique in SKU_DATA. The buyer 'Cindy Lo' appears in two different rows. In fact, for these sample data, all of the buyers occur in two different rows.

In truth, a determinant is unique in a relation only if it determines every other column in the relation. For the SKU_DATA relation, SKU determines all of the other columns. Similarly, SKU_Description determines all of the other columns. Hence, they both are unique. Buyer, however, only determines the Department column. It does not determine SKU or SKU_Description.

The determinants in ORDER_ITEM are (OrderNumber, SKU) and (Quantity, Price). Because (OrderNumber, SKU) determines all of the other columns, it will be unique in the relation. The composite (Quantity and Price) only determines ExtendedPrice. Therefore, it will not be unique in the relation.

This fact means that you cannot find the determinants of all functional dependencies simply by looking for unique values. Some of the determinants will be unique, but some will not. Instead, to determine if column A determines column B, look at the data and ask, "Every time a value of column A appears, is it matched with the same value of Column B?" If so, it can be a determinant of B. Again, however, sample data can be incomplete, so the best strategies are to think about the nature of the business activity from which the data arise and to ask the users.

### Keys

The relational model has more keys than a locksmith. There are candidate keys, composite keys, primary keys, surrogate keys, and foreign keys. In this section, we will define each of these types of keys. Because key definitions rely on the concept of functional dependency, make sure you understand that concept before reading on.

In general, a **key** is a combination of one or more columns that is used to identify particular rows in a relation. Keys that have two or more columns are called **composite keys**.

## Candidate Keys

A **candidate key** is a determinant that determines all of the other columns in a relation. The SKU_DATA relation has two candidate keys: SKU and SKU_Description. Buyer is a determinant, but it is not a candidate key because it determines only Department.

The ORDER_ITEM table has just one candidate key: (OrderNumber, SKU). The other determinant in this table, (Quantity, Price), is not a candidate key because it determines only ExtendedPrice.

Candidate keys identify a unique row in a relation. Given the value of a candidate key, we can find one and only one row in the relation that has that value. For example, given the SKU value of 100100, we can find one and only one row in SKU_DATA. Similarly, given the OrderNumber and SKU values (2000, 101100), we can find one and only one row in ORDER_ITEM.

## Primary Keys

When designing a database, one of the candidate keys is selected to be the **primary key**. This term is used because this key will be defined to the database management system (DBMS), and the DBMS will use it as its primary means for finding rows in a table. A table has only one primary key. The primary key can have one column, or it can be a composite.

In this text, to clarify discussions we will sometimes indicate table structure by showing the name of a table followed by the names of the table's columns enclosed in parentheses. When we do this, we will underline the column(s) that comprise the primary key. For example, we can show the structure of SKU_DATA and ORDER_ITEM as follows:

**SKU_DATA (<u>SKU</u>, SKU_Description, Department, Buyer)**

**ORDER_ITEM (<u>OrderNumber</u>, <u>SKU</u>, Quantity, Price, ExtendedPrice)**

This notation indicates that SKU is the primary key of SKU_DATA and that (OrderNumber, SKU) is the primary key of ORDER_ITEM.

In order to function properly, a primary key, whether it is a single column or a composite key, *must* have unique data values inserted into every row of the table. Although this fact may seem obvious, it is significant enough to be named the **entity integrity constraint** and is a fundamental requirement for the proper functioning of a relational database.

> **BY THE WAY**    What do you do if a table has no candidate keys? In that case, define the primary key as the collection of all of the columns in the table. Because there are no duplicate rows in a stored relation, the combination of all of the columns of the table will always be unique. Again, although tables generated by SQL manipulation may have duplicate rows, the tables that you design to be stored should never be constructed to have data duplication. Thus, the combination of all columns is always a candidate key.

## Surrogate Keys

A **surrogate key** is an artificial column that is added to a table to serve as the primary key. The DBMS assigns a unique value to a surrogate key when the row is created. The assigned value never changes. Surrogate keys are used when the primary key is large and unwieldy. For example, consider the relation RENTAL_PROPERTY:

**RENTAL_PROPERTY (<u>Street</u>, <u>City</u>, <u>State/Province</u>, <u>ZIP/PostalCode</u>, <u>Country</u>, Rental_Rate)**

The primary key of this table is (Street, City, State/Province, ZIP/PostalCode, Country). As we will discuss further in Chapter 6, for good performance, a primary key should be short and, if possible, numeric. The primary key of RENTAL_PROPERTY is neither.

In this case, the designers of the database would likely create a surrogate key. The structure of the table would then be:

**RENTAL_PROPERTY (PropertyID, Street, City, State/Province, ZIP/PostalCode, Country, Rental_Rate)**

The DBMS can then be used to assign a numeric value to PropertyID when a row is created (exactly *how* this is done depends upon which DBMS product is being used). Using that key will result in better performance than using the original key. Note that surrogate key values are artificial and have no meaning to the users. In fact, surrogate key values are normally hidden in forms and reports.

For another example, let's look at the Cape Codd BUYER table as we created it in Chapter 2. The structure of the BUYER table is:

**BUYER (BuyerName, Department, Position, *Supervisor*)**

The primary key is BuyerName, Supervisor is a foreign key referencing BuyerName in a recursive relationship as discussed in Chapter 2, and the data in the table is:

|   | BuyerName | Department | Position | Supervisor |
|---|-----------|-----------|----------|------------|
| 1 | Cindy Lo | Purchasing | Buyer 2 | Mary Smith |
| 2 | Jerry Martin | Purchasing | Buyer 1 | Cindy Lo |
| 3 | Mary Smith | Purchasing | Manager | NULL |
| 4 | Nancy Meyers | Purchasing | Buyer 1 | Pete Hansen |
| 5 | Pete Hansen | Purchasing | Buyer 3 | Mary Smith |

But a primary key must be unique, and BuyerName is only unique because we have so few records in this table—for example, Mary Smith is a common name, and we could easily have multiple Mary Smiths working at Cape Codd as buyers. Another problem is that the BuyerName column actually holds two pieces of data: the Buyer's first name and the Buyer's last name. Good database design dictates that we should split this column into two separate columns: BuyerFirstName and BuyerLastName. Using these two columns as a composite primary key doesn't solve the problem of possible name duplication.

The solution is to use a surrogate primary key and split BuyerName into its components. Thus we get a revised structure of the BUYER table as:

**BUYER (BuyerID, BuyerFirstName, BuyerLastName, Department, Position, *Supervisor*)**

Note that because we are now using the surrogate primary key BuyerID, the Supervisor column must now hold the numeric values that point to the appropriate BuyerID! Our data in the table now looks like this:

|   | BuyerID | BuyerFirstName | BuyerLastName | Department | Position | Supervisor |
|---|---------|----------------|---------------|------------|----------|------------|
| 1 | 1 | Mary | Smith | Purchasing | Manager | NULL |
| 2 | 2 | Pete | Hansen | Purchasing | Buyer 3 | 1 |
| 3 | 3 | Nancy | Meyers | Purchasing | Buyer 1 | 2 |
| 4 | 4 | Cindy | Lo | Purchasing | Buyer 2 | 1 |
| 5 | 5 | Jerry | Martin | Purchasing | Buyer 1 | 4 |

For the time being, we will continue to use the original BUYER table as the basis for our discussions in this chapter. The techniques we would use to convert the original BUYER table into the redesigned BUYER table are discussed in Chapter 8 on database redesign.

## Foreign Keys

A **foreign key** is a column or composite of columns that is the primary key of a table other than the one in which it appears. The term arises because it is a key of a table *foreign* to the one in which it appears as the primary key. In the following two tables, DEPARTMENT. DepartmentName is the primary key of DEPARTMENT, and EMPLOYEE.Department is a foreign key. In this text, we will show foreign keys in italics:

**DEPARTMENT (<u>DepartmentName</u>, BudgetCode, OfficeNumber, DepartmentPhone)**

**EMPLOYEE (<u>EmployeeNumber</u>, LastName, FirstName, *Department*)**

Foreign keys express relationships between rows of tables. In this example, the foreign key EMPLOYEE.Department stores the relationship between an employee and his or her department. Note that the foreign key does *not* need to have the same name as the primary key it references—it only has to contain the same type of data!

Consider the SKU_DATA and ORDER_ITEM tables. SKU_DATA.SKU is the primary key of SKU_DATA, and ORDER_ITEM.SKU is a foreign key.

**SKU_DATA (<u>SKU</u>, SKU_Description, Department, Buyer)**

**ORDER_ITEM (<u>OrderNumber</u>, <u>SKU</u>, Quantity, Price, ExtendedPrice)**

Notice that ORDER_ITEM.SKU is both a foreign key and part of the primary key of ORDER_ITEM. This condition sometimes occurs, but it is not required. In the earlier example, EMPLOYEE.Department is a foreign key, but it is not part of the EMPLOYEE primary key. You will see some uses for foreign keys later in this chapter and the next, and you will study them at length in Chapter 6.

In most cases, we need to ensure that the values of a foreign key match a valid value of a primary key. For the SKU_DATA and ORDER_ITEM tables, we need to ensure that all of the values of ORDER_ITEM.SKU match a value of SKU_DATA.SKU. To accomplish this, we create a **referential integrity constraint**, which is a statement that limits the values of the foreign key. In this case, we create the constraint:

**SKU in ORDER_ITEM must exist in SKU in SKU_DATA**

This constraint stipulates that every value of SKU in ORDER_ITEM must match a value of SKU in SKU_DATA.

Note that we can have a referential integrity constraint on a recursive relationship between two columns in the same table. The referential integrity constraint for the redesigned BUYER table (the one with BuyerID) discussed earlier in this chapter is:

**Supervisor in BUYER must exist in BuyerID in BUYER**

> **BY THE WAY**   While we have defined a *referential integrity constraint* to require a corresponding primary key value in the linked table, the technical definition of the referential integrity constraint allows for one other option—that the foreign key cell in the table is *empty* and *does not have a value*.[2] If a cell in a table does not have a value, it is said to have a **null value**—for example, see the null value for Mary Smith's Supervisor in the BUYER tables earlier (where it appears in all uppercase as NULL). We will discuss null values in Chapter 4.
>
> Except for recursive relationships like the one in the BUYER table, it is difficult to imagine a foreign key having null values in a real database when the referential integrity constraint is actually in use, and we will stick with our basic definition of the referential integrity constraint in this book. At the same time, be aware that the complete formal definition of the referential integrity constraint does allow for null values in foreign key columns and that this can and will occur in recursive relationships—our BUYER table data provides one example of how this can happen.

---

[2] For example, see the Wikipedia article on referential integrity at *http://en.wikipedia.org/wiki/Referential_integrity* (accessed October 2020).

> **BY THE WAY**   We have defined three constraints so far in our discussion:
>
> - The *domain integrity constraint*
> - The *entity integrity constraint*
> - The *referential integrity constraint*
>
> The purpose of these three constraints, taken as a whole, is to create **data integrity**, which means that the data in our database will be useful, meaningful data.[3]

# Normal Forms

All relations are not equal. Some are easy to process, and others are problematic. Relations are categorized into **normal forms** based on the kinds of problems that they have. Knowledge of these normal forms will help you create appropriate database designs. To understand normal forms, we need first to define modification anomalies.

## Modification Anomalies

Consider the EQUIPMENT_REPAIR relation in Figure 3-10, which stores data about manufacturing equipment and equipment repairs. Suppose we delete the data for repair number 2100. When we delete this row (the second one in Figure 3-10), we remove not only data about the repair, but also data about the machine itself. We will no longer know, for example, that the machine was a Lathe and that its AcquisitionCost was 4750.00. When we delete one row, the structure of this table forces us to lose facts about two different things: a machine and a repair. This condition is called a **deletion anomaly**.

Now suppose we want to enter the first repair for a piece of equipment. To enter repair data, we need to know not just RepairNumber, RepairDate, and RepairCost but also ItemNumber, EquipmentType, and AcquisitionCost. If we work in the repair department, this is a problem because we are unlikely to know the value of AcquisitionCost. The structure of this table forces us to enter facts about two entities when we just want to enter facts about one. This condition is called an **insertion anomaly**.

Finally, suppose we want to change existing data. If we alter a value of RepairNumber, RepairDate, or RepairCost, there is no problem. But if we alter a value of ItemNumber, EquipmentType, or AcquisitionCost, we may create a data inconsistency. To see why, suppose we update the last row of the table in Figure 3-10 using the data (100, 'Drill Press', 5500, 2500, '08/17/18', 275).

Figure 3-11 shows the table after this erroneous update. The drill press has two different AcquisitionCosts. Clearly, this is an error. Equipment cannot be acquired at two different costs. If there were, say, 10,000 rows in the table, however, it might be very difficult to detect this error. This condition is called an **update anomaly**.

**FIGURE 3-10**

The EQUIPMENT_REPAIR Table

|   | ItemNumber | Equipment Type | AcquisitionCost | RepairNumber | RepairDate | RepairCost |
|---|------------|----------------|-----------------|--------------|------------|------------|
| 1 | 100 | Drill Press | 3500.00 | 2000 | 2021-05-05 | 375.00 |
| 2 | 200 | Lathe | 4750.00 | 2100 | 2021-05-07 | 255.00 |
| 3 | 100 | Drill Press | 3500.00 | 2200 | 2021-06-19 | 178.00 |
| 4 | 300 | Mill | 27300.00 | 2300 | 2021-06-19 | 1875.00 |
| 5 | 100 | Drill Press | 3500.00 | 2400 | 2021-07-05 | 0.00 |
| 6 | 100 | Drill Press | 3500.00 | 2500 | 2021-08-17 | 275.00 |

---

[3] For more information and discussion, see the Wikipedia article on data integrity (accessed October 2020) at *http://en.wikipedia.org/wiki/Data_integrity* and the articles linked to that article.

**FIGURE 3-11**

The EQUIPMENT_REPAIR
Table after an Incorrect
Update

| | ItemNumber | EquipmentType | AcquisitionCost | RepairNumber | RepairDate | RepairCost |
|---|---|---|---|---|---|---|
| 1 | 100 | Drill Press | 3500.00 | 2000 | 2021-05-05 | 375.00 |
| 2 | 200 | Lathe | 4750.00 | 2100 | 2021-05-07 | 255.00 |
| 3 | 100 | Drill Press | 3500.00 | 2200 | 2021-06-19 | 178.00 |
| 4 | 300 | Mill | 27300.00 | 2300 | 2021-06-19 | 1875.00 |
| 5 | 100 | Drill Press | 3500.00 | 2400 | 2021-07-05 | 0.00 |
| 6 | 100 | Drill Press | 5500.00 | 2500 | 2021-08-17 | 275.00 |

**BY THE WAY**    Notice that the EQUIPMENT_REPAIR table in Figures 3-10 and 3-11 duplicates data. For example, the AcquisitionCost of the same item of equipment appears several times. Any table that duplicates data is susceptible to update anomalies like the one in Figure 3-11. A table that has such inconsistencies is said to have **data integrity problems**.

As we will discuss further in Chapter 4, to improve query speed, we sometimes design a table to have duplicated data. Be aware, however, that any time we design a table this way, we open the door to data integrity problems.

## A Short History of Normal Forms

When Codd defined the relational model, he noticed that some tables had modification anomalies. In his second paper,[4] he defined first normal form, second normal form, and third normal form. He defined **first normal form (1NF)** as the *set of conditions for a relation*, shown in Figure 3-4. Any table meeting the conditions in Figure 3-4 is therefore a relation in 1NF.

This definition, however, brings us back to the "To Key or Not to Key" discussion. Codd's set of conditions for a relation does not require a primary key, but one is clearly implied by the condition that all rows must be unique. Thus, there are various opinions on whether a relation has to have a defined primary key to be in 1NF.[5]

For practical purposes, we will define 1NF as it is used in this book as a table that:

1. Meets the set of conditions for a relation and
2. Has a defined primary key.[6]

Codd also noted that some tables (or, interchangeably in this book, relations) in 1NF had modification anomalies. He found that he could remove some of those anomalies by applying certain conditions. A relation that met those conditions, which we will discuss later in this chapter, was said to be in **second normal form (2NF)**. He also observed, however, that relations in 2NF could also have anomalies, and so he defined **third normal form (3NF)**, which is a set of conditions that removes even more anomalies and which we will also discuss later in this chapter. As time went by, other researchers found still other ways that anomalies can occur, and the conditions for **Boyce-Codd Normal Form (BCNF)** were defined.

These normal forms are defined so that a relation in BCNF is in 3NF, a relation in 3NF is in 2NF, and a relation in 2NF is in 1NF. Thus, if you put a relation into BCNF, it is automatically in the lesser normal forms.

---

[4] E. F. Codd and A. L. Dean, "Proceedings of 1971 ACM-SIGFIDET Workshop on Data Description," *Access and Control*, San Diego, California, November 11-12, 1971 ACM 1971.

[5] For a review of some of the discussion, see the Wikipedia article at *http://en.wikipedia.org/wiki/First_normal_form* (accessed October 2020).

[6] Some definitions of 1NF also state that there can be "no repeating groups." This refers to the *multivalue, multicolumn problem* we discuss in Chapter 4 and also deal with in our discussion of *multivalued dependencies* later in this chapter.

Normal forms 2NF through BCNF concern anomalies that arise from functional dependencies. Other sources of anomalies were found later. They led to the definition of **fourth normal form (4NF)** and **fifth normal form (5NF)**, both of which we will discuss later in this chapter. So it went, with researchers chipping away at modification anomalies, each one improving on the prior normal form.

In 1982, Ronald Fagin published a paper that took a different tack.[7] Instead of looking for just another normal form, Fagin asked, "What conditions need to exist for a relation to have no anomalies?" In that paper, he defined **domain/key normal form (DK/NF)** (and, no, that is *not* a typo–the slash appears between *domain* and *key* in the complete name but between *DK* and *NF* in the acronym). Fagin ended the search for normal forms by showing that a relation in DK/NF has no modification anomalies and, further, that a relation that has no modification anomalies is in DK/NF. DK/NF is discussed in more detail later in this chapter.

## Normalization Categories

As shown in Figure 3-12, normalization theory can be divided into three major categories. Some anomalies arise from functional dependencies, some arise from multivalued dependencies, and some arise from data constraints and odd conditions.

2NF, 3NF, and BCNF are all concerned with anomalies that are caused by functional dependencies. A relation that is in BCNF has no modification anomalies from functional dependencies. It is also automatically in 2NF and 3NF, and, therefore, we will focus on transforming relations into BCNF. However, it is instructive to work through the progression of normal forms from 1NF to BCNF in order to understand how each normal form deals with anomalies, and we will do this later in this chapter.[8]

As shown in the second row of Figure 3-12, some anomalies arise because of another kind of dependency called a multivalued dependency. Those anomalies can be eliminated by placing each multivalued dependency in a relation of its own, a condition known as 4NF. You will see how to do that in the last section of this chapter.

The third source of anomalies is esoteric. These problems involve specific, rare, and even strange data constraints. Accordingly, we will not discuss them in this text.

## From First Normal Form to Boyce-Codd Normal Form Step-by-Step

As we discussed earlier in this chapter, a table is in 1NF if and only if (1) it meets the *definition of a relation* in Figure 3-4 and (2) it has a *defined primary key*. From Figure 3-4 this means that the following must hold: the cells of a table must be a single value, and neither repeating groups nor arrays are allowed as values; all entries in a column must be of the same data

**FIGURE 3-12**

The EQUIPMENT_REPAIR Table after an Incorrect Update

| Source of Anomaly | Normal Forms | Design Principles |
|---|---|---|
| Functional dependencies | 1NF, 2NF, 3NF, BCNF | BCNF: Design tables so that every determinant is a candidate key. |
| Multivalued dependencies | 4NF | 4NF: Move each multivalued dependency to a table of its own. |
| Data constraints and oddities | 5NF, DK/NF | DK/NF: Make every constraint a logical consequence of candidate keys and domains. |

---

[7] Ronald Fagin, "A Normal Form for Relational Databases That Is Based on Domains and Keys," *ACM Transactions on Database Systems*, September 1981, pp. 387–415. A PDF version of the paper (accessed October 2020) is available at *https://www.researchgate.net/publication/215697522_A_normal_form_for_relational_database_that_is_based_on_domains_and_keys*.

[8] See Christopher J. Date, *An Introduction to Database Systems*, 8th ed. (New York: Addison-Wesley, 2003) for a complete discussion of normal forms.

type; each column must have a unique name, but the order of the columns in the table is not significant; and no two rows in a table may be identical, but the order of the rows is not significant. To this, we add the requirement of having a primary key defined for the table.

## Second Normal Form

When Codd discovered anomalies in 1NF tables, he defined 2NF to eliminate some of these anomalies. A relation is in 2NF if and only if *it is in 1NF* and *all non-key attributes are determined by the entire primary key*. This means that if the primary key is a composite primary key, then no non-key attribute can be determined by an attribute or set of attributes that make up only part of the key. Thus, if you have a relation **R (A, B, N, O, P)** with the composite key **(A, B)**, then none of the non-key attributes **N, O,** or **P** can be determined by just **A** or just **B**.

Note that the only way a non-key attribute can be dependent on part of the primary key is if there is a *composite primary key*. This means that relations with *single-attribute primary keys* are automatically in 2NF.

For example, consider the STUDENT_ACTIVITY relation:

**STUDENT_ACTIVITY (StudentID, Activity, ActivityFee)**

The STUDENT_ACTIVITY relation is in 1NF and is shown with sample data in Figure 3-13. Note that STUDENT_ACTIVITY has the composite primary key (StudentID, Activity), which allows us to determine the fee a particular student will have to pay for a particular activity. However, because fees are determined by activities, ActivityFee is also functionally dependent on just Activity itself, and we can say that ActivityFee is **partially dependent** on the key of the table. The set of functional dependencies is therefore:

**(StudentID, Activity) → ActivityFee**

**Activity → ActivityFee**

Thus, there is a non-key attribute determined by part of the composite primary key, and the STUDENT_ACTIVITY relation is *not* in 2NF. What do we do in this case? We will have to move the columns of the functional dependency based on the partial primary key attribute into a separate relation while leaving the determinant in the original relation as a foreign key. We will end up with two relations:

**STUDENT_ACTIVITY (StudentID, *Activity*)**

**ACTIVITY_FEE (Activity, ActivityFee)**

The Activity column in STUDENT_ACTIVITY becomes a foreign key. The new relations are shown in Figure 3-14. Now, are the two new relations in 2NF? Yes. STUDENT_ACTIVITY still has a composite primary key, but now has no attributes that are dependent on only a part of this composite key. ACTIVITY_FEE has a set of attributes (just one each in this case) that are dependent on the entire primary key.

**FIGURE 3-13**

The STUDENT_ACTIVITY Relation

**STUDENT_ACTIVITY**

|   | StudentID | Activity | ActivityFee |
|---|---|---|---|
| 1 | 100 | Golf | 65.00 |
| 2 | 100 | Skiing | 200.00 |
| 3 | 200 | Skiing | 200.00 |
| 4 | 200 | Swimming | 50.00 |
| 5 | 300 | Skiing | 200.00 |
| 6 | 300 | Swimming | 50.00 |
| 7 | 400 | Golf | 65.00 |
| 8 | 400 | Swimming | 50.00 |

**FIGURE 3-14**

The 2NF STUDENT_ACTIVITY
and ACTIVITY_FEE Relations

**STUDENT_ACTIVITY**

|   | StudentID | Activity |
|---|-----------|----------|
| 1 | 100 | Golf |
| 2 | 100 | Skiing |
| 3 | 200 | Skiing |
| 4 | 200 | Swimming |
| 5 | 300 | Skiing |
| 6 | 300 | Swimming |
| 7 | 400 | Golf |
| 8 | 400 | Swimming |

**ACTIVITY_FEE**

|   | Activity | ActivityFee |
|---|----------|-------------|
| 1 | Golf | 65.00 |
| 2 | Skiing | 200.00 |
| 3 | Swimming | 50.00 |

### Third Normal Form

However, the conditions necessary for 2NF do not eliminate all anomalies. To deal with additional anomalies, Codd defined 3NF. A relation is in 3NF if and only if *it is in 2NF and there are no non-key attributes determined by another non-key attribute*. The technical name for a non-key attribute determined by another non-key attribute is **transitive dependency**.[9] We can therefore restate the definition of 3NF: a relation is in 3NF if and only if *it is in 2NF and it has no transitive dependencies*. Thus, in order for our relation **R (A, B, N, O, P)** to be in 3NF, none of the non-key attributes **N, O,** or **P** can be determined by **N, O,** or **P**.

For example, consider the relation STUDENT_HOUSING shown in Figure 3-15. The STUDENT_HOUSING relation is in 2NF, and the table schema is:

**STUDENT_HOUSING (StudentID, Building, BuildingFee)**

Here we have a single-attribute primary key, StudentID, so the relation is in 2NF because there is no possibility of a non-key attribute being dependent on only part of the primary key. Furthermore, if we know the student, we can determine the building where he or she is residing, so:

**StudentID → Building**

However, the building fee is independent of which student is housed in the building, and, in fact, the same fee is charged for every room in a building. Therefore, Building determines BuildingFee:

**Building → BuildingFee**

**FIGURE 3-15**

The STUDENT_HOUSING
Relation

**STUDENT_HOUSING**

|   | StudentID | Building | BuildingFee |
|---|-----------|----------|-------------|
| 1 | 100 | Randoplh | 3200.00 |
| 2 | 200 | Ingersoll | 3400.00 |
| 3 | 300 | Randoplh | 3200.00 |
| 4 | 400 | Randoplh | 3200.00 |
| 5 | 500 | Pitkin | 3500.00 |
| 6 | 600 | Ingersoll | 3400.00 |
| 7 | 700 | Ingersoll | 3400.00 |
| 8 | 800 | Pitkin | 3500.00 |

---

[9] In terms of functional dependencies, a transitive dependency is defined as: IF A → B and B → C, THEN A → C.

FIGURE 3-16

The 3NF
STUDENT_HOUSING and
HOUSING_FEE Relations

**STUDENT_HOUSING**

| | StudentID | Building |
|---|---|---|
| 1 | 100 | Randoplh |
| 2 | 200 | Ingersoll |
| 3 | 300 | Randoplh |
| 4 | 400 | Randoplh |
| 5 | 500 | Pitkin |
| 6 | 600 | Ingersoll |
| 7 | 700 | Ingersoll |
| 8 | 800 | Pitkin |

**HOUSING_FEE**

| | Building | BuildingFee |
|---|---|---|
| 1 | Ingersoll | 3400.00 |
| 2 | Pitkin | 3500.00 |
| 3 | Randoplh | 3200.00 |

Thus, a non-key attribute (BuildingFee) is functionally determined by another non-key attribute (Building), and the relation is *not* in 3NF.

To put the relation into 3NF, we will have to move the columns of the functional dependency into a separate relation while leaving the determinant in the original relation as a foreign key. We will end up with two relations:

**STUDENT_HOUSING (StudentID, *Building*)**

**BUILDING_FEE (Building, BuildingFee)**

The Building column in STUDENT_HOUSING becomes a foreign key. The two relations are now in 3NF (work through the logic yourself to make sure you understand 3NF) and are shown in Figure 3-16.

## Boyce-Codd Normal Form

Some database designers normalize their relations to 3NF. Unfortunately, there are still anomalies due to functional dependences in 3NF. Together with Raymond Boyce, Codd defined BCNF to fix this situation. A relation is in BCNF if and only if *it is in 3NF* and *every determinant is a candidate key*.

For example, consider the relation STUDENT_ADVISOR shown in Figure 3-17, where a student (StudentID) can have one or more majors (Major), a major can have one or more faculty advisors (AdvisorName), and a faculty member advises in only one major area. Note that the figure shows two students (StudentIDs 700 and 800) with double majors (both students show Majors of Math and Psychology) and two Subjects (Math and Psychology) with two Advisors.

Because students can have several majors, StudentID does not determine Major. Moreover, because students can have several advisors, StudentID does not determine AdvisorName. Therefore, StudentID by itself cannot be a key. However, the composite key (StudentID, Major) determines AdvisorName, and the composite key (StudentID, AdvisorName)

FIGURE 3-17

The STUDENT_ADVISOR
Relation

**STUDENT_ADVISOR**

| | StudentID | Major | AdvisorName |
|---|---|---|---|
| 1 | 100 | Math | Cauchy |
| 2 | 200 | Psychology | Jung |
| 3 | 300 | Math | Riemann |
| 4 | 400 | Math | Cauchy |
| 5 | 500 | Psychology | Perls |
| 6 | 600 | English | Austin |
| 7 | 700 | Psychology | Perls |
| 8 | 700 | Math | Riemann |
| 9 | 800 | Math | Cauchy |
| 10 | 800 | Psychology | Jung |

determines Major. This gives us (StudentID, Major) and (StudentID, AdvisorName) as two candidate keys. We can select either of these as the primary key for the relation. Thus, two STUDENT_ADVISOR schemas with different candidate keys are possible:

STUDENT_ADVISOR (**StudentID**, **Major**, AdvisorName)

and

STUDENT_ADVISOR (**StudentID**, Major, **AdvisorName**)

Note that STUDENT_ADVISOR is in 2NF because it has no non-key attributes in the sense that every attribute is a part of *at least one* candidate key. This is a subtle condition, based on the fact that technically the definition of 2NF states that no *non-prime attribute* can be partially dependent on a candidate key, where a **non-prime attribute** is an attribute that is not contained in *any* candidate key. Furthermore, STUDENT_ADVISOR is in 3NF because there are no transitive dependencies in the relation.

The two candidate keys for this relation are **overlapping candidate keys** because they share the attribute StudentID. When a table in 3NF has overlapping candidate keys, it can still have modification anomalies based on functional dependencies. In the STUDENT_ADVISOR relation, there will be modification anomalies because there is one other functional dependency in the relation. Because a faculty member can be an advisor for only one major area, AdvisorName determines Major. Therefore, AdvisorName is a determinant but not a candidate key.

Suppose that we have a student (StudentID = 300) majoring in psychology (Major = Psychology) with faculty advisor Perls (AdvisorName = Perls). Further, assume that this row is the only one in the table with the AdvisorName value of Perls. If we delete this row, we will lose all data about Perls. This is a deletion anomaly. Similarly, we cannot insert the data to represent the Economics advisor Keynes until a student majors in Economics. This is an insertion anomaly. Situations like this led to the development of BCNF.

What do we do with the STUDENT_ADVISOR relation? As before, we move the functional dependency creating the problem to another relation while leaving the determinant in the original relation as a foreign key. In this case, we will create the relations:

STUDENT_ADVISOR (**StudentID**, *AdvisorName*)

ADVISOR_MAJOR (**AdvisorName**, Major)

The AdvisorName column in STUDENT_ADVISOR is the foreign key, and the two final relations are shown in Figure 3-18.

Note that a relation in 3NF *may also already be* in BCNF. The only way a relation in 3NF can have problems actually requiring further normalization work to get it into BCNF is if it has *overlapping composite candidate keys*. If the relation (1) does *not* have composite candidate keys or (2) has *non-overlapping* composite candidate keys, then it is *already in BCNF* once it is in 3NF.

**FIGURE 3-18**

The BCNF
STUDENT_ADVISOR
and ADVISOR_SUBJECT
Relations

STUDENT_ADVISOR

|    | StudentID | AdvisorName |
|----|-----------|-------------|
| 1  | 100       | Cauchy      |
| 2  | 200       | Jung        |
| 3  | 300       | Riemann     |
| 4  | 400       | Cauchy      |
| 5  | 500       | Perls       |
| 6  | 600       | Austin      |
| 7  | 700       | Perls       |
| 8  | 700       | Riemann     |
| 9  | 800       | Cauchy      |
| 10 | 800       | Jung        |

ADVISOR_SUBJECT

|   | AdvisorName | Major      |
|---|-------------|------------|
| 1 | Austin      | English    |
| 2 | Cauchy      | Math       |
| 3 | Riemann     | Math       |
| 4 | Jung        | Psychology |
| 5 | Perls       | Psychology |

## Normalization Example 4

Consider the following table that stores data about student activities:

**STUDENT_ACTIVITY (StudentID, StudentName, Activity, ActivityFee, AmountPaid)**

where StudentID is a student identifier, StudentName is student name, Activity is the name of a club or other organized student activity, ActivityFee is the cost of joining the club or participating in the activity, and AmountPaid is the amount the student has paid toward the ActivityFee. Figure 3-24 shows sample data for this table.

StudentID is a unique student identifier, so we know that:

**StudentID → StudentName**

However, does the following functional dependency exist?

**StudentID → Activity**

It does if a student belongs to just one club or participates in just one activity, but it does not if a student belongs to more than one club or participates in more than one activity. Looking at the data, student Davis with StudentID 200 participates in both Skiing and Swimming, so StudentID does *not* determine Club. StudentID does not determine ActivityFee or AmountPaid, either.

Now consider the StudentName column. Does StudentName determine StudentID? Is, for example, the value 'Jones' always paired with the same value of StudentID? No, there are two students named 'Jones', and they have different StudentID values. StudentName does not determine any other column in this table either.

Considering the next column, Activity, we know that many students can belong to a club. Therefore, Activity does not determine StudentID or StudentName. Does Activity determine ActivityFee? Is the value 'Skiing', for example, always paired with the same value of ActivityFee? From these data, it appears so, and using just this sample data, we can conclude that Activity determines ActivityFee.

However, this data is just a sample. Logically, it is possible for students to pay different costs, perhaps because they select different levels of activity participation. If that were the case, then we would say that:

**(StudentID, Activity) → ActivityFee**

To find out, we need to check with the users. Here, assume that all students pay the same fee for a given activity. The last column is AmountPaid, and it does not determine anything.

So far, we have two functional dependencies:

**StudentID → StudentName**

**Activity → ActivityFee**

**FIGURE 3-24**

Sample Data for the STUDENT_ACTIVITY Relation

**STUDENT_ACTIVITY**

|   | StudentID | StudentName | Activity | ActivityFee | AmountPaid |
|---|-----------|-------------|----------|-------------|------------|
| 1 | 100 | Jones | Golf | 65.00 | 65.00 |
| 2 | 100 | Jones | Skiing | 200.00 | 0.00 |
| 3 | 200 | Davis | Skiing | 200.00 | 0.00 |
| 4 | 200 | Davis | Swimming | 50.00 | 50.00 |
| 5 | 300 | Garrett | Skiing | 200.00 | 100.00 |
| 6 | 300 | Garrett | Swimming | 50.00 | 50.00 |
| 7 | 400 | Jones | Golf | 65.00 | 65.00 |
| 8 | 400 | Jones | Swimming | 50.00 | 50.00 |

Are there other functional dependencies with composite determinants? No single column determines AmountPaid, so consider possible composite determinants for it. AmountPaid is dependent on both the student and the club the student has joined. Therefore, it is determined by the combination of the determinants StudentID and Activity. Thus, we can say:

**(StudentID, Activity) → AmountPaid**

So far, we have three determinants: StudentID, Activity, and (StudentID, Activity). Are any of these candidate keys? Do any of these determinants identify a unique row? From the data, it appears that (StudentID, Activity) identifies a unique row and is a candidate key. Again, in real situations, we would need to check this assumption out with the users.

STUDENT_ACTIVITY_PAYMENT is not in BCNF because columns StudentID and Activity are both determinants but neither is a candidate key. StudentID and Activity are only part of the candidate key (StudentID, Activity).

> **BY THE WAY**   Both StudentID and Activity are *part of* the candidate key (StudentID, Activity). This, however, is not good enough. A determinant must have *all* of the same columns to be the same as a candidate key.

To normalize this table, we need to construct tables so that every determinant is a candidate key. We can do this by creating a separate table for each functional dependency as we did before. The result is:

**STUDENT (StudentID, StudentName)**

**ACTIVITY (Activity, ActivityFee)**

**PAYMENT (*StudentID*, *Activity*, AmountPaid)**

with referential integrity constraints:

**PAYMENT.StudentID must exist in STUDENT.StudentID**

and

**PAYMENT.Activity must exist in ACTIVITY.Activity**

These tables are in BCNF and will have no anomalies from functional dependencies. The sample data for the normalized tables are shown in Figure 3-25.

**FIGURE 3-25**

The Normalized STUDENT, ACTIVITY, and PAYMENT Relations

**STUDENT**

|   | StudentID | StudentName |
|---|-----------|-------------|
| 1 | 100 | Jones |
| 2 | 200 | Davis |
| 3 | 300 | Garrett |
| 4 | 400 | Jones |

**ACTIVITY**

|   | Activity | ActivityFee |
|---|----------|-------------|
| 1 | Golf | 65.00 |
| 2 | Skiing | 200.00 |
| 3 | Swimming | 50.00 |

**PAYMENT**

|   | StudentID | Activity | AmountPaid |
|---|-----------|----------|------------|
| 1 | 100 | Golf | 65.00 |
| 2 | 100 | Skiing | 0.00 |
| 3 | 200 | Skiing | 0.00 |
| 4 | 200 | Swimming | 50.00 |
| 5 | 300 | Skiing | 100.00 |
| 6 | 300 | Swimming | 50.00 |
| 7 | 400 | Golf | 65.00 |
| 8 | 400 | Swimming | 50.00 |

## Normalization Example 5

Now consider a normalization process that requires two iterations of step 3 in the procedure in Figure 3-19. To do this, we will extend the SKU_DATA relation by adding the budget code of each department. We call the revised relation SKU_DATA_3 and define it as follows:

**SKU_DATA_3 (SKU, SKU_Description, Department, DeptBudgetCode, Buyer)**

Sample data for this relation are shown in Figure 3-26. SKU_DATA_3 has the following functional dependencies:

**SKU → (SKU_Description, Department, DeptBudgetCode, Buyer)**

**SKU_Description → (SKU, Department, DeptBudgetCode, Buyer)**

**Buyer → (Department, DeptBudgetCode)**

**Department → DeptBudgetCode**

**DeptBudgetCode → Department**

Of the five determinants, both SKU and SKU_Description are candidate keys, but Buyer, Department, and DeptBudgetCode are not candidate keys. Therefore, this relation is not in BCNF.

To normalize this table, we must transform it into two or more tables that are in BCNF. In this case, there are two problematic functional dependencies. According to the note at the end of the procedure in Figure 3-19, we take the functional dependency whose determinant is not a candidate key and has the largest number of columns first. In this case, we take the columns of:

**Buyer → (Department, DeptBudgetCode)**

and place them in a table of their own.

Next, we make the determinant the primary key of the new table, remove all columns except Buyer from SKU_DATA_3, and make Buyer a foreign key of the new version of SKU_DATA_3, which we will name SKU_DATA_4. We can also now assign SKU as the primary key of SKU_DATA_4. The results are (using the name BUYER_3 to distinguish this relation from the other versions of BUYER discussed earlier in this chapter):

**BUYER_3 (Buyer, Department, DeptBudgetCode)**

**SKU_DATA_4 (SKU, SKU_Description, *Buyer*)**

FIGURE 3-26

Sample Data for the
SKU_DATA_3 Relation

**SKU_DATA_3**

| | SKU | SKU_Description | Department | DeptBudgetCode | Buyer |
|---|---|---|---|---|---|
| 1 | 100100 | Std. Scuba Tank, Yellow | Water Sports | BC-100 | Pete Hansen |
| 2 | 100200 | Std. Scuba Tank, Magenta | Water Sports | BC-100 | Pete Hansen |
| 3 | 100300 | Std. Scuba Tank, Light Blue | Water Sports | BC-100 | Pete Hansen |
| 4 | 100400 | Std. Scuba Tank, Dark Blue | Water Sports | BC-100 | Pete Hansen |
| 5 | 100500 | Std. Scuba Tank, Light Green | Water Sports | BC-100 | Pete Hansen |
| 6 | 100600 | Std. Scuba Tank, Dark Green | Water Sports | BC-100 | Pete Hansen |
| 7 | 101100 | Dive Mask, Small Clear | Water Sports | BC-100 | Nancy Meyers |
| 8 | 101200 | Dive Mask, Med Clear | Water Sports | BC-100 | Nancy Meyers |
| 9 | 201000 | Half-dome Tent | Camping | BC-200 | Cindy Lo |
| 10 | 202000 | Half-dome Tent Vestibule | Camping | BC-200 | Cindy Lo |
| 11 | 203000 | Half-dome Tent Vestibule - Wide | Camping | BC-200 | Cindy Lo |
| 12 | 301000 | Light Fly Climbing Harness | Climbing | BC-300 | Jerry Martin |
| 13 | 302000 | Locking carabiner, Oval | Climbing | BC-300 | Jerry Martin |

We also create the referential integrity constraint:

**SKU_DATA_4.Buyer must exist in BUYER_3.Buyer**

The functional dependencies from SKU_DATA_4 are:

**SKU → (SKU_Description, Buyer)**

**SKU_Description → (SKU, Buyer)**

Because every determinant of SKU_DATA_4 is also a candidate key, the relationship is now in BCNF. Looking at the functional dependencies from BUYER_3, we find:

**Buyer → (Department, DeptBudgetCode)**

**Department → DeptBudgetCode**

**DeptBudgetCode → Department**

BUYER_3 is *not* in BCNF because neither of the determinants Department and DeptBudget-Code are candidate keys. In this case, we must move (Department, DeptBudgetCode) into a table of its own. Following the procedure in Figure 3-19 and breaking BUYER_3 into two tables (DEPARTMENT and BUYER_4) gives us a set of three tables (where *SKU* as a surrogate key is the logical for primary key fir SKU_DATA_4 and *Department* is the logical primary key for DEPARTMENT because other columns are semantically descriptors of the department):

**DEPARTMENT (Department, DeptBudgetCode)**

**BUYER_4 (Buyer, *Department*)**

**SKU_DATA_4 (SKU, SKU_Description, *Buyer*)**

These tables have the referential integrity constraints:

**SKU_DATA_4.Buyer must exist in BUYER_4.Buyer**

**BUYER_4.Department must exist in DEPARTMENT.Department**

The functional dependencies from all three of these tables are:

**Department → DeptBudgetCode**

**DeptBudgetCode → Department**

**Buyer → Department**

**SKU → (SKU_Description, Buyer)**

**SKU_Description → (SKU, Buyer)**

At last, every determinant is a candidate key, and all three of the tables are in BCNF. The resulting relations from these operations are shown in Figure 3-27.

## Eliminating Anomalies from Multivalued Dependencies

All of the anomalies in the last section were due to functional dependencies, and when we normalize relations to BCNF, we eliminate these anomalies. However, anomalies can also arise from another kind of dependency: the multivalued dependency. A **multivalued dependency** occurs when a determinant is matched with a particular *set* of values.

Examples of multivalued dependencies are:

**EmployeeName → → EmployeeDegree**

**EmployeeName → → EmployeeSibling**

**PartKitName → → Part**

**DEPARTMENT**

| | Department | DeptBudgetCode |
|---|---|---|
| 1 | Camping | BC-200 |
| 2 | Climbing | BC-300 |
| 3 | Water Sports | BC-100 |

**BUYER_2**

| | Buyer | Department |
|---|---|---|
| 1 | Cindy Lo | Camping |
| 2 | Jerry Martin | Climbing |
| 3 | Nancy Meyers | Water Sports |
| 4 | Pete Hansen | Water Sports |

**FIGURE 3-27**

The Normalized
DEPARTMENT, BUYER_2,
and SKU_DATA_4 Relations

**SKU_DATA_4**

| | SKU | SKU_Description | Buyer |
|---|---|---|---|
| 1 | 100100 | Std. Scuba Tank, Yellow | Pete Hansen |
| 2 | 100200 | Std. Scuba Tank, Magenta | Pete Hansen |
| 3 | 100300 | Std. Scuba Tank, Light Blue | Pete Hansen |
| 4 | 100400 | Std. Scuba Tank, Dark Blue | Pete Hansen |
| 5 | 100500 | Std. Scuba Tank, Light Green | Pete Hansen |
| 6 | 100600 | Std. Scuba Tank, Dark Green | Pete Hansen |
| 7 | 101100 | Dive Mask, Small Clear | Nancy Meyers |
| 8 | 101200 | Dive Mask, Med Clear | Nancy Meyers |
| 9 | 201000 | Half-dome Tent | Cindy Lo |
| 10 | 202000 | Half-dome Tent Vestibule | Cindy Lo |
| 11 | 203000 | Half-dome Tent Vestibule - Wide | Cindy Lo |
| 12 | 301000 | Light Fly Climbing Harness | Jerry Martin |
| 13 | 302000 | Locking carabiner, Oval | Jerry Martin |

In each case, the determinant is associated with a set of values, and example data for each of these multivalued dependencies are shown in Figure 3-28. Such expressions are read as "EmployeeName multidetermines EmployeeDegree" and "EmployeeName multidetermines EmployeeSibling" and "PartKitName multidetermines Part." Note that multideterminants are shown with a double arrow rather than a single arrow.

Employee Jones, for example, has degrees AA and BA. Employee Green has degrees BS, MS, and PhD. Employee Chau has just one degree, BS. Similarly, employee Jones has siblings (brothers and sisters) Fred, Sally, and Frank. Employee Green has sibling Nikki, and employee Chau has siblings Jonathan and Eileen. Finally, PartKitName Bike Repair has parts Wrench, Screwdriver, and Tube Fix. Other kits have parts as shown in Figure 3-28.

Unlike functional dependencies, the determinant of a multivalued dependency can never be the primary key. In all three of the tables in Figure 3-28, the primary key consists of the composite of the two columns in each table. For example, the primary key of the EMPLOYEE_DEGREE table is the composite key (EmployeeName, EmployeeDegree).

**FIGURE 3-28**

Three Examples of
Multivalued Dependencies

**EMPLOYEE_DEGREE**

| | EmployeeName | EmployeeDegree |
|---|---|---|
| 1 | Chau | BS |
| 2 | Green | BS |
| 3 | Green | MS |
| 4 | Green | PhD |
| 5 | Jones | AA |
| 6 | Jones | BA |

**EMPLOYEE_SIBLING**

| | EmployeeName | EmployeeSibling |
|---|---|---|
| 1 | Chau | Eileen |
| 2 | Chau | Jonathan |
| 3 | Green | Nikki |
| 4 | Jones | Frank |
| 5 | Jones | Fred |
| 6 | Jones | Sally |

**PARTKIT_PART**

| | PartKitName | Part |
|---|---|---|
| 1 | Bike Repair | Screwdriver |
| 2 | Bike Repair | Tibe Fix |
| 3 | Bike Repair | Wench |
| 4 | First Aid | Aspirin |
| 5 | First Aid | Bandaids |
| 6 | First Aid | Elastic Band |
| 7 | First Aid | Ibuprofin |
| 8 | Toolbox | Drill |
| 9 | Toolbox | Drill Bits |
| 10 | Toolbox | Hammer |
| 11 | Toolbox | Saw |
| 12 | Toolbox | Screwdriver |

**FIGURE 3-29**

EMPLOYEE_DEGREE_SIBLING
Relation with Two Multivalued
Dependencies

**EMPLOYEE_DEGREE_SIBLING**

|   | EmployeeName | EmployeeDegree | EmployeeSibling |
|---|---|---|---|
| 1 | Chau | BS | Eileen |
| 2 | Chau | BS | Jonathan |
| 3 | Green | BS | Nicki |
| 4 | Green | MS | Nicki |
| 5 | Green | PhD | Nicki |
| 6 | Jones | AA | Frank |
| 7 | Jones | AA | Fred |
| 8 | Jones | AA | Sally |
| 9 | Jones | BA | Frank |
| 10 | Jones | BA | Fred |
| 11 | Jones | BA | Sally |

Multivalued dependencies pose no problem as long as they exist in tables of their own. None of the tables in Figure 3-28 has modification anomalies. However, if A → → B, then any relation that contains A, B, and one or more additional columns will have modification anomalies.

For example, consider the situation if we combine the employee data in Figure 3-28 into a single EMPLOYEE_DEGREE_SIBLING table with three columns (EmployeeName, EmployeeDegree, EmployeeSibling), as shown in Figure 3-29.

Now, what actions need to be taken if employee Jones earns an MBA? We must add three rows to the table. If we do not, if we only add the row ('Jones', 'MBA', 'Fred'), it will appear as if Jones is an MBA with her brother Fred, but not with her sister Sally or her other brother Frank. However, suppose Green earns an MBA. Then we need only add one row ('Green', 'MBA', 'Nikki'). But, if Chau earns an MBA, we need to add two rows. These are insertion anomalies. There are equivalent modification and deletion anomalies as well.

In Figure 3-29, we combined two multivalued dependencies into a single table and thereby created modification anomalies. Unfortunately, we will also get anomalies if we combine a multivalued dependency with any other column, even if that other column has no multivalued dependency.

Figure 3-30 shows what happens when we combine the multivalued dependency:

**PartKitName → → Part**

**FIGURE 3-30**

PARTKIT_PART_PRICE
Relation with a Functional
Dependency and a
Multivalued Dependency

**PARTKIT_PART_PRICE**

|   | PartKitName | Part | PartKitPrice |
|---|---|---|---|
| 1 | Bike Repair | Screwdriver | 14.95 |
| 2 | Bike Repair | Tibe Fix | 14.95 |
| 3 | Bike Repair | Wench | 14.95 |
| 4 | First Aid | Aspirin | 24.95 |
| 5 | First Aid | Bandaids | 24.95 |
| 6 | First Aid | Elastic Band | 24.95 |
| 7 | First Aid | Ibuprofin | 24.95 |
| 8 | Toolbox | Drill | 74.95 |
| 9 | Toolbox | Drill Bits | 74.95 |
| 10 | Toolbox | Hammer | 74.95 |
| 11 | Toolbox | Saw | 74.95 |
| 12 | Toolbox | Screwdriver | 74.95 |

with the functional dependency:

**PartKitName → PartKitPrice**

For the data to be consistent, we must repeat the value of price for as many rows as each kit has parts. For this example, we must add three PARTKIT_PART_PRICE rows for the Bike Repair kit, four rows for the First Aid kit, and five rows for the Toolbox kit. The result is duplicated data that can cause data integrity problems.

Now you also know the problem with the relation in Figure 3-2. Anomalies exist in that table because it contains two multivalued dependencies:

**BuyerName → → SKU_Managed**

**BuyerName → → CollegeMajor**

Fortunately, it is easy to deal with multivalued dependencies: put them into a table of their own. None of the tables in Figure 3-28 has modification anomalies because each table consists of only the columns in a single, multivalued dependency. Thus, to fix the table in Figure 3-2, we must move BuyerName and SKU_Managed into one table and BuyerName and CollegeMajor into a second table:

**PRODUCT_BUYER_SKU (BuyerName, SKU_Managed)**

**PRODUCT_BUYER_MAJOR (_BuyerName_, CollegeMajor)**

The results are shown in Figure 3-31. If we want to maintain strict equivalence between these tables, we would also add the referential integrity constraint:

**PRODUCT_BUYER_MAJOR.BuyerName must exist in**

**PRODUCT_BUYER_SKU.BuyerName**

This referential integrity constraint may not be necessary, depending on the requirements of the application.

Notice that when you put multivalued dependencies into a table of their own, they disappear. The result is just a table with two columns, and the primary key (and sole candidate key) is the composite of those two columns. When multivalued dependencies have been isolated in this way, the table is said to be in *fourth normal form* (4NF).

**FIGURE 3-31**

Placing the Two Multivalued Dependencies in Figure 3-2 into Separate Relations

**PRODUCT_BUYER_SKU**

| | BuyerName | SKU_Managed |
|---|---|---|
| 1 | Cindy Lo | 201000 |
| 2 | Cindy Lo | 202000 |
| 3 | Cindy Lo | 203000 |
| 4 | Jenny Martin | 301000 |
| 5 | Jenny Martin | 302000 |
| 6 | Nancy Meyers | 101100 |
| 7 | Nancy Meyers | 101200 |
| 8 | Pete Hansen | 100100 |
| 9 | Pete Hansen | 100200 |
| 10 | Pete Hansen | 100300 |
| 11 | Pete Hansen | 100400 |
| 12 | Pete Hansen | 100500 |
| 13 | Pete Hansen | 100600 |

**PRODUCT_BUYER_MAJOR**

| | BuyerName | CollegeMajor |
|---|---|---|
| 1 | Cindy Lo | History |
| 2 | Jenny Martin | Business Administration |
| 3 | Jenny Martin | English Literature |
| 4 | Nancy Meyers | Art |
| 5 | Nancy Meyers | Info Systems |
| 6 | Pete Hansen | Business Administration |

The hardest part of multivalued dependencies is finding them. Once you know they exist in a table, just move them into a table of their own. Whenever you encounter tables with odd anomalies, especially anomalies that require you to insert, modify, or delete different numbers of rows to maintain integrity, check for multivalued dependencies.

> **BY THE WAY**    You will sometimes hear people use the term *normalize* in phrases like "that table has been normalized" or "check to see if those tables are normalized." Unfortunately, not everyone means the same thing with these words. Some people do not know about BCNF, and they will use it to mean tables in 3NF, which is a lesser form of normalization, one that allows for anomalies from functional dependencies that BCNF does not allow. Others use it to mean tables that are both BCNF and 4NF. Others may mean something else. The best choice is to use the term *normalize* to mean tables that are in both BCNF and 4NF.

## Fifth Normal Form

There is a fifth normal form (5NF), also known as **Project-Join Normal Form (PJ/NF)**, which involves an anomaly where a table can be split apart but not correctly joined back together. However, the conditions under which this happens are complex, and generally if a relation is in 4NF, it is in 5NF. We will not deal with 5NF in this book. For more information about 5NF, start with the works cited earlier in this chapter and the Wikipedia article at *http://en.wikipedia.org/wiki/Fifth_normal_form*.

## Domain/Key Normal Form

As discussed earlier in this chapter, in 1982 Ronald Fagin published a paper that defined domain/key normal form (DK/NF). Fagin asked, "What conditions need to exist for a relation to have no anomalies?" He showed that a relation in DK/NF has no modification anomalies and, further, that a relation that has no modification anomalies is in DK/NF.

But what does this mean? Basically, DK/NF requires that all the constraints on the data values be logical implications of the definitions of domains and keys. To the level of detail in this text, and to the level of detail experienced by 99 percent of all database practitioners, this can be restated as follows: every determinant of a functional dependency must be a candidate key. This, of course, is simply our definition of BCNF, and, for practical purposes, relations in BCNF are in DK/NF as well.

## Summary

Databases arise from three sources: from existing data, from new systems development, and from the redesign of existing databases. This chapter and the next are concerned with databases that arise from existing data. Even though a table is a simple concept, certain tables can lead to surprisingly difficult processing problems. This chapter uses the concept of normalization to understand and possibly solve those problems. Figure 3-3 lists terms you should be familiar with.

A relation is a special case of a table; all relations are tables, but not all tables are relations. Relations are tables that have the properties listed in Figure 3-4. Three sets of terms are used to describe relation structure: (relation, attribute, tuple); (table, column, row); and (file, field, and record). Sometimes these terms are mixed and matched. In practice, the terms *table* and *relation* are commonly used synonymously, and we will do so for the balance of this text.

In a functional dependency, the value of one attribute, or attributes, determines the value of another. In the functional dependency $A \rightarrow B$, attribute A is called the determinant. Some functional dependencies arise from equations, but many others do not. The purpose of a database is, in fact, to store instances of functional dependencies that do not arise from equations.

Determinants that have more than one attribute are called composite determinants. If $A \rightarrow (B, C)$, then $A \rightarrow B$ and $A \rightarrow C$ (decomposition rule). However, if $(A, B) \rightarrow C$, then, in general, neither $A \rightarrow C$ nor $B \rightarrow C$. It is true that if $A \rightarrow B$ and $A \rightarrow C$, then $A \rightarrow (B, C)$ (union rule).

If $A \rightarrow B$, the values of A may or may not be unique in a relation. However, every time a given value of A appears, it will be paired with the same value of B. A determinant is unique in a relation only if it determines every other attribute of the relation. You cannot always rely on determining functional dependencies from sample data. The best idea is to verify your conclusions with the users of the data.

A key is a combination of one or more columns used to identify one or more rows. A composite key is a key with two or more attributes. A determinant that determines every other attribute is called a candidate key. A relation may have more than one candidate key. One of them is selected to be used by the DBMS for finding rows and is called the primary key. A surrogate key is an artificial attribute used as a primary key. The value of a surrogate key is supplied by the DBMS and has no meaning to the user. A foreign key is a key in one table that references the primary key of a second table. A referential integrity constraint is a limitation on data values of a foreign key that ensures that every value of the foreign key has a match to a value of a primary key.

The three kinds of modification anomalies are insert, update, and delete. Codd and others defined normal forms for describing different table structures that lead to anomalies. A table that meets the conditions listed in Figure 3-4 is in 1NF. Some anomalies arise from functional dependencies. Three forms—2NF, 3NF, and BCNF—are used to treat such anomalies.

In this text, we are only concerned with the best of these forms, BCNF. If a relation is in BCNF, then no anomalies from functional dependencies can occur. A relation is in BCNF if every determinant is a candidate key.

Relations can be normalized using either a "Step-by-Step" method or a "Straight-to-BCNF" method. Which method to use is a matter of personal preference, and both methods produce the same results.

Some anomalies arise from multivalued dependencies. A multidetermines B, or $A \rightarrow \rightarrow B$, if A determines a set of values. If A multidetermines B, then any relation that contains A, B, and one or more other columns will have modification anomalies. Anomalies due to multivalued dependencies can be eliminated by placing the multivalued dependency in a table of its own. Such tables are in 4NF.

There is a 5NF, but generally tables in 4NF are in 5NF. DK/NF has been defined, but in practical terms, the definition of DK/NF is the same as the definition of BCNF.

# Key Terms

attribute
Boyce-Codd Normal Form (BCNF)
candidate key
composite determinant
composite key
data integrity
data integrity problems
decomposition rule
deletion anomaly

determinant
domain
domain integrity constraint
domain/key normal form (DK/NF)
entity
entity integrity constraint
fifth normal form (5NF)
first normal form (1NF)
foreign key

fourth normal form (4NF)
functional dependency
functionally dependent
insertion anomaly
key
multivalued dependency
non-prime attribute
normal forms
null value

overlapping candidate key
partially dependent
primary key
Project-Join Normal Form (PJ/NF)
referential integrity constraint

relation
second normal form (2NF)
SKU (stock keeping unit)
surrogate key
third normal form (3NF)

transitive dependency
tuple
union rule
update anomaly

# Review Questions

**3.1** Name three sources for databases.

**3.2** What is the basic premise of this chapter?

**3.3** Explain what is wrong with the table in Figure 3-2.

**3.4** Define each of the terms listed in Figure 3-3.

**3.5** Describe the characteristics of a table that make it a relation. Define the term *domain* and explain the significance of the *domain integrity constraint* to a relation.

**3.6** Give an example of two tables that are not relations.

**3.7** Suppose that two columns in two different tables have the same column name. What convention is used to give each a unique name?

**3.8** Must all the values in the same column of a relation have the same length?

**3.9** Explain the three different sets of terms used to describe tables, columns, and rows.

**3.10** Explain the difference between functional dependencies that arise from equations and those that do not.

**3.11** Explain the intuitive meaning of the functional dependency:

**PartNumber → PartWeight**

**3.12** Explain the following statement: "The only reason for having relations is to store instances of functional dependencies."

**3.13** Explain the meaning of the expression:

**(FirstName, LastName) → Phone**

**3.14** What is a composite determinant?

**3.15** If (A, B) → C, then can we also say that A → C?

**3.16** If A → (B, C), then can we also say that A → B?

**3.17** For the SKU_DATA table in Figure 3-1, explain why Buyer determines Department but Department does not determine Buyer.

**3.18** For the SKU_DATA table in Figure 3-1, explain why:

**SKU_Description → (SKU, Department, Buyer)**

**3.19** If it is true that:

**PartNumber → PartWeight**

does that mean that PartNumber will be unique in a relation?

**3.20** Under what conditions will a determinant be unique in a relation?

**3.21** What is the best test for determining whether a determinant is unique?

**3.22** What is a composite key?

**3.23** What is a candidate key?

**3.24** What is a primary key? Explain the significance of the *entity integrity constraint* to a primary key.

**3.25** Explain the difference between a candidate key and a primary key.

**3.26** What is a surrogate key?

**3.27** Where does the value of a surrogate key come from?

**3.28** When would you use a surrogate key?

**3.29** What is a foreign key? Explain the significance of the *referential integrity constraint* to a foreign key.

**3.30** The term *domestic key* is not used. If it were used, however, what do you think it would mean?

**3.31** What is a normal form?

**3.32** Illustrate deletion, modification, and insertion anomalies on the STUDENT_ACTIV-ITY relation in Figure 3-24.

**3.33** Explain why duplicated data lead to data integrity problems.

**3.34** What relations are in 1NF?

**3.35** Which normal forms are concerned with functional dependencies?

**3.36** What conditions are required for a relation to be in 2NF?

**3.37** What conditions are required for a relation to be in 3NF?

**3.38** What conditions are required for a relation to be in BCNF?

**3.39** If a relation is in BCNF, what can we say about it with regard to 2NF and 3NF?

**3.40** What normal form is concerned with multivalued dependencies?

**3.41** What is the premise of Fagin's work on DK/NF?

**3.42** Summarize the three categories of normalization theory.

**3.43** In general, how can you transform a relation not in BCNF into ones that are in BCNF?

**3.44** What is a referential integrity constraint? Define the term, and give an example of its use. Are null values allowed in foreign key columns with a referential integrity constraint? How does the referential integrity constraint contribute to *data integrity*?

**3.45** Explain the role of referential integrity constraints in normalization.

**3.46** Why is an un-normalized relation like a paragraph with multiple themes?

**3.47** In normalization example 3, why is the EXTENDED_PRICE relation "silly"?

**3.48** In normalization example 4, describe the conditions where the functional dependency:

**(StudentID, Activity) → ActivityFee**

would be more accurate than:

**Activity → ActivityFee**

**3.49** If a determinant is part of a candidate key, is that good enough for BCNF?

**3.50** For normalization example 5, why are the following two tables not a correct solution to the problem of normalizing SKU_DATA_3?

DEPARTMENT (**Department**, DeptBudgetCode, Buyer)

SKU_DATA_4 (**SKU**, SKU_Description, *Department*)

**3.51** How does a multivalued dependency differ from a functional dependency?

**3.52** Consider the relation:

PERSON (**Name, Sibling, ShoeSize**)

Assume that the following functional dependencies exist:

Name → → Sibling

Name → ShoeSize

Describe deletion, modification, and insertion anomalies for this relation.

**3.53** Place the PERSON relation in Review Question 3.52 into 4NF.

**3.54** Consider the relation:

PERSON_2 (**Name, Sibling, ShoeSize, Hobby**)

Assume that the following functional dependencies exist:

Name → → Sibling

Name → ShoeSize

Name → → Hobby

Describe deletion, modification, and insertion anomalies for this relation.

**3.55** Place the PERSON_2 relation in Review Question 3.54 into 4NF.

**3.56** What is 5NF?

**3.57** How do the conditions for DK/NF correspond to the conditions for BCNF?

# Exercises

**3.58** Consider the table:

STAFF_MEETING (**EmployeeName, ProjectName, Date**)

The rows of this table record the fact that an employee from a particular project attended a meeting on a given date. Assume that a project meets at most once per day. Also, assume that only one employee represents a given project but that employees can be assigned to multiple projects.

**A.** State the functional dependencies in STAFF_MEETING.

**B.** Transform this table into one or more tables in BCNF. State the primary keys, candidate keys, foreign keys, and referential integrity constraints.

**C.** Is your design in part B an improvement over the original table? What advantages and disadvantages does it have?

| PurchaseItem | PurchasePrice | PurchaseDate | Vendor | Phone |
|---|---|---|---|---|
| Antique Desk | 1,800.00 | 7-Nov-20 | European Specialties | 206-325-7866 |
| Antique Desk | 1,750.00 | 7-Nov-20 | European Specialties | 206-325-7866 |
| Antique Candle Holders | 210.00 | 7-Nov-20 | European Specialties | 206-325-7866 |
| Antique Candle Holders | 200.00 | 7-Nov-20 | European Specialties | 206-325-7866 |
| Dining Table Linens | 600.00 | 14-Nov-20 | Linens and Things | 206-325-6755 |
| Candles | 30.00 | 14-Nov-20 | Linens and Things | 206-325-6755 |
| Desk Lamp | 150.00 | 14-Nov-20 | Lamps and Lighting | 206-325-8977 |
| Floor Lamp | 300.00 | 14-Nov-20 | Lamps and Lighting | 206-325-8977 |
| Dining Table Linens | 450.00 | 21-Nov-20 | Linens and Things | 206-325-6755 |
| Candles | 27.00 | 21-Nov-20 | Linens and Things | 206-325-6755 |
| Book Shelf | 150.00 | 21-Nov-20 | Harrison, Denise | 425-746-4322 |
| Antique Desk | 1,000.00 | 28-Nov-20 | Lee, Andrew | 425-746-5433 |
| Antique Desk Chair | 300.00 | 28-Nov-20 | Lee, Andrew | 425-746-5433 |
| Antique Chair | 750.00 | 28-Nov-20 | New York Brokerage | 206-325-9088 |
| Antique Chair | 1,050.00 | 28-Nov-20 | New York Brokerage | 206-325-9088 |

**FIGURE 3-34**

Sample Purchase Data for The Queen Anne Curiosity Shop

2. CUSTOMER (<u>LastName</u>, <u>FirstName</u>, Phone, EmailAddress, InvoiceDate, InvoiceItem, Price, Tax, Total)

3. CUSTOMER (LastName, FirstName, <u>Phone</u>, EmailAddress, InvoiceDate, InvoiceItem, Price, Tax, Total)

4. CUSTOMER (<u>LastName</u>, <u>FirstName</u>, Phone, EmailAddress, <u>InvoiceDate</u>, InvoiceItem, Price, Tax, Total)

5. CUSTOMER (<u>LastName</u>, <u>FirstName</u>, Phone, EmailAddress, InvoiceDate, <u>InvoiceItem</u>, Price, Tax, Total)

6. CUSTOMER (<u>LastName</u>, <u>FirstName</u>, Phone, EmailAddress)

   and

   SALE (<u>InvoiceDate</u>, InvoiceItem, Price, Tax, Total)

7. CUSTOMER (<u>LastName</u>, <u>FirstName</u>, Phone, EmailAddress, *InvoiceDate*)

   and

   SALE (<u>InvoiceDate</u>, InvoiceItem, Price, Tax, Total)

8. CUSTOMER (<u>LastName</u>, <u>FirstName</u>, Phone, EmailAddress, *InvoiceDate*, *InvoiceItem*)

   and

   SALE (<u>InvoiceDate</u>, <u>InvoiceItem</u>, Price, Tax, Total)

C. Modify what you consider to be the best design in part B to include surrogate ID columns called CustomerID and SaleID. How does this improve the design?

**D.** Modify the design in part C by breaking SALE into two relations named SALE and SALE_ITEM. Modify columns and add columns as you think necessary. How does this improve the design?

**E.** Given your assumptions, comment on the appropriateness of the following designs:

  **1.** PURCHASE (**PurchaseItem, PurchasePrice**, PurchaseDate, Vendor, Phone)

  **2.** PURCHASE (**PurchaseItem, PurchasePrice**, PurchaseDate, Vendor, Phone)

  **3.** PURCHASE (**PurchaseItem**, PurchasePrice, **PurchaseDate**, Vendor, Phone)

  **4.** PURCHASE (**PurchaseItem**, PurchasePrice, PurchaseDate, **Vendor**, Phone)

  **5.** PURCHASE (**PurchaseItem**, PurchasePrice, **PurchaseDate**)

  and

  VENDOR (**Vendor**, Phone)

  **6.** PURCHASE (**PurchaseItem**, PurchasePrice, **PurchaseDate**, Vendor)

  and

  VENDOR (**Vendor**, Phone)

  **7.** PURCHASE (**PurchaseItem**, PurchasePrice, **PurchaseDate**, *Vendor*)

  and

  VENDOR (**Vendor**, Phone)

**F.** Modify what you consider to be the best design in part E to include surrogate ID columns called PurchaseID and VendorID. How does this improve the design?

**G.** The relations in your design from part D and part F are not connected. Modify the database design so that sales data and purchase data are related.

# Morgan Importing Project Questions

James Morgan keeps a table of data about the stores from which he purchases the products he imports and sells. The stores are located in different countries and have different specialties.

**A.** Consider the following relation:

STORE (**StoreName, City, Country, OwnerName, Specialty**)

Explain the conditions under which each of the following is true:

  **1.** StoreName → City
  **2.** City → StoreName
  **3.** City → Country
  **4.** (StoreName, Country) → (City, OwnerName)
  **5.** (City, Specialty) → StoreName
  **6.** OwnerName → → StoreName
  **7.** StoreName → → Specialty

**B.** With regard to the relation in part A:

    **1.** Specify which of the dependencies in part A seem most appropriate for a small import-export business.

    **2.** Given your assumptions in B.1, transform the STORE table into a set of tables that are in both 4NF and BCNF. Indicate the primary keys, candidate keys, foreign keys, and referential integrity constraints.

**C.** Consider the relation:

SHIPMENT (ShipmentNumber, ShipperName, ShipperContact, ShipperFax, DepartureDate, ArrivalDate, CountryOfOrigin, Destination, ShipmentCost, InsuranceValue, Insurer)

    **1.** Write a functional dependency that expresses the fact that the cost of a shipment between two cities is always the same.

    **2.** Write a functional dependency that expresses the fact that the insurance value is always the same for a given shipper.

    **3.** Write a functional dependency that expresses the fact that the insurance value is always the same for a given shipper and country of origin.

    **4.** Describe two possible multivalued dependencies in SHIPMENT.

    **5.** State what you believe are reasonable functional dependencies for the SHIPMENT relation for a small import-export business.

    **6.** State what you believe are reasonable multivalued dependencies for the SHIPMENT relation.

    **7.** Using your assumptions in 5 and 6, transform SHIPMENT into a set of tables in BCNF and 4NF. Indicate the primary keys, candidate keys, foreign keys, and referential integrity constraints.

# 4

# Database Design Using Normalization

## Chapter Objectives

- To design updatable databases to store data received from another source
- To use SQL to access table structure
- To understand the advantages and disadvantages of normalization
- To understand denormalization
- To design read-only databases to store data from updatable databases

- To recognize and be able to correct common design problems:
  - The multivalue, multicolumn problem
  - The inconsistent values problem
  - The missing values problem
  - The general-purpose remarks column problem

**In Chapter 3,** we defined the relational model, described modification anomalies, and discussed normalization using BCNF and 4NF. In this chapter, we apply those concepts to the design of databases that are created from existing data.

The premise of this chapter, as it was in Chapter 3, is that you have received, from some source, one or more tables of data that are to be stored in a new database. The question is: Should that data be stored as is, or should it be transformed in some way before it is stored? Normalization theory plays an important role, as you will see.

## Assess Table Structure

When someone gives you a set of tables and asks you to construct a database to store them, your first step should be to assess the tables' structure and content. General guidelines for assessing a table's structure are summarized in Figure 4-1.

As shown in Figure 4-1, you should examine the data and determine the functional dependencies, multivalued dependencies, candidate keys, and each table's primary key. Also, look for possible foreign keys. Again, you can base your conclusions on sample data, but that data might not have all of the possible data cases. Therefore, verify your assumptions and conclusions with the users.

For example, suppose you receive data for the following SKU_DATA and BUYER tables (with only the primary keys logically determined at this point):

**SKU_DATA (SKU, SKU_Description, Department, Buyer)**

**BUYER (BuyerName, Department, Position, Supervisor)**

Begin by counting the number of rows in each table using the **SQL COUNT(*) function**. Then, to determine the number and type of the table's columns, use an **SQL SELECT * statement**. If your table has thousands or millions of rows, however, a full query will take considerable time. One way to limit the results of this query is to use the **SQL TOP {NumberOfRows} function** as discussed in Chapter 2. (This is the Microsoft SQL Server statement–Oracle Database and MySQL use different statements.) For example, to obtain all columns for the first five rows of the SKU_DATA table, you would code:

```
/* *** SQL-Query-CH04-01 *** */

SELECT     TOP 5 *
FROM       SKU_DATA;
```

This query will show you all columns and data for five rows, as shown in the following results. If you want the top 50 rows, just use TOP 50 instead of TOP 5, and so on. At this point you should confirm the primary key and determine the data type of each of the columns in the table.

|   | SKU | SKU_Description | Department | Buyer |
|---|-----|-----------------|------------|-------|
| 1 | 100100 | Std. Scuba Tank, Yellow | Water Sports | Pete Hansen |
| 2 | 100200 | Std. Scuba Tank, Magenta | Water Sports | Pete Hansen |
| 3 | 100300 | Std. Scuba Tank, Light Blue | Water Sports | Pete Hansen |
| 4 | 100400 | Std. Scuba Tank, Dark Blue | Water Sports | Pete Hansen |
| 5 | 100500 | Std. Scuba Tank, Light Green | Water Sports | Pete Hansen |

With regard to foreign keys, it is risky to assume that referential integrity constraints have been enforced on the data. Instead, check it yourself. Suppose that, after investigation, you

**FIGURE 4-1**

Guidelines for Assessing Table Structure

| Guidelines for Assessing Table Structure |
|---|
| • Count rows and examine columns |
| • Examine data values and interview users to determine: |
| Multivalued dependencies |
| Functional dependencies |
| Candidate keys |
| Primary keys |
| Foreign keys |
| • Assess validity of assumed referential integrity constraints |

confirm that SKU is the primary key of SKU_DATA and that BuyerName is the primary key of BUYER. You also think that SKU_DATA.Buyer is likely a foreign key to BUYER.BuyerName. The question is whether the following referential integrity constraint holds:

**SKU_DATA.Buyer must exist in BUYER.BuyerName**

You can use SQL to determine whether this is true. The following query will return any values of the foreign key that violate the constraint:

```
/* *** SQL-Query-CH04-02 *** */
SELECT     Buyer
FROM       SKU_DATA
WHERE      Buyer NOT IN
           (SELECT     BuyerName
            FROM       BUYER);
```

The subquery finds all values of BUYER.BuyerName. If there is any value of Buyer that is not in this subquery, then that value will be displayed in the results of the main query. All such values violate the referential integrity constraint. In the following actual results of the query on the data in our dataset as shown in Figure 2-6, we get an **empty set**—there are *no* values returned in response to the query—which means that there are *no* foreign key values that violate the referential integrity constraint.

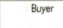

After you have assessed the input tables, your next steps depend on whether you are creating an updatable database or a read-only database. We will consider updatable databases first.

## Designing Updatable Databases

Updatable databases are typically the operational databases of a company, such as the **online transaction processing (OLTP) system** discussed for Cape Codd Outdoor Sports at the beginning of Chapter 2. If you are constructing an updatable database, then you need to be concerned about modification anomalies and inconsistent data. Consequently, you must carefully consider normalization principles. Before we begin, let's first review the advantages and disadvantages of normalization.

### Advantages and Disadvantages of Normalization

Figure 4-2 summarizes the advantages and disadvantages of normalization. On the positive side, normalization eliminates modification anomalies and reduces data duplication. Reduced data duplication eliminates the possibility of data integrity problems due to inconsistent data values. It also saves file space.

> **BY THE WAY**  Why do we say *reduce* data duplication rather than *eliminate* data duplication? The answer is that we cannot eliminate all duplicated data because we must duplicate data in foreign keys. We cannot eliminate Buyer, for example, from the SKU_DATA table because we would then not be able to relate BUYER and SKU_DATA rows. Values of Buyer are thus duplicated in the BUYER and SKU_DATA tables.
>
> This observation leads to a second question: If we only *reduce* data duplication, how can we claim to *eliminate* inconsistent data values? Data duplication in foreign keys will not cause inconsistencies because referential integrity constraints prohibit them. As long as we enforce such constraints, the duplicate foreign key values will cause no inconsistencies.

## Choosing Not to Use BCNF

Although in most cases the tables in an updatable database should be placed in BCNF, in some situations BCNF is just too pure. The classic example of unneeded normalization involves U.S. ZIP codes and similar postal codes in other countries (although, in fact, ZIP codes *do not* always determine city and state). Consider the following table for customers in the United States:

**CUSTOMER (CustomerID, LastName, FirstName, Street, City, State, ZIP)**

The functional dependencies of this table are:

**CustomerID → (LastName, FirstName, Street, City, State, ZIP)**
**ZIP → (City, State)**

This table is not in BCNF because ZIP is a determinant that is not a candidate key. We can normalize this table as follows:

**CUSTOMER_2 (CustomerID, LastName, FirstName, Street, ZIP)**
**ZIP_CODE (ZIP, City, State)**

with referential integrity constraint:

**CUSTOMER_2.ZIP must exist in ZIP_CODE.ZIP**

The tables CUSTOMER_2 and ZIP_CODE are in BCNF, but consider these tables in light of the advantages and disadvantages of normalization listed in Figure 4-2. Normalization eliminates modification anomalies, but how often does ZIP code data change? How often does the post office change the city and state assigned to a ZIP code value? Almost never. The consequences on every business and person would be too severe. So, even though the design allows anomalies to occur, in practice, they will not occur because the data never change. Consider the second advantage: normalization reduces data duplication and hence improves data integrity. In fact, data integrity problems can happen in the single-table example if someone enters the wrong value for City, State, or ZIP. In that case, the database will have inconsistent ZIP values. But normal business processes will cause ZIP code errors to be noticed, and they will be corrected without a problem.

Now consider the disadvantages of normalization. Using two separate tables will require application programs to use more complex SQL. They also require the DBMS to process two tables, which may make the applications slow. Weighing the advantages and disadvantages, most practitioners would say that the normalized data are just too pure. ZIP code data would therefore be left in the original table.

In summary, when you design an updatable database from existing tables, examine every table to determine if it is in BCNF. If it is not, then the table is susceptible to modification anomalies and inconsistent data. In almost all cases, transform the table into tables that are in BCNF. However, if the data are never modified and if data inconsistencies will be easily corrected via the normal operation of business activity, then you may choose not to place the table into BCNF.

## Multivalued Dependencies

Unlike functional dependencies, the anomalies from multivalued dependencies are so serious that multivalued dependencies should always be eliminated. Unlike BCNF, there is no gray area. Just place the columns of a multivalued dependency in tables of their own.

As shown in the last section, using SQL statements to create and populate normalized tables is not difficult. It does mean that application programmers will have to write subqueries and joins to re-create the original data. Writing subqueries and joins, however, is *nothing* compared with the complexity of code that must be written to handle the anomalies due to multivalued dependencies.

Some experts might object to such a hard-and-fast rule, but it is justifiable. Although there may be a few rare, obscure, and weird cases in which multivalued dependencies are not problematic, such cases are not worth remembering. Until you have years of database design experience, always eliminate multivalued dependencies from any updatable table.

## Designing Read-Only Databases

Read-only databases are used in **business intelligence (BI) systems** for producing information for assessment, analysis, planning, and control, as we discussed for Cape Codd Outdoor Sports in Chapter 2 and will return to again when we discuss BI in depth in Chapter 12, "Data Warehouses and Business Intelligence Systems." Read-only databases are commonly used in a **data warehouse**, which we also introduced in Chapter 2. The extracted sales data that we used for Cape Codd Outdoor Sports in Chapter 2 is a small but typical example of a read-only database. Because such databases are updated by carefully controlled and timed procedures, the design guidelines and design priorities are different from those for operational databases that are frequently updated.

In the course of your career, you will likely be given tables of data and asked to create a read-only database. In fact, this task is commonly assigned to beginning database administrators.

For several reasons, normalization is seldom an advantage for a read-only database. For one, if a database is never updated, then no modification anomalies can occur. Hence, considering Figure 4-2, the main reason to normalize a read-only database is to reduce data duplication. However, with no update activity, there is no risk of data integrity problems, so the only remaining reason to avoid duplicated data is to save file space.

Today, however, file space is exceedingly cheap—nearly free. So unless the database is enormous, the cost of storage is minimal. It is true that the DBMS will take longer to find and process data in large tables, so data might be normalized to speed up processing. But even that advantage is not clear-cut. If data are normalized, then data from two or more tables may need to be read, and the time required for the join may overwhelm the time savings of searching in small tables. In almost all cases, normalization of the tables in a read-only database is a bad idea.

### Denormalization

Often the data for a read-only database are extracted from operational databases. Because such databases are updatable, they are probably normalized. Hence, you will likely receive the extracted data in normalized form. In fact, if you have a choice, ask for normalized data. For one, normalized data are smaller in size and can be transmitted to you more quickly. Also, if the data are normalized, it will be easier for you to reformat the data for your particular needs.

According to the last section, you probably do not want to leave the data in normalized form for a read-only database. If that is the case, you will need to **denormalize**, or join, the data prior to storage.

Consider the example in Figure 4-5. This is a copy of the normalized STUDENT, ACTIVITY, and PAYMENT data in Figure 3-25. Suppose that you are creating a read-only database that will be used to report amounts due for student activity payments. If you store the data in this three-table form, every time someone needs to compare AmountPaid with ActivityFee and report student names of students still owing ActivityFee payments, he or she must join the three tables together. To do this, that person will need to know how to write a three-table join, and the DBMS will need to perform the join every time the report is prepared.

You can reduce the complexity of the SQL required to read these data and also reduce DBMS processing by joining the tables once and storing the joined result as a single table. First use the techniques discussed in Chapter 7 to create a new table named

**FIGURE 4-5**

The Normalized STUDENT, ACTIVITY, and PAYMENT Relations

**STUDENT**

|   | StudentID | StudentName |
|---|-----------|-------------|
| 1 | 100 | Jones |
| 2 | 200 | Davis |
| 3 | 300 | Garrett |
| 4 | 400 | Jones |

**ACTIVITY**

|   | Activity | ActivityFee |
|---|----------|-------------|
| 1 | Golf | 65.00 |
| 2 | Skiing | 200.00 |
| 3 | Swimming | 50.00 |

**PAYMENT**

|   | StudentID | Activity | AmountPaid |
|---|-----------|----------|------------|
| 1 | 100 | Golf | 65.00 |
| 2 | 100 | Skiing | 0.00 |
| 3 | 200 | Skiing | 0.00 |
| 4 | 200 | Swimming | 50.00 |
| 5 | 300 | Skiing | 100.00 |
| 6 | 300 | Swimming | 50.00 |
| 7 | 400 | Golf | 65.00 |
| 8 | 400 | Swimming | 50.00 |

STUDENT_ACTIVITY_PAYMENT that will hold the results. The following SQL statement will join the three tables together and store them in STUDENT_ACTIVITY_PAYMENT:

```
/* *** SQL-INSERT-CH04-03 *** */
INSERT INTO STUDENT_ACTIVITY_PAYMENT
    SELECT      STUDENT.StudentID, StudentName,
                ACTIVITY.Activity, ActivityFee,
                AmountPaid
    FROM        STUDENT, PAYMENT, ACTIVITY
    WHERE       STUDENT.StudentID = PAYMENT.StudentID
        AND     PAYMENT.Activity = ACTIVITY.Activity;
```

As shown in Figure 4-6, the STUDENT_ACTIVITY_PAYMENT_DATA table that results from this join has the same data as the original STUDENT_ACTIVITY table shown in Figure 3-24.

As you can see, denormalization is simple. Just join the data together and store the joined result as a table. By doing this, when you place the data into the read-only database, you save the application programmers from having to code joins for each application, and you also save the DBMS from having to perform joins and subqueries every time the users run a query or create a report.

## Customized Duplicated Tables

Because there is no danger of data integrity problems in a read-only database and because the cost of storage today is minuscule, read-only databases are often designed with many copies of the same data, each copy customized for a particular application.

**FIGURE 4-6**

The Denormalized STUDENT_ACTIVITY_PAYMENT Relation

**STUDENT_ACTIVITY_PAYMENT**

|   | StudentID | StudentName | Activity | ActivityFee | AmountPaid |
|---|-----------|-------------|----------|-------------|------------|
| 1 | 100 | Jones | Golf | 65.00 | 65.00 |
| 2 | 100 | Jones | Skiing | 200.00 | 0.00 |
| 3 | 200 | Davis | Skiing | 200.00 | 0.00 |
| 4 | 200 | Davis | Swimming | 50.00 | 50.00 |
| 5 | 300 | Garrett | Skiing | 200.00 | 100.00 |
| 6 | 300 | Garrett | Swimming | 50.00 | 50.00 |
| 7 | 400 | Jones | Golf | 65.00 | 65.00 |
| 8 | 400 | Jones | Swimming | 50.00 | 50.00 |

**FIGURE 4-7**

Columns in the PRODUCT
Table

| Product |
|---|
| • SKU (Primary Key) |
| • PartNumber (Candidate key) |
| • SKU_Description (Candidate key) |
| • VendorNumber |
| • VendorName |
| • VendorContact_1 |
| • VendorContact_2 |
| • VendorStreet |
| • VendorCity |
| • VendorState |
| • VendorZIP |
| • QuantitySoldPastYear |
| • QuantitySoldPastQuarter |
| • QuantitySoldPastMonth |
| • DetailPicture |
| • ThumbNailPicture |
| • MarketingShortDescription |
| • MarketingLongDescription |
| • PartColor |
| • UnitsCode |
| • BinNumber |
| • ProductionKeyCode |

For example, suppose a company has a large PRODUCT table with the columns listed in Figure 4-7. The columns in this table are used by different business processes. Some are used for purchasing, some are used for sales analysis, some are used for displaying parts on a Web site, some are used for marketing, and some are used for inventory control.

The values of some of these columns, such as those for the picture images, are large. If the DBMS is required to read all of these data for every query, processing is likely to be slow. Accordingly, the organization might create several customized versions of this table for use by different applications. In an updatable database, so much duplicated data would risk severe data integrity problems, but for a read-only database, there is no such risk.

Suppose for this example that the organization designs the following tables:

**PRODUCT_PURCHASING (SKU, SKU_Description, VendorNumber, VendorName, VendorContact_1, VendorContact_2, VendorStreet, VendorCity, VendorState, VendorZIP)**

**PRODUCT_USAGE (<u>SKU</u>, SKU_Description, QuantitySoldPastYear, QuantitySoldPastQuarter, QuantitySoldPastMonth)**

**PRODUCT_WEB (<u>SKU</u>, DetailPicture, ThumbnailPicture, MarketingShortDescription, MarketingLongDescription, PartColor)**

**PRODUCT_INVENTORY (<u>SKU</u>, PartNumber, SKU_Description, UnitsCode, BinNumber, ProductionKeyCode)**

You can create these tables using the graphical design facilities of Access or another DBMS. Once the tables are created, they can be filled using INSERT commands similar to those already discussed. The only tricks are to watch for duplicated data and to use DISTINCT where necessary.

# Common Design Problems

Although normalization and denormalization are the primary considerations when designing databases from existing data, there are four additional practical problems to consider. These are summarized in Figure 4-8.

### The Multivalue, Multicolumn Problem

The table in Figure 4-7 illustrates the first common problem, the **multivalue, multicolumn problem**. Notice the columns VendorContact_1 and VendorContact_2. These columns store the names of two contacts at the part vendor. If the company wanted to store the names of three or four contacts using this strategy, it would add columns VendorContact_3, VendorContact_4, and so forth.

Consider another example for an employee parking application. Suppose the EMPLOYEE_AUTO table includes basic employee data plus columns for license numbers for up to three cars. The following is the typical table structure:

**EMPLOYEE (<u>EmployeeNumber</u>, EmployeeLastName, EmployeeFirstName, EmailAddress, Auto1_LicenseNumber, Auto2_LicenseNumber, Auto3_LicenseNumber)**

Other examples of this strategy are to store employees' children's names in columns such as Child_1, Child_2, Child_3, and so forth, for as many children as the designer of the table thinks appropriate, to store a picture of a house in a real estate application in columns labeled Picture_1, Picture_2, Picture_3, and so forth.

Storing multiple values in this way is convenient, but it has two serious disadvantages. The more obvious one is that the number of possible items is fixed. What if there are three contacts at a particular vendor? Where do we put the third name if only columns VendorContact_1 and VendorContact_2 are available? Or if there are only three columns for child names, where do we put the name of the fourth child? And so forth.

**FIGURE 4-8**

Practical Problems in Designing Databases from Existing Data

| Practical Problems in Designing Databases from Existing Data |
| --- |
| The multivalue, multicolumn problem |
| Inconsistent values |
| Missing values |
| General-purpose remarks column |

The second disadvantage occurs when querying the data. Suppose we have the following EMPLOYEE table:

**EMPLOYEE (<u>EmployeeNumber</u>, EmployeeLastName, EmployeeFirstName, EmailAddress, Child_1, Child_2, Child_3, . . . {other data})**

Further, suppose we want to know the names of employees who have a child with the first name Gretchen. If there are three child name columns as shown in our EMPLOYEE table, we must write:

```
/* *** EXAMPLE CODE - DO NOT RUN *** */
/* *** SQL-Query-CH04-03 *** */
SELECT    *
FROM      EMPLOYEE
WHERE     Child_1 = 'Gretchen'
   OR     Child_2 = 'Gretchen'
   OR     Child_3 = 'Gretchen';
```

Of course, if there are seven child names…well, you get the picture.

These problems can be eliminated by using a second table to store the multivalued attribute. For the employee–child case, the tables are:

**EMPLOYEE (<u>EmployeeNumber</u>, EmployeeLastName, EmployeeFirstName, EmailAddress, . . . {other data})**

**CHILD (<u>*EmployeeNumber*</u>, <u>ChildFirstName</u>, . . . {other data})**

Using this second structure, employees can have an unlimited number of children, and storage space will be saved for employees who have no children at all. Additionally, to find all of the employees who have a child named Gretchen, we can code:

```
/* *** EXAMPLE CODE - DO NOT RUN *** */
/* *** SQL-Query-CH04-04 *** */
SELECT    *
FROM      EMPLOYEE
WHERE     EmployeeNumber IN
          (SELECT    EmployeeNumber
           FROM      CHILD
           WHERE     ChildFirstName = 'Gretchen');
```

This second query is easier to write and understand and will work regardless of the number of children that an employee has. Another advantage of the new design is that we avoid storing a large number of NULLs in the database. For example, if employees can have up to three cars, but 99 percent of employees only have one car, then a lot of space will be wasted storing NULLs for those employees' nonexistent second and third cars.

The alternative design does require the DBMS to process two tables, and if the tables are large and performance is a concern, one can argue that the original design is better. In such cases, storing multiple values in multiple columns may be preferred. Another, less valid objection to the two-table design is as follows: "We only need space for three cars because university policy restricts each employee to registering no more than three cars." The problem with this statement is that databases often outlive policies. Next year that policy may change, and, if it does, the database will need to be redesigned. As we will discuss in

Chapter 8, database redesign is tricky, complex, and expensive. It is better to avoid the need for a database redesign.

---

**BY THE WAY**    A few years ago, people argued that only three phone number columns were needed per person: Home, Office, and Fax. Later they said, "Well, OK, maybe we need four: Home, Office, Fax, and Mobile." Today, who would want to guess the maximum number of phone numbers a person might have? Rather than guess, just store Phone in a separate table; such a design will allow each person to have from none to an unlimited number of phone numbers.

---

You are likely to encounter the multivalue, multicolumn problem when creating databases from nondatabase data. It is particularly common in spreadsheet and text data files. Fortunately, the preferred two-table design is easy to create, and the SQL for moving the data to the new design is easy to write.

---

**BY THE WAY**    The multivalue, multicolumn problem is just another form of a multivalued dependency. For the parking application, for example, rather than store multiple rows in EMPLOYEE for each auto, multiple named columns are created in the table. The underlying problem is the same, however.

---

### Inconsistent Values

**Inconsistent values** are a serious problem when creating databases from existing data. Inconsistencies occur because different users or different data sources may use slightly different forms of the same data value. These slight differences may be hard to detect and will create inconsistent and erroneous information.

One of the hardest such problems occurs when different users have coded the same entries differently. One user may have coded a SKU_Description as *Corn, Large Can*; another may have coded the same item as *Can, Corn, Large*; and another may have coded the entry as *Large Can Corn*. Those three entries all refer to the same SKU, but they will be exceedingly difficult to reconcile. These examples are not contrived; such problems frequently occur, especially when combining data from different database, spreadsheet, and file sources.

A related but simpler problem occurs when entries are misspelled. One user may enter *Coffee*; another may enter *Coffeee*. They will appear as two separate products.

Inconsistent data values are particularly problematic for primary and foreign key columns. Relationships will be missing or wrong when foreign key data are coded inconsistently or misspelled.

Two techniques can be used to find such problems. One is the same as the check for referential integrity as discussed on pages 199-200. This check will find values for which there is no match and will find misspellings and other inconsistencies.

Another technique is to use GROUP BY on the suspected column. For example, if we suspect that there are inconsistent values in the SKU_Description column in the SKU_DATA table, we can use the SQL query:

```
/* *** SQL-Query-CH04-05 *** */
SELECT    SKU_Description, COUNT(*) as SKU_Description_Count
FROM      SKU_DATA
GROUP BY  SKU_Description;
```

The result of this query for the SKU_DATA values we have been using is:

| | SKU_Description | SKU_Description_Count |
|---|---|---|
| 1 | Dive Mask, Med Clear | 1 |
| 2 | Dive Mask, Small Clear | 1 |
| 3 | Half-dome Tent | 1 |
| 4 | Half-dome Tent Vestibule | 1 |
| 5 | Half-dome Tent Vestibule - Wide | 1 |
| 6 | Light Fly Climbing Harness | 1 |
| 7 | Locking Carabiner, Oval | 1 |
| 8 | Std. Scuba Tank, Dark Blue | 1 |
| 9 | Std. Scuba Tank, Dark Green | 1 |
| 10 | Std. Scuba Tank, Light Blue | 1 |
| 11 | Std. Scuba Tank, Light Green | 1 |
| 12 | Std. Scuba Tank, Magenta | 1 |
| 13 | Std. Scuba Tank, Yellow | 1 |

In this case, there are no inconsistent values, but if there were, they would stand out. If the list resulting from the select is too long, groups can be selected that have just one or two elements using HAVING. Neither check is foolproof. Sometimes, you just have to read the data.

When working with such data, it is important to develop an error reporting and tracking system to ensure that inconsistencies that users do find are recorded and fixed. Users grow exceedingly impatient with data errors that persist after they have been reported.

## Missing Values

**Missing values** are a third problem that occurs when creating databases from existing data. A missing value, or **null value** (which typically appears in a database table in all uppercase letters as **NULL**), is a value that has never been provided. It is not the same as a blank value because a blank value is a value that is known to be blank. A null value is not known to be anything.

The problem with null values is ambiguity. A null value can indicate one of three conditions: the value is inappropriate; the value is appropriate but unknown; or the value is appropriate and known, but no one has entered it into the database. Unfortunately, we cannot tell from a null value which of these conditions is true.

Consider, for example, a null value for the column DateOfLastChildbirth in a PATIENT table. If a row represents a male patient, then the null occurs because the value is inappropriate; a male cannot give birth. Alternatively, if the patient is a female, but the patient has never been asked for the data, then the value is appropriate but unknown. Finally, the null value could also mean that a date value is appropriate and known, but no one has recorded it into the database.

You can use the SQL comparison operator IS NULL, as discussed in Chapter 2, to check for null values. For example, to find the number of null values of Quantity in the ORDER_ITEM table, you can code:

```
/* *** SQL-Query-CH04-06 *** */
SELECT    COUNT (*) as QuantityNullCount
FROM      ORDER_ITEM
WHERE     Quantity IS NULL;
```

The result of this query for the ORDER_ITEM values we have been using is:

| | QuantityNullCount |
|---|---|
| 1 | 0 |

In this case, there are no NULL values, but if there were, we would know how many, and then we could use a SELECT * statement to find the data of any row that has a NULL value.

When creating a database from existing data, if you try to define a column that has null values as the primary key, the DBMS will generate an error message. You will have to remove the nulls before creating the primary key. Also, you can tell the DBMS that a given column is not allowed to have null values, and when you import the data, if any row has a null value in that column, the DBMS will generate an error message. The particulars depend on the DBMS in use. See Chapter 10A for Microsoft SQL Server 2019, Chapter 10B for Oracle Database, and Chapter 10C for MySQL 8.0. You should form the habit of checking for null values in all foreign keys. Any row with a null foreign key will not participate in the relationship. That may or may not be appropriate—you will need to ask the users to find out. Also, null values can be problematic when implementing referential integrity while creating and populating a new database. We will discuss the implications of allowing null values in foreign keys in Chapter 7.

A final warning about null values: users who provide you with data will have often used other terms or data values when they should have used NULLs. Search for column values such as "unknown," "NULL," the empty string, a string of blanks, or a nonsensical value (e.g., a negative number for a salary), and you may find additional places that should use NULL.

## The General-Purpose Remarks Column

The **general-purpose remarks column** problem is common, serious, and very difficult to solve. Columns with names such as Remarks, Comments, and Notes often contain important data that are stored in an inconsistent, verbal, and verbose manner. Learn to be wary of columns with any such names.

To see why, consider customer data for a company that sells expensive items such as airplanes, rare cars, boats, or paintings. In a typical setting, someone has used a spreadsheet to track customer data. That person used a spreadsheet not because it was the best tool for such a problem, but rather because he or she had a spreadsheet program and knew how to use it (although perhaps "*thought* he or she knew how to use it" would be more accurate).

The typical spreadsheet has columns like LastName, FirstName, Email, Phone, Address, and so forth. It almost always includes a column titled Remarks, Comments, Notes, or something similar. The problem is that needed data are usually buried in such columns and nearly impossible to dig out. Suppose you want to create a database for a customer contact application for an airplane broker. Assume your design contains the two tables:

**CONTACT (ContactID, ContactLastName, ContactFirstName,**
   **Address, . . . {other data}, Remarks, *AirplaneModelID*)**

**AIRPLANE_MODEL (AirplaneModelID, AirplaneModelName,**
   **AirplaneModelDescription, . . . {other airplane model data})**

where CONTACT.AirplaneModelID is a foreign key to AIRPLANE_MODEL.AirplaneModelID. You want to use this relationship to determine who owns, has owned, or is interested in buying a particular model of airplane.

In the typical situation, the data for the foreign key have been recorded in the Remarks column. If you read the Remarks column data in CONTACT, you will find entries like: 'Wants to buy a Piper Seneca II', 'Owner of a Piper Seneca II', and 'Possible buyer for a turbo Seneca'. All three of these rows should have a value of AirplaneModelID (the foreign key in CONTACT) that equals the value of AIRPLANE_MODEL.AirplaneModelID for the AirplaneModelName of 'Piper Seneca II', but without the proper foreign key value, you would pull your hair out making that determination.

Another problem with general-purpose remarks columns is that they are used inconsistently and contain multiple data items. One user may have used the column to store the name of the spouse of the contact, another may have used it to store airplane models as just described, and a third may have used it to store the date the customer was last contacted. Or the same user may have used it for all three purposes at different times!

The best solution in this case is to identify all of the different purposes of the remarks column, create new columns for each of those purposes, and then extract the data and store it in the new columns as appropriate. However, this solution can seldom be automated.

In practice, all solutions require patience and hours of labor. Learn to be wary of such columns, and don't take such jobs on a fixed-price basis!

## Summary

When constructing a database from existing data, the first step is to assess the structure and content of the input tables. Count the number of rows and use the SQL SELECT TOP {NumberOfRows} * statement for SQL Server (or the equivalent SQL statement in other DBMS products) to learn the columns in the data. Then examine the data and determine functional dependencies, multivalued dependencies, candidate keys, each table's primary key, and foreign keys. Check out the validity of possible referential integrity constraints.

Design principles differ depending on whether an updatable or read-only database is being constructed. If the former, then modification anomalies and inconsistent data are concerns. The advantages of normalization are elimination of modification anomalies, reduced data duplication, and the elimination of data inconsistencies. The disadvantages are that more complex SQL will be required and application performance may be slower.

For updatable databases, most of the time the problems of modification anomalies are so great that all tables should be placed in BCNF. SQL for normalization is easy to write. In some cases, if the data will be updated infrequently and if inconsistencies are readily corrected by business processes, then BCNF may be too pure and the tables should not be normalized. The problems of multivalued dependencies are so great that they should always be removed.

Read-only databases are created for reporting, querying, and data mining applications. Creating such a database is a task commonly assigned to beginners. When designing read-only databases, normalization is less desired. If input data is normalized, it frequently needs to be denormalized by joining it together and storing the joined result. Also, sometimes many copies of the same data are stored in tables customized for particular applications.

Four common problems occur when creating databases from existing data. The multivalue, multicolumn design sets a fixed number of repeating values and stores each in a column of its own. Such a design limits the number of items allowed and results in awkward SQL query statements. A better design results from putting multiple values in a table of their own.

Inconsistent values result when data arise from different users and applications. Inconsistent foreign key values create incorrect relationships. Data inconsistencies can be detected using SQL statements, as illustrated in this chapter. A null, or missing, value is not the same as a blank. A null value is not known to be anything. Null values are a problem because they are ambiguous. They can mean that a value is inappropriate, unknown, or known but not yet entered into the database.

The general-purpose remarks column is a column that is used for different purposes. It collects data items in an inconsistent and verbose manner. Such columns are especially problematic if they contain data needed for a foreign key. Even if they do not, they often contain data for several different columns. Automated solutions are not possible, and the correction requires patience and labor.

Write the SQL statements needed for filling the EMPLOYEE and DEPARTMENT tables with data from EMPLOYEE_DEPARTMENT.

**4.11**  Summarize the reasons explained in this chapter for not placing ZIP code values into BCNF.

**4.12**  Describe a situation, other than the one for ZIP codes, in which one would choose not to place tables into BCNF. Justify your decision not to use BCNF.

**4.13**  According to this text, under what situations should you choose not to remove multivalued dependencies from a relation?

**4.14**  Compare the difficulty of writing subqueries and joins with the difficulty of dealing with anomalies caused by multivalued dependencies.

**4.15**  Describe three uses for a read-only database.

**4.16**  How does the fact that a read-only database is never updated influence the reasons for normalization?

**4.17**  For read-only databases, how persuasive is the argument that normalization reduces file space?

**4.18**  What is denormalization?

**4.19**  Suppose you are given the DEPARTMENT and EMPLOYEE tables in Review Question 4.10 and asked to denormalize them into the EMPLOYEE_DEPARTMENT relation. Show the design of the EMPLOYEE_DEPARTMENT relation. Write an SQL statement to fill this table with data.

**4.20**  Summarize the reasons for creating customized duplicated tables.

**4.21**  Why are customized duplicated tables not used for updatable databases?

**4.22**  List four common design problems when creating databases from existing data.

**4.23**  Give an example of a multivalue, multicolumn table other than one discussed in this chapter.

**4.24**  Explain the problems caused by the multivalue, multicolumn table in your example in Review Question 4.23.

**4.25**  Show how to represent the relation in your answer to Review Question 4.23 with two tables.

**4.26**  Show how the tables in your answer to Review Question 4.25 solve the problems you identified in Review Question 4.24.

**4.27**  Explain the following statement: "The multivalue, multicolumn problem is just another form of multivalued dependency." Show how this is so.

**4.28**  Explain ways in which inconsistent values arise.

**4.29**  Why are inconsistent values in foreign keys particularly troublesome?

**4.30**  Describe two ways to identify inconsistent values. Are these techniques certain to find all inconsistent values? What other step can be taken?

**4.31**  What is a null value?

**4.32**  How does a null value differ from a blank value?

**4.33**  What are three interpretations of null values? Use an example in your answer that is different from the one in this book.

**4.34**  Show SQL for determining the number of null values in the column EmployeeFirstName of the table EMPLOYEE.

**4.35** Describe the general-purpose remarks column problem.

**4.36** Give an example in which the general-purpose remarks column makes it difficult to obtain values for a foreign key.

**4.37** Give an example in which the general-purpose remarks column causes difficulties when multiple values are stored in the same column. How is this problem solved?

**4.38** Why should one be wary of general-purpose remarks columns?

# Exercises

The Quincy Bay Sports Club owns and operates three sports club facilities in Boston, Cambridge, and Quincy, Massachusetts. Each facility has a large selection of modern exercise equipment, weight rooms, and rooms for yoga and other exercise classes. Quincy Bay offers 3-month and 1-year memberships. Members can use the facilities at any of the three club locations.

Quincy Bay maintains a roster of personal trainers who operate as independent consultants. Approved trainers can schedule appointments with clients at Quincy Bay facilities as long as their client is a member of the club. Trainers also teach yoga, Pilates, and other classes. Answer the following questions, assuming you have been provided the following three tables of data (PT stands for personal trainer):

> **PT_SESSION (Trainer, Phone, EmailAddress, Fee, ClientLastName, ClientFirstName, ClientPhone, ClientEmailAddress, Date, Time)**
>
> **CLUB_MEMBERSHIP (ClientNumber, ClientLastName, ClientFirstName, ClientPhone, ClientEmailAddress, MembershipType, EndingDate, Street, City, State, ZIP)**
>
> **CLASS (ClassName, Trainer, StartDate, EndDate, Time, DayOfWeek, Cost)**

**4.39** Identify possible multivalued dependencies in these tables.

**4.40** Identify possible functional dependencies in these tables.

**4.41** Determine whether each table is either in BCNF or in 4NF. State your assumptions.

**4.42** Modify each of these tables so that every table is in BCNF and 4NF. Use the assumptions you made in your answer to Question 4.41. Do *not* indicate primary or foreign keys.

**4.43** Using these tables and your assumptions, recommend a design, including primary and foreign keys, for an updatable database.

**4.44** Add a table to your answer to Question 4.43 that would allow Quincy Bay to assign members to particular classes. Include an AmountPaid column in your new table.

**4.45** Recommend a design for a read-only database that would support the following needs:

   **A.** Enable trainers to ensure that their clients are members of the club.

   **B.** Enable the club to assess the popularity of various trainers.

   **C.** Enable the trainers to determine if they are assisting the same client.

   **D.** Enable class instructors to determine if the attendees to their classes have paid.

# Case Questions

### Marcia's Dry Cleaning Case Questions

Marcia Wilson, the owner of Marcia's Dry Cleaning, is in the process of creating databases to support the operation and management of her business. For the past year, she and her staff have been using a cash register system that collects the following data:

**SALE (InvoiceNumber, DateIn, DateOut, Total, Phone, FirstName, LastName)**

Unfortunately, during rush times, not all of the data are entered, and there are many null values in Phone, FirstName, and LastName. In some cases, all three are null; in other cases, one or two are null. InvoiceNumber, DateIn, and Total are never null. DateOut has a few null values. Also, occasionally during a rush, phone number and name data have been entered incorrectly. To help create her database, Marcia purchased a mailing list from a local business bureau. The mailing list includes the following data:

**HOUSEHOLD (Phone, FirstName, LastName, Street, City, State, ZIP, Apartment)**

In some cases, a phone number has multiple names. The primary key is thus the composite (Phone, FirstName, LastName). There are no null values in Phone, FirstName, and LastName, but there are some null values in the address data.

There are many names in SALE that are not in HOUSEHOLD, and there are many names in HOUSEHOLD that are not in SALE.

**A.** Design an updatable database for storing customer and sales data. Explain how to deal with the problems of missing data. Explain how to deal with the problems of incorrect phone and name data.

**B.** Design a read-only database for storing customer and sales data. Explain how to deal with the problems of missing data. Explain how to deal with the problems of incorrect phone and name data.

# The Queen Anne Curiosity Shop Project Questions

The Queen Anne Curiosity Shop project questions in Chapter 3 asked you to create a set of relations to organize and link the Queen Anne Curiosity Shop typical sales data shown in Figure 3-33 and the typical purchase data shown in Figure 3-34. The set of relations may look similar to the following, although some additional columns have been added to the CUSTOMER relation to more closely match the Queen Anne Curiosity Shop database schema shown in the project questions for Chapter 2:

**CUSTOMER (CustomerID, LastName, FirstName, EmailAddress,**
     **EncryptedPassword, Address, City, State, ZIP, Phone, ReferredBy)**
**SALE (SaleID, CustomerID, InvoiceDate, PreTaxTotal, Tax, Total)**
**SALE_ITEM (SaleID, SaleItemID, PurchaseID, SalePrice)**
**PURCHASE (PurchaseID, PurchaseItem, PurchasePrice, PurchaseDate,**
     **VendorID)**
**VENDOR (VendorID, Vendor, Phone)**

**Use these relations and the data in Figures 3-33 and 3-34 (which do *not* contain all the data for all the columns shown in this schema) to answer the following questions.**

A. Follow the procedure shown in Figure 4-1 to assess these data.

1. List all functional dependencies.
2. List any multivalued dependencies.
3. List all candidate keys.
4. List all primary keys
5. List all foreign keys.
6. State any assumptions you make as you list these components.

B. List questions you would ask the owners of the Queen Anne Curiosity Shop to verify your assumptions.

C. If there are any multivalued dependencies, create the tables needed to eliminate these dependencies.

D. Do these data have the multivalue, multicolumn problem? If so, how will you deal with it?

E. Do these data have the inconsistent data problem? If so, how will you deal with it?

F. Do these data have a null (missing) value data problem? If so, how will you deal with it?

G. Do these data have the general-purpose remarks problem? If so, how will you deal with it?

# Morgan Importing Project Questions

Phillip Morgan, the owner of Morgan Importing, makes periodic buying trips to various countries. During the trips, he keeps notes about the items he purchases and basic data about their shipments. He hired a college student as an intern, and she transformed his notes into the spreadsheets in Figure 4-9. These are just sample data. Phillip has purchased hundreds of items over the years, and they have been shipped in dozens of different shipments.

**Phillip wants to enter the information age, so he has decided to develop a database of his inventory. He wants to keep track of the items he has purchased, their shipments, and eventually customers and sales. To get started, he has asked you to create a database for the data in Figure 4-9.**

A. Follow the procedure shown in Figure 4-1 to assess these data.

1. List all functional dependencies.
2. List any multivalued dependencies.
3. List all candidate keys.
4. List all primary keys.
5. List all foreign keys.
6. State any assumptions you make as you list these components.

B. List questions you would ask Phillip to verify your assumptions.

C. If there are any multivalued dependencies, create the tables needed to eliminate these dependencies.

| | A | B | C | D | E | F | G | H | I |
|---|---|---|---|---|---|---|---|---|---|
| 1 | ShipmentNumber | Shipper | Phone | Contact | From | Departure | Arrival | Contents | InsuredValue |
| 2 | 49100300 | Wordwide | 800-123-4567 | Jose | Philippines | 5/5/2021 | 6/17/1999 | QE dining set, large bureau, porcelain lamps | $27,500 |
| 3 | 488955 | Intenational | 800-123-8898 | Marilyn | Singapore | 6/2/2021 | | Miscellaneous linen, large masks, 14 setting Willow design china | $7,500 |
| 4 | 84899440 | Wordwide | 800-123-4567 | Jose | Peru | 7/3/2021 | 7/28/2021 | Woven goods, antique leather chairs | |
| 5 | 399400 | Intenational | 800-123-8898 | Marilyn | Singaporeee | 8/5/2021 | 9/11/2021 | Large bureau, brass lamps, willow design serving dishes | $18,000 |
| 6 | | | | | | | | | |
| 7 | | | | | | | | | |
| 8 | | | | | | | | | |
| 9 | | Item | Date | City | Store | Salesperson | Price | | |
| 10 | | QE Dining Set | 4/7/2021 | Manila | E. Treasures | Gracielle | $14,300 | | |
| 11 | | Willow Serving Dishes | 7/15/2021 | Singapore | Jade Antiques | Swee Lai | $4,500 | | |
| 12 | | Large bureau | 7/17/2021 | Singapore | Eastern Sales | Jeremey | $9,500 | | |
| 13 | | Brass lamps | 7/20/2021 | Singapore | Jade Antiques | Mr. James | $1,200 | | |
| 14 | | | | | | | | | |
| 15 | | | | | | | | | |

**FIGURE 4-9**

**Spreadsheet from Morgan Importing**

**D.** The relationship between shipment and item data could possibly be inferred by matching values in the From cells to values in the City cells. Describe two problems with that strategy.

**E.** Describe a change to this spreadsheet that does express the shipment–item relationship.

**F.** Assume that Phillip wishes to create an updatable database from these data. Design tables you think are appropriate. State all referential integrity constraints.

**G.** Assume that Phillip wishes to create a read-only database from these data. Design tables you think are appropriate. State all referential integrity constraints.

**H.** Do these data have the multivalue, multicolumn problem? If so, how will you deal with it?

**I.** Do these data have the inconsistent data problem? If so, how will you deal with it?

**J.** Do these data have a null (missing) value data problem? If so, how will you deal with it?

**K.** Do these data have the general-purpose remarks problem? If so, how will you deal with it?

# 5

# Data Modeling with the Entity-Relationship Model

## Chapter Objectives

- To understand the two-phase data modeling/database design process
- To understand the purpose of the data modeling process
- To understand entity-relationship (E-R) diagrams
- To be able to determine entities, attributes, and relationships
- To be able to create entity identifiers
- To be able to determine minimum and maximum cardinalities
- To understand variations of the E-R model
- To understand and be able to use ID-dependent and other weak entities
- To understand and be able to use supertype/subtype entities
- To understand and be able to use strong entity relationship patterns

- To understand and be able to use the ID-dependent association relationship pattern
- To understand and be able to use the ID-dependent multivalued attribute relationship pattern
- To understand and be able to use the ID-dependent archetype/instance relationship pattern
- To understand and be able to use the line-item pattern
- To understand and be able to use the for-use-by subtype patterns
- To understand and be able to use recursive relationship patterns
- To understand the iterative nature of the data modeling process
- To be able to apply the data modeling process

**In this chapter** and the next, we consider the design of databases that arise from the development of new information systems. As you will learn, such databases are designed by analyzing requirements and creating a data model, or blueprint, of a database that will meet those requirements. The data model is then transformed into a database design.

This chapter addresses the creation of data models using the entity-relationship data model, the most popular modeling technique. This chapter consists of three major sections. First, we explain the major elements of the entity-relationship model and briefly describe several variations on that model. Next, we examine a number of patterns in forms, reports, and data models that you will encounter when data modeling. We then illustrate the data modeling process using the example of a small database at a university. Before starting, however, you need to understand the purpose of a data model.

Data modeling occurs in the **requirements analysis** step of the **systems development life cycle (SDLC)** in the **systems analysis and design** process. For an introduction to systems analysis and design and to the SDLC, see Appendix B, "Getting Started with Systems Analysis and Design."

## The Purpose of a Data Model

A **data model** is a plan, or blueprint, for a database design—it is a *generalized, non-DBMS-specific* design. By analogy, consider the construction of your dorm or apartment building. The contractor did not just buy some lumber, call for the concrete trucks, and start work. Instead, an architect constructed plans and blueprints for that building long before construction began. If, during the planning stage, it was determined that a room was too small or too large, the blueprint could be changed simply by redrawing the lines. If, however, the need for change occurs after the building is constructed, the walls, electrical system, plumbing, and so on, will need to be rebuilt at great expense and loss of time. It is easier, simpler, and faster to change the plan than it is to change a constructed building.

The same argument applies to data models and databases. Changing a relationship during the data modeling stage is just a matter of changing the diagram and related documentation. Changing a relationship after the database and applications have been constructed, however, is much more difficult. Data must be migrated to the new structure, SQL statements will need to be changed, forms and reports will need to be altered, and so forth.

---

**BY THE WAY**    Books on systems analysis and design often identify three design stages:

- Conceptual design (conceptual schema)
- Logical design (logical schema)
- Physical design (physical schema)

The *data model* we are discussing is equivalent to the *conceptual design* as defined in these books.

---

## The Entity-Relationship Model

Dozens of different tools and techniques for constructing data models have been defined over the years. They include the hierarchical data model, the network data model, the ANSI/SPARC data model, the entity-relationship data model, the semantic object model, and many others. Of these, the entity-relationship data model has emerged as the standard data model, and we will consider only that data model in this chapter.

The entity-relationship data model is commonly known as the **entity-relationship (E-R) model** and was first published by Peter Chen in 1976.[1] In this paper, Chen set out the basic elements of the model. Subtypes (discussed later) were added to the E-R model to create the **extended E-R model**,[2] and today it is the extended E-R model that most people mean when they use the term *E-R model*. In this text, we will use the extended E-R model.

---

[1] Peter P. Chen, "The Entity-Relationship Model—Towards a Unified View of Data," *ACM Transactions on Database Systems*, January 1976, pp. 9–36. For information on Peter Chen, see *http://en.wikipedia.org/wiki/Peter_Chen*, and for a copy of the article, see *http://www2.cis.gsu.edu/dmcdonald/cis8040/Chen.pdf*.

[2] T. J. Teorey, D. Yang, and J. P. Fry, "A Logical Design Methodology for Relational Databases Using the Extended Entity-Relationship Model," *ACM Computing Surveys*, June 1986, pp. 197–222.

FIGURE 5-1

CUSTOMER Entity and Two
Entity Instances

CUSTOMER Entity

**CUSTOMER**

CustomerNumber
CustomerName
Street
City
State
ZIP
ContactName
EmailAddress

Two CUSTOMER Instances

| | |
|---|---|
| 1234<br>Ajax Manufacturing<br>123 Elm Street<br>Memphis<br>TN<br>32455<br>Peter Schwartz<br>Peter@ajax.com | 99890<br>Jones Brothers<br>434 10th Street<br>Boston<br>MA<br>01234<br>Fritz Billingsley<br>Fritz@JB.com |

## Entities

An **entity** is something that users want to track. It is something that is readily identified in the users' work environment. Example entities are EMPLOYEE Mary Lai, CUSTOMER 12345, SALES-ORDER 1000, SALESPERSON Wally Smith, and PRODUCT A4200. Entities of a given type are grouped into an **entity class**. Thus, the EMPLOYEE entity class is the collection of all EMPLOYEE entities. In this text, entity classes are shown in capital letters.

It is important to understand the differences between an entity class and an entity instance. An entity class is a collection of entities and is described by the structure of the entities in that class. An **entity instance** of an entity class is an occurrence of a particular entity, such as CUSTOMER 12345. An entity class usually has many instances of an entity. For example, the entity class CUSTOMER has many instances—one for each customer represented in the database. The CUSTOMER entity class and two of its instances are shown in Figure 5-1.

## Attributes

Entities have **attributes** that describe their characteristics. Examples of attributes are EmployeeNumber, EmployeeName, Phone, and Email. In this text, attributes are written in both uppercase and lowercase letters. The E-R model assumes that all instances of a given entity class have the same attributes.

Figure 5-2 shows two different ways of displaying the attributes of an entity. Figure 5-2(a) shows attributes in ellipses that are connected to the entity. This style was used in the original E-R model prior to the advent of data modeling software products. Figure 5-2(b) shows the rectangle style that is commonly used by data modeling software products today.

## Identifiers

Entity instances have **identifiers**, which are attributes that name, or identify, entity instances. For example, EMPLOYEE instances can be identified by EmployeeNumber, SocialSecurityNumber, or EmployeeName (as long as no two employees have the same name). EMPLOYEE instances are not likely to be identified by attributes such as Salary or

**FIGURE 5-2**

Variations on Entity
Diagram Attribute
Displays in
E-R Models

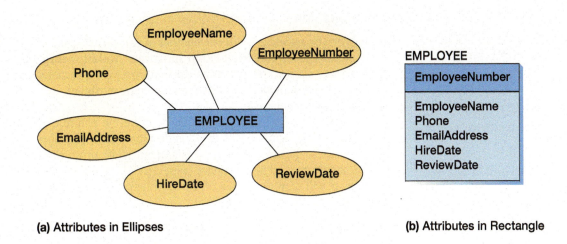

(a) Attributes in Ellipses

(b) Attributes in Rectangle

HireDate because these attributes are not normally used in a naming role. Similarly, customers can be identified by CustomerNumber or CustomerName, and sales orders can be identified by OrderNumber.

The identifier of an entity instance consists of one or more of the entity's attributes. Identifiers that consist of two or more attributes are called **composite identifiers**. Examples are (AreaCode, LocalNumber), (ProjectName, TaskName), and (FirstName, LastName, DateOfHire).

> **BY THE WAY**  Notice the correspondence between identifiers and keys. The term *identifier* is used in a data model, and the term *key* (which we have already introduced in our discussion of relational databases in Chapter 3) is used in a database design. Thus, entities have identifiers, and tables (or relations) have keys. Identifiers serve the same role for entities that keys serve for tables.

As shown in Figure 5-3, entities can be portrayed at three levels of detail in a data model. As shown in Figure 5-3(a), sometimes the entity and all of its attributes are displayed. In such cases, the identifier of the attribute is shown at the top of the entity and a horizontal line is drawn under the identifier. However, in a large data model, so much detail can make the data model diagrams unwieldy. In those cases, the entity diagram is abbreviated by showing just the identifier, as in Figure 5-3(b), or by showing just the name of the entity in a rectangle, as shown in Figure 5-3(c). All three techniques are used in practice; the more abbreviated form in Figure 5-3(c) is used to show the big picture and overall entity relationships. The more detailed view in Figure 5-3(a) is frequently used during database design. Most data modeling software products have the ability to show all three displays.

**FIGURE 5-3**

Variations on Level of Entity
Attribute Displays

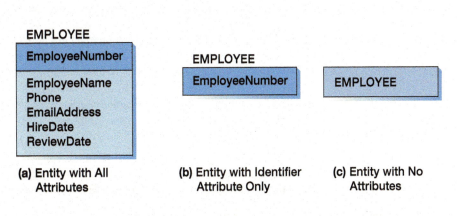

(a) Entity with All Attributes

(b) Entity with Identifier Attribute Only

(c) Entity with No Attributes

## Relationships

Entities can be associated with one another in **relationships**. The E-R model contains both relationship classes and relationship instances.[3] **Relationship classes** are associations among entity classes, and **relationship instances** are associations among entity instances. In the original E-R model, relationships could have attributes. Today, that feature is less common, and we will not use it.

Relationships are given names that describe the nature of the relationship, as shown in Figure 5-4. In Figure 5-4(a), the Qualification relationship shows which employees have which skills. In Figure 5-4(b), the Assignment relationship shows which combinations of clients, architects, and projects have been created. To avoid unnecessary complexity, in this chapter we will show the names of relationships only if there is a chance of ambiguity.

> **BY THE WAY**   Your instructor may believe that it is important to always show the name of a relationship. If so, be aware that you can name a relationship from the perspective of either of the entities or both of the entities. For example, you can name the relationship between DEPARTMENT and EMPLOYEE as Department Consists Of; or you can name it as Employee Works In; or you can name it both ways, using a slash between the two names, Department Consists Of/Employee Works In. Relationship names are a necessity when there are two different relationships between the same two entities.

A relationship class can involve two or more entity classes. The number of entity classes in the relationship is the **degree** of the relationship. In Figure 5-4(a), the Qualification relationship is of degree two because it involves two entity classes: EMPLOYEE and SKILL. In Figure 5-4(b), the Assignment relationship is of degree three because it involves three entity classes: CLIENT, ARCHITECT, and PROJECT. Relationships of degree two are referred to as **binary relationships**. Similarly, relationships of degree three are called **ternary relationships**.

When transforming a data model into a relational database design, relationships of all degrees are treated as combinations of binary relationships. The Assignment relationship in Figure 5-4(b), for example, is decomposed into three binary relationships (can you spot them?). Most of the time, this strategy is not a problem. However, some nonbinary relationships need additional work, as you will learn in Chapter 6. All data modeling software products require you to express relationships as binary relationships.

> **BY THE WAY**   At this point, you may be wondering, "What's the difference between an entity and a table?" So far, they seem like different terms for the same thing. *The principal difference between an entity and a table is that you can express a relationship between entities without using foreign keys.* In the E-R model, you can specify a relationship just by drawing a line connecting two entities. Because you are doing logical data modeling and not physical database design, you need not worry about primary and foreign keys, referential integrity constraints, and the like. Most data modeling products will allow you to consider such details if you choose to, but they do not require it.
>
> This characteristic makes entities easier to work with than tables, especially early in a project when entities and relationships are fluid and uncertain. You can show relationships between entities before you even know what the identifiers are. For example, you can say that a DEPARTMENT relates to many EMPLOYEEs before you know any of the attributes of either EMPLOYEE or DEPARTMENT. This characteristic enables you to work from the general to the specific. First, identify the entities, then think about relationships, and, finally, determine the attributes.

---

[3] For brevity, we sometimes drop the word *instance* or *class* when the context makes it clear whether an instance or a class is involved. This is true of both entities and relationships.

FIGURE 5-4

Binary Versus Ternary
Relationships

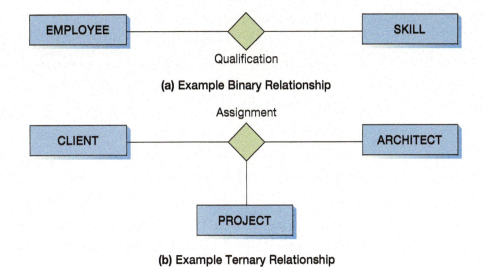

(a) Example Binary Relationship

(b) Example Ternary Relationship

In the entity-relationship model, relationships are classified by their **cardinality**, a word that means "count." The **maximum cardinality** is the maximum number of relationship instances in which an entity can participate. The **minimum cardinality** is the minimum number of relationship instances in which an entity must participate.

## Maximum Cardinality

In Figure 5-5, the maximum cardinality is shown inside the diamond that represents the relationship. The three parts of this figure show the three basic maximum cardinalities in the E-R model.

Figure 5-5(a) shows a **one-to-one (abbreviated 1:1) relationship**. In a 1:1 relationship, an entity instance of one type is related to, at most, one entity instance of the other type. The Employee_Identity relationship in Figure 5-5(a) associates one EMPLOYEE instance with one BADGE instance. According to this diagram, no employee has more than one badge, and no badge is assigned to more than one employee.

The Computer_Assignment relationship in Figure 5-5(b) illustrates a **one-to-many (abbreviated 1:N) relationship**. Here a single instance of EMPLOYEE can be associated with many instances of COMPUTER, but a COMPUTER instance is associated with, at most, one instance of EMPLOYEE. According to this diagram, an employee can be associated with several computers, but a computer is assigned to just one employee.

FIGURE 5-5

Three Types of Maximum
Cardinality

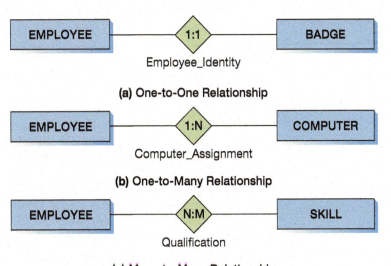

(a) One-to-One Relationship

(b) One-to-Many Relationship

(c) Many-to-Many Relationship

The positions of the 1 and the N are significant. The 1 is close to the line connecting EMPLOYEE, which means that the 1 refers to the EMPLOYEE side of the relationship. The N is close to the line connecting COMPUTER, which means that the N refers to the COMPUTER side of the relationship. If the 1 and the N were reversed and the relationship was written N:1, an EMPLOYEE would have one COMPUTER, and a COMPUTER could be assigned to many EMPLOYEEs.

When discussing one-to-many relationships, the terms **parent** and **child** are sometimes used. The *parent* is the entity on the 1 side of the relationship, and the *child* is the entity on the many side of the relationship. Thus, in a 1:N relationship between DEPARTMENT and EMPLOYEE, DEPARTMENT is the parent and EMPLOYEE is the child (one DEPARTMENT has many EMPLOYEEs).

Figure 5-5(c) shows a **many-to-many (abbreviated N:M) relationship**. According to the Qualification relationship, an EMPLOYEE instance can be associated with many SKILL instances, and a SKILL instance can be associated with many EMPLOYEE instances. This relationship documents the fact that an employee may have many skills and a skill may be held by many employees.

Sometimes students wonder why we do not write many-to-many relationships as N:N or M:M. The reason is that cardinality in one direction may be different from the cardinality in the other direction. In other words, in an N:M relationship, N need not equal M. An EMPLOYEE can have five skills, for example, but one of those skills can have three employees. Writing the relationship as N:M highlights the possibility that the cardinalities may be different.

Sometimes the maximum cardinality is an exact number. For example, for a sports team, the number of players on the roster is limited to some fixed number, say, 15. In that case, the maximum cardinality between TEAM and PLAYER would be set to 15 rather than to the more general N.

---

**BY THE WAY**    Relationships like those in Figure 5-5 are sometimes called **HAS-A relationships**. This term is used because each entity instance has a relationship to a second entity instance. An employee has a badge, and a badge has an employee. If the maximum cardinality is greater than one, then each entity has a set of other entities. An employee has a set of skills, for example, and a skill has a set of employees who have that skill.

---

## Minimum Cardinality

The minimum cardinality is the number of entity instances that *must* participate in a relationship. Generally, minimums are stated as either zero or one. If zero, then participation in the relationship is **optional**. If one, then every entity instance must participate in the relationship, which is called **mandatory** participation. In E-R diagrams, an optional relationship is represented by a small circle on the relationship line; a mandatory relationship is represented by a hash mark or line across the relationship line.

To better understand these terms, consider Figure 5-6. In the Employee_Identity relationship in Figure 5-6(a), the hash marks indicate that an EMPLOYEE is required to have a BADGE, and a BADGE must be allocated to an EMPLOYEE. Such a relationship is referred to as a **mandatory-to-mandatory (M-M) relationship** because entities are required on both sides. The complete specification for the Employee_Identity relationship is that it is a 1:1, M-M relationship.

In Figure 5-6(b), the two small circles indicate that the Computer_Assignment relationship is an **optional-to-optional (O-O) relationship**. This means that an EMPLOYEE need not have a COMPUTER and a COMPUTER need not be assigned to an EMPLOYEE. The Computer_Assignment relationship is thus a 1:N, O-O relationship.

Finally, in Figure 5-6(c), the combination of a circle and a hash mark indicates an **optional-to-mandatory (O-M) relationship**. Here an EMPLOYEE must be assigned

**FIGURE 5-6**

Examples of Three Types of
Minimum Cardinality

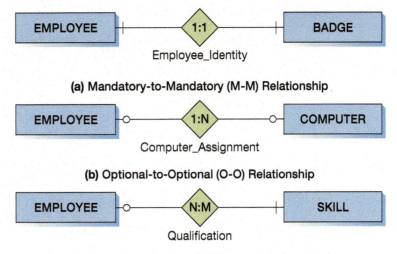

**(a) Mandatory-to-Mandatory (M-M) Relationship**

**(b) Optional-to-Optional (O-O) Relationship**

**(c) Optional-to-Mandatory (O-M) Relationship**

to at least one SKILL, but a SKILL may not necessarily be related to any EMPLOYEE. The complete specification for the Qualification relationship is thus an N:M, O-M relationship. The positions of the circle and the hash mark are important. Because the circle is next to EMPLOYEE, it means that the employee is optional in the relationship.

> **BY THE WAY**   Sometimes when interpreting diagrams like Figure 5-6(c) students become confused about which entity is optional and which is required. An easy way to clarify this situation is to imagine that you are standing in the diamond on the relationship line. Imagine looking toward one of the entities. If you see an oval in that direction, then that entity is optional; if you see a hash mark, then that entity is required. Thus, in Figure 5-6(c), if you stand on the diamond and look toward SKILL, you see a hash mark. This means that SKILL is required in the relationship. If you then turn around and look toward EMPLOYEE, you see a circle. This means that EMPLOYEE is optional in the relationship.

A fourth option, a **mandatory-to-optional (M-O) relationship**, is not shown in Figure 5-6. But if we exchange the circle and the hash mark in Figure 5-6(c), then Qualification becomes an M-O relationship. In that case, an EMPLOYEE need not have a SKILL, but a SKILL must have at least one EMPLOYEE.

As with maximum cardinalities, in rare cases the minimum cardinality is a specific number. To represent the relationship between PERSON and MARRIAGE, for example, the minimum cardinality would be 2: Optional.

## Entity-Relationship Diagrams and Their Versions

The diagrams in Figure 5-5 and Figure 5-6 are sometimes referred to as **entity-relationship (E-R) diagrams**. The original E-R model specified that such diagrams use diamonds for relationships, rectangles for entities, and connected ellipses for attributes, as shown in Figure 5-2. You may still see examples of such E-R diagrams, and it is important for you to be able to interpret them.

For two reasons, however, this original notation is seldom used today. First, there are a number of different versions of the E-R model, and these versions use different symbols. Second, data modeling software products use different techniques. For example, the erwin Data Modeler product uses one set of symbols, and Microsoft Visio uses a second set.

## Variations of the E-R Model

At least three different versions of the E-R model are in use today. One of them, the **Information Engineering (IE) model**, was developed by James Martin in 1990. This model uses crow's feet to show the many side of a relationship, and it is called the **IE Crow's Foot model**. It is easy to understand, and we will use it throughout this text. In 1993, the National Institute of Standards and Technology announced another version of the E-R model as a national standard. This version is called **Integrated Definition 1, Extended (IDEF1X)**.[4] This standard incorporates the basic ideas of the E-R model but uses different graphical symbols. Although this model is a national standard, it is difficult to understand and use. As a national standard, however, it is used in government, and thus it may become important to you. Therefore, the fundamentals of the IDEF1X model are described in Appendix C.

Meanwhile, to add further complications, a newer object-oriented development methodology called the **Unified Modeling Language (UML)** adopted the E-R model but introduced its own symbols while putting an object-oriented programming spin on it. UML notation is summarized in Appendix C.

> **BY THE WAY**    In addition to differences due to different versions of the E-R model, there are differences due to software products. For example, two products that both implement the IE Crow's Foot model may do so in different ways. The result is a mess. When creating a data model diagram, you need to know not just the version of the E-R model you are using but also the idiosyncrasies of the data modeling product you use.

## E-R Diagrams Using the IE Crow's Foot Model

Figure 5-7 shows two versions of a one-to-many, optional-to-mandatory relationship. Figure 5-7(a) shows the original E-R model version. Figure 5-7(b) shows the crow's foot model using common crow's foot symbols. Notice that the relationship is drawn as a dashed line. The reason for this will be explained later in this chapter. For now, notice the **crow's foot symbol** used to show the many side of the relationship.

The crow's foot model uses the notation shown in Figure 5-8 to indicate the relationship cardinality. The symbol closest to the entity shows the maximum cardinality, and the other symbol shows the minimum cardinality. A hash mark indicates one (and therefore

**FIGURE 5-7**

Two Versions of a 1:N O-M Relationship

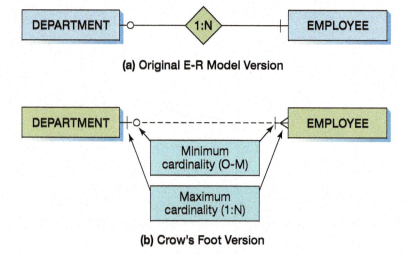

(a) Original E-R Model Version

(b) Crow's Foot Version

---

[4] *Integrated Definition for Information Modeling (IDEF1X)*, Federal Information Processing Standards Publication 184, 1993.

**FIGURE 5-8**

Crow's Foot Notation

| Symbol | Meaning | Numeric Meaning |
|---|---|---|
| ⊢⊢ | Mandatory—One | Exactly one |
| ⊢< | Mandatory—Many | One or more |
| ○⊣ | Optional—One | Zero or one |
| ○< | Optional—Many | Zero or more |

also mandatory), a circle indicates zero (and thus optional), and the crow's foot symbol indicates many. Note that, as indicated in Figure 5-8, we can read the symbols in either purely numeric ("exactly one") or seminumeric ("Mandatory-One") terms, and which reading is used is a matter of preference.

Thus, the diagram in Figure 5-7(b) means that a DEPARTMENT has one or more EMPLOYEEs (the symbol shows many and mandatory), and an EMPLOYEE belongs to zero or one DEPARTMENTs (the symbol shows one and optional).

A 1:1 relationship would be drawn in a similar manner, but the line connecting to each entity should be similar to the connection shown for the one side of the 1:N relationship in Figure 5-7(b).

Figure 5-9 shows two versions of an N:M, optional-to-mandatory relationship. Modeling N:M relationships presents some complications. According to the original E-R model diagram shown in Figure 5-9(a), an EMPLOYEE must have at least one SKILL and may have several. At the same time, although a SKILL may or may not be held by any EMPLOYEE, a SKILL may also be held by several EMPLOYEEs. The crow's foot version in Figure 5-9(b) shows the N:M maximum cardinalities using the notation in Figure 5-8. The crow's foot symbols also indicate the minimum cardinalities for the N:M relationship.

Except for our discussions of alternate modeling symbologies in Appendices C (IDEF1X and UML) and G (the Semantic Object Model), we will use the IE Crow's Foot model for E-R diagrams for the rest of this text. There are no completely standard symbols for the crow's foot notation, and we explain our symbols and notation when we first use them. You can obtain various modeling products that will produce crow's foot models, and they are easily

**FIGURE 5-9**

Two Versions of a N:M O-M
Relationship

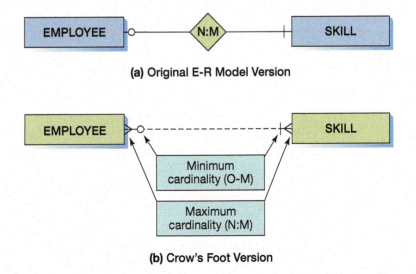

(a) Original E-R Model Version

(b) Crow's Foot Version

understood and related to the original E-R model. Be aware that those other products may use the oval, hash mark, crow's foot, and other symbols in slightly different ways. Further, your instructor may have a favorite modeling tool for you to use. If that tool does not support crow's feet, you will have to adapt the data models in this text to your tool.

> **BY THE WAY**  A number of modeling products are available, and each will have its own idiosyncrasies. Erwin produces erwin Data Modeler, a commercial data modeling product that handles both data modeling and database design tasks. You can use erwin Data Modeler to produce either crow's foot or IDEF1X data models.
>
> You can also try ER-Assistant, which is free and downloadable from Software Informer.
>
> Microsoft Visio 2019 is also a possibility. A trial version is available from the Microsoft Web site. See Appendix E for a full discussion of using Microsoft Visio 2019 for data models.
>
> Finally, Oracle is continuing development of the MySQL Workbench, as described in this book in Chapters 2 and 10C, and a free version is available at the MySQL development Web site. (If you are using a Microsoft operating system, you should install the MySQL Workbench by downloading and running the MySQL Installer for Windows). Although it is better at database designs than data models, it is a very useful tool, and the database designs it produces can be used with any DBMS, not just MySQL. See Appendix D for a full discussion of using MySQL Workbench for database designs.

## Strong Entities and Weak Entities

A **strong entity** is an entity that represents something that can exist on its own. For example, PERSON is a strong entity—we consider people to exist as individuals in their own right. Similarly, AUTOMOBILE is a strong entity. In addition to strong entities, the original version of the E-R model included the concept of a **weak entity**, which is defined as any entity whose existence depends on the presence of another entity.

## ID-Dependent Entities

The E-R model includes a special type of weak entity called an **ID-dependent entity**. An ID-dependent entity is an entity whose identifier includes the identifier of another entity. Consider, for example, an entity for a student apartment in a building, as shown in Figure 5-10(a).

The identifier of such an entity is a composite (BuildingName, ApartmentNumber), where BuildingName is the identifier of the entity BUILDING. ApartmentNumber by itself is insufficient to tell someone where you live. If you say you live in apartment number 5, they must ask you, "In what building?" Therefore, APARTMENT is ID-dependent on BUILDING.

Figure 5-10 shows three different ID-dependent entities. In addition to APARTMENT (which is ID-dependent on BUILDING), the entity PRINT in Figure 5-10(b) is ID-dependent on PAINTING, and the entity EXAM in Figure 5-10(c) is ID-dependent on PATIENT.

In each of these cases, the ID-dependent entity cannot exist unless the parent (the entity on which it depends) also exists. Thus, the minimum cardinality from the ID-dependent entity to the parent is always one.

However, whether the parent is required to have an ID-dependent entity depends on the application requirements. In Figure 5-10, both APARTMENT and PRINT are optional, but EXAM is required. These restrictions arise from the nature of the application and not from any logical requirement.

As shown in Figure 5-10, in our E-R models we use an entity with rounded corners to represent the ID-dependent entity. We also use a solid line to represent the relationship between the ID-dependent entity and its parent. This type of relationship is called an **identifying relationship**. A relationship drawn with a dashed line (refer to Figure 5-7) is used between strong entities and is called a **nonidentifying relationship** because there are no ID-dependent entities in the relationship (ID-dependent entities may participate in

**FIGURE 5-10**

Example ID-Dependent
Entities

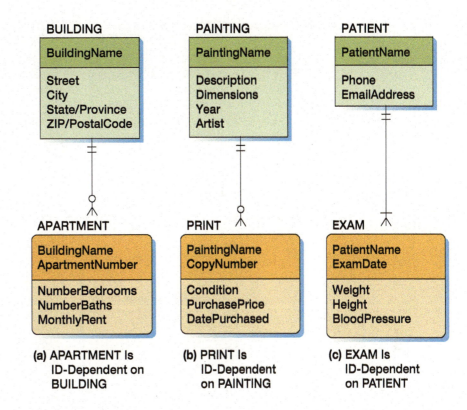

(a) APARTMENT Is
    ID-Dependent on
    BUILDING

(b) PRINT Is
    ID-Dependent
    on PAINTING

(c) EXAM Is
    ID-Dependent
    on PATIENT

other, nonidentifying relationships in addition to their identifying relationships—Figure 5-33 shows an example).

ID-dependent entities pose restrictions on the processing of the database that is constructed from them. Namely, the row that represents the parent entity must be created before any ID-dependent child row can be created. Further, when a parent row is deleted, all child rows must be deleted as well.

ID-dependent entities are common. Another example is the entity VERSION in the relationship between PRODUCT and VERSION, where PRODUCT is a software product and VERSION is a release of that software product. The identifier of PRODUCT is ProductName, and the identifier of VERSION is (ProductName, ReleaseNumber). Yet another example is EDITION in the relationship between TEXTBOOK and EDITION. The identifier of TEXTBOOK is Title, and the identifier of EDITION is (Title, EditionNumber).

---

**BY THE WAY**    The *parent entity* of a *child ID-dependent entity* is sometimes referred to as an **owner entity**. For example, a BUILDING is the *owner* of the APARTMENTs within it.

---

## Non-ID-Dependent Weak Entities

All ID-dependent entities are weak entities. But according to the original E-R model, some entities that are weak are not ID-dependent. Consider the AUTO_MODEL and VEHICLE entity classes in the database of a car manufacturer, such as Ford or Honda, as shown in Figure 5-11.

In Figure 5-11(a), each VEHICLE is assigned a sequential number as it is manufactured. So, for the manufacturer's "Super SUV" AUTO_MODEL, the first VEHICLE manufactured gets a ManufacturingSeqNumber of 1, the next gets a ManufacturingSeqNumber of 2, and so on. This is clearly an ID-dependent relationship because ManufacturingSeqNumber is based on the Manufacturer and Model.

Now let's assign VEHICLE an identifier that is independent of the Manufacturer and Model. We will use a VIN (vehicle identification number), as shown in Figure 5-11(b). Now

FIGURE 5-11

Example of a Non-ID-
Dependent Weak Entity

(a) ID-Dependent Entity     (b) Non-ID-Dependent
                                    Weak Entity

the VEHICLE has a unique identifier of its own and does not need to be identified by its relation to AUTO_MODEL.

This is an interesting situation. VEHICLE has an identity of its own and therefore is not ID-dependent. Yet the VEHICLE is an AUTO_MODEL, and if that particular AUTO_MODEL did not exist, the VEHICLE itself would never have existed. Therefore, VEHICLE is now a *weak but non-ID-dependent entity*.

Consider *your* car—let's say it is a Ford Mustang just for the sake of this discussion. Your individual Mustang is a VEHICLE, and it exists as a physical object and is identified by the VIN that is required for each licensed automobile. It is *not* ID-dependent on AUTO_MODEL, which in this case is Ford Mustang, for its identity. However, if the Ford Mustang had never been created as an AUTO_MODEL—a logical concept that was first designed on paper—your car would never have been built because *no* Ford Mustangs would ever have been built! Therefore, your physical individual VEHICLE would not exist without a logical AUTO_MODEL of Ford Mustang, and in a data model (which *is* what we're talking about), a VEHICLE cannot exist without a related AUTO_MODEL. This makes VEHICLE a weak but non-ID-dependent entity. Most data modeling tools cannot model non-ID-dependent weak entities. So, to indicate such situations, we will use a non-identifying relationship with a note added to the data model indicating that the entity is weak, as shown in Figure 5-11(b). In addition, in this text, we will use an orange color for all weak entities, whether ID-dependent or not.

## The Ambiguity of the Weak Entity

Unfortunately, an ambiguity is hidden in the definition of a *weak entity*, and this ambiguity is interpreted differently by different database designers (as well as different textbook authors). The ambiguity is that in a strict sense, if a weak entity is defined as any entity whose presence

**FIGURE 5-12**

Summary of ID-Dependent
and Non-ID-Dependent
Weak Entities

| Weak Entity Summary |
|---|
| A weak entity is an entity whose existence depends on another entity. |
| An ID-dependent entity is a weak entity whose identifier includes the identifier of another entity. |
| Identifying relationships are used to represent ID-dependent entities. |
| Some entities are weak but not ID-dependent. Using data modeling tools, they are shown with nonidentifying relationships, with separate documentation indicating they are weak. |

in the database depends on another entity, then any entity that participates in a relationship with a minimum cardinality of one to a second entity is a weak entity. Thus, in an academic database, if a STUDENT must have an ADVISER, then STUDENT is a weak entity because a STUDENT entity cannot be stored without an ADVISER.

This interpretation seems too broad to some people. A STUDENT is not physically dependent on an ADVISER (unlike an APARTMENT to a BUILDING), and a STUDENT is not logically dependent on an ADVISER (despite how it might appear to either the student or the adviser), and, therefore, STUDENT should be considered a strong entity.

To avoid such situations, some people interpret the definition of weak entity more narrowly. They say that to be a weak entity, an entity must logically depend on another entity. According to this definition, APARTMENT is a weak entity, but STUDENT is not. An APARTMENT cannot exist without a BUILDING in which it is located. However, a STUDENT can logically exist without an ADVISER, even if a business rule requires it.

We agree with the latter approach. Characteristics of ID-dependent and non-ID-dependent weak entities, as used in this book, are summarized in Figure 5-12.

## Subtype Entities

The extended E-R model introduced the concept of *subtypes*. A **subtype** entity is a special case of another entity called its **supertype**. Students, for example, may be classified as undergraduate or graduate students. In this case, STUDENT is the supertype, and UNDER-GRADUATE and GRADUATE are the subtypes.

Alternatively, a student could be classified as a freshman, sophomore, junior, or senior. In that case, STUDENT is the supertype, and FRESHMAN, SOPHOMORE, JUNIOR, and SENIOR are the subtypes.

As illustrated in Figure 5-13, in our E-R models we use a circle with a line under it as a subtype symbol to indicate a supertype–subtype relationship. Think of this as a symbol for an optional (the circle), 1:1 (the line) relationship. In addition, we use a solid line and rounded corners to represent an ID-dependent subtype entity because each subtype is ID-dependent on the supertype. Also note that none of the line end symbols shown in Figure 5-8 are used on the connecting lines.

In some cases, an attribute of the supertype indicates which of the subtypes is appropriate for a given instance. An attribute that determines which subtype is appropriate is called a **discriminator**. In Figure 5-13(a), the attribute named isGradStudent (which has only the values Yes and No) is the discriminator. In our E-R diagrams, the discriminator is shown next to the subtype symbol, as illustrated in Figure 5-13(a). Not all supertypes have a discriminator. Where a supertype does not have a discriminator, application code must be written to determine which subtype an entity belongs to.

Subtypes can be exclusive or inclusive (also referred to as *disjoint* and *overlapping*, respectively). With **exclusive subtypes**, a supertype instance is related to, at most, one subtype. With **inclusive subtypes**, a supertype instance can relate to one or more subtypes.

FIGURE 5-13

Examples of Subtype
Entities

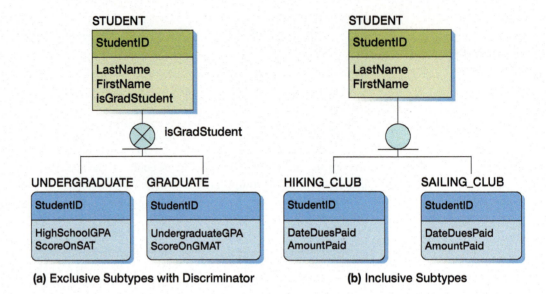

(a) Exclusive Subtypes with Discriminator          (b) Inclusive Subtypes

In Figure 5-13(a), the X in the circle means that the UNDERGRADUATE and GRADU-ATE subtypes are exclusive. Thus, a STUDENT can be either an UNDERGRADUATE or a GRADUATE but not both. Figure 5-13(b) shows that a STUDENT can join either the HIK-ING_CLUB or the SAILING_CLUB or both. These subtypes are inclusive (note there is no X in the circle). Because a supertype may relate to more than one subtype, inclusive subtypes do not have a discriminator.

Some models include another dimension to subtypes, called the *total* or *partial* distinction. For example, in Figure 5-13(b), can there be students who are in *neither* club? If so, the subtype/supertype relationship is **partial**—if not, it is **total**. To indicate a total requirement, we would put a hash mark on the relationship line just below the supertype entity to indicate that the supertype entity itself, and thus at least one of the subtypes, is mandatory in the relationship.

The most important (some would say the only) reason for creating subtypes in a data model is to avoid value-inappropriate nulls. Undergraduate students take the SAT exam and report that score, whereas graduate students take the GMAT and report their score on that exam. Thus, the SAT score would be NULL in all STUDENT entities for graduates, and the GMAT score would be NULL for all undergraduates. Such null values can be avoided by creating subtypes. Another reason for creating subtypes is that in some databases one subtype may participate in relationships that another subtype does not participate it.

> **BY THE WAY** The relationship that connects a supertype and a subtype is called an **IS-A relationship** because a subtype is the same entity as the supertype. Because this is so, the identifier of a supertype and all its subtypes must be the same; they all represent different aspects of the same entity. Contrast this with HAS-A relationships, in which an entity has a relationship to another entity but the identifiers of the two entities are different.

The elements of the entity-relationship model and their IE Crow's Foot representation are summarized in Figure 5-14. The identifier and attributes are shown only in the first example. Note that for 1:1 and 1:N nonidentifying relationships, a relationship to a parent entity may be optional. For identifying relationships, the parent is always required.

| | |
|---|---|
| **DEPARTMENT**<br>DepartmentName<br>BudgetCode<br>OfficeNumber | DEPARTMENT entity; DepartmentName is identifier; BudgetCode and OfficeNumber are attributes. |
| A                    B | 1:1, nonidentifying relationship. A relates to zero or one B; B relates to exactly one A. Identifier and attributes not shown. |
| A                    B | 1:N, nonidentifying relationship. A relates to one or many Bs; B relates to zero or one A. Identifier and attributes not shown. |
| A                    B | Many-to-many, nonidentifying relationship. A relates to zero or more Bs; B relates to one or more As. Identifier and attributes not shown. |
| A                    B | 1:N identifying relationship. A relates to zero, one, or many Bs. B relates to exactly one A. Identifier and attributes not shown. For identifying relationships, the child must always relate to exactly one parent. The parent may relate to any combination of minimum and maximum cardinalities. |
| A<br><br>C        D | A is supertype, C and D are exclusive subtypes. An entity may be a C or a D but not both. Discriminator not shown. Identifier and attributes not shown. |
| A<br><br>C        D | A is supertype, C and D are inclusive subtypes. An entity may be a C or a D or both. Identifier and attributes not shown. |

**FIGURE 5-14**

IE Crow's Foot Symbol
Summary

## Patterns in Forms, Reports, and E-R Models

A data model is a representation of how users view their world. Unfortunately, you cannot walk up to most computer users and ask questions like "What is the maximum cardinality between the EMPLOYEE and SKILL entities?" Few users would have any idea of what you mean. Instead, you must infer the data model indirectly from user documents and from users' conversations and behavior.

One of the best ways to infer a data model is to study the users' forms and reports. From such documents, you can learn about entities and their relationships. In fact, the structure of forms and reports determines the structure of the data model, and the structure of the data model determines the structure of forms and reports. This means that you can examine a form or report and determine the entities and relationships that underlie it.

You can also use forms and reports to validate the data model. Rather than showing the data model to the users for feedback, an alternative is to construct a form or report that reflects the structure of the data model and obtain user feedback on that form or report. For example, if you want to know if an ORDER has one or many SALESPERSONs, you can show the users a form that has a space for entering just one salesperson's name. If the user asks, "Where do I put the name of the second salesperson?" then you know that orders have at least two and possibly many salespeople. Sometimes, when no appropriate form or report exists, teams create a prototype form or report for the users to evaluate.

All of this means that you must understand how the structure of forms and reports determines the structure of the data model and the reverse. Fortunately, many forms and reports fall into common patterns. If you learn how to analyze these patterns, you will be well on your way to understanding the logical relationship between forms and reports and the data model. Accordingly, in the next sections, we will discuss the most common patterns in detail.

### Strong Entity Relationship Patterns

Three basic relationship types are possible between two strong entities: 1:1, 1:N, and N:M. When modeling such relationships, you must determine both the maximum and minimum cardinalities. The maximum cardinality often can be determined from forms and reports. In most cases, to determine the minimum cardinality, you will have to ask the users.

#### 1:1 Strong Entity Relationships

Figure 5-15 shows a data entry form and a report that indicate a one-to-one relationship between the entities CLUB_MEMBER and LOCKER. The Club Member Locker form in Figure 5-15(a) shows data for an athletic club member, and it lists just one locker for that member. This form indicates that a club member has, at most, one locker. The report in Figure 5-15(b) shows the lockers in the club and indicates the member who has been allocated that locker. Each locker is assigned to one club member.

The form and report in Figure 5-15 thus suggest that a CLUB_MEMBER has one LOCKER and a LOCKER is assigned to one CLUB_MEMBER. Hence, the relationship between them is 1:1. To model that relationship, we draw a nonidentifying relationship (meaning neither entity is ID-dependent) between the two entities, as shown in Figure 5-16.

**FIGURE 5-15**

Form and Report Indicating a 1:1 Relationship

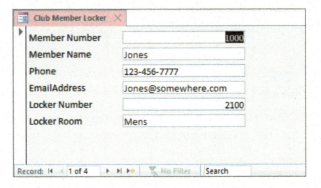

(a) Club Membership Data Entry Form

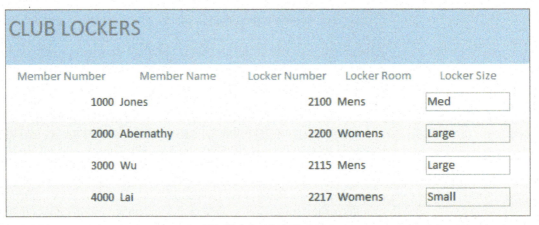

(b) Club Locker Report

FIGURE 5-16

Data Model for the 1:1
Relationship in Figure 5-15

We then set the maximum cardinality to 1:1. You can tell that this is a nonidentifying relationship because the relationship line is dashed. Also, the absence of a crow's foot indicates that the relationship is 1:1.

Regarding minimum cardinality, every club member shown in the form has a locker, and every locker shown in the report is assigned to a club member, so it appears that the relationship is mandatory to mandatory. However, this form and report are just instances; they may not show every possibility. If the club allows social, nonathletic memberships, then not every club member will have a locker. Furthermore, it is unlikely that every locker is occupied; there are likely some lockers that are unused and nonallocated. Accordingly, Figure 5-16 shows this relationship as optional to optional, as indicated by the small circles on the relationship lines.

---

**BY THE WAY**    How do you recognize strong entities? You can use two major tests. First, does the entity have an identifier of its own? If it shares a part of its identifier with another entity, then it is an ID-dependent entity and is therefore weak. Second, does the entity seem to be logically different from and separate from the other entities? Does it stand alone, or is it part of something else? In this case, a CLUB_MEMBER and a LOCKER are two very different, separate things; they are not part of each other or of something else. Hence, they are strong.

Note also that a form or report shows only one side of a relationship. Given entities A and B, a form can show the relationship from A to B, but it cannot show the relationship from B to A at the same time. To learn the cardinality from B to A, you must examine a second form or report, ask the users, or take some other action.

Finally, it is seldom possible to infer minimum cardinality from a form or report. Generally, you must ask the users.

---

### 1:N Strong Entity Relationships

Figure 5-17 shows a form and report that list the uniforms issued to the club members. A club member may have many uniforms, so the maximum cardinality from CLUB_MEMBER to CLUB_UNIFORM is N (or alternatively we will actually use the notation M if the relationship turns out to be many-to-many). But what about the opposite direction? To determine if a uniform relates to one or many (which we will then notate as N in the N:M relationship) club members, we need to examine a form or report that shows the relationship from a uniform to a club member. Alternatively, we can talk to the people at the club who manage the uniforms. We cannot ignore the issue because we need to know whether the relationship is 1:N or N:M.

In such a case, we must ask the users or at least make a determination by thinking about the nature of the business setting. Can a uniform be shared by more than one club member at one time? Because team uniforms have numbers on them to identify the team members, and because this number is generally issued for an entire season (think about your favorite baseball, basketball, or football team), this seems unlikely. Therefore, we can reasonably

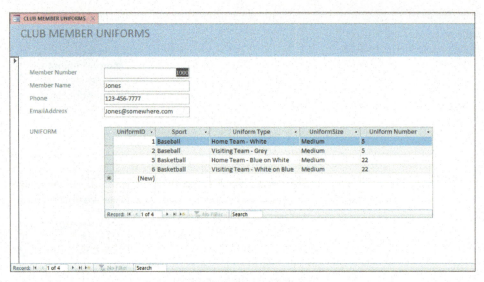

**(a) CLUB MEMBER UNIFORM Form**

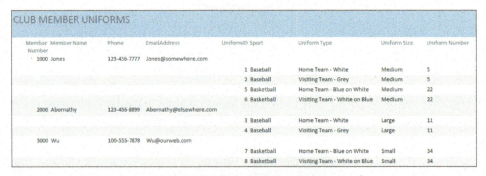

**(b) CLUB MEMBER UNIFORM Report**

assume that a CLUB_UNIFORM relates to just one CLUB_MEMBER. Thus, we conclude the relationship is 1:N. Figure 5-18 shows the resulting data model. Note that the many side of the relationship is indicated by the crow's foot next to CLUB_UNIFORM.

Considering minimum cardinality, it seems reasonable that a CLUB_MEMBER may not be on a team and, therefore, is not required to have a uniform. Similarly, it seems reasonable that some uniforms may not be issued during a particular season. We will definitely need to confirm this by asking the users. Figure 5-18 depicts the situation in which a CLUB_MEM-BER does not need to have a CLUB_UNIFORM and where a CLUB_UNIFORM does not have to be issued to a CLUB_MEMBER.

### N:M Strong Entity Relationships

Figure 5-19(a) shows a form with data about a supplier and the parts it is prepared to supply. Figure 5-19(b) shows a report that summarizes parts and lists the companies that can supply those parts. In both cases, the relationship is many: a COMPANY supplies many PARTs, and a PART is supplied by many COMPANYs. Thus, the relationship is N:M.

Figure 5-20 shows a data model that shows this relationship. A supplier is a company, so we show the supplier entity as a COMPANY.

Because not all companies are suppliers, the relationship from COMPANY to PART must be optional. However, every part must be supplied from somewhere, so the relationship from PART to COMPANY is mandatory.

In summary, the three types of strong entity relationships are 1:1, 1:N, and N:M. You can infer the maximum cardinality in one direction from a form or report. You must examine a second form or report to determine the maximum cardinality in the other direction. If no form or report that shows the relationship is available, you must ask the users. Generally, it is not possible to determine minimum cardinality from forms and reports.

**FIGURE 5-19**

**Form and Report Indicating an N:M Relationship**

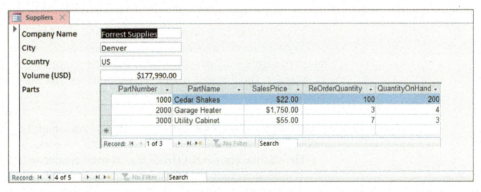

(a) Suppliers Form

| Part Number | Part Name | Sales Price | ROQ | QOH | Company Name | City | Country |
|---|---|---|---|---|---|---|---|
| **PART** | | | | | | | |
| 1000 | Cedar Shakes | $22.00 | 100 | 200 | | | |
| | | | | | Bristol Systems | Manchester | England |
| | | | | | ERS Systems | Vancouver | Canada |
| | | | | | Forrest Supplies | Denver | US |
| 2000 | Garage Heater | $1,750.00 | 3 | 4 | | | |
| | | | | | Bristol Systems | Manchester | England |
| | | | | | ERS Systems | Vancouver | Canada |
| | | | | | Forrest Supplies | Denver | US |
| | | | | | Kyoto Importers | Kyoto | Japan |
| 3000 | Utility Cabinet | $55.00 | 7 | 3 | | | |
| | | | | | Ajax Manufacturing | Sydney | Australia |
| | | | | | Forrest Supplies | Denver | US |

(b) Part Report

**FIGURE 5-20**

Data Model for the N:M
Relationship in Figure 5-19

## ID-Dependent Relationship Patterns

Three principal patterns use ID-dependent entities: multivalued attribute, archetype/instance (also called *version/instance*), and association. Because the association pattern is often confused with the N:M strong entity relationships just discussed, we will look at that pattern first.

### The Association Pattern and the Associative Entity

An **association pattern** is subtly and confusingly similar to an N:M strong relationship. To see why, examine the report in Figure 5-21 and compare it with the report in Figure 5-19(b).

What is the difference? If you look closely, you'll see that the only difference is that the report in Figure 5-21 contains Price, which is the price quotation for a part from a particular supplier. The first line of this report indicates that the part Cedar Shakes is supplied by Bristol Systems for $14.00.

Price is neither an attribute of COMPANY nor an attribute of PART. It is an attribute of the combination of a COMPANY with a PART. Figure 5-22 shows the appropriate data model for such a case.

Here a third entity, QUOTATION, has been created to hold the Price attribute. This entity, which links the other two entities in the data model, is called an **associative entity** (or **association entity**). The identifier of QUOTATION is the combination of PartNumber and CompanyName. Note that PartNumber is the identifier of PART and CompanyName is the identifier of COMPANY. Hence, QUOTATION is ID-dependent on *both* PART and COMPANY.

**FIGURE 5-21**

Report Indicating an
Association Pattern

### PART QUOTATIONS

| PartNumber | PartName | SalesPrice | ROQ | QOH | CompanyName | City | Country | Price |
|---|---|---|---|---|---|---|---|---|
| 1000 | Cedar Shakes | $22.00 | 100 | 200 | | | | |
| | | | | | Bristol Systems | Manchester | England | $14.00 |
| | | | | | ERS Systems | Vancouver | Canada | $12.50 |
| | | | | | Forrest Supplies | Denver | US | $15.50 |
| 2000 | Garage Heater | $1,750.00 | 3 | 4 | | | | |
| | | | | | Bristol Systems | Manchester | England | $950.00 |
| | | | | | ERS Systems | Vancouver | Canada | $875.00 |
| | | | | | Forrest Supplies | Denver | US | $915.00 |
| | | | | | Kyoto Importers | Kyoto | Japan | $1,100.00 |
| 3000 | Utility Cabinet | $55.00 | 7 | 3 | | | | |
| | | | | | Ajax Manufacturing | Sydney | Australia | $37.50 |
| | | | | | Forrest Supplies | Denver | US | $42.50 |

FIGURE 5-22

Association Pattern Data
Model for the Report in
Figure 5-21

In Figure 5-22, then, the relationships between PART and QUOTATION and between COMPANY and QUOTATION are both identifying. This fact is shown in Figure 5-22 by the solid, nondashed lines that represent these relationships.

As with all identifying relationships, the parent entities are required. Thus, the minimum cardinality from QUOTATION to PART is one, and the minimum cardinality from QUOTATION to COMPANY also is one. The minimum cardinality in the opposite direction is determined by business requirements. Here a PART must have a QUOTATION, but a COMPANY need not have a QUOTATION.

> **BY THE WAY**  Consider the differences between the data models in Figure 5-20 and Figure 5-22. The only difference between the two is that in the latter the relationship between COMPANY and PART has an attribute, Price. Remember this example whenever you model an N:M relationship. Is there a missing attribute that pertains to the combination and not just to one of the entities? If so, you are dealing with an association, ID-dependent pattern and not an N:M, strong entity pattern.

Associations can occur among more than two entity types. Figure 5-23, for example, shows a data model for the assignment of a particular client to a particular architect for a particular project. The attribute of the assignment is HoursWorked. This data model shows how the ternary relationship in Figure 5-4(b) can be modeled as a combination of three binary relationships.

### The Multivalued Attribute Pattern

In the E-R model as used today,[5] attributes must have a single value. If the COMPANY entity has PhoneNumber and Contact attributes, then a company can have, at most, one value for phone number and, at most, one value for contact.

In practice, however, companies can have more than one phone number and one contact. Consider, for example, the data entry form in Figure 5-24. This particular company has three phone numbers; other companies might have one or two or four or whatever. We need to create a data model that allows companies to have multiple phones and placing the attribute PhoneNumber in COMPANY will not do it.

---

[5] The original E-R model allowed for multivalued attributes. Over time, that feature has been ignored, and today most people assume that the E-R model requires single-valued attributes. We will do so in this text.

**FIGURE 5-23**

Association Pattern Data
Model for the Ternary
Relationship in Figure 5-4

**FIGURE 5-24**

Data Entry Form with a
Multivalued Attribute

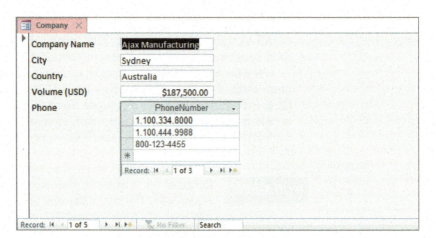

**FIGURE 5-25**

Data Model for the Form
with a Multivalued Attribute
in Figure 5-24

Figure 5-25 shows the solution. Instead of including PhoneNumber as an attribute of
COMPANY, we create an ID-dependent entity, PHONE, that contains the attribute
PhoneNumber. The relationship from COMPANY to PHONE is 1:N, so a company can have
multiple phone numbers. Because PHONE is an ID-dependent entity, its identifier includes
both CompanyName and PhoneNumber.

Company   ✕

| Company Name | Ajax Manufacturing |
|---|---|
| City | Sydney |
| Country | Australia |
| Volume (USD) | $187,500.00 |

Phone

| PhoneNumber ▾ |
|---|
| 1.100.334.8000 |
| 1.100.444.9988 |
| 800-123-4455 |
| * |

Record: I◀ ◀ 1 of 3 ▶ ▶I ▶✱

Contact

| Contact ▾ |
|---|
| Alfred |
| Jackson |
| Lynda |
| Swee |
| * |

Record: I◀ ◀ 1 of 4 ▶ ▶I ▶✱

Record: I◀ ◀ 1 of 5 ▶ ▶I ▶✱   No Filter   Search

We can extend this strategy for as many multivalued attributes as necessary. The COMPANY data entry form in Figure 5-26 has multivalued Phone and multivalued Contact attributes. In this case, we just create a separate ID-dependent entity for each multivalued attribute, as shown in Figure 5-27.

In Figure 5-27, PhoneNumber and Contact are independent. PhoneNumber is the phone number of the company and not necessarily the phone number of a contact. If PhoneNumber is not a general company phone number, but rather the phone number of a particular person at that company, then the data entry form would appear as in Figure 5-28. Here, for example, Alfred has one phone number and Jackson has another.

In this case, the attributes PhoneNumber and Contact belong together. Accordingly, we place them into a single ID-dependent entity, as shown in Figure 5-29. Notice that the identifier of PHONE_CONTACT is Contact and CompanyName. This arrangement means that a given Contact name can appear only once per company. Contacts can share phone numbers, however, as shown for employees Lynda and Swee. If the identifier of PHONE_CONTACT was PhoneNumber and CompanyName, then a phone number could occur only once per company, but contacts could have multiple numbers. Work through these examples to ensure that you understand them.

COMPANY

| CompanyName |
|---|
| City<br>Country<br>Volume |

PHONE

| CompanyName<br>PhoneNumber |
|---|
|  |

CONTACT

| CompanyName<br>Contact |
|---|
|  |

A similar change may occur to the YACHT entity. Although the manufacturer of a yacht may refer to it by specifying the hull number of a given design, the local tax authority may refer to it by State and LicenseNumber. If we change the identifier of YACHT from (HullNumber, DesignName) to (LicenseNumber, State), then YACHT is no longer ID-dependent; it becomes a weak, non-ID-dependent entity.

Similarly, although the home builder may think of a home as the third house constructed according to the Cape Codd design, everyone else will refer to it by its address. When we change the identifier of HOUSE from (HouseNumber, ModelName) to (Street, City, State, ZIP), then HOUSE becomes a weak, non-ID-dependent entity. All of these changes are shown in Figure 5-31.

---

**BY THE WAY**   Data modelers continue to debate the importance of weak, non-ID-dependent entities. Everyone agrees that they exist, but not everyone agrees that they are important.

First, understand that existence dependence influences the way we write database applications. For the CLASS/SECTION example in Figure 5-31, we must insert a new CLASS before we can add a SECTION for that class. Additionally, when we delete a CLASS, we must delete all of the SECTIONs for that CLASS. This is one reason that some data modelers believe that weak, non-ID-dependent entities are important.

Skeptics say that although weak, non-ID-dependent entities may exist, they are not necessary. They say that we can obtain the same result by calling SECTION strong and making CLASS required. Because CLASS is required, the application will need to insert a CLASS before a SECTION is created and delete dependent SECTIONs when deleting a CLASS. So, according to that viewpoint, there is no practical difference between a weak, non-ID-dependent entity and a strong entity with a required relationship.

Others disagree. Their argument goes something like this: The requirement that a SECTION must have a CLASS comes from a logical necessity. It has to be that way—it comes from the nature of reality. The requirement that a strong entity must have a relationship to another strong entity arises from a business rule. Initially, we say that an ORDER must have a CUSTOMER (both strong entities), and then the application requirements change and we say that we can have cash sales, meaning that an ORDER no longer has to have a CUSTOMER. Business rules frequently change, but logical necessity never changes. We need to model weak, non-ID-dependent entities so that we know the strength of the required parent rule.

And so it goes. You, with the assistance of your instructor, can make up your own mind. Is there a difference between a weak, non-ID-dependent entity and a strong entity with a required relationship? In Figure 5-31, should we call the entities SECTION, YACHT, and HOUSE strong as long as their relationships are required? We think not— we think there is a difference. Others think differently, however.

---

## Mixed Identifying and Nonidentifying Relationship Patterns

Some patterns involve both identifying and nonidentifying relationships. The classic example is the line-item pattern, but there are other instances of mixed patterns as well. We begin with line items.

### The Line-Item Pattern

Figure 5-32 shows a typical sales order, or invoice. Such forms usually have data about the order itself, such as the order number and order date, data about the customer, data about the salesperson, and then data about the items on the order. A data model for a typical sales order or invoice is shown in Figure 5-33.

In Figure 5-33, CUSTOMER, SALESPERSON, and SALES_ORDER are all strong entities, and they have the nonidentifying relationships you would expect. The relationship from CUSTOMER to SALES_ORDER is 1:N, and the relationship from SALESPERSON

**FIGURE 5-32**

Data Entry Form for a
Sales Order

to SALES_ORDER also is 1:N. According to this model, a SALES_ORDER must have a
CUSTOMER and may or may not have a SALESPERSON. All of this is readily understood.

The interesting relationships concern the line items on the order. Examine the data grid
in the form in Figure 5-32. Some of the data values belong to the order itself, but other data
values belong to items in general. In particular, Quantity and ExtendedPrice belong to the
SALES_ORDER, but ItemNumber, Description, and UnitPrice belong to ITEM. The lines on

**FIGURE 5-33**

Data Model for the Sales
Order in Figure 5-32

an order do not have their own identifier. No one ever says, "Give me the data for line 12." Instead, they say, "Give me the data for line 12 of order 12345." Hence, the identifier of a line is a composite of the identifier of a particular line and the identifier of a particular order. Thus, entries for line items are always ID-dependent on the order in which they appear. In Figure 5-33, ORDER_LINE_ITEM is ID-dependent on SALES_ORDER. The identifier of the ORDER_LINE_ITEM entity is (SalesOrderNumber, LineNumber).

Now, and this is the part that is sometimes confusing for some students, ORDER_LINE_ITEM is not existence dependent on ITEM. It can exist even if no item has yet been assigned to it. This is indicated in Figure 5-33 by the optional-one relationship symbol on ITEM—it allows the existence of a new record in ORDER_LINE_ITEM without the need to simultaneously specify the corresponding ITEM. (We will discuss this type of situation in detail in Chapter 6.) Further, if an ITEM is deleted, we do not want the line item to be deleted with it. The deletion of an ITEM may make the value of ItemNumber and other data invalid, but it should not cause the line item itself to disappear.

Now consider what happens to a line item when an order is deleted. Unlike with the deletion of an item, which only causes data items to become invalid, the deletion of the order removes the existence of the line item. Logically, a line item cannot exist if its order is deleted. Hence, line items are existence dependent on orders.

Work through each of the relationships in Figure 5-33 and ensure that you understand their type and their maximum and minimum cardinalities. Also understand the implications of this data model. For example, do you see why this sales order data model is unlikely to be used by a company in which salespeople are on commission?

## Other Mixed Relationship Patterns

Mixed identifying and nonidentifying relationships occur frequently. Learn to look for a mixed pattern when a strong entity has a multivalued composite group and when one of the elements in the composite group is an identifier of a second strong entity.

Consider, for example, baking recipes. Each recipe calls for a certain amount of a specific ingredient, such as flour, sugar, or butter. The ingredient list is a multivalued composite group, but one of the elements of that group, the name of the ingredient, is the identifier of a strong entity. As shown in Figure 5-34, the recipe and the ingredients are strong entities, but the amount and instructions for using each ingredient are ID-dependent on RECIPE.

Or consider employees' skill proficiencies. The name of the skill (which is currently not listed in EMPLOYEE_SKILL but will be added as a foreign key in the conversion to a database design in Chapter 6), the proficiency levels, and the courses taken by the employee are a multivalued group, but the skill itself is a strong entity, as shown in Figure 5-35. Dozens of other examples are possible.

**FIGURE 5-34**

Mixed Relationship Pattern for Baking Recipes

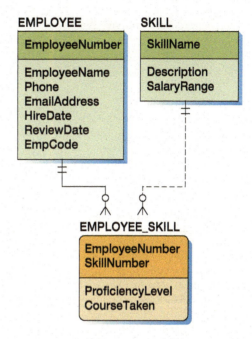

**FIGURE 5-35**

Mixed Relationship Pattern
for Employee Skills

Before continuing, compare the models in Figure 5-33, Figure 5-34, and 5-35 with the association pattern in Figure 5-22. Make sure that you understand the differences and why the model in Figure 5-22 has two identifying relationships and the models in Figure 5-33, Figure 5-34, and Figure 5-35 have just one.

### The For-Use-By Subtype Pattern

As stated earlier in this chapter, the major reason for using subtypes in a database design is to avoid value-inappropriate nulls. Some forms suggest the possibility of such nulls when they show blocks of data fields that are grayed out and labeled "For Use by *someone/something* Only." For example, Figure 5-36 shows two sections shaded in a darker color, one for commercial fishers and another for sport fishers. The presence of these shaded sections indicates the need for subtype entities.

The data model for this form is shown in Figure 5-37. Observe that each grayed-out section has a subtype. Notice that the subtypes differ not only in their attributes, but that one has a relationship that the other does not have. Sometimes the only differences between subtypes are differences in the relationships they have.

**FIGURE 5-36**

Data Entry Form Suggesting
the Need for Subtypes

| **Resident Fishing License**<br>2021 Season | | **License No:**<br>**03-1123432** |
|---|---|---|
| Name: | | |
| Street: | | |
| City: | State: | ZIP: |
| For Use by Commercial Fishers Only | For Use by Sport Fishers Only | |
| Vessel Number: | Number Years at<br>This Address: | |
| Vessel Name: | Prior Year License<br>Number: | |
| Vessel Type: | | |
| Tax ID: | | |

FIGURE 5-37

Data Model for Form in
Figure 5-36

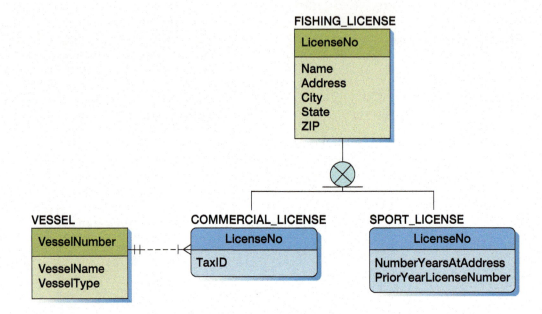

The nonidentifying relationship from VESSEL to COMMERCIAL_LICENSE is shown as 1:N, mandatory to mandatory. In fact, this form does not have sufficient data for us to conclude that the maximum cardinality from VESSEL to COMMERCIAL_LICENSE is N. This fact was determined by interviewing users and learning that one boat is sometimes used by more than one commercial fisher. The minimum cardinalities indicate a commercial fisher must have a vessel and that only vessels that are used for licenses are to be stored in this database.

The point of this example is to illustrate how forms often suggest the need for subtypes. Whenever you see a grayed-out or otherwise distinguished section of a form with the words "For use by . . . ," think "subtype."

## Recursive Relationship Patterns

A **recursive relationship**, also called a **unary relationship**, occurs when an entity type has a relationship to itself. The classic examples of recursive relationships occur in manufacturing applications, but there are many other examples as well. As with strong entities, three types of recursive relationships are possible: 1:1, 1:N, and N:M. Let's consider each.

### 1:1 Recursive Relationships

Suppose you are asked to construct a database for a railroad, and you need to make a model of a freight train. You know that one of the entities is BOXCAR, but how are BOXCARs related? To answer that question, envision a train, as shown in Figure 5-38. Except for the first boxcar, each has one boxcar in front, and, except for the last boxcar, each boxcar has one boxcar in back. Thus, the relationship is 1:1 between boxcars, with an optional relationship for the first and last cars.

> **BY THE WAY**   If you are a casual observer of trains, you may be thinking that a freight train of all boxcars is unrealistic—what about the refrigerator cars, flat cars, tank cars, and so on? However, as any railfan or trainspotter (the British term) knows, *unit trains* consisting of only one type of freight car are common. Examples are unit trains of *grain cars* carrying wheat, *hopper cars* carrying coal, *tank cars* carrying oil products, and *container cars* transporting the ubiquitous shipping containers.

Figure 5-39 shows a data model in which each BOXCAR has a 1:1 relationship to the BOXCAR behind. The BOXCAR entity at the head of the train has a 1:1 relationship to ENGINE. (This model assumes a train has just one engine. To model trains with multiple

**FIGURE 5-38**

Freight Train Relationships

First Boxcar
Relationship

Next Boxcar
Relationship

Next Boxcar
Relationship

engines, create a second recursive relationship among engines. Construct that relationship just like the boxcar behind relationship.)

Note that the 1:1 relationship between the ENGINE entity and the BOXCAR entity is optional-optional (O-O). This is because the BOXCAR entity represents *all* the BOXCARs in the train. Although the first BOXCAR *must be* connected directly to the ENGINE, the second BOXCAR is *not* connected to the engine. Therefore, the relationship from ENGINE to BOXCAR is optional because the ENGINE is directly connected to at most one BOXCAR, and the relationship from BOXCAR to ENGINE is optional because *each* BOXCAR does *not* have to be connected to the ENGINE (only one will be, and all the others will be connected to another BOXCAR).

Also note that several years ago we would have needed a CABOOSE entity to bring up the rear of the train. Today, railroads are permitted to use an *end-of-train marker light* on the last freight car, and there are few cabooses to be seen.

An alternative model is to use the relationship to represent the BOXCAR ahead. Either model works. Other examples of 1:1 recursive relationships are the succession of U.S. presidents, the succession of college deans, and the order of passengers on a waiting list.

### 1:N Recursive Relationships

The classic example of a 1:N recursive relationship occurs in organizational charts, in which an employee has a manager who may, in turn, manage several other employees. Figure 5-40 shows an example organizational chart. Note that the relationship between employees is 1:N.

Figure 5-41 shows a data model for the managerial relationship. The crow's foot indicates that a manager may manage more than one employee. The relationship is optional to optional because one manager (the president) has no manager and because some employees manage no one.

**FIGURE 5-39**

Data Model for a 1:1
Recursive Relationship

ENGINE

EngineNumber

Railroad
Type
EngineModel
HorsePower

First Boxcar

BOXCAR

BoxCarNumber

Railroad
BoxCarType
Capacity

Boxcar Behind

FIGURE 5-40

Organizational Chart
Relationships

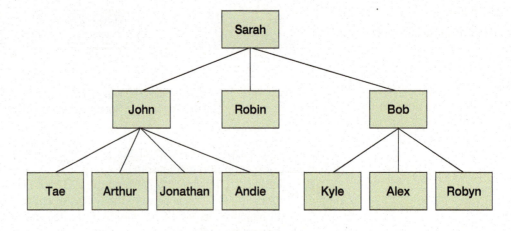

FIGURE 5-41

Data Model for the
Management Structure
in Figure 5-40 as a 1:N
Recursive Relationship

Another example of a 1:N recursive relationship concerns maps. For example, a world map has a relationship to many continent maps, each continent map has a relationship to many nation maps, and so forth. A third example concerns biological parents where the relationship from PERSON to PERSON is shown by tracing either mother or father (but not both).

### N:M Recursive Relationships

N:M recursive relationships occur frequently in manufacturing applications, where they are used to represent bills of materials. Figure 5-42 shows an example.

The key idea of a bill of materials is that one part is composed of other parts. A child's red wagon, for example, consists of a handle assembly, a body, and a wheel assembly, each of which is a part. The handle assembly, in turn, consists of a handle, a bolt, a washer, and a nut. The wheel assembly consists of wheels, axles, washers, and nuts. The relationship among the parts is N:M because a part can be made up of many parts and because a part (such as washers and nuts) can be used in many parts.

The data model for a bill of materials is shown in Figure 5-43. Notice that each part has an N:M relationship to other parts. Because a part need not have any component parts and because a part need not have any parts that contain it, the minimum cardinality is optional to optional.

---

**BY THE WAY**    What would happen to the data model if the diagram showed how many of each part are used? Suppose, for example, that the wheel assembly requires four washers and the handle assembly requires just one. The data model in Figure 5-43 will not be correct for this circumstance. In fact, adding Quantity to this N:M relationship is analogous to adding Price to the N:M relationship in Figure 5-22. See Exercise 5.63.

**FIGURE 5-42**

Bill of Materials

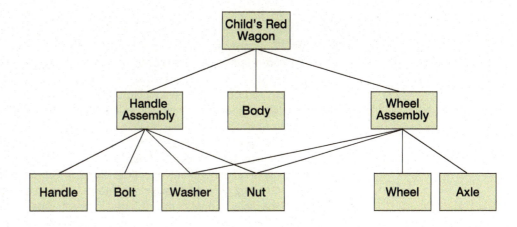

**FIGURE 5-43**

Data Model for the Bill of Materials in Figure 5-42 as an N:M Recursive Relationship

N:M recursive relationships can be used to model directed networks, such as the flow of documents through organizational departments or the flow of gas through a pipeline. They also can be used to model the succession of parents, in which mothers, fathers, and stepparents are included.

If recursive structures seem hard to comprehend, don't fret. They may seem strange at first, but they are not difficult. Work through some data examples to gain confidence. Make up a train and see how the model in Figure 5-39 applies, or change the example in Figure 5-40 from employees to departments and see how the model in Figure 5-41 needs to be adjusted. Once you have learned to identify recursive patterns, you'll find it easy to create models for them.

## The Data Modeling Process

During the data modeling process, the development team analyzes user requirements and constructs a data model from forms, reports, data sources, and user interviews. The process is always iterative; a model is constructed from one form or report and then supplemented and adjusted as more forms and reports are analyzed. Periodically, users are asked for additional information, such as that needed to assess minimum cardinality. Users also review and validate the data model. During that review, prototype databases evidencing data model constructs may need to be constructed to help users see how the database would work. (Microsoft Access 2019 is often used for this purpose.)

To give you an idea of the iterative nature of data modeling, we will consider the development of a simple data model for a university. As you read this example, strive to appreciate how the model evolves as more and more requirements are analyzed. For a more detailed version of this data modeling exercise, combined with an overview of the systems analysis and design process, see Appendix B.

> **BY THE WAY**  One of the authors worked on a large data model for the U.S. Army's logistical system. The model contained more than 500 different entity types, and it took a team of seven people more than a year to develop, document, and validate it. On some occasions, the analysis of a new requirement indicated that the model had been conceived incorrectly, and days of work had to be redone. The most difficult aspect of the project was managing complexity. Knowing which entities related to which; whether an entity had already been defined; and whether a new entity was strong, weak, a supertype, or a subtype required a global understanding of the model. Memory was of poor help because an entity created in July could be a subtype of an entity created hundreds of entities earlier in February. To manage the model, the team used many different administrative tools. Keep this example in mind as you read through the development of the Highline University data model.

Suppose the administration at a hypothetical university named Highline University wants to create a database to track colleges, departments, faculty, and students. To do this, a data modeling team has collected a series of reports as part of its requirements determination. In the next sections, we will analyze these reports to produce a data model.

## The College Report

Figure 5-44 shows an example report from Highline University about one college within the university, the College of Business. This example is one instance of this report; Highline University has similar reports about other colleges, such as the College of Engineering and the College of Social Sciences. The data modeling team needs to gather enough examples to form a representative sample of all the college reports. Here assume that the report in Figure 5-44 is representative.

Examining the report, we find data specific to the college—such as the name, dean, telephone number, and campus address—and also facts about each department within the college. These data suggest that the data model should have COLLEGE and DEPARTMENT entities with a relationship between them, as shown in Figure 5-45.

The relationship in Figure 5-45 is nonidentifying. This relationship is used because DEPARTMENT is not ID-dependent and, logically, a DEPARTMENT is independent of a COLLEGE. We cannot tell from the report in Figure 5-44 whether a department can belong to many colleges. To answer this question, we need to ask the users or look at other forms and reports.

Assume that we know from the users that a department belongs to just one college, and the relationship is thus 1:N from COLLEGE to DEPARTMENT. The report in Figure 5-44 does not show us the minimum cardinalities. Again, we must ask the users. Assume we learn from the users that a college must have at least one department and a department must be assigned to exactly one college.

**FIGURE 5-44**

Highline University Sample College Report

| College of Business Mary B. Jefferson, Dean | | | |
|---|---|---|---|
| Phone: 232-1187 | | Campus Address: Business Building, Room 100 | |
| Department | Chairperson | Phone | Total Majors |
| Accounting | Jackson, Seymour P. | 232-1841 | 318 |
| Finance | HeuTeng, Susan | 232-1414 | 211 |
| Info Systems | Brammer, Nathaniel D. | 236-0011 | 247 |
| Management | Tuttle, Christine A. | 236-9988 | 184 |
| Production | Barnes, Jack T. | 236-1184 | 212 |

**FIGURE 5-45**

Data Model for the College
Report in Figure 5-44

## The Department Report

The Department Report shown in Figure 5-46 contains departmental data along with a list of the professors who are assigned to that department. This report contains data concerning the department's campus address. Because these data do not appear in the DEPARTMENT entity in Figure 5-45, we need to add them, as shown in Figure 5-47. This is typical of the data modeling process. That is, entities and relationships are adjusted as additional forms, reports, and other requirements are analyzed. Figure 5-47(a) also adds the relationship between DEPARTMENT and PROFESSOR.

We initially model the DEPARTMENT to PROFESSOR relationship as an N:M relationship because a professor might have a joint appointment. The data modeling team must further investigate the requirements to determine whether joint appointments are allowed. If not, the relationship can be redefined as a nonidentifying 1:N, as shown in Figure 5-47(b).

Another possibility regarding the N:M relationship is that some attribute about the combination of a professor and a department is missing. If so, then an association pattern is more appropriate. At Highline, suppose the team finds a report that describes the title and employment terms for each professor in each department. Figure 5-47(c) shows an entity for such a report, named APPOINTMENT. As you would expect from the association pattern, APPOINTMENT is ID-dependent on both DEPARTMENT and PROFESSOR.

A chairperson is a professor, so another improvement on the model is to remove the Chairperson data from DEPARTMENT and replace it with a chairperson relationship. This has been done in Figure 5-47(d). In the Chairs/Chaired By relationship, a professor can be the chair of zero or one departments, and a department must have exactly one professor as chair.

With the Chairs/Chaired By relationship, the attribute Chairperson is no longer needed in DEPARTMENT, so it is removed. Normally, a chairperson has his or her office in the department office; if this is the case, Phone, Building, and Room in DEPARTMENT duplicate Phone, Building, and OfficeNumber in PROFESSOR. Consequently, it might be possible to remove Phone, Building, and Room from DEPARTMENT. However, a professor may have a different phone from the official department phone, and the professor may also have an office outside of the department's office. Because of this possibility, we will leave Phone, Building, and Room in DEPARTMENT.

**FIGURE 5-46**

Highline University Sample
Department Report

| Information Systems Department | | |
|---|---|---|
| **College of Business** | | |
| Chairperson: | Brammer, Nathaniel D | |
| Phone: | 236-0011 | |
| Campus Address: | Social Science Building, Room 213 | |

| Professor | Office | Phone |
|---|---|---|
| Jones, Paul D. | Social Science, 219 | 232-7713 |
| Parks, Mary B | Social Science, 308 | 232-5791 |
| Wu, Elizabeth | Social Science, 207 | 232-9112 |

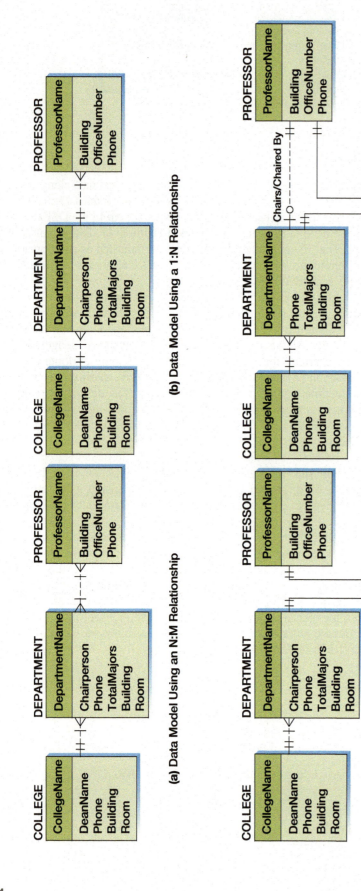

**(a) Data Model Using an N:M Relationship**

**(b) Data Model Using a 1:N Relationship**

**(c) Data Model Using an Association Pattern**

**(d) Data Model Using an Association Pattern and a 1:1 Relationship**

FIGURE 5-47

Alternate Data Models
for the DEPARTMENT-to-
PROFESSOR Relationship

**FIGURE 5-48**

Highline University Sample
Department Student Report

| Student Major List<br>Information Systems Department | | |
| --- | --- | --- |
| Chairperson:   Brammer, Nathaniel D     Phone:  236-0011 | | |
| Major's Name | Student Number | Phone |
| Jackson, Robin R. | 12345 | 237-8713 |
| Lincoln, Fred J. | 48127 | 237-8924 |
| Madison, Janice A. | 37512 | 237-9035 |

## The Department/Major Report

Figure 5-48 shows a report of a department and the students who major in that department. This report indicates the need for a new entity called STUDENT. Because students
are not ID-dependent on departments, the relationship between DEPARTMENT and
STUDENT is nonidentifying, as shown in Figure 5-49. We cannot determine the minimum cardinality from Figure 5-48, but we assume that interviews with users indicate that
a STUDENT must have a MAJOR but no MAJOR need have any students. Also, using the
contents of this report as a guide, attributes StudentNumber, StudentName, and Phone are
placed in STUDENT.

There are two subtleties in this interpretation of the report in Figure 5-48. First, observe
that Major's Name was changed to StudentName when the attribute was placed in STU-
DENT. This was done because StudentName is more generic. Major's Name has no meaning
outside the context of the Major relationship. Additionally, the report heading in Figure 5-48
has an ambiguity. Is the phone number for the department a value of DEPARTMENT.Phone
or a value of PROFESSOR.Phone? The team needs to investigate this further with the users.
Most likely, it is a value of DEPARTMENT.Phone.

## The Student Acceptance Letter

Figure 5-50 shows the acceptance letter that Highline sends to its incoming students. The
data items in this letter that need to be represented in the data model are shown in boldface.
In addition to data concerning the student, this letter contains data regarding the student's
major department as well as data about the student's adviser.

**FIGURE 5-49**

Data Model with **STUDENT**
Entity

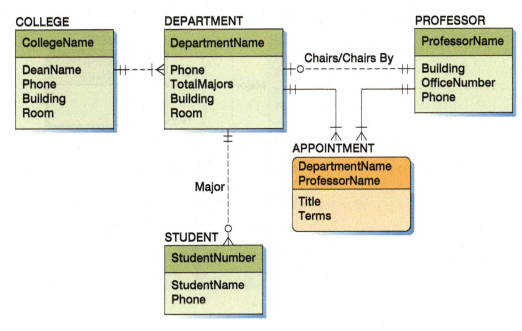

**5.61** Consider the three reports in Figure 5-59. The data are samples of data that would appear in the reports like these.

**A.** Make a list of as many potential entities as these reports suggest.

**B.** Examine your list to determine whether any entities are synonyms. If so, consolidate your list.

**C.** Construct an IE Crow's Foot model showing relationships among your entities. Name each relationship and specify cardinalities. Indicate which cardinalities you can justify on the basis of these reports and which you will need to check out with the users.

**FIGURE 5-59**
**Cereal Product Reports**

# KELLY'S

# RICE

# Cereal

### Nutrition Information

SERVING SIZE: 1 OZ. (28.4 g, ABOUT 1 CUP)
SERVINGS PER PACKAGE:                    13

| | CEREAL | WITH 1/2 CUP VITAMINS A & D SUM MILK |
|---|---|---|
| CALORIES | 110 | 150* |
| PROTEIN | 2 g | 6g |
| CARBOHYDRATE | 25 g | 31g |
| FAT | 0 g | 0g* |
| CHOLESTEROL | 0 mg | 0mg* |
| SODIUM | 290 mg | 350mg |
| POTASSIUM | 35 mg | 240mg |

#### PERCENTAGE OF U.S. RECOMMENDED DAILY ALLOWANCES (U.S. RDA)

| | | |
|---|---|---|
| PROTEIN | 2 | 10 |
| VITAMIN A | 25 | 30 |
| VITAMIN C | 25 | 25 |
| THIAMIN | 35 | 40 |
| RIBOFLAVIN | 35 | 45 |
| NIACIN | 35 | 35 |
| CALCIUM | ** | 15 |
| IRON | 10 | 10 |
| VITAMIN D | 10 | 25 |
| VITAMIN B$_6$ | 35 | 35 |
| FOLIC ACID | 35 | 35 |
| PHOSPHORUS | 4 | 15 |
| MAGNESIUM | 2 | 6 |
| ZINC | 2 | 6 |
| COPPER | 2 | 4 |

*WHOLE MILK SUPPLIES AN ADDITIONAL 30 CALORIES, 4 g FAT, AND 15 mg CHOLESTEROL
**CONTAINS LESS THAN 2% OF THE U.S. RDA OF THIS NUTRIENT

INGREDIENTS: RICE, SUGAR, SALT, CORN SYRUP

VITAMINS AND IRON: VITAMIN C (SODIUM ASCORBATE AND ASCORBIC ACID), NIACINAMIDE, IRON, VITAMIN B$_6$ (PYRIDOXINE HYDROCHLORIDE), VITAMIN A (PALMITATE), VITAMIN B$_2$ (RIBOFLAVIN), VITAMIN B$_1$ (THIAMIN HYDROCHLORIDE), FOLIC ACID, AND VITAMIN D.

**FDA REPORT #6272**
**Date:** June 30, 2020
**Issuer:** Kelly's Corporation
**Report Title: Product Summary by Ingredient**

| | |
|---|---|
| **Corn** | Kelly's Corn Cereal |
| | Kelly's Multigrain Cereal |
| | Kelly's Crunchy Cereal |
| **Corn syrup** | Kelly's Corn Cereal |
| | Kelly's Rice Cereal |
| | Kelly's Crunchy Cereal |
| **Malt** | Kelly's Corn Cereal |
| | Kelly's Crunchy Cereal |
| **Wheat** | Kelly's Multigrain Cereal |
| | Kelly's Crunchy Cereal |

**SUPPLIERS LIST**
**Date:** June 30, 2020

| Ingredient | Supplier | Price |
|---|---|---|
| Corn | Wilson | 2.80 |
| | J. Perkins | 2.72 |
| | Pollack | 2.83 |
| | McKay | 2.80 |
| Wheat | Adams | 1.19 |
| | Kroner | 1.19 |
| | Schmidt | 1.22 |
| Barley | Wilson | 0.85 |
| | Pollack | 0.84 |

**West Side Story**
Based on a conception of Jerome Robbins

Book by ARTHUR LAURENTS
Music by LEONARD BERNSTEIN
Lyrics by STEPHEN SONDHEIM

Entire Original Production Directed
and Choreographed by JEROME ROBBINS

Originally produced on Broadway by Robert E. Griffith and Harold S. Prince
by arrangement with Roger L. Stevens
Orchestration by Leonard Bernstein with Sid Ramin and Irwin Kostal

**HIGHLIGHTS FROM THE COMPLETE RECORDING**

Maria . . . . . . . . . . . . . . . . . KIRI TE KANAWA
Tony . . . . . . . . . . . . . . . JOSE CARRERAS
Anita . . . . . . . . . . . . . TATIANA TROYANOS
Riff . . . . . . . . . . . . . . . . . . . KURT OLLMAN
and MARILYN HORNE singing "Somewhere"

| | |
|---|---|
| Rosalia . . . . . . . . . Louise Edeiken | Diesel . . . . . . . . . . . . Marty Nelson |
| Consuela . . . . . . . . Stella Zambalis | Baby John . . . . . Stephen Bogardus |
| Fancisca . . . . . . . . Angelina Reaux | A-rab . . . . . . . . . . . . . . Peter Thom |
| Action . . . . . . . . . David Livingston | Snowboy . . . . . . . . . . . Todd Lester |
| Bernardo . . . . Richard Harrell | |

| # | Song | |
|---|---|---|
| 1 | Jet Song<br>(Riff, Action, Baby John, A-rab, Chorus) | [3'13] |
| 2 | Something's Coming<br>(Tony) | [2'33] |
| 3 | Maria<br>(Tony) | [2'56] |
| 4 | Tonight<br>(Maria, Tony) | [5'27] |
| 5 | America<br>(Anita, Rosalia, Chorus) | [4'47] |
| 6 | Cool<br>(Riff, Chorus) | [4'37] |
| 7 | One Hand, One Heart<br>(Tony, Maria) | [5'38] |
| 8 | Tonight (Ensemble)<br>(Entire Cast) | [3'40] |
| 9 | I Feel Pretty<br>(Maria, Chorus) | [3'22] |
| 10 | Somewhere<br>(A Girl) | [2'34] |
| 11 | Gee Officer Krupke<br>(Action, Snowboy, Diesel, A-rab, Baby John, Chorus) | [4'18] |
| 12 | A Boy Like That<br>(Anita, Maria) | [2'05] |
| 13 | I Have a Love<br>(Maria, Anita) | [3'30] |
| 14 | Taunting Scene<br>(Orchestra) | [1'21] |
| 15 | Finale<br>(Maria, Tony) | [2'40] |

**FIGURE 5-60**

CD Cover

**5.62** Before music downloading and streaming, there were compact diskettes (CDs)—silver plastic disks that came in plastic boxes with covers. Consider the CD cover in Figure 5-60.

    **A.** Specify identifiers and attributes for the entities CD, ARTIST, ROLE, and SONG.

    **B.** Construct a crow's foot model showing relationships among these four entities. Name each relationship and specify cardinalities. Indicate which cardinalities you can justify on the basis of the CD cover and which you will need to check out with the users.

    **C.** Consider a CD that does not involve a musical, so there is no need for ROLE. However, the entity SONG_WRITER is needed. Create a crow's foot model for CD, ARTIST, SONG, and SONG_WRITER. Assume that an ARTIST can either be a group or an individual. Assume that some artists record individually and as part of a group.

    **D.** Combine the models you developed in your answers to B and C. Create new entities if necessary but strive to keep your model as simple as possible. Specify identifiers and attributes of new entities, name new relationships, and indicate their cardinalities.

**5.63** Consider the data model in Figure 5-43. How should this model be altered if the users want to keep track of how many of each part are used? Suppose, for example, that the wheel assembly requires four washers and the handle assembly requires just one, and the database must store these quantities. (*Hint:* Adding Quantity to this N:M relationship is analogous to adding Price to the N:M relationship in Figure 5-22.)

**5.64** The data model in Figure 5-52 uses the attribute Room in COLLEGE and DEPARTMENT but uses OfficeNumber in PROFESSOR. These attributes have the same kind of data, even though they have different names. Examine Figure 5-46 and explain how this situation came to be. Do you think having different names for the same attribute types is rare? Do you think it is a problem? Why or why not?

# Case Questions

## Writer's Patrol Case Questions

Consider the Writer's Patrol traffic citation shown in Figure 5-61. The rounded corners on this form provide graphical hints about the boundaries of the entities represented.

**A.** Create the entities for an E-R data model based on the traffic citation form. Use five entities and use the data items on the form to specify identifiers and attributes for those entities. In which of these entities should you place the unique Notice Number that is the unique identifier for this notice?

**B.** Complete the E-R data model by specifying relationships among the entities. Use IE Crow's Foot E-R symbols as shown in Figure 5-8. Name the relationships and specify the relationship types and cardinalities. Justify the decisions you make regarding minimum and maximum cardinalities, indicating which cardinalities can be inferred from data on the form and which need to be checked out with systems users.

## Highline University Mentor Program Case Questions

Highline University is a four-year undergraduate school located in the Puget Sound region of Washington State. A discussion of the design of a college information system for Highline University appears in this chapter on pages 251–257 as an example of creating data models, and a variant of that discussion is used in Appendix B.

**FIGURE 5-61**

Writer's Patrol Traffic Citation

**WRITER'S PATROL CORRECTION NOTICE**

In this set of case questions, we will consider a different information system for Highline University, one that will be used by the Highline University Mentor Program. The Highline University Mentor Program recruits business professionals as mentors for Highline University students. The mentors are unpaid volunteers who work together with the students' advisers to ensure that the students in the mentoring program learn needed and relevant management skills. In this case study, you will develop a data model for the Mentor Program Information System.

Highline University, like many colleges and universities in the Pacific Northwest (see the Wikipedia article on *Pacific_Northwest*), is accredited by the Northwest Commission on Colleges and Universities (NWCCU–see the NWCCU Web site). Like all the colleges and universities accredited by the NWCCU, Highline University must be reaccredited at approximately five-year intervals. Additionally, the NWCCU requires annual status-update reports.

Highline University is made up of five colleges: the College of Business, the College of Social Sciences and Humanities, the College of Performing Arts, the College of Sciences and Technology, and the College of Environmental Sciences. Jan Smathers is the president of Highline University, and Dennis Endersby is the provost. (A provost is a vice president of academics; the deans of the colleges report to the provost.) Highline University is a fictional university and should not be confused with Highline Community College located in Des Moines, Washington. Any resemblance between Highline University and Highline Community College is unintentional and purely coincidental.

**A.** Draw an E-R data model for the Highline University Mentor Program Information System (MPIS). Use the IE Crow's Foot E-R model for your E-R diagrams. Justify the decisions you make regarding minimum and maximum cardinalities.

Your model should track students, advisers, and mentors. Additionally, Highline University needs to track alumni because the program administrators view alumni as potential mentors.

**1.** Create separate entities for students, alumni, faculty advisers, and mentors.

- At Highline University, all students are required to live on campus and are assigned Highline University ID numbers and email accounts in the format *FirstName.LastName@students.hu.edu*. The student entity should track student last name, student first name, student University ID number, student email address, dorm name, dorm room number, and dorm phone number.

- At Highline University, all faculty advisers have on-campus offices and are assigned Highline University ID numbers and email accounts in the format *FirstName.LastName@hu.edu*. The faculty entity should track faculty last name, faculty first name, faculty University ID number, faculty email address, department, office building name, office building room number, and office phone number.

- Highline University alumni live off campus and were previously assigned Highline University ID numbers. Alumni have private email accounts in the format *FirstName.LastName@somewhere.com*. The alumni entity should track alumnus last name, alumnus first name, alumnus former student number, email address, home address, home city, home state, home ZIP code, and phone number.

- Highline University mentors work for companies and use their company address, phone, and email address for contact information. They do not have Highline University ID numbers as mentors. Email addresses are in the format *FirstName.LastName@companyname.com*. The mentor entity should track mentor last name, mentor first name, mentor email address, company name, company address, company city, company state, company ZIP code, and company phone number.

**2.** Create relationships between entities based on the following facts:

- Each student is assigned one and only one faculty adviser and must have an adviser. One faculty member may advise several students, but faculty members are not required to advise students. Only the fact of this assignment is to be recorded in the data model, not possible related data (such as the date the adviser was assigned to the student).
- Each student may be assigned one and only one mentor, but students are not required to have a mentor. One mentor may mentor several students, and a person may be listed as a mentor before he or she is actually assigned students to mentor. Only the fact of this assignment is to be recorded in the data model, not possible related data (such as the date the mentor was assigned to the student).
- Each mentor is assigned to work and coordinate with one and only one faculty member, and each mentor must work with a faculty member. One faculty member may work with several mentors, but faculty members are not required to work with mentors. Only the fact of this assignment is to be recorded in the data model, not possible related data (such as the date the faculty member was assigned to the mentor).
- Each mentor may be an alumnus, but mentors are not required to be alumni. Alumni cannot, of course, be required to become mentors.

**B.** Revise the E-R data model you created in part A to create a new E-R data model based on the fact that students, faculty, alumni, and mentors are all a PERSON. Use the IE Crow's Foot E-R model for your E-R diagrams. Justify the decisions you make regarding minimum and maximum cardinalities. Note that:

- A person may be a current student, an alumnus, or both because Highline University does have alumni return for further study
- A person may be a faculty member or a mentor but not both
- A person may be a faculty member and an alumnus
- A person may be a mentor and an alumnus
- A current student cannot be a mentor
- Each mentor may be an alumnus, but mentors are not required to be alumni
- Alumni cannot, of course, be required to become mentors

*Hint:* If there are any constraints that cannot be represented directly in your data model, write them down so they can be implemented in the database design phase. ER diagrams cannot capture every possibility.

**C.** Extend and modify the E-R data model you created in part B to allow more data to be recorded in the MPIS system. Use the IE Crow's Foot E-R model for your E-R diagrams. Justify the decisions you make regarding minimum and maximum cardinalities. The MPIS needs to record:

- The date a student enrolled at Highline University, the date the student graduated, and the degree the student received
- The date an adviser was assigned to a student and the date the assignment ended
- The date an adviser was assigned to work with a mentor and the date the assignment ended
- The date a mentor was assigned to a student and the date the assignment ended

**D.** Write a short discussion of the differences between the three data models you have created. How does data model B differ from data model A, and how does data model C differ from data model B? What additional features of the E-R data model were introduced when you created data models B and C?

# The Queen Anne Curiosity Shop Project Questions

The Queen Anne Curiosity Shop wants to expand its database applications beyond the current recording of sales. The company still wants to maintain data on customers, employees, vendors, sales, and items, but it wants to (a) modify the way it handles inventory and (b) simplify the storage of customer and employee data.

Currently, each item is considered unique, which means the item must be sold as a whole, and multiple units of the item in stock must be treated as separate items in the ITEM table. The Queen Anne Curiosity Shop management wants the database modified to include an inventory system that will allow multiple units of an item to be stored under one ItemID. The system should allow for a quantity on hand, a quantity on order, and an order due date. If the identical item is stocked by multiple vendors, the item should be orderable from any of these vendors. The SALE_ITEM table should then include Quantity and ExtendedPrice columns to allow for sales of multiple units of an item.

The Queen Anne Curiosity Shop management has noticed that some of the fields in CUSTOMER and EMPLOYEE store similar data. Under the current system, when an employee buys something at the store, his or her data has to be reentered into the CUSTOMER table. The managers would like to have the CUSTOMER and EMPLOYEE tables redesigned using subtypes.

**A.** Draw an E-R data model for The Queen Anne Curiosity Shop database schema shown in Chapter 3's The Queen Anne Curiosity Shop project questions. Use the IE Crow's Foot E-R model for your E-R diagrams. Justify the decisions you make regarding minimum and maximum cardinalities.

**B.** Extend and modify the E-R data model by adding only The Queen Anne Curiosity Shop's inventory system requirements. Use the IE Crow's Foot E-R model for your E-R diagrams. Create appropriate identifiers and attributes for each entity. Justify the decisions you make regarding minimum and maximum cardinalities.

**C.** Extend and modify the E-R data model by adding only The Queen Anne Curiosity Shop's need for more efficient storage of CUSTOMER and EMPLOYEE data. Use the IE Crow's Foot E-R model for your E-R diagrams. Create appropriate identifiers and attributes for each entity. Justify the decisions you make regarding minimum and maximum cardinalities.

**D.** Combine the E-R data models from parts B and C to meet all of The Queen Anne Curiosity Shop's new requirements, making additional modifications as needed. Use the IE Crow's Foot E-R model for your E-R diagrams.

**E.** Describe how you would go about validating your data model in part D.

# Morgan Importing Project Questions

James Morgan of Morgan Importing has decided to expand his business and needs to staff and support a *procurement system*[6] to acquire the items sold at Morgan Importing. Suppose that you have been hired to create and implement a database application to support a procurement information system. Data in this procurement information system will include:

- The purchasing agents employed at Morgan Importing
- The receiving clerks employed at Morgan Importing

---

[6] If you are not familiar with the concept of a procurement system, see the Wikipedia article **Procurement** at *https://en.wikipedia.org/wiki/Procurement* (accessed October 2020).

- The stores where the purchasing agents buy items
- The purchases themselves at the store
- The shippers used to ship the purchases to Morgan Importing
- The shipments made by the shippers
- The receipt of the shipments at Morgan Importing by the receiving clerks

James Morgan and his wife Susan often make purchases themselves while traveling to various countries (and, therefore, even though they are not purchasing agents per se, they need to be listed as purchasing agents in the system when data is entered). Purchases may be made at the stores themselves or by Internet or phone. Sometimes several items are purchased from a store on a single visit, but do not assume that all of the items are placed on the same shipment. Shipping must track each item in a shipment and assign a separate insurance value to each item. Receiving must track the arrival date and time of a shipment, who accepted receipt of the shipment on behalf of Morgan Importing, and the condition of each item upon receipt.

A.  Using your knowledge, create a data model for the Morgan Importing procurement information system. Name each entity, describe its type, and indicate all attributes and identifiers. Name each relationship, describe its type, and specify minimum and maximum cardinalities.

B.  List any item in your answer to A that you believe should be checked out with James Morgan and/or his employees.

# 6

# Transforming Data Models into Database Designs

## Chapter Objectives

- To understand how to transform data models into database designs
- To be able to identify primary keys and understand when to use a surrogate key
- To understand the use of referential integrity constraints
- To understand the use of referential integrity actions
- To be able to represent ID-dependent, 1:1, 1:N, and N:M relationships as tables

- To be able to represent weak entities as tables
- To be able to represent supertype/subtypes as tables
- To be able to represent recursive relationships as tables
- To be able to represent ternary relationships as tables
- To be able to implement referential integrity actions required by minimum cardinalities

**This chapter explains** the transformation of entity-relationship data models into relational database designs. This transformation consists of three primary tasks: (1) replacing entities and attributes with tables and columns; (2) representing relationships and maximum cardinalities by placing foreign keys; and (3) representing minimum cardinality by defining actions to constrain activities on values of primary and foreign keys. Steps 1 and 2 are relatively easy to understand and accomplish; step 3 may be easy or difficult, depending on the minimum cardinality type. In this chapter, we will create database designs, and we will implement a database design in Chapter 7 when we build a database using SQL DDL and DML.

Database design occurs in the **component design** step of the **systems development life cycle (SDLC)** in the **systems analysis and design** process. For an introduction to systems analysis and design and to the SDLC, see Appendix B, "Getting Started with Systems Analysis and Design."

## The Purpose of a Database Design

A **database design** is a set of database specifications that can actually be implemented as a database in a DBMS. The *data model* we discussed in Chapter 5 is a *generalized, non-DBMS-specific* design. A database design, on the other hand, is a *DBMS-specific* design intended to be implemented in a DBMS product such as Microsoft SQL Server 2019 or Oracle Database.

Because each DBMS product has its own way of doing things, even if based on the same relational database model and the same SQL standards, each database design must be created for a particular DBMS product. The same data model will result in slightly different database designs depending upon the intended DBMS product.

---

**BY THE WAY**   Books on systems analysis and design often identify three design stages:

- Conceptual design (conceptual schema)
- Logical design (logical schema)
- Physical design (physical schema)

The *database design* we are discussing is basically equivalent to the *logical design*, which is defined in these books as the conceptual design implemented in a specific DBMS product. The *physical design* deals with aspects of the database encountered when it is actually implemented in the DBMS (as we will discuss in Chapter 10A for Microsoft SQL Server 2019, in Chapter 10B for Oracle Database, and in Chapter 10C for MySQL 8.0), such as physical record and file structure and organization, indexing, and query optimization. However, our discussion of database design *will* include data type specifications, which is often considered a physical design issue in systems analysis and design.

---

## Create a Table for Each Entity

We begin the database design by creating a **table** for each entity using the steps shown in Figure 6-1. In most cases, the table is assigned the same name as the entity. Each attribute of the entity becomes a column of the table. The identifier of the entity becomes the **primary key** of the table. The example in Figure 6-2 shows the creation of the EMPLOYEE table from the EMPLOYEE entity. In this text, to differentiate entities from tables, we will show entities with shadowed boxes and tables with nonshadowed boxes. This notation will help clarify our discussion, but be aware that it is not standard notation across the industry.

Be certain that you understand the difference between these similar-looking graphics. The shadowed rectangle in Figure 6-2(a) represents a logical structure that has no physical existence. It is a blueprint. The nonshadowed rectangle in Figure 6-2(b) represents a database table. It is the same as the following notation that we used in Chapters 3 and 4:

EMPLOYEE (**EmployeeNumber**, EmployeeName, Phone, EmailAddress, HireDate, ReviewDate, EmpCode)

Note, too, the key symbol next to EmployeeNumber. It documents the fact that EmployeeNumber is the table key, just as the underline does in the notation used in Chapters 3 and 4.

### Selecting the Primary Key

The selection of the primary key is important. The DBMS will use the primary key to facilitate searching and sorting of table rows, and some DBMS products use it to organize table storage. DBMS products almost always create indexes and other data structures using the values of the primary key.

**FIGURE 6-1**

Steps for Transforming a
Data Model into a Database
Design

| Transforming a Data Model into a Database Design |
| --- |
| **1. Create a table for each entity:** |
| – Specify the primary key (consider surrogate keys, as appropriate) |
| – Specify alternate keys |
| – Specify properties for each column: |
| • Null status |
| • Data type |
| • Default value (if any) |
| • Data constraints (if any) |
| – Verify normalization |
| **2. Create relationships by placing foreign keys:** |
| – Relationships between strong entities (1:1, 1:N, N:M) |
| – Identifying relationships with ID-dependent entities (intersection tables, association patterns, multivalued attributes, archetype/instance patterns) |
| – Relationships between a strong entity and a weak but non-ID-dependent entity (1:1, 1:N, N:M) |
| – Mixed relationships |
| – Relationships between supertype/subtype entities |
| – Recursive relationships (1:1, 1:N, N:M) |
| **3. Specify logic for enforcing minimum cardinality:** |
| – O-O relationships |
| – M-O relationships |
| – O-M relationships |
| – M-M relationships |

**FIGURE 6-2**

Transforming an Entity to a
Table

EMPLOYEE

| EmployeeNumber |
| --- |
| EmployeeName |
| Phone |
| EmailAddress |
| HireDate |
| ReviewDate |
| EmpCode |

**(a) EMPLOYEE Entity**

EMPLOYEE

| 🔑 EmployeeNumber |
| --- |
| EmployeeName |
| Phone |
| EmailAddress |
| HireDate |
| ReviewDate |
| EmpCode |

**(b) EMPLOYEE Table**

The ideal primary key is short, numeric, and fixed. EmployeeNumber in Figure 6-2 meets all of these conditions and is acceptable. Beware of primary keys such as Employee-Name, EmailAddress, (AreaCode, PhoneNumber), (Street, City, State, ZIP), and other long character columns. In cases like these, when the identifier is not short, numeric, or fixed, consider using another candidate key as the primary key. If there are no additional candidate keys, or if none of them is any better, consider using a surrogate key.

A **surrogate key** is a DBMS-supplied identifier of each row of a table. Surrogate key values are unique within the table, and they never change. They are assigned when the row is created, and they are destroyed when the row is deleted. Surrogate key values are the best possible primary keys because they are designed to be short, numeric, and fixed. Because of these advantages, some organizations have gone so far as to require that surrogates be used for the primary key of every table.

Before endorsing such a policy, however, consider two disadvantages of surrogate keys. First, their values have no meaning to a user. Suppose you want to determine the department to which an employee is assigned. If DepartmentName is a foreign key in EMPLOYEE, then when you retrieve an employee row, you obtain a value such as 'Accounting' or 'Finance'. That value may be all that you need to know about department.

Alternatively, if you define the surrogate key DepartmentID as the primary key of DEPARTMENT, then DepartmentID will also be the foreign key in EMPLOYEE. When you retrieve a row of EMPLOYEE, you will get back a number such as 123499788 for the DepartmentID, a value that has no meaning to you at all. You have to perform a second query on DEPARTMENT to obtain DepartmentName.

The second disadvantage of surrogate keys arises when data are shared among different databases. Suppose, for example, that a company maintains three different SALES databases, one for each of three different product lines. Assume that each of these databases has a table called SALES_ORDER that has a surrogate key called ID. The DBMS assigns values to IDs so they are unique within a particular table within a database. It does not, however, assign ID values so they are unique across the three different databases. Thus, it is possible for two different SALES_ORDER rows, in two different databases, to have the same ID value.

This duplication is not a problem until data from the different databases are merged. When that happens, to prevent duplicates, ID values will need to be changed. However, if ID values are changed, then foreign key values may need to be changed as well, and the result is a mess, or at least a lot of work to prevent a mess.

It is, of course, possible to construct a scheme using different starting values for surrogate keys in different databases. Such a policy ensures that each database has its own range of surrogate key values. This requires careful management and procedures, however; and if the starting values are too close to one another, the ranges will overlap, and duplicate surrogate key values will still result.

---

**BY THE WAY**   Some database designers take the position that, for consistency, if one table has a surrogate key, all of the tables in the database should have a surrogate key. Others think that such a policy is too rigid; after all, there are good data keys, such as ProductSKU (which would use SKU codes, discussed in Chapter 2). If such a key exists, it should be used instead of a surrogate key. Your organization may have standards on this issue that you should follow.

Be aware that DBMS products vary in their support for surrogate keys. Microsoft Access 2019, Microsoft SQL Server 2019, and MySQL 8.0 provide them. Microsoft SQL Server 2019 allows the designer to pick the starting value and increment of the key, and MySQL 8.0 allows the designer to pick the starting value. Oracle's Oracle Database, however, does not provide direct support for surrogate keys, but you can obtain the essence of them in a rather backhanded way, as discussed in Chapter 10B.

We use surrogate keys unless there is some strong reason not to. In addition to the advantages described here, the fact that they are fixed simplifies the enforcement of minimum cardinality, as you will learn in the last section of this chapter.

**FIGURE 6-3**

Representing Alternate Keys

**EMPLOYEE**

🔑 EmployeeNumber

EmployeeName
Phone
EmailAddress (AK1.1)
HireDate
ReviewDate
EmpCode

**(a) EMPLOYEE Table**

**CUSTOMER**

🔑 CustomerNumber

Name (AK1.1)
City (AK1.2)
Phone
EmailAddress (AK2.1)

**(b) CUSTOMER Table**

**FIGURE 6-3**

Representing Alternate Keys

## Specifying Alternate Keys

The next step in creating a table is to specify the alternate keys. As discussed in Chapter 3, a **candidate key** is an identifier of the unique rows in a table. There may be several candidate keys in a table, and we ultimately choose one of them to be the *primary key* of the table. Each of the *remaining* candidate keys then becomes an **alternate key (AK)** (note that they can still be also referred to as *candidate keys*, in the sense that they uniquely identify the rows in the tables and could be used as the primary key if we choose to). Figure 6-3 illustrates the use of alternate keys, using AK notation.

Figure 6-3(a) shows EMPLOYEE with a primary key of EmployeeNumber and a candidate, or alternate, key of EmailAddress. In Figure 6-3(b), CustomerNumber is the primary key of CUSTOMER, and both the composite (Name, City) and EmailAddress are candidate keys. In these diagrams, the symbol AK*n.m* means the *n*th alternate key and the *m*th column of that alternate key. In the EMPLOYEE table, EmailAddress is labeled AK1.1 because it is the first alternate key and the first column of that key. CUSTOMER has two alternate keys. The first is a composite of two columns, which are labeled AK1.1 and AK1.2. The nomenclature Name (AK1.1) means that Name is the first column of the first alternate key, and City (AK1.2) means that City is the second column of the first alternate key. In CUSTOMER, EmailAddress is marked as AK2.1 because it is the first (and only) column of the second alternate key.

## Specifying Column Properties

The next step in the creation of a relation is to specify the column properties. Four properties are shown in Figure 6-1: null status, data type, default value, and data constraints.

### Null Status

**Null status** refers to whether the column can have a null value. Typically, null status is specified by using the phrase NULL if nulls are allowed and NOT NULL if not. Thus, NULL does not mean that the column is always null; it means that null values are allowed. Because of this possible confusion, some people prefer the term NULL ALLOWED rather than NULL. Figure 6-4 shows the null status of each of the columns in the EMPLOYEE table.

**FIGURE 6-4**

Table Display Showing Null
Status

**EMPLOYEE**

🔑 EmployeeNumber: NOT NULL

EmployeeName: NOT NULL
Phone: NULL
EmailAddress: NULL (AK1.1)
HireDate: NOT NULL
ReviewDate: NULL
EmpCode: NULL

**BY THE WAY** The EMPLOYEE table in Figure 6-4 contains a subtlety. EmployeeNumber, the primary key, is marked NOT NULL, but EmailAddress, the alternate key, is marked NULL. It makes sense that EmployeeNumber should not be allowed to be null. If it were, and if more than one row had a null value, then EmployeeNumber would not identify a unique row. Why, however, if (1) an alternate key is a candidate key and (2) a candidate key must uniquely identify a row, should EmailAddress be allowed to have null values?

The answer is that alternate keys often are used *just to ensure uniqueness*. Marking EmailAddress as a (possibly null) alternate key means that EmailAddress need not have a value, but, if it has one, then that value will be unique and different from all other values of EmailAddress in the EMPLOYEE table.

This answer is dissatisfying because it means that alternate keys used in this manner are not truly alternate *primary* keys, and thus neither are they true *candidate* keys! Alas, that's the way it is. Just know that primary keys can never be null but that alternate keys can be.

### Data Type

The next step is to define the data type for each column. For a database design, data types are *DBMS specific*. Unfortunately, each DBMS provides a different set of data types. For example, to record currency values, Microsoft Access has a data type called Currency, and Microsoft SQL Server has a data type called Money, but Oracle Database has no data type for currency. Instead, with Oracle, you use the numeric data type for currency values.

Once you know which DBMS you will be using to create the database, use that DBMS product's data types in your design. Figure 6-5 illustrates the display of data types in a table using the data types for SQL Server (e.g., *Char*, *Varchar*, and *Date* are Microsoft SQL Server data types). A summary of data types for Microsoft SQL Server 2019, Oracle Database, and MySQL 8.0 is shown in Figure 6-6.

In fact, with many data modeling products, such as the erwin Data Modeler, you can specify the DBMS you will use, and the data modeling product will supply the appropriate set of data types. Other products are DBMS specific. For example, Oracle's MySQL Workbench is intended to design databases for MySQL and therefore uses MySQL-specific data types.

If you do not know which DBMS product you will be using or if you want to preserve independence from a particular DBMS, you can specify the data types in a generic way. The SQL standard defines many standard data types. Typical character string data types are *CHAR(n)* for a fixed-length character string of length *n*, *VARCHAR(n)* for a variable-length character string with a maximum length *n*, and *NVARCHAR(n)* for a variable-length Unicode character string with a maximum length *n*. Date/Time data types include *DATE* and *TIME*, and numeric data types include *INTEGER (or INT)*, *FLOAT*, *NUMERIC(m,n)*, and *DECIMAL(m,n)* [for NUMERIC and DECIMAL, the designation (m,n) means having a maximum length of *m* digits with *n* digits displayed to the right of the decimal place]. If you work for a larger organization, that company probably has its own generic data standards. If so, you should use those data standards.

**FIGURE 6-5**

Table Display Showing Data Types

**EMPLOYEE**

🔑 **EmployeeNumber: Int**

EmployeeName: Varchar(50)
Phone: Char(15)
EmailAddress: Nvarchar(100) (AK1.1)
HireDate: Date
ReviewDate: Date
EmpCode: Char(18)

| Numeric Data Types | Description |
|---|---|
| Bit | 1-bit integer. Values of only **0, 1,** or **NULL**. |
| Tinyint | 1-byte integer. Range is from **0** to **255**. |
| Smallint | 2-byte integer. Range is from $-2^{(15)}$ (**−32,768**) to $+2^{(15)} -1$ (**+32,767**). |
| Int | 4-byte integer. Range is from $-2^{(31)}$ (**−2,147,483,468**) to $+2^{(31)} -1$ (**+2,147,483,467**). |
| Bigint | 8-byte integer. Range is from $-2^{(63)}$ (**−9,223,372,036,854,775,808**) to $+2^{(63)} -1$ (**+9,223,372,036,854,775,807**). |
| Decimal (p[,s]) | Fixed precision (p) and scale (s) numbers. Range is from $-10^{38} +1$ to $10^{38} -1$ with maximum precision (p) of 38. Precision ranges from 1 to 38, and default precision is 18. Scale (s) indicates the number of digits to the right of the decimal place. Default scale value is 0, and scale values range from 0 to p, where $0 \le s \le p$. |
| Numeric (p[,s]) | Numeric works identically to Decimal. |
| Smallmoney | 4-byte money. Range is from **−214,748.3648** to **+214,748.3647** with accuracy of one ten-thousandth of a monetary unit. Use decimal point to separate digits. |
| Money | 9-byte money. Range is from **−922,337,203,685,477.5808** to **+922,337,203,685,477.5807** with accuracy of one ten-thousandth of a monetary unit. Use decimal point to separate digits. |
| Float (n) | n-bit storage of the mantissa in scientific floating-point notation. The value of n ranges from 1 to 53, and the default is 53. |
| Real | Equivalent to Float (24). |
| **Date and Time Data Types** | **Description** |
| Date | 3-bytes fixed. Default format YYYY-MM-DD. Range is from **January 1, 1** (0001-01-01) to **December 31, 9999** (9999-12-31). |
| Time | 5-bytes fixed is default with 100 nanosecond precision (.0000000). Default format is HH:MM:SS.NNNNNNN. Range is from **00:00:00.0000000** to **23:59:59.9999999**. |
| Smalldatetime | 4-bytes fixed. Restricted date range and rounds time to nearest second. Range is from **January 1, 1900 00:00:00 AM** (1900-01-01 00:00:00) to **June 6, 2079 23:59.59 PM** (2079-06-06 23:59.59). |
| Datetime | 8-bytes fixed. Basically combines Date and Time, but spans fewer dates and has less time precision (rounds to .000, .003, or .007 seconds). Use DATETIME2 for more precision. Date range is from **January 1, 1753** (1753-01-01) to **December 31, 9999** (9999-12-31). |
| Datetime2 | 8-bytes fixed. Combines Date and Time with full precision. Use instead of DATETIME. Range is from **January 1, 1 00:00:00.0000000 AM** (0001-01-01 00:00:00.0000000) to **December 31, 9999 23:59.59.9999999 PM** (9999-12-31 23:59.59.9999999). |
| Datetimeoffset | 10-byte fixed-length default with 100 nanosecond precision (.0000000). Uses 24-hour clock, based on Coordinated Universal Time (UTC). UTC is a refinement of Greenwich Mean Time (GMT), based on the prime meridian at Greenwich, England, which defines when midnight (00:00:00.0000000) occurs. Offset is the time zone difference from the Greenwich time zone. Default format is YYYY-MM-DD HH:MM:SS.NNNNNNN (+|−)HH:MM. Range is from **January 1, 1 00:00:00.0000000 AM** (0001-01-01 00:00:00.0000000) to **December 31, 9999 23:59.59.9999999 PM** (9999-12-31 23:59.59.9999999) with an **offset of −14:59 to +14:59**. Use for 24-hour time. |
| Timestamp | See documentation. |

**(a) Common Data Types in SQL Server 2019**

**FIGURE 6-6**

SQL Data Types in DBMS
Products

| String Data Types | Description |
|---|---|
| Char (n) | n-byte fixed-length string data (non-Unicode). Range of n is from **1** to **8000**. |
| Varchar (n \| max) | n-byte variable-length string data (non-Unicode). Range of n is from **1** to **8000**. Max creates a maximum $+2^{(31)}-1$ bytes (2 GBytes). |
| Text | Use VARCHAR(max). See documentation. |
| Nchar (n) | (n x 2)-byte fixed-length **Unicode** string data. Range of n is from **1** to **4000**. |
| Nvarchar (n \| max) | (n x 2)-byte variable-length **Unicode** string data. Range of n is from **1** to **4000**. Max creates a maximum $+2^{(31)}-1$ bytes (2 GBytes). |
| Ntext | Use NVARCHAR(max). See documentation. |
| Binary (n) | n-byte fixed-length binary data. Range of n is from **1** to **8000**. |
| **Other Data Types** | **Description** |
| Varbinary (n \| max) | Variable-length binary data. Range of n is from **1** to **8000**. Max creates a maximum $+2^{(31)}-1$ bytes (2 GBytes). |
| Image | Use VARBINARY(max). See documentation. |
| Uniqueidentifier | 16-byte Globally Unique Identifier (GUID). See documentation. |
| hierarchyid | See documentation. |
| Cursor | See documentation. |
| Table | See documentation. |
| XML | Use for storing XML data. See documentation. |
| Sql_variant | See documentation. |

(a) Continued - Common Data Types in SQL Server 2019

| Numeric Data Types | Description |
|---|---|
| SMALLINT | Synonym for INTEGER, implemented as **NUMBER(38,0)**. |
| INT | Synonym for INTEGER, implemented as **NUMBER(38,0)**. |
| INTEGER | When specified as a data type, it is implemented as **NUMBER(38,0)**. |
| NUMBER (p[,s]) | 1 to 22 bytes. Fixed precision (p) and scale (s) numbers. Range is from $-10^{38}+1$ to $10^{38}-1$ with maximum precision (p) of 38. Precision ranges from **1** to **38**, and default precision is **18**. Scale (s) indicates the number of digits to the right of the decimal place. Default scale value is **0,** and scale values range from **–84** to **127**, where s can be greater than p. |
| FLOAT (p) | 1 to 22 bytes. Implemented as NUMBER(p). The value of p ranges from **1** to **126** bits. |
| BINARY_FLOAT | 5-byte 32-bit floating-point number. |
| BINARY_LONG | 9-byte 64-bit floating-point number. |
| RAW (n) | n-byte fixed-length raw binary data. Range of n is from **1** to **2000**. |
| LONG RAW | Raw variable-length binary data. Maximum is 2 GBytes. |
| BLOB | Maximum **[(4-GByte – 1)x(database block size)]** binary large object. |
| BFILE | See documentation. |

(b) Common Data Types in Oracle Database

**FIGURE 6-6**

Continued

| Date and Time Data Types | Description |
|---|---|
| DATE | 7-bytes fixed. Default format is set explicitly with the NLS_DATE_FORMAT parameter. Range is from **January 1, 4712 BC** to **December 31, 9999 AD**. It contains the fields YEAR, MONTH, DAY, HOUR, MINUTE, and SECOND (no fractional seconds). It does not include a time zone. |
| TIMESTAMP (p) | Includes fractional seconds based on a precision of p. Default of p is 6, and the range is 0 to 9. 7 to 11-bytes fixed, based on precision. Default format is set explicitly with the NLS_TIMESTAMP_FORMAT parameter. Range is from **January 1, 4712 BC** to **December 31, 9999 AD**. It contains the fields YEAR, MONTH, DAY, HOUR, MINUTE, and SECOND. It contains fractional seconds. It does not include a time zone. |
| TIMESTAMP (p) WITH TIME ZONE | Includes fractional seconds based on a precision of p. Default of p is 6, and the range is 0 to 9. 13-bytes fixed. Default format is set explicitly with the NLS_TIMESTAMP_FORMAT parameter. Range is from **January 1, 4712 BC** to **December 31, 9999 AD**. It contains the fields YEAR, MONTH, DAY, TIMEZONE_HOUR, TIMEZONE_MINUTE, and TIMEZONE_SECOND. It contains fractional seconds. It includes a time zone. |
| TIMESTAMP (p) WITH LOCAL TIME ZONE | Basically the same as TIMESTAMP WITH TIME ZONE, with the following modifications: (1) data is stored with times based on the database time zone when stored, and (2) users view data in session time zone. |
| INTERVAL YEAR [p(year)] TO MONTH | See documentation. |
| INTERVAL DAY [p(day)] TO SECOND [p(seconds)] | See documentation. |
| **String Data Types** | **Description** |
| CHAR (n[BYTE \| CHAR]) | n-byte fixed-length string data (non-Unicode). Range of n is from **1** to **2000**. BYTE and CHAR refer to the semantic usage. See documentation. |
| VARCHAR2 (n[BYTE \| CHAR]) | n-byte variable-length string data (non-Unicode). Range of n is from **1** to **4000** BYTEs or CHARACTERs. BYTE and CHAR refer to the semantic usage. See documentation. |
| NCHAR (n) | (n x 2)-byte fixed-length **Unicode** string data. Up to (n x 3)-bytes for UTF8 encoding. Maximum size is **2000** bytes. |
| NVARCHAR2 (n) | Variable-length **Unicode** string data. Up to (n x 3)-bytes for UTF8 encoding. Maximum size is **4000** bytes. |
| LONG | Variable-length string data (non-Unicode) with maximum a maximum $2^{(31-1)}$ bytes (2 GBytes). See documentation. |
| CLOB | Maximum **[(4-GByte – 1)x(database block size)]** character large object (non-Unicode). Supports fixed-length and variable-length character sets. |
| NCLOB | Maximum **[(4-GByte – 1)x(database block size)]** Unicode character large object. Supports fixed-length and variable-length character sets. |
| **Other Data Types** | **Description** |
| ROWID | See documentation. |
| UROWID | See documentation. |
| HTTPURIType | See documentation. |
| XMLType | Use for storing XML data. See documentation. |
| SDO_GEOMETRY | See documentation. |

**(b) Continued - Common Data Types in Oracle Database**

**FIGURE 6-6**

Continued

| NumericData Type | Description |
|---|---|
| BIT (M) | M = **1** to **64**. |
| TINYINT | Range is from **–128** to **127**. |
| TINYINT UNSIGNED | Range is from **0** to **255**. |
| BOOLEAN | **0 = FALSE, 1 = TRUE**. Synonym for TINYINT(1). |
| SMALLINT | Range is from **–32,768** to **32,767**. |
| SMALLINT UNSIGNED | Range is from **0** to **65,535**. |
| MEDIUMINT | Range is from **–8,388,608** to **8,388,607**. |
| MEDIUMINT UNSIGNED | Range is from **0** to **16,777,215**. |
| INT or INTEGER | Range is from **–2,147,483,648** to **2,147,483,647**. |
| INT UNSIGNED or INTEGER UNSIGNED | Range is from **0** to **4,294,967,295**. |
| BIGINT | Range is from **–9,223,372,036,854,775,808** to **9,223,372,036,854,775,807**. |
| BIGINT UNSIGNED | Range is from **0** to **18,446,744,073,709,551,616**. |
| FLOAT (P) | P = Precision; Range is from **0** to **53**. |
| FLOAT or REAL (M, D) | Small (single-precision) **4-byte** floating-point number: M = Display width          D = Number of digits after the decimal point |
| DOUBLE (M, D) | Normal (double-precision) **8-byte** floating-point number: M = Display width          D = Number of digits after decimal point |
| DEC (M[,D]) or DECIMAL (M[,D]) or FIXED (M[,D]) or NUMERIC (M[,D]) | Fixed-point number: M = Total number or digits D = Number of digits after the decimal point. |
| **Date and Time Data Types** | **Description** |
| DATE | YYYY-MM-DD : Range is from **1000-01-01** to **9999-12-31**. |
| DATETIME | YYYY-MM-DD HH:MM:SS. Range is from **1000-01-01 00:00:00** to **9999-12-31 23:59:59**. |
| TIMESTAMP | Range is from **1970-01-01 00:00:01** to **2038-01-19 03:14:07**. |
| TIME | HH:MM:SS : Range is from **–838:59:59:000000** to **838:59:59:000000**. |
| YEAR (M) | Range is from **1901** to **2155**. |
| **String Data Types** | **Description** |
| CHAR (M) | Fixed length character string. M = **0** to **255** bytes. |
| VARCHAR (M) | Variable length character string. M = **0** to **65,535** bytes. |
| BLOB (M) | BLOB = Binary Large Object: maximum **65,535** characters. |
| TEXT (M) | Maximum **65,535** characters. |
| TINYBLOB, TINYTEXT | See documentation. |
| MEDIUMBLOB, MEDIUMTEXT | See documentation. |
| LONGBLOB, LONGTEXT | See documentation. |
| ENUM ('value1', 'value2', . . . ) | An enumeration. Only one value, but chosen from list. See documentation. |
| SET ('value1', 'value2', . . . ) | A set. Zero or more values, all chosen from list. See documentation. |

(c) Common Data Types in MySQL 8.0

**FIGURE 6-6**

Continued

FIGURE 6-7

Table Display Showing Null
Status and Data Types

**EMPLOYEE**

🔑 **EmployeeNumber: Int NOT NULL**

EmployeeName: Varchar(50) NOT NULL
Phone: Char(15) NULL
EmailAddress: Nvarchar(100) NULL (AK1.1)
HireDate: Date NOT NULL
ReviewDate: Date NULL
EmpCode: Char(18) NULL

Figure 6-7 shows the EMPLOYEE table showing both data type and null status. The display becomes crowded, however, and from now on we will show tables with just column names. With most products, you can turn such displays on or off depending on the work you are doing.

> **BY THE WAY**    The fact that a design tool is dedicated to one DBMS product does *not* mean that it cannot be used to design databases for other DBMSs. For example, an SQL Server database can be designed in MySQL Workbench, and most of the design will be correct. You will, however, have to understand the relevant differences in the DBMS products and make adjustments when creating the actual database.

## Default Value

A **default value** is a value supplied by the DBMS when a new row is created. The value can be a constant, such as the string 'New Hire' for the EmpCode column in EMPLOYEE, or it can be the result of a function, such as the date value of the computer's clock for the HireDate column.

In some cases, default values are computed using more complicated logic. The default value for a price, for example, might be computed by applying a markup to a default cost and then reducing that marked-up price by a customer's discount. In such a case, an application component or a trigger (discussed in Chapter 7) will be written to supply such a value.

It is possible to use the data modeling tool to record default values, but such values often are shown in separate design documentation. Figure 6-8, for example, shows one way that default values are documented.

FIGURE 6-8

Sample Documentation for
Default Values

| Table | Column | Default Value |
|-------|--------|---------------|
| ITEM | ItemNumber | Surrogate key |
| ITEM | Category | None |
| ITEM | ItemPrefix | If Category = 'Perishable' then 'P'<br>If Category = 'Imported' then 'I'<br>If Category = 'One-off' then 'O'<br>Otherwise = 'N' |
| ITEM | ApprovingDept | If ItemPrefix = 'I' then<br>    'SHIPPING/PURCHASING'<br>Otherwise = 'PURCHASING' |
| ITEM | ShippingMethod | If ItemPrefix = 'P' then 'Next Day'<br>Otherwise = 'Ground' |

### Data Constraints

**Data constraints** are limitations on data values. There are several different types. **Domain constraints** limit column values to a particular set of values. For example, EMPLOYEE.EmpCode could be limited to 'New Hire', 'Hourly', 'Salary', or 'Part Time'. **Range constraints** limit values to a particular interval of values. EMPLOYEE.Hire-Date, for example, could be limited to dates between January 1, 1990, and December 31, 2025.

An **intrarelation constraint** limits a column's values in comparison with other columns in the same table. The constraint that EMPLOYEE.ReviewDate be at least three months after EMPLOYEE.HireDate is an intrarelation constraint. An **interrelation constraint** limits a column's values in comparison with other columns in other tables. An example for the CUSTOMER table is that CUSTOMER.Name must not be equal to BAD_CUSTOMER.Name, where BAD_CUSTOMER is a table that contains a list of customers with credit and balance problems.

Referential integrity constraints, which we discussed in Chapter 3, are one type of inter-relation constraint. Because they are so common, sometimes they are documented only when they are not enforced. For example, to save work, a design team might say that every foreign key is assumed to have a referential integrity constraint to the table that it references and that only exceptions to this rule are documented.

### Verify Normalization

The last task in step 1 of Figure 6-1 is to verify table normalization. When data models are developed using forms and reports as guides, they generally result in normalized entities. This occurs because the structures of forms and reports usually reflect how users think about their data. Boundaries of a form, for example, often show the range of a functional dependency. If this is hard to understand, think of a functional dependency as a theme. A well-designed form or report will bracket themes using lines, colors, boxes, or other graphical elements. Those graphical hints will have been used by the data modeling team to develop entities, and the result will be normalized tables.

All of this, however, should be verified. You need to ask whether the resulting tables are in Boyce-Codd Normal Form (BCNF) and whether all multivalued dependencies have been removed. If not, the tables should probably be normalized. However, as we discussed in Chapter 4, sometimes normalization is undesirable. Thus, you should also examine your tables to determine if any normalized ones should be denormalized.

## Create Relationships

The result of step 1 is a set of complete, but independent, tables. The next step is to create relationships. In general, we create relationships by placing foreign keys into tables. The way in which this is done and the properties of the foreign key columns depend on the type of relationship. In this section, we consider each of the relationships described in Chapter 5: nonidentifying relationships between strong entities, identifying relationships between ID-dependent entities, relationships in mixed entity patterns, relationships between a supertype and its subtypes, and recursive relationships. We conclude this section with a discussion of special cases of ternary relationships.

### Relationships Between Strong Entities

As you learned in Chapter 5, nonidentifying relationships between strong entities are characterized by their maximum cardinality. There are three types of these relationships: 1:1, 1:N, and N:M.

#### 1:1 Relationships Between Strong Entities

After the tables corresponding to the strong entities have been designed, a 1:1 relationship between these entities can be represented in one of two ways. You can place the primary key of the first table in the second as a foreign key, or you can place the primary key of the second table in the first as a foreign key. Figure 6-9 shows the representation of the 1:1 nonidentifying relationship between CLUB_MEMBER and LOCKER. In Figure 6-9(a), MemberNumber is placed in LOCKER as a foreign key. In Figure 6-9(b), LockerNumber is placed in CLUB_MEMBER as a foreign key.

Either of these designs will work. If you have a club member's number and want his or her locker, then, using the design in Figure 6-9(a), you can query the LOCKER table for the given value of MemberNumber. But if you have the LockerNumber and want the club member's data, then, still using the design in Figure 6-9(a), you can query the LOCKER table for the LockerNumber, obtain the MemberNumber, and use that value to query the CLUB_MEMBER table for the rest of the club member's data.

Follow a similar procedure to verify that the design in Figure 6-9(b) works as well. However, one data constraint applies to both designs. Because the relationship is 1:1, a given value of a foreign key can appear only once in the table. For example, in the design in Figure 6-9(a), a given value of MemberNumber can appear just once; each value must be unique in the LOCKER table. If a value of MemberNumber were to appear in two rows, then a member would be assigned to two lockers, and the relationship would not be 1:1.

To cause the DBMS to enforce the required uniqueness of the foreign key value, we define the foreign key column as unique. This can be done either directly in the column definition of the foreign key (in which case there is no designation in the table diagram) or by defining the foreign key as an alternate key. This latter technique, though common, is a bit confusing because, logically, MemberNumber is not an alternate key for LOCKER. We are just using the fact that alternate keys are unique to document the uniqueness of the foreign key in a 1:1 relationship. Depending on the database design software being used, the alternate key designation may appear in the database design of the tables and the relationship, and this is illustrated in Figure 6-9(a). A similar technique is used on the foreign key LockerNumber in Figure 6-9(b).

Figure 6-9 shows the minimum cardinalities of the relationship as optional-optional (O-O), and in this case either of the designs in Figure 6-9 will work, though the design team many prefer one over the other. However, if the minimum cardinalities of the relationship are either mandatory-optional (M-O) or optional-mandatory (O-M), then one design will be *greatly* preferred, as you will learn in the section on minimum cardinality design later in this chapter. Also, application requirements may mean that one design is faster than the other.

To summarize, to represent a 1:1 strong entity relationship, place the key of one table in the other table. Enforce the maximum cardinality by defining the foreign key as unique (or as an alternate key).

**FIGURE 6-9**

The Two Alternatives for the Transformation of a 1:1 Relationship Between Strong Entities

**(a) With Foreign Key in LOCKER**

**(b) With Foreign Key in CLUB_MEMBER**

## 1:N Relationships Between Strong Entities

After the tables corresponding to the strong entities have been designed, a 1:N relationship between the entities is represented by placing the primary key of the table on the *one* side into the table on the *many* side as a foreign key. Recall from Chapter 5 that the term *parent* is used to refer to the table on the one side, and the term *child* is used to refer to the table on the many side. Using this terminology, you can summarize the design of 1:N relationships by saying, "Place the primary key of the parent in the child as a foreign key." This is illustrated in Figure 6-10.

Figure 6-10(a) shows an E-R diagram for the 1:N relationship between the CLUB_MEMBER and CLUB_UNIFORM entities. The relationship is represented in the database design in Figure 6-10(b) by placing the primary key of the parent (MemberNumber) in the child (CLUB_UNIFORM) as a foreign key. Because parents have many children (the relationship is 1:N), there is no need to make the foreign key unique.

For 1:N relationships between strong entities, that's all there is to it. Just remember: "Place the primary key of the parent in the child as a foreign key."

## N:M Relationships Between Strong Entities

Again, we must first create the database design tables from the data model entities and then create the relationship. However, the situation for N:M relationships is more complicated. The problem is that there is no place in either table in an N:M relationship in which to place the foreign key. Consider the example in Figure 6-11(a), which shows a relationship between COMPANY and PART that specifies which companies can supply which parts. A COMPANY may supply many PARTs, and a PART may be supplied by many different COMPANYs.

Suppose we try to represent this relationship by placing the primary key of one table as a foreign key in the second table, as we did for 1:N relationships. Say we place the primary key of PART in COMPANY as follows:

**COMPANY (<u>CompanyName</u>, City, Country, Volume, *PartNumber*)**

**PART (<u>PartNumber</u>, PartName, SalesPrice, ReOrderQuantity, QuantityOnHand)**

With this design, a given PartNumber may appear in many rows of COMPANY so that many companies can supply the part. But how do we show that a company can supply many parts? There is only space to show one part. We do not want to duplicate the entire row for a company just to show a second part; such a strategy would result in unacceptable data duplication and data integrity problems. Therefore, this is not an acceptable solution, and a

**FIGURE 6-10**

Transformation of a 1:N Relationship Between Strong Entities

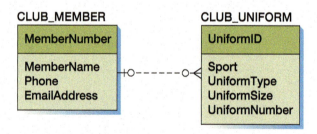

**(a) 1:N Relationship Between Strong Entities**

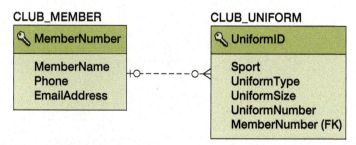

**(b) Placing the Primary Key of the Parent in the Child as a Foreign Key**

**FIGURE 6-11**

Transformation of a N:M
Relationship Between Strong
Entities

**(a) The Foreign Key Has No Place in Either Table**

**(b) Foreign Keys Placed in ID-Dependent Intersection Table**

similar problem will occur if we try to place the primary key of COMPANY, CompanyName, into PART as a foreign key.

The solution is to create a third table, called an **intersection table**.[1] Such a table shows the correspondences of a given company and a given part. It holds only the primary keys of the two tables as foreign keys, and this combination of keys serves as the composite primary key of the intersection table itself. The intersection holds only the key data; it contains no other user data. For the example in Figure 6-11(a) we create the following intersection table:

**COMPANY_PART_INT** (*CompanyName*, *PartNumber*)

The COMPANY_PART_INT table has one row for each company–part combination. Notice that both columns are part of the composite primary key (CompanyName, PartNumber) and that each column is also a foreign key to a different table. Because both columns are keys of other tables, intersection tables are always ID-dependent on both of their parent tables, and the relationships with the parent tables are identifying relationships.

Thus, the database design in Figure 6-11(b) is drawn with an ID-dependent COMPANY_PART_INT intersection table and identifying relationship lines. Like all ID-dependent tables, the parent tables are required–COMPANY_PART_INT requires both a COMPANY and PART. The parents may or may not require an intersection table row, depending on application requirements. In Figure 6-11(b), a COMPANY need not supply a PART, but a PART must be supplied by at least one COMPANY.

[1]Although we use the term *intersection table* in this book, this table structure is known by many other names. In fact, Wikipedia currently lists 15 alternate names, including *intersection table, junction table, bridge table,* and *association table*. We reserve the term *association table* for an *association relationship* (as explained later in this chapter), but your instructor may prefer one of the other terms for this table structure. For more information, see the Wikipedia article *Junction table* at https://en.wikipedia.org/wiki/Associative_entity.

> **BY THE WAY**  The problem for the data models of N:M relationships between strong entities is that they have no direct representation. N:M relationships must *always* be decomposed into two 1:N relationships using an intersection table in the database design. This is why products like MySQL Workbench are unable to represent N:M relationships in a data model. These products force you to make the transformation to two 1:N relationships ahead of time during modeling. As stated in Chapter 5, however, most data modelers consider this requirement to be a nuisance because it adds complexity to data modeling when the whole purpose of data modeling is to reduce complexity to the logical essentials.

## Relationships Using ID-Dependent Entities

Figure 6-12 summarizes the four uses for ID-dependent entities. We have already described the first use shown in Figure 6-12: the representation of N:M relationships. As shown in Figure 6-11, an ID-dependent intersection table is created to hold the foreign keys of the two tables participating in the relationship, and identifying 1:N relationships are created between each table and the intersection table.

The other three uses shown in Figure 6-12 were discussed in Chapter 5, and here we will describe the creation of tables and relationships for each of these three uses.

### Association Relationships

As we discussed in Chapter 5, an **association relationship** is subtly close to an N:M relationship between two strong entities. The only difference between the two types of relationships is that an association relationship has one or more attributes that pertain to the relationship *between the entities* and not to either of the entities themselves. These attributes must be added to what would otherwise be the intersection table in the N:M relationship. In Chapter 5, we described this added entity as an **associative entity** (or **association entity**). Figure 6-13(a) shows the association relationship data model created in Figure 5-22. In this example, the association of a company and a part carries an attribute named Price, which is stored in an associative entity named QUOTATION.

The representation of such a relationship is straightforward: start by creating an *intersection table* that is ID-dependent on both of its parents, and then convert it to an **association table** by adding the nonidentifier attributes from the associative entity to that table. The result for the example in Figure 6-13(a) is the association table:

**QUOTATION (*CompanyName*, *PartNumber*, Price)**

This table appears in the database design in Figure 6-13(b). Like all ID-dependent relationships, the parents of an association table are required. The parents may or may not require the rows of the association table, depending on application requirements. In Figure 6-13(b), a COMPANY need not have any QUOTATION rows, but a PART must have at least one QUOTATION row.

**FIGURE 6-12**

Four Uses for ID-Dependent Entities

| Four Uses for ID-Dependent Entities |
|---|
| Representing N:M relationships |
| Representing association relationships |
| Storing multivalued attributes |
| Representing archetype/instance relationships |

> **BY THE WAY**   The table that represents the association entity looks very much like an intersection table; the only difference is the presence of the Price attribute. Because of the attribute, the need for association tables, such as QUOTATION, will appear in user requirements. Somewhere there will be a form or a report that has the attribute Price. However, the need for intersection tables never appears in the users' world. Such tables are an artifact of the relational model, and no form, report, or other user requirement will indicate the need for one.
>
>   Intersection tables complicate the construction of applications. They must be processed to obtain related rows, but they never directly appear on a form or report. In Microsoft Access, they are frustratingly difficult to mangle into the form and report design tools. You will see more about this in later chapters. In any case, for now understand the key difference between association and intersection tables: association tables have user data, but intersection tables do not.

**FIGURE 6-13**

Transformation of
ID-Dependent Entities in an
Association Relationship

**(a) Association Pattern Data Model from Figure 5-22**

**(b) Association Pattern Database Design**

As shown in Figure 6-14, associative entities sometimes connect more than two entity types. Figure 6-14(a) shows the association relationship among the CLIENT, ARCHITECT, and PROJECT entities from the data model we created in Figure 5-23. When there are several participants in the association, the strategy just shown is simply extended. The association table will have the key of each of its parents, as shown in Figure 6-14(b). In this case, the ASSIGNMENT table has three foreign keys and one non-key attribute, HoursWorked.

In both of these examples, it is only coincidence that the association tables have only one non-key attribute. In general, an association table can have as many non-key attributes as necessary to meet user requirements.

**FIGURE 6-14**

Transformation of
ID-Dependent Entities in an
Association Relationship
Among Three Entities

**(a) Association Pattern Data Model from Figure 5-23**

**(b) Association Pattern Database Design**

## Multivalued Attributes

The third use for ID-dependent entities is to represent multivalued entity attributes, as illustrated in Figure 6-15. Figure 6-15(a) is a copy of Figure 5-29. Here COMPANY has a multivalued composite, (Contact, PhoneNumber), that is represented by the ID-dependent entity PHONE_CONTACT.

As shown in Figure 6-15(b), representing the PHONE_CONTACT entity is straightforward. Just replace it with a table and replace each of its attributes with a column. In this example, the CompanyName attribute is both a part of the primary key and a foreign key.

Like all ID-dependent tables, PHONE_CONTACT must have a parent row in COMPANY. However, a COMPANY row may or may not have a required PHONE_CONTACT, depending on application requirements.

> **BY THE WAY** As you can see from these examples, it is not much work to transform an ID-dependent entity into a table. All that is necessary is to transform the entity into a table and copy the attributes into columns.
>
> Why is it so simple? There are two reasons. First, all identifying relationships are 1:N. If they were 1:1, there would be no need for the ID-dependent relationship. The attributes of the child entity could just be placed in the parent entity. Second, given that the relationship is 1:N, the design principle is to place the key of the parent into the child. However, the definition of an ID-dependent relationship is that part of its identifier is an identifier of its parent. Thus, by definition, the key of the parent is already in the child. Hence, it is not necessary to create a foreign key; that work has already been done during data modeling.

## Archetype/Instance Pattern

As illustrated in Figure 6-16, the fourth use for ID-dependent entities and identifying relationships is the archetype/instance pattern (also referred to as the *version/instance* pattern). Figure 6-16(a), which is a copy of Figure 5-30, shows the CLASS/SECTION archetype/instance example from Chapter 5, and Figure 6-16(b) shows the relational design.

As noted in the previous chapter, however, sometimes the instances of an archetype/instance pattern are given identifiers of their own. In that case, the instance entity becomes a weak but not ID-dependent entity. When this occurs, the relationship must be transformed using the rules of a 1:N relationship between a strong entity and a weak but non-ID-dependent entity. However, this transformation is the same as a 1:N relationship between two

**FIGURE 6-15**

Transformation of ID-Dependent Entities to Store Multivalued Attributes

(a) Data Model with Multivalued Attributes from Figure 5-29

(b) Database Design to Store Multivalued Attributes

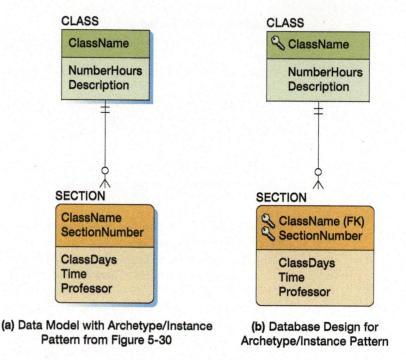

**(a) Data Model with Archetype/Instance
Pattern from Figure 5-30**

**(b) Database Design for
Archetype/Instance Pattern**

strong entities. This just means that the primary key of the parent table should be placed in the child table as a foreign key. Figure 6-17(a) shows a copy of the data model in Figure 5-31 in which SECTION has been given the identifier ReferenceNumber. In the relational database design in Figure 6-17(b), ClassName (the primary key of the parent CLASS table) has been placed in SECTION (the child table) as a foreign key.

Keep in mind, however, that even though SECTION is no longer ID-dependent, it is still weak. SECTION requires a CLASS for its existence. This means that a SECTION must always have a CLASS as its parent, and this restriction arises from logical necessity, not just from application requirements. The fact that SECTION is weak should be recorded in design documentation.

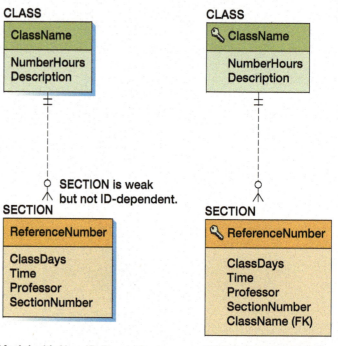

**(a) Data Model with Non-ID-Dependent
Weak Entity from Figure 5-31**

**(b) Database Design for
Non-ID-Dependent Weak Entity**

## Relationships with a Weak Non-ID-Dependent Entity

As you learned in Chapter 5, a relationship between a strong entity and a weak but non-ID-dependent entity behaves just the same as a relationship between two strong entities. The relationship is a nonidentifying relationship, and, again, these relationships are characterized by their maximum cardinality. The previous discussion of 1:1, 1:N, and N:M relationships between strong entities also applies to these types of relationships between a strong entity and a weak but non-ID-dependent entity.

For example, what happens when the identifier of the parent of an ID-dependent entity is replaced with a surrogate key? Consider the example of BUILDING and APARTMENT, in which the identifier of APARTMENT is the composite of an apartment number and a building identifier.

Suppose that the identifier of BUILDING is (Street, City, State/Province, Country). In this case, the identifier of APARTMENT is (Street, City, State/Province, Country, Apartment-Number). This design can be improved by replacing the long BUILDING identifier with a surrogate key. Suppose that we replace the key of BUILDING with BuildingID, a surrogate.

Now, with a surrogate key for BUILDING, what is the key of APARTMENT? When we place the key of the parent in the child, we obtain (BuildingID, ApartmentNumber). But this combination has no meaning to the user. What does an identifier of (10045898, '5C') mean to a user? Nothing! The key became meaningless when Street, City, State/Province, and Country were replaced by BuildingID in BUILDING.

We can improve the design by using the following principle: when replacing the identifier of the parent of an ID-dependent entity with a surrogate key, replace the identifier of the ID-dependent entity with its own surrogate key. The resulting table will be weak but not ID-dependent (we will use this principle later in this chapter as we create a database design for the View Ridge Gallery—you can see the changes in Figure 6-38 and Figure 6-39, where WORK becomes a weak but not ID-dependent table in the relationship with ARTIST).

## Relationships in Mixed Entity Designs

As you might guess, the design of mixed entity patterns is a combination of strong entity and ID-dependent entity designs. Consider the example of employees and skills in Figure 6-18. Figure 6-18(a) is a copy of Figure 5-35. Here the entity EMPLOYEE_SKILL is ID-dependent on EMPLOYEE, but it has a nonidentifying relationship to SKILL.

**FIGURE 6-18**

Transformation of the Mixed Entity Pattern

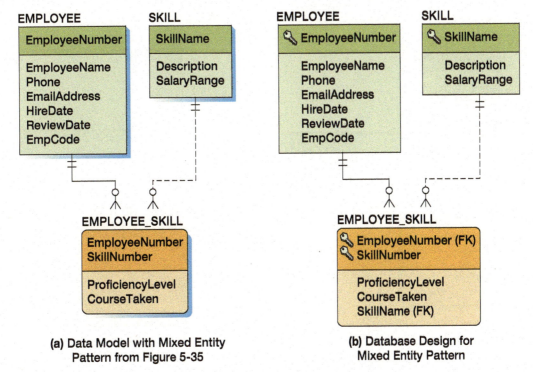

(a) Data Model with Mixed Entity
Pattern from Figure 5-35

(b) Database Design for
Mixed Entity Pattern

The database design of the E-R model for the data model in Figure 6-18(a) is shown in Figure 6-18(b). Notice that EmployeeNumber is both a part of the primary key of EMPLOYEE_SKILL and a foreign key to EMPLOYEE. The 1:N nonidentifying relationship between SKILL and EMPLOYEE_SKILL is represented by placing the key of SKILL, which is SkillName, in EMPLOYEE_SKILL. Note that EMPLOYEE_SKILL.SkillName is a foreign key but not part of the primary key of EMPLOYEE_SKILL.

A similar strategy is used to transform the SALES_ORDER data model in Figure 6-19. Figure 6-19(a) is a copy of the SALES_ORDER data model originally shown in Figure 5-33. In Figure 6-19(b), the ID-dependent table, ORDER_LINE_ITEM, has SalesOrderNumber as part of its primary key and as a foreign key. It has ItemNumber as a foreign key only.

> **BY THE WAY**   The design transformation process for all HAS-A relationships can be sum-
> marized by the phrase, "Place the primary key of the parent in the child as
> a foreign key." For strong entities, a 1:1 relationship can have either entity as the parent,
> and therefore the foreign key can go in either table. For 1:N relationships, the primary
> key of the parent goes in the child as the foreign key. For N:M relationships, decom-
> pose the model into two 1:N relationships by defining an intersection table and place
> the parent key of the parent in the child as a foreign key for each.
>
> For identifying relationships, the primary key of the parent is already in the child, so
> there is nothing more to do. For mixed relationships, on the identifying side, the primary
> key of the parent is already in the child. On the nonidentifying side, place the primary
> key of the parent in the child. In short, if you're going to memorize just a few rules for
> creating relationships, the first one is "HAS-A: Place the primary key of the parent in the
> child as the foreign key."

**FIGURE 6-19**

Transformation of the
SALES_ORDER Pattern

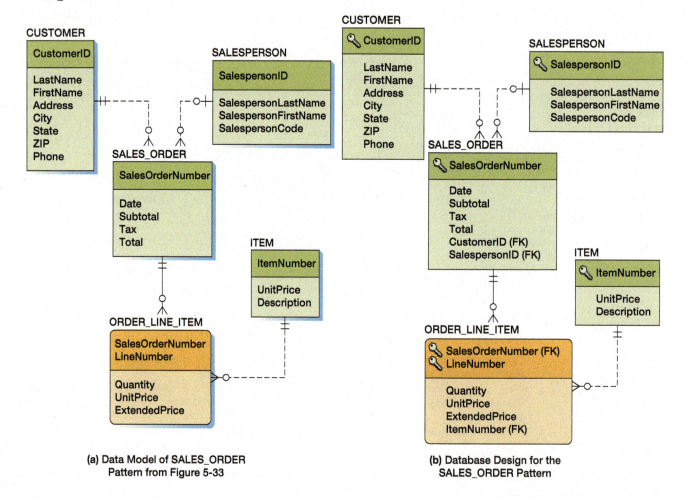

(a) Data Model of SALES_ORDER
Pattern from Figure 5-33

(b) Database Design for the
SALES_ORDER Pattern

## Relationships Between Supertype and Subtype Entities

Representing relationships between supertype entities and their subtypes is easy. Recall that these relationships are also called IS-A relationships because a subtype and its supertype are representations of the same underlying entity. A MANAGER (subtype) is an EMPLOYEE (supertype), and a SALESCLERK (subtype) is also an EMPLOYEE (supertype). Because of this equivalence, the keys of all subtype tables are identical to the key of the supertype table.

Figure 6-20(a) shows the data model in Figure 5-13(a), an example for two subtypes of STUDENT. Notice that the key of STUDENT is StudentID and that the key of each of the subtypes also is StudentID. UNDERGRADUATE.StudentID and GRADUATE.StudentID are both primary keys and foreign keys to their supertype.

Although we are showing the transformation of a set of exclusive subtypes (with the discriminator attribute isGradStudent), the transformation of a set of inclusive subtypes is done exactly the same way. Note that discriminator attributes cannot be represented in relational designs. In Figure 6-20(b), we can do nothing with isGradStudent except note in the design documentation that isGradStudent determines subtype. Application programs will need to be written to use isGradStudent to determine which subtype pertains to a given STUDENT.

## Recursive Relationships

The representation of recursive relationships is just an extension of the techniques used for representing relationships between strong entities. These techniques may be a bit difficult to comprehend at first because they appear strange, but they involve principles that you have already learned.

### 1:1 Recursive Relationships

Consider the 1:1 recursive BOXCAR relationship in Figure 6-21(a), which is the same data model we developed in Figure 5-39. To represent the relationship, we create a foreign key in BOXCAR that contains the identifier of the boxcar behind, as shown in Figure 6-21(b). Because the relationship is 1:1, we make the foreign key unique by defining it as unique (shown here as an alternate key). This restriction enforces the fact that a boxcar can have, at most, one boxcar behind it.

**FIGURE 6-20**

Transformation of
Supertype/Subtype Entities

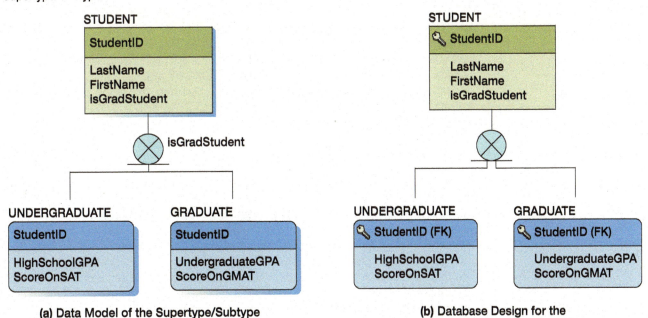

(a) Data Model of the Supertype/Subtype
Relationship from Figure 5-13(a)

(b) Database Design for the
Supertype/Subtype Relationship

**FIGURE 6-21**

Transformation of 1:1
Recursive Relationships

**(a) Data Model for a 1:1 Recursive
Relationship in Figure 5-38**

**(b) Database Design for a 1:1
Recursive Relationship**

Notice that both sides of the relationship are optional. This occurs because the last car on the train has no other car behind it and because the first car on the train is behind no other car. If the data structure were circular, this restriction would not be necessary. For example, if you wanted to represent the sequence of names of the calendar months and you wanted December to lead to January, then you could have a 1:1 recursive structure with required children.

> **BY THE WAY**  If you find the concept of recursive relationships confusing, try this trick. Assume that you have two entities, BOXCAR_AHEAD and BOX-CAR_BEHIND, each having the same attributes. Notice that there is a 1:1 relationship between these two entities. Replace each entity with its table. Like all 1:1 strong entity relationships, you can place the key of either table as a foreign key in the other table. For now, place the key of BOXCAR_BEHIND into BOXCAR_AHEAD.
>
> Now realize that BOXCAR_BEHIND only duplicates data that reside in BOXCAR_AHEAD. The data are unnecessary. So discard BOXCAR_BEHIND and you will have the same design as shown in Figure 6-21(b).

### 1:N Recursive Relationships

As with all 1:N relationships, 1:N recursive relationships are represented by placing the primary key of the parent in the child as a foreign key. Consider the Manages relationship in Figure 6-22(a), which is the data model we developed in Figure 5-41. In this case, we place the name of the manager in each employee's row. Thus, in Figure 6-22(b), the Employee-NameMgr has been added to the EMPLOYEE table.

Notice that both the parent and the child are optional. This is true because the lowest-level employees manage no one and because the highest-level person, the CEO or other most senior person, has no manager. If the data structure were circular, this would not be the case.

**FIGURE 6-22**

Transformation of 1:N
Recursive Relationships

(a) Data Model for a 1:N Recursive
Relationship in Figure 5-41

(b) Database Design for a 1:N
Recursive Relationship

**FIGURE 6-23**

Transformation of N:M
Recursive Relationships

(a) Data Model for an N:M
Recursive Relationship
in Figure 5-43

(b) Database Design for an N:M
Recursive Relationship

### N:M Recursive Relationships

The trick for representing N:M recursive relationships is to decompose the N:M relationship into two 1:N relationships. We do this by creating an intersection table, just as we did for N:M relationships between strong entities.

Figure 6-23(a) is the data model we developed in Figure 5-43. It shows the solution to an example for a bill-of-materials problem. Each part has potentially many subordinate parts, and each part can be used as a component in potentially many other parts. To represent this relationship, create an intersection table that shows the correspondence of a part/part use. You can model upward or downward. If the former, the intersection table will carry the correspondence of a part and where that part is used. If the latter, the intersection table will carry the correspondence of a part and the parts that it contains. Figure 6-23(b) shows the intersection table for modeling downward in the bill of materials.

> **BY THE WAY**   Again, if you find this to be confusing, assume that you have two different tables, one called PART and a second called CONTAINED_PART. Create the intersection table between the two tables. Note that CONTAINED_PART duplicates the attributes in PART and is thus unnecessary. Eliminate the table and you will have the design in Figure 6-23(b).

### Representing Ternary and Higher-Order Relationships

As we discussed in Chapter 5, ternary and higher-order relationships can be represented by multiple binary relationships, and such a representation usually works without any problems. However, in some cases, certain constraints add complexity to the situation.

For example, consider the ternary relationship among the entities ORDER, CUSTOMER, and SALESPERSON. Assume that the relationship from CUSTOMER to ORDER is 1:N and that the relationship from SALESPERSON to ORDER also is 1:N. We can represent the three-part relationship among ORDER:CUSTOMER:SALESPERSON as two separate binary relationships: one between ORDER and CUSTOMER and a second between SALESPERSON and CUSTOMER. The design of the tables will be:

CUSTOMER (<u>CustomerNumber</u>, {non-key data attributes})

SALESPERSON (<u>SalespersonNumber</u>, {non-key data attributes})

ORDER (<u>OrderNumber</u>, {non-key data attributes}, *CustomerNumber, SalespersonNumber*)

Suppose, however, that the business has a rule that each CUSTOMER can place orders only with a particular SALESPERSON. In this case, the ternary relationship ORDER:CUSTOMER:SALESPERSON is constrained by an additional binary 1:N relationship between SALESPERSON and CUSTOMER. To represent the constraint, we need to add the key of SALESPERSON to CUSTOMER. The three tables will now be:

CUSTOMER (<u>CustomerNumber</u>, {non-key data attributes}, *SalespersonNumber*)

SALESPERSON (<u>SalespersonNumber</u>, {non-key data attributes})

ORDER (<u>OrderNumber</u>, {non-key data attributes}, *CustomerNumber, SalespersonNumber*)

The constraint that a particular CUSTOMER is sold to by a particular SALESPERSON means that only certain combinations of CustomerNumber and SalespersonNumber can exist together in ORDER. Unfortunately, this constraint cannot be expressed in a relational model. It must be documented in the design, however, and enforced by program code, as shown in Figure 6-24.

A constraint that requires one entity to be combined with another entity is called a **MUST constraint**. Other similar constraints are the MUST NOT constraint and the MUST COVER constraint. In a **MUST NOT constraint**, the binary relationship indicates combinations that are not allowed to occur in the ternary relationship. For example, the ternary relationship PRESCRIPTION:DRUG:CUSTOMER shown in Figure 6-25 can be constrained

**FIGURE 6-24**

Ternary Relationship with a MUST Constraint

**SALESPERSON Table**

| SalespersonNumber | Other non-key data |
|---|---|
| 10 | |
| 20 | |
| 30 | |

**CUSTOMER Table**

| CustomerNumber | Other non-key data | SalespersonNumber |
|---|---|---|
| 1000 | | 10 |
| 2000 | | 20 |
| 3000 | | 30 |

Binary MUST Constraint

**ORDER Table**

| OrderNumber | Other non-key data | SalespersonNumber | CustomerNumber |
|---|---|---|---|
| 100 | | 10 | 1000 |
| 200 | | 20 | 2000 |
| 300 | | 10 | 1000 |
| 400 | | 30 | 3000 |
| 500 | | | 2000 |

Only 20 is allowed here

**FIGURE 6-25**

Ternary Relationship with
MUST NOT Constraint

**DRUG Table**

| DrugNumber | Other non-key data |
|---|---|
| 10 | |
| 20 | |
| 30 | |
| 45 | |
| 70 | |
| 90 | |

**ALLERGY Table**

| CustomerNumber | DrugNumber | Other non-key data |
|---|---|---|
| 1000 | 10 | |
| 1000 | 20 | |
| 2000 | 20 | |
| 2000 | 45 | |
| 3000 | 30 | |
| 3000 | 45 | |
| 3000 | 70 | |

Binary MUST NOT Constraint

**PRESCRIPTION Table**

| PrescriptionNumber | Other non-key data | DrugNumber | CustomerNumber |
|---|---|---|---|
| 100 | | 45 | 1000 |
| 200 | | 10 | 2000 |
| 300 | | 70 | 1000 |
| 400 | | 20 | 3000 |
| 500 | | | 2000 |

Neither 20 nor 45 can appear here

by a binary relationship in the ALLERGY table that lists the drugs that a customer is not allowed to take.

In a **MUST COVER constraint**, the binary relationship indicates all combinations that must appear in the ternary relationship. For example, consider the relationship AUTO_REPAIR:REPAIR:TASK in Figure 6-26. Suppose that a given REPAIR consists of a number of TASKs, all of which must be performed for the REPAIR to be successful. In this case, in the table AUTO_REPAIR, when a given AUTO_REPAIR has a given REPAIR, then all of the TASKs for that REPAIR must appear as rows in that table.

None of the three types of binary constraints discussed here can be represented in the relational design. Instead, they are documented in the design and implemented in application code.

### Relational Representation of the Highline University Data Model

Let's consider the data model we created for Highline University in Chapter 5. Our final data model for Highline University is shown in Figure 6-27.

Using the principles we have discussed in this chapter, we can turn this into a relational database design, and the resulting database design is a straightforward application of the principles described in this chapter. The database design for Highline University is shown in Figure 6-28.

You should review Figure 6-28 to ensure that you understand the representation of every relationship. Note that there are actually two foreign key references to a DepartmentName primary key column in STUDENT. The first is DepartmentName (FK), which is the foreign key linking to the DepartmentName primary key in DEPARTMENT. This relationship has the following referential integrity constraint:

**DepartmentName in STUDENT must exist in DepartmentName in DEPARTMENT**

FIGURE 6-26

Ternary Relationship with
MUST COVER Constraint

**REPAIR Table**

| RepairNumber | Other non-key data |
|---|---|
| 10 | |
| 20 | |
| 30 | |
| 40 | |

**TASK Table**

| TaskNumber | Other non-key data | *RepairNumber* |
|---|---|---|
| 1001 | | 10 |
| 1002 | | 10 |
| 1003 | | 10 |
| 2001 | | 20 |
| 2002 | | 20 |
| 3001 | | 30 |
| 4001 | | 40 |

— Binary MUST COVER Constraint —

**AUTO_REPAIR Table**

| InvoiceNumber | RepairNumber | TaskNumber | Other non-key data |
|---|---|---|---|
| 100 | 10 | 1001 | |
| 100 | 10 | 1002 | |
| 100 | 10 | 1003 | |
| 200 | 20 | 2001 | |
| 200 | 20 | | |

— 2002 must appear here —

FIGURE 6-27

Data Model for Highline
University in Figure 5-52

**FIGURE 6-28**

**Database Design for Highline University**

The second is ProfessorDepartment (FK), which is part of the composite foreign key (ProfessorDepartment, ProfessorFirstName, ProfessorLastName). This foreign key links to the primary key (DepartmentName, ProfessorFirstName, ProfessorLastName) in APPOINTMENT and has the following referential integrity constraint:

**(ProfessorDepartment, ProfessorFirstName, ProfessorLastName) in STUDENT must exist in (DepartmentName, ProfessorFirstName, ProfessorLastName) in APPOINTMENT**

Note that we had to change DepartmentName in APPOINTMENT to ProfessorDepartment in STUDENT because we cannot have two columns named DepartmentName in STUDENT and we had already used DepartmentName as the foreign key linking to DEPARTMENT. Further, recall that professors can be in more than one department, and having different column names in these tables helps distinguish the different references.

This illustrates that a foreign key does not need to have the same name as the primary key it links to. As long as the referential integrity constraints are correctly specified, the foreign key name can be whatever we want it to be.

In addition to the two referential integrity constraints discussed earlier in our database design, we will have the following:

**CollegeName in DEPARTMENT must exist in CollegeName in COLLEGE**

**(ProfessorFirstName, ProfessorLastName) in DEPARTMENT must exist in (ProfessorFirstName, ProfessorLastName) in PROFESSOR**

**DepartmentName in APPOINTMENT must exist in DepartmentName in DEPARTMENT**

**(ProfessorFirstName, ProfessorLastName) in APPOINTMENT must exist in (ProfessorFirstName, ProfessorLastName) in PROFESSOR**

# Design for Minimum Cardinality

The third and last step of transforming data models into database designs is to create a plan for enforcing minimum cardinality. Unfortunately, this step can be considerably more complicated than the first two design steps. Relationships that have required children entities are particularly problematic because we cannot enforce such constraints with database structures. Instead, as you will see, we must design procedures for execution by the DBMS or by applications.

Relationships can have one of four minimum cardinalities: **parent optional and child optional (O-O)**, **parent mandatory and child optional (M-O)**, **parent optional and child mandatory (O-M)**, or **parent mandatory and child mandatory (M-M)**. As far as enforcing minimum cardinality is concerned, no action needs to be taken for O-O relationships, and we need not consider them further. The remaining three relationships pose restrictions on insert, update, and delete activities.

Figure 6-29 summarizes the actions needed to enforce minimum cardinality. Figure 6-29(a) shows needed actions when the parent row is required (M-O and M-M relationships), and Figure 6-29(b) shows needed actions when the child row is required (O-M and M-M relationships). In these figures and the accompanying discussion, the term **action** means **minimum cardinality enforcement action**. We use the shorter term *action* for ease of discussion.

To discuss these rules, we will use the database design for storing data on several companies shown in Figure 6-30. In this diagram, we have a 1:N, M-O relationship between COMPANY and DEPARTMENT and between DEPARTMENT and EMPLOYEE and a 1:N, M-M relationship between COMPANY and PHONE_CONTACT. In the COMPANY-to-DEPARTMENT relationship, COMPANY (on the 1 side of the relationship) is the parent entity, and DEPARTMENT (on the N side of the relationship) is the child entity. In the DEPARMENT-to-EMPLOYEE relationship, DEPARTMENT (on the 1 side of the relationship) is the parent entity,

**FIGURE 6-29**

Summary of Actions to Enforce Minimum Cardinality

| Parent Required | Action on Parent | Action on Child |
|---|---|---|
| Insert | None. | Get a parent. Prohibit. |
| Modify key or foreign key | Change children's foreign key values to match new value (cascade update). Prohibit. | OK, if new foreign key value matches existing parent. Prohibit. |
| Delete | Delete children (cascade delete). Prohibit. | None. |

(a) Actions When the Parent Is Required

| Child Required | Action on Parent | Action on Child |
|---|---|---|
| Insert | Get a child. Prohibit. | None. |
| Modify key or foreign key | Update the foreign key of (at least one) child. Prohibit. | If not last child, OK. If last child, prohibit or find a replacement. |
| Delete | None. | If not last child, OK. If last child, prohibit or find a replacement. |

(b) Actions When the Child Is Required

**FIGURE 6-30**

Database Design for Data on Several Companies

and EMPLOYEE (on the N side of the relationship) is the child entity. In the COMPANY-to-PHONE_CONTACT relationship, COMPANY (on the 1 side of the relationship) is the parent entity, and PHONE_CONTACT (on the N side of the relationship) is the child entity.

## Actions When the Parent Is Required

When the parent is required, we need to ensure that every row of the child table has a valid, non-null value of the foreign key. To accomplish this, we must restrict actions to update or delete the parent's primary key and actions to create or modify the child's foreign key. We will consider actions on the parent first.

### Actions on the Parent Row when the Parent Is Required

According to Figure 6-29(a), when a new parent is created, nothing needs to be done. No child row can yet be dependent upon the new row. In our example, we can create a new DEPARTMENT and not worry about minimum cardinality enforcement in EMPLOYEE.

However, consider what happens if we attempt to change the value of an existing parent row's primary key. If that row has children, then those children have a foreign key value that matches the current primary key value. If the primary key of the parent changes, then any existing children will become orphans; their foreign key values will no longer match a parent row. To prevent the creation of orphans, either the foreign key values must be changed to match the new value of the parent's primary key or the modification to the parent's primary key must be prohibited.

In our example, if a DEPARTMENT attempts to change its DepartmentName from 'Info Sys' to 'Information Systems', then any child rows in EMPLOYEE that have a foreign key value of 'Info Sys' will no longer match a parent and will be orphans. To prevent orphans, either the values of the foreign key in EMPLOYEE must also be changed to 'Information Systems' or the update to the primary key in DEPARTMENT must be prohibited. The policy of propagating a change from the parent's primary key to the children's foreign key is called **cascading updates**.

Now consider what happens when there is an attempt to delete a parent. If that row has children and if the deletion is allowed, then the children will become orphans. Hence, when such a delete attempt is made, either the children must be deleted as well or the deletion must be prohibited. Deleting the children along with the parent is called **cascading deletions**. In our example, when an attempt is made to delete a DEPARTMENT, either all related rows in EMPLOYEE must be deleted as well or the deletion must be disallowed.

> **BY THE WAY**  Generally, cascading deletions are not chosen for relationships between strong entities. The deletion of a DEPARTMENT row should not force the deletion of EMPLOYEE rows. Instead, the deletion should be disallowed. To remove a DEPARTMENT row, the EMPLOYEE rows would be reassigned to a new DEPARTMENT and then the DEPARTMENT row would be deleted.
>
> However, cascading deletions are almost always chosen for weak child entities. For example, when you delete a COMPANY, you should always delete all of the weak PHONE_NUMBER rows that depend on that COMPANY.

### Actions on the Child Row When the Parent Is Required

Now consider actions on the child row. If the parent is required, then when a new child row is created, the new row must have a valid foreign key value. When we create a new EMPLOYEE, for example, if DEPARTMENT is required, then the new EMPLOYEE row must have a valid value for DepartmentName. If not, the insert must be disallowed. Usually there is a default policy for assigning parents to a new row. In our example, when a new row is added to EMPLOYEE, the default policy could be to add the new employee to the department named 'Human Resources'.

With regard to modifications to the foreign key, the new value must match a value of the primary key in the parent. In EMPLOYEE, if we change DepartmentName from 'Accounting' to 'Finance', then there must already be a DEPARTMENT row with the primary key value of 'Finance'. If not, the modification must be prohibited.

If the parent row is required, there are no restrictions on the deletion of the child row. The child can go away without consequence on the parent.

> **BY THE WAY**  When the parent has a surrogate key, the enforcement actions for updates are different between the parent and the child. On the parent side, the surrogate key will never change, and hence update actions can be ignored. On the child side, however, the foreign key can change if the child switches to a new parent. Hence, on the parent side, you can ignore actions when the key is a surrogate. On the child side, however, you must consider update actions even when the parent's key is a surrogate.

### Actions When the Child Is Required

When the child is required, we need to ensure that there is at least one child row for the parent at all times. The last child cannot leave the parent. For example, in the DEPARTMENT-to-EMPLOYEE relationship, if a DEPARTMENT requires an EMPLOYEE, then the last EMPLOYEE cannot leave the DEPARTMENT. This has ramifications on actions on the child, as shown in Figure 6-29(b).

Enforcing required children is much more difficult than enforcing required parents. To enforce a required parent, we just need to check for a match between primary key and foreign key values. To enforce a required child, we must count the number of children that a parent has. This difference forces us to write code to enforce required children. To begin, consider the required child actions from the perspective of the parent.

### Actions on the Parent Row When the Child Is Required

If the child is required, then we cannot create a new parent without also creating a relationship to a child. This means that either we must find an existing child row and change its foreign key to match that of the new parent or we must create a new child row at the same time the parent is created. If neither action can be taken, then the insertion of the new parent must be prohibited. These rules are summarized in the first row of Figure 6-29(b).

If the child is required, then to modify the parent's primary key, either the key of at least one child must also be changed or the update must be disallowed. This restriction never applies to parents with surrogate keys because their values never change.

Finally, if the child is required and the parent is deleted, no action need be taken. Because it is the child that is required, and not the parent, the parent can disappear without any consequence.

### Actions on the Child Row When the Child Is Required

As shown in Figure 6-29(b), if the child is required, then no special action needs to be taken when inserting a new child. The child comes into existence without influencing any parent.

However, there are restrictions on updating the foreign key of a required child. In particular, if the child is the last child of its current parent, then the update cannot occur. If it were to occur, the current parent would be childless, and that is not allowed. Thus, a procedure must be written to determine the number of children of the current parent. If that number is two or greater, then the child foreign key value can be changed. Otherwise, the update is prohibited.

A similar restriction pertains to the deletion of required children. If the child is the last child to the parent, then the deletion is not allowed. Otherwise, the child can be deleted without restriction.

Figure 6-31 summarizes the application of the actions in Figure 6-29 for each type of minimum cardinality. As stated earlier, O-O relationships pose no restrictions and need not be considered.

### Implementing Actions for M-O Relationships

M-O relationships require that the actions in Figure 6-29(a) be enforced. We need to make sure that every child has a parent and that operations on either parent or child rows never create orphans.

Fortunately, these actions are easy to enforce using facilities available in most DBMS products. It turns out that we can enforce these actions with just two limitations. First, we need to define a referential integrity constraint that ensures that every foreign key value has a match in the parent table. Second, we make the foreign key column NOT NULL. With these two restrictions, all of the actions in Figure 6-29(a) will be enforced.

Consider the DEPARTMENT-to-EMPLOYEE example. If we define the referential integrity constraint as follows:

**DepartmentName in EMPLOYEE must exist in DepartmentName in DEPARTMENT**

FIGURE 6-31

Actions to Apply to Enforce Minimum Cardinality

| Relationship Minimum Cardinality | Action to Apply | Remarks |
|---|---|---|
| O-O | Nothing | |
| M-O | Parent-required actions [Figure 6-29(a)] | Easily enforced by DBMS; define referential integrity constraint and make foreign key NOT NULL. |
| O-M | Child-required actions [Figure 6-29(b)] | Difficult to enforce. Requires use of triggers or other application code. |
| M-M | Parent-required actions and child-required actions [Figures 6-29(a) and 6-29(b)] | Very difficult to enforce. Requires a combination of complex triggers. Triggers can lock each other out. Many problems! |

then we know that every value of DepartmentName in EMPLOYEE will match a value in DEPARTMENT. If we then make DepartmentName required, we know that every row in EMPLOYEE will have a valid DEPARTMENT.

Almost every DBMS product has facilities for defining referential integrity constraints. You will learn how to write SQL statements for that purpose in the next chapter. In those statements, you will have the option of declaring whether updates and deletions are to cascade or are to be prohibited. Once you have defined the constraint and made the foreign key NOT NULL, the DBMS will take care of all of the actions in Figure 6-29(a) for you.

> **BY THE WAY**    Recall that in a 1:1 relationship between strong entities, the key of either table can be placed in the other table. If the minimum cardinality of such a relationship is either M-O or O-M, it is generally best to place the key in the optional table. This placement will make the parent required, which is easier to enforce. With a required parent, all you have to do is define the referential integrity constraint and set the foreign key to NOT NULL. However, if you place the foreign key so that the child is required, let the work begin! You will have your hands full, as you are about to see.

## Implementing Actions for O-M Relationships

Unfortunately, if the child is required, the DBMS does not provide much help. No easy mechanism is available to ensure that appropriate child foreign keys exist, nor is there any easy way to ensure that valid relationships stay valid when rows are inserted, updated, or deleted. You are on your own.

In most cases, required children constraints are enforced using **triggers**, which are modules of code that are invoked by the DBMS when specific events occur. Almost all DBMS products have triggers for insert, update, and delete actions. Triggers are defined for these actions on a particular table. Thus, you can create a trigger on *CUSTOMER INSERT* or a trigger on *EMPLOYEE UPDATE*, and so forth. You will learn more about triggers in Chapter 7.

To see how you would use triggers to enforce required children, consider Figure 6-29(b) again. On the parent side, we need to write a trigger on insert and update on the parent row. These triggers either create the required child or they steal an existing child from another parent. If they are unable to perform one of these actions, they must cancel the insert or update.

On the child side, a child can be inserted without problem. Once a child gets a parent, however, it cannot leave that parent if it is the last or only child. Hence, we need to write update and delete triggers on the child that have the following logic: If the foreign key is null, the row has no parent, and the update or delete can proceed. If the foreign key does have a value, however, check whether the row is the last child. If the row *is* the last child, then the trigger must do one of the following:

- Delete the parent.
- Find a substitute child.
- Disallow the update or delete.

None of these actions will be automatically enforced by the DBMS. Instead, you must write code to enforce these rules. You will see generic examples of such code in the next chapter and real examples for Microsoft SQL Server 2019 in Chapter 10A, Oracle Database in Chapter 10B, and MySQL 8.0 in Chapter 10C.

## Implementing Actions for M-M Relationships

It is very difficult to enforce M-M relationships. All of the actions in both Figure 6-29(a) and Figure 6-29(b) must be enforced simultaneously. We have a needy parent and a needy child, and neither will let go of the other.

Consider, for example, what would happen if we change the relationship between DEPARTMENT and EMPLOYEE in Figure 6-30 to M-M, and the effect that would have on the creation of new rows in DEPARTMENT and EMPLOYEE. On the DEPARTMENT side, we must write an insert department trigger that tries to insert a new EMPLOYEE for the new DEPARTMENT. However, the EMPLOYEE table will have its own insert trigger. When we try to insert the new EMPLOYEE, the DBMS calls the insert employee trigger, which will prevent the insertion of an EMPLOYEE unless it has a DEPARTMENT row. But the new DEPARTMENT row does not yet exist because it is trying to create the new EMPLOYEE row, which does not exist because the new DEPARTMENT row does not yet exist, and 'round and 'round we go!

Now consider a deletion in this same M-M relationship. Suppose we want to delete a DEPARTMENT. We cannot delete a DEPARTMENT that has any EMPLOYEE children. So, before deleting the DEPARTMENT, we must first reassign (or delete) all of the employees in that department. However, when we try to reassign the last EMPLOYEE, an EMPLOYEE update trigger will be fired that will not allow the last employee to be reassigned. (The trigger is programmed to ensure that every DEPARTMENT has at least one EMPLOYEE.) We have a stalemate; the last employee cannot get out of the department, and the department cannot be deleted until all employees are gone!

This problem has several solutions, but none is particularly satisfying. In the next chapter, we will show one solution using SQL Views. That solution is complicated and requires careful programming that is difficult to test and fix. The best advice is to avoid M-M relationships if you can. If you cannot avoid them, budget your time with foreknowledge that a difficult task lies ahead.

## Designing Special Case M-M Relationships

Not all M-M relationships are as bad as the last section indicates. Although M-M relationships between strong entities generally are as complicated as described, M-M relationships between strong and weak entities are often easier. For example, consider the relationship between COMPANY and PHONE_CONTACT in Figure 6-30. Because PHONE_CONTACT is an ID-dependent weak entity, it must have a COMPANY parent. In addition, assume that application requirements indicate that each COMPANY row must have at least one row in PHONE_CONTACT. Hence, the relationship is M-M.

However, transactions are almost always initiated from the side of the strong entity. A data entry form will begin with a COMPANY and then, somewhere in the body of the form, the data from the PHONE_CONTACT table will appear. Hence, all insert, update, and deletion activity on PHONE_CONTACT will come as a result of some action on COMPANY. Given this situation, we can ignore the Action on Child columns in Figure 6-29(a) and Figure 6-29(b) because no one will ever try to insert, modify, or delete a new PHONE_CONTACT except in the context of inserting, modifying, or deleting a COMPANY.

Because the relationship is M-M, however, we must take all of the actions in the Action on Parent columns of both Figure 6-29(a) and Figure 6-29(b). With regard to inserts on parents, we must always create a child. We can meet this need by writing a COMPANY INSERT trigger that automatically creates a new row of PHONE_CONTACT with null values for Contact and PhoneNumber.

With regard to updates and deletions, all we need to do is cascade all of the remaining actions in Figure 6-29(a) and Figure 6-29(b). Changes to COMPANY.CompanyName will be propagated to PHONE_CONTACT.CompanyName. The deletion of a COMPANY will automatically delete that company's PHONE_CONTACT rows. This makes sense; if we no longer want data about a company, we certainly no longer want its contact and phone data.

> **BY THE WAY**  Because of the difficulty in enforcing M-M relationships, developers look for special circumstances to ease the task. Such circumstances usually exist for relationships between strong and weak entities, as described. For relationships between strong entities, such special circumstances may not exist. In this case, the M-M cardinality is sometimes just ignored. Of course, this cannot be done for applications such as financial management or operations that require careful records management, but for an application such as airline reservations, where seats are overbooked anyway, it might be better to redefine the relationship as M-O.

## Documenting the Minimum Cardinality Design

Because enforcing minimum cardinality can be complicated and because it often involves the creation of triggers or other procedures, clear documentation is essential. Because the design for the enforcement of required parents is easier than that for required children, we will use different techniques for each.

### Documenting Required Parents

Database modeling and design tools such as the erwin Data Modeler and Oracle's MySQL Workbench allow you to define **referential integrity (RI) actions** on each table. These definitions are useful for documenting the actions necessary for a required parent. According to Figure 6-29(a), three design decisions are necessary for required parents: (1) determining whether updates to the parent's primary key should cascade or be prohibited, (2) determining whether deletions of the parent should cascade or be prohibited, and (3) identifying how a parent row is to be selected on the insert of a child.

> **BY THE WAY**  In theory, referential integrity actions can be used to document the actions taken to enforce required children as well as required parents. When they are used for both purposes, however, they become confusing and ambiguous. In an M-M relationship, for example, a child may have one set of rules for insert because of its required parent and another set of rules for insert because it is a required child. The insert referential integrity action will be overloaded with these two purposes, and its meaning will be ambiguous at best. Hence, in this text, we will use referential integrity actions only for documenting required parents. We will use another technique, described next, for documenting required children.

### Documenting Required Children

One easy and unambiguous way to define the actions to enforce a required child is to use Figure 6-29(b) as a boilerplate document. Create a copy of this figure for each relationship that has a required child, and fill in the specific actions for insert, update, and delete operations.

For example, consider Figure 6-32, which shows the O-M relationship between DEPARTMENT and EMPLOYEE. A given department must have at least one employee, but an employee does not have to be assigned to a specific department. For example, the company may have an employee who is an expediter (whose job is to solve problems throughout the company and in whichever department is experiencing a problem) who is not formally assigned to a department. DEPARTMENT has a surrogate key, DepartmentID, and other columns as shown in Figure 6-32.

Because the DEPARTMENT-to-EMPLOYEE relationship has a required child, we will fill out the table in Figure 6-29(b). Figure 6-33 shows the result. Here triggers are described

**FIGURE 6-32**

DEPARTMENT-to–
EMPLOYEE O-M
Relationship

**FIGURE 6-33**

Actions to Enforce the
O-M Relationship Between
DEPARTMENT and
EMPLOYEE

| EMPLOYEE Is Required Child | Action on DEPARTMENT | Action on EMPLOYEE |
|---|---|---|
| Insert | Trigger to create row in EMPLOYEE when inserting DEPARTMENT. Disallow DEPARTMENT insert if EMPLOYEE data are not available. | None. |
| Modify key or foreign key | Not possible, surrogate key. | Trigger needed: If not last EMPLOYEE, OK. If last EMPLOYEE, prohibit or assign another EMPLOYEE |
| Delete | None. | Trigger needed: If not last EMPLOYEE, OK. If last EMPLOYEE, prohibit or assign another EMPLOYEE |

for DEPARTMENT insert, EMPLOYEE modification (update), and EMPLOYEE deletion. DEPARTMENT modification (update) actions are unneeded because DEPARTMENT has a surrogate key.

## An Additional Complication

You should be aware of an additional complication that is beyond the scope of this text. A table can participate in many relationships. In fact, there can be multiple relationships between the same two tables. You need to specify a design for the minimum cardinality of every relationship. The minimum cardinality of each relationship will vary. Some will be O-M, some will be M-O, and some will be M-M. Some of the relationships will require triggers, which may mean that you have several sets of insert, update, and delete triggers per table. This array of triggers is not only complicated to write and test; the actions of different triggers may interfere with one another during execution. You will need more experience and knowledge to design, implement, and test such complex arrays of trigger code and DBMS constraints. For now, just be aware that these problems exist.

| Relationship Minimum Cardinality | Design Decisions to Be Made | Design Documentation |
|---|---|---|
| M-O | • Update cascade or prohibit?<br>• Delete cascade or prohibit?<br>• Policy for obtaining parent on insert of child | Referential integrity (RI) actions plus documentation for policy on obtaining parent for child insert. |
| O-M | • Policy for obtaining child on insert of parent<br>• Primary key update cascade or prohibit?<br>• Policy for update of child foreign key<br>• Policy for deletion of child | Use Figure 6-29(b) as a boilerplate. |
| M-M | All decisions for M-O and O-M above, plus how to process trigger conflict on insertion of first instance of parent/child and deletion of last instance of parent/child. | For mandatory parent, RI actions plus documentation for policy on obtaining parent for child insert. For mandatory child, use Figure 6-29(b) as a boilerplate. Add documentation on how to process trigger conflict. |

**FIGURE 6-34**

Summary of Design Decisions for Minimum Cardinality

### Summary of Minimum Cardinality Design

Figure 6-34 summarizes the design for relationship minimum cardinality. It shows each type of relationship, the design decisions that need to be made, and the documentation that should be created. Use this figure as a guide.

## The View Ridge Gallery Database

We conclude this chapter with an example database design problem. This design will be used throughout the rest of the text, so take the time to understand it. This particular problem was chosen because it has typical relationships and moderate complexity. It has enough challenges to make it interesting, but not so many as to make it overwhelming.

### View Ridge Gallery Database Summary of Requirements

The View Ridge Gallery (View Ridge or VRG) is a small art gallery that sells contemporary European and North American fine art, including lithographs, high-quality reproduction prints, original paintings and other artwork, and photographs. All of the lithographs, prints, and photos are signed and numbered, and the original art is usually signed. View Ridge also provides art framing services. It creates a custom frame for each artwork (rather than selling standardized, premade frames) and is known for its excellent collection of frame stock. The View Ridge Gallery Web site is shown in Figure 6-35.

View Ridge emphasizes reproduction artworks of European Impressionist, Abstractionist, and Modernist artists such as Wassily Kandinsky and Henri Matisse. For original art, View Ridge concentrates on Northwest School artists, such as Mark Tobey, Morris Graves, Guy Anderson, and Paul Horiuchi, and produces shows of contemporary artists who work in the Northwest School tradition or in Northwest Maritime art. The price of new reproduction prints ranges up to $1,000, and prices for contemporary artists range from $500 to $10,000. The price of art from the Northwest School artists varies considerably, depending on the artwork itself. Small pencil, charcoal, or watercolor sketches may sell for as little as $2,000, whereas major works can range from $10,000 to $100,000. Very occasionally, View Ridge may carry Northwest School art priced up to $500,000, but art priced above $250,000 is more likely to be sold at auction by a major art auction house.

View Ridge has been in business for 30 years and has one full-time owner, three salespeople, and two workers who make frames, hang art in the gallery, and prepare artwork for shipment. View Ridge holds openings and other gallery events to attract customers to the gallery. View Ridge owns all of the art that it acquires and sells—even the sale of contemporary artwork is treated as a purchase by View Ridge that then is resold to a customer. View Ridge does not take items on a consignment basis.

**FIGURE 6-35**

View Ridge Gallery Web Site
Home Page

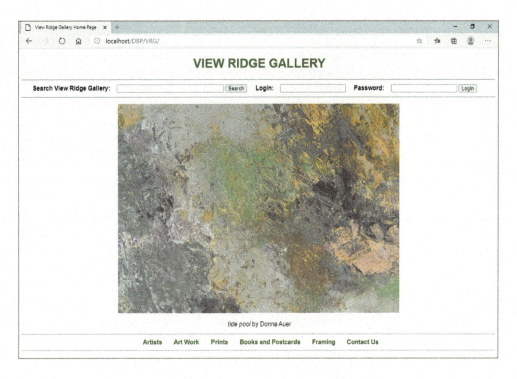

Note that this is *not* a sales order database as illustrated in Figure 6-19. Rather, it is an *artwork acquisitions* database, designed to record each acquisition of a piece of art work by the View Ridge Gallery, and then to record the details of the sale of the piece of art. This system is necessary because a single piece of art may be acquired and resold more than once, and the View Ridge Gallery needs a database designed to meet these specialized data and information requirements.

The View Ridge Gallery does sell other products and services besides artwork. For example, framing services, selected books on art and artists, and specialized postcards are all available at the View Ridge Gallery. For these products and services, however, there is a sale order system that interfaces with the acquisition database.

The requirements for the View Ridge acquisition application are summarized in Figure 6-36. First, both the owner and the salespeople want to keep track of customers' names, addresses, phone numbers, and email addresses. They also want to know which artists have appeal to which customers. The salespeople use this information to determine whom to contact when new art arrives and to personalize verbal and email communications with their customers.

**FIGURE 6-36**

Summary of View
Ridge Gallery Database
Requirements

| Summary of View Ridge Gallery Database Requirements |
|---|
| Track customers and their interest in specific artists |
| Record the gallery's purchases |
| Record customers' purchases |
| Report how fast an artist's works have sold and at what margin |
| Show the artists represented by the gallery on a Web page |
| Show current inventory on a Web page |
| Show all the works of art that have appeared in the gallery on Web pages |

When the gallery purchases new art, data about the artist, the nature of the work, the acquisition date, and the acquisition price are recorded. Also, on occasion, the gallery repurchases art from a customer and resells it; thus, a work may appear in the gallery multiple times. When art is repurchased, the artist and work data are not reentered, but the most recent acquisition date and price are recorded. In addition, when art is sold, the purchase date, sales price, and identity of the purchasing customer are stored in the database.

Salespeople want to examine past purchase data so they can devote more time to the most active buyers. They also sometimes use the purchase records to identify the location of artworks they have sold in the past.

For marketing purposes, View Ridge wants its database application to provide a list of artists and works that have appeared in the gallery. The owner also would like to be able to determine how fast an artist's work sells and at what sales margin. The database application also should display current inventory on a Web page that customers can access via the Internet.

## The View Ridge Data Model

Figure 6-37 shows a data model for the View Ridge database. This model has two strong entities: CUSTOMER and ARTIST. In addition, the entity WORK is ID-dependent on ARTIST, and the entity TRANS is ID-dependent on WORK. There is also a nonidentifying relationship from CUSTOMER to TRANS.

Note that we are using the entity name TRANS instead of TRANSACTION. We are doing this because *transaction* is a **DBMS reserved word** in most (if not all) DBMS products. Using DBMS reserved words such as *table*, *column*, or other names can create problems. Similarly, we cannot use the reserved word *tran*. The word *trans*, however, is not a DBMS reserved word, and we can use it without problems. We will discuss this problem more when we discuss Microsoft SQL Server 2019 in Chapter 10A, Oracle Database in Chapter 10B, and MySQL 8.0 in Chapter 10C.

In the View Ridge data model, an artist may be recorded in the database even if none of his or her works has appeared in the gallery. This is done to record customer preferences for artists whose works might appear in the future. Thus, an artist may have from zero to many works.

The identifier of WORK is the composite (Title, Copy) because, in the case of lithographs and photos, there may be many copies of a given title. Also, the requirements indicate that a work may appear in the gallery many times, so there is a need for potentially many TRANS entities for each WORK. Each time a work appears in the gallery, the acquisition date and price must be recorded. Thus, each WORK must have at least one TRANS row.

A customer may purchase many works; this is recorded in the 1:N relationship from CUSTOMER to TRANS. Note that this relationship is optional in both directions. Finally,

**FIGURE 6-37**

View Ridge Gallery Data Model

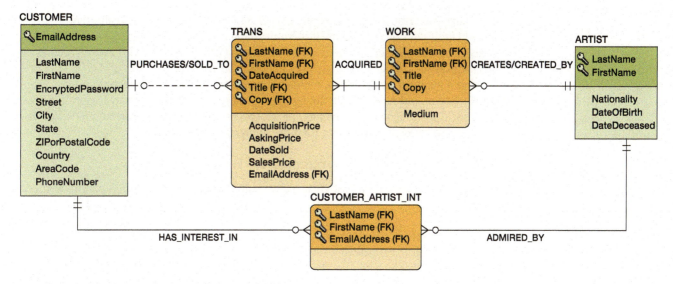

**FIGURE 6-38**

Initial View Ridge Gallery
Database Design

there is an N:M relationship between CUSTOMERs and ARTISTs. This is an N:M relationship between strong entities—the team searched in vain for a missing attribute that would indicate an association pattern rather than an N:M relationship.

### Database Design with Data Keys

A database design for the data model in Figure 6-37 is shown in Figure 6-38. This design uses data keys, and every primary key except the composite (ARTIST.LastName, ARTIST. FirstName) has problems. The keys for WORK and TRANS are huge, and the key for CUSTOMER is doubtful; many customers may not have an email address. Because of these problems, this design cries out for surrogate keys.

### Surrogate Key Database Design

The database design for the View Ridge database using surrogate keys is shown in Figure 6-39. Notice that two identifying relationships (TRANS-to-WORK) and (WORK-to-ARTIST) have been changed to nonidentifying relationships represented by dashed lines. This was done because once ARTIST has a surrogate key, there is no need to keep ID-dependent keys in WORK and TRANS. Realize that WORK and TRANS are both weak entities even though they are no longer ID-dependent.

**FIGURE 6-39**

Final View Ridge Gallery
Database Design

Notice that (LastName, FirstName) in ARTIST has been defined as an alternate key. This notation indicates that (LastName, FirstName) has a UNIQUE constraint, which ensures that artists are not duplicated in the database. Similarly, (Title, Copy) in WORK is defined as an alternate key so that a given work cannot appear more than once.

The foreign key placement is a straightforward application of the techniques described in this chapter, but note that the foreign key CustomerID in TRANS can have null values. This specification allows the creation of a TRANS row when a work is acquired, before any customer has purchased the work. All other foreign keys are required.

## Minimum Cardinality Enforcement for Required Parents

According to Figure 6-29(a), for each relationship that involves a required parent, we need to decide:

- Whether to cascade or prohibit updates of the parent's primary key
- Whether to cascade or prohibit deletions of the parent
- How to obtain a parent when a new child is created

Because there is no consistent means of documenting these actions in commercial database design products, we will use the templates in Figure 6-29 to document our decisions. Figure 6-40 summarizes the relationships in the View Ridge database design.

Because all tables have surrogate keys, there is no need for any update cascade behavior for any parent. However, some update actions on child tables must be restricted. For example, once a WORK (child) is assigned to an ARTIST (parent), it is never to change to another parent. Because this database is used to record purchases and sales, View Ridge management never wants to delete any data that are related to a transaction. From time to time, it may remove a prior year's data in bulk, but it will do that using bulk data transfer and not as part of any application.

Hence, any CUSTOMER, WORK, or ARTIST row that is related to a TRANS row is never to be deleted. Note, however, that rows of CUSTOMERs who have never made a purchase and rows of ARTISTs whose works have never been carried in the gallery can be deleted. If either a CUSTOMER or ARTIST is deleted under these circumstances, the deletion will cascade to rows in the intersection table CUSTOMER_ARTIST_INT.

Finally, referential integrity actions are necessary for obtaining a parent WORK when a TRANS record is created and a parent ARTIST when a WORK record is created. In both cases, the policy will be for the application program to provide the ID of the required parent at the time the WORK or TRANS record is created.

All these actions are documented in Figure 6-41, where each part is based on the template for required children shown in Figure 6-29(a). Note that there is no diagram for the CUSTOMER-to-TRANS relationship because that is an O-O relationship without a required parent (or child).

**FIGURE 6-40**

Summary of View Ridge Database Design Relationships

| Relationship | | Cardinality | | |
|---|---|---|---|---|
| **Parent** | **Child** | **Type** | **MAX** | **MIN** |
| ARTIST | WORK | Nonidentifying | 1:N | M-O |
| WORK | TRANS | Nonidentifying | 1:N | M-M |
| CUSTOMER | TRANS | Nonidentifying | 1:N | O-O |
| CUSTOMER | CUSTOMER_ARTIST_INT | Identifying | 1:N | M-O |
| ARTIST | CUSTOMER_ARTIST_INT | Identifying | 1:N | M-O |

**FIGURE 6-41**

Actions to Enforce Minimum
Cardinality for Required
Parents

| ARTIST Is Required Parent | Action on ARTIST (Parent) | Action on WORK (Child) |
|---|---|---|
| Insert | None. | Get a parent. |
| Modify key or foreign key | Prohibit—ARTIST uses a surrogate key. | Prohibit—ARTIST uses a surrogate key. |
| Delete | Prohibit if WORK exists— data about a work and its related transaction is never deleted (business rule). Allow if no WORK exists (business rule). | None. |

**(a) For the ARTIST-to-WORK Relationship**

| WORK Is Required Parent | Action on WORK (Parent) | Action on TRANS (Child) |
|---|---|---|
| Insert | None. | Get a parent. |
| Modify key or foreign key | Prohibit—WORK uses a surrogate key. | Prohibit—WORK uses a surrogate key. |
| Delete | Prohibit—data about a work and its related transaction is never deleted (business rule). | None. |

**(b) For the WORK-to-TRANS Relationship**

| CUSTOMER Is Required Parent | Action on CUSTOMER (Parent) | Action on CUSTOMER_ARTIST_INT (Child) |
|---|---|---|
| Insert | None. | Get a parent. |
| Modify key or foreign key | Prohibit—CUSTOMER uses a surrogate key. | Prohibit—CUSTOMER uses a surrogate key. |
| Delete | Prohibit if a transaction related to this CUSTOMER exists—data related to a transaction is never deleted (business rule). Allow if no transaction related to this CUSTOMER exists—(business rule)— cascade delete children. | None. |

**(c) For the CUSTOMER-to-CUSTOMER_ARTIST_INT Relationship**

| ARTIST Is Required Parent | Action on ARTIST (Parent) | Action on CUSTOMER_ARTIST_INT (Child) |
|---|---|---|
| Insert | None. | Get a parent. |
| Modify key or foreign key | Prohibit—ARTIST uses a surrogate key. | Prohibit—ARTIST uses a surrogate key. |
| Delete | Prohibit if a transaction related to a work by this ARTIST exists—data related to a transaction is never deleted (business rule). Allow if no transaction related to a work by this ARTIST exists—(business rule)—cascade delete children. | None. |

**(d)** For the ARTIST-to-CUSTOMER_ARTIST_INT Relationship

## Minimum Cardinality Enforcement for the Required Child

As shown in the summary in Figure 6-40, TRANS is the only required child in the database design in Figure 6-39. The actions to enforce that required child are documented in Figure 6-42, which is based on the template in Figure 6-29(b).

According to this document, an INSERT trigger on WORK will be written to create the required child. This trigger will be fired whenever a work is first introduced at the gallery. At that time, a new TRANS row will be created to store the values for DateAcquired and AcquisitionPrice.

Changes to the primary key in WORK will not occur because it has a surrogate key. Changes to the foreign key in TRANS will not be allowed because a TRANS never switches to another work. As stated earlier, the gallery has the policy that no transaction or related data will ever be deleted. Consequently, deletions of either WORK or TRANS are not allowed.

**FIGURE 6-42**

Actions to Enforce Minimum Cardinality for Required Children—For the WORK-to-TRANS Relationship

| TRANS Is Required Child | Action on WORK (Parent) | Action on TRANS (Child) |
|---|---|---|
| Insert | INSERT trigger on WORK to create row in TRANS. TRANS will be given data for DateAcquired and AcquisitionPrice. Other columns will be null. | Will be created by INSERT trigger on WORK. |
| Modify key or foreign key | Prohibit—surrogate key. | Prohibit—TRANS must always refer to the WORK associated with it. |
| Delete | Prohibit—data related to a transaction is never deleted (business rule). | Prohibit—data related to a transaction is never deleted (business rule). |

## Column Properties for the View Ridge Database Design Tables

As we discussed at the beginning of this chapter, besides naming the columns in each table, we must specify the column properties summarized in Figure 6-1 for each column: null status, data type, default value (if any), and data constraints (if any). These are shown in Figure 6-43, where surrogate keys are shown using the **SQL Server IDENTITY({StartValue}, {Increment}) property** to specify the values the surrogate key

**FIGURE 6-43**

Column Properties for the View Ridge Database Design

ARTIST

| Column Name | Type | Key | NULL Status | Remarks |
|---|---|---|---|---|
| ArtistID | Int | Primary Key | NOT NULL | Surrogate Key IDENTITY (1,1) |
| LastName | Char (25) | Alternate Key | NOT NULL | Unique (AK1.1) |
| FirstName | Char (25) | Alternate Key | NOT NULL | Unique (AK1.2) |
| Nationality | Char (30) | No | NULL | IN ('Canadian', 'English', 'French', 'German', 'Mexican', 'Russian', 'Spanish', 'United States') |
| DateOfBirth | Numeric (4) | No | NULL | (DateOfBirth < DateDeceased) (BETWEEN 1900 and 2999) |
| DateDeceased | Numeric (4) | No | NULL | (BETWEEN 1900 and 2999) |

**(a)** Column Characteristics for the ARTIST Table

WORK

| Column Name | Type | Key | NULL Status | Remarks |
|---|---|---|---|---|
| WorkID | Int | Primary Key | NOT NULL | Surrogate Key IDENTITY (500,1) |
| Title | Char (35) | Alternate Key | NOT NULL | Unique (AK1.1) |
| Copy | Char (12) | Alternate Key | NOT NULL | Unique (AK1.2) |
| Medium | Char (35) | No | NULL | |
| Description | Varchar (1000) | No | NULL | DEFAULT value = 'Unknown provenance' |
| ArtistID | Int | Foreign Key | NOT NULL | |

**(b)** Column Characteristics for the WORK Table

TRANS

| Column Name | Type | Key | NULL Status | Remarks |
|---|---|---|---|---|
| TransactionID | Int | Primary Key | NOT NULL | Surrogate Key IDENTITY (100,1) |
| DateAcquired | Date | No | NOT NULL | |
| AcquisitionPrice | Numeric (8,2) | No | NOT NULL | |
| AskingPrice | Numeric (8,2) | No | NULL | |
| DateSold | Date | No | NULL | (DateAcquired <= DateSold) |
| SalesPrice | Numeric (8,2) | No | NULL | (SalesPrice > 0) AND (SalesPrice <= 500000) |
| CustomerID | Int | Foreign Key | NULL | |
| WorkID | Int | Foreign Key | NOT NULL | |

**(c) Column Characteristics for the TRANS Table**

CUSTOMER

| Column Name | Type | Key | NULL Status | Remarks |
|---|---|---|---|---|
| CustomerID | Int | Primary Key | NOT NULL | Surrogate Key IDENTITY (1000,1) |
| LastName | Char (25) | No | NOT NULL | |
| FirstName | Char (25) | No | NOT NULL | |
| EmailAddress | Varchar (100) | Alternate Key | NULL | Unique (AK 1.1) |
| EncryptedPassword | Varchar(50) | No | NULL | |
| Street | Char (30) | No | NULL | |
| City | Char (35) | No | NULL | |
| State | Char (2) | No | NULL | |
| ZIPorPostalCode | Char (9) | No | NULL | |
| Country | Char (50) | No | NULL | |
| AreaCode | Char (3) | No | NULL | |
| PhoneNumber | Char (8) | No | NULL | |

**(d) Column Characteristics for the CUSTOMER Table**

**FIGURE 6-43**

Continued

will use. We will describe how to implement surrogate keys in our discussion of Microsoft SQL Server 2019 in Chapters 7 and 10A, for Oracle Database in Chapter 10B, and for MySQL 8.0 in Chapter 10C.

With this step, we have completed our database design for the View Ridge Gallery database, and now we are ready to create it as an actual, functioning database in a DBMS product. We will do so in many of the following chapters, so be certain that you understand the View Ridge Gallery database design we have built.

CUSTOMER_ARTIST_INT

| Column Name | Type | Key | NULL Status | Remarks |
|---|---|---|---|---|
| ArtistID | Int | Primary Key, Foreign Key | NOT NULL | |
| CustomerID | Int | Primary Key, Foreign Key | NOT NULL | |

**(e) Column Characteristics for the CUSTOMER_ARTIST_INT Table**

**FIGURE 6-43**

Continued

## Summary

This chapter discusses the process of transforming a data model (as discussed in Chapter 5) into a database design. Figure 6-44 summarizes the various aspects of data models and database designs, how they relate to each other, and how they relate to the systems analysis and design process in general and to the systems development life cycle (SDLC) in particular. For more information about systems analysis and design and the SDLC, see Appendix B.

Transforming a data model into a database design requires three major tasks: replacing each entity with a table and each attribute with a column, representing relationships and maximum cardinality by placing foreign keys, and representing minimum cardinality by defining actions to constrain activities on values of primary and foreign keys.

During database design, each entity is replaced by a table. The attributes of the entity become columns of the table. The identifier of the entity becomes the primary key of the table, and candidate keys in the entity become candidate keys in the table. A good primary key is short, numeric, and fixed. If a good primary key is not available, a surrogate key may be used instead. Some organizations choose to use surrogate keys for all of their tables. An alternate key is the same as a candidate key and is used to ensure unique values in a column. The notation AK$n.m$ refers to the $n$th alternative key and the $m$th column in that key.

Four properties need to be specified for each table column: null status, data type, default value, and data constraints. A column can be NULL or NOT NULL. Primary keys are always NOT NULL; alternate keys can be NULL. Data types depend on the DBMS to be used. Generic data types include CHAR(n), VARCHAR(n), NVARCHAR(n), DATE, TIME, INTEGER, FLOAT, NUMERIC, and DECIMAL. A default value is a value to be supplied by the DBMS when a new row is created. It can be a simple value or the result of a function. Sometimes triggers are needed to supply values of more complicated expressions.

Data constraints include domain constraints, range constraints, intrarelation constraints, and interrelation constraints. Domain constraints specify a set of values that a column may have, range constraints specify an interval of allowed values, intrarelation constraints involve comparisons among columns in the same table, and interrelation constraints involve comparisons among columns in different tables. A referential integrity constraint is an example of an interrelation constraint.

Once the tables, keys, and columns have been defined, they should be checked against normalization criteria. Usually the tables will already be normalized, but they should be checked in any case. Also, it may be necessary to denormalize some tables.

The second step in database design is to create relationships by placing foreign keys appropriately. For 1:1 strong relationships, the key of either table can go in the other table as a foreign key; for 1:N strong relationships, the key of the parent must go in the child; and for N:M strong relationships, a new table, called an intersection table, is constructed that has the keys of both tables. Intersection tables never have non-key data.

| | Data Model (Chapter 5) | Database Design (Chapter 6) |
|---|---|---|
| SDLC Stage | Requirements Analysis | Component Design |
| SA&D Reference | Conceptual Design/Schema | |
| | | Logical Design/Schema |
| | | Physical Design (Data Types) |
| Data Structure | Entity | Table (Relation) |
| Relationship Structure | Relationship | Relationship with Foreign Keys |
| Level of Generality | Generic | DBMS Specific |
| Relationships: | | |
| 1:1 | Yes | Yes |
| 1:N | Yes | Yes |
| 1:N ID-Dependent | Yes | Yes |
| N:M | Yes | No—See Intersection Table |
| Intersection Table with two 1:N ID-Dependent Relationships | No—See N:M Relationships | Yes |
| Association Table with two 1: N ID-Dependent Relationships | Yes (Associative Entity) | Yes |
| SuperType/SubType | Yes Depends on Data Modeling Software | Yes Depends on Data Modeling Software |
| Recursive | Yes | Yes |
| Software Tools: (used in this book) | Microsoft Visio 2019 | MySQL Workbench |

**FIGURE 6-44**

Summary of the Database Design Process

Four uses for ID-dependent entities are N:M relationships, association relationships, multivalued attributes, and archetype/instance relationships. An association relationship differs from an intersection table because the ID-dependent entity has non-key data. In all ID-dependent entities, the key of the parent is already in the child. Therefore, no foreign key needs to be created. When an instance entity of the archetype/instance pattern is given a non-ID-dependent identifier, it changes from an ID-dependent entity to a weak entity. The tables that represent such entities must have the key of the parent as a foreign key. They remain weak entities, however. When the parent of an ID-dependent entity is given a surrogate key, the ID-dependent entity is also given a surrogate key. It remains a weak entity, however.

Mixed entities are represented by placing the key of the parent of the nonidentifying relationship into the child. The key of the parent of the identifying relationship will already be in the child. Subtypes are represented by copying the key from the supertype into the subtype(s) as a foreign key. Recursive relationships are represented in the same ways that 1:1, 1:N, and N:M relationships are represented. The only difference is that the foreign key references rows in the table in which it resides.

Ternary relationships are decomposed into binary relationships. However, sometimes binary constraints must be documented. Three such constraints are MUST, MUST NOT, and MUST COVER.

The third step in database design is to create a plan for enforcing minimum cardinality. Figure 6-29 shows the actions that need to be taken to enforce minimum cardinality for required parents and required children. The actions in Figure 6-29(a) must be taken for M-O and M-M relationships; the actions in Figure 6-29(b) must be taken for O-M and M-M relationships.

Enforcing mandatory parents can be done by defining the appropriate referential integrity constraint and by setting the foreign key to NOT NULL. The designer must specify whether updates to the parent's primary key will cascade or be prohibited, whether deletions to the parent will cascade or be prohibited, and what policy will be used for finding a parent when a new child is created.

Enforcing mandatory children is difficult and requires the use of triggers or application code. The particular actions that need to be taken are shown in Figure 6-29(b). Enforcing M-M relationships can be very difficult. Particular challenges concern the creation of the first parent/child rows and the deletion of the last parent/child rows. The triggers on the two tables interfere with one another. M-M relationships between strong and weak entities are not as problematic as those between strong entities.

In this text, the actions to enforce required parents are documented using referential integrity actions on the table design diagrams. The actions to enforce required children are documented by using Figure 6-29(b) as a boilerplate document. An additional complication is that a table can participate in many relationships. Triggers written to enforce the minimum cardinality on one relationship may interfere with triggers written to enforce the minimum cardinality on another relationship. This problem is beyond the scope of this text but be aware that it exists. The principles for enforcing minimum cardinality are summarized in Figure 6-34.

A database design for the View Ridge Gallery is shown in Figures 6-39, 6-40, 6-41, 6-42, and 6-43. You should understand this design because it will be used throughout the remainder of this book.

## Key Terms

action
alternate key (AK)
association entity
association relationship
association table
associative entity
candidate key
cascading deletion
cascading update
component design
data constraint
database design
DBMS reserved word
default value

domain constraint
interrelation constraint
intersection table
intrarelation constraint
minimum cardinality enforcement action
MUST constraint
MUST COVER constraint
MUST NOT constraint
null status
parent mandatory and child mandatory (M-M)
parent mandatory and child optional (M-O)

parent optional and child mandatory (O-M)
parent optional and child optional (O-O)
primary key
range constraint
referential integrity (RI) action
SQL Server IDENTITY ({StartValue}, {Increment}) property
surrogate key
systems analysis and design
systems development life cycle (SDLC)
table
trigger

## Review Questions

**6.1** Identify the three major tasks for transforming a data model into a database design.

**6.2** What is the relationship between entities and tables? Between attributes and columns?

**6.3** Why is the choice of the primary key important?

**6.4** What are the three characteristics of an ideal primary key?

**6.5** What is a surrogate key? What are its advantages?

**6.6** When should you use a surrogate key?

**6.7** Describe two disadvantages of surrogate keys.

**6.8** What is the difference between an alternate key and a candidate key?

**6.9** What does the notation LastName (AK2.2) mean?

**6.10** Name four column properties.

**6.11** Explain why primary keys may never be null but alternate keys can be null.

**6.12** List five generic data types.

**6.13** Describe three ways that a default value can be assigned.

**6.14** What is a domain constraint? Give an example.

**6.15** What is a range constraint? Give an example.

**6.16** What is an intrarelation constraint? Give an example.

**6.17** What is an interrelation constraint? Give an example.

**6.18** What tasks should be accomplished when verifying normalization of a database design?

**6.19** Describe two ways to represent a 1:1 strong entity relationship. Give an example other than one in this chapter.

**6.20** Describe how to represent a 1:N strong entity relationship. Give an example other than one in this chapter.

**6.21** Describe how to represent an N:M strong entity relationship. Give an example other than one in this chapter.

**6.22** What is an intersection table? Why is it necessary?

**6.23** What is the difference between the table that represents an ID-dependent association entity and an intersection table?

**6.24** List four uses for ID-dependent entities.

**6.25** Describe how to represent an association entity relationship. Give an example other than one in this chapter.

**6.26** Describe how to represent a multivalued attribute entity relationship. Give an example other than one in this chapter.

**6.27** Describe how to represent an archetype/instance entity relationship. Give an example other than one in this chapter.

**6.28** What happens when an instance entity is given a non-ID-dependent identifier? How does this change affect relationship design?

**6.29** What happens when the parent in an ID-dependent relationship is given a surrogate key? What should the key of the child become?

**6.30** Describe how to represent a mixed entity relationship. Give an example other than one in this chapter.

**6.31** Describe how to represent a supertype/subtype entity relationship. Give an example other than one in this chapter.

**6.32** Describe two ways to represent a 1:1 recursive relationship. Give an example other than one in this chapter.

**6.33** Describe how to represent a 1:N recursive relationship. Give an example other than one in this chapter.

**6.34** Describe how to represent an N:M recursive relationship. Give an example other than one in this chapter.

**6.35** In general, how are ternary relationships represented? Explain how a binary constraint may affect such a relationship.

**6.36** Describe a MUST constraint. Give an example other than one in this chapter.

**6.37** Describe a MUST NOT constraint. Give an example other than one in this chapter.

**6.38** Describe a MUST COVER constraint. Give an example other than one in this chapter.

**6.39** Explain in general terms what needs to be done to enforce minimum cardinality.

**6.40** Explain the need for each of the actions in Figure 6-29(a).

**6.41** Explain the need for each of the actions in Figure 6-29(b).

**6.42** State which of the actions in Figure 6-29 must be applied for M-O relationships, O-M relationships, and M-M relationships.

**6.43** Explain what must be done for the DBMS to enforce required parents.

**6.44** What design decisions must be made to enforce required parents?

**6.45** Explain why the DBMS cannot be used to enforce required children.

**6.46** What is a trigger? How can triggers be used to enforce required children?

**6.47** Explain why the enforcement of M-M relationships is particularly difficult.

**6.48** Explain the need for each of the design decisions in Figure 6-34.

**6.49** Explain the implications of each of the minimum cardinality specifications in Figure 6-40.

**6.50** Explain the rationale for each of the entries in the table in Figure 6-42.

# Exercises

**6.51** Answer Exercise 5.56 if you have not already done so. Design a database for your model in Exercise 5.56(b). Your design should include a specification of tables and attributes as well as primary, candidate, and foreign keys. Also specify how you will enforce minimum cardinality. Document your minimum cardinality enforcement using referential integrity actions for a required parent, if any, and the form in Figure 6-29(b) for a required child, if any.

**6.52** Answer Exercise 5.57 if you have not already done so. Design a database for your model in Exercise 5.57(c). Your design should include a specification of tables and attributes as well as primary, candidate, and foreign keys. Also specify how you will enforce minimum cardinality. Document your minimum cardinality enforcement using referential integrity actions for required parents, if any, and the form in Figure 6-29(b) for required children, if any.

**6.53** Answer Exercise 5.58 if you have not already done so. Design a database for your model in Exercise 5.58(d). Your design should include a specification of tables and attributes as well as primary, candidate, and foreign keys. Also specify how you will enforce minimum cardinality. Document your minimum cardinality enforcement using referential integrity actions for required parents, if any, and the form in Figure 6-29(b) for required children, if any.

**6.54** Answer Exercise 5.59 if you have not already done so. Design databases for your model in Exercise 5.59(a) and for the model in Figure 5-57. Your designs should include a specification of tables and attributes as well as primary, candidate, and foreign keys. Also specify how you will enforce minimum cardinality. Document your minimum cardinality enforcement using referential integrity actions for required parents, if any, and the form in Figure 6-29(b) for required children, if any.

**6.55** Answer Exercise 5.60 if you have not already done so. Design a database for your model in Exercise 5.60(e). Your design should include a specification of tables and attributes as well as primary, candidate, and foreign keys. Also specify how you will enforce minimum cardinality. Document your minimum cardinality enforcement using referential integrity actions for required parents, if any, and the form in Figure 6-29(b) for required children, if any.

**6.56** Answer Exercise 5.61 if you have not already done so. Design a database for your model in Exercise 5.61(c). Your design should include a specification of tables and attributes as well as primary, candidate, and foreign keys. Also specify how you will enforce minimum cardinality. Document your minimum cardinality enforcement using referential integrity actions for required parents, if any, and the form in Figure 6-29(b) for required children, if any.

**6.57** Answer Exercise 5.62 if you have not already done so. Design a database for your model in Exercise 5.62(d). Your design should include a specification of tables and attributes as well as primary, candidate, and foreign keys. Also specify how you will enforce minimum cardinality. Document your minimum cardinality enforcement using referential integrity actions for required parents, if any, and the form in Figure 6-29(b) for required children, if any.

# Case Questions

## Writer's Patrol Case Questions

Answer the Writer's Patrol case questions in Chapter 5 if you have not already done so. Design a database for your data model from Chapter 5.

**A.** Convert this data model to a database design. Specify tables, primary keys, and foreign keys. Using Figure 6-43 as a guide, specify column properties.

**B.** Describe how you have represented weak entities, if any exist.

**C.** Describe how you have represented supertype and subtype entities, if any exist.

**D.** Create a visual representation of your database design as a Crow's Foot E-R diagram similar to the one in Figure 6-39.

**E.** Document your minimum cardinality enforcement using referential integrity actions for required parents, if any, and the form in Figure 6-29(b) for required children, if any.

## San Juan Sailboat Charters Case Questions

San Juan Sailboat Charters (SJSBC) is an agency that leases (charters) sailboats. SJSBC does not own the boats. Instead, SJSBC leases boats on behalf of boat owners who want to earn income from their boats when they are not using them, and SJSBC charges the owners a fee for this service. SJSBC specializes in boats that can be used for multiday or weekly charters. The smallest sailboat available is 28 feet in length, and the largest is 51 feet in length.

Each sailboat is fully equipped at the time it is leased. Most of the equipment is provided at the time of the charter. Most of the equipment is provided by the owners, but some is provided by SJSBC. The owner-provided equipment includes equipment that is attached to the boat, such as radios, compasses, depth indicators and other instrumentation, stoves, and refrigerators. Other owner-provided equipment, such as sails, lines, anchors, dinghies, life preservers, and equipment in the cabin (dishes, silverware, cooking utensils, bedding, and so on), is not physically attached to the boat. SJSBC provides consumable supplies, such as charts, navigation books, tide and current tables, soap, dish towels, toilet paper, and similar items. The consumable supplies are treated as equipment by SJSBC for tracking and accounting purposes.

Keeping track of equipment is an important part of SJSBC's responsibilities. Much of the equipment is expensive, and those items not physically attached to the boat can be easily damaged, lost, or stolen. SJSBC holds the customer responsible for all of the boat's equipment during the period of the charter.

SJSBC likes to keep accurate records of its customers and charters, and customers are required to keep a log during each charter. Some itineraries and weather conditions are more dangerous than others, and the data from these logs provide information about the customer experience. This information is useful for marketing purposes as well as for evaluating a customer's ability to handle a particular boat and itinerary.

Sailboats need maintenance. Note that two definitions of boat are (1) "break out another thousand" and (2) "a hole in the water into which one pours money." SJSBC is required by its contracts with the boat owners to keep accurate records of all maintenance activities and costs.

A data model of a proposed database to support an information system for SJSBC is shown in Figure 6-45. Note that because the OWNER entity allows for owners to be companies as well as individuals, SJSBC can be included as an equipment owner (note that the cardinalities in the diagram allow SJSBC to own equipment while not owning any boats). Also note that this model relates EQUIPMENT to CHARTER rather than BOAT even when the equipment is physically attached to the boat. This is only one possible way to handle EQUIPMENT, but it is satisfactory to the managers of SJSBC.

**A.** Convert this data model to a database design. Specify tables, primary keys, and foreign keys. Using Figure 6-43 as a guide, specify column properties.

**B.** Describe how you have represented weak entities, if any exist.

**C.** Describe how you have represented supertype and subtype entities, if any exist.

**D.** Create a visual representation of your database design as a Crow's Foot E-R diagram similar to the one in Figure 6-39.

**E.** Document your minimum cardinality enforcement using referential integrity actions for required parents, if any, and the form in Figure 6-29(b) for required children, if any.

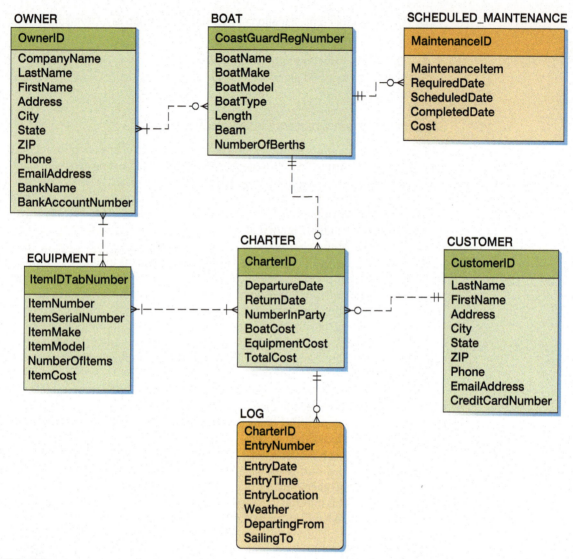

**FIGURE 6-45**

Data Model for San Juan
Sailboat Charters

# The Queen Anne Curiosity Shop Project Questions

**If you have not already done so, complete the Queen Anne Curiosity Shop project questions at the end of Chapter 5.**

**A.** Convert this data model to a database design. Specify tables, primary keys, and foreign keys. Using Figure 6-43 as a guide, specify column properties.

**B.** Describe how you have represented weak entities, if any exist.

**C.** Describe how you have represented supertype and subtype entities, if any exist.

**D.** Create a visual representation of your database design as a Crow's Foot E-R diagram similar to the one in Figure 6-39.

**E.** Document your minimum cardinality enforcement using referential integrity actions for required parents, if any, and the form in Figure 6-29(b) for required children, if any.

# Morgan Importing Project Questions

If you have not already done so, complete the Morgan Importing project questions at the end of Chapter 5.

A. Convert this data model to a database design. Specify tables, primary keys, and foreign keys. Using Figure 6-43 as a guide, specify column properties.

B. Describe how you have represented weak entities, if any exist.

C. Describe how you have represented supertype and subtype entities, if any exist.

D. Create a visual representation of your database design as a Crow's Foot E-R diagram similar to the one in Figure 6-39.

E. Document your minimum cardinality enforcement using referential integrity actions for required parents, if any, and the form in Figure 6-29(b) for required children, if any.

# PART 3

# Database Implementation

In Chapter 5, we discussed how to create a data model for a new database, and in Chapter 6, we demonstrated how to transform that data model into a database design that we can use to build an actual database in a relational DBMS. We used the View Ridge Gallery (VRG) database as our example in Chapter 6 and finished with a complete set of specifications for the VRG database. In Part 3, we will implement the VRG database design in Microsoft SQL Server 2019 (with versions for Oracle Database and MySQL 8.0 shown in Chapters 10B and 10C, respectively, and several different versions implemented in ArangoDB in Chapter 10D to illustrate non-relational document database designs and queries).

Part 3 consists of two chapters. Chapter 7 presents SQL data definition language statements for constructing database components and describes the SQL data manipulation statements for inserting, updating, and deleting data. You will also learn how to construct and use SQL views. The chapter concludes with an introduction to embedding SQL statements in application programs and SQL/Persistent Stored Modules (SQL/PSM), which leads to a discussion of SQL user-defined functions, triggers, and stored procedures.

Chapter 8 presents the use of SQL statements to redesign databases. It presents SQL correlated subqueries and then introduces SQL statements using the SQL EXISTS and NOT EXISTS keywords. Both of these advanced SQL statements are needed for database redesign. Chapter 8 also describes database reverse engineering, surveys common database redesign problems, and shows how to use SQL to solve database redesign problems.

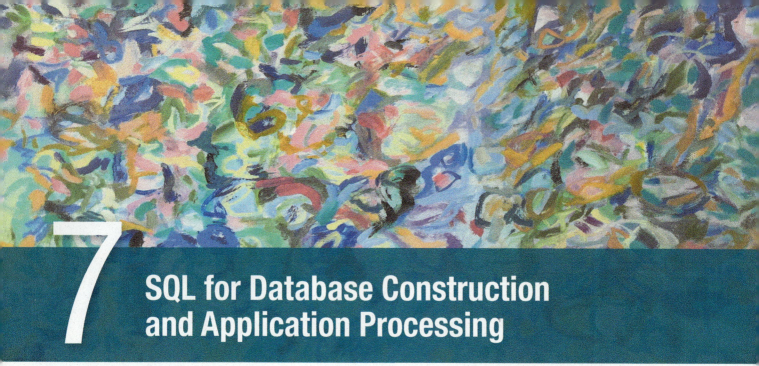

# 7 SQL for Database Construction and Application Processing

## Chapter Objectives

- To create and manage table structures using SQL statements
- To understand how referential integrity actions are implemented in SQL statements
- To create and execute SQL constraints
- To understand several uses for SQL views
- To use SQL statements to create, use, and manage views

- To understand how SQL is used in application programming
- To understand SQL/Persistent Stored Modules (SQL/PSM)
- To understand how to create and use functions
- To understand how to create and use triggers
- To understand how to create and use stored procedures

**In Chapter 2,** we introduced SQL and classified SQL statements into five categories:

- **Data definition language (DDL)** statements, which are used for creating tables, relationships, and other database structures
- **Data manipulation language (DML)** statements, which are used for querying, inserting, updating, and deleting data
- **SQL/Persistent Stored Modules (SQL/PSM)** statements, which extend SQL by adding procedural programming capabilities, such as variables and flow-of-control statements, that provide some programmability within the SQL framework
- **Transaction control language (TCL)** statements, which are used to mark transaction boundaries and control transaction behavior
- **Data control language (DCL)** statements, which are used to grant database permissions (or to revoke those permissions) to users and groups so the users or groups can perform various operations on the data in the database

In Chapter 2, we discussed only DML query statements. This chapter describes and illustrates SQL DDL statements for constructing databases; SQL DML statements for inserting, modifying, and deleting data; and SQL statements to create and use SQL views. We also discuss how to embed SQL statements into application programs and SQL/PSM and how to use SQL/PSM to create functions, triggers, and stored procedures. SQL TCL and SQL DCL statements are discussed in Chapter 9.

In this chapter, we use a DBMS product to create the database that we designed as a **database design** in Chapter 6 based on a **data model** from Chapter 5. We are now in the **implementation** step of the **systems development life cycle (SDLC)** in the **systems analysis and design** process. This is the SDLC step that we have been working toward all along—building and implementing the database and management information system application that uses that database. (For an introduction to systems analysis and design and to the SDLC, see Appendix B, "Getting Started with Systems Analysis and Design.")

The knowledge in this chapter is important whether you become a database administrator or an application programmer. Even if you will not construct SQL user-defined functions, triggers, or stored procedures yourself, it is important that you know what they are, how they work, and how they influence database processing.

## The Importance of Working with an Installed DBMS Product

In order to fully understand the DBMS concepts and features we discuss and illustrate in the chapter, you need to work with them in an installed DBMS product. This *hands-on* experience is necessary so that you move from an abstract understanding of these concepts and features to a practical knowledge of them and how they are used and implemented.

The topics in this chapter, as well as topics in Chapters 9 and 10, outline this material as it relates to the three major DBMS products discussed in this text.

The specific information you need to download, install, and use these DBMS products is found in three online chapters available at *www.pearsonhighered.com/kroenke/*. Microsoft SQL Server 2019 is discussed in online Chapter 10A, Oracle Database and Oracle Database 18c Express Edition (referred to as Oracle Database XE) are discussed in online Chapter 10B, and MySQL 8.0 is discussed in online Chapter 10C. As described in the introductory Chapter 10, portions of these chapters parallel the discussion in this chapter and illustrate the actual use of the concepts and features in each DBMS product.

To get the most out of this chapter, you should download and install the DBMS product(s) of your choice and then follow your work in each section by working thorough the corresponding sections in the chapter for your DBMS product.

## The View Ridge Gallery Database

In Chapter 6, we introduced the View Ridge Gallery, a small art gallery that sells contemporary North American and European fine art and provides art framing services. We also developed a data model and database design for a database for the View Ridge Gallery. Our final database design for the View Ridge Gallery is shown in Figure 7-1. You should review the database design, table column characteristics, and relationship specifications as described in Chapter 6. In this chapter, we will use SQL to build a database for the View Ridge Gallery, named VRG, based on that design. The SQL scripts needed to create the VRG database are available at *www.pearsonhighered.com/kroenke*.

## SQL DDL and DML

Figure 7-2 summarizes the new SQL DDL and DML statements described in this chapter. We begin with SQL DDL statements for managing table structures, including CREATE TABLE, ALTER TABLE, DROP TABLE, and TRUNCATE TABLE. Using these statements, we will build

CUSTOMER

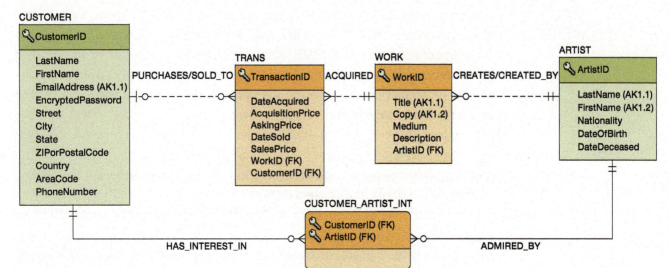

**FIGURE 7-1**

VRG Database Design for the View Ridge Gallery Database

the table structure for the View Ridge database. Then we present the four SQL DML statements for managing data: INSERT, UPDATE, DELETE, and MERGE. Next, we will discuss the SQL statements used to create, use, and manage SQL views. We will end the chapter with a discussion of SQL/Persistent Stored Modules (SQL/PSM) and of functions, triggers, and stored procedures.

**FIGURE 7-2**

SQL Elements

| SQL Elements Discussed in this Chapter |
|---|
| • SQL Data Definition Language (DDL) |
| — CREATE TABLE |
| — ALTER TABLE |
| — DROP TABLE |
| — TRUNCATE TABLE |
| • SQL Data Manipulation Language (DML) |
| — INSERT |
| — UPDATE |
| — DELETE |
| — MERGE |
| • SQL Views |
| — CREATE VIEW |
| — ALTER VIEW |
| — DROP VIEW |
| • SQL/Persistent Stored Modules (SQL/PSM) |
| — Functions |
| — Triggers |
| — Stored Procedures |

# Managing Table Structure with SQL DDL

The **SQL CREATE TABLE statement** is used to construct tables, define columns and column constraints, and create relationships. Most DBMS products provide graphical tools for performing these tasks, and you may be wondering why you need to learn SQL to perform the same work. There are four reasons. First, creating tables and relationships with SQL is quicker than with graphical tools. Once you know how to use the SQL CREATE TABLE statement, you will be able to construct tables faster and more easily than by fussing around with buttons and graphical gimmickry. Second, some applications, particularly those for reporting, querying, and data mining, require you to create the same table repeatedly. You can do this efficiently if you create an SQL script text file with the necessary SQL CREATE TABLE statements. You then just execute the SQL script when you need to re-create a table. Third, some applications require you to create temporary tables during application work. The discussion of RFM reports (RFM is the name a sales analysis report, where R refers to how *recently* a sale was made, F refers to how *frequently* the customer buys from the company, and M refers to how much *money* that customer spends), in Appendix J shows one such application. The only way to create tables from program code is to use SQL. Finally, SQL DDL is standardized and DBMS independent. With the exception of some data types, the same CREATE TABLE statement will work with SQL Server, Oracle Database, DB2, or MySQL.

## Creating the VRG Database

Of course, before you can create any tables, you have to create the database. The SQL-92 and subsequent standards include an SQL statement for creating databases, but it is seldom used. Instead, most developers use special commands or graphical tools for creating a database. These techniques are DBMS specific, and we describe them in context for SQL Server 2019 in Chapter 10A, for Oracle Database in Chapter 10B, for MySQL 8.0 in Chapter 10C, and for Microsoft Access 2019 in Appendix A.

At this point, we highly recommend that you read the section on creating a new database in the DBMS product you are using and use the appropriate steps to create a new database for the View Ridge Gallery named VRG. For illustrative purposes, we will use Microsoft SQL Server 2019 in this chapter, and our SQL code will be the correct code for that product. The correct SQL statements for other DBMS products will be similar, but they will vary slightly. The correct SQL statements for Oracle Database and MySQL 8.0 can be found in Chapters 10B and 10C, respectively. Figure 7-3 shows the VRG database in the Microsoft SQL Server 2019 Management Studio.

## Using SQL Scripts

Each DBMS product has a **graphical user interface (GUI)** utility program that is used to create, edit, and store SQL script files. An **SQL script file** or **SQL script** is a separately stored plain-text file, and it usually uses a file name extension of *.sql*. An SQL script can be opened and run as an SQL command (or set of commands). SQL scripts are used to create and populate databases and to store a query or set of queries. They are also used to store the SQL statements to create SQL elements that we will discuss later in this chapter: SQL views and SQL/PSM functions, triggers, and stored procedures. We recommend that you use SQL scripts to edit and store any work you do in SQL in this chapter (as well as any SQL work in general).

The GUI utilities that we will use to create SQL scripts are:

- **Microsoft SQL Server Management Studio** for use with Microsoft SQL Server 2019 (see Chapter 10A for a discussion of Microsoft SQL Server Management Studio)
- **Oracle SQL Developer** for use with Oracle Database and Oracle Database XE (see Chapter 10B for a discussion of Oracle SQL Developer)
- **Oracle MySQL Workbench** for use with Oracle MySQL 8.0 (see Chapter 10C for a discussion of Oracle MySQL Workbench)

## Implementing 1:1 Relationships

SQL for implementing 1:1 relationships is almost identical to that for 1:N relationships, as just shown. The only difference is that the foreign key must be declared as unique. For example, if the relationship were 1:1 between ARTIST and WORK (i.e., each artist could have only one work at the View Ridge Gallery), then in Figure 7-9 we would add the following constraint to the WORK table:

```
CONSTRAINT    UniqueWork    UNIQUE (ArtistID)
```

Note that the ARTIST-to-WORK relationship in Figure 7-1 is, of course, *not* 1:1, so we will *not* specify this constraint in our current SQL statements. As before, if the parent is required, then the foreign key should be set to NOT NULL. Otherwise, it should be NULL.

## Casual Relationships

Sometimes it is appropriate to create a foreign key column but not specify a FOREIGN KEY constraint. In that case, the foreign key value may or may not match a value of the primary key in the parent. If, for example, you define the column DepartmentName in EMPLOYEE but do not specify a FOREIGN KEY constraint, then a row may have a value of Department-Name that does not match a value of DepartmentName in the DEPARTMENT table.

Such relationships, which are called **casual relationships**, occur frequently in applications that process tables with missing data. For example, you might buy consumer data that include names of consumers' employers. Assume that you have an EMPLOYER table that does not contain all of the possible companies for which the consumers might work. You want to use the relationship if you happen to have the values, but you do not want to require having those values. In that case, create a casual relationship by placing the key of EMPLOYER in the consumer data table but do *not* define a FOREIGN KEY constraint.

Figure 7-10 summarizes the techniques for creating relationships using FOREIGN KEY, NULL, NOT NULL, and UNIQUE constraints in 1:N, 1:1, and casual relationships.

## Creating Default Values and Data Constraints with SQL

Figure 7-11 shows an example default value and example data constraints for the VRG database. The Description column in the WORK table is given the default value of 'Unknown provenance'. The ARTIST and TRANS tables are assigned various data constraints.

In the ARTIST table, Nationality is limited to the values in the domain constraint shown, and DateOfBirth is limited by the **intrarelation constraint** (within the same table) that DateOfBirth occurs before DateDeceased. Further, DateOfBirth and DateDeceased, which as noted earlier

**FIGURE 7-10**

Summary of Relationship Definitions Using the SQL CREATE TABLE Statement

| Relationship Type | CREATE TABLE Constraints |
|---|---|
| 1:N relationship, parent optional | Specify FOREIGN KEY constraint. Set foreign key NULL. |
| 1:N relationship, parent required | Specify FOREIGN KEY constraint. Set foreign key NOT NULL. |
| 1:1 relationship, parent optional | Specify FOREIGN KEY constraint. Specify foreign key UNIQUE constraint. Set foreign key NULL. |
| 1:1 relationship, parent required | Specify FOREIGN KEY constraint. Specify foreign key UNIQUE constraint. Set foreign key NOT NULL. |
| Casual relationship | Create a foreign key column, but do not specify FOREIGN KEY constraint. If relationship is 1:1, specify foreign key UNIQUE. |

FIGURE 7-11

Default Values and Data
Constraints for the VRG
Database

| Table | Column | Default Value | Constraint |
|-------|--------|---------------|------------|
| WORK | Description | 'Unknown provenance' | |
| ARTIST | Nationality | | IN ('Candian', 'English', 'French', 'German', 'Mexican', 'Russian', 'Spanish', 'United States'). |
| ARTIST | DateOfBirth | | Less than DateDeceased. |
| ARTIST | DateOfBirth | | Four digits—1 or 2 is first digit, 0 to 9 for remaining three digits. |
| ARTIST | DateDeceased | | Four digits—1 or 2 is first digit, 0 to 9 for remaining three digits. |
| TRANS | SalesPrice | | Greater than 0 and less than or equal to 500,000. |
| TRANS | DateAcquired | | Less than or equal to DateSold. |

are years, are limited to the domain defined by specifying that the first digit be a 1 or a 2 and the remaining three digits be any decimal numbers. Thus, they can have any value between 1000 and 2999. SalesPrice in the TRANS table is limited by a range constraint to a value greater than 0 but less than or equal to $500,000, and PurchaseDate is limited by an intrarelation constraint that the DateSold be no earlier than the DateAcquired (i.e., DateAcquired is less than or equal to DateSold).

Figure 7-11 shows no **interrelation constraints** between tables. Although the SQL-92 specification defined facilities for creating such constraints, no DBMS vendor has implemented those facilities. Such constraints must be implemented in triggers. An example of this is shown later in this chapter. Figure 7-12 shows the SQL statements to create the ARTIST and WORK tables modified with the appropriate default values and data constraints.

### Implementing Default Values

Default values are created by specifying the DEFAULT keyword in the column definition just after the NULL/NOT NULL specification in SQL Server and MySQL. (In Oracle Database, DEFAULT is placed just *before* NULL/NOT NULL.) Note how in Figure 7-12 the Description column in the WORK table is given the default value of 'Unknown provenance' using this technique.

### Implementing Data Constraints

The data constraints are created using the SQL CHECK constraint. The format for the CHECK constraint is the word CONSTRAINT followed by a developer-provided constraint name, followed by the word CHECK and then by the constraint specification in parentheses. Expressions in CHECK constraints are akin to those used in the WHERE clause of SQL statements. Thus, the SQL IN keyword is used to provide a list of valid values. The SQL NOT IN keyword also can be used for negatively expressed domain constraints (not shown in this example). The SQL LIKE keyword is used for the specification of decimal places, or for string matching for character data. Range checks are specified using comparison operators such as the less than (<) and greater than (>) symbols. Because interrelation constraints are unsupported, comparisons can only be made as intrarelation constraints between columns in the rows of the same table.

> **BY THE WAY**   DBMS products are inconsistent in their implementation of CHECK constraints. The *ValidBirthYear* and *ValidDeathYear* constraints in Figure 7-12, for example, will not work with Oracle Database. However, Oracle Database implements other types of constraints with or without the LIKE keyword. Unfortunately, you must learn the peculiarities of the DBMS you use to know how best to implement constraints.

```
CREATE TABLE ARTIST (
        ArtistID                Int                 NOT NULL IDENTITY(1,1),
        LastName                Char(25)            NOT NULL,
        FirstName               Char(25)            NOT NULL,
        Nationality             Char(30)            NULL,
        DateOfBirth             Numeric(4)          NULL,
        DateDeceased            Numeric(4)          NULL,
        CONSTRAINT              ArtistPK            PRIMARY KEY(ArtistID),
        CONSTRAINT              ArtistAK1           UNIQUE(LastName, FirstName),
        CONSTRAINT              NationalityValues   CHECK
                                    (Nationality IN
                                        ('Canadian', 'English', 'French',
                                        'German', 'Mexican', 'Russian', 'Spanish',
                                        'United States')),
        CONSTRAINT              BirthValuesCheck    CHECK (DateOfBirth < DateDeceased),
        CONSTRAINT              ValidBirthYear      CHECK
                                    (DateOfBirth LIKE '[1-2][0-9][0-9][0-9]'),
        CONSTRAINT              ValidDeathYear      CHECK
                                    (DateDeceased LIKE '[1-2][0-9][0-9][0-9]')
        );

CREATE TABLE WORK (
        WorkID                  Int                 NOT NULL IDENTITY(500,1),
        Title                   Char(35)            NOT NULL,
        [Copy]                  Char(12)            NOT NULL,
        Medium                  Char(35)            NULL,
        [Description]           Varchar(1000)       NULL DEFAULT 'Unknown provenance',
        ArtistID                Int                 NOT NULL,
        CONSTRAINT              WorkPK              PRIMARY KEY(WorkID),
        CONSTRAINT              WorkAK1             UNIQUE(Title, Copy),
        CONSTRAINT              ArtistFK            FOREIGN KEY(ArtistID)
                                    REFERENCES ARTIST(ArtistID)
                                        ON UPDATE NO ACTION
                                        ON DELETE NO ACTION
        );
```

**FIGURE 7-12**

The SQL Statements to Create the VRG Database ARTIST and WORK Tables with Default Values and Data Constraints

## Creating the VRG Database Tables

Figure 7-13 shows SQL for creating all of the tables in the VRG database documented at the end of Chapter 6. Read each line and be certain that you understand its function and purpose. Notice that deletions cascade for the relationships between CUSTOMER and CUSTOMER_ARTIST_INT and between ARTIST and CUSTOMER_ARTIST_INT.

Any DBMS reserved words[4] used as table or column names need to be enclosed in square brackets ([ and ]) and thus converted to delimited identifiers. We have already decided to use the table name TRANS instead of TRANSACTION so we do not use the *transaction* reserved word. The table name WORK is also a potential problem; the word *work* is a reserved word in some DBMS products, as are the column names *Description* in the WORK table and *State* in the TRANS table. Enclosing such terms in brackets[5] signifies to the SQL parser that these terms have been provided by the developer and are not to be used in the standard way. Ironically, whereas SQL Server chokes on the word TRANSACTION, Oracle Database has no problem with it.

You can find a list of reserved words in the documentation for the DBMS product that you use, and we deal with some specific cases in the chapters dedicated to Microsoft SQL Server 2019, Oracle Database, and MySQL 8.0. Be assured that if you use any keyword from the SQL syntax, such as SELECT, FROM, WHERE, LIKE, ORDER, ASC, or DESC, for table or column names, you will have problems. Enclose such words in square brackets for

---

[4]Consult the documentation for the DBMS you are using. For Microsoft SQL Server 2019, which we are using in this chapter, see *https://docs.microsoft.com/en-us/sql/t-sql/language-elements/reserved-keywords-transact-sql* (accessed October 2020).

[5]Brackets are used in Microsoft SQL Server, which is the DBMS we using for our examples in this chapter. Oracle Database uses double quotes, while MySQL 8.0 uses backward single quotes. As usual, always consult the documentation for the DBMS you are using.

```
/**********************************************************************/
/*                                                                  */
/*      Kroenke, Auer, and Vandenberg                               */
/*      Database Processing (16th Edition) Chapters 07/10A           */
/*                                                                  */
/*      The View Ridge Gallery (VRG) Database - Create Tables        */
/*                                                                  */
/*      These are the Microsoft SQL Server 2017/2019 SQL code solutions */
/*                                                                  */
/**********************************************************************/

USE VRG
GO

CREATE TABLE ARTIST (
        ArtistID            Int             NOT NULL IDENTITY(1,1),
        LastName            Char(25)        NOT NULL,
        FirstName           Char(25)        NOT NULL,
        Nationality         Char(30)        NULL,
        DateOfBirth         Numeric(4)      NULL,
        DateDeceased        Numeric(4)      NULL,
        CONSTRAINT          ArtistPK        PRIMARY KEY(ArtistID),
        CONSTRAINT          ArtistAK1       UNIQUE(LastName, FirstName),
        CONSTRAINT          NationalityValues  CHECK
                                (Nationality IN
                                    ('Canadian', 'English', 'French',
                                    'German', 'Mexican', 'Russian', 'Spanish',
                                    'United States')),
        CONSTRAINT          BirthValuesCheck   CHECK (DateOfBirth < DateDeceased),
        CONSTRAINT          ValidBirthYear     CHECK
                                (DateOfBirth LIKE '[1-2][0-9][0-9][0-9]'),
        CONSTRAINT          ValidDeathYear     CHECK
                                (DateDeceased LIKE '[1-2][0-9][0-9][0-9]')
        );

CREATE TABLE WORK (
        WorkID              Int             NOT NULL IDENTITY(500,1),
        Title               Char(35)        NOT NULL,
        [Copy]              Char(12)        NOT NULL,
        Medium              Char(35)        NULL,
        [Description]       Varchar(1000)   NULL DEFAULT 'Unknown provenance',
        ArtistID            Int             NOT NULL,
        CONSTRAINT          WorkPK          PRIMARY KEY(WorkID),
        CONSTRAINT          WorkAK1         UNIQUE(Title, Copy),
        CONSTRAINT          ArtistFK        FOREIGN KEY(ArtistID)
                                REFERENCES ARTIST(ArtistID)
                                    ON UPDATE NO ACTION
                                    ON DELETE NO ACTION
        );

CREATE TABLE CUSTOMER (
        CustomerID          Int             NOT NULL IDENTITY(1000,1),
        LastName            Char(25)        NOT NULL,
        FirstName           Char(25)        NOT NULL,
        EmailAddress        Varchar(100)    NULL,
        EncryptedPassword   VarChar(50)     NULL,
        Street              Char(30)        NULL,
        City                Char(35)        NULL,
        [State]             Char(2)         NULL,
        ZIPorPostalCode     Char(9)         NULL,
        Country             Char(50)        NULL,
        AreaCode            Char(3)         NULL,
        PhoneNumber         Char(8)         NULL,
        CONSTRAINT          CustomerPK      PRIMARY KEY(CustomerID),
        CONSTRAINT          EmailAK1        UNIQUE(EmailAddress)
        );
```

**FIGURE 7-13**

The SQL Statements to Create the VRG Database Table Structure

```
CREATE TABLE TRANS (
        TransactionID          Int              NOT NULL IDENTITY(100,1),
        DateAcquired           Date             NOT NULL,
        AcquisitionPrice       Numeric(8,2)     NOT NULL,
        AskingPrice            Numeric(8,2)     NULL,
        DateSold               Date             NULL,
        SalesPrice             Numeric(8,2)     NULL,
        CustomerID             Int              NULL,
        WorkID                 Int              NOT NULL,
        CONSTRAINT         TransPK                  PRIMARY KEY(TransactionID),
        CONSTRAINT         TransWorkFK              FOREIGN KEY(WorkID)
                      REFERENCES WORK(WorkID)
                          ON UPDATE NO ACTION
                          ON DELETE NO ACTION,
        CONSTRAINT         TransCustomerFK          FOREIGN KEY(CustomerID)
                      REFERENCES CUSTOMER(CustomerID)
                          ON UPDATE NO ACTION
                          ON DELETE NO ACTION,
        CONSTRAINT         SalesPriceRange          CHECK
                      ((SalesPrice > 0) AND (SalesPrice <=500000)),
        CONSTRAINT         ValidTransDate     CHECK (DateAcquired <= DateSold)
        );

CREATE TABLE CUSTOMER_ARTIST_INT(
        ArtistID               Int              NOT NULL,
        CustomerID             Int              NOT NULL,
        CONSTRAINT         CAIntPK                  PRIMARY KEY(ArtistID, CustomerID),
        CONSTRAINT         CAInt_ArtistFK           FOREIGN KEY(ArtistID)
                      REFERENCES ARTIST(ArtistID)
                          ON UPDATE NO ACTION
                          ON DELETE CASCADE,
        CONSTRAINT         CAInt_CustomerFK         FOREIGN KEY(CustomerID)
                      REFERENCES CUSTOMER(CustomerID)
                          ON UPDATE NO ACTION
                          ON DELETE CASCADE
        );
```

**FIGURE 7-13**

Continued

Microsoft SQL Server or in the equivalent markers in other DBMS products. And, of course, your life will be easier if you can avoid using such terms for tables or columns altogether.

> **BY THE WAY** Every now and then, the DBMS might generate bizarre syntax-error messages. For example, suppose you define a table with the name ORDER. When you submit the statement SELECT * FROM ORDER;, you will get very strange messages back from the DBMS because ORDER is an SQL reserved word.
>
> If you do receive odd messages back from statements that you know are coded correctly, think about reserved words. If a term might be reserved, enclose it in brackets and see what happens when you submit it to the DBMS. No harm is done by enclosing SQL terms in brackets.
>
> If you want to torture your DBMS, you can submit queries like:
>
> ```
> SELECT [SELECT] FROM [FROM] WHERE [WHERE] < [NOT FIVE];
> ```
>
> Most likely, you have better ways to spend your time, however. Without a doubt, the DBMS has better ways to spend its time!

Running the SQL statements in Figure 7-13 (or the specific variant for Oracle Database in Chapter 10B or for MySQL 8.0 in Chapter 10C) with your DBMS will generate all of the tables, relationships, and constraints for the VRG database. Figure 7-14 shows the completed

**FIGURE 7-14**

**Microsoft SQL Server 2019 VRG Database Diagram**

table structure in SQL Server 2019 as a database diagram. It is far easier to create these tables and relationships using SQL code than by using GUI displays, which are discussed for Microsoft SQL Server in Chapter 10A, for Oracle Database in Chapter 10B, and for MySQL 8.0 in Chapter 10C.

> ### Does Not Work with Microsoft Access ANSI-89 SQL
>
> Microsoft Access 2019 ANSI-89 SQL unfortunately does not support a number of standard SQL features we have examined in this discussion. However, you can run a basic SQL CREATE TABLE statement in ANSI-89 SQL and then use the Microsoft Access GUI display to finish building the tables and relationships. Specifically:
>
> 1. Although Microsoft Access supports a Number data type, it does not support the ( ) extension to specify the number of digits and the number of digits to the right of the decimal place.
>
>    Solution: You can set these values in the table Design view after the column is created.
>
> 2. Although Microsoft Access does support an AutoNumber data type, it starts at 1 and increments by 1. Further, AutoNumber can be used as an SQL data type.
>
>    Solution: Set AutoNumber data type manually after the table is created. Any other numbering system must be supported manually or by application code.
>
> 3. Microsoft Access ANSI-89 SQL does not support the UNIQUE and CHECK column constraints or the DEFAULT keyword.
>
>    Solution: Equivalent constraints and initial values can be set in the GUI table Design view.
>
> 4. Microsoft Access does not completely support foreign key CONSTRAINT phrases. Although the basic referential integrity constraint can be created using SQL, the ON UPDATE and ON DELETE clauses are not supported.
>
>    Solution: ON UPDATE and ON DELETE actions can be set manually after the relationship is created.
>
> 5. Unlike SQL Server, Oracle Database, and MySQL, Microsoft Access does not support SQL scripts.
>
>    Solution: You can still create tables by using the SQL CREATE command and insert data by using the SQL INSERT command (discussed later in this chapter), but you must do so one command at a time.

## The SQL ALTER TABLE Statement

The **SQL ALTER TABLE statement** is an SQL DDL statement that is used to change the structure of an existing table. It can be used to add, remove, or change columns. It also can be used to add or remove constraints.

### Adding and Dropping Columns

The following statement will add a column named MyColumn to the CUSTOMER table by using the **SQL ADD clause** in the SQL ALTER TABLE statement:

```
/* *** SQL-ALTER-TABLE-CH07-01 *** */

ALTER TABLE CUSTOMER

    ADD MyColumn Char(5) NULL;
```

You can drop an existing column by using the **SQL DROP COLUMN clause** in the SQL ALTER TABLE statement:

```
/* *** SQL-ALTER-TABLE-CH07-02 *** */

ALTER TABLE CUSTOMER

    DROP COLUMN MyColumn;
```

Note the asymmetry in syntax; the keyword COLUMN is used in the DROP COLUMN clause but not in the ADD clause. You can also use the ALTER TABLE statement to change column properties, as you will see in the next three chapters.

### Adding and Dropping Constraints

The ALTER TABLE statement can be used with an **SQL ADD CONSTRAINT clause** to add a constraint as follows:

```
/* *** SQL-ALTER-TABLE-CH07-03 *** */

ALTER TABLE CUSTOMER

    ADD CONSTRAINT MyConstraint CHECK

        (LastName NOT IN ('RobertsNoPay'));
```

You can also use the ALTER TABLE statement with an **SQL DROP CONSTRAINT clause** to DROP a constraint:

```
/* *** SQL-ALTER-TABLE-CH07-04 *** */

ALTER TABLE CUSTOMER

    DROP CONSTRAINT MyConstraint;
```

> **BY THE WAY**    The SQL ALTER TABLE statement can be used to add or drop any of the SQL constraints. You can use it to create primary keys and alternate keys, to set null status, to create referential integrity constraints, and to create data constraints. In fact, another SQL coding style uses CREATE TABLE only to declare the table's columns; all constraints are added using ALTER TABLE. We do not use that style in this text, but be aware that it does exist and that your employer might require it.

## The SQL DROP TABLE Statement

It is very easy to remove a table in SQL. In fact, it is far too easy. The following **SQL DROP TABLE statement** will drop the TRANS table *and all of its data*:

```
/* *** EXAMPLE CODE - DO NOT RUN *** */
/* *** SQL-DROP-TABLE-CH07-01 *** */
DROP TABLE TRANS;
```

Because this simple statement drops the table and all of its data, be very careful when using it. Do not code this statement on the wrong table!

The DBMS will not drop a table that is the parent in a FOREIGN KEY constraint. It will not do so even if there are no children or even if you have coded DELETE CASCADE. Instead, to drop such a table, you must first either drop the foreign key constraint or drop the child table. Then you can delete the parent table. As mentioned earlier, parent tables must be first in and last out.

The following statements are needed to drop the CUSTOMER table:

```
/* *** EXAMPLE CODE - DO NOT RUN *** */
/* *** SQL-DROP-TABLE-CH07-02 *** */
DROP TABLE CUSTOMER_ARTIST_INT;
DROP TABLE TRANS;
DROP TABLE CUSTOMER;
```

Alternatively, you could drop CUSTOMER with:

```
/* *** EXAMPLE CODE - DO NOT RUN *** */
/* *** SQL-ALTER-TABLE-CH07-05 *** */
ALTER TABLE CUSTOMER_ARTIST_INT
    DROP CONSTRAINT CAInt_CustomerFK;
ALTER TABLE TRANS
    DROP CONSTRAINT TransCustomerFK;
/* *** SQL-DROP-TABLE-CH07-03 *** */
DROP TABLE CUSTOMER;
```

## The SQL TRUNCATE TABLE Statement

The **SQL TRUNCATE TABLE statement** was officially added in the SQL:2008 standard, so it is one of the latest additions to SQL. It is used to remove all data from a table while leaving the table structure itself in the database. The SQL TRUNCATE TABLE statement does not use an SQL WHERE clause to specify conditions for the data deletion—*all* the data in the table is *always* removed when TRUNCATE is used. Although similar to the SQL DELETE statement discussed later in this chapter, there are two important differences between the two commands. First, the DELETE statement *does* allow the use of the SQL WHERE CLAUSE. Second, the TRUNCATE resets any surrogate key values back to the *initial value*, whereas the DELETE statement does not.

The following statement could be used to remove all the data in the CUSTOMER_ARTIST_INT table:

```
/* *** EXAMPLE CODE - DO NOT RUN *** */
/* *** SQL-TRUNCATE-TABLE-CH07-01 *** */
TRUNCATE TABLE CUSTOMER_ARTIST_INT;
```

The TRUNCATE TABLE statement *cannot* be used with a table that is referenced by a foreign key constraint because this could create foreign key values that have no corresponding primary key value. Thus, although we can use TRUNCATE TABLE with the CUSTOMER_ARTIST_INT table, we *cannot* use it with the CUSTOMER table.

## The SQL CREATE INDEX Statement

An **index** is a special data structure that is created to improve database performance. SQL Server automatically creates an index on all primary and foreign keys. A developer can also direct SQL Server to create an index on other columns that are frequently used in WHERE clauses or on columns that are used for sorting data when sequentially processing a table for queries and reports. Indexing concepts are discussed in Appendix F, "Physical Database Design and Data Structures for Database Processing."

SQL DDL includes an **SQL CREATE INDEX statement** to create indexes, an **SQL ALTER INDEX statement** to modify existing database indexes, and an **SQL DROP INDEX statement** to remove indexes from the database. Because each DBMS product implements indexing in different ways, we discuss the specific implementation of indexing in each DBMS as part of our detailed discussions of each DBMS product:

- Microsoft SQL Server 2019 in Chapter 10A
- Oracle Database in Chapter 10B
- MySQL 8.0 in Chapter 10C

---

**BY THE WAY**    Books on systems analysis and design often identify three design stages:

- Conceptual design (conceptual schema)
- Logical design (logical schema)
- Physical design (physical schema)

The creation and use of indexes is a part of the *physical design*, which is defined in these books as the aspects of the database that are actually implemented in the DBMS. Besides indexes, this includes physical record and file structure and organization and query optimization. We discuss some of these issues for Microsoft SQL Server 2019 in Chapter 10A, for Oracle Database in Chapter 10B, and for MySQL 8.0 in Chapter 10C.

---

## SQL DML Statements

At this point, you have learned how to query tables using SQL SELECT statements (in Chapter 2), and you should know how to create, alter, and drop tables, columns, and constraints. You do not yet know, however, how to use SQL statements to insert, modify, and delete data. We consider those statements next.

### The SQL INSERT Statement

The **SQL INSERT statement** is used to add rows of data to a table. The statement has a number of different options.

### The SQL INSERT Statement Using Column Names

The standard version of the INSERT statement is used to name the table, name the columns for which you have data, and then list the data in the following format:

```
/* *** EXAMPLE CODE - DO NOT RUN *** */
/* *** SQL-INSERT-CH07-01 *** */
INSERT INTO ARTIST
    (LastName, FirstName, Nationality, DateOfBirth, DateDeceased)
    VALUES ('Miro', 'Joan', 'Spanish', 1893, 1983);
```

Note that both column names and values are enclosed in parentheses and that DBMS-populated surrogate keys are not included in the statement. If you are providing data for all of the columns, if that data is in the same order as the columns in the table, and if you have no surrogate keys, then you can omit the column list.

```
/* *** EXAMPLE CODE - DO NOT RUN *** */
/* *** SQL-INSERT-CH07-02 *** */
INSERT INTO ARTIST VALUES
    ('Miro', 'Joan', 'Spanish', 1893, 1983);
```

Further, you need not provide the values in the same order as the columns in the table. If for some reason you want to provide Nationality first, you can revise the column names and the data value, as shown in the following example:

```
/* *** EXAMPLE CODE - DO NOT RUN *** */
/* *** SQL-INSERT-CH07-03 *** */
INSERT INTO ARTIST
    (Nationality, LastName, FirstName, DateOfBirth, DateDeceased)
    VALUES ('Spanish', 'Miro', 'Joan', 1893, 1983);
```

If you have partial values, just code the names of the columns for which you have data. For example, if you have only LastName, FirstName, and Nationality for an artist, you would use the following SQL statement:

```
/* *** EXAMPLE CODE - DO NOT RUN *** */
/* *** SQL-INSERT-CH07-04 *** */
INSERT INTO ARTIST
    (LastName, FirstName, Nationality)
    VALUES ('Miro', 'Joan', 'Spanish');
```

You must, of course, have values for all NOT NULL columns. Columns not specifically named in the INSERT statement will have values set to NULL.

## Bulk INSERT

One of the most often used forms of INSERT uses an SQL SELECT statement to provide values. Suppose you have the names, nationalities, birth dates, and dates deceased of a number of artists in a table named IMPORTED_ARTIST. In this case, you can add those data to the ARTIST table with the following statement:

```
/* *** EXAMPLE CODE - DO NOT RUN *** */
/* *** SQL-INSERT-CH07-05 *** */
INSERT INTO ARTIST
    (LastName, FirstName, Nationality, DateOfBirth, DateDeceased)
    SELECT    LastName, FirstName, Nationality,
              DateOfBirth, DateDeceased
    FROM      IMPORTED_ARTIST;
```

Note that the SQL keyword VALUES is not used with this form of insert. This syntax should seem familiar. We used it for normalization and denormalization examples in Chapters 3 and 4.

## Populating the VRG Database Tables

Now that we know how to use the SQL INSERT statement to add rows of data to a table, we can put data into the VRG database. Sample data for the VRG database is shown in Figure 7-15. (Note that the rows of the CUSTOMER table have been split apart in Figure 7-15(a) for ease of presentation on the page—they are not split in the database.)

| CustomerID | LastName | FirstName | EmailAddress | EncryptedPassword |
|---|---|---|---|---|
| 1000 | Janes | Jeffrey | Jeffrey.Janes@somewhere.com | ng76tG9E |
| 1001 | Smith | David | David.Smith@somewhere.com | ttr67i23 |
| 1015 | Twilight | Tiffany | Tiffany.Twilight@somewhere.com | gr44t5uz |
| 1033 | Smathers | Fred | Fred.Smathers@somewhere.com | mnF3D00Q |
| 1034 | Frederickson | Mary Beth | MaryBeth.Frederickson@somewhere.com | Nd5qr4Tv |
| 1036 | Warning | Selma | Selma.Warning@somewhere.com | CAe3Gh98 |
| 1037 | Wu | Susan | Susan.Wu@somewhere.com | Ues3thQ2 |
| 1040 | Gray | Donald | Donald.Gray@somewhere.com | NULL |
| 1041 | Johnson | Lynda | NULL | NULL |
| 1051 | Wilkens | Chris | Chris.Wilkens@somewhere.com | 45QZjx59 |

| CustomerID | LastName | FirstName | Street | City | State | ZIPorPostalCode |
|---|---|---|---|---|---|---|
| 1000 | Janes | Jeffrey | 123 W. Elm St | Renton | WA | 98055 |
| 1001 | Smith | David | 813 Tumbleweed Lane | Loveland | CO | 81201 |
| 1015 | Twilight | Tiffany | 88 1st Avenue | Langley | WA | 98260 |
| 1033 | Smathers | Fred | 10899 88th Ave | Bainbridge Island | WA | 98110 |
| 1034 | Frederickson | Mary Beth | 25 South Lafayette | Denver | CO | 80201 |
| 1036 | Warning | Selma | 205 Burnaby | Vancouver | BC | V6Z 1W2 |
| 1037 | Wu | Susan | 105 Locust Ave | Atlanta | GA | 30322 |
| 1040 | Gray | Donald | 55 Bodega Ave | Bodega Bay | CA | 94923 |
| 1041 | Johnson | Lynda | 117 C Street | Washington | DC | 20003 |
| 1051 | Wilkens | Chris | 87 Highland Drive | Olympia | WA | 98508 |

| CustomerID | LastName | FirstName | Country | AreaCode | PhoneNumber |
|---|---|---|---|---|---|
| 1000 | Janes | Jeffrey | USA | 425 | 543-2345 |
| 1001 | Smith | David | USA | 970 | 654-9876 |
| 1015 | Twilight | Tiffany | USA | 360 | 765-5566 |
| 1033 | Smathers | Fred | USA | 206 | 876-9911 |
| 1034 | Frederickson | Mary Beth | USA | 303 | 513-8822 |
| 1036 | Warning | Selma | Canada | 604 | 988-0512 |
| 1037 | Wu | Susan | USA | 404 | 653-3465 |
| 1040 | Gray | Donald | USA | 707 | 568-4839 |
| 1041 | Johnson | Lynda | USA | 202 | 438-5498 |
| 1051 | Wilkens | Chris | USA | 360 | 876-8822 |

**(a) CUSTOMER Table Data**

**FIGURE 7-15**

Sample Data for the VRG
Database

| ArtistID | LastName | FirstName | Nationality | DateOfBirth | DateDeceased |
|----------|----------|-----------|-------------|-------------|--------------|
| 1 | Miro | Joan | Spanish | 1893 | 1983 |
| 2 | Kandinsky | Wassily | Russian | 1866 | 1944 |
| 3 | Klee | Paul | German | 1879 | 1940 |
| 4 | Matisse | Henri | French | 1869 | 1954 |
| 5 | Chagall | Marc | French | 1887 | 1985 |
| 11 | Sargent | John Singer | United States | 1856 | 1925 |
| 17 | Tobey | Mark | United States | 1890 | 1976 |
| 18 | Horiuchi | Paul | United States | 1906 | 1999 |
| 19 | Graves | Morris | United States | 1920 | 2001 |

**(b)** ARTIST Table Data

| ArtistID | CustomerID |
|----------|------------|
| 1 | 1001 |
| 1 | 1034 |
| 2 | 1001 |
| 2 | 1034 |
| 4 | 1001 |
| 4 | 1034 |
| 5 | 1001 |
| 5 | 1034 |
| 5 | 1036 |
| 11 | 1001 |
| 11 | 1015 |
| 11 | 1036 |
| 17 | 1000 |
| 17 | 1015 |

| ArtistID | CustomerID |
|----------|------------|
| 17 | 1033 |
| 17 | 1040 |
| 17 | 1051 |
| 18 | 1000 |
| 18 | 1015 |
| 18 | 1033 |
| 18 | 1040 |
| 18 | 1051 |
| 19 | 1000 |
| 19 | 1015 |
| 19 | 1033 |
| 19 | 1036 |
| 19 | 1040 |
| 19 | 1051 |

**(c)** CUSTOMER_ARTIST_INT Table Data                    (*continued*)

**FIGURE 7-15**

Continued

| WorkID | Title | Copy | Medium | Description | ArtistID |
|--------|-------|------|--------|-------------|----------|
| 500 | Memories IV | Unique | Casein rice paper collage | 31 × 24.8 in. | 18 |
| 511 | Surf and Bird | 142/500 | High Quality Limited Print | Northwest School Expressionist style | 19 |
| 521 | The Tilled Field | 788/1000 | High Quality Limited Print | Early Surrealist style | 1 |
| 522 | La Lecon de Ski | 353/500 | High Quality Limited Print | Surrealist style | 1 |
| 523 | On White II | 435/500 | High Quality Limited Print | Bauhaus style of Kandinsky | 2 |
| 524 | Woman with a Hat | 596/750 | High Quality Limited Print | A very colorful Impressionist piece | 4 |
| 537 | The Woven World | 17/750 | Color lithograph | Signed | 17 |
| 548 | Night Bird | Unique | Watercolor on Paper | 50 × 72.5 cm. — Signed | 19 |
| 551 | Der Blaue Reiter | 236/1000 | High Quality Limited Print | The Blue Rider—Early Pointilism influence | 2 |
| 552 | Angelus Novus | 659/750 | High Quality Limited Print | Bauhaus style of Klee | 3 |
| 553 | The Dance | 734/1000 | High Quality Limited Print | An Impressionist masterpiece | 4 |
| 554 | I and the Village | 834/1000 | High Quality Limited Print | Shows Belarusian folk-life themes and symbology | 5 |
| 555 | Claude Monet Painting | 684/1000 | High Quality Limited Print | Shows French Impressionist influence of Monet | 11 |
| 561 | Sunflower | Unique | Watercolor and ink | 33.3 × 16.1 cm. — Signed | 19 |
| 562 | The Fiddler | 251/1000 | High Quality Limited Print | Shows Belarusian folk-life themes and symbology | 5 |
| 563 | Spanish Dancer | 583/750 | High Quality Limited Print | American realist style—From work in Spain | 11 |
| 564 | Farmer's Market #2 | 267/500 | High Quality Limited Print | Northwest School Abstract Expressionist style | 17 |

**(d)** WORK Table Data

**FIGURE 7-15**
Continued

352

| WorkID | Title | Copy | Medium | Description | ArtistID |
|---|---|---|---|---|---|
| 565 | Farmer's Market #2 | 268/500 | High Quality Limited Print | Northwest School Abstract Expressionist style | 17 |
| 566 | Into Time | 323/500 | High Quality Limited Print | Northwest School Abstract Expressionist style | 18 |
| 570 | Untitled Number 1 | Unique | Monotype with tempera | 4.3 × 6.1 in.—Signed | 17 |
| 571 | Yellow covers blue | Unique | Oil and collage | 71 × 78 in.—Signed | 18 |
| 578 | Mid-Century Hibernation | 362/500 | High Quality Limited Print | Northwest School Expressionist style | 19 |
| 580 | Forms in Progress I | Unique | Color aquatint | 19.3 × 24.4 in.—Signed | 17 |
| 581 | Forms in Progress II | Unique | Color aquatint | 19.3 × 24.4 in.—Signed | 17 |
| 585 | The Fiddler | 252/1000 | High Quality Limited Print | Shows Belarusian folk-life themes and symbology | 5 |
| 586 | Spanish Dancer | 588/750 | High Quality Limited Print | American Realist style—From work in Spain | 11 |
| 587 | Broadway Boggie | 433/500 | High Quality Limited Print | Northwest School Abstract Expressionist style | 17 |
| 588 | Universal Field | 114/500 | High Quality Limited Print | Northwest School Abstract Expressionist style | 17 |
| 589 | Color Floating in Time | 487/500 | High Quality Limited Print | Northwest School Abstract Expressionist style | 18 |
| 590 | Blue Interior | Unique | Tempera on card | 43.9 × 28 in. | 17 |
| 593 | Surf and Bird | Unique | Gouache | 26.5 × 29.75 in.—Signed | 19 |
| 594 | Surf and Bird | 362/500 | High Quality Limited Print | Northwest School Expressionist style | 19 |
| 595 | Surf and Bird | 365/500 | High Quality Limited Print | Northwest School Expressionist style | 19 |
| 596 | Surf and Bird | 366/500 | High Quality Limited Print | Northwest School Expressionist style | 19 |

**(d) continued - WORK Table Data**

**FIGURE 7-15**
Continued

353

| TransactionID | DateAcquired | AcquisitionPrice | AskingPrice | DateSoldID | SalesPrice | CustomerID | WorkID |
|---|---|---|---|---|---|---|---|
| 100 | 11/4/2017 | $30,000.00 | $45,000.00 | 12/14/2017 | $42,500.00 | 1000 | 500 |
| 101 | 11/7/2017 | $250.00 | $500.00 | 12/19/2017 | $500.00 | 1015 | 511 |
| 102 | 11/17/2017 | $125.00 | $250.00 | 1/18/2018 | $200.00 | 1001 | 521 |
| 103 | 11/17/2017 | $250.00 | $500.00 | 12/12/2018 | $400.00 | 1034 | 522 |
| 104 | 11/17/2017 | $250.00 | $250.00 | 1/18/2018 | $200.00 | 1001 | 523 |
| 105 | 11/17/2017 | $200.00 | $500.00 | 12/12/2018 | $400.00 | 1034 | 524 |
| 115 | 3/3/2018 | $1,500.00 | $3,000.00 | 6/7/2018 | $2,750.00 | 1033 | 537 |
| 121 | 9/21/2018 | $15,000.00 | $30,000.00 | 11/28/2018 | $27,500.00 | 1015 | 548 |
| 125 | 11/21/2018 | $125.00 | $250.00 | 12/18/2018 | $200.00 | 1001 | 551 |
| 126 | 11/21/2018 | $200.00 | $400.00 | NULL | NULL | NULL | 552 |
| 127 | 11/21/2018 | $125.00 | $500.00 | 12/22/2018 | $400.00 | 1034 | 553 |
| 128 | 11/21/2018 | $125.00 | $250.00 | 3/16/2019 | $225.00 | 1036 | 554 |
| 129 | 11/21/2018 | $125.00 | $250.00 | 3/16/2019 | $225.00 | 1036 | 555 |
| 151 | 5/7/2019 | $10,000.00 | $20,000.00 | 6/28/2019 | $17,500.00 | 1036 | 561 |
| 152 | 5/18/2019 | $125.00 | $250.00 | 8/15/2019 | $225.00 | 1001 | 562 |
| 153 | 5/18/2019 | $200.00 | $400.00 | 8/15/2019 | $350.00 | 1001 | 563 |
| 154 | 5/18/2019 | $250.00 | $500.00 | 9/28/2019 | $400.00 | 1040 | 564 |
| 155 | 5/18/2019 | $250.00 | $500.00 | NULL | NULL | NULL | 565 |
| 156 | 5/18/2019 | $250.00 | $500.00 | 9/27/2019 | $400.00 | 1040 | 566 |
| 161 | 6/28/2019 | $7,500.00 | $15,000.00 | 9/29/2019 | $13,750.00 | 1033 | 570 |
| 171 | 8/23/2019 | $35,000.00 | $60,000.00 | 9/29/2019 | $55,000.00 | 1000 | 571 |
| 175 | 9/29/2019 | $40,000.00 | $75,000.00 | 12/18/2019 | $72,500.00 | 1036 | 500 |
| 181 | 10/11/2019 | $250.00 | $500.00 | NULL | NULL | NULL | 578 |
| 201 | 2/28/2020 | $2,000.00 | $3,500.00 | 4/26/2020 | $3,250.00 | 1040 | 580 |
| 202 | 2/28/2020 | $2,000.00 | $3,500.00 | 4/26/2020 | $3,250.00 | 1040 | 581 |
| 225 | 6/8/2020 | $125.00 | $250.00 | 9/27/2020 | $225.00 | 1051 | 585 |
| 226 | 6/8/2020 | $200.00 | $400.00 | NULL | NULL | NULL | 586 |
| 227 | 6/8/2020 | $250.00 | $500.00 | 9/27/2020 | $475.00 | 1051 | 587 |
| 228 | 6/8/2020 | $250.00 | $500.00 | NULL | NULL | NULL | 588 |
| 229 | 6/8/2020 | $250.00 | $500.00 | NULL | NULL | NULL | 589 |
| 241 | 8/29/2020 | $2,500.00 | $5,000.00 | 9/27/2020 | $4,750.00 | 1015 | 590 |
| 251 | 10/25/2020 | $25,000.00 | $50,000.00 | NULL | NULL | NULL | 593 |
| 252 | 10/27/2020 | $250.00 | $500.00 | NULL | NULL | NULL | 594 |
| 253 | 10/27/2020 | $250.00 | $500.00 | NULL | NULL | NULL | 595 |
| 254 | 10/27/2020 | $250.00 | $500.00 | NULL | NULL | NULL | 596 |

**FIGURE 7-15**    (e) TRANS Table Data

Continued

However, we need to be careful about exactly how we enter these data into the VRG database. Notice that in the SQL CREATE TABLE statements in Figure 7-13 CustomerID, ArtistID, WorkID, and TransactionID are all surrogate keys with values automatically inserted by the DBMS. This will produce sequential numbers. For example, if we insert the ARTIST table data shown in Figure 7-15(b) using the automatic ArtistID numbering from IDENTITY(1, 1), the ArtistID numbers for the nine artists will be (1, 2, 3, 4, 5, 6, 7, 8, 9). But in Figure 7-15(b), the ArtistID numbers are (1, 2, 3, 4, 5, 11, 17, 18, 19).

This happens because the View Ridge Gallery data shown in Figure 7-15 is *sample data*, not the complete data for the VRG database. Therefore, the primary key numbers for CustomerID, ArtistID, WorkID, and TransactionID in the data set are *not* sequential.

This, of course, raises the question of how to override DBMS mechanisms that provide automatic surrogate key numbering. The answer to this question varies among DBMS products (as does the method for generating the surrogate values). A discussion of this topic specific to each DBMS product used in this book and the complete set of SQL INSERT statements needed to enter the VRG data can be found for SQL Server 2019 in Chapter 10A, for Oracle Database in Chapter 10B, and for MySQL 8.0 in Chapter 10C. At this point, we recommend that you read the appropriate section for the DBMS product you are using and populate the VRG database in your DBMS.

## The SQL UPDATE Statement

The **SQL UPDATE statement** is used to change values of existing rows. For example, the following statement will change the value of City to 'New York City' for the View Ridge Gallery customer whose CustomerID is 1000 (Jeffrey Janes):

```
/* *** EXAMPLE CODE - DO NOT RUN *** */

/* *** SQL-UPDATE-CH07-01 *** */

UPDATE      CUSTOMER
   SET      City = 'New York City'
   WHERE    CustomerID = 1000;
```

To change the value of both City and State, we would use the following SQL statement:

```
/* *** EXAMPLE CODE - DO NOT RUN *** */

/* *** SQL-UPDATE-CH07-02 *** */

UPDATE      CUSTOMER
   SET      City = 'New York City', State = 'NY'
   WHERE    CustomerID = 1000;
```

The DBMS will enforce all referential integrity constraints when processing UPDATE commands. For the VRG database, all keys are surrogate keys, but for tables with data keys, the DBMS will cascade or disallow (NO ACTION) updates according to the specification in the FOREIGN KEY constraint. Also, if there is a FOREIGN KEY constraint, the DBMS will enforce the referential integrity constraint on updates to a foreign key.

### Bulk Updates

It is quite easy to make bulk updates with the UPDATE statement. It is so easy, in fact, that it is dangerous. Consider the following SQL UPDATE statement:

```
/* *** EXAMPLE CODE - DO NOT RUN *** */

/* *** SQL-UPDATE-CH07-03 *** */

UPDATE      CUSTOMER
   SET      City = 'New York City';
```

This statement will change the value of City for every row of the CUSTOMER table. If we had intended to change just the value for customer 1000, we would have an unhappy result—every customer would have the value 'New York City'. (Data recovery methods are discussed in Chapter 9.)

You can also perform bulk updates using an SQL WHERE clause that finds multiple rows. If, for example, we wanted to change the AreaCode for every customer who lives in Denver, we would code:

```
/* *** EXAMPLE CODE - DO NOT RUN *** */
/* *** SQL-UPDATE-CH07-04 *** */
UPDATE      CUSTOMER
   SET      AreaCode = '303'
   WHERE    City = 'Denver';
```

### Updating Using Values from Other Tables

The SQL UPDATE statement can set a column equal to the value of a column in a different table. The VRG database has no appropriate example for this operation, so suppose instead that we have a table named TAX_TABLE with columns (Tax, City), where Tax is the appropriate tax rate for the City.

Now suppose we have a table named PURCHASE_ORDER that includes the columns TaxRate and City. We can update all rows for purchase orders in the city of Bodega Bay with the following SQL statement:

```
/* *** EXAMPLE CODE - DO NOT RUN *** */
/* *** SQL-UPDATE-CH07-05 *** */
UPDATE      PURCHASE_ORDER
   SET      TaxRate =
            (SELECT   Tax
             FROM     TAX_TABLE
             WHERE    TAX_TABLE.City = 'Bodega Bay')
   WHERE    PURCHASE_ORDER.City = 'Bodega Bay';
```

More likely, we want to update the value of the tax rate for a purchase order without specifying the city. Say we want to update the TaxRate for purchase order number 1000. In that case, we use the slightly more complex SQL statement:

```
/* *** EXAMPLE CODE - DO NOT RUN *** */
/* *** SQL-UPDATE-CH07-06 *** */
UPDATE      PURCHASE_ORDER
   SET      TaxRate =
            (SELECT   Tax
             From     TAX_TABLE
             WHERE    TAX_TABLE.City = PURCHASE_ORDER.City)
   WHERE    PURCHASE_ORDER.Number = 1000;
```

SQL SELECT statements can be combined with UPDATE statements in many different ways. We need to move on to other topics, but try these and other variations of UPDATE on your own.

### The SQL MERGE Statement

The **SQL MERGE statement** (not available in Microsoft Access 2019 ANSI-89 SQL) was introduced in SQL:2003 and, like the previously discussed SQL TRUNCATE TABLE statement, is one of the newer additions to SQL. The SQL MERGE statement essentially combines the SQL INSERT and SQL UPDATE statements into one statement that can either insert or update data depending upon whether some condition is met.

For example, suppose that before VRG staff insert data into the ARTIST table, they carefully research data about each artist and store it in a table named ARTIST_DATA_RESEARCH. Data on new artists is initially stored in ARTIST_DATA_RESEARCH, along with corrections to data on artists already in ARTIST. The VRG business rule is that ARTIST names are never changed after they have been entered, but if errors in Nationality, DateOfBirth, or Date-Deceased are discovered, these errors will be corrected. In this case, new ARTIST data can be inserted and ARTIST data updated by using the following SQL MERGE statement:

```
/* *** EXAMPLE CODE - DO NOT RUN *** */
/* *** SQL-MERGE-CH07-01 *** */
MERGE INTO ARTIST AS A USING ARTIST_DATA_RESEARCH AS ADR
     ON  (A.LastName = ADR.LastName
         AND
         A.FirstName = ADR.FirstName)
     WHEN MATCHED THEN
         UPDATE SET
              A.Nationality = ADR.Nationality,
              A.DateOfBirth = ADR.DateOfBirth,
              A.DateDeceased = ADR.DateDeceased
     WHEN NOT MATCHED THEN
         INSERT (LastName, FirstName, Nationality,
                 DateOfBirth, DateDeceased)
         VALUES (ADR.LastName, ADR.FirstName,
                 ADR.Nationality, ADR.DateOfBirth, ADR.DateDeceased);
```

### The SQL DELETE Statement

The **SQL DELETE statement** is also quite easy to use. The following SQL statement will delete the row for a customer with a CustomerID of 1000:

```
/* *** EXAMPLE CODE - DO NOT RUN *** */
/* *** SQL-DELETE-CH07-01 *** */
DELETE    FROM CUSTOMER
WHERE     CustomerID = 1000;
```

Of course, if you omit the WHERE clause, you will delete *every* customer row, so be careful with this command as well. Note that the DELETE statement without the WHERE clause is the logical equivalent of the SQL TRUNCATE TABLE statement previously discussed. However, the two statements use different methods to remove the data from the table and are *not* identical. For example, the DELETE statement *may* fire a trigger (as discussed later in this chapter), but the TRUNCATE TABLE statement never fires triggers. Further, the TRUNCATE resets any surrogate key values back to the *initial value*, whereas the DELETE statement does not.

The DBMS will enforce all referential integrity constraints when processing DELETE commands. For example, in the VRG database, you will be unable to delete a CUSTOMER row if that row has any TRANS children. Further, if a row with no TRANS children is deleted, any existing CUSTOMER_ARTIST_INT children will be deleted as well. This latter action occurs because of the CASCADE DELETE specification on the relationship between CUSTOMER and CUSTOMER_ARTIST_INT.

## Using SQL Views

An **SQL View** is a virtual table that is constructed from other tables or views. A view has no data of its own but obtains data from tables or other views. Views are constructed from SQL SELECT statements using the **SQL CREATE VIEW statement**, and view names are then used just as table names would be in the FROM clause of other SQL SELECT statements.

SQL views are a very important part of application development for both Web client–based applications and smartphone apps, as shown in Figure 7-16. The design principle is that when an application requests information from a server to be displayed in the user's client program, the request should be as simple as possible. In Appendix B, we define **data** as recorded facts and numbers. Based on this definition, we can now define **information**[6] as:

- Knowledge derived from data
- Data presented in a meaningful context
- Data processed by summing, ordering, averaging, grouping, comparing, or other similar operations

In general, application programmers prefer that the work of transforming *database data* into the *information* that will be used in and presented by the application be done by the DBMS itself. SQL views are the main DBMS tool for this work. The basic principle is that all *summing, averaging, grouping, comparing, and similar operations* should be done in SQL views and that it is the final result as it appears in the SQL view that is passed to the application program for use. This is the process illustrated in Figure 7-16.

In the SQL-92 standard, the only limitation on the SQL statements that are used to create views was that they could not contain an ORDER BY clause. In this case, the sort order must be provided by the SELECT statement that processes the view.

However, the methodology for how views are actually implemented varies by DBMS product. For example, Oracle Database and MySQL allow views to include ORDER BY, whereas SQL Server will only allow ORDER BY if the SQL phrase TOP 100 PERCENT is included in the SELECT clause of an SQL query statement. In this case, the included ORDER BY clause determines a default sorting order, which may be modified by including another ORDER BY clause in the SELECT statement that processes the view.

**FIGURE 7-16**

SQL Views as the Basis for Application Reports

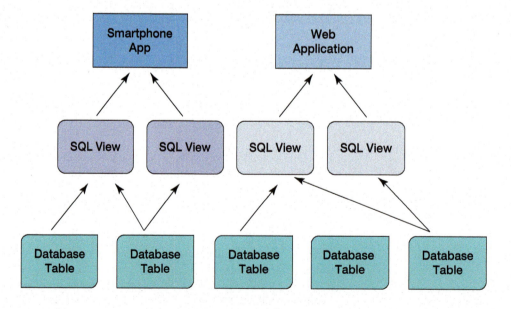

---

[6]These definitions are from David M. Kroenke and Randall J. Boyle's books *Using MIS* (11th ed., Upper Saddle River, NJ: Prentice-Hall, 2020) and *Experiencing MIS* (9th ed., Upper Saddle River: Prentice-Hall, 2021). See these books for a full discussion of these definitions, as well as a discussion of a fourth definition, "a difference that makes a difference."

> **BY THE WAY**   Views are a standard and popular SQL construct. Microsoft Access, how-
> ever, does not support them. Instead, in Microsoft Access, you can create
> a view-equivalent *query*, name it, and then save it. You can then process the query in
> the same ways that we process views in the following discussion. SQL Server, Oracle
> Database, and MySQL all support views, and they are an important structure with
> many uses. Do not conclude from Microsoft Access's lack of support that views are
> unimportant. Read on, and, if possible, use SQL Server, Oracle Database, or MySQL to
> process the statements in this section.

We will begin our discussion of SQL views by defining a view named Customer-
NameView on the CUSTOMER table that displays the customer's LastName and FirstName
data, but relabeling as CustomerLastName and CustomerFirstName:

```
/* *** SQL-CREATE-VIEW-CH07-01 *** */
CREATE VIEW CustomerNameView AS
    SELECT    LastName AS CustomerLastName,
              FirstName AS CustomerFirstName
    FROM      CUSTOMER;
```

Note that the results from executing this statement will be only a system message stating the
action completed. With GUI utilities such as SQL Server Management Studio, an appropriately named object will also be created.[7]

Once the view is created, it can be used in the FROM clause of SELECT statements just
like a table. The following obtains a list of customer names in sorted order:

```
/* *** SQL-Query-View-CH07-01 *** */
SELECT     *
FROM       CustomerNameView
ORDER BY   CustomerLastName, CustomerFirstName;
```

The result for the sample data in Figure 7-15 is:

|    | CustomerLastName | CustomerFirstName |
|----|------------------|-------------------|
| 1  | Frederickson     | Mary Beth         |
| 2  | Gray             | Donald            |
| 3  | Janes            | Jeffrey           |
| 4  | Johnson          | Lynda             |
| 5  | Smathers         | Fred              |
| 6  | Smith            | David             |
| 7  | Twilight         | Tiffany           |
| 8  | Warning          | Selma             |
| 9  | Wilkens          | Chris             |
| 10 | Wu               | Susan             |

[7]The current versions of SQL Server, Oracle Database, and MySQL all process the CREATE VIEW statements
as written here without difficulty. However, an earlier version of SQL Server, SQL Server 2000, had a quirk: to
create views, you had to remove the semicolon from the CREATE VIEW statement. We have no idea why SQL
Server 2000 accepted a semicolon for all other SQL statements but would not accept one for SQL statements
that create views. If by chance you are still using SQL Server 2000, be aware that you must remove the semicolon
when writing CREATE VIEW statements. Even better, upgrade your version of SQL Server—Microsoft stopped
supporting SQL Server 2000 in April 2013, and important security updates are no longer being provided!

Note that the number of columns returned in the result depends on the number of columns in the view, not on the number of columns in the underlying table. In this example, the SELECT clause produces just two columns because CustomerNameView itself has just two columns.

Also notice that the columns LastName and FirstName in the CUSTOMER table have been renamed to CustomerLastName and CustomerFirstName in the view. Because of this, the ORDER BY phrase in the SELECT statement uses CustomerLastName and CustomerFirstName, not LastName and FirstName. Also, the DBMS uses the labels CustomerLastName and CustomerFirstName when producing results.

---

**BY THE WAY**  If you need to change an SQL view after you have created it, use the **SQL ALTER VIEW statement**. For example, if you wanted to reverse the order of LastName and FirstName in the CustomerNameView, you would use the following SQL statement:

```
/* *** EXAMPLE CODE - DO NOT RUN *** */
/* *** SQL-ALTER-VIEW-CH07-01 *** */
ALTER VIEW CustomerNameView AS
  SELECT    FirstName AS CustomerFirstName,
            LastName AS CustomerLastName,
  FROM      CUSTOMER;
```

Further, starting with SQL Server 2016 SP1 and now with SQL Server 2019, in Microsoft SQL Server you can use the **SQL CREATE OR ALTER VIEW statement** to create or change a view:

```
/* *** EXAMPLE CODE - DO NOT RUN *** */
/* *** SQL-CREATE-OR-ALTER-VIEW-CH07-01 *** */
CREATE OR ALTER VIEW CustomerNameView AS
  SELECT    FirstName AS CustomerFirstName,
            LastName AS CustomerLastName,
  FROM      CUSTOMER;
```

This allows you to modify the stored view without using a separate SQL ALTER VIEW syntax.

If you are using Oracle Database or MySQL 8.0, you can also use the **SQL CREATE OR REPLACE VIEW statement** in place of the SQL CREATE VIEW syntax. Again, this allows you to modify the stored view without using a separate SQL ALTER VIEW syntax.

---

Figure 7-17 lists the uses for SQL views. SQL views can hide columns or rows. They also can be used to display the results of computed columns, to hide complicated SQL syntax, and to layer the use of built-in functions to create results that are not possible with a single SQL statement. Additionally, SQL views can provide an alias for table names and thus hide the true table names from applications and users. SQL views also are used to assign different processing permissions and different triggers to different views of the same table. We will show examples for each of these.

**FIGURE 7-17**

Uses of SQL Views

| Uses of SQL Views |
| --- |
| Hide columns or rows. |
| Display results of computations. |
| Hide complicated SQL syntax. |
| Layer built-in functions. |
| Provide level of isolation between table data and users' view of data. |
| Assign different processing permissions to different views of the same table. |
| Assign different triggers to different views of the same table. |

## Using SQL Views to Hide Columns and Rows

SQL views can be used to hide columns to simplify results or to prevent the display of sensitive data. For example, suppose the users at the View Ridge Gallery want a simplified list of customers that has just names and phone numbers. The following SQL statement defines a view, BasicCustomerDataView, which will produce that list:

```
/* *** SQL-CREATE-VIEW-CH07-02 *** */
CREATE VIEW CustomerBasicDataView AS
    SELECT   LastName AS CustomerLastName,
             FirstName AS CustomerFirstName,
             AreaCode, PhoneNumber
    FROM     CUSTOMER;
```

To use this view, we can run the following SQL statement:

```
/* *** SQL-Query-View-CH07-02 *** */
SELECT     *
FROM       CustomerBasicDataView
ORDER BY   CustomerLastName, CustomerFirstName;
```

The result is:

| | CustomerLastName | CustomerFirstName | AreaCode | PhoneNumber |
| --- | --- | --- | --- | --- |
| 1 | Frederickson | Mary Beth | 303 | 513-8822 |
| 2 | Gray | Donald | 707 | 568-4839 |
| 3 | Janes | Jeffrey | 425 | 543-2345 |
| 4 | Johnson | Lynda | 202 | 438-5498 |
| 5 | Smathers | Fred | 206 | 876-9911 |
| 6 | Smith | David | 970 | 654-9876 |
| 7 | Twilight | Tiffany | 360 | 765-5566 |
| 8 | Warning | Selma | 604 | 988-0512 |
| 9 | Wilkens | Chris | 360 | 876-8822 |
| 10 | Wu | Susan | 404 | 653-3465 |

If the management of the View Ridge Gallery wants to hide the columns Acquisition-Price and SalesPrice in TRANS, it can define a view that does not include those columns. One use for such a view is to populate a Web page.

SQL views also can hide rows by providing a WHERE clause in the view definition. The next SQL statement defines a view of customer name and phone data for all customers with an address in Washington State:

```
/* *** SQL-CREATE-VIEW-CH07-03 *** */
CREATE VIEW CustomerBasicDataWAView AS
    SELECT    LastName AS CustomerLastName,
              FirstName AS CustomerFirstName,
              AreaCode, PhoneNumber
    FROM      CUSTOMER
    WHERE     State='WA';
```

To use this view, we can run the following SQL statement:

```
/* *** SQL-Query-View-CH07-03 *** */
SELECT        *
FROM          CustomerBasicDataWAView
ORDER BY      CustomerLastName, CustomerFirstName;
```

The result is:

| | CustomerLastName | CustomerFirstName | AreaCode | PhoneNumber |
|---|---|---|---|---|
| 1 | Janes | Jeffrey | 425 | 543-2345 |
| 2 | Smathers | Fred | 206 | 876-9911 |
| 3 | Twilight | Tiffany | 360 | 765-5566 |
| 4 | Wilkens | Chris | 360 | 876-8822 |

As desired, only customers who live in Washington are shown in this view. This limitation is not obvious from the results because State is not included in the view. This characteristic is good or bad, depending on the use of the view. It is good if this view is used in a setting in which only Washington customers matter; it is bad if the view miscommunicates that these customers are the only View Ridge Gallery customers.

## Using SQL Views to Display Results of Computed Columns

Another purpose of views is to show the results of computed columns without requiring the user to enter the computation expression. For example, the following view combines the AreaCode and PhoneNumber columns and formats the result:

```
/* *** SQL-CREATE-VIEW-CH07-04 *** */
CREATE VIEW CustomerPhoneView AS
    SELECT    LastName AS CustomerLastName,
              FirstName AS CustomerFirstName,
              ('(' + AreaCode + ') ' + PhoneNumber) AS CustomerPhone
    FROM      CUSTOMER;
```

When the view user executes the following SQL statement:

```
/* *** SQL-Query-View-CH07-04 *** */
SELECT      *
FROM        CustomerPhoneView
ORDER BY    CustomerLastName, CustomerFirstName;
```

the results[8] will be:

|    | CustomerLastName | CustomerFirstName | CustomerPhone |
|----|------------------|-------------------|---------------|
| 1  | Frederickson     | Mary Beth         | (303) 513-8822 |
| 2  | Gray             | Donald            | (707) 568-4839 |
| 3  | Janes            | Jeffrey           | (425) 543-2345 |
| 4  | Johnson          | Lynda             | (202) 438-5498 |
| 5  | Smathers         | Fred              | (206) 876-9911 |
| 6  | Smith            | David             | (970) 654-9876 |
| 7  | Twilight         | Tiffany           | (360) 765-5566 |
| 8  | Warning          | Selma             | (604) 988-0512 |
| 9  | Wilkens          | Chris             | (360) 876-8822 |
| 10 | Wu               | Susan             | (404) 653-3465 |

Placing computations in views has two major advantages. First, it saves users from having to know or remember how to write an expression to get the results they want. Second, it ensures consistent results. If each developer who uses a computation writes his or her own SQL expression, that developer may write it differently and obtain inconsistent results.

## Using SQL Views to Hide Complicated SQL Syntax

Another use of SQL views is to hide complicated SQL syntax. Using a view, developers need not enter a complex SQL statement when they want a particular result. Also, such views give the benefits of complicated SQL statements to developers who do not know how to write such statements. This use of views also ensures consistency.

For example, suppose that the View Ridge Gallery salespeople want to see which customers are interested in which artists, and they want to see the names of both the customers and artists. To display these interests, two joins are necessary: one to join CUSTOMER to CUSTOMER_ARTIST_INT and another to join that result to ARTIST. We can code an SQL statement that constructs these joins and define it as an SQL view to create the CustomerInterestsView:

```
/* *** SQL-CREATE-VIEW-CH07-05 *** */
CREATE VIEW CustomerInterestsView AS
   SELECT   C.LastName AS CustomerLastName,
            C.FirstName AS CustomerFirstName,
            A.LastName AS ArtistName
   FROM     CUSTOMER AS C JOIN CUSTOMER_ARTIST_INT AS CAI
         ON C.CustomerID = CAI.CustomerID
            JOIN        ARTIST AS A
                ON      CAI.ArtistID = A.ArtistID;
```

---

[8]As you might expect, different DBMS products use different operators for the concatenation operation in the CustomerPhoneView definition. For example, in Oracle Database, the plus sign (+) must be replaced by double vertical bars ( ‖ ) for string concatenation, whereas MySQL uses the CONCAT( ) string function. See the example in Chapter 2 and the documentation for your DBMS for more details.

While Oracle Database does use the SQL AS keyword when specifying column aliases, it does *not* use it when specifying table aliases. Thus, for Oracle Database we would use:

```
/* *** SQL-CREATE-VIEW-CH07-05-ORACLE-DATABASE *** */
CREATE VIEW CustomerInterestsView AS
  SELECT      C.LastName AS CustomerLastName,
              C.FirstName AS CustomerFirstName,
              A.LastName AS ArtistName
  FROM        CUSTOMER C JOIN CUSTOMER_ARTIST_INT CAI
        ON    C.CustomerID = CAI.CustomerID
              JOIN          ARTIST A
                  ON        CAI.ArtistID = A.ArtistID;
```

Notice the aliasing of C.LastName to CustomerLastName and A.LastName to ArtistLastName. We *must* use at least one of these column aliases, for without them the resulting table has two columns named LastName. The DBMS would not be able to distinguish one LastName from the other and would generate an error when an attempt is made to create such a view.

This is a complicated SQL statement to write, but once the view is created, the result of this statement can be obtained with a simple SELECT statement. For example, the following statement shows the results sorted by CustomerLastName and CustomerFirstName:

```
/* *** SQL-Query-View-CH07-05 *** */
SELECT       *
FROM         CustomerInterestsView
ORDER BY     CustomerLastName, CustomerFirstName;
```

Figure 7-18 displays the fairly large result set. Clearly, using the view is much simpler than constructing the join syntax. Even developers who know SQL well will appreciate having a simpler SQL view with which to work.

## Layering Built-in Functions

Recall from Chapter 2 that you cannot use a computation or a built-in function as part of an SQL WHERE clause. You can, however, construct a view that computes a variable and then write an SQL statement on that view that uses the computed variable in a WHERE clause. To understand this, consider the SQL view definition for the ArtistWorkNetView:

```
/* *** SQL-CREATE-VIEW-CH07-06 *** */
CREATE VIEW ArtistWorkNetView AS
    SELECT      LastName AS ArtistLastName,
                FirstName AS ArtistFirstName,
                W.WorkID, Title, Copy, DateSold,
                AcquisitionPrice, SalesPrice,
                (SalesPrice - AcquisitionPrice) AS NetProfit
    FROM        TRANS AS T JOIN WORK AS W
          ON    T.WorkID = W.WorkID
                JOIN          ARTIST AS A
                    ON        W.ArtistID = A.ArtistID;
```

| | CustomerLastName | CustomerFirstName | ArtistName |
|---|---|---|---|
| 1 | Frederickson | Mary Beth | Chagall |
| 2 | Frederickson | Mary Beth | Kandinsky |
| 3 | Frederickson | Mary Beth | Miro |
| 4 | Frederickson | Mary Beth | Matisse |
| 5 | Gray | Donald | Tobey |
| 6 | Gray | Donald | Horiuchi |
| 7 | Gray | Donald | Graves |
| 8 | Janes | Jeffrey | Graves |
| 9 | Janes | Jeffrey | Horiuchi |
| 10 | Janes | Jeffrey | Tobey |
| 11 | Smathers | Fred | Tobey |
| 12 | Smathers | Fred | Horiuchi |
| 13 | Smathers | Fred | Graves |
| 14 | Smith | David | Chagall |
| 15 | Smith | David | Matisse |
| 16 | Smith | David | Kandinsky |
| 17 | Smith | David | Miro |
| 18 | Smith | David | Sargent |
| 19 | Twilight | Tiffany | Sargent |
| 20 | Twilight | Tiffany | Tobey |
| 21 | Twilight | Tiffany | Horiuchi |
| 22 | Twilight | Tiffany | Graves |
| 23 | Warning | Selma | Chagall |
| 24 | Warning | Selma | Graves |
| 25 | Warning | Selma | Sargent |
| 26 | Wilkens | Chris | Tobey |
| 27 | Wilkens | Chris | Graves |
| 28 | Wilkens | Chris | Horiuchi |

This SQL view joins TRANS, WORK, and ARTIST and creates the computed column NetProfit. We can now use NetProfit in an SQL WHERE clause in a query as follows:

```
/* *** SQL-Query-View-CH07-06 *** */
SELECT      ArtistLastName, ArtistFirstName,
            WorkID, Title, Copy, DateSold, NetProfit
FROM        ArtistWorkNetView
WHERE       NetProfit > 5000
ORDER BY    DateSold;
```

Here we are using the named result of a computation in a WHERE clause, something that is not allowed in a single SQL statement (the *results* of a computation can be used in a WHERE clause, but *not by name*). The result of the SQL SELECT statement is:

| | Artist Last Name | Artist First Name | Work ID | Title | Copy | Date Sold | Net Profit |
|---|---|---|---|---|---|---|---|
| 1 | Horiuchi | Paul | 500 | Memories IV | Unique | 2017-12-14 | 12500.00 |
| 2 | Graves | Morris | 548 | Night Bird | Unique | 2018-11-28 | 12500.00 |
| 3 | Graves | Morris | 561 | Sunflower | Unique | 2019-06-28 | 7500.00 |
| 4 | Tobey | Mark | 570 | Untitled Number 1 | Unique | 2019-09-29 | 6250.00 |
| 5 | Horiuchi | Paul | 571 | Yellow Covers Blue | Unique | 2019-09-29 | 20000.00 |
| 6 | Horiuchi | Paul | 500 | Memories IV | Unique | 2019-12-18 | 32500.00 |

Such layering can be continued over many levels. We can define another view with another computation on the computation in the first view. For example, note that in the results just shown, the Horiuchi work *Memories IV* has been acquired and sold more than once by the View Ridge Gallery, and then consider the SQL view ArtistWorkTotalNetView, which will calculate the total net profit from *all* sales of each work:

```
/* *** SQL-CREATE-VIEW-CH07-07 *** */

CREATE VIEW ArtistWorkTotalNetView AS
    SELECT      ArtistLastName, ArtistFirstName,
                WorkID,Title, Copy,
                SUM(NetProfit) AS TotalNetProfit
    FROM        ArtistWorkNetView
    GROUP BY    ArtistLastName, ArtistFirstName,
                WorkID, Title, Copy;
```

Now we can use TotalNetProfit in an SQL WHERE clause on the ArtistWorkTotalNet view as follows:

```
/* *** SQL-Query-View-CH07-07 *** */
SELECT      *
FROM        ArtistWorkTotalNetView
WHERE       TotalNetProfit > 5000
ORDER BY    TotalNetProfit;
```

In this SELECT, we are using an SQL view on an SQL view and a built-in function on a computed variable in the WHERE clause. The results are as follows:

| | Artist Last Name | Artist First Name | Work ID | Title | Copy | Total Net Profit |
|---|---|---|---|---|---|---|
| 1 | Tobey | Mark | 570 | Untitled Number 1 | Unique | 6250.00 |
| 2 | Graves | Morris | 561 | Sunflower | Unique | 7500.00 |
| 3 | Graves | Morris | 548 | Night Bird | Unique | 12500.00 |
| 4 | Horiuchi | Paul | 571 | Yellow Covers Blue | Unique | 20000.00 |
| 5 | Horiuchi | Paul | 500 | Memories IV | Unique | 45000.00 |

## Using SQL Views for Isolation, Multiple Permissions, and Multiple Triggers

SQL views have three other important uses. First, they can isolate source data tables from application code. To see how, suppose we define the following view:

```
/* *** SQL-CREATE-VIEW-CH07-08 *** */
CREATE VIEW CustomerTableBasicDataView AS
    SELECT    *
    FROM      CUSTOMER;
```

This view assigns the alias CustomerTableBasicDataView to the CUSTOMER table, and when we query this view we can simply select all the data in the view:

```
/* *** SQL-Query-View-CH07-08 *** */
SELECT    *
FROM      CustomerTableBasicDataView;
```

The result (shown on the next page), as expected, is the data in the CUSTOMER table itself. If all application code uses the CustomerTableBasicDataView view as the data source in SQL statements, then the true source of the data is hidden from application programmers.

| | CustomerID | LastName | FirstName | EmailAddress | EncryptedPassword | Street | City | State | ZIPorPostalCode | Country | AreaCode | PhoneNumber |
|---|---|---|---|---|---|---|---|---|---|---|---|---|
| 1 | 1000 | Janes | Jeffrey | Jeffrey.Janes@somewhere.com | ng7&G9E | 123 W. Elm St | Renton | WA | 98055 | USA | 425 | 543-2345 |
| 2 | 1001 | Smith | David | David.Smith@somewhere.com | ttr6723 | 813 Tumbleweed Lane | Loveland | CO | 81201 | USA | 970 | 654-9876 |
| 3 | 1015 | Twilight | Tiffany | Tiffany.Twilight@somewhere.com | gr44t5uz | 88 1st Avenue | Langley | WA | 98260 | USA | 360 | 765-5566 |
| 4 | 1033 | Smathers | Fred | Fred.Smathers@somewhere.com | mnF3D00Q | 10899 88th Ave | Bainbridge Island | WA | 98110 | USA | 206 | 876-9911 |
| 5 | 1034 | Frederickson | Mary Beth | MaryBeth.Frederickson@somewhere.com | Nd5qr4Tv | 25 South Lafayette | Denver | CO | 80201 | USA | 303 | 513-8822 |
| 6 | 1036 | Warning | Selma | Selma.Warning@somewhere.com | CAe3Gh98 | 205 Burnaby | Vancouver | BC | V6Z 1W2 | Canada | 604 | 988-0512 |
| 7 | 1037 | Wu | Susan | Susan.Wu@somewhere.com | Ues3hQ2 | 105 Locust Ave | Atlanta | GA | 30322 | USA | 404 | 653-3465 |
| 8 | 1040 | Gray | Donald | Donald.Gray@somewhere.com | NULL | 55 Bodega Ave | Bodega Bay | CA | 94923 | USA | 707 | 568-4839 |
| 9 | 1041 | Johnson | Lynda | NULL | NULL | 117 C Street | Washington | DC | 20003 | USA | 202 | 438-5498 |
| 10 | 1051 | Wilkens | Chris | Chris.Wilkens@somewhere.com | 45QZjx59 | 87 Highland Drive | Olympia | WA | 98508 | USA | 360 | 876-8822 |

Such table isolation provides flexibility to the database administration staff. For example, suppose that at some future date the source of customer data is changed to a different table (perhaps one that is imported from a different database) named NEW_CUSTOMER. In this situation, all the database administrator needs to do is redefine CustomerTableBasicData-View using the SQL ALTER VIEW statement as follows:

```
/* *** EXAMPLE CODE - DO NOT RUN *** */
/* *** SQL-ALTER-VIEW-CH07-08 *** */
ALTER VIEW CustomerTableBasicDataView AS
    SELECT    *
    FROM      NEW_CUSTOMER;
```

All of the application code that uses CustomerTableBasicDataView will now run on the new data source without any problem (assuming that the column names, data types, and other table characteristics have not been changed).

Another important use for SQL views is to give different sets of processing permissions to the same table. We will discuss security in more detail in Chapters 9, 10, 10A, 10B, and 10C, but for now understand that it is possible to limit insert, update, delete, and read permissions on tables and views.

For example, an organization might define a view of CUSTOMER called *Customer-TableReadView* with read-only permissions on CUSTOMER and a second view of CUSTOMER called *CustomerTableUpdateView* with both read and update permissions. Applications that need not update the customer data would work with CustomerTableReadView, whereas those that need to update these data would work with CustomerTableUpdateView.

The final use of SQL views is to enable the definition of multiple sets of triggers on the same data source. This technique is commonly used for enforcing O-M and M-M relationships. In this case, one view has a set of triggers that prohibits the deletion of a required child and another view has a set of triggers that deletes a required child as well as the parent. The views are assigned to different applications, depending on the authority of those applications.

```
CREATE FUNCTION dbo.NameConcatenation

-- These are the input parameters
(
        @FirstName    CHAR(25),
        @LastName     CHAR(25)
)
RETURNS VARCHAR(60)
AS
BEGIN
        -- This is the variable that will hold the value to be returned
        DECLARE @FullName VARCHAR(60);

        -- SQL statements to concatenate the names in the proper order
        SELECT @FullName = RTRIM(@LastName) + ', ' + RTRIM(@FirstName);

        -- Return the concatentate name
        RETURN @FullName;
END;
```

The Oracle Database version of this function, which uses Oracle's PL/SQL, is discussed in Chapter 10B, and the MySQL version, which uses the MySQL SQL/PSM standards, is discussed in Chapter 10C.

Now that we have created and stored the user-defined function, we can use it in SQL-Query-CH07-02:

```
/* *** SQL-Query-CH07-02 *** */

SELECT       dbo.NameConcatenation(FirstName, LastName) AS
             CustomerName,  AreaCode, PhoneNumber, EmailAddress
FROM         CUSTOMER
ORDER BY     CustomerName;
```

Now we have a function that produces the results we want, which, of course, are identical to the results for SQL-Query-CH07-01 earlier:

| | CustomerName | AreaCode | PhoneNumber | EmailAddress |
|---|---|---|---|---|
| 1 | Frederickson, Mary Beth | 303 | 513-8822 | MaryBeth.Frederickson@somewhere.com |
| 2 | Gray, Donald | 707 | 568-4839 | Donald.Gray@somewhere.com |
| 3 | Janes, Jeffrey | 425 | 543-2345 | Jeffrey.Janes@somewhere.com |
| 4 | Johnson, Lynda | 202 | 438-5498 | NULL |
| 5 | Smathers, Fred | 206 | 876-9911 | Fred.Smathers@somewhere.com |
| 6 | Smith, David | 970 | 654-9876 | David.Smith@somewhere.com |
| 7 | Twilight, Tiffany | 360 | 765-5566 | Tiffany.Twilight@somewhere.com |
| 8 | Warning, Selma | 604 | 988-0512 | Selma.Warning@somewhere.com |
| 9 | Wilkens, Chris | 360 | 876-8822 | Chris.Wilkens@somewhere.com |
| 10 | Wu, Susan | 404 | 653-3465 | Susan.Wu@somewhere.com |

The advantage of having a user-defined function is that we can now use it whenever we need to without having to re-create the code. For example, our previous query used data in the View Ridge Gallery CUSTOMER table, but we could just as easily use the function with the data in the ARTIST table:

```
/* *** SQL-Query-CH07-03 *** */

SELECT       dbo.NameConcatenation(FirstName, LastName) AS ArtistName,
             DateofBirth, DateDeceased
FROM         ARTIST
ORDER BY     ArtistName;
```

This query produces the expected result:

| | ArtistName | DateOfBirth | DateDeceased |
|---|---|---|---|
| 1 | Chagall, Marc | 1887 | 1985 |
| 2 | Graves, Morris | 1920 | 2001 |
| 3 | Horiuchi, Paul | 1906 | 1999 |
| 4 | Kandinsky, Wassily | 1866 | 1944 |
| 5 | Klee, Paul | 1879 | 1940 |
| 6 | Matisse, Henri | 1869 | 1954 |
| 7 | Miro, Joan | 1893 | 1983 |
| 8 | Sargent, John Singer | 1856 | 1925 |
| 9 | Tobey, Mark | 1890 | 1976 |

We can even use the function multiple times in the same SQL statement, as shown in SQL-Query-CH07-04, which is a variant on the SQL query we used to create the SQL view CustomerInterestsView in our discussion of SQL views:

```
/* *** SQL-Query-CH07-04 *** */
SELECT      dbo.NameConcatenation(C.FirstName, C.LastName) AS
            CustomerName, dbo.NameConcatenation(A.FirstName,
            A.LastName) AS ArtistName
FROM        CUSTOMER AS C JOIN CUSTOMER_ARTIST_INT AS CAI
   ON       C.CustomerID = CAI.CustomerID
        JOIN    ARTIST AS A
           ON    CAI.ArtistID = A.ArtistID
ORDER BY    CustomerName, ArtistName;
```

This query produces the expected large result that is shown in Figure 7-22, where we see that both CustomerName and ArtistName display the names in the LastName, First-Name syntax produced by the *NameConcatenation* user-defined function. Compare the results in this figure to those in Figure 7-18, which presents essentially the same results, but without the formatting provided by the *NameConcatenation* function.

## Using SQL Triggers

A **trigger** is a stored program that is executed by the DBMS whenever a specified event occurs. Triggers for Oracle Database are written in Java or in Oracle's PL/SQL. Microsoft SQL Server triggers are written in Microsoft .NET Common Language Runtime (CLR) languages, such as Visual Basic .NET (VB.NET), or Microsoft's T-SQL. MySQL triggers are written in MySQL's variant of SQL. In this chapter, we will discuss triggers in a generic manner without considering the particulars of those languages. We will discuss triggers written in DBMS-specific SQL variants for T-SQL in Chapter 10A, for PL/SQL in Chapter 10B, and for MySQL SQL in Chapter 10C.

A trigger is attached to a table or a view. A table or a view may have many triggers, but a trigger is associated with just one table or view. A trigger is invoked by an SQL DML INSERT, UPDATE, or DELETE request on the table or view to which it is attached. Figure 7-23 summarizes the triggers available for SQL Server 2019, Oracle Database, and MySQL 8.0.

Oracle Database and Oracle Database XE both support three kinds of triggers: BEFORE, INSTEAD OF, and AFTER. As you would expect, BEFORE triggers are executed before the DBMS processes the insert, update, or delete request. INSTEAD OF triggers are executed in place of any DBMS processing of the insert, update, or delete request. AFTER triggers are executed after the insert, update, or delete request has been processed. All together, nine trigger types are possible: BEFORE (INSERT, UPDATE, DELETE); INSTEAD OF (INSERT, UPDATE, DELETE); and AFTER (INSERT, UPDATE, DELETE).

**FIGURE 7-22**

Result of SQL Query Using
the NameConcatenation
User-Defined Function

| | CustomerName | ArtistName |
|---|---|---|
| 1 | Frederickson, Mary Beth | Chagall, Marc |
| 2 | Frederickson, Mary Beth | Kandinsky, Wassily |
| 3 | Frederickson, Mary Beth | Matisse, Henri |
| 4 | Frederickson, Mary Beth | Miro, Joan |
| 5 | Gray, Donald | Graves, Morris |
| 6 | Gray, Donald | Horiuchi, Paul |
| 7 | Gray, Donald | Tobey, Mark |
| 8 | Janes, Jeffrey | Graves, Morris |
| 9 | Janes, Jeffrey | Horiuchi, Paul |
| 10 | Janes, Jeffrey | Tobey, Mark |
| 11 | Smathers, Fred | Graves, Morris |
| 12 | Smathers, Fred | Horiuchi, Paul |
| 13 | Smathers, Fred | Tobey, Mark |
| 14 | Smith, David | Chagall, Marc |
| 15 | Smith, David | Kandinsky, Wassily |
| 16 | Smith, David | Matisse, Henri |
| 17 | Smith, David | Miro, Joan |
| 18 | Smith, David | Sargent, John Singer |
| 19 | Twilight, Tiffany | Graves, Morris |
| 20 | Twilight, Tiffany | Horiuchi, Paul |
| 21 | Twilight, Tiffany | Sargent, John Singer |
| 22 | Twilight, Tiffany | Tobey, Mark |
| 23 | Warning, Selma | Chagall, Marc |
| 24 | Warning, Selma | Graves, Morris |
| 25 | Warning, Selma | Sargent, John Singer |
| 26 | Wilkens, Chris | Graves, Morris |
| 27 | Wilkens, Chris | Horiuchi, Paul |
| 28 | Wilkens, Chris | Tobey, Mark |

**FIGURE 7-23**

Summary of SQL Triggers by
DBMS Product

| Trigger Type / DML Action | BEFORE | INSTEAD OF | AFTER |
|---|---|---|---|
| INSERT | Oracle Database<br><br>MySQL | Oracle Database<br>SQL Server | Oracle Database<br>SQL Server<br>MySQL |
| UPDATE | Oracle Database<br><br>MySQL | Oracle Database<br>SQL Server | Oracle Database<br>SQL Server<br>MySQL |
| DELETE | Oracle Database<br><br>MySQL | Oracle Database<br>SQL Server | Oracle Database<br>SQL Server<br>MySQL |

Since SQL Server 2005, SQL Server supports DDL triggers (triggers on such SQL DDL statements as CREATE, ALTER, and DROP) as well as DML triggers. We will only deal with the DML triggers here, which for SQL Server 2019 are INSTEAD OF and AFTER triggers on INSERT, UPDATE, and DELETE. (Microsoft includes the FOR keyword, but this is a synonym for AFTER in Microsoft syntax.) Thus, we have six possible trigger types.

MySQL 8.0 supports only BEFORE and AFTER triggers–thus, like SQL Server 2019, it supports only six trigger types. Other DBMS products support triggers differently. See the documentation of your product to determine which trigger types it supports.

When a trigger is invoked, the DBMS makes the data involved in the triggering action available to the trigger code. For an insert, the DBMS will supply the values of columns for the row that is being inserted. For deletions, the DBMS will supply the values of columns for the row that is being deleted. For updates, it will supply both the old and the new values.

The way in which this is done depends on the DBMS product. For now, assume that new values are supplied by prefixing a column name with the expression *new:*. Thus, during an insert on CUSTOMER, the variable new:LastName is the value of LastName for the row being inserted. For an update, new:LastName has the value of LastName after the update takes place. Similarly, assume that old values are supplied by prefixing a column name with the expression *old:*. Thus, for a deletion, the variable old:LastName has the value of LastName for the row being deleted. For an update, old:LastName has the value of Name prior to the requested update. This, in fact, is the basic strategy (with slight syntactic differences) used by Oracle PL/SQL and MySQL SQL–you will see the equivalent SQL Server strategy in Chapter 10A.

Triggers have many uses. In this chapter, we consider the four uses summarized in Figure 7-24:

- Providing default values
- Enforcing data constraints
- Updating SQL views
- Performing referential integrity actions

### Using Triggers to Provide Default Values

Earlier in this chapter, you learned to use the SQL DEFAULT keyword to provide initial column values. DEFAULT works only for simple expressions, however, and if the computation of a default value requires complicated logic, then an INSERT trigger must be used instead.

For example, suppose that there is a policy at View Ridge Gallery to set the value of AskingPrice equal either to twice the AcquisitionPrice or to the AcquisitionPrice plus the average net gain for sales of this art in the past, whichever is greater. The AFTER trigger in Figure 7-25 implements this policy. Note that the code in Figure 7-25, although resembling Oracle Database PL/SQL, is *generic pseudocode*. You will learn how to write specific code for SQL Server in Chapter 10A, for Oracle Database in Chapter 10B, and for MySQL in Chapter 10C.

After declaring program variables, the trigger reads the TRANS table to find out how many TRANS rows exist for this work. Because this is an AFTER trigger, the new TRANS row for the work will have already been inserted. Thus, the count will be one if this is the first

| Uses of SQL Triggers |
| --- |
| Provide default values. |
| Enforce data constraints. |
| Update views. |
| Perform referential integrity actions. |

```
/* *** EXAMPLE CODE - DO NOT RUN ***                                */

CREATE TRIGGER TRANS_AskingPriceInitialValue
      AFTER INSERT ON TRANS

DECLARE
      rowCount          Int;
      sumNetProfit      Numeric(10,2);
      avgNetProfit      Numeric(10,2);
BEGIN
      /* First find if work has been here before              */

      SELECT     Count(*) INTO rowCount
      FROM       TRANS AS T
      WHERE      new:WorkID = T.WorkID;

      IF (rowCount = 1)
      THEN
         /* This is first time work has been in gallery        */

         new:AskingPrice = 2 * new:AcquisitionPrice;

      ELSE
         IF rowCount > 1
         THEN
            /* Work has been here before                       */

            SELECT     SUM(NetProfit) into sumNetProfit
            FROM       ArtistWorkNetView AWNV
            WHERE      AWNV.WorkID = new:WorkID;

            avgNetProfit = sumNetProfit / (rowCount - 1);

            /* Now choose larger value for the new AskingPrice  */

            IF ((new:AcquisitionPrice + avgNetProfit)
                  > (2 * new:AcquisitionPrice))
            THEN
               new:AskingPrice = (new:AcquisitionPrice + avgNetProfit);
            ELSE
               new:AskingPrice = (2 * new:AcquisitionPrice);
            END IF;
         ELSE
            /* Error, rowCount cannot be less than 1            */
            /* Do something!                                    */
         END IF;
      END IF;
END;
```

**FIGURE 7-25**

Trigger Code to Insert a
Default Value

time the work has been in the gallery. If so, the new value of SalesPrice is set to twice the AcquisitionPrice.

If the user variable *rowCount* is greater than one, then the work has been in the gallery before. To compute the average gain for this work, the trigger uses the ArtistWorkNetView described on page 364 to compute SUM(NetProfit) for this work. The sum is placed in the variable sumNetProfit. Notice that the WHERE clause limits the rows to be used in the view to this particular work. The average is then computed by dividing this sum by *rowCount* minus one.

You may be wondering, why not use AVG(NetProfit) in the SQL statement? The answer is that the default SQL average function would have counted the new row in the computation of the average. We do not want that row to be included, so we subtract one from *rowCount* when the average is computed. Once the value of avgNetProfit has been computed, it is compared with twice the AcquisitionPrice; the larger result is used for the new value of AskingPrice.

## Using Triggers to Enforce Data Constraints

A second purpose of triggers is to enforce data constraints. Although SQL CHECK constraints can be used to enforce domain, range, and intrarelation constraints, no DBMS vendor has implemented the SQL-92 features for interrelation CHECK constraints, which are called *ASSERTIONs* in the SQL standard. Consequently, such constraints are implemented in triggers.

Suppose, for example, that the gallery has a special interest in Mexican painters and never discounts the price of their works. Thus, the SalesPrice of a work must always be at least the AskingPrice. To enforce this rule, the gallery database has an insert and update trigger on TRANS that checks to see if the work is by a Mexican painter. If so, the SalesPrice is checked against the AskingPrice. If it is less than the AskingPrice, the SalesPrice is reset to the AskingPrice. This, of course, must happen when the artwork is actually being sold and the customer charged the full amount! This is *not* a postsale accounting adjustment.

Figure 7-26 shows *generic trigger code* that implements this rule. This trigger will be fired after any insert or update on a TRANS row. The trigger first checks to determine if the

**FIGURE 7-26**

**Trigger Code to Enforce an Interrelation Data Constraint**

```
/* *** EXAMPLE CODE - DO NOT RUN ***                                        */

CREATE TRIGGER TRANS_CheckSalesPrice
      AFTER INSERT, UPDATE ON TRANS

DECLARE

      artistNationality   Char (30);

BEGIN
      /* First determine if work is by a Mexican artist */

      SELECT    Nationality into artistNationality
      FROM      ARTIST AS A JOIN WORK AS W
          ON A.ArtistID = W.ArtistID
      WHERE     W.WorkID = new:WorkID;

      IF (artistNationality <> 'Mexican')
      THEN
         Exit Trigger;
      ELSE

         /* Work is by a Mexican artist - enforce constraint          */

         IF (new:SalesPrice < new:AskingPrice)
         THEN

            /* Sales Price is too low, reset it                       */

            UPDATE    TRANS
            SET       SalesPrice = new:AskingPrice
            WHERE     TransactionID = new:TransactionID;

            /* Note:  The above update will cause a recursive call on this */
            /* trigger. The recursion will stop the second time through    */
            /* because SalesPrice will be = AskingPrice.                   */

            /* At this point send a message to the user saying what's been */
            /* done so that the customer has to pay the full amount        */

         ELSE
            /* new:SalesPrice >= new:AskingPrice                      */
         Exit Trigger;
         END IF;
      END IF;
END;
```

work is by a Mexican artist. If not, the trigger is exited. Otherwise, the SalesPrice is checked against the AskingPrice; if it is less than the AskingPrice, the SalesPrice is set equal to the AskingPrice.

This trigger will be called recursively; the update statement in the trigger will cause an update on TRANS, which will cause the trigger to be called again. The second time, however, the SalesPrice will be equal to the AskingPrice, no more updates will be made, and the recursion will stop.

### Using Triggers to Update Views

As stated earlier, the DBMS can update some views but not others, depending on the way the view is constructed. Applications can sometimes update the views that the DBMS cannot update by applying logic that is particular to a given business setting. In this case, the application-specific logic for updating the view is placed in an INSTEAD OF trigger.

When an INSTEAD OF trigger is declared on a view, the DBMS performs no action other than to call the trigger. Everything else is up to the trigger. If you declare an INSTEAD OF INSERT trigger on view MyView and if your trigger does nothing but send an email message, then that email message becomes the result of an INSERT on the view. INSERT MyView means "send an email" and nothing more.

More realistically, consider the SQL view CustomerInterestsView on page 363 and the result of that view in Figure 7-18. This view is the result of two joins across the intersection table between CUSTOMER and ARTIST. Suppose that this view populates a grid on a user form, and further suppose that users want to make customer name corrections when necessary on this form. If such changes are not possible, the users will say something like, "But, hey, the name is right there. Why can't I change it?" Little do they know the trials and tribulations the DBMS went through to display those data!

In any case, if, for example, the customer LastName value happens to be unique within the database, the view has sufficient information to update the customer's last name. Figure 7-27 shows *generic trigger code* for such an update. The code just counts the number of customers that have the old value of LastName. If only one customer has that value, then the update is made; otherwise, an error message is generated. Notice that the update activity is on one of the tables that underlie the view. The view, of course, has no real data. Only actual tables can be updated.

### Using Triggers to Implement Referential Integrity Actions

The fourth use of triggers is to implement referential integrity actions. Consider, for example, the 1:N relationship between DEPARTMENT and EMPLOYEE. Assume that the relationship is M-M and that EMPLOYEE.DepartmentName is a foreign key to DEPARTMENT.

To enforce this constraint, we will construct two views, both based on EMPLOYEE. The first view, DeleteEmployeeView, will delete an EMPLOYEE row only if that row is not the last child in the DEPARTMENT. The second view, DeleteEmployeeDepartmentView, will delete an EMPLOYEE row, and if that row is the last EMPLOYEE in the DEPARTMENT, it will also delete the DEPARTMENT row.

An organization would make the view DeleteEmployeeView available to applications that do not have permission to delete a row in DEPARTMENT. The view DeleteEmployeeDepartmentView would be given to applications that have permission to delete both employees and departments that have no employees. At the same time, the organization would disallow all deletions directly on the EMPLOYEE and DEPARTMENT tables.

Both of the views DeleteEmployeeView and DeleteEmployeeDepartmentView have the identical structure:

```
/* *** EXAMPLE CODE - DO NOT RUN *** */
/* *** SQL-CREATE-VIEW-CH07-09 *** */
CREATE VIEW DeleteEmployeeView AS
    SELECT  *
    FROM    EMPLOYEE;
```

```
/* *** EXAMPLE CODE - DO NOT RUN ***                                      */

CREATE TRIGGER CustomerInterestView_UpdateCustomerLastName
        INSTEAD OF UPDATE ON CustomerInterestView

DECLARE

        rowCount          Int;

BEGIN

        SELECT      COUNT(*) into rowCount
        FROM        CUSTOMER
        WHERE       CUSTOMER.LastName = old:LastName;

        IF (rowCount = 1)
        THEN

            /* If get here, then only one customer has this last name.   */
            /* Make the name change.                                     */

            UPDATE      CUSTOMER
            SET         CUSTOMER.LastName = new:LastName
            WHERE       CUSTOMER.LastName = old:LastName;

        ELSE

            IF (rowCount > 1 )
            THEN

                /* Send a message to the user saying cannot update because */
                /* there are too many customers with this last name.       */

            ELSE
                /* Error, if rowcount <= 0 there is an error!              */
                /* Do something!                                          */
            END IF;
        END IF;
    END;
```

**FIGURE 7-27**

Trigger Code to Update an
SQL View

```
/* *** EXAMPLE CODE - DO NOT RUN *** */

/* *** SQL-CREATE-VIEW-CH07-10 *** */

CREATE VIEW DeleteEmployeeDepartmentView AS

    SELECT    *
    FROM      EMPLOYEE;
```

The trigger on DeleteEmployeeView, shown in Figure 7-28, determines if the employee is the last employee in the department. If not, the EMPLOYEE row is deleted. If, however, the employee *is* the last employee in the department, *nothing* is done. Note again that the DBMS does nothing when an INSTEAD OF trigger is declared on the deletion. All activity is up to the trigger. If the employee is the last employee, then this trigger does nothing, which means that no change will be made to the database because the DBMS left all processing tasks to the INSTEAD OF trigger.

The trigger on DeleteEmployeeDepartmentView, shown in Figure 7-29, treats the employee deletion a bit differently. First, the trigger checks to determine if the employee is the last employee in the department. If so, the EMPLOYEE is deleted, and then the DEPART-MENT itself is deleted. Notice that the row in EMPLOYEE is deleted in either case.

Triggers such as those in Figures 7-28 and 7-29 are used to enforce the referential integrity actions for O-M and M-M relationships, as described at the end of Chapter 6. (Note that a full implementation of those actions would also have to deal with insertions of departments.) You will learn how to write them for SQL Server 2019 in Chapter 10A, for Oracle Database in Chapter 10B, and for MySQL 8.0 in Chapter 10C.

**FIGURE 7-28**

**Trigger Code to
Delete All but Last
Child**

```
/* *** EXAMPLE CODE - DO NOT RUN ***                                        */

CREATE TRIGGER EMPLOYEE_DeleteCheck
      INSTEAD OF DELETE ON DeleteEmployeeView

DECLARE

      rowCount          Int;

BEGIN

      /*  First determine if this is the last employee in the department */

      SELECT    Count(*) into rowCount
      FROM      EMPLOYEE
      WHERE     EMPLOYEE.EmployeeNumber = old:EmployeeNumber;

      IF (rowCount > 1)
      THEN

         /* Not last employee, allow deletion                             */

         DELETE    EMPLOYEE
         WHERE     EMPLOYEE.EmployeeNumber = old:EmployeeNumber;

      ELSE

         /* Send a message to user saying that the last employee          */
         /* in a department cannot be deleted.                            */

      END IF;

   END;
```

**FIGURE 7-29**

**Trigger Code
to Delete Last
Child and
Parent When
Necessary**

```
/* *** EXAMPLE CODE - DO NOT RUN ***                                         */

CREATE TRIGGER EMPLOYEE_DEPARTMENT_DeleteCheck
      INSTEAD OF DELETE ON DeleteEmployeeDepartmentView
DECLARE

      rowCount          Int;

BEGIN

      /*  First determine if this is the last employee in the department    */

      SELECT    Count(*) into rowCount
      FROM      EMPLOYEE
      WHERE     EMPLOYEE.EmployeeNumber = old:EmployeeNumber;

      /* Delete Employee row regardless of whether Department is deleted    */

      DELETE    EMPLOYEE
      WHERE     EMPLOYEE.EmployeeNumber = old:EmployeeNumber;

      IF (rowCount = 1)
      THEN

         /* Last employee in Department, delete Department                  */

         DELETE    DEPARTMENT
         WHERE     DEPARTMENT.DepartmentName = old:DepartmentName;

      END IF;

END;
```

## Using Stored Procedures

A **stored procedure** is a program that is stored within the database and compiled when used. In Oracle Database, stored procedures can be written in PL/SQL or in Java. With Microsoft SQL Server 2019, stored procedures are written in T-SQL or a .NET CLR language, such as Visual Basic .NET (VB.NET), Visual C#, or Visual C++ .NET (all included in the Microsoft Visual Studio Integrated Development Environment (IDE) and supported by the .NET Framework discussed in Chapter 11). With MySQL, stored procedures are written in MySQL's variant of SQL.

Stored procedures can receive input parameters and return results. Unlike triggers, which are attached to a given table or view, stored procedures are attached to the database. They can be executed by any process using the database that has permission to use the procedure. Differences between triggers and stored procedures are summarized in Figure 7-30.

Stored procedures are used for many purposes. Although database administrators use them to perform common administration tasks, their primary use is within database applications. They can be invoked from application programs written in languages such as COBOL, C, Java, C#, or C++. They also can be invoked from Web pages (as we will see in Chapter 11) using VBScript, JavaScript, or PHP. Ad-hoc users can run them from DBMS management products such as SQL*Plus or SQL Developer in Oracle Database, SQL Server Management Studio in SQL Server, or the MySQLWorkbench in MySQL.

## Advantages of Stored Procedures

The advantages of using stored procedures are listed in Figure 7-31. Unlike application code, stored procedures are never distributed to client computers. They always reside in the database and are processed by the DBMS on the database server. Thus, they are more secure than distributed application code, and they also reduce network traffic. Increasingly, stored procedures are the preferred mode of processing application logic over the Internet or corporate intranets. Another advantage of stored procedures is that their SQL statements can be optimized by the DBMS compiler.

When application logic is placed in a stored procedure, many different application programmers can use that code. This sharing results not only in less work but also in standardized processing. Further, the developers best suited for database work can create the stored procedures while other developers, say, those who specialize in Web-tier programming,

**FIGURE 7-30**

Triggers Versus Stored Procedures

| Triggers Versus Stored Procedures |
|---|
| **Trigger** |
| Module of code that is called by the DBMS when INSERT, UPDATE, or DELETE commands are issued. |
| Assigned to a table or view. |
| Depending on the DBMS, may have more than one trigger per table or view. |
| Triggers may issue INSERT, UPDATE, and DELETE commands and thereby may cause the invocation of other triggers. |
| **Stored Procedure** |
| Module of code that is called by a user or database administrator. |
| Assigned to a database, but not to a table or a view. |
| Can issue INSERT, UPDATE, DELETE, and MERGE commands. |
| Used for repetitive administration tasks or as part of an application. |

FIGURE 7-31

Advantages of Stored
Procedures

| Advantages of Stored Procedures |
| --- |
| Greater security. |
| Decreased network traffic. |
| SQL can be optimized. |
| Code sharing. |
| Less work. |
| Standardized processing. |
| Specialization among developers. |

can do other work. Because of these advantages, it is likely that stored procedures will see increased use in the future.

### The WORK_AddWorkTransaction Stored Procedure

Figure 7-32 shows a stored procedure that records the acquisition of a work in the VRG database. Again, this code is generic, but the code style in Figure 7-32 is closer to that used in Microsoft SQL Server T-SQL rather than the Oracle Database PL/SQL style that was used for the trigger examples in the prior section. If you compare the pseudocode examples in both sections, you can gain a sense of the differences between code written in PL/SQL and T-SQL.

The WORK_addWorkTransaction procedure receives five input parameters and returns none. In a more realistic example, a return parameter would be passed back to the caller to indicate the success or failure of the operation. That discussion takes us away from database concepts, however, and we will omit it here. This code does not assume that the value of ArtistID that is passed to it is a valid ID. Instead, the first step in the stored procedure is to check whether the ArtistID value is valid. To do this, the first block of statements counts the number of rows that have the given ArtistID value. If the count is zero, then the ArtistID value is invalid, and the procedure writes an error message and returns.

Otherwise,[9] the procedure then checks to determine if the work has been in the View Ridge Gallery before. If so, the WORK table will already contain a row for this ArtistID, Title, and Copy. If no such row exists, the procedure creates a new WORK row. Once that has been done, it then uses a SELECT to obtain a value for the WorkID value. If the WORK row was just created, this statement is necessary to obtain the new value of the WorkID surrogate key. If the work was not created, the SELECT on WorkID is necessary to obtain the WorkID of the existing row. Once a value of WorkID has been obtained, the new row is inserted into TRANS. Notice that the system function GetDate() is used to supply a value for DateAcquired in the new row.

This procedure illustrates how SQL is embedded in stored procedures. It is not complete because we need to do something to ensure that either all updates originating in the stored procedures are made to the database or none of them are. You will learn how to do this in Chapter 9. For now, just concentrate on how SQL can be used as part of a database application.

### Comparing User-Defined Functions, Triggers, and Stored Procedures

User-defined functions, triggers, and stored procedures are all modules of programming code that are stored and used with a database. They differ in their intended use and in their ability to perform specific actions within the database. Figure 7-33 summarizes these three components of SQL/PSM.

---

[9]This code does not check for more than one row having the given ArtistID because ArtistID is a surrogate key.

```
/* *** EXAMPLE CODE - DO NOT RUN ***                                          */

CREATE PROCEDURE WORK_AddWorkTransaction
        (
        @ArtistID             Int,   -- Artist must already exist in database  */
        @Title                Char(25),
        @Copy                 Char(8),
        @Description          Varchar(1000),
        @AcquisitionPrice     Numeric(6,2) )


/* Stored procedure to record the acquisition of a work.  If the work has      */
/* never been in the gallery before, add a new WORK row.  Otherwise, use       */
/* the existing WORK row.  Add a new TRANS row for the work and set            */
/* DateAcquired to the system date.                                           */

AS
BEGIN

        DECLARE    @rowCount    AS Int,
                   @WorkID      AS Int


        /* Check that the ArtistID is valid                                    */
        SELECT     @rowCount = COUNT(*)
        FROM       ARTIST AS A
        WHERE      A.ArtistID = @ArtistID;

        IF (@rowCount = 0)
            /* The Artist does not exist in the database                */
            BEGIN
                Print 'No artist with ID of ' + CONVERT(Char(6), @artistID)
                Print 'Processing terminated.'
                RETURN
            END

        /* Check to see if the work is in the database                        */

        SELECT     @rowCount = COUNT(*)
        FROM       WORK AS W
        WHERE      W.ArtistID = @ArtistID and
           AND     W.Title = @Title and
           AND     W.Copy = @Copy;

        IF (@rowCount = 0)
        /* The Work is not in database, so put it in.                         */
            BEGIN
                INSERT INTO WORK (Title, Copy, Description, ArtistID)
                    VALUES (@Title, @Copy, @Description, @ArtistID);
            END

        /* Get the work surrogate key WorkID value                            */

        SELECT     @WorkID = W.WorkID
        FROM       WORK AS W
        WHERE      W.ArtistID = @ArtistID
           AND     W.Title = @Title
           AND     W.Copy = @Copy;

        /* Now put the new TRANS row into database.                           */

        INSERT INTO TRANS (DateAcquired, AcquisitionPrice, WorkID)
            VALUES (GetDate(), @AcquisitionPrice, @WorkID);

        RETURN
    END
```

**FIGURE 7-32**

Stored Procedure to Record
the Acquisition of a Work

SQL statements can be embedded in program code in functions, triggers, stored procedures, and application code. To do so, there must be a way to associate SQL table columns with program variables. Also, there is a paradigm mismatch between SQL and programs. Most SQL statements return sets of rows; an application expects to work on one row at a time. To resolve this mismatch, the results of SQL statements are processed as pseudofiles using a cursor. Web database applications are a good example of SQL statements embedded in application program code.

SQL/PSM is the portion of the SQL standard that provides for storing reusable modules of program code within a database. SQL/PSM specifies that SQL statements will be embedded in user-defined functions, triggers, and stored procedures in a database. It also specifies SQL variables, cursors, control-of-flow statements, and output procedures.

A user-defined function accepts input parameter values from an SQL statement, processes the parameter values, and returns a result value back to the calling statement. User-defined functions may be written to return a single value based on row values (a scalar-valued function), a table of values based on row values (a table-valued function), or a single value based on grouped column values (an aggregate function).

A trigger is a stored program that is executed by the DBMS whenever a specified event occurs on a specified table or view. In Oracle, triggers can be written in Java or in a proprietary Oracle language called PL/SQL. In SQL Server, triggers can be written in a propriety SQL Server language called TRANSACT-SQL, or T-SQL, and in Microsoft CLR languages, such as Visual Basic .NET, C# .NET, and C++ .NET. With MySQL, triggers can be written in MySQL's variant of SQL.

Possible triggers are BEFORE, INSTEAD OF, and AFTER. Each type of trigger can be declared for insert, update, and delete actions, so nine types of triggers are possible. Oracle supports all nine trigger types, SQL Server supports only INSTEAD OF and AFTER triggers, and MySQL supports the BEFORE and AFTER triggers. When a trigger is fired, the DBMS supplies old and new values for the update. New values are provided for inserts and updates, and old values are provided for updates and deletions. How these values are provided to the trigger depends on the DBMS in use.

Triggers have many uses. This chapter discussed four: setting default values, enforcing interrelation data constraints, updating views, and enforcing referential integrity actions.

A stored procedure is a program that is stored within the database and compiled when used. Stored procedures can receive input parameters and return results. Unlike triggers, their scope is database-wide; they can be used by any process that has permission to run the stored procedure.

Stored procedures can be called from programs written in the same languages used for triggers. They also can be called from DBMS SQL utilities. The advantages of using stored procedures are summarized in Figure 7-31.

A summary and comparison of user-defined functions, triggers, and stored procedures is shown in Figure 7-33.

# Key Terms

aggregate function
casual relationship
CHECK
cursor
data
data control language (DCL)
data definition language (DDL)
data manipulation language (DML)
data model
database design

DEFAULT keyword
graphical user interface (GUI)
FOREIGN KEY
IDENTITY({StartValue}, {Increment}) property
implementation
index
information
interrelation constraint
intrarelation constraint

Microsoft SQL Server Management Studio (SSMS)
NOT NULL
NULL
Oracle MySQL Workbench
Oracle SQL Developer
PRIMARY KEY
procedural programming language
Procedural Language/SQL (PL/SQL)
pseudofile

scalar-valued function
SQL ADD clause
SQL ADD CONSTRAINT clause
SQL ALTER INDEX statement
SQL ALTER TABLE statement
SQL ALTER VIEW statement
SQL CREATE FUNCTION statement
SQL CREATE INDEX statement
SQL CREATE OR ALTER VIEW
   statement
SQL CREATE OR REPLACE VIEW
   statement
SQL CREATE TABLE statement

SQL CREATE VIEW statement
SQL DELETE statement
SQL DROP COLUMN clause
SQL DROP CONSTRAINT clause
SQL DROP INDEX statement
SQL DROP TABLE statement
SQL INSERT statement
SQL MERGE statement
SQL ON DELETE clause
SQL ON UPDATE clause
SQL/Persistent Stored Modules (SQL/
   PSM)
SQL script

SQL script file
SQL TRUNCATE TABLE statement
SQL UPDATE statement
SQL view
stored procedure
systems analysis and design
systems development life cycle (SDLC)
table-valued function
transaction control language (TCL)
Transact-SQL (T-SQL)
trigger
UNIQUE
user-defined function (stored function)

# Review Questions

**7.1** What does DDL stand for? List the SQL DDL statements.

**7.2** What does DML stand for? List the SQL DML statements.

**7.3** Explain the meaning of the following expression: IDENTITY (4000, 5).

For this set of Review Questions, we will create and use a database with a set of tables that will allow us to compare variations in **SQL CREATE TABLE** and **SQL INSERT** statements. The purpose of these questions is to illustrate different situations that call for specific uses of various **SQL CREATE TABLE** and **SQL INSERT** options.

The database will be named **CH07_RQ_TABLES** and will contain the following six tables:

CUSTOMER_01 (<u>**EmailAddress**</u>, **LastName, FirstName**)

CUSTOMER_02 (<u>**CustomerID**</u>, **EmailAddress, LastName, FirstName**)

CUSTOMER_03 (<u>**CustomerID**</u>, **EmailAddress, LastName, FirstName**)

CUSTOMER_04 (<u>**CustomerID**</u>, **EmailAddress, LastName, FirstName**)

SALE_01 (<u>**SaleID**</u>, **DateOfSale,** *EmailAddress,* **SaleAmount**)

SALE_02 (<u>**SaleID**</u>, **DateOfSale,** *CustomerID,* **SaleAmount**)

EmailAddress is a text column containing an email address and is therefore not a surrogate key. CustomerID is a surrogate key that starts at 1 and increments by 1. SaleID is a surrogate key that starts at 20210001 and increases by 1.

The CH07_RQ_TABLES database has the following referential integrity constraints:

**EmailAddress in SALE_01 must exist in EmailAddress in CUSTOMER_01**

**CustomerID in SALE_02 must exist in CustomerID in CUSTOMER_04**

The relationship from SALE_01 to CUSTOMER_01 is N:1, O-M.
The relationship from SALE_02 to CUSTOMER_04 is N:1, O-M.
The column characteristics for these tables are shown in Figures 7-35 (CUSTOMER_01), 7-36 (CUSTOMER_02, CUSTOMER_03, and CUSTOMER_04), 7-37 (SALE_01), and 7-38 (SALE_02) . The data for these tables are shown in Figures 7-39 (CUSTOMER_01), 7-40 (CUSTOMER_02), 7-41 (CUSTOMER_04), 7-42 (SALE_01), and 7-43 (SALE_02).

**FIGURE 7-35**

Column Characteristics
for the CH07-RQ-TABLES
Database CUSTOMER_01
Table

| Column Name | Type | Key | Required | Remarks |
|---|---|---|---|---|
| EmailAddress | Varchar (100) | Primary Key | Yes | |
| LastName | Varchar (25) | No | Yes | |
| FirstName | Varchar (25) | No | Yes | |

**FIGURE 7-36**

Column Characteristics
for the CH07-RQ-TABLES
Database CUSTOMER_02,
CUSTOMER_03, and
CUSTOMER_04 Tables

| Column Name | Type | Key | Required | Remarks |
|---|---|---|---|---|
| CustomerID | Integer | Primary Key | Yes | Surrogate Key: Initial value=1 Increment=1 |
| EmailAddress | Varchar (100) | No | Yes | |
| LastName | Varchar (25) | No | Yes | |
| FirstName | Varchar (25) | No | Yes | |

**FIGURE 7-37**

Column Characteristics
for the CH07-RQ-TABLE
Database SALE_01 Table

| Column Name | Type | Key | Required | Remarks |
|---|---|---|---|---|
| SaleID | Integer | Primary Key | Yes | Surrogate Key: Initial value=1 Increment=1 |
| DateOfSale | Date | No | Yes | |
| EmailAddress | Varchar (100) | Foreign Key | Yes | REF: CUSTOMER_01 |
| SaleAmount | Numeric (7,2) | No | Yes | |

**FIGURE 7-38**

Column Characteristics
for the CH07-RQ-TABLE
Database SALE_02 Table

| Column Name | Type | Key | Required | Remarks |
|---|---|---|---|---|
| SaleID | Integer | Primary Key | Yes | Surrogate Key: Initial value=1 Increment=1 |
| DateOfSale | Date | No | Yes | |
| CustomerID | Integer | Foreign Key | Yes | REF: CUSTOMER_04 |
| SaleAmount | Numeric (7,2) | No | Yes | |

**FIGURE 7-39**

Data for the CH07-RQ-
TABLES Database
CUSTOMER_01 Table

| EmailAddress | LastName | FirstName |
|---|---|---|
| Robert.Shire@somewhere.com | Shire | Robert |
| Katherine.Goodyear@somewhere.com | Goodyear | Katherine |
| Chris.Bancroft@somewhere.com | Bancroft | Chris |

**FIGURE 7-40**

Data for the CH07-RQ-
TABLES Database
CUSTOMER_02 Table

| CustomerID | EmailAddress | LastName | FirstName |
|---|---|---|---|
| 1 | Robert.Shire@somewhere.com | Shire | Robert |
| 2 | Katherine.Goodyear@somewhere.com | Goodyear | Katherine |
| 3 | Chris.Bancroft@somewhere.com | Bancroft | Chris |

**FIGURE 7-41**

Data for the CH07-RQ-
TABLES Database
CUSTOMER_04 Table

| CustomerID | EmailAddress | LastName | FirstName |
|---|---|---|---|
| 17 | Robert.Shire@somewhere.com | Shire | Robert |
| 23 | Katherine.Goodyear@somewhere.com | Goodyear | Katherine |
| 46 | Chris.Bancroft@somewhere.com | Bancroft | Chris |
| 47 | John.Griffith@somewhere.com | Griffith | John |
| 48 | Doris.Tiemey@somewhere.com | Tiemey | Doris |
| 49 | Donna.Anderson@elsewhere.com | Anderson | Donna |

**FIGURE 7-42**

Data for the CH07-RQ-
TABLES Database SALE_01
Table

| SaleID | DateOfSale | EmailAddress | SaleAmount |
|---|---|---|---|
| 20210001 | 2021-01-14 | Robert.Shire@somewhere.com | 234.00 |
| 20210002 | 2021-01-14 | Chris.Bancroft@somewhere.com | 56.50 |
| 20210003 | 2021-01-16 | Robert.Shire@somewhere.com | 123.00 |
| 20210004 | 2021-01-17 | Katherine.Goodyear@somewhere.com | 34.25 |

**FIGURE 7-43**

Data for the CH07-RQ-
TABLES Database SALE_02
Table

| SaleID | DateOfSale | CustomerID | SaleAmount |
|---|---|---|---|
| 20210001 | 2021-01-14 | 17 | 234.00 |
| 20210002 | 2021-01-14 | 46 | 56.50 |
| 20210003 | 2021-01-16 | 17 | 123.00 |
| 20210004 | 2021-01-17 | 23 | 34.25 |
| 20210005 | 2021-01-18 | 49 | 345.00 |
| 20210006 | 2021-01-21 | 46 | 567.35 |
| 20210007 | 2021-01-23 | 47 | 78.50 |

**7.4** If you are using Microsoft SQL Server, Oracle Database, or MySQL, create a folder in your *Documents* folder to save and store the *.sql scripts containing the SQL statements that you are asked to create in the following Review Questions about the CH07_RQ_TABLES database:

■ For SQL Server Management Studio, create a folder named *CH07-RQ-TABLES-Database* in the *Projects* folder in your *SQL Server Management Studio* folder.

- For Oracle SQL Developer, create a folder named *CH07-RQ-TABLES-Database* in your *SQL Developer* folder.
- For SQL Workbench, create a folder named *CH07-RQ-TABLES-Database* in the *Schemas* folder in your *MySQL Workbench* folder.

If you are using Microsoft Access2019, create a folder named *CH07-Databases* in your *DBP-e16-Access-2019-Databases* folder.

**7.5**  Create a database named CH07_RQ_TABLES.

**7.6**  If you are using Microsoft SQL Server, Oracle Database, or MySQL, create and save an SQL script named *CH07-RQ-TABLES-Tables-Data-and-Views.sql* to hold the answers to Review Questions 7.7–7.40. Use *SQL script commenting* (/* and */ symbols) to write your answers to Review Questions that require written answers as comments.

If you are running Microsoft Access 2019, create and save a Microsoft Notepad text file named *CH07-RQ-TABLES-Tables-Data-and-Views.txt* to hold the answers to Review Questions 7.7–7.40. After you run each SQL statement in Microsoft Access 2019, copy your SQL statement to this file.

**7.7**  Write and run an SQL CREATE TABLE statement to create the CUSTOMER_01 table.

**7.8**  Write and run an SQL CREATE TABLE statement to create the CUSTOMER_02 table.

**7.9**  Are there any significant differences between the CUSTOMER_01 and CUS-TOMER_02 tables? If so, what are they?

**7.10**  Write and run an SQL CREATE TABLE statement to create the CUSTOMER_03 table.

**7.11**  Are there any significant differences between the CUSTOMER_02 and CUSTOMER_03 tables? If so, what are they?

**7.12**  Write and run an SQL CREATE TABLE statement to create the CUSTOMER_04 table.

**7.13**  Are there any significant differences between the CUSTOMER_03 and CUSTOMER_04 tables? If so, what are they?

**7.14**  Write and run an SQL CREATE TABLE statement to create the SALE_01 table. Note that the foreign key is EmailAddress, which references CUSTOMER_01. EmailAddress. In this database, CUSTOMER_01 and SALE_01 records are never deleted, so there will be no ON DELETE referential integrity action. However, you will need to decide how to implement the ON UPDATE referential integrity action.

**7.15**  In Review Question 7.14, how did you implement the ON UPDATE referential integrity action? Why?

**7.16**  Are there any significant differences between the CUSTOMER_01 and SALE_01 tables? If so, what are they?

**7.17**  Could we have created the SALE_01 table before creating the CUSTOMER_01 table? If not, why not?

**7.18**  Write and run an SQL CREATE TABLE statement to create the SALE_02 table. Note that the foreign key is CustomerID, which references CUSTOMER_04.CustomerID. In this database, CUSTOMER_04 and SALE_02 records are never deleted, so there will be no ON DELETE referential integrity action. However, you will need to decide how to implement the ON UPDATE referential integrity action.

**7.19**  In Review Question 7.18, how did you implement the ON UPDATE referential integrity action? Why?

**7.20** Are there any significant differences between the SALE_01 and SALE_02 tables? If so, what are they?

**7.21** Could we have created the SALE_02 table before creating the CUSTOMER_04 table? If not, why not?

**7.22** Write and run a set of SQL INSERT statements to populate the CUSTOMER_01 table.

**7.23** Write and run a set of SQL INSERT statements to populate the CUSTOMER_02 table. Do *not* use a bulk INSERT command.

**7.24** Are there any significant differences between the sets of SQL INSERT statements used to populate the CUSTOMER_01 and CUSTOMER_02 tables? If so, what are they?

**7.25** Write and run an SQL INSERT statement to populate the CUSTOMER_03 table. Use a bulk INSERT command and the data in the CUSTOMER_01 table. (*Hint:* In Oracle Database, this requires using a nested query in the FROM clause, which is not covered in the text. See the Oracle Database documentation.)

**7.26** Are there any significant differences between the sets of SQL INSERT statements used to populate the CUSTOMER_02 and CUSTOMER_03 tables? If so, what are they?

**7.27** Write and run a set of SQL INSERT statements to populate rows 1 through 3 in the CUSTOMER_04 table. Note that this question involves nonsequential surrogate key values and is based on techniques for Microsoft SQL Server 2019 in Chapter 10A, for Oracle Database in Chapter 10B, or for MySQL 8.0 in Chapter 10C, depending upon which DBMS product you are using.

**7.28** Are there any significant differences between the sets of SQL INSERT statements used to populate the CUSTOMER_02 table and rows 1 through 3 of the CUSTOMER_04 table? If so, what are they?

**7.29** Write and run a set of SQL INSERT statements to populate rows 4 through 6 in the CUSTOMER_04 table. Note that this question involves sequential surrogate key values and is based on techniques for Microsoft SQL Server 2019 in Chapter 10A, for Oracle Database in Chapter 10B, or for MySQL 8.0 in Chapter 10C, depending upon which DBMS product you are using.

**7.30** Are there any significant differences between the sets of SQL INSERT statements used to populate the CUSTOMER_02 table and rows 4 through 6 of the CUSTOMER_04 table? If so, what are they?

**7.31** Write and run a set of SQL INSERT statements to populate the SALE_01 table.

**7.32** Are there any significant differences between the sets of SQL INSERT statements used to populate the CUSTOMER_01 table and the SALE_01 table? If so, what are they?

**7.33** Could we have populated the SALE_01 table before populating the CUSTOMER_01 table? If not, why not?

**7.34** Write and run a set of SQL INSERT statements to populate the SALE_02 table.

**7.35** Are there any significant differences between the sets of SQL INSERT statements used to populate the SALE_01 table and the SALE_02 table? If so, what are they?

**7.36** Could we have populated the SALE_02 table before populating the CUSTOMER_04 table? If not, why not?

**7.37** Write and run an SQL INSERT statement to insert the additional data shown in Figure 7-44 into the SALE_02 table. What was the result of running this statement? Why did this result occur?

| SaleID | DateOfSale | CustomerID | SaleAmount |
|--------|-----------|-----------|-----------|
| 20210008 | 2021-01-25 | 50 | 890.15 |

**7.38** Write an SQL statement to create a view named Customer01DataView based on the CUSTOMER_01 table. In the view, include the values of EmailAddress, LastName as CustomerLastName, and FirstName as CustomerFirstName. Run this statement to create the view, and then test the view by writing and running an appropriate SQL SELECT statement.

**7.39** Write an SQL statement to create a view named Customer04DataView based on the CUSTOMER_04 table. In the view, include the values of Customer ID, LastName as CustomerLastName, FirstName as CustomerFirstName, and EmailAddress in that order. Run this statement to create the view, and then test the view by writing and running an appropriate SQL SELECT statement.

**7.40** Write an SQL statement to create a view named CustomerSalesView based on the CUSTOMER_04 and SALE_02 tables. In this view, include the values of Customer ID, LastName as CustomerLastName, FirstName as CustomerFirstName, EmailAddress, SaleID, DateOfSale, and SaleAmount in that order. Run this statement to create the view, and then test the view by writing and running an appropriate SQL SELECT statement.

## Wedgewood Pacific Review Questions

For this set of Review Questions, we will create and use a database for Wedgewood Pacific (WP) that is similar to the Microsoft Access database we created and used in Chapters 1 and 2. Founded in 1987 in Seattle, Washington, this company manufactures and sells consumer drone aircraft. This is an innovative and rapidly developing market. In October 2020, the Federal Aviation Administration (FAA) said that over 1,700,000 drones had been registered under the new FAA drone registration rules.[10] Of these, only about 500,000 were commercial drones, and the rest were drones for recreational use! The FAA also reported that over 198,000 remote pilots had been certified.

WP currently produces three drone models: the Alpha III, the Bravo III, and the Delta IV. These products are created by WP's Research and Development group and produced at WP's production facilities. WP manufactures some of the parts used in the drones, but also purchases some parts from other suppliers.

The company is located in two buildings. One building houses the Administration, Legal, Finance, Accounting, Human Resources, and Sales and Marketing departments, and the second houses the Information Systems, Research and Development, and Production departments. The company database contains data about employees; departments; projects; assets, such as finished goods inventory, parts inventory, and computer equipment; and other aspects of company operations.

The database will be named WP and will contain the following four tables:

DEPARTMENT (**DepartmentName**, BudgetCode, OfficeNumber, DepartmentPhone)

EMPLOYEE (**EmployeeNumber**, FirstName, LastName, *Department*, Position, *Supervisor*, OfficePhone, EmailAddress)

PROJECT (**ProjectID**, ProjectName, *Department*, MaxHours, StartDate, EndDate)

ASSIGNMENT (***ProjectID***, ***EmployeeNumber***, HoursWorked)

---

[10]See *https://www.faa.gov/uas/resources/by_the_numbers/* (accessed October 2020).

EmployeeNumber is a surrogate key that starts at 1 and increments by 1. ProjectID is a surrogate key that starts at 1000 and increases by 100. DepartmentName is the text name of the department and is therefore not a surrogate key.

The WP database has the following referential integrity constraints:

**Department in EMPLOYEE must exist in DepartmentName in DEPARTMENT**

**Supervisor in EMPLOYEE must exist in EmployeeNumber in EMPLOYEE**

**Department in PROJECT must exist in DepartmentName in DEPARTMENT**

**ProjectID in ASSIGNMENT must exist in ProjectID in PROJECT**

**EmployeeNumber in ASSIGNMENT must exist in EmployeeNumber in EMPLOYEE**

The relationship from EMPLOYEE to ASSIGNMENT is 1:N, M-O, and the relationship from PROJECT to ASSIGNMENT is 1:N, M-O.

The database also has the following business rules:

- If an EMPLOYEE row is to be deleted and that row is connected to any ASSIGN-MENT, the EMPLOYEE row deletion will be disallowed.
- If a PROJECT row is deleted, then all the ASSIGNMENT rows that are connected to the deleted PROJECT row will also be deleted.

The business sense of these rules is as follows:

- If an EMPLOYEE row is deleted (e.g., if the employee is transferred), then someone must take over that employee's assignments. Thus, the application needs someone to reassign assignments before deleting the employee row.
- If a PROJECT row is deleted, then the project has been canceled, and it is unnecessary to maintain records of assignments to that project.

The column characteristics for these tables are shown in Figures 1-34 (DEPARTMENT), 1-36 (EMPLOYEE), 2-43 (PROJECT), and 2-45 (ASSIGNMENT). The data for these tables are shown in Figures 1-35 (DEPARTMENT), 1-37 (EMPLOYEE), 2-44 (PROJECT), and 2-46 (ASSIGNMENT).

If at all possible, you should run your SQL solutions to the following questions against an actual database. Because we have already created this database in Microsoft Access, you should use an SQL-oriented DBMS such as Microsoft SQL Server 2019, Oracle Database, or MySQL 8.0 in these exercises. Create a database named *WP*, and create a folder in your *Documents* folder to save and store the *.sql scripts containing the SQL statements that you are asked to create in the remaining questions pertaining to the WP database in this section and the following Exercises section.

- For the SQL Server Management Studio, create a folder named *WP-Database* in the *Projects* folder structure in your *SQL Server Management Studio* folder.
- In the Oracle SQL Developer folder structure in your *SQL Developer* folder, create a folder named *WP-Database*.
- For the MySQL Workbench, create a folder named *WP-Database* in the *Schemas* folder in your *MySQL Workbench* folder.

If that is not possible, create a new Microsoft Access database named *WP-CH07.accdb*, and use the SQL capabilities in these exercises. In all the exercises, use the data types appropriate for the DBMS you are using.

Write and save an SQL script named *WP-Create-Tables.sql* that includes the answers to Review Questions 7.41 through 7.50. Use *SQL script commenting* (/* and */ symbols) to write your answers to Review Questions 7.45 and 7.46 as comments so that they cannot be run! Test and run your SQL statements for Review Questions 7.41, 7.42, 7.43, and 7.44 only. After the tables are created, run your answers to Review Questions 7.47 through 7.50. Note that after these four statements have been run, the table structure is exactly the same as it was before you ran them.

**7.41**  Write a CREATE TABLE statement for the DEPARTMENT table.

**7.42**  Write a CREATE TABLE statement for the EMPLOYEE table. Email is required and is an alternate key, and the default value of Department is Human Resources. Cascade updates but not deletions from DEPARTMENT to EMPLOYEE.

**7.43**  Write a CREATE TABLE statement for the PROJECT table. The default value for MaxHours is 100. Cascade updates but not deletions from DEPARTMENT to PROJECT.

**7.44**  Write a CREATE TABLE statement for the ASSIGNMENT table. Cascade only deletions from PROJECT to ASSIGNMENT; do not cascade either deletions or updates from EMPLOYEE to ASSIGNMENT.

**7.45**  Modify your answer to Review Question 7.43 to include the constraint that StartDate be prior to EndDate.

**7.46**  Write an alternate SQL statement that modifies your answer to Review Question 7.44 to make the relationship between EMPLOYEE and ASSIGNMENT a 1:1 relationship.

**7.47**  Write an ALTER statement to add the column AreaCode to EMPLOYEE. Assume that AreaCode is not required.

**7.48**  Write an ALTER statement to remove the column AreaCode from EMPLOYEE.

**7.49**  Write an ALTER statement to make OfficePhone an alternate key in EMPLOYEE.

**7.50**  Write an ALTER statement to drop the constraint that OfficePhone is an alternate key in EMPLOYEE.

**Create SQL scripts to answer Review Questions 7.51 through 7.56. Write the answer to Review Question 7.55 as an SQL text comment, but include it in your script. Write the answer to Review Question 7.56 as an SQL comment so that it *cannot* be run.**

**7.51**  Write INSERT statements to add the data shown in Figure 1-29 to the DEPARTMENT table. Run these statements to populate the DEPARTMENT table. (*Hint:* Write and test an SQL script, and then run the script. Save the script as *WP-Insert-DEPARTMENT-Data.sql* for future use.)

**7.52**  Write INSERT statements to add the data shown in Figure 1-31 to the EMPLOYEE table. Run these statements to populate the EMPLOYEE table. (*Hint:* Write and test an SQL script, and then run the script. Save the script as *WP-Insert-EMPLOYEE-Data.sql* for future use.)

**7.53**  Write INSERT statements to add the data shown in Figure 2-44 to the PROJECT table. Run these statements to populate the PROJECT table. (*Hint:* Write and test an SQL script, and then run the script. Save the script as *WP-Insert-PROJECT-Data.sql* for future use.)

**7.54**  Write INSERT statements to add the data shown in Figure 2-46 to the ASSIGNMENT table. Run these statements to populate the ASSIGNMENT table. (*Hint:* Write and test an SQL script, and then run the script. Save the script as *WP-Insert-ASSIGNMENT-Data.sql* for future use.)

**7.55**  Why were the tables populated in the order shown in Review Questions 7.51 through 7.54?

**7.56**  Assume that you have a table named NEW_EMPLOYEE that has the columns Department, Email, FirstName, and LastName, in that order. Write an INSERT statement to add all of the rows from the table NEW_EMPLOYEE to EMPLOYEE. Do not attempt to run this statement!

**Create and run an SQL script named *WP-Update-Data.sql* to answer Review Questions 7.57 through 7.62. Write the answer to Review Question 7.62 as an SQL comment so that it *cannot* be run.**

**7.57** Write an UPDATE statement to change the phone number of the employee with EmployeeNumber 11 to 360-287-8810. Run this SQL statement.

**7.58** Write an UPDATE statement to change the department of the employee with EmployeeNumber 5 to Finance. Run this SQL statement.

**7.59** Write an UPDATE statement to change the phone number of the employee with EmployeeNumber 5 to 360-287-8420. Run this SQL statement.

**7.60** Combine your answers to Review Questions 7.58 and 7.59 into one SQL statement. Run this statement.

**7.61** Write an UPDATE statement to set the HoursWorked to 60 for every row in ASSIGN-MENT with the value 10 for EmployeeNumber. Run this statement.

**7.62** Assume that you have a table named NEW_EMAIL, which has new values of Email for some employees. NEW_EMAIL has two columns: EmployeeNumber and New-Email. Write a MERGE statement to change the values of Email in EMPLOYEE to those in the NEW_EMAIL table. Do *not* run this statement.

**Create and run an SQL script named *WP-Delete-Data.sql* to answer Review Questions 7.63 and 7.64. Write the answers to Review Questions 7.63 and 7.64 as SQL comments so that they *cannot* be run.**

**7.63** Write one DELETE statement that will delete all data for project '2021 Q3 Production Plan' and all of its rows in ASSIGNMENT. Do *not* run this statement.

**7.64** Write a DELETE statement that will delete the rows for employees with last name 'Smith'. Do *not* run this statement. What happens if one of these employees has rows in ASSIGNMENT?

**7.65** What is an SQL view? What purposes do views serve?

**7.66** What is the limitation on SELECT statements used in SQL views?

**Create and run an SQL script named *WP-Create-Views.sql* to answer Review Questions 7.67 through 7.72.**

**7.67** Write an SQL statement to create a view named EmployeePhoneView that shows the values of EMPLOYEE.LastName as EmployeeLastName, EMPLOYEE.FirstName as EmployeeFirstName, and EMPLOYEE.OfficePhone as EmployeePhone. Run this statement to create the view, and then test the view by writing and running an appropriate SQL SELECT statement.

**7.68** Write an SQL statement to create a view named FinanceEmployeePhoneView that shows the values of EMPLOYEE.LastName as EmployeeLastName, EMPLOYEE. FirstName as EmployeeFirstName, and EMPLOYEE.OfficePhone as EmployeePhone for employees who work in the Finance Department. Run this statement to create the view, and then test the view by writing and running an appropriate SQL SELECT statement.

**7.69** Write an SQL statement to create a view named CombinedNameEmployeePhon-eView that shows the values of EMPLOYEE.LastName, EMPLOYEE.FirstName, and EMPLOYEE.OfficePhone as EmployeePhone but that combines EMPLOYEE.Last-Name and EMPLOYEE.FirstName into one column named EmployeeName that displays the employee name first name first. Run this statement to create the view, and then test the view by writing and running an appropriate SQL SELECT statement.

**7.70** Write an SQL statement to create a view named EmployeeProjectAssignmentView that shows the values of EMPLOYEE.LastName as EmployeeLastName, EMPLOYEE.FirstName as EmployeeFirstName, EMPLOYEE.OfficePhone as EmployeePhone, and PROJECT.ProjectName as ProjectName. Run this statement to create the view, and then test the view by writing and running an appropriate SQL SELECT statement.

**7.71** Write an SQL statement to create a view named DepartmentEmployeeProject-AssignmentView that shows the values of EMPLOYEE.LastName as EmployeeLast-Name, EMPLOYEE.FirstName as EmployeeFirstName, EMPLOYEE.OfficePhone as Employee-Phone, DEPARTMENT.DepartmentName, DEPARTMENT.Department-Phone as DepartmentPhone, and PROJECT.ProjectName as ProjectName. Run this statement to create the view, and then test the view by writing and running an appropriate SQL SELECT statement.

**7.72** Write an SQL statement to create a view named ProjectHoursToDateView that shows the values of PROJECT.ProjectID, PROJECT.ProjectName, PROJECT.Max-Hours as ProjectMaxHours, and the sum of ASSIGNMENT.HoursWorked as ProjectHoursWorkedToDate. Run this statement to create the view, and then test the view by writing and running an appropriate SQL SELECT statement.

**7.73** Describe how views are used to provide aliases for tables. Why is this useful?

**7.74** Explain how views can be used to improve data security.

**7.75** Explain how views can be used to provide additional trigger functionality.

**7.76** Give an example of a view that is clearly updatable.

**7.77** Give an example of a view that is clearly not updatable.

**7.78** Summarize the general idea for determining whether a view is updatable.

**7.79** If a view is missing required items, what action on the view is definitely not allowed?

**7.80** Explain the paradigm mismatch between SQL and programming languages.

**7.81** How is the mismatch in your answer to Review Question 7.80 corrected?

**7.82** Describe the SQL/PSM component of the SQL standard. What are PL/SQL and T-SQL? What is the MySQL equivalent?

**7.83** What is a user-defined function?

**Using the WP database, create an SQL script named *WP-Create-Function-and-View. sql* to answer Review Questions 7.84 and 7.85.**

**7.84** Create and test a user-defined function named FirstNameFirst that combines two parameters named FirstName and LastName into a concatenated value named Full-Name and displays, in order, the FirstName, a space, and the LastName. (*Hint: Steve* and *Smith* would be combined to read *Steve Smith.*)

**7.85** Create and test a view called EmployeeDepartmentDataView that contains the employee name concatenated by the FirstNameFirst user-defined function in a field named EmployeeName, EMPLOYEE.Department, DEPARTMENT.OfficeNum-ber, DEPARTMENT.DepartmentPhone, and EMPLOYEE.OfficePhone as Employee-Phone. Run this statement to create the view, and then test the view by writing and running an appropriate SQL SELECT statement.

**7.86** What is a trigger?

**7.87** What is the relationship between a trigger and a table or view?

**7.88** Name nine possible trigger types.

**7.89** Explain in general terms how new and old values are made available to a trigger.

**7.90**  Describe four uses for triggers.

**7.91**  Assume that the View Ridge Gallery will allow a row to be deleted from WORK if the work has never been sold. Explain in general terms how to use a trigger to accomplish such a deletion. (*Hint:* Check transactions.)

**7.92**  Assume that the Wedgewood Pacific Corporation will allow a row to be deleted from EMPLOYEE if the employee has no project assignments. Explain in general terms how to use a trigger to accomplish such a deletion. (*Hint:* Check assignments.)

**7.93**  What are stored procedures? How do they differ from triggers?

**7.94**  Summarize how to invoke a stored procedure.

**7.95**  Summarize the key advantages of stored procedures.

# Exercises

## Wedgewood Pacific Exercises

These Exercises extend the Wedgewood Pacific database you created and used in the Review Questions with two new tables named COMPUTER and COMPUTER_ASSIGNMENT.

The data model for these modifications is shown in Figure 7-45. The column characteristics for the COMPUTER table are shown in Figure 7-46, and those for the COMPUTER_ASSIGNMENT table are shown in Figure 7-47. Data for the COMPUTER table are shown in Figure 7-48, and data for the COMPUTER_ASSIGNMENT table are shown in Figure 7-49.

**7.96**  Describe the relationships in terms of type (identifying or nonidentifying) and maximum and minimum cardinality.

**7.97**  Explain the need for each of the foreign keys.

**7.98**  Define referential integrity actions (such as ON UPDATE CASCADE) for the COMPUTER-to-COMPUTER_ASSIGNMENT relationship only. Explain the need for these actions.

**FIGURE 7-45**

**WP Database Design Extension**

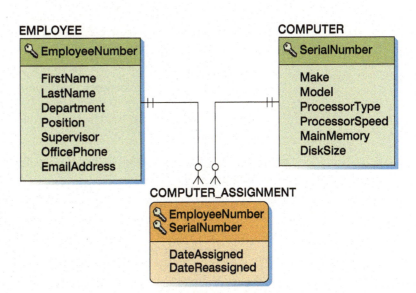

**FIGURE 7-46**

Column Characteristics
for the WP Database
COMPUTER Table

COMPUTER

| ColumnName | Type | Key | Required | Remarks |
|---|---|---|---|---|
| SerialNumber | Integer | Primary Key | Yes | |
| Make | Char (12) | No | Yes | Must be "Dell" or "HP" or "Other" |
| Model | Char (24) | No | Yes | |
| ProcessorType | Char (24) | No | No | |
| ProcessorSpeed | Numeric (3,2) | No | Yes | Between 2.0 and 5.0 |
| MainMemory | Char (15) | No | Yes | |
| DiskSize | Char (15) | No | Yes | |

**FIGURE 7-47**

Column Characteristics
for the WP Database
COMPUTER_ASSIGNMENT
Table

COMPUTER_ASSIGNMENT

| ColumnName | Type | Key | Required | Remarks |
|---|---|---|---|---|
| SerialNumber | Integer | Primary Key, Foreign Key | Yes | REF: COMPUTER |
| EmployeeNumber | Integer | Primary Key, Foreign Key | Yes | REF: EMPLOYEE |
| DateAssigned | Date | No | Yes | |
| DateReassigned | Date | No | No | |

**7.99** Assume that COMPUTER_ASSIGNMENT in the EMPLOYEE-to-COMPUTER_ASSIGNMENT relationship is now mandatory (i.e., every employee must have at least one computer). Use Figure 6-29(b) as a boilerplate to describe triggers for enforcing the required child between EMPLOYEE and COMPUTER_ASSIGNMENT. Define the purpose of any necessary triggers.

**7.100** Explain the interaction between the triggers in your answer to Project Question 7.99 and the COMPUTER-to-COMPUTER_ASSIGNMENT relationship. What, if any, cascading behavior do you want to occur? Explain how you can test to find out if it works the way that you want it to.

Using the WP database, create an SQL script named *WP-Create-New-Tables.sql* to answer Exercise 7.101.

**7.101** Write CREATE TABLE statements for the COMPUTER and COMPUTER_ASSIGNMENT tables in Figure 7-45 using the column characteristics shown in Figures 7-46 and 7-47. Write CHECK constraints to ensure that Make is Dell, HP, or Other. Also, write constraints to ensure that ProcessorSpeed is between 2.0 and 5.0 (these are units of gigahertz). Run these statements on your WP database to extend the database structure.

| SerialNumber | Make | Model | ProcessorType | ProcessorSpeed | MainMemory | DiskSize |
|---|---|---|---|---|---|---|
| 9871234 | HP | ProDesk 600 G5 | Intel i5-9500T | 3.70 | 16.0 GBytes | 1.0 TBytes |
| 9871235 | HP | ProDesk 600 G5 | Intel i5-9500T | 3.70 | 16.0 GBytes | 1.0 TBytes |
| 9871236 | HP | ProDesk 600 G5 | Intel i5-9500T | 3.70 | 16.0 GBytes | 1.0 TBytes |
| 9871237 | HP | ProDesk 600 G5 | Intel i5-9500T | 3.70 | 16.0 GBytes | 1.0 TBytes |
| 9871238 | HP | ProDesk 600 G5 | Intel i5-9500T | 3.70 | 16.0 GBytes | 1.0 TBytes |
| 9871239 | HP | ProDesk 600 G5 | Intel i5-9500T | 3.70 | 16.0 GBytes | 1.0 TBytes |
| 9871240 | HP | ProDesk 600 G5 | Intel i5-9500T | 3.70 | 16.0 GBytes | 1.0 TBytes |
| 9871241 | HP | ProDesk 600 G5 | Intel i5-9500T | 3.70 | 16.0 GBytes | 1.0 TBytes |
| 9871242 | HP | ProDesk 600 G5 | Intel i5-9500T | 3.70 | 16.0 GBytes | 1.0 TBytes |
| 9871243 | HP | ProDesk 600 G5 | Intel i5-9500T | 3.70 | 16.0 GBytes | 1.0 TBytes |
| 6541001 | Dell | OptiPlex 7060 | Intel i7-8700 | 4.60 | 32.0 GBytes | 2.0 TBytes |
| 6541002 | Dell | OptiPlex 7060 | Intel i7-8700 | 4.60 | 32.0 GBytes | 2.0 TBytes |
| 6541003 | Dell | OptiPlex 7060 | Intel i7-8700 | 4.60 | 32.0 GBytes | 2.0 TBytes |
| 6541004 | Dell | OptiPlex 7060 | Intel i7-8700 | 4.60 | 32.0 GBytes | 2.0 TBytes |
| 6541005 | Dell | OptiPlex 7060 | Intel i7-8700 | 4.60 | 32.0 GBytes | 2.0 TBytes |
| 6541006 | Dell | OptiPlex 7060 | Intel i7-8700 | 4.60 | 32.0 GBytes | 2.0 TBytes |
| 6541007 | Dell | OptiPlex 7060 | Intel i7-8700 | 4.60 | 32.0 GBytes | 2.0 TBytes |
| 6541008 | Dell | OptiPlex 7060 | Intel i7-8700 | 4.60 | 32.0 GBytes | 2.0 TBytes |
| 6541009 | Dell | OptiPlex 7060 | Intel i7-8700 | 4.60 | 32.0 GBytes | 2.0 TBytes |
| 6541010 | Dell | OptiPlex 7060 | Intel i7-8700 | 4.60 | 32.0 GBytes | 2.0 TBytes |

**FIGURE 7-48**

WP Database COMPUTER
Table Data

Using the WP database, create an SQL script named *WP-Insert-New-Data.sql* to answer Exercise 7.102.

**7.102** Using the sample data for the COMPUTER table shown in Figure 7-48 and the COMPUTER_ASSIGNMENT table shown in Figure 7-49, write INSERT statements to add this data to these tables in the WP database. Run these INSERT statements to populate the tables.

Using the WP database, create an SQL script named *WP-Create-New-Views-And-Functions.sql* to answer Exercises 7.103 through 7.108.

**7.103** Create a view of COMPUTER named ComputerView that displays SerialNumber and then Make and Model combined as one attribute named ComputerType. Place a colon and a space between Make and Model in the format: *Dell: OptiPlex 7060*. Do *not* create a user-defined function to perform this task. Run the statement to create the view, and then test the view with an appropriate SQL SELECT statement.

FIGURE 7-49

WP Database COMPUTER_
ASSIGNMENT Table Data

| SerialNumber | EmployeeNumber | DateAssigned | DateReassigned |
|---|---|---|---|
| 9871234 | 12 | 15-Sep-21 | 21-Oct-21 |
| 9871235 | 13 | 15-Sep-21 | 21-Oct-21 |
| 9871236 | 14 | 15-Sep-21 | 21-Oct-21 |
| 9871237 | 15 | 15-Sep-21 | 21-Oct-21 |
| 9871238 | 6 | 15-Sep-21 | 21-Oct-21 |
| 9871239 | 7 | 15-Sep-21 | 21-Oct-21 |
| 9871240 | 8 | 15-Sep-21 | 21-Oct-21 |
| 9871241 | 9 | 15-Sep-21 | 21-Oct-21 |
| 9871242 | 16 | 15-Sep-21 | 21-Oct-21 |
| 9871243 | 17 | 15-Sep-21 | 21-Oct-21 |
| 6541001 | 12 | 21-Oct-21 | |
| 6541002 | 13 | 21-Oct-21 | |
| 6541003 | 14 | 21-Oct-21 | |
| 6541004 | 15 | 21-Oct-21 | |
| 6541005 | 6 | 21-Oct-21 | |
| 6541006 | 7 | 21-Oct-21 | |
| 6541007 | 8 | 21-Oct-21 | |
| 6541008 | 9 | 21-Oct-21 | |
| 6541009 | 16 | 21-Oct-21 | |
| 6541010 | 17 | 21-Oct-21 | |
| 9871234 | 1 | 21-Oct-21 | |
| 9871235 | 2 | 21-Oct-21 | |
| 9871236 | 3 | 21-Oct-21 | |
| 9871237 | 4 | 21-Oct-21 | |
| 9871238 | 5 | 21-Oct-21 | |
| 9871239 | 10 | 21-Oct-21 | |
| 9871240 | 11 | 21-Oct-21 | |
| 9871241 | 18 | 21-Oct-21 | |
| 9871242 | 19 | 21-Oct-21 | |
| 9871243 | 20 | 21-Oct-21 | |

**7.104** Create a view called ComputerMakeView that shows the Make and average Processor Speed for all computers. Run the statement to create the view, and then test the view with an appropriate SQL SELECT statement.

**7.105** Create a view called ComputerUserView that has all of the data of COMPUTER and ASSIGNMENT. Run the statement to create the view, and then test the view with an appropriate SQL SELECT statement.

**7.106** Create an SQL SELECT statement to use the view you created called ComputerView to show the computer SerialNumber, ComputerType, and Employee name. Run this statement.

**7.107** Create and test a user-defined function named *ComputerMakeAndModel* to concatenate Make and Model to form the *{Make}:{Model}* character string as you did without a function in Exercise 7.103.

**7.108** Create a view of COMPUTER named ComputerMakeAndModelView that displays SerialNumber and then uses the ComputerMakeAndModel function you created in Exercise 7.107 to display an attribute named ComputerType. Test the view with an appropriate SQL SELECT statement.

**7.109** Suppose you want to use a trigger to automatically place a DateReassigned value in an old row of the COMPUTER_ASSIGNMENT table whenever a new row is inserted into COMPUTER_ASSIGNMENT to record a new computer assignment of an existing computer. Describe in general terms the trigger logic.

**7.110** Suppose you want to use a stored procedure to store a new row in COMPUTER. List the minimum number of parameters that need to be in the procedure. Describe in general terms the logic of the stored procedure.

# Case Questions

## Heather Sweeney Designs Case Questions

Heather Sweeney is an interior designer who specializes in home kitchen design. Her company is named Heather Sweeney Designs. Heather offers a variety of seminars at home shows, kitchen and appliance stores, and other public locations. The seminars are free; she offers them as a way of building her customer base. She earns revenue by selling books and videos that instruct people on kitchen design. She also offers custom-design consulting services.

After someone attends a seminar, Heather wants to leave no stone unturned in attempting to sell that person one of her products or services. She would therefore like to develop a database to keep track of customers, the seminars they have attended, the contacts she has made with them, and the purchases they have made. She wants to use this database to continue to contact her customers and offer them products and services.

The database will be named HSD. For reference, the SQL statements shown here are built from the HSD database design in Figure 7-50, the column characteristics specifications shown in Figure 7-51, and the referential integrity constraint specifications detailed in Figure 7-52.

The SQL statements to create the HSD database for Heather Sweeney Designs are shown in Figure 7-53 in Microsoft SQL Server syntax. The SQL statements to populate the HSD database are shown in Figure 7-54, again in Microsoft SQL Server syntax.

**FIGURE 7-50**

Database Design for the
HSD Database

Write SQL statements and answer questions for this database as follows:

**A.** Create a database named HSD in your DBMS.

**B.** Create a folder in your *Documents* folder to save and store *.sql scripts containing the
SQL statements that you are asked to create in the remaining questions in this section.
  - For the SQL Server Management Studio, create a folder named *HSD-Database* in
    the *Projects* folder structure in your *SQL Server Management Studio* folder.
  - In the Oracle SQL Developer folder structure in your *SQL Developer* folder, create
    a folder named *HSD-Database*.
  - For the MySQL Workbench, create a folder named *HSD-Database* in the *Schemas*
    folder in your *MySQL Workbench* folder.

**C.** Write an SQL script named *HSD-Create-Tables.sql* based on Figure 7-53 to create the
tables and relationships for the HSD database. Save this script, and then execute
the script to create the HSD tables.

**D.** Write an SQL script named *HSD-Insert-Data.sql* based on Figure 7-54 to insert the
data for the HSD database. Save this script, and then execute the script to populate
the HSD tables.

**Using the HSD database, create an SQL script named *HSD-CQ-CH07.sql* to answer
questions E through Q. Include your answer to part Q, but be sure to put it in comment
marks so that it is interpreted as a comment by the DBMS and cannot actually be run!**

**E.** Write SQL statements to list all columns for all tables.

**F.** Write an SQL statement to list LastName, FirstName, and Phone for all customers
who live in Dallas.

**G.** Write an SQL statement to list LastName, FirstName, and Phone for all customers
who live in Dallas and have a LastName that begins with the letter T.

| Column Name | Data Type (Length) | Key | Required | Default Value | Remarks |
|---|---|---|---|---|---|
| SeminarID | Integer | Primary Key | Yes | | DBMS Supplied Surrogate Key: Initial Value=1 Increment=1 |
| SeminarDate | Date | No | Yes | None | Format: yyyy-mm-dd |
| SeminarTime | Time | No | Yes | None | Format: 00:00:00.00 |
| Location | Varchar (100) | No | Yes | None | |
| SeminarTitle | Varchar (100) | No | Yes | None | |

(a) SEMINAR

| Column Name | Data Type (Length) | Key | Required | Default Value | Remarks |
|---|---|---|---|---|---|
| CustomerID | Integer | Primary Key | Yes | | DBMS Supplied Surrogate Key: Initial Value=1 Increment=1 |
| LastName | Char (25) | No | Yes | None | |
| FirstName | Char (25) | No | Yes | None | |
| EmailAddress | Varchar (100) | Alternate Key | Yes | None | AK1.1 |
| EncryptedPassword | Varchar (50) | No | No | None | |
| Phone | Char (12) | No | Yes | None | Format: ###-###-#### |
| StreetAddress | Char(35) | No | No | None | |
| City | Char (35) | No | No | Dallas | |
| State | Char (2) | No | No | TX | Format: AA |
| ZIP | Char (10) | No | No | 75201 | Format: #####-#### |

(b) CUSTOMER

| Column Name | Data Type (Length) | Key | Required | Default Value | Remarks |
|---|---|---|---|---|---|
| SeminarID | Integer | Primary Key, Foreign Key | Yes | None | REF: SEMINAR |
| CustomerID | Integer | Primary Key, Foreign Key | Yes | None | REF: CUSTOMER |

(c) SEMINAR_CUSTOMER

**FIGURE 7-51**

Database Column Specifications for the HSD Database

*(continued)*

| Column Name | Data Type (Length) | Key | Required | Default Value | Remarks |
|---|---|---|---|---|---|
| CustomerID | Integer | Primary Key, Foreign Key | Yes | None | REF: CUSTOMER |
| ContactNumber | Integer | Primary Key | Yes | None | This is not quite a Surrogate Key—for *each* ContactNumber: Start=1 Increment=1 Application logic will be needed to supply the correct value |
| ContactDate | Date | No | Yes | None | Format: yyyy-mm-dd |
| ContactType | Varchar (30) | No | Yes | None | Allowed values: Seminar, FormLetterSeminar, WebAccountCreation, WebPurchase, EmailAccountMessage, EmailSeminarMessage, EmailPurchaseMessage, EmailExchangeMessage, PhoneConversation |
| SeminarID | Integer | Foreign Key | No | None | REF: SEMINAR |

(d) CONTACT

| Column Name | Data Type (Length) | Key | Required | Default Value | Remarks |
|---|---|---|---|---|---|
| InvoiceNumber | Integer | Primary Key | Yes | | DBMS Supplied Surrogate Key: Initial Value=35000 Increment=1 |
| InvoiceDate | Date | No | Yes | None | Format: yyyy-mm-dd |
| CustomerID | Integer | Foreign Key | Yes | None | REF: CUSTOMER |
| PaymentType | Char (25) | No | Yes | Cash | Allowed values: VISA, MasterCard, American Express, PayPal, Check, Cash |
| Subtotal | Numeric (9,2) | No | No | None | |
| Shipping | Numeric (9,2) | No | No | None | |
| Tax | Numeric (9,2) | No | No | None | |
| Total | Numeric (9,2) | No | No | None | |

(e) INVOICE

**FIGURE 7-51**

Continued

| Column Name | Data Type (Length) | Key | Required | Default Value | Remarks |
|---|---|---|---|---|---|
| InvoiceNumber | Integer | Primary Key, Foreign Key | Yes | None | REF: INVOICE |
| LineNumber | Integer | Primary Key | Yes | None | This is not quite a Surrogate Key—for *each* InvoiceNumber: Start=1 Increment=1 Application logic will be needed to supply the correct value |
| ProductNumber | Char (35) | Foreign Key | Yes | None | REF: PRODUCT |
| Quantity | Integer | No | Yes | None | |
| UnitPrice | Numeric (9,2) | No | No | None | |
| Total | Numeric (9,2) | No | No | None | |

**(f) LINE_ITEM**

| Column Name | Data Type (Length) | Key | Required | Default Value | Remarks |
|---|---|---|---|---|---|
| ProductNumber | Char (35) | Primary Key | Yes | None | |
| ProductType | Char (24) | No | Yes | None | Allowed values: Video, Video Companion, Book |
| ProductDescription | Varchar (100) | No | Yes | None | |
| UnitPrice | Numeric (9,2) | No | Yes | None | |
| QuantityOnHand | Integer | No | Yes | None | |

**(g) PRODUCT**

**FIGURE 7-51**

Continued

H. Write an SQL statement to list the INVOICE.InvoiceNumber for sales that include the *Heather Sweeney Seminar Live in Dallas on 25-OCT-19* video. Use a subquery. (*Hint:* The correct solution uses three tables in the query because the question asks for INVOICE.InvoiceNumber. Otherwise, there is a possible solution with only two tables in the query.)

I. Answer part H but use JOIN ON syntax. (*Hint:* The correct solution uses three tables in the query because the question asks for INVOICE.InvoiceNumber. Otherwise, there is a possible solution with only two tables in the query.)

J. Write an SQL statement to list the FirstName, LastName, and Phone of customers (list each name only once) who have attended the Kitchen on a Big D Budget seminar. Sort the results by LastName in descending order and then by FirstName in descending order.

K. Write an SQL statement to list the FirstName, LastName, Phone, ProductNumber, and ProductDescription of customers (list each combination of name and video

| Relationship | | Referential Integrity Constraint | Cascading Behavior | |
|---|---|---|---|---|
| Parent | Child | | On Update | On Delete |
| SEMINAR | SEMINAR_CUSTOMER | SeminarID in SEMINAR_CUSTOMER must exist in SeminarID in SEMINAR | No | No |
| CUSTOMER | SEMINAR_CUSTOMER | CustomerID in SEMINAR_CUSTOMER must exist in CustomerID in CUSTOMER | No | No |
| SEMINAR | CONTACT | SeminarID in CONTACT must exist in SeminarID in SEMINAR | No | No |
| CUSTOMER | CONTACT | CustomerID in CONTACT must exist in CustomerID in CUSTOMER | No | Yes |
| CUSTOMER | INVOICE | CustomerID in INVOICE must exist in CustomerID in CUSTOMER | No | No |
| INVOICE | LINE_ITEM | InvoiceNumber in LINE_ITEM must exist in InvoiceNumber in INVOICE | No | Yes |
| PRODUCT | LINE_ITEM | ProductNumber in LINE_ITEM must exist in ProductNumber in PRODUCT | Yes | No |

**FIGURE 7-52**

Referential Integrity Constraint Enforcement for the HSD Database

product only once) who have purchased a video product. Sort the results by LastName in descending order, then by FirstName in descending order, and then by ProductNumber in descending order. (*Hint:* Video products have a ProductNumber that starts with VK.)

**L.** Write an SQL statement to show the sum of SubTotal (this is the money earned by HSD on products sold exclusive of shipping costs and taxes) for INVOICE as SumOfSubTotal.

**M.** Write an SQL statement to show the average of Subtotal (this is the money earned by HSD on products sold exclusive of shipping costs and taxes) for INVOICE as AverageOfSubTotal.

**N.** Write an SQL statement to show both the sum and the average of Subtotal (this is the money earned by HSD on products sold exclusive of shipping costs and taxes) for INVOICE as SumOfSubTotal and AverageOfSubTotal, respectively.

**O.** Write an SQL statement to modify PRODUCT UnitPrice for ProductNumber VK004 to $34.95 instead of the current UnitPrice of $24.95.

**P.** Write an SQL statement to undo the UnitPrice modification in part O.

**Q. Do not run your answer to the following question in your actual database!** Write the fewest number of DELETE statements possible to remove all the data in your database but leave the table structures intact.

**Using the HSD database, create an SQL script named *HSD-Create-Views-and-Functions.sql* to answer questions R through T.**

**R.** Write an SQL statement to create a view called InvoiceSummaryView that contains INVOICE.InvoiceNumber, INVOICE.InvoiceDate, LINE_ITEM.LineNumber,

```
USE HSD
GO

CREATE  TABLE CUSTOMER(
      CustomerID              Int             NOT NULL IDENTITY (1, 1),
      LastName                Char(25)        NOT NULL,
      FirstName               Char(25)        NOT NULL,
      EmailAddress            VarChar(100)    NOT NULL,
      EncryptedPassword       VarChar(50)     NULL,
      Phone                   Char(12)        NOT NULL,
      StreetAddress           Char(35)        NULL,
      City                    Char(35)        NULL DEFAULT 'Dallas',
      State                   Char(2)         NULL DEFAULT 'TX',
      ZIP                     Char(10)        NULL DEFAULT '75201',
      CONSTRAINT              CUSTOMER_PK     PRIMARY KEY(CustomerID),
      CONSTRAINT              CUSTOMER_EMAIL  UNIQUE(EmailAddress)
      );

CREATE  TABLE SEMINAR(
      SeminarID               Int             NOT NULL IDENTITY (1, 1),
      SeminarDate             Date            NOT NULL,
      SeminarTime             Time            NOT NULL,
      Location                VarChar(100)    NOT NULL,
      SeminarTitle            VarChar(100)    NOT NULL,
      CONSTRAINT              SEMINAR_PK      PRIMARY KEY(SeminarID)
      );

CREATE  TABLE SEMINAR_CUSTOMER(
      SeminarID               Int             NOT NULL,
      CustomerID              Int             NOT NULL,
      CONSTRAINT              S_C_PK          PRIMARY KEY(SeminarID, CustomerID),
      CONSTRAINT              S_C_SEMINAR_FK  FOREIGN KEY(SeminarID)
                                 REFERENCES SEMINAR(SeminarID)
                                    ON UPDATE NO ACTION
                                    ON DELETE NO ACTION,
      CONSTRAINT              S_C_CUSTOMER_FK FOREIGN KEY(CustomerID)
                                 REFERENCES CUSTOMER(CustomerID)
                                    ON UPDATE NO ACTION
                                    ON DELETE NO ACTION
      );

CREATE  TABLE CONTACT(
      CustomerID              Int             NOT NULL,
      ContactNumber           Int             NOT NULL,
      ContactDate             Date            NOT NULL,
      ContactType             VarChar(30)     NOT NULL,
      SeminarID               Int             NULL,
      CONSTRAINT              CONTACT_PK      PRIMARY KEY(CustomerID, ContactNumber),
      CONSTRAINT              CONTACT_ContactType
                                 CHECK (ContactType IN ('Seminar', 'FormLetterSeminar',
                                          'WebAccountCreation', 'WebPurchase',
                                          'EmailAccountMessage', 'EmailSeminarMessage',
                                          'EmailPurchaseMessage', 'EmailMessageExchange',
                                          'PhoneConversation')),
      CONSTRAINT              CONTACT_SEMINAR_FK FOREIGN KEY(SeminarID)
                                 REFERENCES SEMINAR(SeminarID)
                                    ON UPDATE NO ACTION
                                    ON DELETE NO ACTION,
      CONSTRAINT              CONTACT_CUSTOMER_FK FOREIGN KEY(CustomerID)
                                 REFERENCES CUSTOMER(CustomerID)
                                    ON UPDATE NO ACTION
                                    ON DELETE NO ACTION
      );
```

**FIGURE 7-53**

**SQL Statements to Create
the HSD Database**

(continued)

```
CREATE  TABLE PRODUCT(
        ProductNumber             Char(35)          NOT NULL,
        ProductType               Char(24)          NOT NULL,
        ProductDescription        VarChar(100)      NOT NULL,
        UnitPrice                 Numeric(9,2)      NOT NULL,
        QuantityOnHand            Int               NULL,
        CONSTRAINT                PRODUCT_PK        PRIMARY KEY(ProductNumber),
        CONSTRAINT                PRODUCT_ProductType
                      CHECK (ProductType IN ('Video',
                             'Video Companion', 'Book'))

        );

CREATE  TABLE INVOICE(
        InvoiceNumber             Int               NOT NULL IDENTITY (35000, 1),
        InvoiceDate               Date              NOT NULL,
        CustomerID                Int               NOT NULL,
        PaymentType               Char(25)          NOT NULL DEFAULT 'Cash',
        SubTotal                  Numeric(9,2)      NULL,
        Shipping                  Numeric(9,2)      NULL,
        Tax                       Numeric(9,2)      NULL,
        Total                     Numeric(9,2)      NULL,
        CONSTRAINT                INVOICE_PK        PRIMARY KEY (InvoiceNumber),
        CONSTRAINT                INVOICE_PaymentType
                      CHECK (PaymentType IN ('VISA',
                             'MasterCard', 'American Express',
                             'PayPal', 'Check', 'Cash')),
        CONSTRAINT                INVOICE_CUSTOMER_FK FOREIGN KEY(CustomerID)
                      REFERENCES CUSTOMER(CustomerID)
                          ON UPDATE NO ACTION
                          ON DELETE NO ACTION

        );

CREATE  TABLE LINE_ITEM(
        InvoiceNumber             Int               NOT NULL,
        LineNumber                Int               NOT NULL,
        ProductNumber             Char(35)          NOT NULL,
        Quantity                  Int               NOT NULL,
        UnitPrice                 Numeric(9,2)      NULL,
        Total                     Numeric(9,2)      NULL,
        CONSTRAINT                LINE_ITEM_PK      PRIMARY KEY (InvoiceNumber, LineNumber),
        CONSTRAINT                L_I_INVOICE_FK    FOREIGN KEY(InvoiceNumber)
                      REFERENCES INVOICE(InvoiceNumber)
                          ON UPDATE NO ACTION
                          ON DELETE CASCADE,
        CONSTRAINT                L_I_PRODUCT_FK  FOREIGN KEY(ProductNumber)
                      REFERENCES PRODUCT (ProductNumber)
                          ON UPDATE CASCADE
                          ON DELETE NO ACTION

        );
```

**FIGURE 7-53**

Continued

LINE_ITEM.ProductNumber, PRODUCT.ProductDescription, and LINE_ITEM. UnitPrice. Run the statement to create the view, and then test the view with an appropriate SQL SELECT statement.

**S.** Create and test a user-defined function named *FirstNameFirst* that combines two parameters named *FirstName* and *LastName* into a concatenated value named FullName and displays, in order, the FirstName, a space, and the LastName. (*Hint: Steve* and *Smith* would be combined to read *Steve Smith*.)

**T.** Write an SQL statement to create a view called CustomerInvoiceSummaryView that contains INVOICE.InvoiceNumber, INVOICE.InvoiceDate, the concatenated customer name using the *FirstNameFirst* function, CUSTOMER.EmailAddress, and INVOICE.Total. Run the statement to create the view, and then test the view with an appropriate SQL SELECT statement.

```
/*****    CUSTOMER DATA    ***********************************************************/

INSERT INTO CUSTOMER VALUES(
    'Jacobs', 'Nancy', 'Nancy.Jacobs@somewhere.com', 'nf46tG9E', '817-871-8123',
    '1440 West Palm Drive', 'Fort Worth', 'TX', '76110');
INSERT INTO CUSTOMER VALUES(
    'Jacobs', 'Chantel', 'Chantel.Jacobs@somewhere.com', 'b65TG03f', '817-871-8234',
    '1550 East Palm Drive', 'Fort Worth', 'TX', '76112');
INSERT INTO CUSTOMER VALUES(
    'Able', 'Ralph', 'Ralph.Able@somewhere.com', 'm56fGH08', '210-281-7987',
    '123 Elm Street', 'San Antonio', 'TX', '78214');
INSERT INTO CUSTOMER VALUES(
    'Baker', 'Susan', 'Susan.Baker@elsewhere.com', 'PC93fEk9', '210-281-7876',
    '456 Oak Street', 'San Antonio', 'TX', '78216');
INSERT INTO CUSTOMER VALUES(
    'Eagleton', 'Sam', 'Sam.Eagleton@elsewhere.com', 'bnvR44W8', '210-281-7765',
    '789 Pine Street', 'San Antonio', 'TX', '78218');
INSERT INTO CUSTOMER VALUES(
    'Foxtrot', 'Kathy', 'Kathy.Foxtrot@somewhere.com', 'aa8tY4GL', '972-233-6234',
    '11023 Elm Street', 'Dallas', 'TX', '75220');
INSERT INTO CUSTOMER VALUES(
    'George', 'Sally', 'Sally.George@somewhere.com', 'LK8G2tyF', '972-233-6345',
    '12034 San Jacinto', 'Dallas', 'TX', '75223');
INSERT INTO CUSTOMER VALUES(
    'Hullett', 'Shawn', 'Shawn.Hullett@elsewhere.com', 'bu78WW3t', '972-233-6456',
    '13045 Flora', 'Dallas', 'TX', '75224');
INSERT INTO CUSTOMER VALUES(
    'Pearson', 'Bobbi', 'Bobbi.Pearson@elsewhere.com', 'kq6N2O0p', '512-974-3344',
    '43 West 23rd Street', 'Austin', 'TX', '78710');
INSERT INTO CUSTOMER VALUES(
    'Ranger', 'Terry', 'Terry.Ranger@somewhere.com', 'bv3F9Qc4', '512-974-4455',
    '56 East 18th Street', 'Austin', 'TX', '78712');
INSERT INTO CUSTOMER VALUES(
    'Tyler', 'Jenny', 'Jenny.Tyler@somewhere.com', 'Yu4be77Z', '972-233-6567',
    '14056 South Ervay Street', 'Dallas', 'TX', '75225');
INSERT INTO CUSTOMER VALUES(
    'Wayne', 'Joan', 'Joan.Wayne@elsewhere.com', 'JW4TX6g', '817-871-8245',
    '1660 South Aspen Drive', 'Fort Worth', 'TX', '76115');


/*****    SEMINAR    ***********************************************************/

INSERT INTO SEMINAR VALUES(
    '12-OCT-2020', '11:00 AM', 'San Antonio Convention Center',
    'Kitchen on a Budget');
INSERT INTO SEMINAR VALUES(
    '26-OCT-2020', '04:00 PM', 'Dallas Convention Center',
    'Kitchen on a Big D Budget');
INSERT INTO SEMINAR VALUES(
    '02-NOV-2020', '08:30 AM', 'Austin Convention Center',
    'Kitchen on a Budget');
INSERT INTO SEMINAR VALUES(
    '22-MAR-2021', '11:00 AM', 'Dallas Convention Center',
    'Kitchen on a Big D Budget');
INSERT INTO SEMINAR VALUES(
    '23-MAR-2021', '11:00 AM', 'Dallas Convention Center',
    'Kitchen on a Big D Budget');
INSERT INTO SEMINAR VALUES(
    '05-APR-2021', '08:30 AM', 'Austin Convention Center',
    'Kitchen on a Budget');
```

**FIGURE 7-54**

**SQL Statements to Populate
the HSD Database**

*(continued)*

```
/*****    SEMINAR_CUSTOMER DATA   **************************************************/

INSERT INTO SEMINAR_CUSTOMER VALUES(1, 1);
INSERT INTO SEMINAR_CUSTOMER VALUES(1, 2);
INSERT INTO SEMINAR_CUSTOMER VALUES(1, 3);
INSERT INTO SEMINAR_CUSTOMER VALUES(1, 4);
INSERT INTO SEMINAR_CUSTOMER VALUES(1, 5);
INSERT INTO SEMINAR_CUSTOMER VALUES(2, 6);
INSERT INTO SEMINAR_CUSTOMER VALUES(2, 7);
INSERT INTO SEMINAR_CUSTOMER VALUES(2, 8);
INSERT INTO SEMINAR_CUSTOMER VALUES(3, 9);
INSERT INTO SEMINAR_CUSTOMER VALUES(3, 10);
INSERT INTO SEMINAR_CUSTOMER VALUES(4, 6);
INSERT INTO SEMINAR_CUSTOMER VALUES(4, 7);
INSERT INTO SEMINAR_CUSTOMER VALUES(4, 11);
INSERT INTO SEMINAR_CUSTOMER VALUES(4, 12);


/*****    CONTACT DATA    **************************************************/

-- 'Nancy.Jacobs@somewhere.com'
INSERT INTO CONTACT VALUES(1, 1, '12-OCT-2020', 'Seminar', 1);
-- 'Chantel.Jacobs@somewhere.com'
INSERT INTO CONTACT VALUES(2, 1, '12-OCT-2020', 'Seminar', 1);
-- 'Ralph.Able@somewhere.com'
INSERT INTO CONTACT VALUES(3, 1, '12-OCT-2020', 'Seminar', 1);
-- 'Susan.Baker@elsewhere.com'
INSERT INTO CONTACT VALUES(4, 1, '12-OCT-2020', 'Seminar', 1);
-- 'Sam.Eagleton@elsewhere.com'
INSERT INTO CONTACT VALUES(5, 1, '12-OCT-2020', 'Seminar', 1);


-- 'Nancy.Jacobs@somewhere.com',
INSERT INTO CONTACT (CustomerID, ContactNumber, ContactDate,  ContactType)
      VALUES(1, 2, '15-OCT-2020', 'EmailSeminarMessage');
-- 'Chantel.Jacobs@somewhere.com'
INSERT INTO CONTACT (CustomerID, ContactNumber, ContactDate,  ContactType)
      VALUES(2, 2, '15-OCT-2020', 'EmailSeminarMessage');
-- 'Ralph.Able@somewhere.com'
INSERT INTO CONTACT (CustomerID, ContactNumber, ContactDate,  ContactType)
      VALUES(3, 2, '15-OCT-2020', 'EmailSeminarMessage');
-- 'Susan.Baker@elsewhere.com'
INSERT INTO CONTACT (CustomerID, ContactNumber, ContactDate,  ContactType)
      VALUES(4, 2, '15-OCT-2020', 'EmailSeminarMessage');
-- 'Sam.Eagleton@elsewhere.com'
INSERT INTO CONTACT (CustomerID, ContactNumber, ContactDate,  ContactType)
      VALUES(5, 2, '15-OCT-2020', 'EmailSeminarMessage');


-- 'Nancy.Jacobs@somewhere.com',
INSERT INTO CONTACT (CustomerID, ContactNumber, ContactDate,  ContactType)
      VALUES(1, 3, '15-OCT-2020', 'FormLetterSeminar');
-- 'Chantel.Jacobs@somewhere.com'
INSERT INTO CONTACT (CustomerID, ContactNumber, ContactDate,  ContactType)
      VALUES(2, 3, '15-OCT-2020', 'FormLetterSeminar');
-- 'Ralph.Able@somewhere.com'
INSERT INTO CONTACT (CustomerID, ContactNumber, ContactDate,  ContactType)
      VALUES(3, 3, '15-OCT-2020', 'FormLetterSeminar');
```

**FIGURE 7-54**

Continued

```
-- 'Susan.Baker@elsewhere.com'
INSERT INTO CONTACT (CustomerID, ContactNumber, ContactDate,  ContactType)
     VALUES(4, 3, '15-OCT-2020', 'FormLetterSeminar');
-- 'Sam.Eagleton@elsewhere.com'
INSERT INTO CONTACT (CustomerID, ContactNumber, ContactDate,  ContactType)
     VALUES(5, 3, '15-OCT-2020', 'FormLetterSeminar');


-- 'Kathy.Foxtrot@somewhere.com'
INSERT INTO CONTACT VALUES(6, 1, '26-OCT-2020', 'Seminar', 2);
-- 'Sally.George@somewhere.com'
INSERT INTO CONTACT VALUES(7, 1, '26-OCT-2020', 'Seminar', 2);
-- 'Shawn.Hullett@elsewhere.com'
INSERT INTO CONTACT VALUES(8, 1, '26-OCT-2020', 'Seminar', 2);


-- 'Kathy.Foxtrot@somewhere.com'
INSERT INTO CONTACT (CustomerID, ContactNumber, ContactDate,  ContactType)
     VALUES(6, 2, '30-OCT-2020', 'EmailSeminarMessage');
-- 'Sally.George@somewhere.com'
INSERT INTO CONTACT (CustomerID, ContactNumber, ContactDate,  ContactType)
     VALUES(7, 2, '30-OCT-2020', 'EmailSeminarMessage');
-- 'Shawn.Hullett@elsewhere.com'
INSERT INTO CONTACT (CustomerID, ContactNumber, ContactDate,  ContactType)
     VALUES(8, 2, '30-OCT-2020', 'EmailSeminarMessage');


-- 'Kathy.Foxtrot@somewhere.com'
INSERT INTO CONTACT (CustomerID, ContactNumber, ContactDate,  ContactType)
     VALUES(6, 3, '30-OCT-2020', 'FormLetterSeminar');
-- 'Sally.George@somewhere.com'
INSERT INTO CONTACT (CustomerID, ContactNumber, ContactDate,  ContactType)
     VALUES(7, 3, '30-OCT-2020', 'FormLetterSeminar');
-- 'Shawn.Hullett@elsewhere.com'
INSERT INTO CONTACT (CustomerID, ContactNumber, ContactDate,  ContactType)
     VALUES(8, 3, '30-OCT-2020', 'FormLetterSeminar');


-- 'Bobbi.Pearson@elsewhere.com'
INSERT INTO CONTACT VALUES(9, 1, '02-NOV-2020', 'Seminar', 3);
-- 'Terry.Ranger@somewhere.com'
INSERT INTO CONTACT VALUES(10, 1, '02-NOV-2020', 'Seminar', 3);


-- 'Bobbi.Pearson@elsewhere.com'
INSERT INTO CONTACT (CustomerID, ContactNumber, ContactDate,  ContactType)
     VALUES(9, 2, '06-NOV-2020', 'EmailSeminarMessage');
-- 'Terry.Ranger@somewhere.com'
INSERT INTO CONTACT (CustomerID, ContactNumber, ContactDate,  ContactType)
     VALUES(10, 2, '06-NOV-2020', 'EmailSeminarMessage');


-- 'Bobbi.Pearson@elsewhere.com'
INSERT INTO CONTACT (CustomerID, ContactNumber, ContactDate,  ContactType)
     VALUES(9, 3, '06-NOV-2020', 'FormLetterSeminar');
-- 'Terry.Ranger@somewhere.com'
INSERT INTO CONTACT (CustomerID, ContactNumber, ContactDate,  ContactType)
     VALUES(10, 3, '06-NOV-2020', 'FormLetterSeminar');


-- 'Ralph.Able@somewhere.com'
INSERT INTO CONTACT (CustomerID, ContactNumber, ContactDate,  ContactType)
     VALUES(3, 4, '20-FEB-2021', 'WebAccountCreation');
-- 'Ralph.Able@somewhere.com'
INSERT INTO CONTACT (CustomerID, ContactNumber, ContactDate,  ContactType)
     VALUES(3, 5, '20-FEB-2021', 'EmailAccountMessage');
```

*(continued)*

**FIGURE 7-54**

Continued

```
-- 'Kathy.Foxtrot@somewhere.com'
INSERT INTO CONTACT (CustomerID, ContactNumber, ContactDate,  ContactType)
     VALUES(6, 4, '22-FEB-2021', 'WebAccountCreation');
-- 'Kathy.Foxtrot@somewhere.com'
INSERT INTO CONTACT (CustomerID, ContactNumber, ContactDate,  ContactType)
     VALUES(6, 5, '22-FEB-2021', 'EmailAccountMessage');
-- 'Sally.George@somewhere.com'
INSERT INTO CONTACT (CustomerID, ContactNumber, ContactDate,  ContactType)
     VALUES(7, 4, '25-FEB-2021', 'WebAccountCreation');
-- 'Sally.George@somewhere.com'
INSERT INTO CONTACT (CustomerID, ContactNumber, ContactDate,  ContactType)
     VALUES(7, 5, '25-FEB-2021', 'EmailAccountMessage');
-- 'Shawn.Hullett@elsewhere.com'
INSERT INTO CONTACT (CustomerID, ContactNumber, ContactDate,  ContactType)
     VALUES(8, 4, '07-MAR-2021', 'WebAccountCreation');
-- 'Shawn.Hullett@elsewhere.com'
INSERT INTO CONTACT (CustomerID, ContactNumber, ContactDate,  ContactType)
     VALUES(8, 5, '07-MAR-2021', 'EmailAccountMessage');


-- 'Kathy.Foxtrot@somewhere.com'
INSERT INTO CONTACT VALUES(6, 6, '22-MAR-2021', 'Seminar', 4);
-- 'Sally.George@somewhere.com'
INSERT INTO CONTACT VALUES(7, 6, '22-MAR-2021', 'Seminar', 4);
-- 'Jenny.Tyler@somewhere.com'
INSERT INTO CONTACT VALUES(11, 1, '22-MAR-2021', 'Seminar', 4);
-- 'Joan.Wayne@elsewhere.com'
INSERT INTO CONTACT VALUES(12, 1, '22-MAR-2021', 'Seminar', 4);

/*****    PRODUCT DATA    ***********************************************************/

INSERT INTO PRODUCT VALUES(
     'VK001', 'Video', 'Kitchen Remodeling Basics', 14.95, 50);
INSERT INTO PRODUCT VALUES(
     'VK002', 'Video', 'Advanced Kitchen Remodeling', 14.95, 35);
INSERT INTO PRODUCT VALUES(
     'VK003', 'Video', 'Kitchen Remodeling Dallas Style', 19.95, 25);
INSERT INTO PRODUCT VALUES(
     'VK004', 'Video', 'Heather Sweeney Seminar Live in Dallas on 25-OCT-16',
     24.95, 20);
INSERT INTO PRODUCT VALUES(
     'VB001', 'Video Companion', 'Kitchen Remodeling Basics', 7.99, 50);
INSERT INTO PRODUCT VALUES(
     'VB002', 'Video Companion', 'Advanced Kitchen Remodeling I',7.99, 35);
INSERT INTO PRODUCT VALUES(
     'VB003', 'Video Companion', 'Kitchen Remodeling Dallas Style', 9.99, 25);
INSERT INTO PRODUCT VALUES(
     'BK001', 'Book', 'Kitchen Remodeling Basics For Everyone', 24.95, 75);
INSERT INTO PRODUCT VALUES(
     'BK002', 'Book', 'Advanced Kitchen Remodeling For Everyone', 24.95, 75);
INSERT INTO PRODUCT VALUES(
     'BK003', 'Book', 'Kitchen Remodeling Dallas Style For Everyone', 24.95, 75);
```

**FIGURE 7-54**

**Continued**

```
/*****    INVOICE DATA      *********************************************/

/*****     Invoice 35000    *********************************************/
-- 'Ralph.Able@somewhere.com'
INSERT INTO INVOICE VALUES(
        '15-Oct-2020', 3, 'VISA', 22.94, 5.95, 1.31, 30.20);
INSERT INTO LINE_ITEM VALUES(35000, 1, 'VK001', 1, 14.95, 14.95);
INSERT INTO LINE_ITEM VALUES(35000, 2, 'VB001', 1, 7.99, 7.99);

/*****     Invoice 35001    *********************************************/
-- 'Susan.Baker@elsewhere.com'
INSERT INTO INVOICE VALUES(
        '25-Oct-2020', 4, 'MasterCard', 47.89, 5.95, 2.73, 56.57);
INSERT INTO LINE_ITEM VALUES(35001, 1, 'VK001', 1, 14.95, 14.95);
INSERT INTO LINE_ITEM VALUES(35001, 2, 'VB001', 1, 7.99, 7.99);
INSERT INTO LINE_ITEM VALUES(35001, 3, 'BK001', 1, 24.95, 24.95);

/*****     Invoice 35002    *********************************************/
-- 'Sally.George@somewhere.com'
INSERT INTO INVOICE VALUES(
        '20-Dec-2020', 7, 'VISA', 24.95, 5.95, 1.42, 32.32);
INSERT INTO LINE_ITEM VALUES(35002, 1, 'VK004', 1, 24.95, 24.95);

/*****     Invoice 35003    *********************************************/
-- 'Susan.Baker@elsewhere.com'
INSERT INTO INVOICE VALUES(
        '25-Mar-2021', 4, 'MasterCard', 64.85, 5.95, 3.70, 74.50);
INSERT INTO LINE_ITEM VALUES(35003, 1, 'VK002', 1, 14.95, 14.95);
INSERT INTO LINE_ITEM VALUES(35003, 2, 'BK002', 1, 24.95, 24.95);
INSERT INTO LINE_ITEM VALUES(35003, 3, 'VK004', 1, 24.95, 24.95);

/*****     Invoice 35004    *********************************************/
-- 'Kathy.Foxtrot@somewhere.com'
INSERT INTO INVOICE VALUES(
        '27-Mar-2021', 6, 'MasterCard', 94.79, 5.95, 5.40, 106.14);
INSERT INTO LINE_ITEM VALUES(35004, 1, 'VK002', 1, 14.95, 14.95);
INSERT INTO LINE_ITEM VALUES(35004, 2, 'BK002', 1, 24.95, 24.95);
INSERT INTO LINE_ITEM VALUES(35004, 3, 'VK003', 1, 19.95, 19.95);
INSERT INTO LINE_ITEM VALUES(35004, 4, 'VB003', 1, 9.99, 9.99);
INSERT INTO LINE_ITEM VALUES(35004, 5, 'VK004', 1, 24.95, 24.95);

/*****     Invoice 35005    *********************************************/
-- 'Sally.George@somewhere.com'
INSERT INTO INVOICE VALUES(
        '27-Mar-2021', 7, 'MasterCard', 94.80, 5.95, 5.40, 106.15);
INSERT INTO LINE_ITEM VALUES(35005, 1, 'BK001', 1, 24.95, 24.95);
INSERT INTO LINE_ITEM VALUES(35005, 2, 'BK002', 1, 24.95, 24.95);
INSERT INTO LINE_ITEM VALUES(35005, 3, 'VK003', 1, 19.95, 19.95);
INSERT INTO LINE_ITEM VALUES(35005, 4, 'VK004', 1, 24.95, 24.95);

/*****     Invoice 35006    *********************************************/
-- 'Bobbi.Pearson@elsewhere.com'
INSERT INTO INVOICE VALUES(
        '31-Mar-2021', 9, 'VISA', 47.89,      5.95, 2.73, 56.57);
INSERT INTO LINE_ITEM VALUES(35006, 1, 'BK001', 1, 24.95, 24.95);
INSERT INTO LINE_ITEM VALUES(35006, 2, 'VK001', 1, 14.95, 14.95);
INSERT INTO LINE_ITEM VALUES(35006, 3, 'VB001', 1, 7.99, 7.99);
```

*(continued)*

**FIGURE 7-54**

Continued

```
/*****      Invoice 35007     ***********************************************/
-- 'Jenny.Tyler@somewhere.com'
INSERT INTO INVOICE VALUES(
       '03-Apr-2021', 11, 'MasterCard', 109.78, 5.95, 6.26, 121.99);
INSERT INTO LINE_ITEM VALUES(35007, 1, 'VK003', 2, 19.95, 39.90);
INSERT INTO LINE_ITEM VALUES(35007, 2, 'VB003', 2, 9.99, 19.98);
INSERT INTO LINE_ITEM VALUES(35007, 3, 'VK004', 2, 24.95, 49.90);


/*****      Invoice 35008     ***********************************************/
-- 'Sam.Eagleton@elsewhere.com'
INSERT INTO INVOICE VALUES(
       '08-Apr-2021', 5, 'MasterCard', 47.89, 5.95, 2.73, 56.57);
INSERT INTO LINE_ITEM VALUES(35008, 1, 'BK001', 1, 24.95, 24.95);
INSERT INTO LINE_ITEM VALUES(35008, 2, 'VK001', 1, 14.95, 14.95);
INSERT INTO LINE_ITEM VALUES(35008, 3, 'VB001', 1, 7.99, 7.99);


/*****      Invoice 35009     ***********************************************/
-- 'Nancy.Jacobs@somewhere.com'
INSERT INTO INVOICE VALUES(
       '08-Apr-2021', 1, 'VISA', 47.89,      5.95, 2.73, 56.57);
INSERT INTO LINE_ITEM VALUES(35009, 1, 'BK001', 1, 24.95, 24.95);
INSERT INTO LINE_ITEM VALUES(35009, 2, 'VK001', 1, 14.95, 14.95);
INSERT INTO LINE_ITEM VALUES(35009, 3, 'VB001', 1, 7.99, 7.99);


/*****      Invoice 35010     ***********************************************/
-- 'Ralph.Able@somewhere.com'
INSERT INTO INVOICE VALUES(
       '23-Apr-2021', 3, 'VISA', 24.95,      5.95, 1.42, 32.32);
INSERT INTO LINE_ITEM VALUES(35010, 1, 'BK001', 1, 24.95, 24.95);


/*****      Invoice 35011     ***********************************************/
-- 'Bobbi.Pearson@elsewhere.com'
INSERT INTO INVOICE VALUES(
       '07-May-2021', 9, 'VISA', 22.94,      5.95, 1.31, 30.20);
INSERT INTO LINE_ITEM VALUES(35011, 1, 'VK002', 1, 14.95, 14.95);
INSERT INTO LINE_ITEM VALUES(35011, 2, 'VB002', 1, 7.99, 7.99);


/*****      Invoice 35012     ***********************************************/
-- 'Shawn.Hullett@elsewhere.com'
INSERT INTO INVOICE VALUES(
       '21-May-2021', 8, 'MasterCard', 54.89, 5.95, 3.13, 63.97);
INSERT INTO LINE_ITEM VALUES(35012, 1, 'VK003', 1, 19.95, 19.95);
INSERT INTO LINE_ITEM VALUES(35012, 2, 'VB003', 1, 9.99, 9.99);
INSERT INTO LINE_ITEM VALUES(35012, 3, 'VK004', 1, 24.95, 24.95);


/*****      Invoice 35013     ***********************************************/
-- 'Ralph.Able@somewhere.com'
INSERT INTO INVOICE VALUES(
       '05-Jun-2021', 3, 'VISA', 47.89,      5.95, 2.73, 56.57);
INSERT INTO LINE_ITEM VALUES(35013, 1, 'VK002', 1, 14.95, 14.95);
INSERT INTO LINE_ITEM VALUES(35013, 2, 'VB002', 1, 7.99, 7.99);
INSERT INTO LINE_ITEM VALUES(35013, 3, 'BK002', 1, 24.95, 24.95);
```

**FIGURE 7-54**

Continued

```
/*****    Invoice 35014    **********************************************/
-- 'Jenny.Tyler@somewhere.com'
INSERT INTO INVOICE VALUES(
       '05-Jun-2021', 11, 'MasterCard', 45.88, 5.95, 2.62, 54.45);
INSERT INTO LINE_ITEM VALUES(35014, 1, 'VK002', 2, 14.95, 29.90);
INSERT INTO LINE_ITEM VALUES(35014, 2, 'VB002', 2, 7.99, 15.98);


/*****    Invoice 35015    **********************************************/
-- 'Joan.Wayne@elsewhere.com'
INSERT INTO INVOICE VALUES(
       '05-Jun-2021', 12, 'MasterCard', 94.79, 5.95, 5.40, 106.14);
INSERT INTO LINE_ITEM VALUES(35015, 1, 'VK002', 1, 14.95, 14.95);
INSERT INTO LINE_ITEM VALUES(35015, 2, 'BK002', 1, 24.95, 24.95);
INSERT INTO LINE_ITEM VALUES(35015, 3, 'VK003', 1, 19.95, 19.95);
INSERT INTO LINE_ITEM VALUES(35015, 4, 'VB003', 1, 9.99, 9.99);
INSERT INTO LINE_ITEM VALUES(35015, 5, 'VK004', 1, 24.95, 24.95);


/*****    Invoice 35016    **********************************************/
-- 'Ralph.Able@somewhere.com'
INSERT INTO INVOICE VALUES(
       '05-Jun-2021', 3, 'VISA', 45.88,        5.95, 2.62, 54.45);
INSERT INTO LINE_ITEM VALUES(35016, 1, 'VK001', 1, 14.95, 14.95);
INSERT INTO LINE_ITEM VALUES(35016, 2, 'VB001', 1, 7.99, 7.99);
INSERT INTO LINE_ITEM VALUES(35016, 3, 'VK002', 1, 14.95, 14.95);
INSERT INTO LINE_ITEM VALUES(35016, 4, 'VB002', 1, 7.99, 7.99);


/************************************************************************/
```

**FIGURE 7-54**

Continued

# The Queen Anne Curiosity Shop Project Questions

Assume that the Queen Anne Curiosity Shop designs a database with the following tables:

CUSTOMER (CustomerID, LastName, FirstName, EmailAddress, EncryptedPassword, Address, City, State, ZIP, Phone, *ReferredBy*)

EMPLOYEE (EmployeeID, LastName, FirstName, Position, *Supervisor*, OfficePhone, EmailAddress)

VENDOR (VendorID, CompanyName, ContactLastName, ContactFirstName, Address, City, State, ZIP, Phone, Fax, EmailAddress)

ITEM (ItemID, ItemDescription, PurchaseDate, ItemCost, ItemPrice, *VendorID*)

SALE (SaleID, *CustomerID*, *EmployeeID*, SaleDate, SubTotal, Tax, Total)

SALE_ITEM (*SaleID*, SaleItemID, *ItemID*, ItemPrice)

The referential integrity constraints are:

ReferredBy in CUSTOMER must exist in CustomerID in CUSTOMER

Supervisor in EMPLOYEE must exist in EmployeeID in EMPLOYEE

CustomerID in SALE must exist in CustomerID in CUSTOMER

VendorID in ITEM must exist in VendorID in VENDOR

EmployeeID in SALE must exist in EmployeeID in EMPLOYEE

SaleID in SALE_ITEM must exist in SaleID in SALE

ItemID in SALE_ITEM must exist in ItemID in ITEM

Assume that CustomerID of CUSTOMER, EmployeeID of EMPLOYEE, VendorID of VENDOR, ItemID of ITEM, and SaleID of SALE are all surrogate keys with values as follows:

| | | |
|---|---|---|
| **CustomerID** | **Start at 1** | **Increment by 1** |
| **EmployeeID** | **Start at 1** | **Increment by 1** |
| **VendorID** | **Start at 1** | **Increment by 1** |
| **ItemID** | **Start at 1** | **Increment by 1** |
| **SaleID** | **Start at 1** | **Increment by 1** |

A vendor may be an individual or a company. If the vendor is an individual, the CompanyName field is left blank, whereas the ContactLastName and ContactFirstName fields must have data values. If the vendor is a company, the company name is recorded in the CompanyName field, and the name of the primary contact at the company is recorded in the ContactLastName and ContactFirstName fields.

**A.** Specify NULL/NOT NULL constraints for each table column.

**B.** Specify alternate keys, if any.

**C.** State relationships as implied by foreign keys, and specify the maximum and minimum cardinalities of each relationship. Justify your choices.

**D.** Explain how you will enforce the minimum cardinalities in your answer to part C. Use referential integrity actions for required parents, if any. Use Figure 6-29(b) as a boilerplate for required children, if any.

**E.** Create a database named QACS in your DBMS.

**F.** Create a folder in your *Documents* folder to save and store *.sql scripts containing the SQL statements that you are asked to create in the remaining questions in this section.

- For the SQL Server Management Studio, create a folder named QACS-*Database* in the *Projects* folder structure in your *SQL Server Management Studio* folder.
- In the Oracle SQL Developer folder structure in your *SQL Developer* folder, create a folder named QACS-*Database*.
- For the MySQL Workbench, create a folder named QACS-*Database* in the *Schemas* folder in your *MySQL Workbench* folder.

**Using the QACS database, create an SQL script named *QACS-Create-Tables.sql* to answer parts G and H. Your answer to part H should be in the form of an SQL comment in the script.**

**G.** Write CREATE TABLE statements for each of the tables using your answers to parts A through D, as necessary. Set the surrogate key values as shown earlier. Use FOREIGN KEY constraints to create appropriate referential integrity constraints. Set UPDATE and DELETE behavior in accordance with your referential integrity action design. Run these statements to create the QACS tables.

**H.** Explain how you would enforce the data constraint that SALE_ITEM.UnitPrice be equal to ITEM.ItemPrice, where SALE_ITEM.ItemID = ITEM.ItemID.

**Using the QACS database, create an SQL script named *QACS-Insert-Data.sql* to answer part I.**

**I.** Write INSERT statements to insert the data shown in Figures 7-55, 7-56, 7-57, 7-58, 7-59, and 7-60.

**Using the QACS database, create an SQL script named *QACS-DML-CH07.sql* to answer parts J and K.**

**J.** Write an UPDATE statement to change values of ITEM.ItemDescription from *Desk Lamp* to *Desk Lamps*.

| CustomerID | LastName | FirstName | EmailAddress | EncyptedPassword | Address | City | State | ZIP | Phone | Referred By |
|---|---|---|---|---|---|---|---|---|---|---|
| 1 | Shire | Robert | Robert.Shire@somewhere.com | 56gHjj8w | 6225 Evanston Ave N | Seattle | WA | 98103 | 206-524-2433 | |
| 2 | Goodyear | Katherine | Katherine.Goodyear@somewhere.com | fkJU0K24 | 7335 11th Ave NE | Seattle | WA | 98105 | 206-524-3544 | 1 |
| 3 | Bancroft | Chris | Chris.Bancroft@somewhere.com | 98bpT4vw | 12605 NE 6th Street | Bellevue | WA | 98005 | 425-635-9788 | |
| 4 | Griffith | John | John.Griffith@somewhere.com | mnBh88t4 | 335 Aloha Street | Seattle | WA | 98109 | 206-524-4655 | 1 |
| 5 | Tierney | Doris | Doris.Tierney@somewhere.com | as87PP3z | 14510 NE 4th Street | Bellevue | WA | 98005 | 425-635-8677 | 2 |
| 6 | Anderson | Donna | Donna.Anderson@elsewhere.com | 34Gf7e0t | 1410 Hillcrest Parkway | Mt. Vernon | WA | 98273 | 360-538-7566 | 3 |
| 7 | Svane | Jack | Jack.Svane@somewhere.com | wpv7FF9q | 3211 42nd Street | Seattle | WA | 98115 | 206-524-5766 | 1 |
| 8 | Walsh | Denesha | Denesha.Walsh@somewhere.com | D7gb7T84 | 6712 24th Avenue NE | Redmond | WA | 98053 | 425-635-7566 | 5 |
| 9 | Enquist | Craig | Craig.Enquist@elsewhere.com | gg7ER53t | 534 15th Street | Bellingham | WA | 98225 | 360-538-6455 | 6 |
| 10 | Anderson | Rose | Rose.Anderson@elsewhere.com | vx67gH8W | 6823 17th Ave NE | Seattle | WA | 98105 | 206-524-6877 | 3 |

FIGURE 7-55

Sample Data for the QACS
Database CUSTOMER Table

417

| PurchaseItemID | StoreID | PurchasingAgentID | PurchaseDate | ItemDescription | Category | PriceUSD |
|---|---|---|---|---|---|---|
| 500 | 1050 | 101 | 12/10/2020 | Antique Large Bureaus | Furniture | $ 13,415.00 |
| 505 | 1050 | 102 | 12/12/2020 | Porcelain Lamps | Lamps | $ 13,300.00 |
| 510 | 1200 | 104 | 12/15/2020 | Gold Rim Design China | Tableware | $ 38,500.00 |
| 515 | 1200 | 104 | 12/16/2020 | Gold Rim Design Serving Dishes | Tableware | $ 3,200.00 |
| 520 | 1050 | 102 | 4/7/2021 | QE Dining Set | Furniture | $ 14,300.00 |
| 525 | 1100 | 103 | 5/18/2021 | Misc Linen | Linens | $ 88,545.00 |
| 530 | 1000 | 103 | 5/19/2021 | Large Masks | Decorations | $ 22,135.00 |
| 535 | 1100 | 104 | 5/20/2021 | Willow Design China | Tableware | $ 147,575.00 |
| 540 | 1100 | 104 | 5/20/2021 | Willow Design Serving Dishes | Tableware | $ 12,040.00 |
| 545 | 1150 | 102 | 6/14/2021 | Woven Goods | Decorations | $ 1,200.00 |
| 550 | 1150 | 101 | 6/16/2021 | Antique Leather Chairs | Furniture | $ 5,375.00 |
| 555 | 1100 | 104 | 7/15/2021 | Willow Design Serving Dishes | Tableware | $ 4,500.00 |
| 560 | 1000 | 103 | 7/17/2021 | Large Bureau | Furniture | $ 9,500.00 |
| 565 | 1100 | 104 | 7/20/2021 | Brass Lamps | Lamps | $ 1,200.00 |

**FIGURE 7-63**

Sample Data for the MI Database PURCHASE_ITEM Table

**Using the MI database, create an SQL script named *MI-DML-CH07.sql* to answer parts K and L.**

K. Write an UPDATE statement to change values of STORE.City from *New York City* to *NYC*.

L. Create new data records to record a SHIPMENT and the SHIPMENT_ITEMs for that SHIPMENT. Write the INSERT statements necessary to add these records to the MI database, and then write a DELETE statement(s) to delete that SHIPMENT and all of the items on that SHIPMENT. How many DELETE statements did you have to use? Why?

**Using the MI database, create an SQL script named *MI-Create-Views-and-Functions.sql* to answer parts M through S.**

M. Write an SQL statement to create a view called EmployeeSupervisorView that shows who, if anyone, supervises each employee at the Queen Anne Curiosity Shop, and which contains E1.LastName as EmployeeLastName, E1.FirstName as EmployeeFirstName, E1.Position, E2.Lastname as SupervisorLastName, and E2.FirstName as SupervisorFirstName. E1 and E2 are two aliases for the EMPLOYEE table and are required to run a query on a recursive relationship. Include employees who do not have a supervisor. Run the statement to create the view, and then test the view with an appropriate SQL SELECT statement.

**FIGURE 7-64**

Sample Data for the MI Database SHIPPER Table

N. Write an SQL statement to create a view called PurchaseSummaryView that shows only PURCHASE_ITEM.PurchaseItemID, PURCHASE_ITEM.PurchaseDate,

| ShipperID | ShipperName | Phone | Fax | EmailAddress | Contact |
|---|---|---|---|---|---|
| 1 | ABC Trans-Oceanic | 800-234-5656 | 800-234-5659 | Sales@ABCTransOceanic.com | Jonathan |
| 2 | International | 800-123-8898 | 800-123-8899 | Sales@International.com | Marylin |
| 3 | Worldwide | 800-123-4567 | 800-123-4569 | Sales@worldwide.com | Jose |

| ShipmentID | ShipperID | PurchasingAgentID | ShipperInvoiceNumber | Origin | Destination | ScheduledDepartureDate | ActualDepartureDate | EstimatedArrivalDate |
|---|---|---|---|---|---|---|---|---|
| 100 | 1 | 103 | 2017651 | Manila | Los Angeles | 10-Dec-20 | 10-Dec-20 | 15-Mar-21 |
| 101 | 1 | 104 | 2018012 | Hong Kong | Seattle | 10-Jan-21 | 12-Jan-21 | 20-Mar-21 |
| 102 | 3 | 103 | 49100300 | Manila | Los Angeles | 05-May-21 | 05-May-21 | 17-Jun-21 |
| 103 | 2 | 104 | 399400 | Singapore | Portland | 02-Jun-21 | 04-Jun-21 | 17-Jul-21 |
| 104 | 3 | 103 | 84899440 | Lima | Los Angeles | 10-Jul-21 | 10-Jul-21 | 28-Jul-21 |
| 105 | 2 | 104 | 488955 | Singapore | Portland | 05-Aug-21 | 09-Aug-21 | 11-Sep-21 |

FIGURE 7-65

Sample Data for the MI
Database SHIPMENT Table

427

| ShipmentID | ShipmentItemID | PurchaseItemID | InsuredValue |
|------------|----------------|----------------|--------------|
| 100 | 1 | 500 | $15,000.00 |
| 100 | 2 | 505 | $15,000.00 |
| 101 | 1 | 510 | $40,000.00 |
| 101 | 2 | 515 | $3,500.00 |
| 102 | 1 | 520 | $15,000.00 |
| 103 | 1 | 525 | $90,000.00 |
| 103 | 2 | 530 | $25,000.00 |
| 103 | 3 | 535 | $150,000.00 |
| 103 | 4 | 540 | $12,500.00 |
| 104 | 1 | 545 | $12,500.00 |
| 104 | 2 | 550 | $5,500.00 |
| 105 | 1 | 555 | $4,500.00 |
| 105 | 2 | 560 | $10,000.00 |
| 105 | 3 | 565 | $1,500.00 |

PURCHASE_ITEM.ItemDescription, and PURCHASE_ITEM.PriceUSD. Run the statement to create the view, and then test the view with an appropriate SQL SELECT statement.

**O.** Create and test a user-defined function named *StoreContactAndPhone* that combines two parameters named *StoreContact* and *ContactPhone* into a concatenated data field formatted *StoreContact: ContactPhone* (including the colon and space).

**P.** Write an SQL statement to create a view called StorePurchaseHistoryView that shows STORE.StoreName, STORE.Phone, STORE.Contact, PURCHASE_ITEM. PurchaseItemID, PURCHASE_ITEM.PurchaseDate, PURCHASE_ITEM. ItemDescription, and PURCHASE_ITEM.PriceUSD. Run the statement to create the view, and then test the view with an appropriate SQL SELECT statement.

**Q.** Write an SQL statement to create a view called StoreContactPurchaseHistoryView that shows STORE.StoreName, the concatenated result of STORE.Phone and STORE.Contact from the *StoreContactAndPhone* function, PURCHASE_ITEM. PurchaseItemID, PURCHASE_ITEM.PurchaseDate, PURCHASE_ITEM.Item-Description, and PURCHASE_ITEM.PriceUSD. Run the statement to create the view, and then test the view with an appropriate SQL SELECT statement.

**R.** Write an SQL statement to create a view called StoreHistoryView that sums the PriceUSD column of StorePurchaseHistoryView for each store into a column named TotalPurchases. Run the statement to create the view, and then test the view with an appropriate SQL SELECT statement. (*Hint:* Assume unique store names.)

**S.** Write an SQL statement to create a view called MajorSources that uses StoreHistory View and selects only those stores that have TotalPurchases greater than 100000. Run the statement to create the view, and then test the view with an appropriate SQL SELECT statement.

**T.** Explain in general terms how you would use triggers to enforce minimum cardinality actions as required by your design. You need not write the triggers; just specify which triggers you need and describe their logic in general terms.

| ReceiptNumber | ShipmentID | PurchaseItemID | ReceivingAgentID | ReceiptDate | ReceiptTime | ReceiptQuantity | isReceivedUndamaged | DamageNotes |
|---|---|---|---|---|---|---|---|---|
| 200001 | 100 | 500 | 105 | 17-Mar-21 | 10:00 AM | 3 | Yes | NULL |
| 200002 | 100 | 505 | 105 | 17-Mar-21 | 10:00 AM | 50 | Yes | NULL |
| 200003 | 101 | 510 | 105 | 23-Mar-21 | 3:30 PM | 100 | Yes | NULL |
| 200004 | 101 | 515 | 105 | 23-Mar-21 | 3:30 PM | 10 | Yes | NULL |
| 200005 | 102 | 520 | 106 | 19-Jun-21 | 10:15 AM | 1 | No | One leg on one chair broken. |
| 200006 | 103 | 525 | 106 | 20-Jul-21 | 2:20 AM | 1000 | Yes | NULL |
| 200007 | 103 | 530 | 106 | 20-Jul-21 | 2:20 AM | 100 | Yes | NULL |
| 200008 | 103 | 535 | 106 | 20-Jul-21 | 2:20 AM | 100 | Yes | NULL |
| 200009 | 103 | 540 | 106 | 20-Jul-21 | 2:20 AM | 10 | Yes | NULL |
| 200010 | 104 | 545 | 105 | 29-Jul-21 | 9:00 PM | 100 | Yes | NULL |
| 200011 | 104 | 550 | 105 | 29-Jul-21 | 9:00 PM | 5 | Yes | NULL |
| 200012 | 105 | 555 | 106 | 14-Sep-21 | 2:45 PM | 4 | Yes | NULL |
| 200013 | 105 | 560 | 106 | 14-Sep-21 | 2:45 PM | 1 | Yes | NULL |
| 200014 | 105 | 565 | 106 | 14-Sep-21 | 2:45 PM | 10 | No | Base of one lamp scratched |

FIGURE 7-67

Sample Data for the MI Database SHIPMENT_ RECEIPT Table

# 8 Database Redesign

## Chapter Objectives

- To understand the need for database redesign
- To be able to use correlated subqueries
- To be able to use the SQL EXISTS and NOT EXISTS comparison operators in correlated subqueries
- To understand reverse engineering
- To be able to use dependency graphs
- To be able to change table names
- To be able to change table columns
- To be able to change relationship cardinalities
- To be able to change relationship properties
- To be able to add and delete relationships

**As stated in** Chapter 1, database design and implementation are needed for three reasons. Databases can be created (1) from existing data (such as spreadsheets and database tables), (2) for a new systems development project, or (3) for a database redesign. We have discussed the first two sources in Chapters 2–7. In this chapter, we will discuss the last source: database redesign.

We begin with a discussion of the need for database redesign, and then we will describe two important SQL statements: correlated subqueries and EXISTS. These statements play an important role when analyzing data prior to redesign. They also can be used for advanced queries and are important in their own right. After that discussion, we will turn to a variety of common database redesign tasks.

## The Need for Database Redesign

You may be wondering, "Why do we have to redesign a database? If we build it correctly the first time, why would we ever need to redesign it?" This question has two answers. First, it is not easy to build a database correctly the first time, especially databases that arise from the development of new systems. Even if we obtain all of the users' requirements and build a correct data model, the transformation of that data model into a correct database design is difficult. For large databases, the tasks are daunting and may require several stages of development. During those stages, some aspects of the database will need to be redesigned. Also, inevitably, mistakes will be made that must be corrected.

The second answer to this question is the more important one. Reflect for a moment on the relationship between information systems and the organizations that use them. It is tempting to say that they influence each other; that is, that information systems influence organizations and that organizations influence information systems.

In truth, however, the relationship is much stronger than that. Information systems and organizations do not just influence each other; they *create* each other. When a new information system is installed, the users can behave in new ways. As the users behave in those new ways, they will want changes to the information system to accommodate their new behaviors. As those changes are made, the users will have more new behaviors, they will request more changes to the information system, and so forth, in a never-ending cycle.

We are now in the **system maintenance** step of the **systems development life cycle (SDLC)** in the **systems analysis and design** process. This is the SDLC step where we face the fact that revising an information system is a natural step in using and maintaining that information system. (For an introduction to systems analysis and design and to the SDLC, see Appendix B.) The system maintenance step may therefore result in the need for a redesigned and reimplemented system and thus start a new iteration of the SDLC. This circular process means that changes to an information system are not the sad consequence of a poor implementation but rather a natural outcome of information system use. Therefore, the need for change to information systems never goes away; it neither can nor should be removed by better requirements definition, better initial design, better implementation, or anything else. Instead, change is part and parcel of information systems use. Thus, we need to plan for it. In the context of database processing, this means we need to know how to perform database redesign.

## SQL Statements for Checking Functional Dependencies

Database redesign is not terribly difficult if the database has no data. The serious difficulties arise when we have to change a database that has data and when we want to make changes with minimum impact on existing data. Telling the users that the system now works the way they want but that all of their data were lost while making the change is not acceptable.

Often, we need to know whether certain conditions or assumptions are valid in the data before we can proceed with a change. For example, we may know from user requirements that Department functionally determines DeptPhone, but we may not know whether that functional dependency is correctly represented in all of the data.

Recall from Chapter 3 that if Department determines DeptPhone, every value of Department must be paired with the same value of DeptPhone. If, for example, Accounting has a DeptPhone value of 834-1100 in one row, it should have that value in every row in which it appears. Similarly, if Finance has a DeptPhone of 834-2100 in one row, it should have that value in all rows in which it appears. Figure 8-1 shows data that violate this assumption. In the third row, the DeptPhone for Finance is different than for the other rows; it has too many zeroes. Most likely, someone made a keying mistake when entering DeptPhone. Such errors are typical.

Now, before we make a database change, we need to find all such violations and correct them. For the small table shown in Figure 8-1, we can just look at the data, but what if the EMPLOYEE table has 4,000 rows? Two SQL statements are particularly helpful in this regard: correlated subqueries and their cousins, the SQL EXISTS and NOT EXISTS keywords. We will consider each of these in turn.

**FIGURE 8-1**

Table Showing Constraint
Assumption Violation

| EmployeeNumber | LastName | EmailAddress | Department | DeptPhone |
|---|---|---|---|---|
| 100 | Johnson | JJ@somewhere.com | Accounting | 834-1100 |
| 200 | Abernathy | MA@somewhere.com | Finance | 834-2100 |
| 300 | Smathers | LS@somewhere.com | Finance | 834-21000 |
| 400 | Caruthers | TC@somewhere.com | Accounting | 834-1100 |
| 500 | Jackson | TJ@somewhere.com | Production | 834-4100 |
| 600 | Caldera | EC@somewhere.com | Legal | 834-3100 |
| 700 | Bandalone | RB@somewhere.com | Legal | 834-3100 |

## What Is a Correlated Subquery?

A **correlated subquery** looks very much like the noncorrelated subqueries we discussed in Chapter 2, but, in actuality, correlated subqueries are very different. To understand the difference, consider the following noncorrelated subquery, which is like those in Chapter 2:

```
/* *** SQL-Query-CH08-01 *** */
SELECT          A.FirstName, A.LastName
FROM            ARTIST AS A
WHERE           A.ArtistID IN
                (SELECT     W.ArtistID
                 FROM       WORK AS W
                 WHERE      W.Title = 'Blue Interior');
```

The DBMS can process such subqueries from the bottom up; that is, it can first find all of the values of ArtistID in WORK that have the title 'Blue Interior' and then process the upper query using that set of values. There is no need to move back and forth between the two SELECT statements. The result of this query is the artist Mark Tobey, as we would expect based on the data in Figure 7-15:

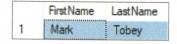

## Searching for Multiple Rows with a Given Title

Now, to introduce correlated subqueries, suppose that someone at View Ridge Gallery proposes that the Title column of WORK be an alternate key. If you look at the data in Figure 7-15(d), you can see that although there is only one copy of 'Blue Interior', there are two or more copies of other titles, such as 'Surf and Bird'. Therefore, Title cannot be an alternate key, and we can determine this by simply looking at the dataset.

However, if the WORK table had 10,000 or more rows, this would be difficult to determine. In that case, we need a query that examines the WORK table and displays the Title and Copy of any works that share the same title.

If we were asked to write a program to perform such a query, our logic would be as follows: Take the value of Title from the first row in WORK and examine all of the other rows in the table. If we find a row that has the same title as the one in the first row, we know there are duplicates, so we print the Title and Copy of the first work. We continue searching for duplicate title values until we come to the end of the WORK table.

Then we take the value of Title in the second row and compare it with all other rows in the WORK table, printing out the Title and Copy of any duplicate works. We proceed in this way until all rows of WORK have been examined.

### A Correlated Subquery that Finds Rows with the Same Title

The following correlated subquery performs the action just described:

```
/* *** SQL-Query-CH08-02 *** */
SELECT      W1.Title, W1.Copy
FROM        WORK AS W1
WHERE       W1.Title IN
            (SELECT     W2.Title
             FROM       WORK AS W2
             WHERE      W1.Title = W2.Title
             AND        W1.WorkID <> W2.WorkID);
```

The result of this query for the data in Figure 7-15(d) is:

| | Title | Copy |
|---|---|---|
| 1 | Farmer's Market #2 | 267/500 |
| 2 | Farmer's Market #2 | 268/500 |
| 3 | Spanish Dancer | 583/750 |
| 4 | Spanish Dancer | 588/750 |
| 5 | Surf and Bird | 142/500 |
| 6 | Surf and Bird | 362/500 |
| 7 | Surf and Bird | 365/500 |
| 8 | Surf and Bird | 366/500 |
| 9 | Surf and Bird | Unique |
| 10 | The Fiddler | 251/1000 |
| 11 | The Fiddler | 252/1000 |

Looking at these results, it is easy to see the nonunique, duplicated Title data that prevents Title from being used as an alternate key. When you are interpreting these results, note that a value of *Unique* in the Copy column indicates the original piece of art itself, which is, by definition, unique. Numbers such as *142/500* indicate one numbered print from a set of numbered reproduction prints of that artwork.

This subquery, which is a correlated subquery, looks deceptively similar to a regular, noncorrelated subquery. To the surprise of many students, this subquery and the one earlier are drastically different. Their similarity is only superficial.

Before learning why, first notice the notation in the correlated subquery. The WORK table is used in both the upper and the lower SELECT statements. In the upper statement, it is given the alias W1; in the lower SELECT statement, it is given the alias W2.

In essence, when we use this notation, it is as if we have made two copies of the WORK table. One copy is called W1, and the second copy is called W2. Therefore, in the last two lines of the correlated subquery, values in the W1 copy of WORK are compared with values in the W2 copy.

### What Is the Difference Between Regular and Correlated Subqueries?

Now consider what makes this subquery so different. Unlike with a regular, noncorrelated subquery, the DBMS cannot run the bottom SELECT by itself, obtain a set of Titles, and then use that set to execute the upper query. The reason for this appears in the last two lines of the query:

```
WHERE       W1.Title = W2.Title
AND         W1.WorkID <> W2.WorkID);
```

In these expressions, W1.Title (from the top SELECT statement) is being compared with W2.Title (from the bottom SELECT statement). The same is true for W1.WorkID and W2.WorkID. Because of this fact, the DBMS cannot process the subquery portion independent of the upper SELECT.

Instead, the DBMS must process this statement as a subquery that is *nested* within the main query. The logic is as follows: Take the first row from W1. Using that row, evaluate the second query. To do that, for each row in W2, compare W1.Title with W2.Title and W1.WorkID with W2.WorkID. If the titles are equal and the values of WorkID are not equal, return the value of W2.Title to the upper query. Do this for every row in W2.

Once all of the rows in W2 have been evaluated for the first row in W1, move to the second row in W1 and evaluate it against all the rows in W2. Continue in this way until all rows of W1 have been compared with all of the rows of W2.

If this is not clear to you, write out two copies of the WORK data from Figure 7-15(d) on a piece of scratch paper. Label one of them W1 and the second W2, and then work through the logic as described. From this, you will see that correlated subqueries always require nested processing.

### A Common Trap

By the way, do not fall into the following common trap:

```
/* *** SQL-Query-CH08-03 *** */
SELECT      W1.Title, W1.Copy
FROM        WORK AS W1
WHERE       W1.WorkID IN
            (SELECT      W2.WorkID
             FROM        WORK AS W2
             WHERE       W1.Title = W2.Title
               AND       W1.WorkID <> W2.WorkID);
```

The logic here seems correct, but it is not. Compare SQL-Query-CH08-03 to SQL-Query-CH08-02, and note the differences between the two SQL statements. The result of SQL-Query-CH08-03 when run on the View Ridge Gallery data in Figure 7-15(d) is an empty set:

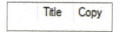

In fact, *no row will ever be displayed by this query*, regardless of the underlying data (see if you can figure out why this is so before continuing to the next paragraph).

The bottom query will indeed find all rows that have the same title and different WorkIDs. If one is found, it will produce the W2.WorkID of that row. But that value will then be compared with W1.WorkID. *These two values will always be different because of the condition*

```
W1.WorkID <> W2.WorkID
```

No rows are returned because the values of the two unequal WorkIDs are used in the subquery SELECT statement called by WHERE W1.WorkID IN phrase instead of the values of the two equal Titles.

### Using Correlated Subqueries to Check Functional Dependencies

Correlated subqueries can be used to your advantage during database redesign. As mentioned, one application of correlated subqueries is to verify functional dependencies. For example, suppose we have EMPLOYEE data like that in Figure 8-1 in a database and we want to know whether the data conform to the following functional dependency:

Department → DeptPhone

If so, every time a given value of Department occurs in the table, that value will be matched with the same value of DeptPhone.

The following correlated subquery will find any rows that violate this assumption:

```
/* *** SQL-Query-CH08-04 *** */
SELECT      E1.EmployeeNumber, E1.Department, E1.DeptPhone
FROM        EMPLOYEE AS E1
WHERE       E1.Department IN
            (SELECT     E2.Department
             FROM       EMPLOYEE AS E2
             WHERE      E1.Department = E2.Department
             AND        E1.DeptPhone <> E2.DeptPhone);
```

The results of this query for the data in Figure 8-1 are:

| | EmployeeNumber | Department | DeptPhone |
|---|---|---|---|
| 1 | 200 | Finance | 834-2100 |
| 2 | 300 | Finance | 834-21000 |

A listing like this can readily be used to find and fix any rows that violate the functional dependency.

### SQL Correlated Subqueries Using the EXISTS and NOT EXISTS Comparison Operators

In Chapter 2, we discussed a set of SQL comparison operators, and these are summarized in Figure 2-23. To this set we will now add the **SQL EXISTS comparison operator** and the **SQL NOT EXISTS comparison operator**, as shown in Figure 8-2. When we use the EXIST or NOT EXISTS operator in a query, we are creating another form of correlated subquery.

These operators simply test whether *any* values are returned by the subquery, which indicates there are values meeting its conditions. If one or more values are returned, then values from the subquery are used to run the top-level query. If no values are returned, the top-level query produces an empty set as the result.

For example, we can rewrite the SQL-Query-CH08-4 correlated subquery using the SQL EXISTS keyword as follows:

```
/* *** SQL-Query-CH08-05 *** */
SELECT      E1.EmployeeNumber, E1.Department, E1.DeptPhone
FROM        EMPLOYEE AS E1
WHERE       EXISTS
            (SELECT     E2.Department
             FROM       EMPLOYEE AS E2
             WHERE      E1.Department = E2.Department
             AND        E1.DeptPhone <> E2.DeptPhone);
```

**FIGURE 8-2**

SQL Comparison Operators
EXISTS and NOT EXISTS

| SQL Comparison Operators | |
|---|---|
| **Operator** | **Meaning** |
| EXISTS | Is a non-empty set of values |
| NOT EXISTS | Is an empty set |

Because using EXISTS creates a form of a correlated subquery, the processing of the SELECT statements is nested. The first row of E1 is input to the subquery. If the subquery finds any row in E2 for which the department names are the same and the department phone numbers are different, then the EXISTS is *true* (returns a nonempty set of values) and the Department and DeptPhone for the first row are selected. Next, the second row of E1 is input to the subquery, the SELECT is processed, and the EXISTS is evaluated. If true, the Department and DeptPhone of the second row are selected. This process is repeated for all of the rows in E1.

The results of SQL-Query-CH08-05 are identical to the previous results from SQL-Query-CH08-04:

| | Employee Number | Department | Dept Phone |
|---|---|---|---|
| 1 | 200 | Finance | 834-2100 |
| 2 | 300 | Finance | 834-21000 |

## Using NOT EXISTS in a Double Negative

The SQL EXISTS operator will be true (will return a nonempty set of values) if *any* row in the subquery *meets the condition*. The SQL NOT EXISTS operator will be true (will return an empty set) only if *all* rows in the subquery *fail to meet the condition*. Consequently, the double use of NOT EXISTS can be used to find rows that do not *not match a condition*. And, yes, the word *not* is supposed to be there twice—this is a *double negative*.

Because of the logic of a double negative, if a row does not *not match any row*, then it *matches every row*! For example, suppose that at View Ridge the users want to know the name of any artist that *every* customer is interested in. We can proceed as follows:

- First, produce the set of all customers who are interested in a particular artist.
- Then take the complement of that set, which will be the customers who are *not* interested in that artist.
- If that complement is an empty set, then *all* customers are interested in the given artist.

> **BY THE WAY** The doubly nested NOT EXISTS pattern is famous in one guise or another among SQL practitioners. It is often used as a test of SQL knowledge in job interviews and in bragging sessions, and it can be used to your advantage when assessing the desirability of certain database redesign possibilities, as you will see in the last section of this chapter. Therefore, even though this example involves some serious study, it is worth your while to understand it.

## The Double NOT EXISTS Query

The following SQL statement implements the strategy just described:

```
/* *** SQL-Query-CH08-06 *** */
SELECT      A.FirstName, A.LastName
FROM        ARTIST AS A
WHERE       NOT EXISTS
            (SELECT    C.CustomerID
             FROM      CUSTOMER AS C
             WHERE     NOT EXISTS
                       (SELECT    CAI.CustomerID
                        FROM      CUSTOMER_ARTIST_INT AS CAI
                        WHERE     C.CustomerID = CAI.CustomerID
                          AND     A.ArtistID = CAI.ArtistID));
```

The result of this query is an empty set, indicating that there is *no* artist that *every* customer is interested in:

Let's see how this works. The bottom SELECT (the third SELECT in the SQL statement) finds all of the customers who are interested in a particular artist. As you read this SELECT (the last SELECT in the query), keep in mind that this is a correlated subquery; this SELECT is nested inside the query on CUSTOMER, which is nested inside the query on ARTIST. C.CustomerID is coming from the SELECT on CUSTOMER in the middle, and A.ArtistID is coming from the SELECT on ARTIST at the top.

Now the NOT EXISTS in the sixth line of the query will find the customers who are *not* interested in the given artist. If *all* customers are interested in the given artist, the result of the middle SELECT will be *null*. If the result of the middle SELECT is null, the NOT EXISTS in the third line of the query will be *true* and the name of that artist will be produced, just as we want.

Consider what happens for artists who do not qualify in this query. Suppose that every customer except Tiffany Twilight is interested in the artist Joan Miro. (This is *not* the case for the data in Figure 7-15, but assume that it were true.) Now, for the preceding query, when Miro's row is considered, the bottom SELECT will retrieve every customer *except* Tiffany Twilight. In this case, because of the NOT EXISTS in the sixth line of the query, the middle SELECT will produce the CustomerID for Tiffany Twilight (because her row is the only one that does not appear in the bottom SELECT). Now, because there *is* a result from the middle SELECT, the NOT EXISTS in the top SELECT is *false*, and the name Joan Miro will *not* be included in the output of the query. This is correct because there is a customer who is not interested in Joan Miro.

Again, take some time to study this pattern. It is a famous one, and if you become a database professional, you will certainly see it again in one form or another. In fact, you will *not not* see it again!

## How Do I Analyze an Existing Database?

Before we proceed with a discussion of database redesign, reflect for a moment on what this task means for a real company whose operations are dependent on the database. Suppose, for example, that you work for a company such as Amazon.com. Further suppose that you have been tasked with an important database redesign assignment—say, to change the primary key of the vendor table.

To begin, you may wonder, why would Amazon want to do this? It could be that in the early days, when it only sold books, Amazon used company names for vendors. But as Amazon began to sell more types of products, company name was no longer sufficient. Perhaps there are too many duplicates, and Amazon may have decided to switch to an Amazon-created VendorID.

Now, what does it mean to switch primary keys? Besides adding the new data to the correct rows, what else does it mean? Clearly, if the old primary key has been used as a foreign key, all of the foreign keys need to be changed as well. So we need to know all of the relationships in which the old primary key was used. But what about views? Do any views use the old primary key? If so, they will need to be changed. What about triggers and stored procedures? Do any of them use the old primary key? Not to mention any application code that may break when the old key is removed.

Now, to create a nightmare, what happens if you get partway through the change process and something fails? Suppose you encounter unexpected data and receive errors from the DBMS while trying to add the new primary key. Amazon cannot change its Web site to display, "Sorry, our database is broken—come back tomorrow (we hope)!"

This nightmare brings up many topics, most of which relate to systems analysis and design. (See Appendix B for a brief introduction to systems analysis and design.) But with regard to database processing, three principles become clear. First, as carpenters say, "Measure twice and cut once." Before we attempt any structural changes to a database, we must clearly understand the current structure and contents of the database, and we must know what depends on what. Second, before we make any structural changes to an operational database, we must test those changes on a realistically sized test database that has all of the important test data cases. Finally, if at all possible, we need to create a complete backup of the operational database prior to making any structural changes. If all goes awry, the backup can be used to restore the database while problems are corrected. We will consider each of these important topics next.

## Reverse Engineering

Reverse engineering is the process of reading a database schema and producing a data model from it. The data model produced is not truly a logical model because entities will be generated for every table, including entities for intersection tables that have no nonkey data and should not appear in a logical model at all. The model generated by reverse engineering is a thing unto itself, a table-relationship diagram that is dressed in entity-relationship clothes. In this text, we will call it the **reverse engineered (RE) data model**.

Figure 8-3 shows the RE data model of the View Ridge Gallery VRG database produced by the MySQL Workbench from a MySQL 8.0 version of the VRG database created in Chapter 7. Note that due to the limitations of the MySQL Workbench, this is a physical database design rather than a logical data model. Nonetheless, it illustrates the reverse engineering technique we are discussing.

We used the MySQL Workbench because of its general availability. The MySQL Workbench, as discussed in Appendix E, "Getting Started with the MySQL Workbench Data Modeling Tools," uses standard IE Crow's Foot database modeling notation. Figure 6-37 shows the VRG data model, and Figure 6-39 shows the VRG database design.

**FIGURE 8-3**

Reverse Engineered VRG
Data Model

If you compare these to the VRG RE data model in Figure 8-3, you will see that the MySQL Workbench came close to duplicating the VRG database design rather than the VRG data model. The MySQL Workbench:

- Contains the final *primary keys* and *foreign keys*, rather than the data model entity identifiers.
- Contains the *customer_artist_int* table, rather than the N:M relationship between CUSTOMER and ARTIST shown in the data model.
- Contains wrong *minimum cardinality* values. All of the many sides of the 1:N relationships should be optional except for the WORK-to-TRANS relationship, based on the VRG database design.

All in all, however, this is a reasonable representation of the View Ridge Gallery database design.

Although the MySQL Workbench produces only a database design and not a data model, some other design software, such as erwin's erwin Data Modeler, can create both logical (data model) and physical (database design) versions of the database structure. In addition to tables and views, some data modeling products will capture constraints, triggers, and stored procedures from the database. (In fact, the MySQL Workbench can capture some of these, although we have not included them in Figure 8-3.)

These constructs are not interpreted, but their program code and other text is imported into the data model. With some products, the relationship of the text to the items it references also is obtained. The redesign of constraints, triggers, and stored procedures is beyond the scope of our discussion here. You should realize that they, too, are part of the database, however, and are subject to redesign.

## Dependency Graphs

Before making changes to database structures, it is vitally important to understand the dependencies of those structures. What changes will affect what? For example, consider changing the name of a table. Where is the table name used? In which triggers? In which stored procedures? In which relationships? Because of the need to know all of the dependencies, many database redesign projects begin by making a **dependency graph**.

The term *graph* arises from the mathematical topic of graph theory. Dependency graphs are not graphical displays like bar charts; rather, they are diagrams that consist of nodes and arcs (or lines) that connect those nodes.

Figure 8-4 shows a partial dependency graph that was drawn using the results of the RE model but manually interpreting views and triggers we developed in Chapter 7. For simplicity, this graph does not show the views and triggers of CUSTOMER, nor does it show CUSTOMER_ARTIST_INT and related structures. Also, the stored procedure WORK_AddWorkTransaction is not shown, nor are the constraints.

Even this partial diagram reveals the complexity of dependencies among database constructs. You can see that it would be wise to tread lightly, for example, when changing anything in the TRANS table. The consequences of such a change need to be assessed against two relationships, two triggers, and two views. Again, measure twice and cut once!

## Database Backup and Test Databases

Because of the potential damage that can be done to a database during redesign, a complete backup of the operational database should be made prior to making any changes. Equally important, it is essential that any proposed changes be thoroughly tested. Not only must structural changes proceed successfully, but all triggers, stored procedures, and applications must also run correctly on the revised database.

Typically, at least three different copies of the database schema are used in the redesign process. One is a small test database that can be used for initial testing. The second is a large test database, which may even be a full copy of the operational database. Sometimes, there are several large test databases. Finally, there is the operational database.

At this point, tests should be run against the database to verify that all changes have been made correctly. After that, stored procedures and applications that use WORK can be changed to run against the new table name.[1] If all is correct, then the foreign key constraint TransWorkFK and the WORK table can be dropped with the following:

```
/* *** EXAMPLE CODE - DO NOT RUN *** */
/* *** SQL-ALTER-TABLE-CH08-01 *** */
ALTER TABLE TRANS
    DROP CONSTRAINT TransWorkFK;
/* *** SQL-DROP-TABLE-CH08-01 *** */
DROP TABLE WORK;
```

The TransWorkFK constraint then can be added back to TRANS using the new name for the WORK table:

```
/* *** EXAMPLE CODE - DO NOT RUN *** */
/* *** SQL-ALTER-TABLE-CH08-02 *** */
ALTER TABLE TRANS
    ADD CONSTRAINT        TransWorkFK        FOREIGN KEY(WorkID)
                          REFERENCES WORK_VERSION2(WorkID)
                              ON UPDATE NO ACTION
                              ON DELETE NO ACTION;
```

Clearly, there is more to changing a table name than you would think. You now can see why some organizations do not allow programmers or users to employ the true name of a table. Instead, views are described that serve as table aliases, as explained in Chapter 7. If this were done here, only the views that define the aliases would need to be changed when the source table name is changed *as long as* the view references all the columns in the table using the asterisk (*) wild card. However, if the view references the columns by name and if any column name has been changed, then more work will be needed to revise the view.

## Adding and Dropping Columns

Adding null columns to a table is straightforward. For example, to add the null column Date-Created to WORK, we simply use the ALTER TABLE statement as follows:

```
/* *** EXAMPLE CODE - DO NOT RUN *** */
/* *** SQL-ALTER-TABLE-CH08-03 *** */
ALTER TABLE WORK
    ADD  DateCreated   Date    NULL;
```

If there are other column constraints, such as DEFAULT or UNIQUE, include them with the column definition, just as you would if the column definition were part of a CREATE TABLE statement. However, if you include a DEFAULT constraint, be aware that the default value will be applied to all new rows, but existing rows will have null values.

---

[1]The timing is important. The WORK_VERSION2 table was created from WORK. If triggers, stored procedures, and applications continue to run against WORK while the verification of WORK_VERSION2 is underway, then WORK_VERSION2 will be out of date. Some action will need to be taken to bring it up to date before switching the stored procedures and applications over to WORK_VERSION2.

Suppose, for example, that you want to set the default value of DateCreated to 1/1/1900 to signify that the value has not yet been entered. In this case, you would use the following ALTER TABLE statement:

```
/* *** EXAMPLE CODE - DO NOT RUN *** */

/* *** SQL-ALTER-TABLE-CH08-04 *** */

ALTER TABLE WORK

    ADD   DateCreated   Date   NULL DEFAULT '01/01/1900';
```

This statement causes DateCreated for new rows in WORK to be set to 1/1/1900 by default. To set existing rows, you would need to execute the following query:

```
/* *** EXAMPLE CODE - DO NOT RUN *** */

/* *** SQL-UPDATE-CH08-01 *** */

UPDATE WORK

    SET       DateCreated = '01/01/1900'

    WHERE     DateCreated IS NULL;
```

### Adding NOT NULL Columns

To add a new NOT NULL column, first add the column as NULL. Then use an UPDATE statement like that just shown to give the column a value in all rows. After the update, the following SQL ALTER TABLE ALTER COLUMN statement can be executed to change DateCreated from NULL to NOT NULL:

```
/* *** EXAMPLE CODE - DO NOT RUN *** */

/* *** SQL-ALTER-TABLE-CH08-05 *** */

ALTER TABLE WORK

    ALTER COLUMN       DateCreated   Date   NOT NULL;
```

Note that this statement will fail if DateCreated has not been given values in all rows.

### Dropping Columns

Dropping nonkey columns is easy. For example, eliminating the DateCreated column from WORK can be done with the following:

```
/* *** EXAMPLE CODE - DO NOT RUN *** */

/* *** SQL-ALTER-TABLE-CH08-06 *** */

ALTER TABLE WORK

    DROP COLUMN DateCreated;
```

To drop a foreign key column, the constraint that defines the foreign key must first be dropped. Making such a change is equivalent to dropping a relationship, and that topic is discussed later in this chapter.

To drop the primary key, the primary key constraint first needs to be dropped. To drop that, however, all foreign keys that use the primary key must first be dropped. Thus, to drop the primary key of WORK and replace it with the composite primary key (Title, Copy, ArtistID), the following steps are necessary:

- Drop the constraint WorkFK from TRANS.
- Drop the constraint WorkPK from WORK.
- Create a new WorkPK constraint using (Title, Copy, ArtistID).
- Create a new WorkFK constraint referencing (Title, Copy, ArtistID) in TRANS.
- Drop the column WorkID.

It is important to verify that all changes have been made correctly before dropping WorkID. Once it is dropped, there is no way to recover it except by restoring the WORK table from a backup.

### Changing a Column Data Type or Column Constraints

To change a column data type or to change column constraints, the column is redefined using the ALTER TABLE ALTER COLUMN command. However, if the column is being changed from NULL to NOT NULL, then all rows must have a value in that column for the change to succeed.

Also, some data type changes may cause data loss. Changing Char(50) to Date, for example, will cause loss of any text field that the DBMS cannot successfully transform into a date value. Or, alternatively, the DBMS may simply refuse to make the column change. The results depend on the DBMS product in use.

Generally, converting numeric to Char or Varchar will succeed. Also, converting Date or Money or other more specific data types to Char or Varchar will usually succeed. Converting Char or Varchar back to Date, Money, or Numeric is risky, and it may or may not be possible.

In the View Ridge schema, if DateOfBirth had been defined as Char(4), then a risky but sensible data type change would be to modify DateOfBirth in the ARTIST table to Numeric(4,0).

This would be a sensible change because all of the values in this column are numeric. Recall the check constraint that was used to define DateOfBirth (refer to Figure 7-13). The following makes that change and simplifies the CHECK constraint:

```
/* *** EXAMPLE CODE - DO NOT RUN *** */
/* *** SQL-ALTER-TABLE-CH08-07 *** */
ALTER TABLE ARTIST
    ALTER COLUMN          DateOfBirth   Numeric(4,0)   NULL;
ALTER TABLE ARTIST
    ADD CONSTRAINT NumericBirthYearCheck
        CHECK (DateOfBirth > 1900 AND DateOfBirth < 2100);
```

The prior check constraints on DateOfBirth should now be deleted.

### Adding and Dropping Constraints

As already shown, constraints can be added and removed using the ALTER TABLE ADD CONSTRAINT and ALTER TABLE DROP CONSTRAINT statements.

## Changing Relationship Cardinalities

Changing cardinalities is a common database redesign task. Sometimes, the need is to change minimum cardinalities from zero to one or from one to zero. Another common task is to change the maximum cardinality from 1:1 to 1:N or from 1:N to N:M. Another possibility, which is less common, is to decrease maximum cardinality from N:M to 1:N or from 1:N to 1:1. This latter change can be made only with data loss, as you will see.

### Changing Minimum Cardinalities

The action to be taken in changing minimum cardinalities depends on whether the change is on the parent side or on the child side of the relationship.

#### Changing Minimum Cardinalities on the Parent Side

If the change is on the parent side, meaning that the child will or will not be required to have a parent, making the change is a matter of changing whether null values are allowed for the foreign key that represents the relationship. For example, suppose that in the 1:N relationship from DEPARTMENT to EMPLOYEE, the foreign key DepartmentNumber appears in the EMPLOYEE table. Changing whether an employee is required to have a department is simply a matter of changing the null status of DepartmentNumber.

If the change is from a minimum cardinality of zero to one, then the foreign key, which would have been null, must be changed to NOT NULL. Changing a column to NOT NULL can be done only if all the rows in the table have a value. In the case of a foreign key, this means that every record must already be related. If not, all records must be changed so that all have a relationship before the foreign key can be made NOT NULL. In the previous example, every employee must be related to a department before DepartmentNumber can be changed to NOT NULL.

Depending on the DBMS product in use, the foreign key constraint that defines the relationship may have to be dropped before the change is made to the foreign key. Then the foreign key constraint can be re-added. The following SQL will work for the preceding example:

```
/* *** EXAMPLE CODE - DO NOT RUN *** */
/* *** SQL-ALTER-TABLE-CH08-08 *** */
ALTER TABLE EMPLOYEE
    DROP CONSTRAINT DepartmentFK;
ALTER TABLE EMPLOYEE
    ALTER COLUMN   DepartmentNumber   Int   NOT NULL;
ALTER TABLE EMPLOYEE
    ADD CONSTRAINT   DepartmentFK   FOREIGN KEY(DepartmentNumber)
                     REFERENCES DEPARTMENT(DepartmentNumber)
                     ON UPDATE CASCADE;
```

Also, cascade behavior for UPDATE and DELETE must be specified when changing the minimum cardinality from zero to one. In this example, updates are to cascade, but deletions will not. (Recall that the default behavior is NO ACTION.)

Changing the minimum cardinality from one to zero is simple. Just change DepartmentNumber from NOT NULL to NULL. You also may want to change the cascade behavior on updates and deletions, if appropriate.

### Changing Minimum Cardinalities on the Child Side

As noted in Chapter 6, the only way to enforce a minimum cardinality other than zero on the child side of a relationship is to write triggers or application code that enforces the constraint. So, to change the minimum cardinality from zero to one, it is necessary to write the appropriate triggers. Design the trigger behavior using Figure 6-29, and then write the triggers. To change the minimum cardinality from one to zero, just drop the triggers that enforce that constraint.

In the DEPARTMENT-to-EMPLOYEE relationship example, to require each DEPARTMENT to have an EMPLOYEE means that triggers would need to be written on INSERT of DEPARTMENT and on UPDATE and DELETE of EMPLOYEE. The trigger code in DEPARTMENT ensures that an EMPLOYEE is assigned to the new DEPARTMENT, and the trigger code in EMPLOYEE ensures that the employee being moved to a new department or the employee being deleted is not the last employee in the relationship to its parent.

This discussion assumes that the required child constraint is enforced by triggers. If the required child constraint is enforced by application programs, then all of those programs also must be changed. Dozens of programs may need to be changed, which is one reason why it is better to enforce such constraints using triggers rather than application code.

### Changing Maximum Cardinalities

The only difficulty when increasing cardinalities from 1:1 to 1:N or from 1:N to N:M is preserving existing relationships. This can be done, but it requires a bit of manipulation, as you will see. When reducing cardinalities, relationship data will be lost. In this case, a policy must be created for deciding which relationships to lose.

### Changing a 1:1 Relationship to a 1:N Relationship

Figure 8-5 shows a 1:1 relationship between EMPLOYEE and PARKING_PERMIT. As we discussed in Chapter 6, the foreign key can be placed in either table for a 1:1 relationship. The action taken depends on whether EMPLOYEE is to be the parent entity in the 1:N relationship or whether PARKING_PERMIT is to be the parent.

If EMPLOYEE is to be the parent (employees are to have multiple parking permits), then the only change necessary is to drop the constraint that PARKING_PERMIT.EmployeeNumber be unique. The relationship will then be 1:N.

If PARKING_PERMIT is to be the parent (e.g., if parking permits are to be allocated to many employees, say, for a carpool), then the foreign key and appropriate values must be moved from PARKING_PERMIT to EMPLOYEE. The following SQL will accomplish this:

```
/* *** EXAMPLE CODE - DO NOT RUN *** */
/* *** SQL-ALTER-TABLE-CH08-09 *** */
ALTER TABLE EMPLOYEE
    ADD    PermitNumber   Int   NULL;
/* *** SQL-UPDATE-CH08-02 *** */
UPDATE EMPLOYEE
    SET EMPLOYEE.PermitNumber =
            (SELECT    PP.PermitNumber
             FROM      PARKING_PERMIT AS PP
             WHERE     PP.EmployeeNumber = EMPLOYEE.EmployeeNumber);
```

Once the foreign key has been moved over to EMPLOYEE, the EmployeeNumber column of PARKING_PERMIT should be dropped. Next, create a new foreign key constraint to define referential integrity. So multiple employees can relate to the same parking permit, the new foreign key must not have a UNIQUE constraint.

### Changing a 1:N Relationship to an N:M Relationship

Suppose that View Ridge Gallery decides that it wants to record multiple purchasers for a given transaction. It may be that some of its art is co-owned between a customer and a bank or trust account, for example; or perhaps it may want to record the names of both owners when a couple purchases art. For whatever reason, this change will require that the 1:N relationship between CUSTOMER and TRANS be changed to an N:M relationship.

Changing a 1:N relationship to an N:M relationship is surprisingly easy.[2] Just create the new intersection table with appropriate foreign key constraints, fill it with data, and drop the old foreign key column. Figure 8-6 shows the View Ridge database design with a new intersection table to support the N:M relationship.

**FIGURE 8-5**

The Employee-to-Parking_ Permit 1:1 Relationship

---

[2]Making the data change is easy. Dealing with the consequences of the data change with regard to views, triggers, stored procedures, and application code will be more difficult. All of these will need to be rewritten to join across a new intersection table. All forms and reports also will need to be changed to portray multiple customers for a transaction; this will mean changing text boxes to grids, for example. All of this work is time-consuming and, hence, expensive.

**FIGURE 8-6**

**VRG Database Design with New N:M Relationship**

We need to create this table and then copy the values of TransactionID and CustomerID from TRANS for rows in which CustomerID is not null. First, create the new intersection table using the following SQL:

```
/* *** EXAMPLE CODE - DO NOT RUN *** */
/* *** SQL-CREATE-TABLE-CH08-01 *** */
CREATE TABLE CUSTOMER_TRANSACTION_INT(
    CustomerID      Int    NOT NULL,
    TransactionID   Int    NOT NULL,
    CONSTRAINT      CustomerTransaction_PK
        PRIMARY KEY(CustomerID, TransactionID),
    CONSTRAINT      Customer_Transaction_Int_Trans_FK
        FOREIGN KEY(TransactionID) REFERENCES TRANS(TransactionID),
    CONSTRAINT      Customer_Transaction_Int_Customer_FK
        FOREIGN KEY(CustomerID) REFERENCES CUSTOMER(CustomerID)
    );
```

Note that there is no cascade behavior for updates because CustomerID is a surrogate key. There is no cascade behavior for deletions because of the business policy never to delete data that involve transactions. The next task is to fill the table with data from the TRANS table using the following SQL statement:

```
/* *** EXAMPLE CODE - DO NOT RUN *** */
/* *** SQL-INSERT-CH08-02 *** */
INSERT INTO CUSTOMER_TRANSACTION_INT (CustomerID, TransactionID)
    SELECT   CustomerID, TransactionID
    FROM     TRANS
    WHERE    CustomerID IS NOT NULL;
```

Once all of these changes have been made, the CustomerID column of TRANS can be dropped.

### Reducing Cardinalities (with Data Loss)

It is easy to make the structural changes to reduce cardinalities. To reduce an N:M relationship to 1:N, we just create a new foreign key in the relation that will be the child and fill it with data from the intersection table. To reduce a 1:N relationship to 1:1, we just make the values of the foreign key of the 1:N relationship unique and then define a unique constraint on the foreign key. In either case, the most difficult problem is deciding which data to lose.

Consider the reduction of N:M to 1:N. Suppose, for example, that the View Ridge Gallery decides to keep just one artist interest for each customer. Thus, the relationship will then be 1:N from ARTIST to CUSTOMER. Accordingly, we add a new foreign key column ArtistID to CUSTOMER and set up a foreign key constraint to ARTIST on that customer. The following SQL will accomplish this:

```
/* *** EXAMPLE CODE - DO NOT RUN *** */
/* *** SQL-ALTER-TABLE-CH08-10 *** */
ALTER TABLE CUSTOMER
    ADD    ArtistID    Int    NULL;
ALTER TABLE CUSTOMER
      ADD CONSTRAINT    ArtistInterestFK    FOREIGN KEY(ArtistID)
                        REFERENCES ARTIST(ArtistID);
```

Updates need not cascade because of the surrogate key, and deletions cannot cascade because the customer may have a valid transaction and ought not to be deleted just because an artist interest goes away.

Now, which of a customer's potentially many artist interests should be preserved in the new relationship? The answer depends on the business policy at the gallery. Here suppose we decide simply to take the first artist interest:

```
/* *** EXAMPLE CODE - DO NOT RUN *** */
/* *** SQL-UPDATE-CH08-03 *** */
UPDATE      CUSTOMER
    SET     ArtistID =
                (SELECT    TOP 1 ArtistID
                 FROM      CUSTOMER_ARTIST_INT AS CAI
                 WHERE     CUSTOMER.CustomerID = CAI.CustomerID);
```

The SQL Top 1 phrase is used to return the first qualifying row.

All views, triggers, stored procedures, and application code need to be changed to account for the new 1:N relationship. Then the constraints defined on CUSTOMER_ ARTIST_INT can be dropped. Finally, the table CUSTOMER_ARTIST_INT can be dropped.

To change a 1:N to a 1:1 relationship, we just need to remove any duplicate values of the foreign key of the relationship and then add a unique constraint on the foreign key. See Review Question 8.51.

## Adding and Deleting Tables and Relationships

Adding new tables and relationships is straightforward. Just add the tables and relationships using CREATE TABLE statements with FOREIGN KEY constraints, as shown before. If an existing table has a child relationship to the new table, add a FOREIGN KEY constraint using the existing table.

For example, if a new table, COUNTRY, were added to the View Ridge database with the primary key Name and if CUSTOMER.Country is to be used as a foreign key in the new table, a new FOREIGN KEY constraint would be defined in CUSTOMER:

```
/* *** EXAMPLE CODE - DO NOT RUN *** */
/* *** SQL-ALTER-TABLE-CH08-11 *** */
ALTER TABLE CUSTOMER
    ADD CONSTRAINT CountryFK FOREIGN KEY(Country)
                     REFERENCES COUNTRY(Name)
                        ON UPDATE CASCADE;
```

Deleting relationships and tables is just a matter of dropping the foreign key constraints and then dropping the tables. Of course, before this is done, dependency graphs must be constructed and used to determine which views, triggers, stored procedures, and application programs will be affected by the deletions.

As described in Chapter 4, another reason to add new tables and relationships or to compress existing tables into fewer tables is for normalization and denormalization. We will not address that topic further in this chapter, except to say that normalization and denormalization are common tasks during database redesign.

## Forward Engineering

You can use a variety of different data modeling products to make database changes on your behalf. To do so, you first reverse engineer the database, make changes to the RE data model, and then invoke the forward engineering functionality of the data modeling tool.

We will not consider forward engineering here because it hides the SQL that you need to learn. Also, the specifics of the forward engineering process are product dependent.

Because of the importance of making data model changes correctly, many professionals are skeptical about using an automated process for database redesign. Certainly, it is necessary to test the results thoroughly before using forward engineering on operational data. Some products will show the SQL they are about to execute for review before making the changes to the database.

Database redesign is one area in which automation may not be the best idea. Much depends on the nature of the changes to be made and the quality of the forward engineering features of the data modeling product. Given the knowledge you have gained in this chapter, you should be able to make most redesign changes by writing your own SQL. There is nothing wrong with that approach!

## Summary

Database design and implementation are needed for three reasons. Databases can be created (1) from existing data (such as spreadsheets and databases tables), (2) for a new systems development project, or (3) for a database redesign. Database redesign is part of the system maintenance step of the SDLC and is necessary both to fix mistakes made during the initial database design and to adapt the database to changes in system requirements. Such changes are common because information systems and organizations do not just influence each other—they create each other. Thus, new information systems cause changes in systems requirements.

Correlated subqueries and SQL EXISTS and NOT EXISTS comparison operators are important tools. They can be used to answer advanced queries. They also are useful during database redesign for determining whether specified data conditions exist. For example, they can be used to determine whether possible functional dependencies exist in the data.

A correlated subquery appears deceptively similar to a regular subquery. The difference is that a regular subquery can be processed from the bottom up. In a regular subquery, results from the lowest query can be determined and then used to evaluate the upper-level queries. In contrast, in a correlated subquery, the processing is nested; that is, a row from an upper-level query statement is compared with rows in a lower-level query. The key distinction of a correlated subquery is that the lower-level SELECT statements use columns from upper-level statements.

The SQL EXISTS and NOT EXISTS keywords create specialized forms of correlated subqueries. When these are used, the upper-level query produces results, depending on the existence or nonexistence of rows in lower-level queries. An EXISTS condition is true if any row in the subquery meets the specified conditions; a NOT EXISTS condition is true only if all rows in the subquery do not meet the specified conditions. NOT EXISTS is useful for queries that involve conditions that must be true for all rows, such as a "customer who has purchased all products." The double use of NOT EXISTS is a famous SQL pattern that often is used to test a person's knowledge of SQL.

Before redesigning a database, the existing database needs to be carefully examined to avoid making the database unusable by partially processing a database change. The rule is to measure twice and cut once. Reverse engineering is used to create a data model of the existing database. This is done to better understand the database structure before proceeding with a change. The data model produced, called a reverse engineered (RE) data model, is not a true data model but is a thing unto itself. Most data modeling tools can perform reverse engineering. The RE data model almost always has missing information; such models should be carefully reviewed.

All of the elements of a database are interrelated. Dependency graphs are used to portray the dependency of one element on another. For example, a change in a table can potentially affect relationships, views, indexes, triggers, stored procedures, and application programs. These impacts need to be known and accounted for before making database changes.

A complete backup must be made to the operational database prior to any database redesign changes. Additionally, such changes must be thoroughly tested, initially on small test databases and later on larger test databases that may even be duplicates of the operational databases. The redesign changes are made only after such extensive testing has been completed.

Database redesign changes can be grouped into different types. One type involves changing table names and table columns. Changing a table name has a surprising number of potential consequences. A dependency graph should be used to understand these consequences before proceeding with the change. Nonkey columns are readily added and deleted. Adding a NOT NULL column must be done in three steps: first, add the column as NULL; then add data to every row; and then alter the column constraint to NOT NULL. To drop a column used as a foreign key, the foreign key constraint must first be dropped.

Column data types and constraints can be changed using the ALTER TABLE ALTER COLUMN statement. Changing the data type to Char or Varchar from a more specific type, such as Date, is usually not a problem. Changing a data type from Char or Varchar to a more specific type, however, can be a problem. In some cases, data will be lost or the DBMS may refuse the change.

Constraints can be added or dropped using the ADD CONSTRAINT and DROP CONSTRAINT with the SQL ALTER TABLE statement. Use of this statement is easier if the developers have provided their own names for all constraints.

Changing minimum cardinalities on the parent side of a relationship is simply a matter of altering the constraint on the foreign key from NULL to NOT NULL or from NOT NULL to NULL. Changing minimum cardinalities on the child side of a relationship can be accomplished only by adding or dropping triggers that enforce the constraint.

Changing maximum cardinality from 1:1 to 1:N is simple if the foreign key resides in the correct table. In that case, just remove the unique constraint on the foreign key column. If the foreign key resides in the wrong table for this change, move the foreign key to the other table and do not place a unique constraint on that table.

Changing a 1:N relationship to an N:M relationship requires building a new intersection table and moving the primary key and foreign key values to the intersection table. This aspect of the change is relatively simple. It is more difficult to change all of the views, triggers, stored procedures, application programs, and forms and reports to use the new intersection table.

Reducing cardinalities is easy, but such changes may result in data loss. Prior to making such reductions, a policy must be determined to decide which data to keep. Changing N:M to 1:N involves creating a foreign key in the child table and moving one value from the intersection table into that foreign key. Changing 1:N to 1:1 requires first eliminating duplicates in the foreign key and then setting a uniqueness constraint on that key. Adding and deleting relationships can be accomplished by defining new foreign key constraints or by dropping existing foreign key constraints.

Most data modeling tools have the capacity to perform forward engineering, which is the process of applying data model changes to an existing database. If forward engineering is used, the results should be thoroughly tested before using it on an operational database. Some tools will show the SQL that they will execute during the forward engineering process. Any SQL generated by such tools should be carefully reviewed. All in all, there is nothing wrong with writing database redesign SQL statements by hand rather than using forward engineering.

# Key Terms

| | | |
|---|---|---|
| correlated subquery | SQL EXISTS comparison operator | system maintenance |
| dependency graph | SQL NOT EXISTS comparison | systems analysis and design |
| reverse engineered (RE) data model | operator | systems development life cycle (SDLC) |

# Review Questions

**8.1** Review the three sources of database design and implementation.

**8.2** Describe why database redesign is necessary.

**8.3** Explain the following statement in your own words: "Information systems and organizations create each other." How does this relate to database redesign?

**8.4** Suppose that a table contains two nonkey columns: AdviserName and AdviserPhone. Further suppose that you suspect that AdviserPhone → AdviserName. Explain how to examine the data to determine if this supposition is true.

**8.5** Write a subquery, other than one in this chapter, that is not a correlated subquery.

**8.6** Explain the following statement: "The processing of correlated subqueries is nested, whereas that of regular subqueries is not."

**8.7** Write a correlated subquery, other than one in this chapter.

**8.8** Explain how the query in your answer to Review Question 8.5 differs from the query in your answer to Review Question 8.7.

**8.9** Explain what is wrong with the correlated subquery SQL-Query-CH08-03 on page 434.

**8.10** Write a correlated subquery to determine whether the data support the supposition in Review Question 8.4.

**8.11** Explain the meaning of the SQL EXISTS comparison operator.

**8.12** Answer Review Question 8.10, but use the SQL EXISTS comparison operator.

**8.13** Explain how the words *any* and *all* pertain to the SQL EXISTS and NOT EXISTS comparison operators.

**8.14** Explain the processing of SQL-Query-CH08-06 on page 436.

**8.15** Using the View Ridge Gallery database, write a query that will display the names of any customers who are interested in all artists.

**8.16** Explain how the query in your answer to Review Question 8.15 works.

**8.17** Why is it important to analyze the database before implementing database redesign tasks? What can happen if this is not done?

**8.18** Explain the process of reverse engineering.

**8.19** Why is it important to carefully evaluate the results of reverse engineering?

**8.20** What is a dependency graph? What purpose does it serve?

**8.21** Explain the dependencies for WORK in the graph in Figure 8-4.

**8.22** What sources are used when creating a dependency graph?

**8.23** Explain two different types of test databases that should be used when testing database redesign changes.

**8.24** Explain the problems that can occur when changing the name of a table.

**8.25** Describe the process of changing a table name.

**8.26** Considering Figure 8-4, describe the tasks that need to be accomplished to change the name of the table WORK to WORK_VERSION2.

**8.27** Explain how views can simplify the process of changing a table name.

**8.28** Under what conditions is the following SQL statement valid?

```
INSERT     INTO T1 (A, B)
     SELECT    (C, D)
     FROM      T2;
```

**8.29** Show an SQL statement to add an integer column C1 to the table T2. Assume that C1 is NULL.

**8.30** Extend your answer to Review Question 8.29 to add C1 when C1 is to be NOT NULL.

**8.31** Show an SQL statement to drop the column C1 from table T2.

**8.32** Describe the process for dropping primary key C1 and making the new primary key C2.

**8.33** Which data type changes are the least risky?

**8.34** Which data type changes are the most risky?

**8.35** Write an SQL statement to change a column C1 to Char(10) NOT NULL. What conditions must exist in the data for this change to be successful?

**8.36** Explain how to change the minimum cardinality when a child that was required to have a parent is no longer required to have one.

**8.37** Explain how to change the minimum cardinality when a child that was not required to have a parent is now required to have one. What condition must exist in the data for this change to work?

**8.38** Explain how to change the minimum cardinality when a parent that was required to have a child is no longer required to have one.

**8.39** Explain how to change the minimum cardinality when a parent that was not required to have a child is now required to have one.

**8.40** Describe how to change the maximum cardinality from 1:1 to 1:N. Assume that the foreign key is on the side of the new child in the 1:N relationship.

**8.41** Describe how to change the maximum cardinality from 1:1 to 1:N. Assume that the foreign key is on the side of the new parent in the 1:N relationship.

**8.42** Assume that tables T1 and T2 have a 1:1 relationship. Assume that T2 has the foreign key. Show the SQL statements necessary to move the foreign key to T1. Make up your own names for the primary and foreign keys.

**8.43** Explain how to transform a 1:N relationship into an N:M relationship.

**8.44** Suppose that tables T1 and T2 have a 1:N relationship. Show the SQL statements necessary to fill an intersection table named T1_T2_INT, in preparation to making the relationship N:M. Make up your own names for the primary and foreign keys.

**8.45** Explain how the reduction of maximum cardinalities causes data loss.

**8.46** Using the tables in your answer to Review Question 8.44, show the SQL statements necessary to change the relationship back to 1:N. Assume that the first row in the qualifying rows of the intersection table is to provide the foreign key. Use the keys and foreign keys from your answer to Review Question 8.44.

**8.47** Using the results of your answer to Review Question 8.46, explain what must be done to convert this relationship to 1:1. Use the keys and foreign keys from your answer to Review Question 8.46.

**8.48** In general terms, what must be done to add a new relationship?

**8.49** Suppose that tables T1 and T2 have a 1:N relationship, with T2 as the child. Show the SQL statements necessary to remove table T1. Make your own assumptions about the names of keys and foreign keys.

**8.50** What are the risks and problems of forward engineering?

# Exercises

**8.51** Suppose that the table EMPLOYEE has a 1:N relationship to the table PHONE_NUMBER. Further suppose that the primary key of EMPLOYEE is EmployeeID and the columns of PHONE_NUMBER are PhoneNumberID (a surrogate key), AreaCode, LocalNumber, and EmployeeID (a foreign key to EMPLOYEE). Alter this design so that EMPLOYEE has a 1:1 relationship to PHONE_NUMBER. For employees with more than one phone number, keep only the first one.

**8.52** Suppose that the table EMPLOYEE has a 1:N relationship to the table PHONE_NUMBER. Further suppose that the key of EMPLOYEE is EmployeeID and the columns of PHONE_NUMBER are PhoneNumberID (a surrogate key), AreaCode, LocalNumber, and EmployeeID (a foreign key to EMPLOYEE). Write all SQL statements necessary to redesign this database so that it has just one table. Explain the difference between the result of Project Question 8.51 and the result of this question.

**8.53** Consider the following table:

> TASK (EmployeeID, EmpLastName, EmpFirstName, Phone, OfficeNumber, ProjectName, Sponsor, WorkDate, HoursWorked)

Also consider the following possible functional dependencies:

> EmployeeID → (EmpLastName, EmpFirstName, Phone, OfficeNumber)
> ProjectName → Sponsor

**A.** Write SQL statements to display the values of any rows that violate these functional dependencies.

**B.** If no data violate these functional dependencies, can we assume that they are valid? Why or why not?

**C.** Assume that these functional dependencies are true and that the data have been corrected, as necessary, to reflect them. Write all SQL statements necessary to redesign this table into a set of tables in BCNF and 4NF. Assume that the table has data values that must be appropriately transformed to the new design.

# Case Questions

## Marcia's Dry Cleaning Case Questions

Marcia Wilson owns and operates Marcia's Dry Cleaning, which is an upscale dry cleaner in a well-to-do suburban neighborhood. Marcia makes her business stand out from the competition by providing superior customer service. She wants to keep track of each of her customers and their orders. Ultimately, she wants to notify them that their clothes are ready via email. Suppose that you have designed a database for Marcia's Dry Cleaning that has the following tables:

CUSTOMER (CustomerID, FirstName, LastName, Phone, EmailAddress)

INVOICE (InvoiceNumber, CustomerID, DateIn, DateOut, Subtotal, Tax, TotalAmount)

INVOICE_ITEM (InvoiceNumber, ItemNumber, ServiceID, Quantity, UnitPrice, ExtendedPrice)

SERVICE (ServiceID, ServiceDescription, UnitPrice)

Assume that all relationships have been defined, as implied by the foreign keys in this table list, and that the appropriate referential integrity constraints are in place. The referential integrity constraints are:

CustomerID in INVOICE must exist in CustomerID in CUSTOMER

InvoiceNumber in INVOICE_ITEM must exist in InvoiceNumber in INVOICE

ServiceID in INVOICE_ITEM must exist in ServiceID in SERVICE

Assume that CustomerID of CUSTOMER, EmployeeID of EMPLOYEE, ItemID of ITEM, SaleID of SALE, and SaleItemID of SALE_ITEM are all surrogate keys with values as follows:

| CustomerID | Start at 100 | Increment by 1 |
| InvoiceNumber | Start at 2021001 | Increment by 1 |

**A.** Create a dependency graph that shows dependencies among these tables. Explain how you need to extend this graph for views and other database constructs, such as triggers and stored procedures.

**B.** Using your dependency graph, describe the tasks necessary to change the name of the INVOICE table to CUST_INVOICE.

**C.** Write all SQL statements to make the name change described in part B.

**D.** Suppose that Marcia decides to allow multiple customers per order (e.g., for customers' spouses). Modify the design of these tables to accommodate this change.

**E.** Code SQL statements necessary to redesign the database, as described in your answer to part D.

**F.** Suppose that Marcia considers changing the primary key of CUSTOMER to (FirstName, LastName). Write correlated subqueries to display any data that indicate that this change is not justifiable.

**G.** Suppose that (FirstName, LastName) can be made the primary key of CUSTOMER. Make appropriate changes to the table design with this new primary key.

**H.** Code all SQL statements necessary to implement the changes described in part G.

# The Queen Anne Curiosity Shop Project Questions

Assume that the Queen Anne Curiosity Shop designs a database with the tables described at the end of Chapter 7:

**CUSTOMER** (**CustomerID**, LastName, FirstName, EmailAddress, EncryptedPassword, Address, City, State, ZIP, Phone, *ReferredBy*)

**EMPLOYEE** (**EmployeeID**, LastName, FirstName, Position, *Supervisor*, OfficePhone, EmailAddress)

**VENDOR** (**VendorID**, CompanyName, ContactLastName, ContactFirstName, Address, City, State, ZIP, Phone, Fax, EmailAddresss)

**ITEM** (**ItemID**, ItemDescription, PurchaseDate, ItemCost, ItemPrice, *VendorID*)

**SALE** (**SaleID**, *CustomerID*, *EmployeeID*, SaleDate, SubTotal, Tax, Total)

**SALE_ITEM** (*SaleID*, **SaleItemID**, *ItemID*, ItemPrice)

The referential integrity constraints are:

**ReferredBy in CUSTOMER must exist in CustomerID in CUSTOMER**

**Supervisor in EMPLOYEE must exist in EmployeeID in EMPLOYEE**

**CustomerID in SALE must exist in CustomerID in CUSTOMER**

**VendorID in ITEM must exist in VendorID in VENDOR**

**EmployeeID in SALE must exist in EmployeeID in EMPLOYEE**

**SaleID in SALE_ITEM must exist in SaleID in SALE**

**ItemID in SALE_ITEM must exist in ItemID in ITEM**

Assume that CustomerID of CUSTOMER, EmployeeID of EMPLOYEE, ItemID of ITEM, SaleID of SALE, and SaleItemID of SALE_ITEM are all surrogate keys with values as follows:

| | | |
|---|---|---|
| **CustomerID** | **Start at 1** | **Increment by 1** |
| **EmployeeID** | **Start at 1** | **Increment by 1** |
| **VendorID** | **Start at 1** | **Increment by 1** |
| **ItemID** | **Start at 1** | **Increment by 1** |
| **SaleID** | **Start at 1** | **Increment by 1** |

A vendor may be an individual or a company. If the vendor is an individual, the Company Name field is left blank, whereas the ContactLastName and ContactFirstName fields must have data values. If the vendor is a company, the company name is recorded in the CompanyName field, and the name of the primary contact at the company is recorded in the ContactLastName and ContactFirstName fields.

**If you want to run these solutions in a DBMS product, first create a version of the QACS database described in Chapter 7 and name it QACS_CH08.**

**A.** Create a dependency graph that shows dependencies among these tables. Explain how you need to extend this graph for views and other database constructs, such as triggers and stored procedures.

**B.** Using your dependency graph, describe the tasks necessary to change the name of the SALE table to CUSTOMER_SALE.

**C.** Write all SQL statements to make the name change described in part B.

**D.** Suppose that the Queen Anne Curiosity Shop owners decide to allow multiple customers per order (e.g., for customers' spouses). Modify the design of these tables to accommodate this change.

**E.** Code SQL statements necessary to redesign the database, as described in your answer to part D.

**F.** Suppose that the Queen Anne Curiosity Shop owners are considering changing the primary key of CUSTOMER to (FirstName, LastName). Write correlated subqueries to display any data that indicate that this change is not justifiable.

**G.** Suppose that (FirstName, LastName) can be made the primary key of CUSTOMER. Make appropriate changes to the table design with this new primary key.

**H.** Code all SQL statements necessary to implement the changes described in part G.

# Morgan Importing Project Questions

Assume that Morgan has created a database with the tables described at the end of Chapter 7 (note that STORE uses the surrogate key StoreID):

**EMPLOYEE (EmployeeID, LastName, FirstName, Department, Position, *Supervisor*, OfficePhone, OfficeFax, EmailAddress)**

**STORE (StoreID, StoreName, City, Country, Phone, Fax, EmailAddress, Contact)**

**PURCHASE_ITEM (PurchaseItemID, *StoreID*, *PurchasingAgentID*, PurchaseDate, ItemDescription, Category, PriceUSD)**

**SHIPMENT** (<u>ShipmentID</u>, *ShipperID*, *PurchasingAgentID*, **ShipperInvoiceNumber,**
**Origin, Destination, ScheduledDepartureDate, ActualDepartureDate,**
**EstimatedArrivalDate)**

**SHIPMENT_ITEM** (<u>ShipmentID</u>, <u>ShipmentItemID</u>, *PurchaseItemID*, **InsuredValue)**

**SHIPPER** (<u>ShipperID</u>, **ShipperName, Phone, Fax, Email, Contact)**

**SHIPMENT_RECEIPT** (<u>ReceiptNumber</u>, *ShipmentID*, *PurchaseItemID*,
*ReceivingAgent*, **ReceiptDate, ReceiptTime, ReceiptQuantity,**
**isReceivedUndamaged, DamageNotes)**

Assume that all relationships have been defined as implied by the foreign keys in this table list. The referential integrity constraints are:

**Supervisor in EMPLOYEE must exist in EmployeeID in EMPLOYEE**

**StoreID in PURCHASE_ITEM must exist in StoreID in STORE**

**PurchasingAgentID in PURCHASE_ITEM must exist in EmployeeID in EMPLOYEE**

**ShipperID in SHIPMENT must exist in ShipperID in SHIPPER**

**PurchasingAgentID in SHIPMENT must exist in EmployeeID in EMPLOYEE**

**PurchaseItemID in SHIPMENT_ITEM must exist in PurchaseItemID in**
**PURCHASE_ITEM**

**ShipmentID in SHIPMENT_RECEIPT must exist in ShipmentID in SHIPMENT**

**PurchaseItemID in SHIPMENT_RECEIPT must exist in PurchaseItemID in**
**PURCHASE_ITEM**

**ReceivingAgentID in SHIPMENT_RECEIPT must exist in EmployeeID in**
**EMPLOYEE**

Assume that EmployeeID of EMPLOYEE, PurchaseItemID of PURCHASE_ITEM, ShipperID of SHIPPER, ShipmentID of SHIPMENT, and ReceiptNumber of SHIPMENT_RECEIPT are all surrogate keys with values as follows:

| | | |
|---|---|---|
| **Store ID** | **Start at 100** | **Increment by 50** |
| **EmployeeID** | **Start at 101** | **Increment by 1** |
| **PurhaseItemID** | **Start at 500** | **Increment by 5** |
| **ShipperID** | **Start at 1** | **Increment by 1** |
| **ShipmentID** | **Start at 100** | **Increment by 1** |
| **ReceiptNumber** | **Start at 200001** | **Increment by 1** |

Values of the Country column in the STORE table are restricted to: Hong Kong, India, Japan, Peru, Philippines, Singapore, and United States.

James Morgan wants to modify the database design of the Morgan Importing procurement information system (MIPIS) to separate the items in PURCHASE_ITEM in a separate table named ITEM. This will allow each item to be tracked as a unique entity throughout its acquisition and sale. The schema for the ITEM table is:

**ITEM** (<u>ItemID</u>, **ItemDescription, Category)**

PURCHASE_ITEM will then be replaced by two tables named INVOICE and INVOICE_LINE_ITEM, linked in a modified sales order configuration as shown in Figure 8-7. (Compare this figure to Figure 6-18(b).)

Similarly, the shipping part of the MIPIS will be modified by changes to the SHIPMENT_ITEM tables as follows:

**SHIPMENT_LINE_ITEM** (<u>ShipmentID</u>, <u>ShipmentLineNumber</u>, *ItemID*,
**InsuredValue)**

**FIGURE 8-7**

The Morgan Importing MIPIS
Modified SALES_ORDER
Configuration

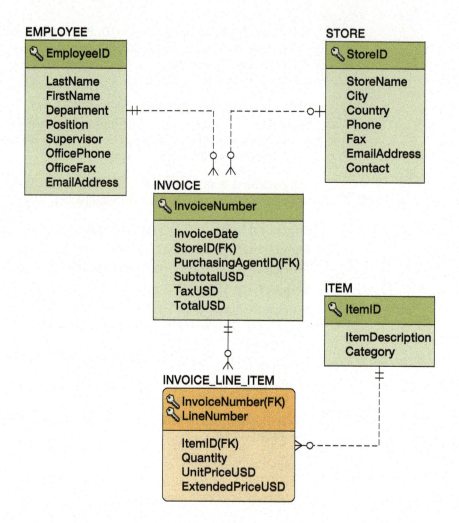

If you want to run these solutions in a DBMS product, first create a version of the MI database described in Chapter 7 and name it MI_CH08.

**A.** Create a dependency graph that shows dependencies among the original set of tables. Explain how you need to extend this graph for views and other database constructs, such as stored procedures.

**B.** Using your dependency graph, describe the tasks necessary to create and populate the ITEM table.

**C.** Write all SQL statements to make the name change described in part B.

**D.** Using your dependency graph, describe the tasks necessary to change the name of the SHIPMENT_ITEM table to SHIPMENT_LINE_ITEM and the needed changes to column names.

**E.** Write all SQL statements to make the name change described in part D.

**F.** Using your dependency graph, describe the tasks necessary to convert the sales order component of the MIPIS to the new configuration.

**G.** Code SQL statements to implement your redesign recommendations in your answer to part F.

# Enterprise Database Processing

The six chapters in Part 4 introduce and discuss the major problems of enterprise and multiuser database processing and describe the features and functions for solving those problems offered by four important DBMS products. We begin in Chapter 9 with a description of database administration and the major tasks and techniques for enterprise and multiuser database management. In Chapter 10, we introduce the topics that are covered in detail in online Chapters 10A, 10B, 10C, and 10D, which are the four chapters that discuss and illustrate the features and functions of Microsoft SQL Server 2019, Oracle Database, MySQL 8.0, and ArangoDB, respectively.

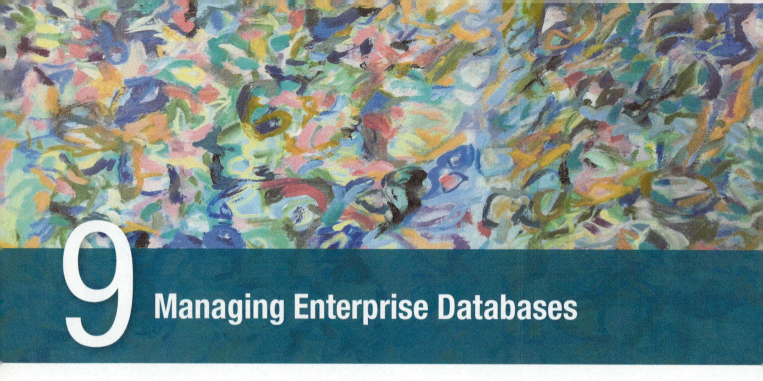

# 9 Managing Enterprise Databases

## Chapter Objectives

- To understand the need for and importance of database administration
- To understand the need for concurrency control, security, backup, and recovery
- To learn about typical problems that can occur when multiple users process a database concurrently
- To understand the use of locking and the problem of deadlock
- To learn the difference between optimistic and pessimistic locking
- To know the meaning of an ACID transaction
- To learn the four ANSI standard isolation levels

- To learn different ways of processing a database using cursors
- To understand the need for security and specific tasks for improving database security
- To know the difference between recovery via reprocessing and recovery via rollback/rollforward
- To understand the nature of the tasks required for recovery using rollback/rollforward
- To know basic administrative and managerial DBA functions
- To learn some of the basic terms and concepts involved in physical database design and query optimization

**Although enterprise databases** offer great value to the organizations that create and use them, they also pose difficult problems for those same organizations. For one, multiuser enterprise databases are complicated to design and develop because they support many overlapping user views.

Additionally, as discussed in the previous chapter, requirements change over time, and those changes necessitate other changes to the database structure. Such structural changes must be carefully planned and controlled so that a change made for one group does not cause problems for another. In addition, when users process a database concurrently, special controls are needed to ensure that the actions of one user do not inappropriately influence the results for another. This topic is both important and complicated, as you will see.

In large organizations, processing rights and responsibilities need to be defined and enforced. What happens, for example, when an employee leaves the firm? When can the employee's records be deleted? For the purposes of payroll processing, records can be deleted after the last pay period. For the purposes of quarterly reporting, they can be deleted at the end of the quarter. For the purposes of end-of-year tax record processing, they can be deleted at the end of the year. Clearly, no department can unilaterally decide when to delete that data. Similar comments pertain to the insertion and changing of data values. For these and other reasons, security systems need to be developed that enable only authorized users to take authorized actions at authorized times.

Databases have become key components of organizational operations and even key components of an organization's value. Unfortunately, database failures and disasters do occur. Thus, effective backup and recovery plans, techniques, and procedures are essential.

Finally, over time, the DBMS itself will need to be changed to improve performance by incorporating new features and releases and to conform to changes made in the underlying operating system. Similarly, specific databases will need to be tuned for performance over time as data and requirements change. All of this requires attentive management.

To ensure that these problems are addressed and solved, most organizations have a database administration office. We begin with a description of the tasks of that office. We then describe the combination of software and manual practices and procedures that are used to perform those tasks.

## The Importance of Working with an Installed DBMS Product

In order to fully understand the DBMS concepts and features we discuss and illustrate in the chapter, you need to work with them in an installed DBMS product. This *hands-on* experience is necessary so that you move from an abstract understanding of these concepts and features to a practical knowledge of them and how they are used and implemented. The information you need to download, install, and use the relational DBMS products discussed in this book is in Chapter 10 (introduction to the DBMS products), Chapter 10A (Microsoft SQL Server 2019), Chapter 10B (Oracle Database), and Chapter 10C (MySQL 8.0). ArangoDB, covered in Chapter 10D, also illustrates many of these topics, but they are best initially learned in a relational setting. Portions of these chapters parallel the discussion in this chapter and illustrate the actual use of the concepts and features in each DBMS product.

To get the most out of this chapter, you should download and install the DBMS product(s) of your choice and then follow along as you work in each section of this chapter by working thorough the corresponding sections of the chapter for your relational DBMS product.

## Database Administration

The terms **data administration** and **database administration** are both used in practice. In some cases, the terms are considered to be synonymous; in other cases, they have different meanings. Most commonly, the term *data administration* refers to a function that applies to an entire organization; it is a management-oriented function that concerns corporate data privacy and security issues. In contrast, the term *database administration* refers to a more technical function that is specific to a particular database, including the applications that process that database. This chapter addresses database administration.

Databases vary considerably in size and scope, ranging from single-user personal databases to large interorganizational databases, such as airline reservation systems. All of these databases have a need for database administration, though the tasks to be accomplished vary in complexity. For personal databases, individuals follow simple procedures for backing up their data, and they keep minimal records for documentation. In this case, the person who uses the database also performs the database administration functions, even though he or she is probably unaware of it.

For enterprise and multiuser database applications, database administration becomes both more important and more difficult. Consequently, it generally has formal recognition. For some applications, one or two people are given this function on a part-time basis. For large Internet or intranet databases, database administration responsibilities are often too time-consuming and too varied to be handled even by a single full-time person. Supporting a database with dozens or hundreds of users requires considerable time as well as both technical knowledge and diplomatic skills. Such support usually is handled by an office of database administration. The manager of the office is often known as the **database administrator**. In this case, the acronym **DBA** refers to either the office or the manager. DBAs usually coordinate with the organization's systems programming staff in installing new versions of the DBMS and applying maintenance fixes from the vendor. The overall responsibility of the DBA is to facilitate the development and use of the database. Usually, this means balancing the conflicting goals of protecting the database and maximizing its availability and benefit to users. Specific tasks are shown in Figure 9-1. We consider each of these tasks in the following sections.

## Managing the Database Structure

Managing the database structure includes participating in the initial database design and implementation as well as controlling and managing changes to the database. Ideally, the DBA is involved early in the development of the database and its applications; participates in the requirements study; helps evaluate alternatives, including the DBMS to be used; and helps design the database structure. For large organizational applications, the DBA usually is a manager who supervises the work of technically oriented database design personnel.

Creating the database involves several different tasks. First, the database is created and disk space is allocated for database files and logs. Then tables are generated, indexes are created, and stored procedures and triggers are written. We will discuss examples of all of these tasks in the next five chapters. Once the database structures are created, the database is filled with data.

### Configuration Control

After a database and its applications have been implemented, changes in requirements are inevitable, as described in Chapter 8. Such changes can arise from new needs, from changes in the business environment, from changes in policy, and from changes in business processes that evolve with system use. When changes to requirements necessitate changes

**FIGURE 9-1**

Summary of Database Administration Tasks

| Summary of Database Administration Tasks |
|---|
| Manage database structure |
| Control concurrent processing |
| Manage processing rights and responsibilities |
| Develop database security |
| Provide for database recovery |
| Manage the DBMS |
| Maintain the data repository |

to the database structure, great care must be used because changes to the database structure seldom involve just one application.

Hence, effective database administration includes procedures and policies by which users can register their needs for changes, the entire database community can discuss the impacts of the changes, and a global decision can be made whether to implement proposed changes. Because of the size and complexity of a database and its applications, changes sometimes have unexpected results. Thus, the DBA must be prepared to repair the database and to gather sufficient information to diagnose and correct the problem that caused the damage. The database is most vulnerable to failure after its structure has been changed.

### Documentation

The DBA's final responsibility in managing the database structure is documentation. It is extremely important to know what changes have been made, how they were made, and when they were made. A change in the database structure may cause an error that is not revealed for six months; without proper documentation of the change, diagnosing the problem is next to impossible. Considerable work may be required to identify the point at which certain symptoms first appeared. For this reason, it also is important to maintain a record of the test procedures and test runs made to verify a change. If standardized test procedures, test forms, and recordkeeping methods are used, recording the test results does not have to be time-consuming.

Although maintaining documentation is tedious and unfulfilling, the effort pays off when disaster strikes and the documentation is the difference between a quick problem solution and a confused muddle of activity. Today, several products are emerging that ease the burden of documentation. Many **computer-aided software engineering (CASE)** tools, for example, can be used to document logical database designs. Version-control software can be used to track changes. Data dictionaries provide reports and other outputs that present database data structures.

Another reason for carefully documenting changes in the database structure is so that historical data are used properly. If, for example, marketing wants to analyze three-year-old sales data that have been in the archives for two years, it will be necessary to know what structure was current at the time the data were last active. Records that show the changes in the structure can be used to answer that question. A similar situation arises when a six-month-old backup copy of data must be used to repair a damaged database. (Although this should not happen, it sometimes does.) The backup copy can be used to reconstruct the database to the state it was in at the time of the backup. Then transactions and structural changes can be made in chronological order to restore the database to its current state. Figure 9-2 summarizes the DBA's responsibilities for managing the database structure.

**FIGURE 9-2**

Summary of DBA's Responsibilities for Managing Database Structure

| Participate in Database and Application Development |
|---|
| Assist in the requirements analysis stage and data model creation |
| Play an active role in database design and creation |
| **Facilitate Changes to Database Structure** |
| Seek communitywide solutions |
| Assess impact on all users |
| Provide configuration control forum |
| Be prepared for problems after changes are made |
| Maintain documentation |

## Physical Database Design and Optimization

Another important consideration for DBAs involves the efficient performance of the DBMS. One basic concept here is that of the **index**, a secondary structure that can speed up access to data for certain types of queries. As an example, if queries requesting employee data based on an employee's name are common, then an index on the EMPLOYEE.Name field could speed up such queries by one or more orders of magnitude (see SQL-Code-Example-CH-09-11). An index is one component of what is called **physical database design**. Other aspects of physical database design include DBA decisions about database usage of primary memory and the sizes of blocks of data that are read into main memory from secondary memory; the DBA must have a good understanding of the relative sizes and speeds of primary and secondary memory in order to create the best physical database design. A DBA may also be able to influence the amount of replication of data; common data storage techniques include **disk mirroring** (maintaining two copies of the data so a disk failure need not result in unavailable data) and various forms of **redundant arrays of independent disks (RAID)** storage, which take advantage of using multiple disks to store a single database, using combinations of duplication of data and spreading data among several disks.

In addition to physical database design issues, which mostly involve a static picture of the database, the DBA must pay careful attention to the performance of specific queries as the database evolves. Every enterprise DBMS has a component called a **query optimizer**, which will evaluate several potential ways to execute a query and will execute the one with the lowest expected execution time. The optimizer will look at things such as different ways of joining several tables (e.g., should we join tables A and B and then join the result to C, or should we join B and C first and then join the result to A?), which algorithm to use to compute a join (there are several), whether to use an existing index to speed up a query, and so on. This all happens automatically, but the DBA can greatly influence the choices available to the optimizer. As a database changes over time, the DBA might decide to create a new index, delete an existing index, alter the amount of memory used by the DBMS, help the query optimizer by providing it with some hints, and so on. The details of physical database design and query processing/optimization are beyond the scope of this book, but it is important to know that these issues can be crucial for the DBA of a large enterprise database. Online Appendix F contains more coverage of physical database design, including file and data structures, and an introduction to multicolumn indexes, clustering, and decomposition techniques for enhancing DBMS performance.

# Concurrency Control

Concurrency control measures are taken to ensure that one user's work does not inappropriately influence another user's work. In some cases, these measures ensure that a user gets the same result when processing with other users that he or she would have received if processing alone. In other cases, it means that the user's work is influenced by other users but in an anticipated way. For example, in an order entry system, a user should be able to enter an order and get the same result, regardless of whether there are no other users or hundreds of other users. In contrast, a user who is printing a report of the most current inventory status may want to obtain in-process data changes from other users, even if there is a danger that those changes may later be canceled.

Unfortunately, no concurrency control technique or mechanism is ideal for every circumstance. All involve trade-offs. For example, a program can obtain very strict concurrency control by locking the entire database, but no other programs will be able to do anything while it runs. This is strict protection, but at a high cost. As you will see, other measures are available that are more difficult to program or enforce but that allow more throughput. Still other measures are available that maximize throughput but have a low level of concurrency control. When designing multiuser database applications, you will need to choose among these trade-offs.

## The Need for Atomic Transactions

In most database applications, users submit work in the form of **transactions**, which are also known as **logical units of work (LUW)**. A transaction (or LUW) is a series of actions to be taken on the database so that either all of them are performed successfully or none of them is performed at all, in which case the database remains unchanged. Such a transaction is sometimes called **atomic** because it is performed as a unit.

Consider the following sequence of database actions that could occur when recording a new order:

1. Change a customer's row, increasing AmountDue.
2. Change a salesperson's row, increasing CommissionDue.
3. Insert a new order row into the database.

Suppose that the last step failed, perhaps because of insufficient file space. Imagine the confusion if the first two changes were made but the third one was not. The customer would be billed for an order they never received, and a salesperson would receive a commission on an order that was never sent to the customer. Clearly, these three actions need to be taken as a unit—either all of them should be done or none of them should be done.

Figure 9-3 compares the results of performing these activities as a series of independent steps (Figure 9-3(a)) and as an atomic transaction (Figure 9-3(b)). Notice that when the steps are carried out atomically and one fails, no changes are made in the database. Also note that the commands Start Transaction, Commit Transaction, and Rollback Transaction are issued by the application program to mark the boundaries of the transaction logic. You will learn more about these commands later in this chapter and in Chapters 10A, 10B, 10C, and 10D.

### Concurrent Transaction Processing

When two transactions are being processed against a database at the same time, they are termed **concurrent transactions**. Although it may appear to the users that concurrent transactions are being processed simultaneously, this cannot be true because the CPU of the machine processing the database can execute only one instruction at a time. Even newer multi-core CPUs are limited in how transactions are processed because only a few **threads** (the smallest sequence of instructions that can be run at a time) can be run concurrently. Usually, transactions are interleaved, which means that the operating system switches CPU services among tasks so that some portion of each transaction is carried out in a given interval. This switching among tasks is done so quickly that two people seated at browsers side by side, processing the same database, may believe that their two transactions are completed simultaneously; in reality, however, the two transactions are interleaved.

Figure 9-4 shows two concurrent transactions. User A's transaction reads Item 100, changes it, and rewrites it in the database. User B's transaction takes the same actions but on Item 200. The CPU processes User A's transactions until it encounters an I/O interrupt or some other delay for User A. The operating system (or DBMS) shifts control to User B. The CPU now processes User B's transactions until an interrupt, at which point the operating system passes control back to User A. To the users, the processing appears to be simultaneous, but it is interleaved, or concurrent.

### The Lost Update Problem

The concurrent processing illustrated in Figure 9-4 poses no problems because the users are processing different data. But suppose that both users want to process Item 100. For example, User A wants to order five units of Item 100, and User B wants to order three units of the same item. Figure 9-5 illustrates the problem.

User A reads a copy of Item 100's record into memory. According to the record, there are 10 items in inventory. Then User B reads another copy of Item 100's record into a different section of memory. Again, according to the record, there are 10 items in inventory. Now User A takes five, decrements the count of items in its copy of the data to five, and rewrites the record for Item 100. Then User B takes three, decrements the count in its copy of the data to seven, and rewrites the record for Item 100. The database now shows, incorrectly, that there

(a) Errors Introduced Without Transaction

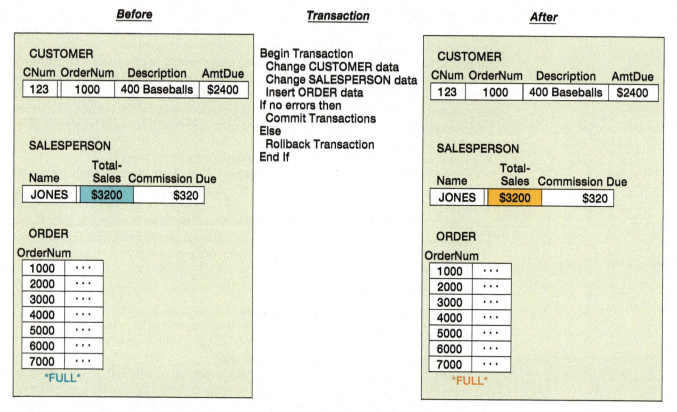

(b) Atomic Transaction Prevents Errors

**FIGURE 9-3**

Transaction Processing
Example

**FIGURE 9-4**

Concurrent-Processing
Example

**User A**

1. Read item 100.
2. Change item 100.
3. Write item 100.

**User B**

1. Read item 200.
2. Change item 200.
3. Write item 200.

**Order of processing at database server**

1. Read item 100 for A.
2. Read item 200 for B.
3. Change item 100 for A.
4. Write item 100 for A.
5. Change item 200 for B.
6. Write item 200 for B.

are seven Item 100s in inventory. To review: we started with 10 in inventory, User A took 5, User B took 3, and the database shows that 7 are in inventory. Clearly, this is a problem.

Both users obtained data that were correct at the time they obtained them. But when User B read the record, User A already had a copy that it was about to update. This situation is called the **lost update problem** or the **concurrent update problem**. A similar problem is the **inconsistent read problem**. With this problem, User A reads data that have been processed by a portion of a transaction from User B. As a result, User A reads incorrect data.

One remedy for the inconsistencies caused by concurrent processing is to prevent multiple applications from obtaining copies of the same record when the record is about to be changed. This remedy is called **resource locking**.

## Resource Locking

One way to prevent concurrent processing problems is to disallow sharing by locking data that are retrieved for update. Figure 9-6 shows the order of processing using a **lock** command.

**FIGURE 9-5**

Lost Update Problem

**User A**

1. Read item 100
   (item count is 10).
2. Reduce count of items by 5.
3. Write item 100.

**User B**

1. Read item 100
   (item count is 10).
2. Reduce count of items by 3.
3. Write item 100.

**Order of processing at database server**

1. Read item 100 (for A).
2. Read item 100 (for B).
3. Set item count to 5 (for A).
4. Write item 100 for A.
5. Set item count to 7 (for B).
6. Write item 100 for B.

Note: The change and write in steps 3 and 4 are lost.

**FIGURE 9-6**

Concurrent Processing with
Explicit Locks

User A

1. Lock item 100.
2. Read item 100.
3. Reduce count by 5.
4. Write item 100.

User B

1. Lock item 100.
2. Read item 100.
3. Reduce count by 3.
4. Write item 100.

Order of processing at database server

A's transaction

1. Lock item 100 for A.
2. Read item 100 for A.
3. Lock item 100 for B; cannot,
   so place B in wait state.
4. Set item count to 5 for A.
5. Write item 100 for A.
6. Release A's lock on item 100.

B's transaction

7. Place lock on item 100 for B.
8. Read item 100 for B.
9. Set item count to 2 for B.
10. Write item 100 for B.
11. Release B's lock on item 100.

Because of the lock, User B's transaction must wait until User A is finished with the Item 100 data. Using this strategy, User B can read Item 100's record only after User A has completed the modification. In this case, the final item count stored in the database is two, as it should be. (We started with 10, User A took 5, and User B took 3, leaving 2.)

### Lock Terminology

Locks can be placed either automatically by the DBMS or by a command issued to the DBMS from the application program. Locks placed by the DBMS are called **implicit locks**, and those placed by command are called **explicit locks**. Today, almost all locking is implicit. The program declares the behavior it wants, and the DBMS places locks accordingly. You will learn how to do that later in this chapter.

In the preceding example, the locks were applied to rows of data. Not all locks are applied at this level, however. Some DBMS products lock groups of rows within a table, some lock entire tables, and some lock the entire database. The size of a lock is referred to as **lock granularity**. Locks with large granularity are easy for the DBMS to administer but frequently cause conflicts. Locks with small granularity are difficult to administer (the DBMS has to track and check many more details), but conflicts are less common.

Locks also vary by type. An **exclusive lock** locks the item from any other access. No other transaction can read or change the data. A **shared lock** locks the item from change but not from read; that is, other transactions can read the item as long as they do not attempt to alter it.

### Serializable Transactions

When two or more transactions are processed concurrently, the results in the database should be logically consistent with the results that would have been achieved had the transactions been processed in an arbitrary, serial fashion. A scheme for processing concurrent transactions in this way is said to be **serializable**.

Serializability can be achieved by a number of different means. One way is to process the transaction using **two-phase locking**. With this strategy, transactions are allowed to obtain locks as necessary, but once the first lock is released, no other lock can be obtained. Transactions thus have a **growing phase**, during which the locks are obtained, and a **shrinking phase**, during which the locks are released. A special case of two-phase locking is used with a number of DBMS products. With it, locks are obtained throughout the transaction, but no lock is released until the COMMIT or ROLLBACK command is issued. This strategy is more restrictive than two-phase locking requires, but it is easier to implement. This is known as **strict two-phase locking**.

Consider an order-entry transaction that processes data in the CUSTOMER, SALES-PERSON, and ORDER tables. To avoid concurrency problems, the order entry transaction issues locks on CUSTOMER, SALESPERSON, and ORDER as needed; makes all database changes; and then releases all locks.

### Deadlock

Although locking solves one problem, it introduces another. Consider what can happen when two users want to order two items from inventory. Suppose that User A wants to order some paper, and if she can get the paper, she wants to order some pencils. Then suppose that User B wants to order some pencils, and if he can get the pencils, he wants to order some paper. The order of processing is shown in Figure 9-7.

In this figure, Users A and B are locked in a condition known as **deadlock** or sometimes as the **deadly embrace**. Each user is waiting for a resource that the other has locked. This problem can be solved either by preventing the deadlock from occurring or by allowing the deadlock to occur and then breaking it.

Deadlock can be prevented in several ways. One way is to require users to issue all lock requests at one time. In Figure 9-7, if User A had locked both the paper and the pencil records at the beginning, deadlock would not occur. A second way to prevent deadlock is to require all application programs to lock resources in the same order.

> **BY THE WAY**   Even if all the applications do not lock resources in the same order, dead-lock will be prevented for those that do. Sometimes this policy is implemented with an organizational programming standard such as "Whenever processing rows from tables in a parent–child relationship, lock the parent row before the child rows." This policy will at least reduce the likelihood of deadlock and thus save the DBMS from having to recover from some deadlocked transactions.

Almost every DBMS has algorithms for breaking deadlock when it does occur. First, the DBMS must detect that it has occurred. Then the typical solution is to cancel one of the transactions and remove its changes from the database. You will see variants of this with Microsoft SQL Server, Oracle Database, MySQL, and ArangoDB in the next five chapters.

**FIGURE 9-7**

**Deadlock Example**

User A
1. Lock paper.
2. Take paper.
3. Lock pencils.

User B
1. Lock pencils.
2. Take pencils.
3. Lock paper.

Order of processing at database server

1. Lock paper for user A.
2. Lock pencils for user B.
3. Process A's requests; write paper record.
4. Process B's requests; write pencil record.
5. Put A in wait state for pencils.
6. Put B in wait state for paper.
   ** Deadlocked **

## Optimistic Versus Pessimistic Locking

Locks can be invoked in two basic styles. With **optimistic locking**, the assumption is made that no conflict will occur. Data are read, the transaction is processed, updates are issued, and then a check is made to see if conflict occurred. If not, the transaction is finished. If conflict did occur, the transaction is repeated until it processes with no conflict. With **pessimistic locking**, the assumption is made that conflict will occur. Locks are issued, the transaction is processed, and then the locks are freed.

Figures 9-8 and 9-9 show examples of each style for a transaction that is reducing the quantity of the pencil row in PRODUCT by 5. (The code in these statements is **pseudo code**, which means that the code, while closely resembling Microsoft SQL Server T-SQL, is *not* written in an actual programming language and is, rather, designed to simply illustrate the code elements that are needed for the actions covered by the code.) Figure 9-8 shows optimistic locking. First, the data are read, and the current value of Quantity of pencils is saved in the variable varOldQuantity. The transaction is then processed, and assuming that all is OK, an SQL statement is issued to update the pencil row to a Quantity equal to varNewQuantity with a WHERE condition that the current value of Quantity equals varOldQuantity. If no other transaction has changed the Quantity of the pencil row, then this UPDATE will be successful. If another transaction has changed the Quantity of the pencil row, the UPDATE will fail. If the transaction failed, the process is repeated until the transaction finishes with no conflict. Notice that no locking occurs in this process. *Optimistic locking,* despite being a widely used term, is somewhat of a misnomer and is often referred to as **optimistic concurrency control** instead to avoid this confusion.

Figure 9-9 shows the logic for the same transaction using pessimistic locking. Here a lock is obtained on PRODUCT (in fact, the lock might be only for the pencil row, or it might be at a larger level of granularity, but the principle is the same) before any work is begun. Then values are read, the transaction is processed, the UPDATE occurs, and PRODUCT is unlocked.

The advantage of optimistic locking is that locks are not required. If few conflicts are expected (i.e., if it will be rare for two transactions to be changing the same data at the same time), then the database will be very efficient as the overhead of locking is avoided. The disadvantage of optimistic locking is that if there is a lot of activity on the pencil row, the transaction may have to be repeated many times. Thus, transactions that involve a lot of activity on a given row (purchasing a popular stock, for example) are poorly suited for optimistic locking.

In general, the Internet is a wild and woolly place, and users are likely to take unexpected actions, such as abandoning transactions in the middle. So unless Internet users have

**FIGURE 9-8**

**Optimistic Locking**

```
/* *** EXAMPLE CODE - DO NOT RUN   *** */
/* *** !!! This is pseudo code !!! *** */
/* *** SQL-Code-Example-CH09-01    *** */

SELECT   varOldQuantity = PRODUCT.Quantity
FROM     PRODUCT
WHERE    PRODUCT.ProductName = 'Pencil';

SET      varNewQuantity = varOldQuantity - 5;

-- Process transaction - take exception action if varNewQuantity < 0, etc.

-- Assuming all is OK:

UPDATE   PRODUCT
         SET    PRODUCT.Quantity = varNewQuantity
         WHERE  PRODUCT.ProductName = 'Pencil'
            AND PRODUCT.Quantity = varOldQuantity;

-- Check to see if update was successful - IF NOT, repeat transaction.
```

**FIGURE 9-9**

**Pessimistic Locking**

```
/* *** EXAMPLE CODE - DO NOT RUN   *** */
/* *** !!! This is pseudo code !!! *** */
/* *** SQL-Code-Example-CH09-02   *** */

LOCK      PRODUCT EXCLUSIVE MODE;

SELECT    varOldQuantity = PRODUCT.Quantity
FROM      PRODUCT
WHERE     PRODUCT.ProductName = 'Pencil';

SET       varNewQuantity = varOldQuantity - 5;

-- Process transaction - take exception action if varNewQuantity < 0, etc.

-- Assuming all is OK:

UPDATE    PRODUCT
          SET     PRODUCT.Quantity = varNewQuantity
          WHERE   PRODUCT.ProductName = 'Pencil'
            AND   PRODUCT.Quantity = varOldQuantity;


UNLOCK    PRODUCT;

-- No need to check to see if update was successful.
```

been prequalified (by enrolling in an online brokerage stock purchase plan, for example), optimistic locking is the better choice in that environment. On intranets, however, the decision is more difficult. Optimistic locking is probably still preferred for many intranet applications unless some characteristic of the application causes substantial activity on particular data or if application requirements make reprocessing transactions particularly undesirable. In the more specialized DBMS environment, however, nearly all enterprise-class DBMSs use primarily pessimistic locking approaches to concurrency control. Microsoft SQL Server provides a mechanism called row versioning to achieve optimistic concurrency control, but by default concurrency is implemented using (pessimistic) locking, Locking is also the default mode of operation in Oracle and MySQL, though it is possible to implement optimistic methods in these systems. ArangoDB uses pessimistic locking for concurrency control.

### SQL Transaction Control Language and Declaring Lock Characteristics

As you can see, concurrency control is a complicated subject; determining the level, type, and placement of the lock is difficult. Sometimes, too, the optimal locking strategy depends on which transactions are active and what they are doing. For these and other reasons, database application programs do not generally explicitly issue locks as shown in Figures 9-8 and 9-9. Instead, they mark transaction boundaries using **SQL Transaction Control Language (TCL)** and then declare the type of locking behavior they want the DBMS to use. In this way, the DBMS can place and remove locks and even change the level and type of locks dynamically.

Figure 9-10 shows the pencil transaction (again in pseudo code) with transaction boundaries marked with the SQL TCL standard commands for controlling transactions:

- The **SQL BEGIN TRANSACTION statement**
- The **SQL COMMIT TRANSACTION statement**
- The **SQL ROLLBACK TRANSACTION statement**

The SQL BEGIN TRANSACTION statement explicitly marks the start of a new transaction, whereas the SQL COMMIT TRANSACTION statement makes any database changes made by the transaction permanent and marks the end of the transaction. If there is a need to undo the changes made during the transaction due to an error in the process, the SQL

During that time, other transactions may attempt to update the AreaCode or ZIPCode fields of CUSTOMER. If the SQL statement is consistent, such update requests will be disallowed. Hence, the update shown in SQL-UPDATE-CH09-03 will apply to the set of rows as they existed at the time the SQL statement started. Such consistency is called **statement-level consistency**.

Now consider a transaction (SQL-Code-Example-CH09-04) that contains two SQL UPDATE statements as part (possibly with other transaction actions) of a transaction marked by SQL transaction boundaries:

```
/* *** EXAMPLE CODE - DO NOT RUN *** */
/* *** SQL-Code-Example-CH09-04 *** */
BEGIN TRANSACTION;
    /* *** SQL-UPDATE-CH09-03 *** */
    UPDATE   CUSTOMER
        SET      AreaCode = '425'
        WHERE    ZIPCode = '98050';
    -- Other transaction work
    /* *** SQL-UPDATE-CH09-04 *** */
    UPDATE   CUSTOMER
        SET      Discount = 0.05
        WHERE    AreaCode = '425';
    -- Other transaction work
COMMIT TRANSACTION;
```

In this context, what does *consistent* mean? Statement-level consistency means that each statement independently processes rows consistently but that changes from other users to these rows might be allowed during the interval between the two SQL statements. **Transaction-level consistency** means that all rows affected by either of the SQL statements are protected from changes during the entire transaction.

Observe that transaction-level consistency is so strong that for some implementations of it, a transaction will not see its own changes. In this example, the SQL statement SQL-Update-CH09-04 may not see rows changed by the SQL statement SQL-Update-CH09-03.

Thus, when you hear the term *consistent*, look further to determine which type of consistency is meant. Be aware as well of the potential trap of transaction-level consistency.

## Transaction Isolation Level

The term *isolated* has several different meanings. To understand those meanings, we need first to define several new terms that describe various problems that can occur when we read data from a database, which are summarized in Figure 9-11.

- A **dirty read** occurs when a transaction reads a row that has been changed but for which the change has not yet been committed to the database. The danger of a dirty read is that the uncommitted change can be rolled back. If so, the transaction that made the dirty read will be processing incorrect data.
- A **nonrepeatable read** occurs when a transaction rereads data it has previously read and finds modifications or deletions caused by a committed transaction.
- A **phantom read** occurs when a transaction rereads data and finds new rows that were inserted by a committed transaction since the prior read.

In order to deal with these potential data read problems, the SQL standard defines four **transaction isolation levels** or **isolation levels** that control which of these problems are

**FIGURE 9-11**

Summary of Data Read
Problems

| Data Read Problem Type | Definition |
|---|---|
| Dirty Read | The transaction reads a row that has been changed, but the change has *not* been committed. If the change is rolled back, the transaction has incorrect data. |
| Nonrepeatable Read | The transaction rereads data that has been changed and finds updates or deletions due to committed transactions. |
| Phantom Read | The transaction rereads data and finds new rows inserted by a committed transaction. |

allowed to occur. Using these SQL-defined isolation levels, the application programmer can declare the type of isolation level he or she wants, and the DBMS will create and manage locks to achieve that level of isolation.

These transaction isolation levels are summarized in Figure 9-12 and can be defined as:

- The **read-uncommitted isolation level** allows dirty reads, nonrepeatable reads, and phantom reads to occur.
- The **read-committed isolation level** allows nonrepeatable reads and phantom reads but disallows dirty reads.
- The **repeatable-read isolation level** allows phantom reads but disallows both dirty reads and nonrepeatable reads.
- The **serializable isolation level** will not allow any of these three data read problems to occur.

Generally, the more restrictive the level, the less the throughput, though much depends on the workload and how the application programs are written. Moreover, not all DBMS products support all of these levels. As usual, the support of SQL transaction isolation levels varies between DBMS products, and you will learn how Microsoft SQL Server 2019, Oracle Database, and MySQL 8.0 support isolation levels in Chapters 10A, 10B, and 10C, respectively.

### SQL Cursors

An **SQL cursor** or **cursor** is a pointer into a set of rows. SQL cursors are usually defined in an **SQL DECLARE CURSOR statement** that defines the cursor by using an SQL SELECT statement. For example, the following DECLARE CURSOR statement defines

**FIGURE 9-12**

Summary of Transaction
Isolation Levels

| | | Isolation Level | | | |
|---|---|---|---|---|---|
| | | Read Uncommitted | Read Committed | Repeatable Read | Serializable |
| Problem Type | Dirty Read | Possible | Not Possible | Not Possible | Not Possible |
| | Nonrepeatable Read | Possible | Possible | Not Possible | Not Possible |
| | Phantom Read | Possible | Possible | Possible | Not Possible |

a cursor named TransCursor that operates over the set of rows indicated by the included SELECT statement:

```
/* *** EXAMPLE CODE - DO NOT RUN *** */
/* *** SQL-Code-Example-CH09-05 *** */
DECLARE CURSOR TransCursor AS
    SELECT         *
    FROM           TRANS
    WHERE          PurchasePrice > 10000;
```

As was explained in Chapter 7, after an application program opens a cursor, it can place the cursor somewhere in the result set. Most commonly, the cursor is placed on the first or last row, but other possibilities exist.

A transaction can open several cursors—either sequentially or simultaneously. Additionally, two or more cursors may be open on the same table—either directly on the table or through an SQL view on that table. Because cursors require considerable memory, having many cursors open at the same time for, say, a thousand concurrent transactions will consume exorbitant memory. One way to reduce cursor burden is to define reduced-capability cursors and use them when a full-capability cursor is not needed.

Figure 9-13 lists four SQL cursor types used in the Microsoft SQL Server 2019 environment. (Cursor types for other systems are similar.) The simplest cursor is the **forward only cursor**. With it, the application can move only forward through the records. Changes made by other cursors in this transaction and by other transactions will be visible only if they occur to rows ahead of the cursor.

The next three types of cursors are called **scrollable cursors** because the application can scroll forward and backward through the records. A **static cursor** takes a snapshot of a relation and processes that snapshot. Changes made using this cursor are visible; changes from other sources are not visible.

A **keyset cursor** combines some of the features of static cursors with some of the features of dynamic cursors. When the cursor is opened, a primary key value is saved for each row. When the application positions the cursor on a row, the DBMS uses the key value to read the current value of the row. Inserts of new rows by other cursors (in this transaction or in other transactions) are not visible. If the application issues an update on a row that has been deleted by a different cursor, the DBMS creates a new row with the old key value and places the updated values in the new row (assuming that all required fields are present). Unless the isolation level of the transaction is dirty read, only committed updates and deletions are visible to the cursor.

A **dynamic cursor** is a fully featured cursor. All inserts, updates, deletions, and changes in row order are visible to a dynamic cursor. As with keyset cursors, unless the isolation level of the transaction is a dirty read, only committed changes are visible.

The amount of overhead and processing required to support a cursor is different for each type. In general, the cost goes up as we move down the cursor types shown in Figure 9-13. To improve DBMS performance, the application developer should create cursors that are just powerful enough to do the job. It is also very important to understand how a particular DBMS implements cursors and whether cursors are located on the server or on the client. In some cases, it might be better to place a dynamic cursor on the client than to have a static cursor on the server. No general rule can be stated because performance depends on the implementation used by the DBMS product and the application requirements.

A word of caution: If you do not specify the isolation level of a transaction or do not specify the type of cursors you open, the DBMS will use a default level and default types. These defaults may be perfect for your application, but they also may be terrible. Thus, even though these issues can be ignored, their consequences cannot be avoided. You must learn the capabilities of your DBMS product.

| CursorType | Description | Comments |
|---|---|---|
| Forward only | Application can only move forward through the recordset. | Changes made by other cursors in this transaction or in other transactions will be visible only if they occur on rows ahead of the cursor. |
| Static | Application sees the data as they were at the time the cursor was opened. | Changes made by this cursor are visible. Changes from other sources are not visible. Backward and forward scrolling allowed. |
| Keyset | When the cursor is opened, a primary key value is saved for each row in the recordset. When the application accesses a row, the key is used to fetch the current values for the row. | Updates from any source are visible. Inserts from sources outside this cursor are not visible (there is no key for them in the keyset). Inserts from this cursor appear at the bottom of the recordset. Deletions from any source are visible. Changes in row order are not visible. If the isolation level is read-uncommitted, then uncommitted updates and deletions are visible; otherwise, only committed updates and deletions are visible. |
| Dynamic | Changes of any type and from any source are visible. | All inserts, updates, deletions, and changes in recordset order are visible. If the isolation level is dirty read, then uncommitted changes are visible. Otherwise, only committed changes are visible. |

## Database Security

The goal of database security is to ensure that only authorized users can perform authorized activities at authorized times. This goal is difficult to achieve, and to make any progress at all, the database development team must determine the processing rights and responsibilities of all users during the project's requirements specification phase. These security requirements can then be enforced using the security features of the DBMS and additions to those features written into the application programs.

### Processing Rights and Responsibilities

Consider, for example, the needs of View Ridge Gallery. The View Ridge database has three types of users: sales personnel, management personnel, and system administrators. View Ridge designed processing rights for each as follows: Sales personnel are allowed to enter new customer and transaction data, to change customer data, and to query any of the data. They are not allowed to enter new artist or work data. They are never allowed to delete data.

Management personnel are allowed all of the permissions of sales personnel, plus they are allowed to enter new artist and work data and to modify transaction data. Even though management personnel have the authority to delete data, they are not given that permission in this application. This restriction is made to prevent the possibility of accidental data loss.

FIGURE 9-14

Processing Rights at View
Ridge Gallery

|  | CUSTOMER | TRANSACTION | WORK | ARTIST |
|---|---|---|---|---|
| **Sales personnel** | Insert, change, query | Insert, query | Query | Query |
| **Management personnel** | Insert, change, query | Insert, change, query | Insert, change, query | Insert, change, query |
| **System administrator** | Grant rights, modify structure | Grant rights, modify structure | Grant rights, modify structure | Grant rights, modify structure |

The system administrator can grant processing rights to other users, and he or she can change the structure of the database elements such as tables, indexes, stored procedures, and the like. The system administrator is not given rights to process the data. Figure 9-14 summarizes these processing rights.

> **BY THE WAY**  You may be wondering what good it does to say that the system administrator cannot process the data when that person has the ability to grant processing rights. He or she can just grant the right to change data to himself or herself. Although this is true, the granting of those rights will leave an audit trail in the database log. Clearly, this limitation is not foolproof, but it is better than just allowing the system administrator (or DBA) full access to all rights in the database.

The permissions in this table are not given to particular people, but rather are given to groups of people. Sometimes these groups are termed **roles** because they describe people acting in a particular capacity. The term **user groups** is also used. Assigning permission to roles (or user groups) is typical but not required. It would be possible to say, for example, that the user identified as "Benjamin Franklin" has certain processing rights. Note, too, that when roles are used, it is necessary to have a way to allocate users to roles. When "Mary Smith" signs on to the computer, there must be some way to determine which role or roles she has. We will discuss this further in the next section.

In this discussion, we have used the phrase **processing rights and responsibilities**. As this phrase implies, responsibilities go with processing rights. If, for example, the manager modifies transaction data, the manager has the responsibility to ensure that these modifications do not adversely affect the gallery's operation, accounting, and so forth.

Processing responsibilities cannot be enforced by the DBMS or by the database applications. Instead, they are encoded in manual procedures and explained to users during systems training. These are topics for a systems development text, and we will not consider them further here—except to reiterate that *responsibilities* go with *rights*. Such responsibilities must be documented and enforced.

According to Figure 9-1, the DBA has the task of managing processing rights and responsibilities. As this implies, these rights and responsibilities will change over time. As the database is used and as changes are made to the applications and to the structure of the DBMS, the need for new or different rights and responsibilities will arise. The DBA is a focal point for the discussion of such changes and for their implementation.

Once processing rights have been defined, they can be implemented at many levels: operating system, network, Web server, DBMS, and application. In the next two sections, we will consider DBMS and application implementation. The other levels are beyond the scope of this text.

## DBMS Security

The terminology, features, and functions of DBMS security depend on the DBMS product in use. Basically, all such products provide facilities that limit certain actions on certain objects to certain users. A general model of DBMS security is shown in Figure 9-15.

**FIGURE 9-15**

A Model of DBMS Security

Eleanore Wu
James Johnson
Richard Ent

Richard Ent has the Accounting role and can read data from the EMPLOYEE table.
Eleanore Wu can execute MonthEnd Stored Procedure.
James Johnson can alter all tables.

Accounting
Tellers
Shop Managers
Unknown Public

Accounting can update CUSTOMER table.

Note: Each PERMISSION *must* be associated with *at least one* USER or ROLE.

A USER can be assigned to one or more ROLEs (or USER GROUPs), and a ROLE can have one or more USERs. An OBJECT is an element of a database, such as a table, view, or stored procedure. PERMISSION is an association entity among an OBJECT and either a USER or a ROLE or BOTH. Hence, the relationships from USER to PERMISSION, ROLE to PERMISSION, and OBJECT to PERMISSION are all 1:N. The relationship from PERMISSION to OBJECT is M-O (parent required), as is at least one of the PERMISSION-USER and PERMISSION-ROLE relationships for each PERMISSION. In addition, though this is not shown in Figure 9-15, each PERMISSION has a type (e.g., SELECT, UPDATE, EXECUTE, etc.) that describes the kind of PERMISSION on the OBJECT that is granted to the USER or ROLE.

Permissions can be managed using **SQL Data Control Language (DCL)** statements:

■ The **SQL GRANT statement** is used to assign permissions to users and groups so that the users or groups can perform various operations on the data in the database.
■ The **SQL REVOKE statement** is used to take existing permissions away from users and groups.

SQL statements to create the Accounting role and give it the ability to update the CUSTOMER table are:

```
/* *** EXAMPLE CODE - DO NOT RUN *** */
/* *** SQL-Code-Example-CH09-06 *** */
CREATE ROLE Accounting;
GRANT UPDATE ON CUSTOMER TO Accounting;
```

The following SQL statements make Richard Ent an Accountant (with all the privileges that role includes) and give him read access to the EMPLOYEE table:

```
/* *** EXAMPLE CODE - DO NOT RUN *** */
/* *** SQL-Code-Example-CH09-07 *** */
GRANT Accounting to RichardEnt;
GRANT SELECT ON EMPLOYEE TO RichardEnt;
```

The SQL REVOKE command can also be used to remove a previously granted privilege. If the DBA no longer wants Richard Ent to see what is in the EMPLOYEE table, the following SQL command will work:

```
/* *** EXAMPLE CODE - DO NOT RUN *** */
/* *** SQL-Code-Example-CH09-08 *** */
REVOKE SELECT ON EMPLOYEE FROM RichardEnt;
```

Although these statements can be used in SQL scripts and with SQL command-line utilities, we will find it much easier to use the GUI DBMS administration utilities provided for use with each of the major DBMS products and will illustrate how to use these utilities for Microsoft SQL Server 2019 in Chapter 10A, Oracle Database in Chapter 10B, for MySQL 8.0 in Chapter 10C, and for ArangoDB in Chapter 10D. Microsoft SQL Server 2019, Oracle Database, and MySQL 8.0 security systems are variations of the model in Figure 9-15.

When a user signs on to the database, the DBMS limits the user's actions to the permissions defined for that user and to the permissions for roles to which that user has been assigned. Determining whether someone actually is who he or she claims to be is a difficult task in general. All commercial DBMS products use some version of username and password verification, even though such security is readily circumvented if users are careless with their identities.

Users can enter their **username** (also called the **login name**) and password, or, in some applications, the name and password are entered on the user's behalf. For example, the Windows username and password can be passed directly to the DBMS. In other cases, an application program provides the username and password. Internet applications usually define a group such as "Unknown Public" and assign anonymous users to that group when they sign on. In this way, companies such as Dell need not enter every potential customer into their security system by username and password.

## DBMS Security Guidelines

Guidelines for improving security in database systems are listed in Figure 9-16. First, the DBMS must always be run behind a firewall. However, the DBA should plan security with the assumption that the firewall has been breached. The DBMS, the database, and all applications should be secure even if the firewall fails.

DBMS vendors, including IBM, Oracle, and Microsoft, are constantly adding product features to improve security and reduce vulnerability. Consequently, organizations using

**FIGURE 9-16**

Summary of DBMS Security Guidelines

- Run DBMS behind a firewall, but plan as though the firewall has been breached

- Apply the latest operating system and DBMS service packs and fixes

- Use the least functionality possible
  - Support the fewest network protocols possible
  - Delete unnecessary or unused system stored procedures
  - Disable default logins and guest users, if possible
  - Unless required, never allow users to log on to the DBMS interactively

- Protect the computer that runs the DBMS
  - No user allowed to work at the computer that runs the DBMS
  - DBMS computer physically secured behind locked doors
  - Visits to the room containing the DBMS computer should be recorded in a log

- Manage accounts and passwords
  - Use a low-privilege user account for the DBMS service
  - Protect database accounts with strong passwords
  - Monitor failed login attempts
  - Frequently check group and role memberships
  - Audit accounts with null passwords
  - Assign accounts the lowest privileges possible
  - Limit DBA account privileges

- Planning
  - Develop a security plan for preventing and detecting security problems
  - Create procedures for security emergencies and practice them

DBMS products should continually check the vendors' Web sites for service packs and fixes; any service packs or fixes that involve security features, functions, and processing should be installed as soon as possible.

The installation of new service packs and fixes is not quite as simple as described here. The installation of a service pack or fix can break some applications, particularly some licensed software that requires specific service packs and fixes to be installed (or not installed). It may be necessary to delay installation of DBMS service packs until vendors of licensed software have upgraded their products to work with the new versions. Sometimes just the possibility that a licensed application *might* fail after a DBMS service pack or fix is applied is sufficient reason to delay the fix. However, the DBMS is still vulnerable during this period. Pick your regret!

Additionally, database features and functions that are not required by the applications should be removed or disabled from the DBMS. For example, if TCP/IP is used to connect to the DBMS, other communications protocols should be removed. This action reduces the pathways by which unauthorized activity can reach the DBMS. Further, all DBMS products are installed with system-stored procedures that provide services such as starting a command file, modifying the system registry, initiating email, and the like. Any of these stored procedures that are not needed should be removed. If all users are known to the DBMS, default logins and guest user accounts should be removed as well. Finally, unless otherwise required, users should never be allowed to log on to the DBMS in interactive mode. They should always access the database via an application.

In addition, the computer(s) that runs the DBMS must be protected. No one other than authorized DBA personnel should be allowed to work at the keyboard of the computer that runs the DBMS. The computer running the DBMS should be physically secured behind locked doors, and access to the facility housing the computer should be controlled. Visits to the DBMS computer room should be recorded in a log.

Accounts and passwords should be assigned carefully and continually managed. The DBMS itself should run on an account that has the lowest possible operating system privileges. In that way, if an intruder were to gain control of the DBMS, the intruder would have limited authority on that local computer or network. Additionally, all accounts within the DBMS should be protected by **strong passwords**. Such passwords have at least 15 characters and contain uppercase and lowercase letters; numbers; special characters, such as +, @, #, *, and unprintable key combinations (certain Alt + key combinations).[1]

The DBA should frequently check the accounts that have been assigned to groups and roles to ensure that all accounts and roles are known, are authorized, and have the correct permissions. Further, the DBA should audit accounts with null passwords. The users of such accounts should be required to protect those accounts with strong passwords. Also, as a general rule, accounts should be granted the lowest privileges possible.

As stated, the privileges for the DBA should normally not include the right to process the users' data. If the DBA grants himself or herself that privilege, the unauthorized grant operation will be visible in the database log.

In the spring of 2003, the Slammer worm invaded thousands of sites running Microsoft SQL Server. Microsoft had previously released a patch to SQL Server that prevented this attack. Sites that had installed the patch had no problems. The moral: Install security patches to your DBMS as promptly as possible. Create a procedure for regularly checking for such patches. More recently, in 2017 ransomware attacks exploiting poor security practices by DBAs affected over 10,000 databases, holding them hostage for money. In this case, the DBMS involved was MongoDB, a popular NoSQL DBMS (see Chapter 13), but it could have happened to any DBMS. The attacks were successful only on databases that were directly connected to the Internet and had no password set for the default administrative user. The DBAs were doing a poor job managing security.

Finally, the DBA should participate in security planning. Procedures for both preventing and detecting security problems should be developed. Furthermore, procedures should be

---

[1]The key to a truly strong password is the number of characters in the password—the more, the better depending on how many characters the system will accept. Thus, a long passphrase such as "itwasacoldandlonelynightandtheboystoodonthedeck" is more secure than a short password such as "Pa$$w0rd".

developed for actions to be taken in case of a security breach. Such procedures should be tested periodically. The importance of security in information systems has increased dramatically in recent years. DBA personnel should regularly search for security information on the Web in general and at the DBMS vendor's Web site.

## Application Security

Although DBMS products such as Oracle Database, Microsoft SQL Server, and MySQL do provide substantial database security capabilities, those capabilities are generic. If the application requires specific security measures, such as "No user can view a row of a table or of a join of a table that has an employee name other than his or her own," the DBMS facilities will not be adequate. In these cases, the security system must be augmented by features in database applications.

For example, as you will learn in Chapter 11, application security in Internet applications is often provided on the Web server. Executing application security on this server means that sensitive security data need not be transmitted over the network.

To understand this better, suppose that an application is written so that when users click a particular button on a browser page, the following query is sent to the Web server and then to the DBMS:

```
/* *** EXAMPLE CODE - DO NOT RUN *** */
/* *** SQL-Code-Example-CH09-09 *** */
SELECT        *
FROM          EMPLOYEE;
```

This statement will, of course, return all EMPLOYEE rows. If the application security policy permits employees to access only their own data, then a Web server could add the following WHERE clause to this query:

```
/* *** EXAMPLE CODE - DO NOT RUN *** */
/* *** SQL-Code-Example-CH09-10 *** */
SELECT        *
FROM          EMPLOYEE
WHERE         EMPLOYEE.Name = '<% = SESSION(("EmployeeName"))%>';
```

An expression like this one will cause the Web server to fill the employee's name into the WHERE clause. For a user signed in under the name 'Benjamin Franklin', the statement that results from this expression is:

```
/* *** EXAMPLE CODE - DO NOT RUN *** */
/* *** SQL-Code-Example-CH09-11 *** */
SELECT        *
FROM          EMPLOYEE
WHERE         EMPLOYEE.Name = 'Benjamin Franklin';
```

Because the name is inserted by a program on the Web server, the browser user does not know that it is occurring and cannot interfere with it even if he or she did.

Such security processing can be done as shown here on a Web server, but it also can be done within the application programs themselves or written as stored procedures or triggers to be executed by the DBMS at the appropriate times.

This idea can be extended by storing additional data in a security database that is accessed by the Web server or by stored procedures and triggers. That security database could contain, for example, the identities of users paired with additional values of WHERE clauses. For example, suppose that the users in the personnel department can access more than just their own data. The predicates for appropriate WHERE clauses could be stored in the security database, read by the application program, and appended to SQL SELECT statements as necessary.

Many other possibilities exist for extending DBMS security with application processing. In general, however, you should use the DBMS security features first. Only if they are inadequate for the requirements should you add to them with application code. The closer the security enforcement is to the data, the less chance there is for infiltration. Also, using the DBMS security features is faster and cheaper and probably results in higher-quality results than developing your own.

### The SQL Injection Attack

Whenever data from the user are used to modify an SQL statement, an **SQL injection attack** is possible. For example, in the prior section, if the value of EmployeeName used in the SELECT statement is not obtained by secure means, such as from the operating system rather than from a Web form, there is the chance that the user can inject SQL into the statement.

For example, suppose that users are asked to enter their names into a Web form textbox. Suppose that a user enters the value *Benjamin Franklin' OR 'x' = 'x* for his or her name. The SQL statement generated by the application will then be the following:

```
/* *** EXAMPLE CODE - DO NOT RUN *** */
/* *** SQL-Code-Example-CH09-12 *** */
SELECT        *
FROM          EMPLOYEE
WHERE         EMPLOYEE.Name = 'Benjamin Franklin' OR 'x' = 'x';
```

Of course, the value of 'x' = 'x' is true for every row, so every row of the EMPLOYEE table will be returned! Note that a user's name would typically be entered into a text box without quotes, the quotes being added by the application program, as in this example. That is why the extra comparison involves a string without an ending quote: the application program will be adding that quote no matter what we type in the text box. As we can see, anytime user input is used to modify an SQL statement, that input must be carefully edited to ensure that only valid input has been received and that no additional SQL syntax has been entered.

Despite being a well-known hacker attack, the SQL injection attack can still be very effective if not defended against. In May 2020, a New York City man was charged with hacking and money laundering conspiracies after using SQL injection to obtain payment card data and other personally identifying information.[2]

## Database Backup and Recovery

Computer systems fail. Hardware breaks. Programs have bugs. Human procedures contain errors, and people make mistakes. All of these failures can and do occur in database applications. Because a database is shared by many people and because it often is a key element of an organization's operations, it is important to recover it as soon as possible.

Several problems must be addressed. First, from a business standpoint, business functions must continue. During the failure, customer orders, financial transactions, and packing lists must be completed somehow, even manually. Later, when the database application is operational again, the data from those activities must be entered into the database. Second, computer operations personnel must restore the system to a usable state as quickly as

---

[2]For more information, see *www.justice.gov/usao-ma/pr/new-york-city-man-charged-hacking-credit-card-trafficking-and-money-laundering.*

possible and as close as possible to what it was when the system crashed. Third, users must know what to do when the system becomes available again. Some work may need to be reentered, and users must know how far back they need to go.

When failures occur, it is impossible simply to fix the problem and resume processing. Even if no data are lost during a failure (which assumes that all types of memory are nonvolatile—an unrealistic assumption), the timing and scheduling of computer processing are too complex to be accurately re-created. Enormous amounts of overhead data and processing would be required for the operating system to be able to restart processing precisely where it was interrupted. It is simply not possible to roll back the clock and put all of the electrons in the same configuration they were in at the time of the failure. Two other approaches are possible: **recovery via reprocessing** and **recovery via rollback/rollforward**.

## Recovery via Reprocessing

Because processing cannot be resumed at a precise point, the next best alternative is to go back to a known point and reprocess the workload from there. The simplest form of this type of recovery is to periodically make a copy of the database (called a **database save** or **database backup** or simply **backup**) and to keep a record of all transactions that have been processed since the save. Then, when there is a failure, the operations staff can restore the database from the save and then reprocess all the transactions. Unfortunately, this simple strategy is normally not feasible. First, reprocessing transactions takes the same amount of time as processing them in the first place did. If the computer is heavily scheduled, the system may never catch up.

Second, when transactions are processed concurrently, events are asynchronous. Slight variations in human activity, such as a user reading an email before responding to an application prompt, can change the order of the execution of concurrent transactions. Therefore, whereas Customer A got the last seat on a flight during the original processing, Customer B may get the last seat during reprocessing. For these reasons, reprocessing is normally not a viable form of recovery from failure in concurrent processing systems.

## Recovery via Rollback/Rollforward

A second approach is to periodically make a copy of the database (the database save or backup) and to keep a log of the changes made by transactions against the database since the save. Then, when there is a failure, one of two methods can be used. Using the first method, called **rollforward**, the database is restored using the saved data, and all valid transactions since the save are reapplied. (We are not reprocessing the transactions because the application programs are not involved in the rollforward. Instead, the processed changes, as recorded in the log, are reapplied.)

The second method is **rollback**. With this method, we undo changes made by erroneous or partially processed transactions by undoing the changes they have made in the database. Then the valid transactions that were in process at the time of the failure are restarted.

Both of these methods require that a **log** of the transaction results be kept. This log contains records of the data changes in chronological order. Transactions must be written to the log before they are applied to the database. That way, if the system crashes between the time a transaction is logged and the time it is applied, at worst there is a record of an unapplied transaction. If, however, the transactions were to be applied before they were logged, it would be possible (as well as undesirable) to change the database but have no record of the change. If this happened, an unwary user might reenter an already completed transaction. In the event of a failure, the log is used both to undo and to redo transactions, as shown in Figure 9-17.

To undo a transaction, the log must contain a copy of every database record (or page) before it was changed. Such records are called **before images**. A transaction is undone by applying before images of all of its changes to the database. To redo a transaction, the log must contain a copy of every database record (or page) after it was changed. These records are called **after images**. A transaction is redone by applying after images of all of its changes to the database. Possible data items in a transaction log are shown in Figure 9-18.

FIGURE 9-17

Undo and Redo Transactions

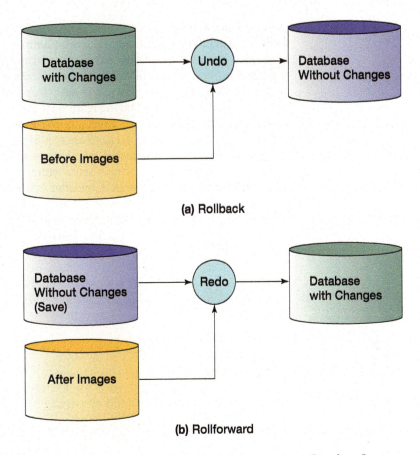

(a) Rollback

(b) Rollforward

In this example log, each transaction has a unique name for identification purposes. Furthermore, all of the images for a given transaction are linked together with pointers. One pointer points to the previous change made by this transaction (the reverse pointer), and the other points to the next change made by this transaction (the forward pointer). A zero in the pointer field means that this is the end of the list. The DBMS recovery subsystem uses these pointers to locate all of the records for a particular transaction. Figure 9-18 shows an

FIGURE 9-18

Example Transaction Log

| Relative Record Number | Transaction ID | Reverse Pointer | Forward Pointer | Time | Type of Operation | Object | Before Image | After Image |
|---|---|---|---|---|---|---|---|---|
| 1 | OT1 | 0 | 2 | 11:42 | START | | | |
| 2 | OT1 | 1 | 4 | 11:43 | MODIFY | CUST 100 | (old value) | (new value) |
| 3 | OT2 | 0 | 8 | 11:46 | START | | | |
| 4 | OT1 | 2 | 5 | 11:47 | MODIFY | SP AA | (old value) | (new value) |
| 5 | OT1 | 4 | 7 | 11:47 | INSERT | ORDER 11 | | (value) |
| 6 | CT1 | 0 | 9 | 11:48 | START | | | |
| 7 | OT1 | 5 | 0 | 11:49 | COMMIT | | | |
| 8 | OT2 | 3 | 0 | 11:50 | COMMIT | | | |
| 9 | CT1 | 6 | 10 | 11:51 | MODIFY | SP BB | (old value) | (new value) |
| 10 | CT1 | 9 | 0 | 11:51 | COMMIT | | | |

example of the linking of log records. Other data items in the log are the time of the action; the type of operation (START marks the beginning of a transaction and COMMIT terminates a transaction, releasing all locks that were in place); the object acted on, such as record type and identifier; and, finally, the before images and the after images.

Given a log with before images and after images, the undo and redo actions are straightforward. To undo the transaction in Figure 9-19, the recovery processor simply replaces each changed record with its before image. For *rollforward*, the *after images* are applied in *forward* time order; for *rollback*, the *before images* are applied in *reverse* time order.

When all of the before images have been restored, the transaction is undone. To redo a transaction, the recovery processor starts with the version of the database at the time the transaction started and applies all of the after images. As stated, this action assumes that an earlier version of the database is available from a database save.

Restoring a database to its most recent save and reapplying all transactions may require considerable processing. To reduce the delay, DBMS products sometimes use checkpoints. A **checkpoint** is a point of synchronization between the database and the transaction log. To perform a checkpoint, the DBMS refuses new requests, finishes processing outstanding requests, and writes its main memory buffers to disk. The DBMS then waits until the operating system notifies it that all outstanding write requests to the database and to the log

**FIGURE 9-19**

Recovery Example

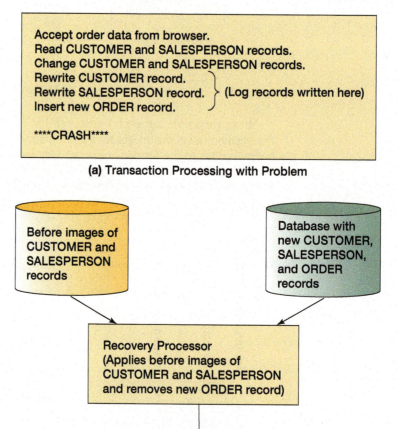

Accept order data from browser.
Read CUSTOMER and SALESPERSON records.
Change CUSTOMER and SALESPERSON records.
Rewrite CUSTOMER record.
Rewrite SALESPERSON record.    } (Log records written here)
Insert new ORDER record.

****CRASH****

(a) Transaction Processing with Problem

Before images of CUSTOMER and SALESPERSON records

Database with new CUSTOMER, SALESPERSON, and ORDER records

Recovery Processor
(Applies before images of CUSTOMER and SALESPERSON and removes new ORDER record)

Database with ORDER transaction removed

(b) Recovery Processing

have been successfully completed. At this point, the log and the database are synchronized. A checkpoint record is then written to the log. Later, the database can be recovered from the checkpoint, and only after images for transactions that started after the checkpoint need be applied. Checkpoints are sometimes inexpensive operations, and it may be feasible to take three or four (or more) per hour. In this way, no more than 15 or 20 minutes of processing need to be recovered. In busier applications, it may not always be feasible to stop accepting new transactions, even for a short period of time, but more sophisticated checkpointing methods are available in enterprise DBMSs. Most DBMS products perform automatic checkpoints, making human intervention unnecessary, but the DBA can often specify their frequency if desired.

You will see specific examples of backup and recovery techniques for Microsoft SQL Server, Oracle Database, MySQL, and ArangoDB in the next five chapters. For now, you only need to understand the basic ideas and to realize that it is the responsibility of the DBA to ensure that adequate backup and recovery plans have been developed and that database saves and logs are generated as required.

## Managing the DBMS

In addition to managing data activity and the database structure, the DBA must manage the DBMS itself. The DBA should compile and analyze statistics concerning the system's performance and identify potential problem areas. Keep in mind that the database is serving many user groups. The DBA needs to investigate all complaints about the system's response time, accuracy, ease of use, and so forth. If changes are needed, the DBA must plan and implement them.

The DBA must periodically monitor the users' activity on the database. DBMS products include features that collect and report statistics. For example, some of these reports may indicate which users have been active, which files—and perhaps which data items—have been used, and which access methods have been employed. Error rates and types also can be captured and reported. The DBA analyzes these data to determine whether a change to the database design is needed to improve performance or to ease the users' tasks. If change is necessary, the DBA will ensure that it is accomplished.

The DBA should analyze run-time statistics on database activity and performance. When a performance problem is identified (by either a report or a user's complaint), the DBA must determine whether a modification of the database structure or system is appropriate. Examples of possible structural modifications are establishing new keys and indexes, purging data, deleting keys, and establishing new relationships among objects.

When the vendor of the DBMS being used announces new product features, the DBA must consider them in light of the overall needs of the user community. If the DBA decides to incorporate the new DBMS features, the developers must be notified and trained in their use. Accordingly, the DBA must manage and control changes in the DBMS as well as in the database structure.

Other changes in the system for which the DBA is responsible vary widely, depending on the DBMS product as well as on other software and hardware in use. For example, changes in other software (such as the operating system or the Web server) may mean that some DBMS features, functions, or parameters must be changed. The DBA must therefore also tune the DBMS product with other software in use.

The DBMS options (such as transaction isolation levels) are initially chosen when little is known about how the system will perform in the particular user environment. Consequently, operational experience and performance analysis over a period of time may reveal that changes are necessary. Even if the performance seems acceptable, the DBA may want to alter the options and observe the effect on performance. This process is referred to as *tuning*, or *optimizing*, the system. Figure 9-20 summarizes the DBA's responsibilities for managing the DBMS product.

DBMS products provide security facilities. Most involve the declaration of users, groups, objects to be protected, and permissions or privileges on those objects. Almost all DBMS products use some form of username and password security. Security guidelines are listed in Figure 9-16. DBMS security can be augmented by application security.

In the event of system failure, the database must be restored to a usable state as soon as possible. Transactions in process at the time of the failure must be reapplied or restarted. Although in some cases recovery can be done by reprocessing, the use of logs and rollback and rollforward is almost always preferred. Checkpoints can be taken to reduce the amount of work that needs to be done after a failure.

In addition to these tasks, the DBA manages the DBMS product itself, measuring database application performance and assessing the need for changes in database structure or DBMS performance tuning. The DBA also ensures that new DBMS features are evaluated and used as appropriate. Finally, the DBA is responsible for maintaining the data repository.

# Key Terms

<table>
<tr><td>ACID transaction</td><td>inconsistent read problem</td><td>serializable</td></tr>
<tr><td>active repository</td><td>index</td><td>serializable isolation level</td></tr>
<tr><td>after image</td><td>isolated</td><td>shared lock</td></tr>
<tr><td>atomic</td><td>isolation level</td><td>shrinking phase</td></tr>
<tr><td>backup</td><td>keyset cursor</td><td>SQL BEGIN TRANSACTION</td></tr>
<tr><td>before image</td><td>lock</td><td>   statement</td></tr>
<tr><td>checkpoint</td><td>lock granularity</td><td>SQL COMMIT TRANSACTION</td></tr>
<tr><td>computer-aided software engineering</td><td>log</td><td>   statement</td></tr>
<tr><td>   (CASE)</td><td>logical unit of work (LUW)</td><td>SQL cursor</td></tr>
<tr><td>concurrent transaction</td><td>login name</td><td>SQL Data Control Language (DCL)</td></tr>
<tr><td>concurrent update problem</td><td>lost update problem</td><td>SQL DECLARE CURSOR</td></tr>
<tr><td>consistent</td><td>nonrepeatable read</td><td>   statement</td></tr>
<tr><td>cursor</td><td>optimistic concurrency control</td><td>SQL GRANT statement</td></tr>
<tr><td>data administration</td><td>optimistic locking</td><td>SQL injection attack</td></tr>
<tr><td>data repository</td><td>passive repository</td><td>SQL REVOKE statement</td></tr>
<tr><td>database administration</td><td>pessimistic locking</td><td>SQL ROLLBACK TRANSACTION</td></tr>
<tr><td>database administrator</td><td>phantom read</td><td>   statement</td></tr>
<tr><td>database backup</td><td>physical database design</td><td>SQL START TRANSACTION</td></tr>
<tr><td>database save</td><td>processing rights and responsibilities</td><td>   statement</td></tr>
<tr><td>DBA</td><td>pseudo code</td><td>SQL Transaction Control Language</td></tr>
<tr><td>deadlock</td><td>query optimizer</td><td>   (TCL)</td></tr>
<tr><td>deadly embrace</td><td>read-committed isolation level</td><td>SQL WORK keyword</td></tr>
<tr><td>dirty read</td><td>read-uncommitted isolation level</td><td>statement-level consistency</td></tr>
<tr><td>disk mirroring</td><td>recovery via reprocessing</td><td>static cursor</td></tr>
<tr><td>durable</td><td>recovery via rollback/rollforward</td><td>strict two-phase locking</td></tr>
<tr><td>dynamic cursor</td><td>redundant arrays of independent</td><td>strong password</td></tr>
<tr><td>exclusive lock</td><td>   disks (RAID)</td><td>threads</td></tr>
<tr><td>explicit COMMIT</td><td>repeatable-read isolation level</td><td>transaction</td></tr>
<tr><td>explicit lock</td><td>resource locking</td><td>transaction isolation level</td></tr>
<tr><td>forward only cursor</td><td>role</td><td>transaction-level consistency</td></tr>
<tr><td>growing phase</td><td>rollback</td><td>two-phase locking</td></tr>
<tr><td>implicit COMMIT</td><td>rollforward</td><td>user group</td></tr>
<tr><td>implicit lock</td><td>scrollable cursor</td><td>username</td></tr>
</table>

# Review Questions

**9.1**   Briefly describe five difficult problems for organizations that create and use multiuser enterprise databases.

**9.2**   Explain the difference between a database administrator and a data administrator.

**9.3**   List seven important DBA tasks.

**9.4**   Summarize the DBA's responsibilities for managing database structure.

**9.5**   What is configuration control? Why is it necessary?

**9.6**   Explain the meaning of the word *inappropriately* in the phrase "one user's work does not inappropriately influence another user's work."

**9.7**   Explain the trade-off that exists in concurrency control.

**9.8**   Define an atomic transaction, and explain why atomicity is important.

**9.9**   Explain the difference between concurrent transactions and simultaneous transactions. How many CPUs are required for simultaneous transactions?

**9.10**   Give an example, other than the one in this text, of the lost update problem.

**9.11**   Explain the difference between an explicit and an implicit lock.

**9.12**   What is lock granularity?

**9.13**   Explain the difference between an exclusive lock and a shared lock.

**9.14**   Explain two-phase locking.

**9.15**   How does releasing all locks at the end of the transaction relate to two-phase locking?

**9.16**   In general, how should the boundaries of a transaction be defined?

**9.17**   What is deadlock? How can it be avoided? How can it be resolved once it occurs?

**9.18**   Explain the difference between optimistic and pessimistic locking.

**9.19**   Explain the benefits of marking transaction boundaries, declaring lock characteristics, and letting the DBMS place locks.

**9.20**   What is SQL Transaction Control Language (TCL)? Explain the use of the SQL BEGIN TRANSACTION, COMMIT TRANSACTION, and ROLLBACK TRANSACTION statements. Why does MySQL also use the SQL START TRANSACTION statement?

**9.21**   What is an *implicit COMMIT*? What is an *explicit COMMIT*? Which of these are used by default with Microsoft SQL Server 2019, Oracle Database, and MySQL 8.0?

**9.22**   Explain the meaning of the expression *ACID transaction*.

**9.23**   Describe statement-level consistency.

**9.24**   Describe transaction-level consistency. What disadvantage can exist with it?

**9.25**   What is the purpose of transaction isolation levels?

**9.26**   Explain the read-uncommitted isolation level. Give an example of its use.

**9.27**   Explain the read-committed isolation level. Give an example of its use.

**9.28**   Explain the repeatable-read isolation level. Give an example of its use.

**9.29**   Explain the serializable isolation level. Give an example of its use.

**9.30** Explain the term *SQL cursor*.

**9.31** Explain why a transaction may have many cursors. Also, how is it possible that a transaction may have more than one cursor on a given table?

**9.32** What is the advantage of using different types of cursors?

**9.33** Explain forward only cursors. Give an example of their use.

**9.34** Explain static cursors. Give an example of their use.

**9.35** Explain keyset cursors. Give an example of their use.

**9.36** Explain dynamic cursors. Give an example of their use.

**9.37** What happens if you do not declare the transaction isolation level and the cursor type to the DBMS? Is this good or bad?

**9.38** What is SQL Data Control Language (DCL)? Explain the necessity of defining processing rights and responsibilities. How are such responsibilities enforced, and what is the role of SQL DCL in enforcing them?

**9.39** Explain the relationships among USER, ROLE, PERMISSION, and OBJECT for a generic database security system.

**9.40** Should the DBA assume a firewall when planning security?

**9.41** What should be done with unused DBMS features and functions?

**9.42** Explain how to protect the computer that runs the DBMS.

**9.43** With regard to security, what actions should the DBA take on user accounts and passwords?

**9.44** List two elements of a database security plan.

**9.45** Describe the advantages and disadvantages of DBMS-provided and application-provided security.

**9.46** What is an SQL injection attack, and how can it be prevented?

**9.47** Explain how a database could be recovered via reprocessing. Why is this generally not feasible?

**9.48** Define *rollback* and *rollforward*.

**9.49** Why is it important to write to the log before changing the database values?

**9.50** Describe the rollback process. Under what conditions should it be used?

**9.51** Describe the rollforward process. Under what conditions should it be used?

**9.52** What is the advantage of taking frequent checkpoints of a database?

**9.53** Summarize the DBA's responsibilities for managing the DBMS.

**9.54** What is a data repository? A passive data repository? An active data repository?

**9.55** Explain why a data repository is important. What is likely to happen if one is not available?

## Exercises

**9.56** Visit *www.oracle.com*, and search for "Oracle Security Guidelines." Read articles at three of the links you find and summarize them. How does the information you find compare with that in Figure 9-15?

**9.57**   Visit *www.msdn.microsoft.com*, and search for "SQL Server Security Guidelines." Read articles at three of the links you find and summarize them. How does the information you find compare with that in Figure 9-15?

**9.58**   Visit *www.mysql.com*, and search for "MySQL Security Guidelines." Read articles at three of the links you find and summarize them. How does the information you find compare with that in Figure 9-15?

**9.59**   Use Google (*www.google.com*) or another search engine, and search the Web for "Database Security Guidelines." Read articles at three of the links you find and summarize them. How does the information you find compare with that in Figure 9-15?

**9.60**   Search the Web for "distributed two-phase locking." Find a tutorial on that topic and explain in general terms how this locking algorithm works.

**9.61**   Answer the following questions for the View Ridge Gallery VRG database discussed in Chapter 7 with the tables shown in Figures 7-13 and 7-14 and the data shown in Figures 7-15.

   **A.**   Suppose that you are developing a stored procedure to record an artist who has never been in the gallery before, a work for that artist, and a row in the TRANS table to record the date acquired and the acquisition price. How will you declare the boundaries of the transaction? What transaction isolation level will you use?

   **B.**   Suppose that you are writing a stored procedure to change values in the CUSTOMER table. What transaction isolation level will you use?

   **C.**   Suppose that you are writing a stored procedure to record a customer's purchase. Assume that the customer's data are new. How will you declare the boundaries of the transaction? What isolation level will you use?

   **D.**   Suppose that you are writing a stored procedure to check the validity of the intersection table. Specifically, for each customer, your procedure should read the customer's transaction and determine the artist of that work. Given the artist, your procedure should then check to ensure that an interest has been declared for that artist in the intersection table. If there is no such intersection row, your procedure should create one. How will you set the boundaries of your transaction? What isolation level will you use? What cursor types (if any) will you use?

# Case Questions

## Marcia's Dry Cleaning Case Questions

Marcia Wilson owns and operates Marcia's Dry Cleaning, which is an upscale dry cleaner in a well-to-do suburban neighborhood. Marcia makes her business stand out from the competition by providing superior customer service. She wants to keep track of each of her customers and their orders. Ultimately, she wants to notify them that their clothes are ready via email. Suppose that Marcia has hired you as a database consultant to develop a database for Marcia's Dry Cleaning that has the following tables:

> CUSTOMER (**CustomerID**, FirstName, LastName, Phone, EmailAddress, *ReferredBy*)
>
> INVOICE (**InvoiceNumber**, *CustomerID*, DateIn, DateOut, Subtotal, Tax, TotalAmount)
>
> INVOICE_ITEM (***InvoiceNumber***, **ItemNumber**, *ServiceID*, Quantity, UnitPrice, ExtendedPrice)
>
> SERVICE (**ServiceID**, ServiceDescription, UnitPrice)

Where

**ReferredBy in CUSTOMER must exist in CustomerID in CUSTOMER**

**CustomerID in INVOICE must exist in CustomerID in CUSTOMER**

**InvoiceNumber in INVOICE_ITEM must exist in InvoiceNumber in INVOICE**

**ServiceID in INVOICE_ITEM must exist in ServiceID in SERVICE**

Assume that all relationships have been defined, as implied by the foreign keys in this table list, and that the appropriate referential integrity constraints are in place. Note that CUSTOMER contains a recursive relationship between ReferredBy and CustomerID, where ReferredBy contains the CustomerID value of the existing customer who referred the new customer to Marcia's Dry Cleaning.

**A.** Assume that Marcia's has the following personnel: two owners, a shift manager, a part-time seamstress, and two salesclerks. Prepare a two- to three-page memo that addresses the following points:

   **1.** The need for database administration.

   **2.** Your recommendation as to who should serve as database administrator. Assume that Marcia's is not sufficiently large to need or afford a full-time database administrator.

   **3.** Using Figure 9-1 as a guide, describe the nature of database administration activities at Marcia's. As an aggressive consultant, keep in mind that you can recommend yourself for performing some of the DBA functions.

**B.** For the employees described in part A, define users, groups, and permissions on data in these four tables. Use the security scheme shown in Figure 9-15 as an example. Create a table like that in Figure 9-14. Don't forget to include yourself.

**C.** Suppose that you are writing a stored procedure to create new records in SERVICE for new services that Marcia's will perform. Suppose that you know that while your procedure is running, another stored procedure that records new or modifies existing customer orders and order line items can also be running. Additionally, suppose that a third stored procedure that records new customer data can be running.

   **1.** Give an example of a dirty read, a nonrepeatable read, and a phantom read among this group of stored procedures.

   **2.** What concurrency control measures are appropriate for the stored procedure that you are creating?

   **3.** What concurrency control measures are appropriate for the two other stored procedures?

# The Queen Anne Curiosity Shop Project Questions

Assume that the owners of the Queen Anne Curiosity Shop have hired you as a database consultant to develop an operational database with the same tables described at the end of Chapter 7:

**CUSTOMER** (<u>CustomerID</u>, LastName, FirstName, EmailAddress, EncryptedPassword, Address, City, State, ZIP, Phone, *ReferredBy*)

**EMPLOYEE** (<u>EmployeeID</u>, LastName, FirstName, Position, *Supervisor*, OfficePhone, EmailAddress)

VENDOR (<u>VendorID</u>, CompanyName, ContactLastName, ContactFirstName, Address, City, State, ZIP, Phone, Fax, EmailAddress)

ITEM (<u>ItemID</u>, ItemDescription, PurchaseDate, ItemCost, ItemPrice, *VendorID*)

SALE (<u>SaleID</u>, *CustomerID*, *EmployeeID*, SaleDate, SubTotal, Tax, Total)

SALE_ITEM (<u>*SaleID*</u>, <u>SaleItemID</u>, *ItemID*, ItemPrice)

**The referential integrity constraints are:**

ReferredBy in CUSTOMER must exist in CustomerID in CUSTOMER

Supervisor in EMPLOYEE must exist in EmployeeID in EMPLOYEE

CustomerID in SALE must exist in CustomerID in CUSTOMER

VendorID in ITEM must exist in VendorID in VENDOR

EmployeeID in SALE must exist in EmployeeID in EMPLOYEE

SaleID in SALE_ITEM must exist in SaleID in SALE

ItemID in SALE_ITEM must exist in ItemID in ITEM

**Assume that CustomerID of CUSTOMER, EmployeeID of EMPLOYEE, ItemID of ITEM, SaleID of SALE, and SaleItemID of SALE_ITEM are all surrogate keys with values as follows:**

| | | |
|---|---|---|
| CustomerID | Start at 1 | Increment by 1 |
| EmployeeID | Start at 1 | Increment by 1 |
| VendorID | Start at 1 | Increment by 1 |
| ItemID | Start at 1 | Increment by 1 |
| SaleID | Start at 1 | Increment by 1 |

**A vendor may be an individual or a company. If the vendor is an individual, the CompanyName field is left blank, whereas the ContactLastName and ContactFirstName fields must have data values. If the vendor is a company, the company name is recorded in the CompanyName field, and the name of the primary contact at the company is recorded in the ContactLastName and ContactFirstName fields.**

**A.** Assume that the Queen Anne Curiosity Shop personnel are the two owners, an office administrator, one full-time salesperson, and two part-time salespeople. The two owners and the office administrator want to process data in all tables. Additionally, the full-time salesperson can enter purchase and sales data. The part-time employees can only read sales data. Prepare a three- to five-page memo for the owner that addresses the following issues:

   **1.** The need for database administration at the Queen Anne Curiosity Shop.

   **2.** Your recommendation as to who should serve as database administrator. Assume that the Queen Anne Curiosity Shop is not sufficiently large that it needs or can afford a full-time database administrator.

   **3.** Using Figure 9-1 as a guide, describe the nature of database administration activities at the Queen Anne Curiosity Shop. As an aggressive consultant, keep in mind that you can recommend yourself for performing some of the DBA functions.

**B.** For the employees described in part A, define users, groups, and permissions on data in these six tables. Use the security scheme shown in Figure 9-15 as an example. Create a table like that in Figure 9-14. Don't forget to include yourself.

**C.** Suppose that you are writing a stored procedure to record new purchases. Suppose that you know that while your procedure is running, another stored procedure that records new customer sales and sale line items can also be running. Additionally, suppose that a third stored procedure that records new customer data can be running.

1. Give an example of a dirty read, a nonrepeatable read, and a phantom read among this group of stored procedures.

2. What concurrency control measures are appropriate for the stored procedure that you are creating?

3. What concurrency control measures are appropriate for the two other stored procedures?

# Morgan Importing Project Questions

Assume that Morgan has hired you as a database consultant to develop an operational database with the same tables described at the end of Chapter 7 (note that STORE uses the surrogate key StoreID):

EMPLOYEE (<u>EmployeeID</u>, LastName, FirstName, Department, Position, *Supervisor*, OfficePhone, OfficeFax, EmailAddress)

STORE (<u>StoreName</u>, City, Country, Phone, Fax, EmailAddress, Contact)

PURCHASE_ITEM (<u>PurchaseItemID</u>, *StoreName*, *PurchasingAgentID*, PurchaseDate, ItemDescription, Category, PriceUSD)

SHIPPER (<u>ShipperID</u>, ShipperName, Phone, Fax, EmailAddress, Contact)

SHIPMENT (<u>ShipmentID</u>, *ShipperID*, *PurchasingAgentID*, ShipperInvoiceNumber, Origin, Destination, ScheduledDepartureDate, ActualDepartureDate, EstimatedArrivalDate)

SHIPMENT_ITEM (<u>*ShipmentID*</u>, <u>ShipmentItemID</u>, *PurchaseItemID*, InsuredValue)

SHIPMENT_RECEIPT (<u>ReceiptNumber</u>, *ShipmentID*, *PurchaseItemID*, *ReceivingAgentID*, ReceiptDate, ReceiptTime, ReceiptQuantity, isReceivedUndamaged, DamageNotes)

The referential integrity constraints are:

Supervisor in EMPLOYEE must exist in EmployeeID in EMPLOYEE

StoreName in PURCHASE_ITEM must exist in StoreName in STORE

PurchasingAgentID in PURCHASE_ITEM must exist in EmployeeID in EMPLOYEE

ShipperID in SHIPMENT must exist in ShipperID in SHIPPER

PurchasingAgentID in SHIPMENT must exist in EmployeeID in EMPLOYEE

ShipmentID in SHIPMENT_ITEM must exist in ShipmentID in SHIPMENT

PurchaseItemID in SHIPMENT_ITEM must exist in PurchaseItemID in PURCHASE_ITEM

ShipmentID in SHIPMENT_RECEIPT must exist in ShipmentID in SHIPMENT

PurchaseItemID in SHIPMENT_RECEIPT must exist in PurchaseItemID in PURCHASE_ITEM

ReceivingAgentID in SHIPMENT_RECEIPT must exist in EmployeeID in EMPLOYEE

Assume that EmployeeID of EMPLOYEE, PurchaseItem.ID of PURCHASE_ITEM, ShipperID of SHIPPER, ShipmentID of SHIPMENT, and ReceiptNumber of SHIPMENT_RECEIPT are all surrogate keys with values as follows:

| | | |
|---|---|---|
| EmployeeID | Start at 101 | Increment by 1 |
| PurchaseItemID | Start at 500 | Increment by 5 |
| ShipperID | Start at 1 | Increment by 1 |
| ShipmentID | Start at 100 | Increment by 1 |
| ReceiptNumber | Start at 200001 | Increment by 1 |

A. Assume that Morgan personnel are the owner (Morgan), an office administrator, one full-time salesperson, and two part-time salespeople. Morgan and the office administrator want to process data in all tables. Additionally, the full-time salesperson can enter purchase and shipment data. The part-time employees can read only shipment data; they are not allowed to see InsuredValue, however. Prepare a three- to five-page memo for the owner that addresses the following issues:

1. The need for database administration at Morgan.

2. Your recommendation as to who should serve as database administrator. Assume that Morgan is not sufficiently large that it needs or can afford a full-time database administrator.

3. Using Figure 9-1 as a guide, describe the nature of database administration activities at Morgan. As an aggressive consultant, keep in mind that you can recommend yourself for performing some of the DBA functions.

B. For the employees described in part A, define users, groups, and permissions on data in these five tables. Use the security scheme shown in Figure 9-15 as an example. Create a table like that in Figure 9-14. Don't forget to include yourself.

C. Suppose that you are writing a stored procedure to record new purchases. Suppose that you know that while your procedure is running, another stored procedure that records shipment data can be running, and a third stored procedure that updates shipper data can also be running.

1. Give an example of a dirty read, a nonrepeatable read, and a phantom read among this group of stored procedures.

2. What concurrency control measures are appropriate for the stored procedure that you are creating?

3. What concurrency control measures are appropriate for the two other stored procedures?

Oracle Database presents a more complex situation. The current version of Oracle Database is Oracle Database 19c. (Version 19.3 is the most recent downloadable version available for all platforms.) If you have Oracle Database 19c available to you (either Standard, Enterprise, or Personal) in a computer lab or other situation where it has been installed for your use in a class or work setting, you will be able to use it for the work in this book. Chapter 10B contains complete instructions for installing and running Oracle Database 18c Express Edition. If no version of Oracle is already installed for you, we recommend you download and use the current version of Oracle Database Express Edition, which is the Oracle Database Express Edition 18c.[3] The Oracle SQL Developer GUI utility discussed later in this chapter will work well with all versions of Oracle Database and will allow you to complete nearly all the exercises in this book. Oracle updates the Express Edition much less frequently than the Enterprise and other editions, so we expect Oracle Database XE to be stable for some time. It contains everything needed to do everything in this book, including the advanced business intelligence and data mining activities described in Chapter 12.

MySQL 8.0 is available in MySQL Community Server 807,[4] but if you are using a Windows operating system, you should download and use the **MySQL Installer for Windows**.[5]

ArangoDB also has multiple editions but is simple to download, install, and manage.

Installing and using one of these DBMS products (or, at a minimum, having **Microsoft Access 2019**) is a necessity for getting the most out of your study of the material in this book—using the material in a real DBMS is an important part of your learning process.

Of course, in order to use a DBMS product, you first have to install it and configure it on your computer. Therefore, we discuss what you need to know to be able to successfully install and use each DBMS product in the relevant online chapter.

## Using the DBMS in the Cloud

Each of these DBMS products is available on one or more **cloud computing service**, such as **Microsoft Azure**, **Amazon Web Services (AWS)**, and others. In the online chapter for each DBMS, we discuss some cloud computing possibilities for that DBMS product.

## Using the DBMS Database Administration and Database Development Utilities

Each of these DBMS products has one or more utility programs that you will use for database administration tasks and for database development. Examples of these utilities are:

- Microsoft SQL Server 2019 uses the **Microsoft SQL Server Management Studio (SSMS)**.[6]
- Oracle Database XE uses **Oracle SQL Developer**.[7]
- MySQL 5.7 uses the **MySQL Workbench**,[8] but if you are using the Windows version, you should install it using the MySQL Installer for Windows.[9]
- ArangoDB 3.7 uses the **Arango Management Interface**, which is Web browser based and installed as part of the ArangoDB installation.

---

[3]Downloadable from *www.oracle.com/database/technologies/xe-downloads.html* (accessed October 2020).

[4]Downloadable from *https://dev.mysql.com/downloads/* (accessed October 2020).

[5]Downloadable from *https://dev.mysql.com/downloads/windows/* (accessed October 2020).

[6]Downloadable from *https://docs.microsoft.com/en-us/sql/ssms/download-sql-server-management-studio-ssms?view= sql-server-ver15* (accessed October 2020).

[7]Downloadable from *http://oracle.com/tools/downloads/sqldev-downloads.html* (accessed October 2020).

[8]Downloadable from *https://dev.mysql.com/downloads/* (accessed October 2020).

[9]Downloadable from *https://dev.mysql.com/downloads/windows/* (accessed October 2020).

In each online chapter, we discuss the appropriate utility programs for each DBMS product and show you how to use them.

## Creating a Database

The first step in working with a specific database in a DBMS is to actually create that database. However, this step is a bit more complicated than it might seem because each DBMS product has different terminology for what we just called a *database!*

- In Microsoft SQL Server 2019 and ArangoDB 3.7 we create a **database**. (That was easy!)
- In Oracle Database 19*c* and Oracle Database XE, we may (but it is not required that we) create a **tablespace** to store the tables and other objects that make up what we are referring to as a database.
- In MySQL 8.0, we create a **schema**.

In each online chapter for the specific DBMS product, we tell you exactly what in that DBMS product constitutes what we have been calling a *database* and the steps to create and name it. In each case, we end up with a usable database named *Cape_Codd* (although the exact name varies depending on the DBMS) for use with the Chapter 2 SQL queries and a second usable database named *VRG* (again the exact name varies depending on the DBMS) for the View Ridge Gallery database project.

## Creating and Running SQL Scripts

Now that we have created the *Cape_Codd* and *VRG* databases, we need to create the table and relationship structures of the databases and then populate the tables with data. For the three relational DBMS products, we prefer to do this with SQL scripts, as we have discussed in Chapter 2 on SQL queries and in Chapter 7 on SQL DDL. ArangoDB does not provide an easy way to execute sequences of commands from a file. (This functionality can be achieved by using Java like SQL-PSM and embedding AQL statements, but that is beyond the scope of this book.) This is not necessarily a drawback, just an indication that some things are done differently in NoSQL databases, where there is less need for such scripts due to the fact that importing JSON files is more common, and so on. In part this is due to JSON being somewhat of a standard NoSQL format, while there is no standard document query language as we have with SQL and relational databases. The tasks using SQL Scripts in the relational setting are performed in different ways in NoSQL databases and will be covered in online Chapter 10D. Therefore, we discuss how to create, store, retrieve, and run SQL scripts using one of the DBMS utilities:

- For Microsoft SQL Server 2019, we use the SQL Server Management Studio.
- For Oracle Database XE, we use SQL Developer.
- For MySQL 8.0, we use the MySQL Workbench.

Further, each relational DBMS product has its own variant of SQL and **SQL/Persistent Stored Modules (SQL/PSM):**

- For Microsoft SQL Server 2019, we have **Transact-SQL (T-SQL).**
- For Oracle Database XE, we have **Procedural Language/SQL (PL/SQL).**
- For MySQL 8.0, there is no separate variant name and we just use SQL and SQL/PSM.

We discuss each of these in the context of its parent DBMS product in the separate online chapters.

## Reviewing the Database Structure in the DBMS GUI Utility

Each DBMS product has also built its GUI utilities with the capability to work with database objects such as tables (or collections, in ArangoDB) in a GUI mode (similar to what we do in Microsoft Access 2019). We discuss how to use specific GUI utilities to do this:

- For Microsoft SQL Server 2019, we use the SQL Server 2019 Management Studio.
- For Oracle Database XE, we use Oracle SQL Developer.
- For MySQL 8.0, we use the MySQL Workbench.
- For ArangoDB, we use the Arango Management Interface

## Creating and Populating the View Ridge Gallery VRG Database Tables

Having created the VRG database and knowing how to use SQL scripts (or AQL queries), we turn to actually creating the VRG tables, referential integrity constraints, and indexes that form the basic structure of the database itself. As you might expect, each DBMS product has its own variation on exactly how this should be done. A good example of these differences is how each DBMS product handles surrogate keys:

- In Microsoft SQL Server 2019, we use the **T-SQL IDENTITY property**.
- For Oracle Database XE, we use the **PL/SQL SEQUENCE object**.
- For MySQL 8.0, we use the **MySQL AUTO_INCREMENT property**.
- In ArangoDB, each new document is automatically given a surrogate key value when it is created. The creator can override this by specifying a value for the key. There is no facility for automatically generating sequential numeric key values, so this would have to be done via application programming if desired.

Once the database structure is created, we discuss how to populate the tables (or collections) with data. Because the VRG data as provided in Figure 7-15 contains noncontinuous surrogate key values, we discuss how to handle this situation when inputting data into tables or collections.

## Creating SQL Views for the View Ridge Gallery VRG Database

In Chapter 7, we discussed the use of SQL views in a database. We now show how to create and use them in each specific relational DBMS. ArangoDB has a concept of views, but they are different and used for different purposes than typical relational views.

## Importing Microsoft Excel Data into a Database Table

When developing a database to support an application, it is very common to find that some (if not all) of the data needed in the database exists as data in user **worksheets** (also called **spreadsheets**). A typical example of this is a Microsoft Excel 2019 worksheet that a user has been maintaining that must now be converted to data stored in the database.

Therefore, we discuss how to import Microsoft Excel 2019 data into a database table. As usual, each DBMS product has its own way of doing this:

- In Microsoft SQL Server 2019, we use the data import tools of SQL Server Management Studio.
- For Oracle Database XE, we use the data import tools of SQL Developer.

- For MySQL 8.0, we have to download and install the **MySQL for Excel** utility,[10] which is also installable with MySQL Installer.
- For ArangoDB 3.7 we can use the Arango Management Interface to import CSV files, which can be created from Microsoft Excel files easily.

## Database Application Logic and SQL/Persistent Stored Modules (SQL/PSM)

In order to be used in an application (such as a Web site application), a database must be accessible from that application, and several application-related problems (such as creating and storing application variables) must be overcome. Although this can be done within an application programming language such as Java; a Microsoft .NET language such as C#.NET, C++.NET, or VB.NET; or the PHP Web scripting language (discussed in Chapter 11), we base our main discussion on how application logic can be embedded in **SQL/Persistent Stored Modules (SQL/PSM)–user-defined functions**, **triggers**, and **stored procedures**.

For each specific relational DBMS product, we examine and explain various SQL/PSM constructs and features:

- Variables
- Parameters
- Control-of-flow statements
  - BEGIN . . . END blocks
  - IF . . . THEN . . . ELSE structures
  - WHILE (looping) structures
  - RETURN {value} statements
- Cursor structures and statements
- SQL transaction control statements
- Output statements

We then use these elements to build DBMS SQL/PSM-specific user-defined functions, stored procedures, and triggers, and we cover these topics in a depth far beyond our coverage in Chapter 7. We build and run several stored procedures and triggers, explaining both the application use of the trigger or stored procedure and additional programming elements that are useful when creating user-defined functions, stored procedures, and triggers.

In non-relational DBMSs such as ArangoDB, SQL/PSM functionality is typically available via programming languages and APIs. In ArangoDB, for example, user-defined functions can be written in JavaScript, using a built-in API to access ArangoDB data. Stored procedure and trigger functionality is available by using the Foxx services framework, which is also based on JavaScript and runs inside the DBMS. We do not cover ArangoDB database application logic in this book.

## DBMS Concurrency Control

We discussed the concept of concurrency control in Chapter 9. As you would expect, each DBMS product implements concurrency **transaction isolation level** and **locking behavior** in its own way, which we examine for each specific DBMS product in the appropriate online chapter.

---

[10]Downloadable as part of the **MySQL Installer for Windows** at *https://dev.mysql.com/downloads/windows/* (accessed October 2020).

## DBMS Security

We discussed security in general terms in Chapter 9. For each specific DBMS product, we summarize how those general ideas pertain to that product, examine the specific server and database security options available, and create users with specific security privileges. We cover these topics in a depth far beyond our coverage in Chapter 7, and when we are done creating the needed database users for the VRG database, we are ready to use these users to provide the needed database security for our Web database applications in Chapter 11.

## DBMS Database Backup and Recovery

As explained in Chapter 9, databases and associated log files should be backed up periodically. When backups are available, it is possible to recover a failed database by restoring it from a prior database save and applying changes in the log. Again, we cover these topics in a depth far beyond our coverage in Chapter 7, and we examine and discuss the specific backup and recovery features and methods of the specific DBMS.

## Other DBMS Topics Not Discussed

Each online chapter covers essential topics for a specific DBMS product, but we cannot possibly cover everything about each DBMS in this book and online chapters. Therefore, we briefly discuss some of the important topics *not* covered in the chapter and point you toward information about those topics.

## Choose Your DBMS Product(s)!

Please see the online chapter for the DBMS product(s) you want to install and use. Download the appropriate online chapter, and study it, as it will be your guide to implementing the concepts discussed in this book in a DBMS, and to really learn these concepts, you need to actually use them in a DBMS.

> **CHAPTER 10A: MANAGING DATABASES WITH MICROSOFT SQL SERVER 2019**
>
> **CHAPTER 10B: MANAGING DATABASES WITH ORACLE DATABASE**
>
> **CHAPTER 10C: MANAGING DATABASES WITH MySQL 8.0**
>
> **AND**
>
> **CHAPTER 10D: MANAGING DOCUMENT DATABASES WITH ARANGODB**
>
> **ARE AVAILABLE ONLINE ON THE**
>
> *DATABASE PROCESSING:*
>
> *FUNDAMENTALS, DESIGN, AND IMPLEMENTATION (16TH EDITION)*
>
> **COMPANION WEBSITE AT**
>
> **www.pearsonhighered.com/kroenke**

# Summary

Online chapters are available at the *Database Processing: Fundamentals, Design, and Implementation (16th Edition)* Companion Web site, accessible at *www.pearsonhighered.com/kroenke*.

These chapters have been placed online to allow us to include more material relevant to each separate DBMS product than the length of this book would otherwise allow. The online materials are in PDF format and require that you have a PDF reader installed. If you need a PDF reader, we suggest you download and install the current version of the free Adobe Acrobat Reader DC.[11]

The material in these chapters describes the basic features and functions of Microsoft SQL Server 2019 in Chapter 10A, Oracle Database XE in Chapter 10B, Oracle MySQL 8.0 in Chapter 10C, and ArangoDB 3.7 in Chapter 10D. The discussion in these chapters uses the *Cape_Codd* database from Chapter 2 and the View Ridge Gallery VRG database from Chapter 7, and it parallels the discussion of SQL DDL, DML, and SQL/PSM in Chapter 7 and the discussion of database administration tasks in Chapter 9.

Topics in each online chapter written to cover each specific DBMS product include:

- Installing the DBMS
- Using the DBMS in the Cloud
- Using the DBMS Database Administration and Database Development Utilities
- Creating a Database
- Creating and Running SQL Scripts (for relational products)
- Reviewing the Database Structure in the DBMS GUI Utility
- Creating and Populating the View Ridge Gallery VRG Database Tables
- Creating SQL Views for the View Ridge Gallery VRG Database (for relational products)
- Importing Microsoft Excel 2019 Data into a Database Table
- Database Application Logic and SQL/Persistent Stored Modules (SQL/PSM) (for relational products)
- DBMS Concurrency Control
- DBMS Security
- DBMS Database Backup and Recovery
- Other DBMS Topics Not Discussed

These chapters build on the material presented in Chapter 7, but coverage of these topics is at a depth far beyond what Chapter 7 provides. Please see the online chapter for the DBMS product you want to install and use.

# Key Terms

Amazon Web Services (AWS)
ArangoDB
ArangoDB Community Edition 3.7
cloud computing service
database
locking behavior
Microsoft Access 2019
Microsoft Azure

Microsoft SQL Server 2019
Microsoft SQL Server 2019 Developer
 Edition
Microsoft SQL Server 2019 Reporting
 Services
Microsoft SQL Server Management
 Studio (SSMS)
MySQL 8.0

MySQL AUTO_INCREMENT property
MySQL Community Server 8.0
MySQL for Excel
MySQL Installer
MySQL Workbench
Oracle Database
Oracle Database 18c Express Edition
Oracle Database 19c

---

[11]Downloadable from *https://get.adobe.com/reader/* (accessed October 2020).

Oracle Database XE
Oracle SQL Developer
PL/SQL SEQUENCE object
Procedural Language/SQL (PL/SQL)
schema
spreadsheets

SQL/Persistent Stored Modules (SQL/
    PSM)
stored procedures
tablespace
Transact-SQL (T-SQL)
transaction isolation level

triggers
T-SQL IDENTITY property
user-defined functions
worksheets

# Exercises

**10.1** Determine which DBMS product or products you will be using while working through the material in this book.

**10.2** Based on your answer to Exercise 10.1, download Chapter 10A, Chapter 10B, Chapter 10C, and/or Chapter 10D as appropriate from the *Database Processing: Fundamentals, Design, and Implementation (16th edition)* Companion Web site at *www.pearsonhighered.com/kroenke*.

**10.3** Based on your answer to Exercise 10.1 and the discussions in Chapter 10A, Chapter 10B, Chapter 10C, and/or Chapter 10D, download and install the DBMS software that you will be using while working through the material in this book. When you have completed this exercise, you should have available for your use a working installation of the DBMS product or products you want to use.

# PART 5

# Database Access Standards and Technology

The three chapters in this section examine standards for database application processing and emerging technologies that are profoundly affecting where and how database systems exist and are used. Each chapter goes beyond the common relational DBMS setting described in Chapters 1–10 by extending our approach into other dimensions.

We begin in Chapter 11 by looking at ways of accessing relational data that typically exist outside the relational DBMS. We discuss database access standards, including ODBC, ADO.NET, and ASP.NET in Microsoft's .NET Framework and the Java-based JDBC and Java Server Pages (JSP) technologies. These standards are used to access relational (and other) databases even though they are in some sense outside the DBMS. Even though some of these standards are no longer on the leading edge of database processing, many applications still use them, and you will likely encounter them in your career. In fact, ODBC is making a comeback as relational DBMS products need to interconnect to Big Data structured storage products (discussed in Chapter 13) and ODBC is an established standard that can handle the task. Chapter 11 then describes the use of the popular PHP scripting language to create Web pages that access the View Ridge Gallery database. This is followed by a discussion of the confluence of database processing and document processing in an introduction to XML.

Chapter 12 extends into a different dimension with an introduction to some of the uses to which relational data can be put that go well beyond standard SQL queries and SQL/PSM code. We discuss business intelligence (BI) systems, including the data warehouse and data mart databases that support them. This is technology that has built on the main relational concepts presented in this book to deliver useful information in the form of various reports and data mining solutions such as market basket analysis and decision trees. In some cases this functionality has been incorporated into the DBMS, but in many cases it has not.

Chapter 13 completes our discussion, taking us in yet another direction by (1) introducing the cloud as another way to manage relational data and (2) leaving the relational model altogether and looking at the relatively recent topic of Big Data and the NoSQL and cloud-based systems designed to manage Big Data. Of course, enterprise relational DBMSs have managed and continue to manage large amounts of data, but there are many application areas that can benefit from relaxing typical relational assumptions about the structure of the data and the amount of consistency required by the system. In addition, these systems are often designed from the ground up with distributed data as the focus.

# 11

# The Web Server Environment

## Chapter Objectives

- To understand the nature and characteristics of the data environment that surrounds Internet technology database applications
- To learn the purpose, features, and facilities of ODBC
- To understand the characteristics of the Microsoft .NET Framework
- To understand the nature and goals of OLE DB
- To learn the characteristics and object model of ADO.NET
- To understand the characteristics of JDBC and the four types of JDBC drivers

- To understand the nature of JSP and know the differences between JSP and ASP.NET
- To understand HTML and PHP
- To be able to construct Web database application pages using PHP
- To understand the importance of XML
- To learn the basic concepts involved in using the SQL SELECT . . . FOR XML statement

**We have now** learned how to design and implement databases. Specifically, we have used the VRG database we have designed and implemented for the View Ridge Gallery as our example throughout most of this book. We started by creating the VRG data model and the VRG database design in Chapter 6 and then implemented that database design in SQL Server 2019 in Chapter 7. We used it as the basis of our discussion of database redesign in Chapter 8 and of database administration in Chapter 9.

Databases, however, do not exist in isolation. Rather, they are created as part of an information system and are used to store the data that the system processes to provide information to the people who use it, as discussed at the beginning of our work in Chapter 1.

In one way or another, today we are usually working with the **World Wide Web (WWW or W3 or Web)**, which is now so ubiquitous and commonly used that everyone takes it for granted. Application clients running in a **Web browser** such as **Microsoft Edge**, **Microsoft Internet Explorer**, **Apple Safari**, **Google Chrome**, or **Mozilla Firefox** are the norm and allow users to shop online and communicate with their friends by posts on Facebook or tweets on Twitter.

The WWW is not a communications network in itself. Instead, the WWW runs on the **Internet**, a system of interconnected smaller networks that now spans the earth and allows computer communication worldwide.

We no longer need a computer to use the Web. In addition to using the Web on their computers, people are using a **mobile phone** (or **cell phone**) over a **cellular network** provided by vendors such as Verizon, T-Mobile, AT&T, and Sprint. The widely used **smartphone** makes use of the data packages available from cellular providers to access the WWW, making smartphones very portable computers.

Another popular form factor is the **tablet**, of which the **Apple iPad** is the best example (although many other tablets running the **Google Android operating system (OS)** are also available). Tablets connecting to the Internet provide another link in the interconnected lifestyle we are living today.

Figure 11-1 illustrates how people use these devices today, in what is technically known as **client-server architecture**. Users actually want some sort of **service**, such as shopping online or communicating on Facebook. To get this service, a user has a hardware **device** (computer, smartphone, or tablet) that runs a software **client** application that provides the user with an interface for a desired service. A Web browser is often the client for a service such as Facebook or Twitter. (A smartphone **app** is also a client for these services.) A service is provided by a special computer called a **server** (because it provides the service). For example, Twitter uses servers to receive, store, and broadcast tweets. The client and the server communicate over the Internet or a cellular data network (which itself will connect to the Internet at some point). Internet hardware such as **routers** running networking software are responsible for the connections between the client and the server.

**FIGURE 11-1**

Client-Server Architecture

DEVICES running SERVICE CLIENT software    INTERNET HARDWARE running NETWORKING software    SERVERS running SERVICE SERVER software    DATABASES

USERS

And supporting all the client/server applications are databases. Every application needs to store, update, read, and delete data, and, as we have learned, that is the purpose of a database. Databases do not exist for their own sake—they exist to be used by applications needing the data they hold and maintain.

In this chapter, we will discuss and demonstrate exactly how databases are used to support the services that users want. This chapter begins by discussing some traditional standard interfaces and some current tools for accessing database servers. *ODBC*, or the Open Database Connectivity standard, was developed in the early 1990s to provide a product-independent interface to relational and other tabular data. Today, it is finding new life because of the new non-relational databases being developed to deal with the *Big Data* environment (which we will discuss in detail in Chapter 13). In the mid-1990s, Microsoft announced *OLE DB*, which is an object-oriented interface that encapsulates data-server functionality. Microsoft then developed *Active Data Objects (ADO)*, which is a set of objects for utilizing OLE DB that is designed for use by any language, including VBScript and JScript/JavaScript. This technology was used in *Active Server Pages (ASP)*, which were the basis of Web database applications. In 2002, Microsoft introduced the .NET Framework, which included *ADO.NET* (the successor to ADO) and *ASP.NET* (the successor to ASP) components. Today, the .NET Framework is the basis for all application development using Microsoft technology.

As an alternative to the Microsoft technologies, Sun Microsystems developed the Java platform in the 1990s, which includes the Java programming language, *Java Database Connectivity (JDBC)*, and *Java Server Pages (JSP)*. Sun Microsystems was purchased by Oracle Corporation in 2010, and the Java platform is now part of the Oracle family.

Although the .NET and Java technologies are important development platforms, additional technologies have been developed by other companies and open source projects. We will use two of these independently developed tools in this chapter: the NetBeans integrated development environment (IDE) and the PHP scripting language.

This chapter also considers one of the most important recent developments in information systems technology. It discusses the confluence of two information technology subject areas: database processing and document processing. For more than 20 years, these two subject areas developed independently of one another. With the advent of the Internet, however, they crashed together in what some industry pundits called a technology train wreck. The result is still being sorted out, with new products, product features, technology standards, and development practices emerging every month.

## A Web Database Application for the View Ridge Gallery

Now that we have created the VRG database, we will use it in this chapter as the basis for developing a Web database application for the View Ridge Gallery. We will call this Web database application the View Ridge Gallery Information System (VRGIS), and the VRGIS will provide both reporting and data input capabilities for the gallery. A screen shot of the VRGIS was used in Figure 6-35 to illustrate our introduction of the View Ridge Gallery. But before we build the VRGIS, we need to understand the underlying basis and process for developing Web database applications.

## Before You Read the Rest of Chapter!

To recreate the examples in this chapter, you need to have first done the following:

1. Created the *VRG-User* account for the VRG database. How to do this is discussed for SQL Server 2019 in online Chapter 10A, for Oracle Database XE in online Chapter 10B, and for MySQL 8.0 in online Chapter 10C.
2. Created the *InsertCustomerAndInterests* stored procedure for the VRG database. How to do this is discussed for SQL Server 2019 in online Chapter 10A, for Oracle Database XE in online Chapter 10B, and for MySQL 8.0 in online Chapter 10C.
3. Installed the appropriate ODBC driver for your DBMS. How to do this is discussed for SQL Server 2019 in online Chapter 10A, for Oracle Database XE in online Chapter 10B, and for MySQL 8.0 in online Chapter 10C.
4. Set up a Web server and supporting applications. How to do all of this is discussed in Appendix G, "Getting Started with Web Servers, PHP, and the NetBeans IDE." While you (or your instructor) may choose to use other components, our setup includes"

   - Setting up a Web server. We are using the Microsoft Internet Information Services (IIS) 10 Web server.
   - Installing the Java support via installing a Java Development Kit (JDK). We are using OpenJDK 14.0.2.
   - Installing the NetBeans integrated development environment (IDE) for creating and editing Web pages. We are using Apache NetBeans 12.0.
   - Installing the PHP Web page scripting language. We are using PHP 7.4.1., which we downloaded and set up using the Microsoft Web Platform Installer 5.1.
   - Installing the appropriate PHP drivers for you DBMS. We are using Microsoft Drivers for PHP for SQL Server 5.8.

If you haven't completed this work yet, we recommend that you complete it now, before continuing on with this chapter!

## The Web Database Processing Environment

The environment in which today's Web database applications reside is rich and complicated. As shown in Figure 11-2, users use Web browsers on their computers to request Web pages from Web servers, which in turn request information from database servers, which use a DBMS to obtain the data from their databases. Various programming languages are used in the process of creating the Web page code that is returned to the Web browser, which formats the Web page and displays it for the user. The final Web page coded may include:

- Scripting language code, such as JavaScript, which runs on the user's computer.
- Code generated by Web server programming languages, such as **PHP**, which controls the code content returned to the Web browser.
- Output from databases generated by Web servers sending requests for DBMS operations using SQL and SQL/PSM.

Although we will not discuss scripting languages in this text, you are undoubtedly familiar with their actions. A familiar example is the "Does not match" message you see every time a Web form requires you to reenter some data such as an email address or new password for validation and you don't retype it exactly. This type of error checking is performed locally on your computer by a Web page scripting language such as JavaScript.

We will discuss the interaction between the Web server and the DBMS. In a Web-based database processing environment, if the Web server and the DBMS can both run on the same computer, the system has a **two-tier architecture**. (One tier is for the Web browsers,

**FIGURE 11-2**

Three-Tier Architecture

and one is for the Web server/DBMS computer.) Alternatively, the Web server and DBMS can run on different computers, in which case the system has a **three-tier architecture**, as illustrated in Figure 11-2. High-performance applications might use many Web server computers, and in some systems several computers can run the DBMS as well. In the latter case, if the DBMS computers are processing the same databases, the system is referred to as a *distributed database*. Distributed databases are discussed later in this chapter.

As shown in Figure 11-3, a typical Web server needs to create Web pages that involve data from dozens of different sources, each with different data types. So far in this text, we have considered only relational databases, but as you can see from this figure, there are many other data types as well.

Consider the problems that the developer of Web server applications has when integrating these data. The developer may need to connect to:

- A relational database created in Microsoft SQL Server or Oracle Database
- A non-relational database, such as *MongoDB* or Neo Technology's *Neo4j*
- File-based data, such as found in spreadsheets like Microsoft Excel
- Email directories

Each one of these products has a different programming interface that the developer must learn. Further, these products evolve; thus, new features and functions will be added over time that will increase the developer's challenge.

**FIGURE 11-3**

The Variety of Data Types in Web Database Applications

# Database Server Access Standards

To solve the problem of communicating with different products, several standard interfaces have been developed for accessing database servers. Every DBMS product has an **application programming interface (API)**. An API is a collection of objects, methods, and properties for executing DBMS functions from program code. Unfortunately, each DBMS has its own API, and APIs vary from one DBMS product to another. To save programmers from having to learn to use many different interfaces, the computer industry has developed standards for database access.

The **Open Database Connectivity (ODBC)** standard was developed in the early 1990s to provide a DBMS-independent means for processing relational database data. In the mid-1990s, Microsoft announced **OLE DB**, which is an object-oriented interface that encapsulates data-server functionality. OLE DB was designed not just for access to relational databases but also for accessing many other types of data as well. As a **Component Object Model (COM)** interface, OLE DB is readily accessible to programmers through the use of programming languages such as C, C#, and Java. However, OLE DB is not as accessible to users of Visual Basic (VB) and scripting languages. Therefore, Microsoft developed **Active Data Objects (ADO)**, which is a set of objects for utilizing OLE DB that is designed for use by any language, including Visual Basic (VB), VBScript, and JScript. ADO has now been followed by **ADO.NET** (pronounced "A-D-O-dot-NET"), which is an improved version of ADO developed as part of Microsoft's .NET (pronounced "dot-NET") initiative and a component of the .NET Framework.

ADO technology is used to build Web pages as part of Microsoft's **Active Server Pages (ASP)**, which are then used to create Web-based database applications. ASP is a combination of Hypertext Markup Language (HTML) and VBScript or JScript that can read and write database data and transmit it over public and private networks using Internet protocols. ASP runs on Microsoft's Web server product, **Internet Information Services (IIS)**. When ADO.NET was introduced, Microsoft also introduced **ASP.NET**. ASP.NET is the successor to ASP and is the preferred Web page technology in the .NET Framework.

Of course, there are other connectivity methods and standards besides those propagated by Microsoft. The main alternatives to ADO.NET technology are based on or associated with Oracle Corporation's **Java platform** and include the **Java programming language**, **Java Database Connectivity (JDBC)**, **Java Data Objects (JDO)**, and **JavaServer Pages (JSP)**.

JSP technology is a combination of HTML and Java that accomplishes the same function as ASP.NET by compiling pages into Java servlets. JSP may connect to databases using JDBC. JSP is often used with Apache Tomcat, which implements JSP in an open source Web server (and is often used in conjunction with the open source **Apache Web server**).

However, the defining characteristic of the Java-related technology is that you must use Java as the programming language. You cannot even use **JavaScript**, Java's somewhat related scripting language cousin. If you know (or want to learn) Java, this is fine.

Although the Microsoft .NET Framework and the Oracle Corporation's Java platform are the two major players in Web database application development, other options are available. One such product is PHP, which is an open source Web page programming language, and another favorite combination of Web developers is the Apache Web server with the MySQL DBMS and the PHP language. This combination is called **AMP** (Apache-MySQL-PHP). When running on the Linux operating system, it is referred to as **LAMP**; when running on the Windows operating system, it is referred to as **WAMP**. And because PHP works with all DBMS products, we will use it in this book. Other possibilities include the Perl and Python languages (both of which can be the "P" in AMP, LAMP, or WAMP) and the Ruby language with its Web development framework called Ruby on Rails.

# The ODBC Standard

The ODBC standard was created to address the data access problem that concerns relational databases and data sources that are table-like, such as spreadsheets. As shown in Figure 11-4, ODBC is an interface between the Web server (or other database application) and the DBMS. It consists of a set of standards by which SQL statements can be issued and results and error messages can be returned. As shown in Figure 11-4, developers can call the DBMS using native DBMS interfaces (which are APIs) if they want to (sometimes they do this to improve performance), but the developer who does not have the time or desire to learn many different DBMS native libraries can use the ODBC instead.

The ODBC standard is an interface by which application programs can access and process databases and tabular data in a DBMS-independent manner. This means, for example, that an application that uses the ODBC interface could process an Oracle Database database, an SQL Server database, a spreadsheet, or any other ODBC-compliant database without making any coding changes. The goal is to allow a developer to create a single application that can access databases supported by different DBMS products without needing to be changed or even recompiled.

ODBC was developed by a committee of industry experts from the X/Open and SQL Access Group committees. Several such standards were proposed, but ODBC emerged as the winner, primarily because it had been implemented by Microsoft and is an important part of Windows. Microsoft's initial interest in support of such a standard was to allow products such as Microsoft Excel to access database data from a variety of DBMS products without having to be recompiled. Of course, Microsoft's interests have changed since the introduction of OLE DB and ADO.NET.

## ODBC Architecture

Figure 11-5 shows the components of the ODBC standard. The application program, driver manager, and DBMS drivers all reside on the application server computer. The drivers send requests to data sources, which reside on the database server. According to the standard, an **ODBC data source** is the database and its associated DBMS, operating system, and network platform. An ODBC data source can be a relational database; it can also be a file server, such as BTrieve, or even a spreadsheet.

**FIGURE 11-4**

Role of the ODBC Standard

Relational Databases:
Oracle Database,
Microsoft SQL Server,
MySQL, Microsoft Access,
IBM DB2 . . .

Nonrelational Databases:
Dynamo, Apache Cassandra,
MongoDB, ArangoDB, Neo4j...

VSAM, ISAM, Other
File Processors

Email, Spreadsheets,
Other Document Types

Pictures, Audio,
Other????

FIGURE 11-5

ODBC Architecture

**Application can process a database using any of the three DBMS products.**

The application issues requests to create a connection with a data source; to issue SQL statements and receive results; to process errors; and to start, commit, and roll back transactions. ODBC provides a standard means for each of these requests, and it defines a standard set of error codes and messages.

The **ODBC driver manager** serves as an intermediary between the application and the DBMS drivers. When the application requests a connection, the driver manager determines the type of DBMS that processes a given ODBC data source and loads that driver into memory (if it is not already loaded). The driver manager also processes certain initialization requests and validates the format and order of ODBC requests that it receives from the application. For Windows, the driver manager is provided by Microsoft.

An **ODBC driver** processes ODBC requests and submits specific SQL statements to a given type of data source. Each data source type has a different driver. For example, there are drivers for SQL Server, for Oracle Database, for MySQL, for Microsoft Access, and for all of the other products whose vendors have chosen to participate in the ODBC standard. Drivers are supplied by DBMS vendors and by independent software companies.

It is the responsibility of the driver to ensure that standard ODBC commands execute correctly. In some cases, if the data source is itself not SQL compliant, the driver may need to perform considerable processing to fill in for a lack of capability at the data source. In other cases, when the data source supports full SQL, the driver need only pass the request through for processing by the data source. The driver also converts data source error codes and messages into the ODBC standard codes and messages.

ODBC identifies two types of drivers: single tier and multiple tier. An **ODBC single-tier driver** processes both ODBC calls and SQL statements. An example of a single-tier driver is shown in Figure 11-6(a). In this example, the data are stored in Xbase files (the format used by FoxPro, dBase, and others). Because Xbase file managers do not process SQL, it is the job of the driver to translate the SQL request into Xbase file-manipulation commands and to transform the results back into SQL form.

An **ODBC multiple-tier driver** processes ODBC calls but passes the SQL requests directly to the database server. Although it may reformat an SQL request to conform to the dialect of a particular data source, it does not process the SQL. An example of the use of a multiple-tier driver is shown in Figure 11-6(b).

## Conformance Levels

The creators of the ODBC standard faced a dilemma. If they chose to describe a standard for a minimal level of capability, many vendors would be able to comply. But if they did so, the standard would represent only a small portion of the complete power and expressiveness of ODBC and SQL. However, if the standard addressed a very high level of capability, only a few vendors would be able to comply with the standard, and it would become unimportant. To deal with this dilemma, the committee wisely chose to define levels of conformance to the standard. The committee defined two types of conformance: ODBC conformance and SQL conformance.

**FIGURE 11-6**

ODBC Driver Types

(a) ODBC Single-Tier Driver

(b) ODBC Multiple-Tier Driver

### ODBC Conformance Level

**ODBC conformance levels** are concerned with the features and functions that are made available through the driver's API. As previously discussed, a driver API is a set of functions that the application can call to receive services. Figure 11-7 summarizes the three levels of ODBC conformance that are addressed in the standard. In practice, almost all drivers provide at least Level 1 API conformance, so the core API level is not too important.

An application can call a driver to determine which level of ODBC conformance it provides. If the application requires a level of conformance that is not present, it can terminate the session in an orderly fashion and generate appropriate messages to the user. Or the application can be written to use higher-level conformance features if they are available and to work around the missing functions if a higher level is not available.

For example, drivers at the Level 2 API must provide a scrollable cursor. Using conformance levels, an application could be written to use cursors if they are available; but if they are not, to work around the missing feature, the application would select needed data using highly restrictive WHERE clauses. Doing this would ensure that only a few rows were returned at a time to the application, and it would process those rows using a cursor that it maintained itself. Performance would likely be slower in the second case, but at least the application would be able to successfully execute.

### SQL Conformance Level

**ODBC SQL conformance levels** specify which SQL statements, expressions, and data types a driver can process. Three SQL conformance levels are defined, as summarized in Figure 11-8. The capability of the minimum SQL grammar is quite limited, and most drivers support at least the core SQL grammar.

As with ODBC conformance levels, an application can call the driver to determine what level of SQL conformance it supports. With that information, the application can then determine which SQL statements can be issued. If necessary, the application can then terminate the session or use alternative, less powerful, means of obtaining the data.

### Creating an ODBC Data Source Name

An ODBC data source is an ODBC data structure that identifies a database and the DBMS that processes it. Data sources identify other types of data, such as spreadsheets and other nondatabase tabular data stores, but we are not concerned with that use here.

FIGURE 11-7

Summary of ODBC
Conformance Levels

| Core API |
| --- |
| Connect to data sources |
| Prepare and execute SQL statements |
| Retrieve data from a result set |
| Commit or roll back transactions |
| Retrieve error information |

| Level 1 API |
| --- |
| Core API |
| Connect to data sources with driver-specific information |
| Send and receive partial results |
| Retrieve catalog information |
| Retrieve information about driver options, capabilities, and functions |

| Level 2 API |
| --- |
| Core and Level 1 API |
| Browse possible connections and data sources |
| Retrieve native form of SQL |
| Call a translation library |
| Process a scrollable cursor |

The three types of data sources are file, system, and user. A **file data source** is a file that can be shared among database users. The only requirement is that the users have the same DBMS driver and privilege to access the database. The data source file can be emailed or otherwise distributed to possible users. A **system data source** is one that is local to a single computer. The operating system and any user on that system (with proper privileges) can use a system data source. A **user data source** is available only to the user who created it.

In general, the best choice for Internet applications is to create a system data source on the Web server. Browser users then access the Web server, which, in turn, uses the system data source to set up a connection with the DBMS and the database.

As our first step in developing the VRGIS, we need to create a system data source for the VRG database so that we can use it in the Web database processing application. We created the VRG database in SQL Server 2019, and the system data source will provide a connection to the SQL Server 2019 DBMS. To create a system data source in a Windows operating system, you use the **ODBC Data Source Administrator**.[1]

---

[1]**Important:** If you are using a 64-bit Windows operating system, be aware that there are two different ODBC Data Source Administrator programs provided—one for 32-bit applications and one for 64-bit applications. The ODBC Data Source Administrator used if you follow the steps in the text is the 64-bit version. However, if you are running a 32-bit program in the Web application set (e.g., a 32-bit Web browser), then you must use the 32-bit version of the ODBC Data Source Administrator. Starting with Windows 8, and Windows Server 2012, the programs are, fortunately, clearly labeled as either 32-bit or 64-bit. Nonetheless, if everything seems to be set up correctly yet the Web pages are not displaying properly, then this is likely to be the problem.

**FIGURE 11-8**

Summary of SQL
Conformance Levels

| Minimum SQL Grammar |
| --- |
| CREATE TABLE, DROP TABLE |
| Simple SELECT (does not include subqueries) |
| INSERT, UPDATE, DELETE |
| Simple expressions (A > B + C) |
| CHAR, VARCHAR, LONGVARCHAR data types |

| Core SQL Grammar |
| --- |
| Minimum SQL Grammar |
| ALTER TABLE, CREATE INDEX, DROP INDEX |
| CREATE VIEW, DROP VIEW |
| GRANT, REVOKE |
| Full SELECT (includes subqueries) |
| Aggregate functions such as SUM, COUNT, MAX, MIN, AVG |
| DECIMAL, NUMERIC, SMALLINT, INTEGER, REAL, FLOAT, DOUBLE PRECISION data types |

| Extended SQL Grammar |
| --- |
| Core SQL Grammar |
| Outer joins |
| UPDATE and DELETE using cursor positions |
| Scalar functions such as SUBSTRING, ABS |
| Literals for date, time, and timestamp |
| Batch SQL statements |
| Stored procedures |

### Opening the ODBC Data Source Administrator in Windows 10

1. Click the **Start** button.
2. **Browse through the applications to** the **Windows Administrative Tools** folder, and click the folder to open it.
3. **Right**-click the **ODBC Data Sources (64-bit)** program to display the shortcut menu.
4. Click **More | Run as administrator** to open the program.

We can now use the ODBC Data Source Administrator to create a system data source named VRG for use with SQL Server 2019:

### Creating the VRG System Data Source

1. In the ODBC Data Source Administrator, click the **System DSN** tab, and then click the **Add** button.

**2.** In the Create New Data Source dialog box, we need to connect to SQL Server 2019, so we select the **Microsoft ODBC Driver 17 for SQL Server**, as shown in Figure 11-9.

**3.** Click the **Finish** button. The Create New Data Source to SQL Server dialog box appears.

**4.** In the Create New Data Source to SQL Server dialog box, enter the information shown for the VRG in Figure 11-10(a) (note that the database server is selected from the Server drop-down list), and then click the **Next** button.

   ■ **NOTE:** If the name of the installed SQL server instance, preceded by the name of the computer on which it is installed, does not appear in the Server drop-down list, enter it manually as **ComputerName\SQLServerName**. You can find the proper name to use in Object Explorer in SQL Server Management Studio, where it appears as the name of the connected SQL Server. If the SQL Server instance is the *default installation* (always named MSSQLSERVER) of SQL Server on the computer, enter *only* **ComputerName**.

**5.** As shown in Figure 11-10(b), in the next page of the Create a New Data Source to SQL Server dialog box, click the radio button that selects SQL Server authentication, and then enter the Login ID of **VRG-User** and the Password of **VRG-User+password** that we created in online Chapter 10A. (See online Chapter 10B for creating users in Oracle Database, and online Chapter 10C for creating users in MySQL 8.0.). After these data have been entered, click the **Next** button.

   ■ **NOTE:** If the Login ID and Password are not correct, an error message will appear. Make sure you have correctly created the SQL Server login as discussed in online Chapter 10A and have entered the correct data here.

**6.** As shown in Figure 11-10(c), click the check box to change the default database, set the default database to **VRG**, and then click the **Next** button.

**7.** As shown in Figure 11-10(d), another group of settings is displayed. There is no need to change any of these settings, so click the **Finish** button to close the Create a New Data Source to SQL Server dialog box.

**FIGURE 11-9**

The Create New Data Source to SQL Server Dialog Box

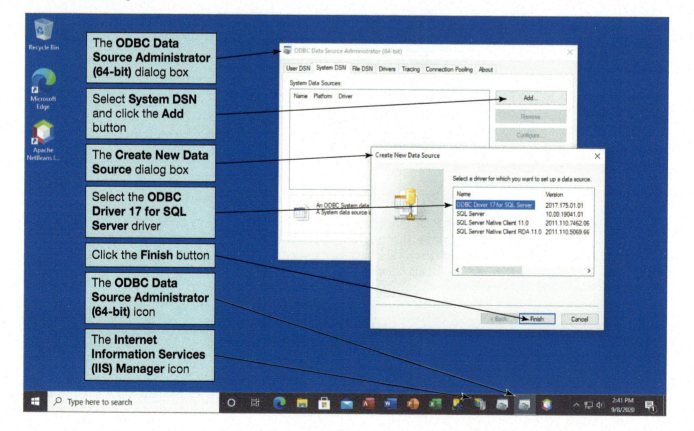

Type in a name for this system DSN

Type in a description

The drop-down list arrow button—Select the server from the drop-down list—if the list is empty, type in the *server name* shown in the SQL Server Management Studio Object Explorer

The **Next** button

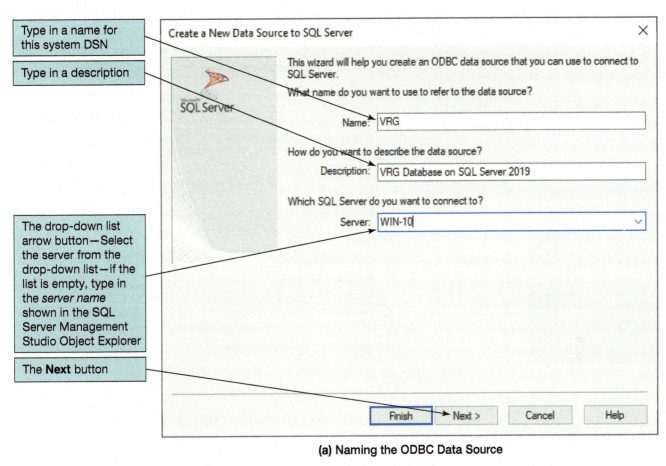

**(a)** Naming the ODBC Data Source

Click this radio button for SQL Server authentication

Type in the user Login ID here

Type in the associated user password here

The **Next** button

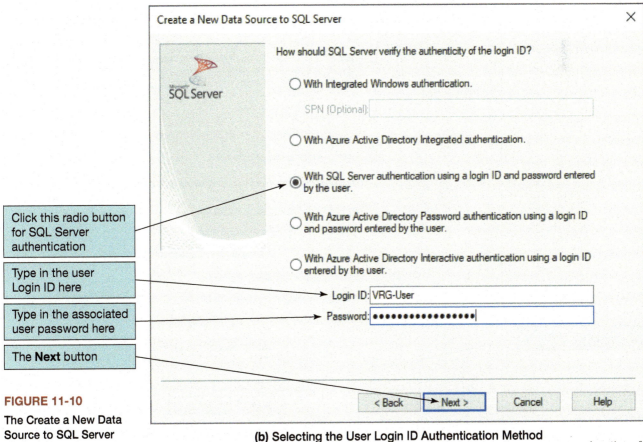

**FIGURE 11-10**

The Create a New Data Source to SQL Server Dialog Box

**(b)** Selecting the User Login ID Authentication Method

*(continued)*

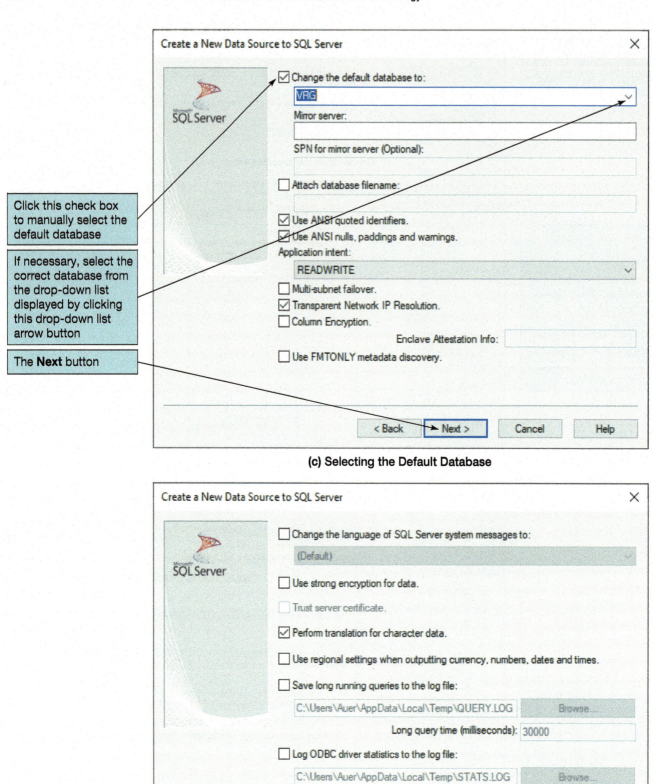

Click this check box to manually select the default database

If necessary, select the correct database from the drop-down list displayed by clicking this drop-down list arrow button

The **Next** button

**(c) Selecting the Default Database**

The **Finish** button

**(d) Additional Setting Options**

FIGURE 11-10
Continued

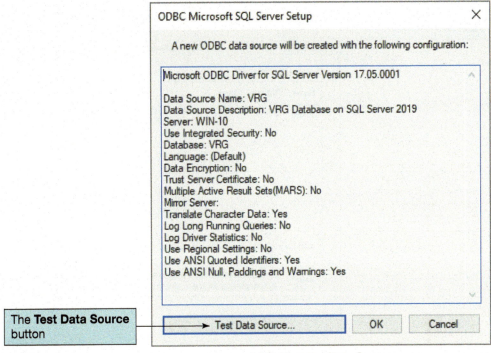

The **Test Data Source** button

**(e) Testing the Data Source**

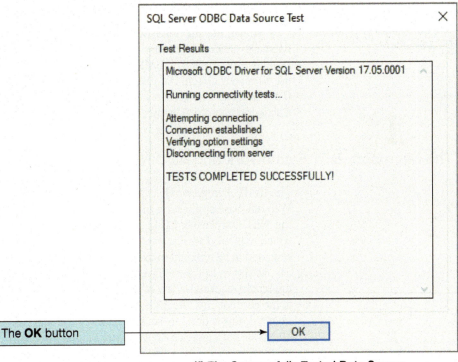

The **OK** button

**FIGURE 11-10**

Continued

**(f) The Successfully Tested Data Source**

8. The ODBC Microsoft SQL Server Setup dialog box is displayed, as shown in Figure 11-10(e). This dialog box is used to summarize the settings to be created for the new ODBC data source. Click the **Test Data Source** button to test the settings.

9. As shown in Figure 11-10(f), the SQL Server ODBC Data Source Test dialog box appears, showing that the tests completed successfully. Click the **OK** button to exit the dialog box and create the ODBC data source.

10. The completed VRG system data source is shown in Figure 11-11. Click the **OK** button to close the ODBC Data Source Administrator.

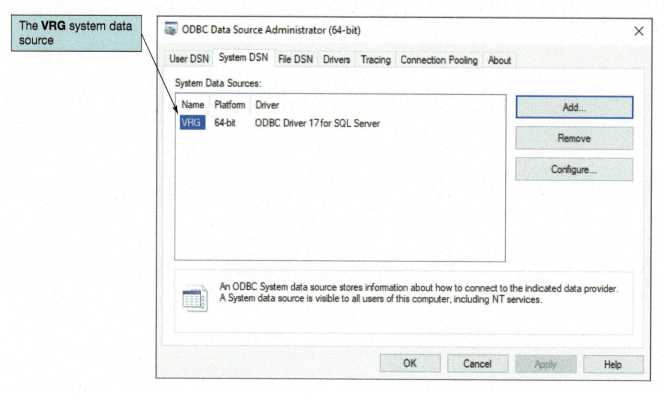

The **VRG** system data source

**FIGURE 11-11**

The Completed VRG System Data Source

We will use the VRG DSN later in this chapter to process the SQL Server 2019 *VRG* database created in online Chapter 10A. Similarly, if you are using either the Oracle Database or MySQL DBMS, you should create an appropriate system data source for use with your Oracle Database or MySQL version of the View Ridge Gallery *VRG* database. (For Oracle Database, see the discussion in online Chapter 10B, and for MySQL, see the discussion in online Chapter 10C.)

## The Microsoft .NET Framework and ADO.NET

The **.NET Framework** is Microsoft's comprehensive application development platform. Web database application tools are included in the .NET Framework. Originally released as the .NET Framework 1.0 in January 2002, the current version is the .NET Framework 4.8, which will be the final version of the .NET Framework. The cross-platform .NET 5 is expected to be released in fall or winter 2020.[2]

As shown in Figure 11-12, the .NET Framework can best be visualized as a set of building blocks stacked on top of each other. Each additional block provides more functionality to the components already existing in previous blocks, and if earlier components need to be updated, this is done by service packs to the older blocks. Thus, .NET Framework 2.0 SP2 and .NET Framework SP2 were included as part of .NET Framework 3.5 SP1. Upgrades to all portions of the .NET Framework are included in .NET Framework 4.0, .NET Framework 4.5, and .NET Framework 4.5.1. The .NET Framework 4.6, .NET Framework 4.6.1, .NET Framework 4.6.2, .NET Framework 4.7, .NET Framework 4.7.1, .NET Framework 4.7.2, and .NET Framework 4.8 each update the .NET Framework for new versions of the Microsoft Windows operating system and provide new enhancements, particularly in the area of network security and cryptography.

Although Figure 11-12 does not show every feature of the .NET Framework 3.5 SP1, the basic structure is easy to see. The .NET Framework 2.0 is now the basic layer and

---

[2]See *Introducing .NET 5* at https://devblogs.microsoft.com/dotnet/introducing-net-5/ (accessed August 2020).

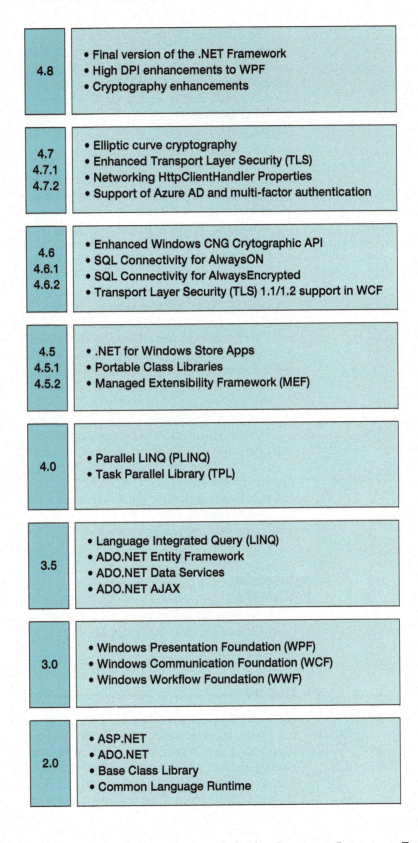

contains the most basic features. These include the **Common Language Runtime (CLR)** and the **Base Class Library**, which support all of the programming languages (e.g., VB.NET and Visual C#.NET) used with the .NET Framework. This layer also includes the ADO.NET and ASP.NET components, which are needed for Web database applications.

The .NET Framework 3.0 added a set of components that are not of interest to us here. We are more concerned with the features added in .NET Framework 3.5 and 3.5 SP1, noting that these features were upgraded, but not replaced, by .NET Framework 4.0. Note that several extensions to ADO.NET were included in .NET Framework 3.5 and 3.5 SP1, such as the **ADO.NET Entity Framework**, which supports Microsoft's emerging **Entity Data Model (EDM)** data modeling technology, as well as the **Language Integrated Query (LINQ)** component, which allows SQL queries to be programmed directly into application programs in a simple manner.

Besides updating existing features, the .NET Framework 4.0 added features needed for parallel processing on clustered servers. These include **Parallel LINQ (PLINQ)** and **Task Parallel Library (TPL)**, but these parallel processing features are beyond the scope of this book. The .NET Framework 4.5 again updated many existing features and added functionality for Windows 8 Apps, including **.NET for Windows Store Apps**, **Portable Class Libraries**, and the **Managed Extensibility Framework (MEF)**. .NET Framework 4.5.1 and .NET Framework 4.5.2 were minor updates distributed with Windows 8.1 and Windows Server 2012 R2.

Requiring Windows Vista SP 2, also known as .NET 2015, added the .NET Framework 4.6 and ASP.NET 5. Included were a just-in-time 64-bit compiler and significant cryptography updates. The Windows Communication Foundation (WCF) introduced in .NET Framework 3.0 **Secure Sockets Layer (SSL)** gained **Transport Layer Security (TLS) 1.1** and **Transport Layer Security (TLS) 1.2**. While dropping support for Windows Vista and Windows Server 2008, .NET Framework 4.6.1 and .NET Framework 4.6.2 added new functionality in cryptography, ADO.NET, and ASP.NET.

Released with the Windows 10 Creators Update, .NET Framework 4.7 and 4.7.1 include elliptic curve cryptography and operating system support for TLS. .NET Framework 4.7.2 added server enhancements to SQL client authentication, including multi-factor authentication, and implementation of HttpClientHandler networking support.

The .NET Framework added new features in the base .NET classes, the Windows Communication Foundation (WCF), the Windows Presentation Foundation (WPF) and the common language runtime (CLR). For more information on changes to .NET Framework, see the Microsoft MSDN Web page.[3] Now that we understand the basic structure of the .NET Framework, we can look at some of the pieces in detail.

> **BY THE WAY**   The Microsoft Entity Data Model (EDM) is similar in concept to the Semantic Object Model discussed in Appendix F, "The Semantic Object Model," of this book. A discussion of the EDM can be found at *http://msdn.microsoft.com/en-us/library/aa697428(VS.80).aspx*.

## OLE DB

ODBC has been a tremendous success and has greatly simplified some database development tasks. However, it does have some disadvantages, and in particular one substantial disadvantage that Microsoft addressed by creating OLE DB. Figure 11-13 shows the relationship among OLE DB, ODBC, and other data types. OLE DB is one of the foundations of data access in the Microsoft world. As such, it is important to understand the fundamental ideas of OLE DB, even if you will only work with the ADO.NET interface that lies on top of it because, as you will see, OLE DB remains as a data provider to ADO.NET. In this section, we present essential OLE DB concepts and use them to introduce some important object-oriented programming topics.

---

[3]Located at *https://docs.microsoft.com/en-us/dotnet/framework/whats-new/index.*

**FIGURE 11-13**

The Role of OLE DB

OLE DB provides an object-oriented interface to data of almost any type. DBMS vendors can wrap portions of their native libraries in OLE DB objects to expose their product's functionality through this interface. OLE DB can also be used as an interface to ODBC data sources. Finally, OLE DB was developed to support the processing of non-relational data as well.

OLE DB is an implementation of the Microsoft **Object Linking and Embedding (OLE)** object standard. OLE DB objects are Component Object Model (COM) objects and support all required interfaces for such objects. Fundamentally, OLE DB breaks the features and functions of a DBMS up into COM objects. Some objects support query operations; others perform updates; others support the creation of database schema constructs, such as tables, indexes, and views; and still others perform transaction management, such as optimistic locking.

This characteristic overcomes a major disadvantage of ODBC. With ODBC, a vendor must create an ODBC driver for almost all DBMS features and functions in order to participate in ODBC at all. This is a large task that requires a substantial investment. With OLE DB, however, a DBMS vendor can implement portions of a product. One could, for example, implement only the query processor, participate in OLE DB, and hence be accessible to customers using ADO.NET. Later, the vendor could add more objects and interfaces to increase OLE DB functionality.

This text does not assume that you are an object-oriented programmer, so we need to develop a few concepts. In particular, you need to understand objects, abstractions, methods, properties, and collections. An **abstraction** is a generalization of something. ODBC interfaces are abstractions of native DBMS access methods. When we abstract something, we lose detail, but we gain the ability to work with a broader range of types.

For example, a **recordset** is an abstraction of a relation. In this abstraction, a recordset is defined to have certain characteristics that will be common to all recordsets. Every recordset, for instance, has a set of columns, which in this abstraction is called Fields. Now, the goal of abstraction is to capture everything important but to omit details that are not needed by users of the abstraction. Thus, Oracle relations may have some characteristics that are not represented in a recordset; the same might be true for relations in SQL Server, in DB2, and in other DBMS products. These unique characteristics will be lost in the abstraction, but if the abstraction is a good one, no one will care.

Moving up a level, a **rowset** is the OLE DB abstraction of a recordset. Now, why does OLE DB need to define another abstraction? Because OLE DB addresses data sources that are not tables but that do have *some* of the characteristics of tables. Consider all of the email addresses in your personal email file. Are those addresses the same as a relation? No, but they do share some of the characteristics that relations have. Each address is a semantically related group of data items. Like rows of a table, it is sensible to go to the first one, move to the next one, and so forth. But unlike relations, they are not all of the same type. Some addresses are for individuals; others are for mailing lists. Thus, any action on a recordset that depends on everything in the recordset being the same kind of thing cannot be used on a rowset.

Working from the top down, OLE DB defines a set of data properties and behaviors for rowsets. Every rowset has those properties and behaviors. Furthermore, OLE DB defines a recordset as a subtype of a rowset. Recordsets have all of the properties and behaviors that rowsets have, plus they have some that are uniquely characteristic of recordsets.

Abstraction is both common and useful. You will hear of abstractions of transaction management or abstractions of querying or abstractions of interfaces. This simply means that certain characteristics of a set of things are formally defined as a type.

An object-oriented programming **object** is an abstraction that is defined by its properties and methods. For example, a recordset object has an AllowEdits property and a RecordsetType property and an EOF property. These **properties** represent characteristics of the recordset abstraction. An object also has actions that it can perform that are called **methods**. A recordset has methods such as Open, MoveFirst, MoveNext, and Close. Strictly speaking, the definition of an object abstraction is called an **object class** or just a *class*. An instance of an object class, such as a particular recordset, is called an *object*. All objects of a class have the same methods and the same properties, but the values of the properties vary from object to object.

The last term we need to address is *collection*. A **collection** is an object that contains a group of other objects. A recordset has a collection of other objects called Fields. The collection has properties and methods. One of the properties of all collections is Count, which is the number of objects in the collection. Thus, recordset.Fields.Count is the number of fields in the collection. In OLE DB, collections are named as the plural of the objects they collect. Thus, there is a Fields collection of Field objects, an Errors collection of Error objects, a Parameters collection of Parameters objects, and so forth. An important method of a collection is an iterator, which is a method that can be used to process each member of the collection or otherwise identify the items in the collection.

## Goals of OLE DB

The major goals for OLE DB are listed in Figure 11-14. First, as mentioned, OLE DB breaks DBMS functionality and services into object pieces. This partitioning means great flexibility for both **data consumers** (users of OLE DB functionality) and **data providers** (vendors of products that deliver OLE DB functionality). Data consumers take only the objects and functionality they need; a wireless device for reading a database can have a very slim footprint. Unlike with ODBC, data providers need only implement a portion of DBMS functionality. This partitioning also means that data providers can deliver capabilities in multiple interfaces.

This last point needs expansion. An **object interface** is a packaging of objects. An **interface** is specified by a set of objects and the properties and methods that they expose. An object need not expose all of its properties and methods in a given interface. Thus, a recordset object would expose only read methods in a query interface but would expose create, update, and delete methods in a modification interface.

How the object supports the interface, or the **implementation**, is completely hidden from the user. In fact, the developers of an object are free to change the implementation whenever they want. Who will know? But they may not ever change the interface without incurring the justifiable disdain of their users!

OLE DB defines standardized interfaces. Data providers, however, are free to add interfaces on top of the basic standards. Such extensibility is essential for the next goal, which is to provide an object interface to any data type. Relational databases can be processed through

**FIGURE 11-14**

The Goals of OLE DB

| Create object interfaces for DBMS functionality pieces |
| --- |
| Query |
| Update |
| Transaction management |
| Other DBMS functionality |
| **Increase flexibility** |
| Allow data consumers to use only the objects they need |
| Allow data providers to expose pieces of DBMS functionality |
| Providers can deliver functionality in multiple interfaces |
| Interfaces are standardized and extensible |
| **Object interface over any type of data** |
| Relational database |
| ODBC or native |
| Nonrelational database |
| VSAM and other files |
| Email |
| Other |
| **Do not force data to be converted or moved from where they are** |

OLE DB objects that use ODBC or that use the native DBMS drivers. OLE DB includes support for the other types as indicated in Figure 11-13.

The net result of these design goals is that data need not be converted from one form to another, nor need they be moved from one data source to another. The Web server shown in Figure 11-13 can utilize OLE DB to process data in any of the formats, right where the data reside. This means that transactions may span multiple data sources and may be distributed on different computers. The OLE DB provision for this is the **Microsoft Transaction Server (MTS)**. However, discussion of the MTS is beyond the scope of this text.

### OLE DB Terminology

As shown in Figure 11-15, OLE DB has two types of data providers. **Tabular data providers** present their data via rowsets. Examples are DBMS products, spreadsheets, and ISAM file processors, such as dBase and FoxPro. Additionally, other types of data, such as email, can be presented in rowsets. Tabular data providers bring data of some type into the OLE DB world.

A **service provider**, in contrast, is a transformer of data. Service providers accept OLE DB data from an OLE DB tabular data provider and transform it in some way. Service providers are both consumers and providers of transformed data. An example of a service provider is one that obtains data from a relational DBMS and then transforms them into XML documents. Both data and service providers process rowset objects. A rowset is equivalent to what we called a **cursor** in Chapter 9, and in fact the two terms are frequently used synonymously.

FIGURE 11-15

Two Types of OLE DB Data
Providers

| Tabular data provider |
| --- |
| Exposes data via rowsets |
| Examples: DBMS, spreadsheets, ISAMs, email |
| **Service provider** |
| Transforms data through OLE DB interfaces |
| Both a consumer and a provider of data |
| Examples: query processors, XML document creator |

For database applications, rowsets are created by processing SQL statements. The results of a query, for example, are stored in a rowset. OLE DB rowsets have dozens of different methods, which are exposed via the interfaces listed in Figure 11-16.

IRowSet provides object methods for forward-only sequential movement through a rowset. When you declare a forward-only cursor in OLE DB, you are invoking the IRowSet interface. The IAccessor interface is used to bind program variables to rowset fields.

The IColumnsInfo interface has methods for obtaining information about the columns in a rowset. IRowSet, IAccessor, and IColumnsInfo are the basic rowset interfaces. Other interfaces are defined for more advanced operations such as scrollable cursors, update operations, direct access to particular rows, explicit locks, and so forth.

## ADO and ADO.NET

Because OLE DB is an object-oriented interface, it is particularly suited to object-oriented languages such as VB.NET and Visual C#.NET. Many database application developers, however, program in scripting languages such as VBScript or JScript (Microsoft's version of JavaScript). To meet the needs of these programmers, Microsoft developed Active Data Objects (ADO) as a cover over OLE DB objects, as shown in Figure 11-17. ADO has enabled programmers to use almost any language to access OLE DB functionality.

ADO is a simple object model that overlies the more complex OLE DB object model. ADO can be called from scripting languages, such as JScript and VBScript, and it can also be

FIGURE 11-16

Rowset Interfaces

| IRowSet |
| --- |
| Methods for sequential iteration through a rowset |
| **IAccessor** |
| Methods for setting and determining bindings between rowset and client program variables |
| **IColumnsInfo** |
| Methods for determining information about the columns in the rowset |
| **Other interfaces** |
| Scrollable cursors |
| Create, update, delete rows |
| Directly access particular rows (bookmarks) |
| Explicitly set locks |
| Additional capabilities |

FIGURE 11-17

The Role of ADO

called from more powerful languages, such as Visual Basic .NET, Visual C#.NET, Visual C++. NET, and even Java. Because ADO is easier to understand and use than OLE DB, ADO was (and still is) often used for database applications.

ADO.NET is a new, improved, and greatly expanded version of ADO that was developed as part of Microsoft's .NET initiative. It incorporates the functionality of ADO and OLE DB but adds much more. In particular, ADO.NET facilitates the transformation of XML documents (discussed later in this chapter) to and from relational database constructs. ADO. NET also provides the ability to create and process in-memory databases called *datasets*. Figure 11-18 shows the role of ADO.NET.

### The ADO.NET Object Model

Now we need to look at ADO.NET in more detail. As shown in Figure 11-19, an **ADO.NET Data Provider** is a class library that provides ADO.NET services. Microsoft-supplied ADO. NET Data Providers are available for ODBC, OLE DB, SQL Server, Oracle Database, and

FIGURE 11-18

The Role of ADO.NET

FIGURE 11-19

Components of an ADO.NET
Data Provider

**ADO.NET Data Providers:**

• OLE DB
• SQL Server Client
• Oracle Database Client
• Others . . .

EDM applications, which means that ADO.NET works not only with the ODBC and OLE DB data access methods we have discussed in this chapter, but directly with SQL Server, Oracle Database, and .NET language applications that use EDM as well. ADO Data Providers from Microsoft and other vendors are listed at *https://docs.microsoft.com/en-us/dotnet/framework/data/adonet/data-providers*.

A simplified version of the ADO.NET object model is shown in Figure 11-20. The ADO.NET object classes are grouped into Data Providers and DataSets.

FIGURE 11-20

The ADO.NET Object
Model

The **ADO.NET Connection object** is responsible for connecting to the data source. It is basically the same as the ADO Connection object, except that ODBC is not used as a data source.

The **ADO.NET DataSet** is a representation of the data stored in the computer memory as a set of data separate from the one in the DBMS. The DataSet is distinct and disconnected from the DBMS data. This allows commands to be run against the DataSet instead of the actual data. DataSet data can be constructed from data in multiple databases, and they can be managed by different DBMS products. The DataSet contains the DataTableCollection and the DataRelationCollection. A more detailed version of the ADO.NET dataset object model is shown in Figure 11-21.

The **DataTableCollection** mimics DBMS tables with **DataTable objects**. DataTable objects include a **DataColumnCollection**, a **DataRowCollection**, and **Constraints**. Data values are stored in DataRow collections in three forms: **original values**, **current values**, and **proposed values**. Each DataTable object has a **PrimaryKey property** to enforce row uniqueness. The Constraints collection uses two constraints. The **ForeignKeyConstraint** supports referential integrity, and the **UniqueConstraint** supports data integrity.

The **DataRelationCollection** stores **DataRelations**, which act as the relational links between tables. Note again that referential integrity is maintained by the ForeignKeyConstraint in the Constraints collection. Relationships among DataSet tables can be processed just as relationships in a database can be processed. A relationship can be used to compute the values of a column, and DataSet tables can also have views.

The **ADO.NET Command object** shown in Figures 11-19 and 11-20 is used as an SQL statement or stored procedure and is run on data in the DataSet. The **ADO.NET DataAdapter object** is the link between a Connection object and a DataSet object. The DataAdapter uses four Command objects: the **SelectCommand object**, the

**FIGURE 11-21**

The ADO.NET DataSet Object Model

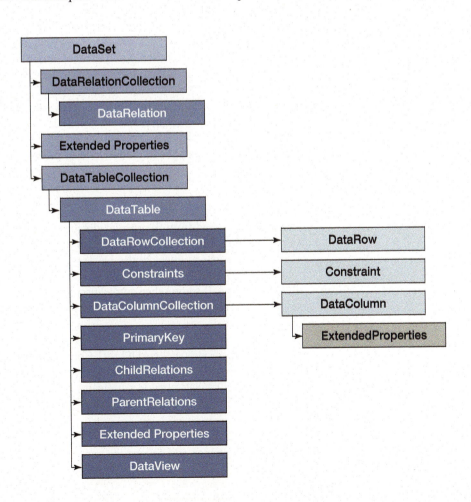

**InsertCommand object**, the **UpdateCommand object**, and the **DeleteCommand object**. The SelectCommand object gets data from a DBMS and places it in a DataSet. The other commands send changes in the DataSet back to the DBMS data.

The **ADO.NET DataReader** is similar to a cursor that provides read-only, forward-only data transfers from a data source and can be used only through an Execute method of a command.

Looking ahead to our discussion of XML later in this chapter, we see some advantages of ADO.NET over ADO. Once a DataSet is constructed, its contents can be formatted as an XML document with a single command. Similarly, an XML Schema document for the DataSet can also be produced with a single command. This process works in reverse as well. An XML Schema document can be used to create the structure of a DataSet, and the DataSet data can then be filled by reading an XML document.

---

**BY THE WAY**    As Microsoft developed .NET technology, it became clear that a generalized means was needed to define and process database views and related structures. Microsoft could have defined a new proprietary technology for this purpose, but thankfully it did not. Instead, it recognized that the concepts, techniques, and facilities used to manage regular databases can be used to manage in-memory databases as well. The benefit to you is that all of the concepts and techniques that you have learned to this point for processing regular databases can also be used to process datasets.

You may be wondering, "Why is all of this necessary? Why do we need an in-memory database?" The answer lies in database views like that shown in the XML discussion in Appendix I, "XML," and, specifically, in Figure I-14. There is no standardized way to describe and process such data structures. Because it involves two multivalued paths through the data, SQL cannot be used to describe the data. Instead, we must execute two SQL statements and somehow patch the results to obtain the view.

Views like that shown in Figure I-14 have been processed for many years, but only by private, proprietary means. Every time such a structure needs to be processed, a developer designs programs for creating and manipulating the data in memory and for saving them to the database. Object-oriented programmers define a class for this data structure and create methods to serialize (transfer from memory representation to persistent disk storage) objects of this class into the database. Other programmers use other means. The problem is that every time a different view is designed, a different scheme must be designed and developed to process the new view.

---

DataSets do have a downside, and a serious one for some applications. Because DataSet data are disconnected from the regular database, only optimistic locking can be used. The data are read from the database, placed into the DataSet, and processed there. No attempt is made to propagate changes in the DataSet back to the database. If, after processing, the application later wants to save all of the DataSet data into a regular database, it needs to use optimistic locking. If some other application has changed the data, either the DataSet will need to be reprocessed or the data change will be forced onto the database, causing the lost update problem.

Thus, DataSets cannot be used for applications in which optimistic locking is problematic. For such applications, the ADO.NET Command object should be used instead. But for applications in which conflict is rare or for those in which reprocessing after conflict can be accommodated, DataSets provide significant value.

---

**BY THE WAY**    Combining Oracle Database with ASP.NET applications is somewhat complex and beyond the scope of this discussion.

> **BY THE WAY**  The only way to use Oracle Database XML facilities is to write in Java, an object-oriented programming language. Further, the only way to process ADO.NET is from one of the .NET languages, all of which, like Visual Basic .NET, are object-oriented languages. Thus, if you do not yet know object-oriented design and programming and if you want to work in the emerging world of database processing, you should run, not walk, to your nearest object-oriented design and programming class!

## The Java Platform

Having looked at the Microsoft .NET Framework in some detail, we will now turn our attention to the Java platform and look at its components.

### JDBC

Originally, and contrary to many sources, JDBC did *not* stand for Java Database Connectivity. According to Sun Microsystems—the inventor of Java and the original source of many Java-oriented products—JDBC was not an acronym; it just stood for JDBC. At this point in time, however, we can even find the name Java Database Connectivity (JDBC) on Oracle's Web site (Oracle Corporation purchased Sun Microsystems in January of 2010)—see *www.oracle.com/technetwork/java/javase/tech/index-jsp-136101.html*! Still, because we use acronyms in this book after introducing the full term, we will use *JDBC*.

A JDBC driver is available for almost every conceivable DBMS product. Some of the drivers are free, and almost all of them have an evaluation edition that can be used for free for a limited period. The Microsoft JDBC driver for SQL Server 2019 is available at *https://docs.microsoft.com/en-us/sql/connect/jdbc/download-microsoft-jdbc-driver-for-sql-server?view=sql-server-ver15*, and the JDBC driver for MySQL is the MySQL Connector/J, which is available at *http://dev.mysql.com/downloads/connector/j/*.

#### Driver Types

As summarized in Figure 11-22, there are four defined JDBC driver types. Type 1 drivers are JDBC–ODBC bridge drivers, which provide an interface between Java and regular ODBC drivers. Most ODBC drivers are written in C or C++. For reasons unimportant to us here, there are incompatibilities between Java and C/C++. Bridge drivers resolve these incompatibilities and allow access to ODBC data sources from Java. Because we use ODBC in the chapter, if you are using MySQL, you will want to download the MySQL Connector/ODBC driver. The MySQL Connector/ODBC is available from *http://dev.mysql.com/downloads/connector/odbc/*.

**FIGURE 11-22**

Summary of JDBC Driver Types

| Summary of JDBC Driver Types | |
| --- | --- |
| **Driver Type** | **Characteristics** |
| 1 | JDBC–ODBC bridge. Provides a Java API that interfaces to an ODBC driver. Enables processing of ODBC data sources from Java. |
| 2 | A Java API that connects to the native library of a DBMS product. The Java program and the DBMS must reside on the same machine, or the DBMS must handle the intermachine communication. |
| 3 | A Java API that connects to a DBMS-independent network protocol. Can be used for servlets and applets. |
| 4 | A Java API that connects to a DBMS-dependent network protocol. Can be used for servlets and applets. |

Note that the MySQL connector for Windows operating systems is included in the MySQL Installer for Windows discussed in Chapter 10C.

Drivers of Types 2 through 4 are written entirely in Java; they differ only in how they connect to the DBMS. Type 2 drivers connect to the native API of the DBMS. For example, they call Oracle Database using the standard (non-ODBC) programming interface to Oracle Database. Drivers of Types 3 and 4 are intended for use over communications networks. A Type 3 driver translates JDBC calls into a DBMS-independent network protocol. This protocol is then translated into the network protocol used by a particular DBMS. Finally, Type 4 drivers translate JDBC calls into DBMS-specific network protocols.

To understand how drivers Types 2 through 4 differ, you must first understand the difference between a *servlet* and an *applet*. As you probably know, Java was designed to be portable. To accomplish portability, Java programs are not compiled into a particular machine language but instead are compiled into machine-independent bytecode. Oracle, Microsoft, and others have written **bytecode interpreters** for each machine environment (Intel Pentium, Intel Core, Alpha, and so on). These interpreters are referred to as **Java virtual machines**.

To run a compiled Java program, the machine-independent bytecode is interpreted by the virtual machine at run time. The cost of this, of course, is that bytecode interpretation constitutes an extra step, so such programs can never be as fast as programs that are compiled directly into machine code. This may or may not be a problem, depending on the application's workload.

An **applet** is a Java bytecode program that runs on the application user's computer. Applet bytecode is sent to the user via HTTP and is invoked using the HTTP protocol on the user's computer. The bytecode is interpreted by a virtual machine, which is usually part of the browser. Because of portability, the same bytecode can be sent to a Windows, a UNIX, or an Apple computer.

A **servlet** is a Java program that is invoked via HTTP on the Web server computer. It responds to requests from browsers. Servlets are interpreted and executed by a Java virtual machine running on the server.

Because they have a connection to a communications protocol, Type 3 and Type 4 drivers can be used in either applet or servlet code. Type 2 drivers can be used only in situations where the Java program and the DBMS reside on the same machine or where the Type 2 driver connects to a DBMS program that handles the communications between the computer running the Java program and the computer running the DBMS.

Thus, if you write code that connects to a database from an applet (two-tier architecture), only a Type 3 or Type 4 driver can be used. In these situations, if your DBMS product has a Type 4 driver, use it; it will be faster than a Type 3 driver.

In three-tier or *n*-tier architecture, if the Web server and the DBMS are running on the same machine, you can use any of the four types of drivers. If the Web server and the DBMS are running on different machines, Type 3 and Type 4 drivers can be used without a problem. Type 2 drivers can also be used if the DBMS vendor handles the communications between the Web server and the DBMS. The MySQL Connector/J is a Type 4 driver.

### Using JDBC

Unlike ODBC, JDBC does not have a separate utility for creating a JDBC data source. Instead, all of the work to define a connection is done in Java code via the JDBC driver. The coding pattern for using a JDBC driver is as follows:

1. Load the driver.
2. Establish a connection to the database.
3. Create a statement.
4. Do something with the statement.

To load the driver, you must first obtain the driver library and install it in a directory. You need to ensure that the directory is named in the CLASSPATH both for the Java compiler and for the Java virtual machine. The name of the DBMS product to be used and the name of the database are provided at step 2. Figure 11-23 summarizes the JDBC components.

**FIGURE 11-23**

JDBC Components

Note that Java is used to create the application shown in the figure, and because Java is an object-oriented programming language, we see a set of objects in the application that are similar to those we have discussed for ADO.NET. The application creates a **JDBC Connection object**, **JDBC Statement objects**, a **JDBC ResultSet object**, and a **JDBC ResultSetMetaData object**. Calls from these objects are routed via the **JDBC DriverManager** to the proper driver. Drivers then process their databases. Notice that the Oracle database in this figure could be processed either via a JDBC–ODBC bridge or via a pure JDBC driver.

> **BY THE WAY**   Most of this technology arose in the Unix operating system world (you will also see the name written in all upper case as UNIX, because that is how it was trademarked—see the Wikipedia article *Unix*). Unix is case sensitive, and almost everything you enter here also is case sensitive. Thus, *jdbc* and *JDBC* are *not* the same.

**Prepared Statement objects** and **Callable Statement objects** can be used to invoke compiled queries and stored procedures in the database. Their use is similar to the use of ADO.NET Command objects discussed previously in this chapter. It is possible to receive values back from procedures as well. Start at *www.oracle.com/technetwork/java/javase/documentation/index.html* for more information.

### Java Server Pages (JSP) and Servlets

Java Server Pages (JSP) technology provides a means to create dynamic Web pages using HTML (and XML) and the Java programming language. With Java, the capabilities of a complete object-oriented language are directly available to the Web page developer. This is similar to what can be done using ASP.NET using the Microsoft .NET languages.

Because Java is machine independent, JSP is also machine independent. With JSP, you are not locked into using Windows and IIS. You can run the same JSP page on a Linux server, on a Windows server, and on others as well. The official specification for JSP can be found at *www.oracle.com/technetwork/java/javaee/jsp/index.html*.

JSP pages are transformed into standard Java language and then compiled just like a regular program. In particular, they are transformed into Java servlets, which means that JSP pages are transformed into subclasses of the HTTPServlet class behind the scenes. JSP code thus has access to the HTTP request and response objects and to their methods and to other HTTP functionality.

## Apache Tomcat

The Apache Web server does not support servlets. However, the Apache Foundation and Sun cosponsored the Jakarta Project that developed a servlet processor named **Apache Tomcat** (now in version 9.0.37, with version 10.0 in development). You can obtain the source and binary code of Tomcat from the Apache Tomcat Web site at *https://tomcat.apache.org/*.

Tomcat is a servlet processor that can work in conjunction with Apache or as a stand-alone Web server. Tomcat has limited Web server facilities, however, so it is normally used in standalone mode only for testing servlets and JSP pages. For commercial production applications, Tomcat should be used in conjunction with Apache. If you are running Tomcat and Apache separately on the same Web server, they need to use different ports. The default port for a Web server is 80, and Apache normally uses it. When used in standalone mode, Tomcat is usually configured to listen to port 8080, though this, of course, can be changed.

Figure 11-24 shows the process by which JSP pages are compiled. When a request for a JSP page is received, a Tomcat (or other) servlet processor finds the compiled version of the page and checks to determine whether it is current. It does this by looking for an uncompiled version of the page with a creation date and time later than the compiled page's creation date and time. If the page is not current, the new page is parsed and transformed into a Java source file, and that source file is then compiled. The servlet is then loaded and executed. If the compiled JSP page is current, then it is loaded into memory, if not already there, and then executed. If it is in memory, it is simply executed.

**FIGURE 11-24**

**JSP Compilation Process**

> **BY THE WAY**   The downside of such automatic compilation is that if you make syntax errors and forget to test your pages, the first user to access your page will receive the compiler errors!
>
> Unlike common gateway interface (CGI) files (see the Wikipedia article *Common_Gateway_Interface*) and some other Web server programs, only one copy of a JSP page can be in memory at a time. Further, pages are executed by one of Tomcat's threads, not by an independent process. This means that much less memory and processor time are required to execute a JSP page than to execute a comparable CGI script.
>
> Nonetheless, developments in JSP pages continues. For example, see the Wikipedia article *Node.js*.

## Web Database Processing with PHP

At this point in our discussion, it is time to build an actual Web database application and apply both some of the knowledge from this chapter and some new techniques yet to be discussed. We have already created an ODBC data source for the View Ridge Gallery database, and now we will use it to look at Web database processing. Although we have introduced technologies such as ADO.NET, ASP.NET, Java, and JSP, these technologies are complex subjects and beyond the scope of this book. Further, these technologies tend to become vendor specific—you are either working in a Microsoft-centric world with .NET technologies and ASPs or an Oracle Corporation-centric world with Java and JSPs.

> **BY THE WAY**   Before working your way through this chapter, you should install and set up the software we will be using—the Microsoft IIS Web server, the Java JRE, PHP, and the NetBeans IDE—on your computer if you do not have the software available for your use in a computer lab or similar facility. Installing and setting up this software correctly, which is complex but straightforward, is described in detail in Appendix H, "Getting Started with Web Servers, PHP, and the NetBeans IDE." We strongly suggest that you read Appendix H now and make sure your computer is completely set up before continuing with the material in this chapter. Then try out each of our examples on your computer to get the most out of this discussion.

In this book, we will take a vendor-neutral approach and use technologies that can be used with any operating system or DBMS. We will use the PHP language. PHP, which is an abbreviation for **PHP: Hypertext Processor** (and which was previously known as the *Personal Hypertext Processor*), is a scripting language that can be embedded in Web pages. Although PHP started as purely a scripting language, it now also has object-oriented programming elements, but we will not cover those in this book.

PHP is extremely popular. In January 2013, there were about 244 million PHP Web sites,[4] and the September 2020 TIOBE Programming Community Index ranked PHP as the eighth most popular programming language (following, in order, C, Java, Python, C++, C#, Visual Basic .NET, and JavaScript).[5] PHP is easy to learn and can be used in most Web server environments and with most databases. As an added bonus, it is an open source product available for free download from the PHP Web site (*www.php.net* and *http://windows.php.net/download/* for the Windows versions).

Although Microsoft would probably prefer that you use ASP.NET for Web applications, there is still good information on using PHP in a Microsoft environment on the Microsoft Web site

---

[4]See *www.php.net/usage.php*. This site does not appear to be updated on a regular basis (accessed August 2020).
[5]See *www.tiobe.com/index.php/content/paperinfo/tpci/index.html* (accessed September 2020).

(e.g., see Running PHP on IIS at *http://php.iis.net*). Both Oracle DBMS products—Oracle Database and MySQL—enthusiastically support PHP. Oracle publishes the *Oracle Database 2 Day + PHP Developer's Guide* (available in both HTML and PDF format for Oracle Database at *http://docs. oracle.com/database/122/TDPPH/toc.htm* and for Oracle Database XE [which is currently based on Oracle Database 18c] at *http://docs.oracle.com/cd/E11882_01/appdev.112/e10811/toc.htm*). Because PHP is often the P in AMP, LAMP, and WAMP, many books are available that discuss the combination of PHP and MySQL, and the MySQL Web site contains basic documentation on using PHP with MySQL (e.g., see *https://dev.mysql.com/doc/apis-php/en/*).

## Web Database Processing with PHP and the NetBeans IDE

To start, we need a Web server to store the Web pages that we will build and use. We could use the Apache HTTP Server (available from the Apache Software Foundation at *www. apache.org*). This is the most widely used Web server, and there is a version that will run on just about every operating system in existence. However, because we have been using the Windows operating system for the DBMS products shown in this book, we will build a Web site using the Microsoft IIS Web server. One advantage of using this Web server for users of the Windows 10 and the Windows Server 2016 operating systems is that IIS is included with the operating system: IIS version 10 is included with both Windows 10 and Windows Server 2019. IIS is installed but not operational by default, but it can easily be made operational at any time. This means that any user can practice creating and using Web pages on his or her own workstation as well as working on a networked Web server. See Appendix G for a detailed discussion of setting up IIS.

> **BY THE WAY**    This discussion of Web database processing has been written to be as widely applicable as possible. With minor adjustments to the following steps, you should be able to use the Apache Web server if you have it available. Whenever possible, we have chosen to use products and technologies that are available for many operating systems.

When IIS is installed, it creates an **inetpub folder** on the C: drive as C:\inetpub. Within the inetpub folder is the **wwwroot folder**, which is where IIS stores the most basic Web pages used by the Web server. Figure 11-25 shows this directory structure in Windows 10 after IIS has been installed, with the files in the wwwroot folder displayed in the file pane.

IIS is managed using a program called **Internet Information Services Manager** as shown in Figure 11-26 for Windows 10. The location of the program icon varies depending on the operating system:

- For Windows 7, open **Control Panel**, then open **System and Security**, and then open **Administrative Tools**. The shortcut icon for Internet Information Services Manager is located in Administrative Tools.
- For Windows 10, press the **Windows Key** to open the menu, then open the **Windows Administrative Tools** folder, In the Windows Administrative Tools folder, open **Internet Information Services (IIS) Manager**.

Note that the files shown in the **Default Web Site folder** in Figure 11-26 are the same files that are in the wwwroot folder in Figure 11-25—they are the default files created by IIS when it is iinstalled. In Windows 7, Windows 8.1, and Windows 10, the file **iisstart. htm** generates the Web page that Internet Explorer (or any other Web browser) contacting this Web server over the Internet will display.

To test the Web server installation, open your Web browser, type in the URL **http:// localhost**, and press the **Enter** key. For Windows 10, the Web page shown in Figure 11-27 (in the Microsoft Edge Web browser) appears. If the appropriate Web page isn't displayed in your Web browser, your Web server is not properly installed.

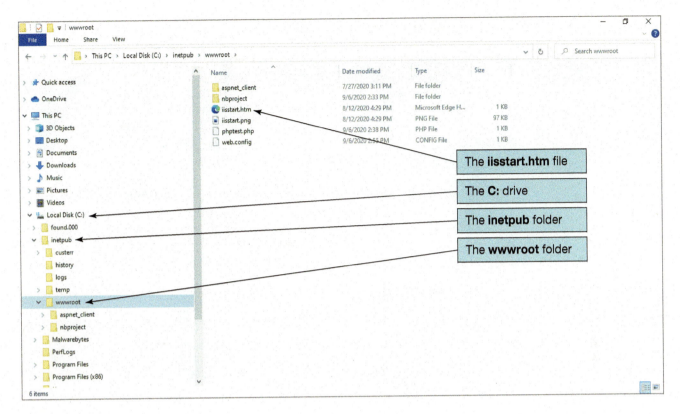

**FIGURE 11-25**

**The IIS wwwroot Folder**

**FIGURE 11-26**

**Managing IIS**

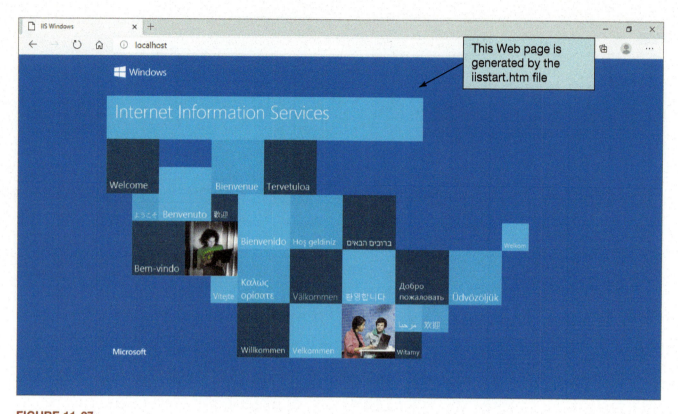

This Web page is generated by the iisstart.htm file

**FIGURE 11-27**

**The Default IIS Web Page**

Now we will set up a small Web site that can be used for Web database processing of the View Ridge Gallery *VRG* database. First, we will create a new folder named *DBP* (Database Processing) under the wwwroot folder. This new folder will be used to hold all the Web pages developed in discussions and exercises in this book. Second, we will create a subfolder of DBP named *VRG*. This folder will hold the View Ridge Gallery Web site. We create these folders using Windows Explorer.

### Getting Started with HTML Web Pages

The most basic Web pages are created using **Hypertext Markup Language (HTML)**. The term *hypertext* refers to the fact that you can include links to other objects, such as Web pages, maps, pictures, and even audio and video files in a Web page, and when you click the link, you are immediately taken to that other object and it is displayed in your Web browser. HTML itself is a standard set of **HTML syntax rules** and **HTML document tags** that can be interpreted by Web browsers to create specific onscreen displays.

Tags are usually paired, with a specific beginning tag and a matching ending tag that includes the slash character (/). Thus, a paragraph of text is tagged as <p>*{paragraph text here}*</p>, and a main heading is tagged as <h1>*{heading text here}*</h1>. Some tags do not need a separate end tag because they are essentially self-contained. For example, to insert a horizontal line on a Web page, you use the horizontal rule tag <hr />. Note that such single, self-contained tags must include the slash character as part of the tag. (In HTML5 these tags can optionally be written without the slash [the horizontal rule tag is just <hr>], but we prefer to use the older form in this book.)

The rules of HTML are defined as standards by the **World Wide Web Consortium (W3C)**, and the details of current and proposed standards can be found at *www.w3c.org* (this site also has several excellent tutorials on HTML[6]). The W3C Web site has current standards

---

[6]To learn more about HTML, go to the Web site of the World Wide Web Consortium (W3C) at *www.w3.org*. For good HTML tutorials, see David Raggett's "Getting Started with HTML" tutorial at *www.w3.org/MarkUp/ Guide*, his "More Advanced Features" tutorial at *www.w3.org/MarkUp/Guide/Advanced.html*, and his "Adding a Touch of Style" tutorial at *www.w3.org/MarkUp/Guide/Style.html*.

for HTML and **Extensible Markup Language (XML)** (which we will discuss later in this chapter). A full discussion of these standards is beyond the scope of this text; this chapter uses the current **HTML5** standard.

In this chapter, we will create a simple HTML home page for the View Ridge Gallery Web site and place it in the VRG folder. We will discuss some of the numerous available Web page editors shortly, but all you really need to create Web pages is a simple text editor. For this first Web page, we will use the Microsoft Notepad ASCII text editor, which has the advantage of being supplied with every version of the Windows operating system.

### The index.html Web Page

The name for the file we are going to create is **index.html**. We need to use the name *index.html* because it is a special name as far as Web servers are concerned. The file name index.html is one of only a few file names that *most* Web servers automatically display when a URL request is made without a specific file reference, and thus it will become the new default display page for our Web database application. However, note the phrase "*most* Web servers" in the last sentence. Although Apache, IIS 7.0 and later versions of IIS (IIS 10 is shown in Figure 11-28) are configured to recognize index.html, IIS 5.1 is not.

### Creating the index.html Web Page

Now we can create the index.html Web page, which consists of the basic HTML statements shown in Figure 11-29. Figure 11-30 shows the HTML code in Microsoft Notepad.

> **BY THE WAY** In the HTML code for index.html, the HTML code segment:
>
> ```
> <!DOCTYPE html>
> ```
>
> is an HTML/XML **document type declaration (DTD)**, which is used to check and validate the contents of the code that you write. DTDs are discussed later in this chapter. For now, just include the code as it is written.

**FIGURE 11-28**

The index.html file in Windows 10 IIS Manager

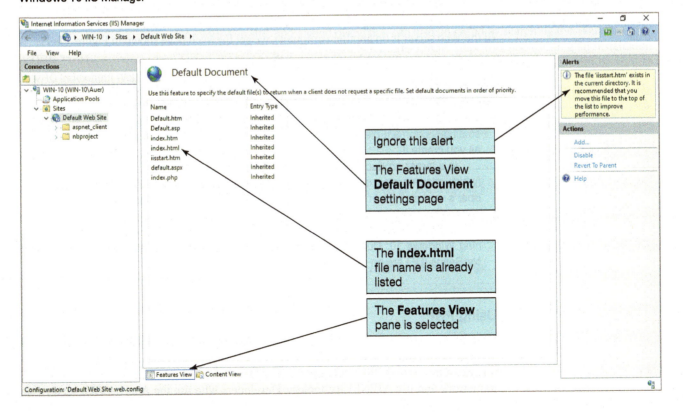

```
                    <p>
                        <input type="submit" value="Add New Artist" />
                        <input type="reset" value="Reset Values" />
                    </p>
                </form>
                <br />
                <hr />
                <p class="footer">
                    <a href="../VRG/index.html">
                        Return to View Ridge Gallery Home Page
                    </a>
                </p>
                <hr />
            </body>
        </html>
```

**FIGURE 11-40**

**Continued**

This tag defines a form section on the page, and the section will be set up to obtain data entry values. This form has only one data entry value: the table name. The **POST method** refers to a process that causes the data in the form (here the last name, the first name, and the selected nationality) to be delivered to the PHP server so they can be used in an array variable named $_POST. Note that $_POST is an array and thus can have multiple values. An alternative method is GET, but POST can carry more data, and this distinction is not too important to us here. The second parameter of the form tag is *action*, which is set to InsertNewArtist.php. This parameter tells the Web server that when it receives the response from this form, it should store the data values in the $_POST array and pass control to the InsertNewArtist.php page.

The rest of the page is standard HTML, with the addition of the <select> . . . </select> structure for creating a drop-down list in the form. Note that the name for the selected value is Nationality.

When the user clicks the Add New Artist button, these data are to be processed by the InsertNewArtist.php page. Figure 11-41 shows the InsertNewArtist.php, the page that will be invoked when the response is received from the form. Note that the variable values for the INSERT statement are obtained from the $_POST[] array. First, we create short variable names for the $_POST version of the name, and then we use these short variable names to create the SQL INSERT statement. Thus:

```
// Create short variable names
$LastName = $_POST["LastName"];
$FirstName = $_POST["FirstName"];
$Nationality = $_POST["Nationality"];

// Create SQL statement
$SQL = "INSERT INTO ARTIST(LastName, FirstName, Nationality) ";
$SQL .= "VALUES('$LastName', '$FirstName', '$Nationality')";
```

Note the use of the **PHP concatenation operator (.=)** (a combination of a period and an equal sign) to combine the two sections of the SQL INSERT statement. As another example, to create a variable named $AllOfUs with the value *me, myself, and I*, we would use:

```
$AllOfUs = "me, ";
$AllOfUs .= "myself, ";
$AllOfUs .= "and I";
```

Most of the code is self-explanatory, but make sure you understand how it works.

```html
<!DOCTYPE html>
<html>
    <head>
        <title>InsertNewArtist</title>
        <meta charset="UTF-8">
        <meta name="viewport" content="width=device-width,
        initial-scale=1.0">
        <style type="text/css">
            h1 {text-align: center; color: blue}
            h2 {font-family: Ariel, sans-serif; text-align: left; color: blue}
            p.footer {text-align: center}
            table.output {font-family: Ariel, sans-serif}
        </style>
    </head>
    <body>
    <?php
        // Get connection
            $DSN = "VRG";
            $User = "VRG-User";
            $Password = "VRG-User+password";

            $Conn = odbc_connect($DSN, $User, $Password);

        // Test connection
        if (!$Conn)
            {
                exit ("ODBC Connection Failed: " . $Conn);
            }
        // Create short variable names
        $LastName = $_POST["LastName"];
        $FirstName = $_POST["FirstName"];
        $Nationality = $_POST["Nationality"];

        // Create SQL statement
        $SQL = "INSERT INTO ARTIST(LastName, FirstName, Nationality) ";
        $SQL .= "VALUES('$LastName', '$FirstName', '$Nationality')";

        // Execute SQL statement
        $Result = odbc_exec($Conn, $SQL);

        // Test existence of result
        echo "<h1>
                The View Ridge Gallery ARTIST Table
            </h1>
            <hr />";
        if ($Result){
            echo "<h2>
                New Artist Added:
            </h2>
```

*(continued)*

**FIGURE 11-41**

**The HTML and PHP Code for InsertNewArtist.php**

## Example 2: Using PHP Data Objects (PDO)

Our next example is an exercise in using PHP Data Objects (PDO). Here we are re-creating the ReadArtist.php page but using PDO to do it. We call the new Web page Read ArtistPDO.php, and it is shown in Figure 11-42. The PHP code to create the page is shown in Figure 11-43, and you should compare this PHP code to the PHP code for ReadArtist. php in Figure 11-33.

The New Customer and Artist Interests Added message is displayed along with the customer and artist interest data

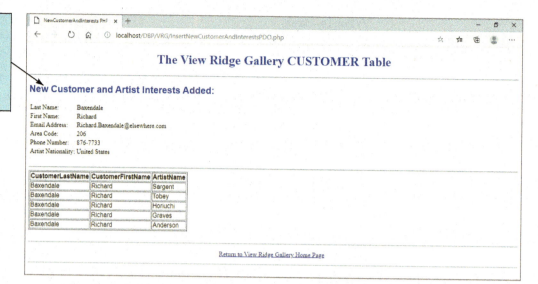

**FIGURE 11-45**

The Added New Acknowledgment Page

```
<!DOCTYPE html>
<html>
    <head>
        <title>NewCustomerAndInterestsForm</title>
        <meta charset="UTF-8">
        <meta name="viewport" content="width=device-width, initial-scale=1.0">
        <style type="text/css">
            h1 {text-align: center; color: blue}
            h2 {font-family: Ariel, sans-serif; text-align: left; color: blue}
            p.footer {text-align: center}
            table.output {font-family: Ariel, sans-serif}
        </style>
    </head>
    <body>
        <form action="InsertNewCustomerAndInterestsPDO.php" method="POST">
            <!--  Page Headers -->
            <h1>
                The View Ridge Gallery New Customer Form
            </h1>
            <hr />
            <br />
            <p>
                <b>Enter customer data:</b>
            </p>
            <table>
                <tr>
                    <td> Last Name:  </td>
                    <td>
                        <input type="text" name="LastName" size="25" />
                    </td>
                </tr>
```

**FIGURE 11-46**

The HTML Code for NewCustomerAnd InterestsForm.html

```
          <tr>
            <td> First Name:  </td>
            <td>
               <input type="text" name="FirstName" size="25" />
            </td>
          </tr>
          <tr>
            <td> Area Code:  </td>
            <td>
               <input type="text" name="AreaCode" size="3" />
            </td>
          </tr>
          <tr>
            <td> Phone:  </td>
            <td>
               <input type="text" name="PhoneNumber" size="8" />
            </td>
          </tr>
          <tr>
            <td> Email:  </td>
            <td>
               <input type="text" name="Email" size="100" />
            </td>
          </tr>
        </table>
        <p>
          <b>Select artist nationality:</b>
        </p>
        <select name="Nationality">
          <option value="Canadian">Canadian</option>
          <option value="English">English</option>
          <option value="French">French</option>
          <option value="German">German</option>
          <option value="Mexican">Mexican</option>
          <option value="Russian">Russian</option>
          <option value="Spanish">Spanish</option>
          <option value="United States">United States</option>
        </select>
        <br />
        <p>
          <input type="submit" value="Add New Customer" />
          <input type="reset" value="Reset Values" />
        </p>
      </form>
      <br />
      <hr />
      <p class="footer">
        <a href="../VRG/index.html">
          Return to View Ridge Gallery Home Page
        </a>
      </p>
      <hr />
    </body>
  </html>
```

**FIGURE 11-46**

Continued

```html
<!DOCTYPE html>
<html>
    <head>
        <title>InsertNewCustomerAndInterestsPDO</title>
        <meta charset="UTF-8">
        <meta name="viewport" content="width=device-width, initial-scale=1.0">
        <style type="text/css">
            h1 {text-align: center; color: blue}
            h2 {font-family: Ariel, sans-serif; text-align: left; color: blue}
            p.footer {text-align: center}
            table.output {font-family: Ariel, sans-serif}
        </style>
    </head>
    <body>
<?php
        // Get connection
        $DSN = "VRG";
        $User = "VRG-User";
        $Password = "VRG-User+password";

        $PDOConnection = new PDO("odbc:$DSN", $User, $Password);

    // Test connection
    if (!$PDOConnection)
    {
        exit ("ODBC Connection Failed: " . $PDOConnection);
    }
    // Create short variable names
    $LastName = $_POST["LastName"];
    $FirstName = $_POST["FirstName"];
    $AreaCode = $_POST["AreaCode"];
    $PhoneNumber = $_POST["PhoneNumber"];
    $EmailAddress = $_POST["EmailAddress"];
    $Nationality = $_POST["Nationality"];

    // Create SQL statement to call the Stored Procedure
    $SQLSP  = "EXEC InsertCustomerAndInterests ";
    $SQLSP .= "'$LastName', '$FirstName', '$AreaCode','$PhoneNumber', ";
    $SQLSP .= "'$EmailAddress', '$Nationality'";

    // Create SQL statement to retrieve additions to
    // CUSTOMER_ARTIST_INT table
    $SQL  = "SELECT * FROM CustomerInterestsView ";
    $SQL .= "WHERE CustomerLastName = '$LastName' ";
    $SQL .= "AND CustomerFirstName = '$FirstName'";

    // Execute SQL Stored Procedure statement
    $Result = $PDOConnection->exec($SQLSP);

    // Test existence of $Result
    if (!$Result)
    {
        exit ("SQL Statement Error: " . $SQL);
    }
```

**FIGURE 11-47**

The HTML and PHP Code for
InsertNewCustomerAnd
InterestsPDO.php

```
// Execute SQL statement
$RecordSet = $PDOConnection->exec($SQL);

// Test existence of $ResultSet
if (!$RecordSet)
    {
        exit ("SQL Statement Error: " . $SQL);
    }


echo "<h1>
        The View Ridge Gallery CUSTOMER Table
    </h1>
    <hr />";

    echo "<h2>
        New Customer and Artist Interests Added:
    </h2>
    <table>
        <tr>";
        echo "<td>Last Name:</td>";
        echo "<td>" . $LastName . "</td>";
        echo "</tr>";
        echo "<tr>";
        echo "<td>First Name:</td>";
        echo "<td>" . $FirstName . "</td>";
        echo "</tr>";
        echo "<tr>";
        echo "<td>Area Code:</td>";
        echo "<td>" . $AreaCode . "</td>";
        echo "</tr>";
        echo "<tr>";
        echo "<td>Phone Number:</td>";
        echo "<td>" . $PhoneNumber . "</td>";
        echo "</tr>";
        echo "<tr>";
        echo "<td>Email Address:</td>";
        echo "<td>" . $EmailAddress . "</td>";
        echo "</tr>";
        echo "<tr>";
        echo "<td>Artist Nationality:</td>";
        echo "<td>" . $Nationality . "</td>";
        echo "</tr>";
    echo "</table><br /><hr />";
    // Table headers
    echo "<table class='output' border='1'>
        <tr>
            <th>CustomerLastName</th>
            <th>CustomerFirstName</th>
            <th>ArtistName</th>
        </tr>";
```

**FIGURE 11-47**
Continued

*(continued)*

## Challenges for Web Database Processing

Web database application processing is complicated by an important characteristic of HTTP.
Specifically, HTTP is stateless; it has no provision for maintaining sessions between requests.
Using HTTP, a client at a browser makes a request of a Web server. The server services the

```
    // Table data
    while($RecordSetRow = odbc_fetch_array($RecordSet))
        {
        echo "<tr>";
        echo "<td>" . $RecordSetRow['CustomerLastName'] . "</td>";
        echo "<td>" . $RecordSetRow['CustomerFirstName'] . "</td>";
        echo "<td>" . $RecordSetRow['ArtistName'] . "</td>";
        echo "</tr>";
        }
    echo "</table>";

    // Close connection
    $PDOConnection = null;
?>
    <br />
    <hr />
    <p class="footer">
        <a href="../VRG/index.html">
            Return to View Ridge Gallery Home Page
        </a>
    </p>
    <hr />
</body>
</html>
```

**FIGURE 11-47**

**Continued**

client request, sends results back to the browser, and forgets about the interaction with that client. A second request from that same client is treated as a new request from a new client. No data are kept to maintain a session or connection with the client.

This characteristic poses no problem for serving content, either static Web pages or responses to queries of a database. However, it is not acceptable for applications that require multiple database actions in an atomic transaction. Recall from Chapter 9 that in some cases, a group of database actions needs to be grouped into a transaction, with all of them committed to the database or none of them committed to the database. In this case, the Web server or other program must augment the base capabilities of HTTP.

For example, IIS provides features and functions for maintaining data about sessions between multiple HTTP requests and responses. Using these features and functions, the application program on the Web server can save data to and from the browser. A particular session will be associated with a particular set of data. In this way, the application program can start a transaction, conduct multiple interactions with the user at the browser, make intermediate changes to the database, and commit or roll back all changes when ending the transaction. Other means are used to provide for sessions and session data with Apache.

In some cases, the application programs must create their own methods for tracking session data. PHP does include support for sessions—see the PHP documentation for more information.

The particulars of session management are beyond the scope of this chapter. However, you should be aware that HTTP is stateless, and, regardless of the Web server, additional code must be added to database applications to enable transaction processing.

### SQL Injection Attacks

When we create Web pages that allow data inserts, updates, or deletes on a database, we may create a vulnerability that allows an *SQL injection attack*. An **SQL injection attack** attempts to issue hacker-modified SQL commands to the DBMS. For example, suppose that a Web page is used to update a user's phone number and thus requires the user to input the new phone number. The Web application would then use PHP code to create and run an SQL statement such as:

```
// Create SQL statement
$varSQL = "UPDATE CUSTOMER SET PHONE = '$NewPhone' ";
$varSQL .= "WHERE CustomerID = '$CustomerID'";
// Execute SQL statement
$RecordSet = odbc_exec($Conn, $varSQL);
```

If the input value of NewPhone is not carefully checked, it may be possible for an attacker to use an input value such as:

```
678-345-1234; DELETE FROM CUSTOMER;
```

If this input value is accepted and the SQL statement is run, we may lose all data in the CUSTOMER table if the Web application has DELETE permissions on the CUSTOMER table. Therefore, Web database applications must be carefully constructed to provide for data checking and to ensure that only necessary database permissions are granted.

## Extensible Markup Language (XML)

XML is a standard means for defining the structure of documents and for transmitting documents from one computer to another. XML is important for database processing because it provides a standardized means of submitting data to a database and for receiving results back from the database. XML is a large, complicated subject that requires several books to explain fully. Here we touch on the fundamentals and further explain why XML is important for database processing.

### The Importance of XML

Database processing and document processing need each other. Database processing needs document processing for transmitting database views; document processing needs database processing for storing and manipulating data. However, even though these technologies need each other, it took the popularity of the Internet to make that need obvious. As Web sites evolved, organizations wanted to use Internet technology to display and update data from organizational databases. Web developers began to take a serious interest in SQL, database performance, database security, and other aspects of database processing.

As the Web developers invaded the database community, database practitioners wondered, "Who are these people, and what do they want?" Database practitioners began to learn about Hypertext Markup Language (HTML), the language used to format documents for display by Web browsers. At first, the database community scoffed at HTML because of its limitations, but it soon learned that HTML was the output of a more robust document markup language called **Standard Generalized Markup Language (SGML)**. SGML was clearly important, just as important to document processing as the relational model was to database processing. Obviously, this powerful language had some role to play in the display of database data, but what role?

In the early 1990s, the two communities began to meet, and the result of their work is a series of standards that concerns a language called Extensible Markup Language (XML). XML is a subset of SGML, but additional standards and capabilities have been added to XML, and today XML technology is a hybrid of document processing and database processing. In fact, as XML standards evolved, it became clear that the communities had been working on different aspects of the same problem for many years. They even used the same terms but with different meanings. You will see later in this chapter how the term *schema* is used in XML for a concept that is completely different from the use of *schema* in the database world.

XML provides a standardized yet customizable way to describe the content of documents. As such, it can be used to describe any database view but in a standardized way. As you will learn in Appendix I, "XML," SQL views have certain limitations, which we can overcome by using XML views.

In addition, when used with the XML Schema standard, XML documents can automatically be generated from database data. Further, database data can automatically be extracted from XML documents. Even more, there are standardized ways of defining how document components are mapped to database schema components, and vice versa.

Meanwhile, the rest of the computing community began to take notice of XML. **SOAP**, which originally meant **Simple Object Access Protocol**, was defined as an XML-based standard for providing remote procedure calls over the Internet. Initially, SOAP assumed the use of HTTP as a transport mechanism. When Microsoft, IBM, Oracle Corporation, and other large companies joined forces in support of the SOAP standard, this assumption was removed, and SOAP was generalized to become a standard protocol for sending messages of any type using any protocol. With this change, SOAP no longer meant Simple Object Access Protocol, so now SOAP is just a name and not an acronym.

Today, XML is used for many purposes. One of the most important is its use as a standardized means to define and communicate documents for processing over the Internet. XML plays a key role in Microsoft's .NET initiative, and in 2001, Bill Gates called XML the "*lingua franca* of the Internet age."

As you read the rest of this chapter and more information on XML in Appendix H, "XML," keep in mind that this area is an important part of database processing. Standards, products, and product capabilities are frequently changing. You can keep abreast of these changes by checking the following Web sites: *www.w3c.org*, *www.xml.org*, *http://msdn.microsoft.com*, *www.oracle.com*, *www.ibm.com*, and *www.mysql.com*. Learning as much as you can about XML and database processing is one of the best ways you can prepare yourself for a successful career in database processing.

## XML as a Markup Language

As a markup language, XML is significantly better than HTML in several ways. For one, XML provides a clean separation between document structure, content, and materialization (rendering for display on a specific device) XML has facilities for dealing with each, and they cannot be confounded, as they are with HTML.

Additionally, XML is standardized, but as its name implies, the standards allow for extension by developers. With XML, you are not limited to a fixed set of elements such as <title>, <H1>, and <p>; you can create your own.

Third, XML eliminates the inconsistent tag use that is possible (and popular) with HTML. For example, consider the following HTML:

```
<H2>Hello World</H2>
```

Although the tag can be used to mark a level-two heading in an outline, it can be used for other purposes, too, such as causing "Hello World" to be displayed in a particular font size, weight, and color. Because a tag has potentially many uses, we cannot rely on tags to discern the structure of an HTML page. Tag use is too arbitrary; it may mean a heading, or it may mean nothing at all.

As you will see, the structure of an XML document can be formally defined. Tags are defined in relationship to one another. In XML, if we find the tag <street>, we know exactly what data we have, where those data belong in the document, and how that tag relates to other tags.

## Creating XML Documents from Database Data

SQL Server, Oracle Database, and MySQL have facilities for generating XML documents from database data. The Oracle Database XML features require the use of Java. Because we do not assume that you are a Java programmer, we will not discuss those features further in this chapter. If you are a Java programmer, you can learn more about Oracle Database's XML features at *www.oracle.com*.

The facilities in SQL Server, Oracle Database, and MySQL are undergoing rapid development. In the case of SQL Server, version 7.0 added the expression FOR XML to SQL SELECT syntax. That expression was carried forward to SQL Server 2000. In 2002, the SQL Server group extended the SQL Server capabilities with the SQLXML class library. SQLXML, which was produced by the SQL Server group, is different from ADO.NET. All of these features and functions were merged together in SQL Server 2005 and are carried forward in SQL Server 2019.

### Using the SQL SELECT . . . FOR XML Statement

SQL Server 2019 uses the **SQL SELECT . . . FOR XML statement** to work with XML. Consider the following SQL statement:

```
/* *** SQL-Query-CH11-01 *** */

SELECT      *

FROM        ARTIST

    FOR     XML RAW;
```

**FIGURE 11-48**

**FOR XML RAW Examples**

Figure 11-48(a) shows an example of a FOR XML RAW query in the Microsoft SQL Server Management Studio. The results of the query are displayed in a single cell. Clicking this

**(a) FOR XML RAW Query**

(continued)

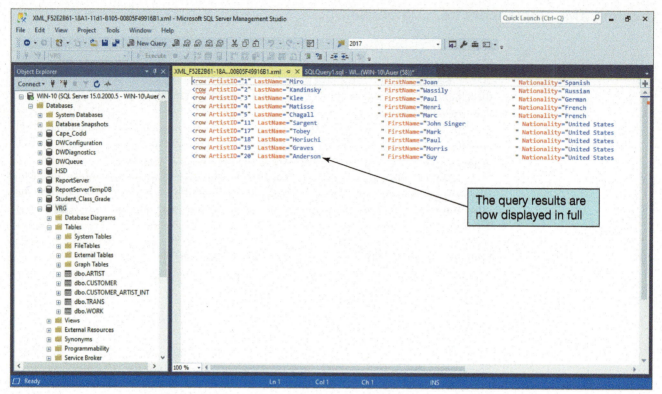

**(b) FOR XML RAW Results in the Microsoft SQL Server Management Studio**

```
<row ArtistID="1" LastName="Miro" FirstName="Joan"
        Nationality="Spanish" DateOfBirth="1893" DateDeceased="1983" />
<row ArtistID="2" LastName="Kandinsky" FirstName="Wassily"
        Nationality="Russian" DateOfBirth="1866" DateDeceased="1944" />
<row ArtistID="3" LastName="Klee" FirstName="Paul"
        Nationality="German" DateOfBirth="1879" DateDeceased="1940" />
<row ArtistID="4" LastName="Matisse" FirstName="Henri"
        Nationality="French" DateOfBirth="1869" DateDeceased="1954" />
<row ArtistID="5" LastName="Chagall" FirstName="Marc"
        Nationality="French" DateOfBirth="1887" DateDeceased="1985" />
<row ArtistID="11" LastName="Sargent" FirstName="John Singer"
        Nationality="United States" DateOfBirth="1856" DateDeceased="1925" />
<row ArtistID="17" LastName="Tobey" FirstName="Mark"
        Nationality="United States" DateOfBirth="1890" DateDeceased="1976" />
<row ArtistID="18" LastName="Horiuchi" FirstName="Paul"
        Nationality="United States" DateOfBirth="1906" DateDeceased="1999" />
<row ArtistID="19" LastName="Graves" FirstName="Morris"
        Nationality="United States" DateOfBirth="1920" DateDeceased="2001" />
<row ArtistID="20" LastName="Anderson" FirstName="Guy"
        Nationality="United States" />
```

**(c) FOR XML RAW Results in XML Document**

**FIGURE 11-48**

**Continued**

cell displays the results as shown in Figure 11-48(b). As expected, each column is placed as an attribute of the element named *row*. The complete output, edited as it would appear in an XML document (and with extra spaces in the attribute values removed), is shown in Figure 11-48(c). We will discuss the FOR XML clause in depth in Appendix I.

# Summary

Today, database applications reside in rich and complicated environments. In addition to relational databases, there are non-relational databases, VSAM and other file-processing data, email, and other types of data. To ease the job of the application programmer, various standards have been developed. The ODBC standard is for relational databases; the OLE DB standard is for relational databases and other data sources. ADO was developed to provide easier access to OLE DB data for the non–object-oriented programmer.

ODBC, or the Open Database Connectivity standard, provides an interface by which database applications can access and process relational data sources in a DBMS-independent manner. ODBC was developed by an industry committee and has been implemented by Microsoft and many other vendors. ODBC consists of an applications program, a driver manager, DBMS drivers, and data source components. Single- and multiple-tier drivers are defined. The three data source names are file, system, and user. System data sources are recommended for Web servers. The process of defining a system data source name involves specifying the type of driver and the identity of the database to be processed.

The Microsoft .NET Framework is Microsoft's comprehensive application development framework. The current version is .NET Framework 4.8 (this is the final version of .NET Framework), which is built on top of the .NET Framework 2.0 and .NET Framework 3.0 (and their service pack updates). It includes ADO.NET, ASP.NET, CLR, and the Base Class Library. Enhancements specific to .NET Framework 3.5 include the ADO.NET Entity Framework, which supports the EDM (Entity Data Model). The .NET Framework 4.0 added Parallel LINQ (PLINQ) and the Task Parallel Library (TPL). The .NET Framework 4.5 added support for Windows 8 Apps, including .NET for Windows Store Apps, Portable class libraries, and the Managed Extensibility Framework (MEF).

.NET Framework 4.6 included a just-in-time 64-bit compiler and significant cryptography updates. The Windows Communication Foundation (WCF) introduced in .NET Framework 3.0 gained TLS 1.1 and TLS 1.2. .NET Framework 4.6.1 and .NET Framework 4.6.2 added new functionality in cryptography, ADO.NET, and ASP.NET among the changes. Released with the Windows 10 Creators Update, .NET Framework 4.7, 4.7.1 and 4.7.2 include elliptic curve cryptography, operating system support for Transport Layer Security (TLS), new networking HyypClientHandler properties, and support of Azure Active Directory and multifactor authentication.

OLE DB is one of the foundations of the Microsoft data access world. It implements the Microsoft OLE and COM standards, and it is accessible to object-oriented programs through those interfaces. OLE DB breaks the features and functions of a DBMS into objects, thus making it easier for vendors to implement portions of functionality. Key object terms are *abstraction, methods, properties,* and *collections.* A rowset is an abstraction of a recordset, which, in turn, is an abstraction of a relation. Objects are defined by properties that specify their characteristics and by methods, which are the actions they can perform. A collection is an object that contains a group of other objects. An interface is a set of objects and the properties and methods they expose in that interface. Objects may expose different properties and methods in different interfaces. An implementation is how an object accomplishes its tasks. Implementations are hidden from the outside world and may be changed without affecting the users of the objects. An interface ought not to be changed ever.

Tabular data providers present data in the form of rowsets. Service providers transform data into another form; such providers are both consumers and providers of data. A rowset is equivalent to a cursor. Basic rowset interfaces are IRowSet, IAccessor, and IColumnsInfo. Other interfaces are defined for more advanced capabilities.

ADO.NET is a new, improved, and greatly expanded version of ADO that was developed for the Microsoft .NET initiative. ADO.NET incorporates all of the functionality of ADO but adds much more. In particular, ADO.NET facilitates the transformation of XML documents to and from database data.

A .NET data provider is a library of classes that provides ADO.NET services. A data provider data reader provides fast, forward-only access to data. A Command object can be processed to execute SQL and to invoke stored procedures in a manner similar to but improved from that in ADO. The major new concept of ADO.NET is the DataSet. A DataSet is an in-memory database that is disconnected from any regular database but that has all the important characteristics of a regular database. DataSets can have multiple tables, relationships, referential integrity rules, referential integrity actions, views, and the equivalent of triggers. DataSet tables may have surrogate key columns (called auto-increment columns) and primary keys and may be declared unique.

DataSets are disconnected from the database(s) from which they are constructed, and they may be constructed from several different databases and possibly managed by different DBMS products. After a DataSet is constructed, an XML document of its contents and an XML Schema of its structure are easily produced. Further, the process works in reverse as well. XML Schema documents can be read to create the structure of the DataSet, and XML documents can be read to fill the DataSet.

DataSets are needed to provide a standardized, nonproprietary means to process database views. They are especially important for the processing of views with multiple multivalued paths, as discussed in Appendix I, "XML." The potential downside of DataSets is that because they are disconnected, any updates against the databases they access must be performed using optimistic locking. In the case of conflict, either the DataSet must be reprocessed or the data change must be forced onto the database, causing the lost update problem.

JDBC is an alternative to ODBC and ADO that provides database access to programs written in Java. A JDBC driver is available for almost every conceivable DBMS product. Sun defines four driver types. Type 1 drivers provide a bridge between Java and ODBC. Types 2, 3, and 4 are written entirely in Java. Type 2 drivers rely on the DBMS product for intermachine communication, if any. Type 3 drivers translate JDBC calls into a DBMS-independent network protocol. Type 4 drivers translate JDBC calls into a DBMS-dependent network protocol.

An applet is a compiled Java bytecode program that is transmitted to a browser via HTTP and is invoked using the HTTP protocol. A servlet is a Java program that is invoked on the server to respond to HTTP requests. Type 3 and Type 4 drivers can be used for both applets and servlets. Type 2 drivers can be used only in servlets, and only then if the DBMS and Web server are on the same machine or if the DBMS vendor handles the intermachine communication between the Web server and the database server.

There are four steps when using JDBC: (1) load the driver, (2) establish a connection to the database, (3) create a statement, and (4) execute the statement.

Java Server Pages (JSP) technology provides a means to create dynamic Web pages using HTML (and XML) and Java. JSP pages provide the capabilities of a full object-oriented language to the page developer. Neither VBScript nor JavaScript can be used in a JSP page. JSP pages are compiled into machine-independent bytecode.

JSP pages are compiled as subclasses of the HTTPServlet class. Consequently, small snippets of code can be placed in a JSP page as well as complete Java programs. To use JSP, the Web server must implement the Java Servlet 2.1+ and JSP 1.0+ specifications. Apache Tomcat, an open source product from the Jakarta Project, implements these specifications. Tomcat can work in conjunction with Apache or as a stand-alone Web server for testing purposes.

When using Tomcat (or any other JSP processor), the JDBC drivers and JSP pages must be located in specified directories. When a JSP page is requested, Tomcat ensures that the most recent page is used. If an uncompiled newer version is available, Tomcat will automatically cause it to be parsed and compiled. Only one JSP page can be in memory at a time, and JSP requests are executed as a thread of the servlet processor, not as a separate process. The Java code in a JSP page can invoke a compiled Java bean, if desired.

PHP (PHP: Hypertext Processor) is a scripting language that can be embedded in Web pages. PHP is extremely popular and easy to learn, and it can be used in most Web server environments and with most databases.

For creating complex pages, you need an integrated development environment (IDE). An IDE gives you the most robust and user-friendly means of creating and maintaining Web pages. Microsoft Visual Studio, NetBeans for Java users, and the open source Eclipse IDE are all good IDEs. The NetBeans IDE provides a framework that can be modified by plug-in modules.

PHP now includes object-oriented features and PHP Data Objects (PDO), which simplify connecting Web pages to databases.

The confluence of database processing and document processing is one of the most important developments in information systems technology today. Database processing and document processing need each other. Database processing needs document processing for the representation and materialization (rendering Web pages for a specific device) of database views. Document processing needs database processing for the permanent storage of data.

SGML is as important to document processing as the relational model is to database processing. XML is a series of standards that were developed jointly by the database processing and document processing communities. XML provides a standardized yet customizable way to describe the contents of documents. XML documents can be automatically generated from database data, and database data can be automatically extracted from XML documents.

Although XML can be used to materialize Web pages, this is one of its least important uses. More important is its use for describing, representing, and materializing database views. XML is on the leading edge of database processing; see *www.w3.org* and *www.xml.org* for the latest developments.

XML is a better markup language than HTML, primarily because XML provides a clear separation between document structure, content, and materialization. Also, XML tags are not ambiguous.

SQL Server, Oracle Database, and MySQL can produce XML documents from database data. The Oracle Database facilities require the use of Java; see *www.oracle.com* for more information. SQL Server supports an add-on expression to the SQL SELECT statement, the FOR XML expression.

# Key Terms

?php and ?
.NET for Windows Store Apps
.NET Framework
abstraction
Active Data Objects (ADO)
Active Server Pages (ASP)
ADO.NET
ADO.NET Command object
ADO.NET Connection object
ADO.NET Data Provider
ADO.NET DataAdapter object
ADO.NET DataReader
ADO.NET DataSet
ADO.NET Entity Framework
AMP
Apache Tomcat
Apache Web server
app
Apple iPad
Apple Safari
applet

application programming interface (API)
ASP.NET
Base Class Library
bytecode interpreter
Callable Statement object
cell phone
cellular network
client
client/server architecture
collection
Common Language Runtime (CLR)
Component Object Model (COM)
Constraints
current values
cursor
data consumer
data provider
DataColumnCollection
DataRelationCollection
DataRelations

DataRowCollection
DataTable object
DataTableCollection
Default Web Site folder
DeleteCommand object
device
document type declaration (DTD)
Entity Data Model (EDM)
Extensible Markup Language (XML)
file data source
ForeignKeyConstraint
Google Android operating system (OS)
Google Chrome
HTML document tags
HTML syntax rules
HTML5
http://localhost
Hypertext Markup Language (HTML)
iisstart.htm
implementation
index.html

```
<!DOCTYPE html>
<html>
     <head>
          <title>DBP-e16 Home Page</title>
          <meta charset="UTF-8">
          <meta name="viewport" content="width=device-width, initial-scale=1.0">
     </head>
     <body>
          <h1 style="text-align: center; color: blue">
               Database Processing (16th Edition) Home Page
          </h1>
          <hr />
          <h3 style="text-align: center">
               Use this page to access Web-based materials from Chapter 11 of:
          </h3>
          <h2 style="text-align: center; color: blue">
               Database Processing (16th Edition)
          </h2>
          <p style="text-align: center; font-weight: bold">
               David M. Kroenke, David J. Auer, and Scott L. Vandenberg
          </p>
          <hr />
          <h3>Chapter 11 Demonstration Pages from Figures in the Text:</h3>
          <p>
               <a href="VRG/index.html">
                    View Ridge Gallery Demonstration Pages
               </a>
          </p>
          <hr />
     </body>
</html>
```

**FIGURE 11-49**

**The HTML Code for the index.html File in the DBP Folder**

```
          <p>Example 4:   
               <a href="NewCustomerWithInterestsForm.html">
                    Add a New Customer to the CUSTOMER Table
               </a>
          </p>
          <hr />
<!-- *********** NEW CODE STARTS HERE ************ -->
          <p style="text-align: center">
               <a href="../index.html">
                    Return to the Database Processing Home Page
               </a>
          </p>
          <hr />
<!-- *********** NEW CODE ENDS HERE ************ -->
     </body>
</html>
```

**FIGURE 11-50**

**HTML Modifications for the index.html File in the VRG Folder**

# Case Questions

### Marcia's Dry Cleaning Case Question

**If you have not already done so, create and populate the Marcia's Dry Cleaning (MDC) database for the DBMS you are using as described in:**

- Chapter 10A for Microsoft SQL Server 2019
- Chapter 10B for Oracle Database
- Chapter 10C for MySQL 8.0

**A.** Add a new folder to the DBP Web site named MDC. Create a Web page for Marcia's Dry Cleaning in this folder, using the file name index.html. Link this page to the DBP Web page.

**B.** Create an appropriate ODBC data source for your database.

**C.** Add a new column Status to the INVOICE table. Assume that Status can have the values ['Waiting', 'In-process', 'Finished', 'Pending'].

**D.** Create a view called CustomerInvoiceView that has the columns LastName, First-Name, Phone, InvoiceNumber, DateIn, DateOut, Total, and Status.

**E.** Code a PHP page to display CustomerInvoiceView. Using your sample database, demonstrate that your page works.

**F.** Code two HTML/PHP pages to receive a date value AsOfDate and to display rows of CustomerInvoiceView for orders having DateIn greater than or equal to AsOfDate. Using your sample database, demonstrate that your pages work.

**G.** Code two HTML/PHP pages to receive customer Phone, LastName, and FirstName and to display rows for customers with that Phone, LastName, and FirstName. Using your sample database, demonstrate that your pages work.

**H.** Write a stored procedure that receives values for InvoiceNumber and NewStatus and that sets the value of Status to NewStatus for the row with the given value of Invoice-Number. Generate an error message if no row has the given value of InvoiceNumber. Using your sample database, demonstrate that your stored procedure works.

**I.** Code two HTML/PHP pages to invoke the stored procedure created in part H. Using your sample database, demonstrate that your page works.

# The Queen Anne Curiosity Shop Project Questions

**If you have not already done so, answer the questions for the Queen Anne Curiosity Shop (QACS) at the end of Chapter 7 (pages 415–422) and for the DBMS you are using as described in:**

- Chapter 10A for Microsoft SQL Server 2019
- Chapter 10B for Oracle Database
- Chapter 10C for MySQL 8.0

**A.** Add a new folder to the DBP Web site named QACS. Create a Web page for the Queen Anne Curiosity Shop in this folder, using the file name index.html. Link this page to the DBP Web page.

**B.** Create an appropriate ODBC data source for your database.

C.  Code a PHP page to display the data in the CUSTOMER table. Using your sample database, demonstrate that your page works.

D.  Create a view called CustomerPurchasesView that has the columns CustomerID, LastName, FirstName, SaleID, SaleDate, SaleItemID, ItemID, ItemDescription, and ItemPrice.

E.  Code a PHP page to display CustomerPurchasesView. Using your sample database, demonstrate that your page works.

F.  Code two HTML/PHP pages to receive a date value AsOfDate and display rows of the CustomerPurchasesView for purchases with SaleDate greater than or equal to AsOfDate. Using your sample database, demonstrate that your pages work.

G.  Write a stored procedure that receives values for SaleItemID and NewItemPrice and sets the value of ItemPrice to NewItemPrice for the row with the given value of SaleItemID. Generate an error message if no row has the given value of SaleItemID. Using your sample database, demonstrate that your stored procedure works.

H.  Code two HTML/PHP pages to invoke the stored procedure created in part G. Using your sample database, demonstrate that your page works.

# Morgan Importing Project Questions

If you have not already done so, answer the questions for Morgan Importing (MI) at the end of Chapter 7 (pages 422–429) and for the DBMS you are using as described in:

- Chapter 10A for Microsoft SQL Server 2019
- Chapter 10B for Oracle Database
- Chapter 10C for MySQL 8.0

A.  Add a new folder to the DBP Web site named MI. Create a Web page for Morgan Importing in this folder, using the file name index.html. Link this page to the DBP Web page.

B.  Create an appropriate ODBC data source for your database.

C.  Create a view called StorePurchasesView that has the columns StoreName, City, Country, Email, Contact, PurchaseDate, ItemDescription, Category, and PriceUSD.

D.  Code a PHP page to display StorePurchasesView. Using your sample database, demonstrate that your page works.

E.  Code two HTML/PHP pages to receive a date value AsOfDate and display rows of Store Purchases for purchases with PurchaseDate greater than or equal to AsOfDate. Using your sample database, demonstrate that your pages work.

F.  Code two HTML/PHP pages to receive values of Country and Category and display rows of StorePurchases with values for input Country and Category values. Using your sample database, demonstrate that your pages work.

G.  Write a stored procedure that receives values for PurchaseItemID and NewPriceUSD and sets the value of PriceUSD to NewPriceUSD for the row with the given value of PurchaseItemID. Generate an error message if no row has the given value of Purchase-ItemID. Using your sample database, demonstrate that your stored procedure works.

H.  Code two HTML/PHP pages to invoke the stored procedure created in part G. Using your sample database, demonstrate that your page works.

# 12

# Data Warehouses and Business Intelligence Systems

## Chapter Objectives

- To learn the basic concepts of business intelligence (BI) systems
- To learn the basic concepts of data warehouses and data marts
- To learn the basic concepts of dimensional databases
- To learn the basic concepts of reporting systems
- To learn how to create RFM reports
- To learn the basic concepts of online analytical processing (OLAP)
- To learn the basic concepts of data mining
- To learn the basic concepts of market basket analysis
- To learn the basic concepts of decision trees

**This chapter introduces** topics that build on the fundamentals you have learned in the other chapters of this book. Now that we have designed and built a database, we are ready to put it to work. In Chapter 11, we built a Web database application for the View Ridge Gallery (VRG) Information System, and in this chapter, we will look at business intelligence (BI) systems applications, which often (but not always) use data warehouse databases to support decision making.

There is often a need for business analysts to have large datasets (such as data warehouses or other large production databases) available for analysis by **business intelligence (BI) systems**, particularly **online analytical processing (OLAP)**, and the data warehouse structures that were designed for their use. These new and often very visible applications and methods are highlighting the problems of dealing with large datasets. This chapter introduces business intelligence activities that often take place in the context of large amounts of data, typically stored in a data warehouse or similar database. Chapter 13 takes these large databases in different directions, looking at issues arising from sheer size, new (non-relational) data models, and cloud-based storage and processing.

# Business Intelligence Systems

Business intelligence (BI) systems are information systems that assist managers and other professionals in the analysis of current and past activities and in the prediction of future events. Unlike transaction processing systems, they do not support operational activities, such as the recording and processing of orders. Instead, BI systems are used to support management assessment, analysis, planning, control, and, ultimately, decision making. BI systems are often built on top of data warehouse databases rather than operational databases.

## The Relationship Between Operational and BI Systems

Figure 12-1 summarizes the relationship between operational and business intelligence systems. **Operational systems**—such as sales, purchasing, and inventory control systems—support primary business activities. They use a DBMS to both read data from and store data in the operational database. They are also known as **transactional systems** or **online transaction processing (OLTP) systems** because they record the ongoing stream of business transactions.

Instead of supporting the primary business activities, BI systems support management's analysis and decision-making activities. BI systems obtain data from three possible sources. First, they read and process data existing in the operational database—they use the operational DBMS to obtain such data, but they do not insert, modify, or delete operational data. Second, BI systems process data that are extracted from operational databases. In this situation, they manage the extracted database using a BI DBMS, which may be the same as or different from the operational DBMS. Finally, BI systems read data purchased from data vendors.

## Reporting Systems and Data Mining Applications

BI systems fall into two broad categories: reporting systems and data mining applications. **Reporting systems** sort, filter, group, and make elementary calculations on operational data. **Data mining applications**, in contrast, perform sophisticated analyses on data, analyses that usually involve complex statistical and mathematical processing. The characteristics of BI applications are summarized in Figure 12-2.

**FIGURE 12-1**

Relationship Between
Operational and BI
Systems

FIGURE 12-2

Characteristics of Business
Intelligence Applications

| Characteristics of Business Intelligence Applications |
|---|
| • Reporting |
|       – Filter, sort, group, and make simple calculations |
|       – Summarize current status |
|       – Compare current status to past or predicted status |
|       – Classify entities (customers, products, employees, etc.) |
|       – Report delivery crucial |
| • Data Mining |
|       – Often employ sophisticated statistical and mathematical techniques |
|       – Used for: |
|            • What-if analyses |
|            • Predictions |
|            • Decisions |
|       – Results often incorporated into some other report or system |

## Reporting Systems

Reporting systems filter, sort, group, and make simple calculations. All reporting analyses can be performed using standard SQL, though extensions to SQL, such as those used for online analytical processing (OLAP), are sometimes used to ease the task of report production.

Reporting systems summarize the current status of business activities and compare that status with past or predicted future activities. Reports must be delivered to the proper users on a timely basis in the appropriate format. For example, reports may be delivered on paper, via a Web browser, or in some other format. Two types of common reporting systems, RFM and OLAP, are described in detail later in this chapter.

## Data Mining Applications

Data mining applications use sophisticated statistical and mathematical techniques to perform what-if analyses, to make predictions, and to facilitate decision making. For example, data mining techniques can analyze past cell phone usage and predict which customers are likely to switch to a competing phone company. Data mining can also be used to analyze past loan behavior to determine which customers are most (or least) likely to default on a loan.

Report delivery is not as important for data mining systems as it is for reporting systems. First, most data mining applications have only a few users, and those users have sophisticated computer skills. Second, the results of a data mining analysis are usually incorporated into some other report, analysis, or information system. In the case of cell phone usage, the characteristics of customers who are in danger of switching to another company, called "customer churn," may be given to the sales department for action; or the parameters of an equation for determining the likelihood of a loan default may be incorporated into a loan approval application.

More details and a brief example of a kind of data mining called clustering are discussed later in this chapter. Two other common kinds of data mining, market basket analysis and decision trees, are described in more detail later in this chapter.

## Data Warehouses and Data Marts

According to Figure 12-1, some BI systems read and process operational data directly from the operational database. Although this is possible for simple reporting systems and small databases, such direct reading of operational data is not feasible for more complex applications or larger databases. Those larger applications usually process a separate database constructed from an extract of the operational database.

Operational data are difficult to read for several reasons. For one, querying data for BI applications can place a substantial burden on the DBMS and unacceptably slow the performance of operational applications. Additionally, operational data have problems that limit their use for BI applications. Further, the creation and maintenance of BI systems require programs, facilities, and expertise that are not normally available from operations-focused departments. Because of these problems, many organizations have chosen to develop data warehouses and data marts to support BI applications. Some organizations will go even farther and create a **data lake**, which is a repository that includes all data relevant to a business, some of it relational and some not (for example, files of any type, photos, documents, and so on). This information can come from databases, web sites, and other applications. Typically, it is used by more sophisticated users for puposes fo advanced analytics, machine learning, data mining, and so on, and not for more standard BI tasks. Amazon.com's AWS service provides data lake capabilities in the cloud.

### Problems with Operational Data

Most operational databases have problems that limit their usefulness to all but the simplest BI applications. Figure 12-3 lists the major problem categories.

First, although data that are critical for successful operations must be complete and accurate, data that are only marginally necessary need not be. For example, some operational systems gather customer demographic data during the ordering process. However, because such data are not needed to fill, ship, or bill orders, the quality of the demographic data may suffer.

Problematic data are termed **dirty data**. Examples are a value of "G" for customer sex and a value of "213" for customer age. Other examples are a value of "999-999-9999" for a U.S. phone number, a part color of "gren," and an email address of "WhyMe@somewhereelse@intheuniverse.who." All of these values pose problems for reporting and data mining purposes.

**FIGURE 12-3**

Problems of Using Transaction Data for Business Intelligence

| Problems of Using Transaction Data for Business Intelligence |
|---|
| • Dirty data |
| • Missing values |
| • Inconsistent data |
| • Data not integrated |
| • Wrong format |
| – Too fine |
| – Not fine enough |
| • Too much data |
| – Too many attributes |
| – Too much volume |

Purchased data often contain missing elements. In fact, most data vendors state the percentage of **missing values** for each attribute in the data they sell. An organization buys such data because, for some uses, some data are better than no data at all. This is especially true for data items whose values are difficult to obtain, such as the number of adults in a household, household income, dwelling type, and the education of the primary income earner. Some missing data are not too much of a problem for reporting applications. For some data mining applications, however, a few missing or erroneous data points can actually be worse than no data at all because they bias the analysis.

**Inconsistent data**, the third problem in Figure 12-3, is particularly common for data that have been gathered over time. When an area code changes, for example, the phone number for a given customer before the change will differ from the customer's phone number after the change. Part codes can change, as can sales territories. Before such data can be used, they must be recoded for consistency over the period of the study. Inconsistencies often come in simpler forms as well—for example, using both "Yes" and "y" to mean the same thing.

Some data inconsistencies occur because of the nature of the business activity. Consider a Web-based order entry system used by customers around the world. When the Web server records the time of order, which time zone does it use? The server's system clock time is irrelevant to an analysis of customer behavior. Any standard time such as Universal Time Coordinate (UTC) time is also meaningless. Somehow, Web server time must be adjusted to the time zone of the customer.

Another problem is **nonintegrated data**. Suppose, for example, that an organization wants to report on customer orders and payment behavior. Unfortunately, order data might be stored in a Microsoft Dynamics CRM system, whereas payment data are recorded in an Oracle PeopleSoft financial management database. To perform the analysis, the data must somehow be integrated.

The next problem is that data can be *inappropriately formatted*. First, data can be too fine. For example, suppose that we want to analyze the placement of graphics and controls on an order entry Web page. It is possible to capture the customers' clicking behavior in what is termed **click-stream data**. However, click-stream data include *everything* the customer does. In the middle of the order stream, there may be data for clicks on the news, email, instant chat, and the weather. Although all of this data might be useful for a study of consumer computer behavior, it will be overwhelming if we just want to know how customers responded to an ad located on the screen. Because the data are too fine, the data analysts must throw millions of extraneous clicks away before they can proceed.

Data can also be too coarse. A file of order totals cannot be used for a market basket analysis, which identifies items that are commonly purchased together. Market basket analyses require item-level data; we need to know which items were purchased with which others. This doesn't mean the order total data are useless; they can be adequate for other analyses, but they just won't do for a market basket analysis.

If the data are too fine, they can be made coarser by summing and combining. An analyst or a computer can sum and combine such data. If the data are too coarse, however, they cannot be separated into their constituent parts.

The final problem listed in Figure 12-3 concerns the issue of *too much data*. We can have an excess of columns, rows, or both. To illustrate the problem of too many columns (a synonym for attributes), suppose that we want to know the attributes that influence customers' responses to a marketing promotion. Between customer data stored within the organization and customer data that can be purchased, we might have a hundred or more different attributes, or columns, to consider. How do we select the ones that really influence a customer's decision? Because of a phenomenon called the **curse of dimensionality**, the more attributes there are, the easier it is to build a model that fits the sample data but becomes worthless as a predictor. For this and other reasons, the number of attributes may need to be reduced, and one of the major activities in data mining concerns the efficient and effective selection of variables (attributes).

Finally, we may have too many instances, or rows, of data. Suppose that we want to analyze click-stream data on CNN.com. How many clicks does this site receive per month?

Millions upon millions! To meaningfully analyze such data, we need to reduce the number of instances. A good solution to this problem is statistical sampling. However, developing a reliable sample requires specialized expertise and information system tools.

## Components of a Data Warehouse

To overcome the problems just described, many organizations have created **data warehouses**, which are database systems that have data, programs, and personnel that specialize in the preparation of data for BI processing. Data warehouse databases differ from operational databases because the data warehouse data is frequently denormalized. Further, that data is never inserted, updated, or deleted by users, but only by data warehouse administrators. Data warehouses vary in scale and scope. They can be as simple as a sole employee processing a data extract on a part-time basis or as complex as a department with dozens of employees maintaining libraries of data and programs.

Figure 12-4 shows the components of a data warehouse. Data are read from operational databases by the **Extract, Transform, and Load (ETL) system**. The ETL system then cleans and prepares the data for BI processing. This can be a complex process.

> **BY THE WAY**   Once problematic operational data have been cleaned in the ETL system, the corrected data can also be used to update the operational system to fix the original data problems.

First, the data may be problematic, as discussed in the previous section. Second, data may need to be changed or transformed for use in a data warehouse. For example, the operational systems may store data about countries using standard two-letter country codes, such as US (United States) and CA (Canada). However, applications using the data warehouse may need to use the country names in full. Thus, the data transformation {**CountryCode → CountryName**} will be needed before the data can be loaded into the data warehouse.

The ETL system stores the extracted data in a data warehouse database using a data warehouse DBMS, which can be different from the organization's operational DBMS. For example, an organization might use Oracle Database for its operational processing but use Microsoft SQL Server 2019 for its data warehouse. Other organizations might use Microsoft SQL Server 2019 for operational processing and data management programs from statistical package vendors such as SAS (SAS Analytics) or IBM (IBM SPSS Statistics) in the data warehouse.

**FIGURE 12-4**

Components of a Data Warehouse

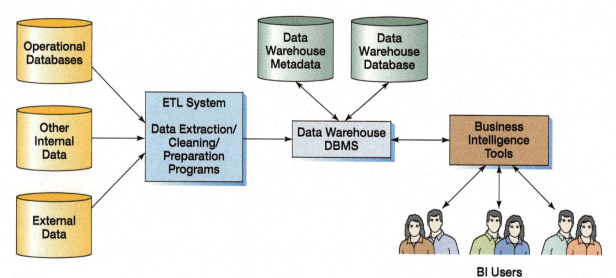

Metadata concerning the data's source, format, assumptions, constraints, and other facts are kept in a **data warehouse metadata database**. The data warehouse DBMS extracts and provides data to BI tools, such as data mining programs.

### Purchasing Data from Vendors

Data warehouses often include data that are purchased from outside sources. A typical example is customer credit data. Figure 12-5 lists some of the consumer data that can be purchased from the KBM Group in their AmeriLINK database of consumer data. An amazing, and from a privacy standpoint frightening, amount of data is available just from this one vendor.

## Data Warehouses Versus Data Marts

You can think of a data warehouse as a distributor in a supply chain. The data warehouse takes data from the data manufacturers (operational systems and purchased data), cleans and processes them, and locates the data on the shelves, so to speak, of the data warehouse. The people who work in a data warehouse are experts at data management, data cleaning, data transformation, and the like. However, they are not usually experts in other, more specific business functions.

A **data mart** is a collection of data that is smaller than that contained in a data warehouse and is used to represent a specific component or functional area of the business. A data mart is like a retail store in a supply chain. Users in the data mart obtain data that pertain to a particular business function from the data warehouse. Such users do not have the data management expertise that data warehouse employees have, but they are knowledgeable analysts for a given business function. Figure 12-6 illustrates these relationships.

**FIGURE 12-5**

AmeriLINK Sells Data on 260-Plus Million Americans

| AmeriLINK Data Categories |
|---|
| • Name, Address, Phone |
| • Age, Gender |
| • Ethnicity, Religion |
| • Income |
| • Education |
| • Marital Status, Life Stage |
| • Health Conditions |
| • Spouse's Name, Birth Date, etc. |
| • Kids' Birth Dates |
| • Voter Registration |
| • Home Ownership |
| • Vehicles |
| • Magazine Subscriptions |
| • Catalog Orders |
| • Hobbies |
| • Attitudes |

**FIGURE 12-6**

Data Warehouses and Data
Marts

This data warehouse takes data from the data producers and distributes it to three data marts. One data mart analyzes click-stream data for the purpose of designing Web pages. The second analyzes store sales data and determines which products tend to be purchased together. This information is used to train salespeople on the best way to up-sell customers. The third data mart analyzes customer order data to assist with reducing labor costs when picking items from the warehouse. Companies like Amazon.com go to great lengths to organize their warehouses to reduce picking times and expenses.

When the data mart structure shown in Figure 12-6 is combined with the data warehouse architecture shown in Figure 12-4, the combined system is known as an **enterprise data warehouse (EDW) architecture**. In this configuration, the data warehouse maintains all enterprise BI data and acts as the authoritative source for data extracts provided to the data marts. The data marts receive all their data from the data warehouse—they do not add or maintain any additional data.

Of course, it is expensive to create, staff, and operate data warehouses and data marts, and only large organizations with deep pockets can afford to operate a system such as an EDW. Smaller organizations operate subsets of such systems. For example, they may have just a single data mart for analyzing marketing and promotion data.

## Dimensional Databases

The databases in a data warehouse or data mart are built to a different type of database design than the normalized relational databases used for operational systems. The data warehouse databases are built in a design called a **dimensional database** that is designed for efficient data queries and analysis. A dimensional database is used to store historical data rather than just the current data stored in an operational database. Figure 12-7 compares operational databases and dimensional databases.

A **dimension** within a dimensional database is a column or set of columns that describes some aspect of the enterprise (for example, a location or a customer). Typically in a data warehouse, a dimension is modeled as a table based on one or more columns from an operational database. An address field, for example, could be expanded into a location dimension table with separate street, city, and state columns.

Because dimensional databases are used for the analysis of historical data, they must be designed to handle data that change over time. In order to track such changes, a dimensional database must have a **date dimension** or **time dimension** as well. For example, a customer may have moved from one residence to another in the same city or may have moved

FIGURE 12-7

Characteristics of
Operational and Dimensional
Databases

| Operational Database | Dimensional Database |
| --- | --- |
| Used for structured transaction data processing | Used for unstructured analytical data processing |
| Current data are used | Current and historical data are used |
| Data are inserted, updated, and deleted by users | Data are loaded and updated systematically, not by users |

to a completely different city and state. This type of data arrangement is called a **slowly changing dimension** because changes to such data are infrequent.

### The Star Schema

Rather than using the normalized database designs used in operational databases, a dimensional database uses a star schema. A **star schema**, so named because, as shown in Figure 12-8, it visually resembles a star, has a **fact table** at the center of the star and **dimension tables** radiating out from the center. The fact table is always fully normalized, but dimension tables may be non-normalized.

> **BY THE WAY**   There is a more complex version of the star schema called the *snowflake schema*. In the snowflake schema, each dimension table is normalized, which may create additional tables attached to the dimension tables.

To illustrate a star schema for a dimensional database, we will build a (very) small data warehouse for Heather Sweeney Designs (HSD), a Texas company specializing in products for kitchen-remodeling services. HSD offers seminars to attract customers and sell books and videos in addition to doing actual design work. For more information about Heather Sweeney Designs, see the Chapter 7 Heather Sweeney Designs Case Questions on pages 401–415. A database design for HSD is shown in Figure 12-9, and a MySQL Workbench database diagram for the HSD database is shown in Figure 12-10. In addition, the Chapter 7 Heather Sweeney Designs Case Questions show the HSD database column specifications in Figure 7-51, HSD database referential integrity constraint enforcement in Figure 7-52, the SQL statements to create the HSD database in Figure 7-53, and the SQL statements to populate the HSD database in Figure 7-54. The HSD database is the operational database for Heather Sweeney Designs. All production data are stored in the HSD database, and that database provides the source data that we will load into a dimensional database for BI work at Heather Sweeney Designs.

FIGURE 12-8

The Star Schema

**FIGURE 12-9**

The HSD Database Design

**FIGURE 12-10**

The HSD Database Diagram

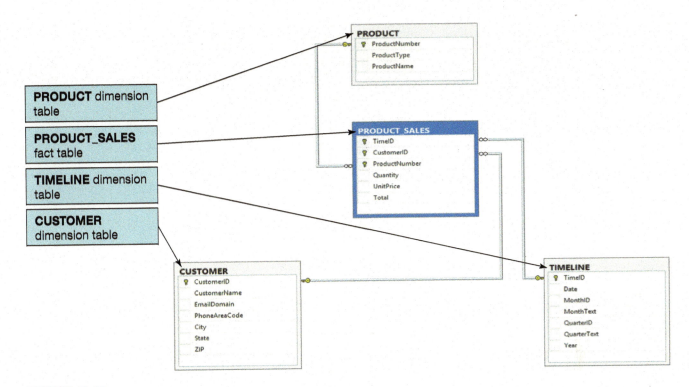

**FIGURE 12-11**

**The HSD_DW Star Schema**

The actual dimensional database for BI use is named *HSD_DW*, and it is shown in Figure 12-11. The SQL statements needed to create the tables in the HSD_DW database are shown in Figure 12-12, and the data for the HSD_DW database are shown in Figure 12-13. Compare the HSD_DW dimensional database model in Figure 12-11 to the HSD database diagram shown in Figure 12-10, and note how data in the HSD database have been used in the HSD_DW schema. For example, some of the details from the LINE_ITEM table are included in the PRODUCT_SALES fact table of the HSD_DW database.

> **BY THE WAY**   You do not need to create the HSD database in order to create and use the HSD_DW database used in this chapter. However, because the HSD_DW database uses data extracted from the HSD database, it is worthwhile to study and understand the structure of the HSD database and data contained in the HSD database to fully appreciate how we transform that data for use in the HSD_DW database.

A fact table is used to store **measures** of business activity, which are quantitative or factual data about the entity represented by the fact table. For example, in the HSD_DW database, the fact table is PRODUCT_SALES:

**PRODUCT_SALES (*TimeID*, *CustomerID*, *ProductNumber*, Quantity, UnitPrice, Total)**

In this table:

- Quantity is quantitative data that record how many of the item were sold.
- UnitPrice is quantitative data that record the dollar price of each item sold.
- Total (= Quantity * UnitPrice) is quantitative data that records the total dollar value of the sale of this item.

```
CREATE TABLE TIMELINE(
        TimeID                  Int                     NOT NULL,
        Date                    Date                    NOT NULL,
        MonthID                 Int                     NOT NULL,
        MonthText               Char(15)                NOT NULL,
        QuarterID               Int                     NOT NULL,
        QuarterText             Char(10)                NOT NULL,
        Year                    Char(10)                NOT NULL,
        CONSTRAINT              TIMELINE_PK     PRIMARY KEY(TimeID)
        );

CREATE TABLE CUSTOMER(
        CustomerID              Int                     NOT NULL,
        CustomerName            Char(75)                NOT NULL,
        EmailDomain             VarChar(100)            NOT NULL,
        PhoneAreaCode           Char(6)                 NOT NULL,
        City                    Char(35)                NULL,
        State                   Char(2)                 NULL,
        ZIP                     Char(10)                NULL,
        CONSTRAINT              CUSTOMER_PK     PRIMARY KEY(CustomerID)
        );

CREATE TABLE PRODUCT(
        ProductNumber           Char(35)                NOT NULL,
        ProductType             Char(25)                NOT NULL,
        ProductName             VarChar(75)             NOT NULL,
        CONSTRAINT              PRODUCT_PK      PRIMARY KEY(ProductNumber)
        );

CREATE TABLE PRODUCT_SALES(
        TimeID                  Int                     NOT NULL,
        CustomerID              Int                     NOT NULL,
        ProductNumber           Char(35)                NOT NULL,
        Quantity                Int                     NOT NULL,
        UnitPrice               Numeric(9,2)            NOT NULL,
        Total                   Numeric(9,2)            NULL,
        CONSTRAINT              SALES_PK
                PRIMARY KEY         (TimeID, CustomerID, ProductNumber),
        CONSTRAINT              PS_TIMELINE_FK FOREIGN KEY(TimeID)
                                        REFERENCES TIMELINE(TimeID)
                                                ON UPDATE NO ACTION
                                                ON DELETE NO ACTION,
        CONSTRAINT              PS_CUSTOMER_FK FOREIGN KEY(CustomerID)
                                        REFERENCES CUSTOMER(CustomerID)
                                                ON UPDATE NO ACTION
                                                ON DELETE NO ACTION,
        CONSTRAINT              PS_PRODUCT_FK FOREIGN KEY(ProductNumber)
                                        REFERENCES PRODUCT(ProductNumber)
                                                ON UPDATE NO ACTION
                                                ON DELETE NO ACTION
        );
```

**FIGURE 12-12**

**The HSD_DW SQL Create Table Statements**

The measures in the PRODUCT_SALES table are for *units of product per customer per day.* We do not use individual sale data (which would be based on InvoiceNumber), but rather data summed for each customer for each day. For example, if you could examine the HSD database INVOICE data for Ralph Able for 6/5/21, you would see that Ralph made two purchases on that date (InvoiceNumber 35013 and InvoiceNumber 35016). In the HSD_DW database, however, these two purchases are summed into the PRODUCT_SALES data for Ralph (CustomerID = 3) for 6/5/21 (TimeID = 44352).

|   | TimeID | Date | MonthID | MonthText | QuarterID | QuarterText | Year |
|---|--------|------|---------|-----------|-----------|-------------|------|
| 1 | 44119 | 2020-10-15 | 10 | October | 3 | Qtr4 | 2020 |
| 2 | 44129 | 2020-10-25 | 10 | October | 3 | Qtr4 | 2020 |
| 3 | 44185 | 2020-12-20 | 12 | December | 3 | Qtr4 | 2020 |
| 4 | 44280 | 2021-03-25 | 3 | March | 1 | Qtr1 | 2021 |
| 5 | 44282 | 2021-03-27 | 3 | March | 1 | Qtr1 | 2021 |
| 6 | 44286 | 2021-03-31 | 3 | March | 1 | Qtr1 | 2021 |
| 7 | 44289 | 2021-04-03 | 4 | April | 2 | Qtr2 | 2021 |
| 8 | 44294 | 2021-04-08 | 4 | April | 2 | Qtr2 | 2021 |
| 9 | 44309 | 2021-04-23 | 4 | April | 2 | Qtr2 | 2021 |
| 10 | 44323 | 2021-05-07 | 5 | May | 2 | Qtr2 | 2021 |
| 11 | 44337 | 2021-05-21 | 5 | May | 2 | Qtr2 | 2021 |
| 12 | 44352 | 2021-06-05 | 6 | June | 2 | Qtr2 | 2021 |

(a) TIMELINE Dimension Table

|   | CustomerID | CustomerName | EmailDomain | PhoneAreaCode | City | State | ZIP |
|---|-----------|--------------|-------------|---------------|------|-------|-----|
| 1 | 1 | Jacobs, Nancy | somewhere.com | 817 | Fort Worth | TX | 76110 |
| 2 | 2 | Jacobs, Chantel | somewhere.com | 817 | Fort Worth | TX | 76112 |
| 3 | 3 | Able, Ralph | somewhere.com | 210 | San Antonio | TX | 78214 |
| 4 | 4 | Baker, Susan | elsewhere.com | 210 | San Antonio | TX | 78216 |
| 5 | 5 | Eagleton, Sam | elsewhere.com | 210 | San Antonio | TX | 78218 |
| 6 | 6 | Foxtrot, Kathy | somewhere.com | 972 | Dallas | TX | 75220 |
| 7 | 7 | George, Sally | somewhere.com | 972 | Dallas | TX | 75223 |
| 8 | 8 | Hullett, Shawn | elsewhere.com | 972 | Dallas | TX | 75224 |
| 9 | 9 | Pearson, Bobbi | elsewhere.com | 512 | Austin | TX | 78710 |
| 10 | 10 | Ranger, Terry | somewhere.com | 512 | Austin | TX | 78712 |
| 11 | 11 | Tyler, Jenny | somewhere.com | 972 | Dallas | TX | 75225 |
| 12 | 12 | Wayne, Joan | elsewhere.com | 817 | Fort Worth | TX | 76115 |

(b) CUSTOMER Dimension Table

|   | ProductNumber | ProductType | ProductName |
|---|---------------|-------------|-------------|
| 1 | BK001 | Book | Kitchen Remodeling Basics For Everyone |
| 2 | BK002 | Book | Advanced Kitchen Remodeling For Everyone |
| 3 | BK003 | Book | Kitchen Remodeling Dallas Style For Everyone |
| 4 | VB001 | Video Companion | Kitchen Remodeling Basics |
| 5 | VB002 | Video Companion | Advanced Kitchen Remodeling I |
| 6 | VB003 | Video Companion | Kitchen Remodeling Dallas Style |
| 7 | VK001 | Video | Kitchen Remodeling Basics |
| 8 | VK002 | Video | Advanced Kitchen Remodeling |
| 9 | VK003 | Video | Kitchen Remodeling Dallas Style |
| 10 | VK004 | Video | Heather Sweeney Seminar Live in Dallas on 25-OCT-19 |

(c) PRODUCT Dimension Table

|   | TimeID | CustomerID | ProductNumber | Quantity | UnitPrice | Total |
|---|--------|-----------|---------------|----------|-----------|-------|
| 1 | 44119 | 3 | VB001 | 1 | 7.99 | 7.99 |
| 2 | 44119 | 3 | VK001 | 1 | 14.95 | 14.95 |
| 3 | 44129 | 4 | BK001 | 1 | 24.95 | 24.95 |
| 4 | 44129 | 4 | VB001 | 1 | 7.99 | 7.99 |
| 5 | 44129 | 4 | VK001 | 1 | 14.95 | 14.95 |
| 6 | 44185 | 7 | VK004 | 1 | 24.95 | 24.95 |
| 7 | 44280 | 4 | BK002 | 1 | 24.95 | 24.95 |
| 8 | 44280 | 4 | VK002 | 1 | 14.95 | 14.95 |
| 9 | 44280 | 4 | VK004 | 1 | 24.95 | 24.95 |
| 10 | 44282 | 6 | BK002 | 1 | 24.95 | 24.95 |
| 11 | 44282 | 6 | VB003 | 1 | 9.99 | 9.99 |
| 12 | 44282 | 6 | VK002 | 1 | 14.95 | 14.95 |
| 13 | 44282 | 6 | VK003 | 1 | 19.95 | 19.95 |
| 14 | 44282 | 6 | VK004 | 1 | 24.95 | 24.95 |
| 15 | 44282 | 7 | BK001 | 1 | 24.95 | 24.95 |
| 16 | 44282 | 7 | BK002 | 1 | 24.95 | 24.95 |
| 17 | 44282 | 7 | VK003 | 1 | 19.95 | 19.95 |
| 18 | 44282 | 7 | VK004 | 1 | 24.95 | 24.95 |
| 19 | 44286 | 9 | BK001 | 1 | 24.95 | 24.95 |
| 20 | 44286 | 9 | VB001 | 1 | 7.99 | 7.99 |
| 21 | 44286 | 9 | VK001 | 1 | 14.95 | 14.95 |
| 22 | 44289 | 11 | VB003 | 2 | 9.99 | 19.98 |
| 23 | 44289 | 11 | VK003 | 2 | 19.95 | 39.90 |
| 24 | 44289 | 11 | VK004 | 2 | 24.95 | 49.90 |
| 25 | 44294 | 1 | BK001 | 1 | 24.95 | 24.95 |
| 26 | 44294 | 1 | VB001 | 1 | 7.99 | 7.99 |
| 27 | 44294 | 1 | VK001 | 1 | 14.95 | 14.95 |
| 28 | 44294 | 5 | BK001 | 1 | 24.95 | 24.95 |
| 29 | 44294 | 5 | VB001 | 1 | 7.99 | 7.99 |
| 30 | 44294 | 5 | VK001 | 1 | 14.95 | 14.95 |
| 31 | 44309 | 3 | BK001 | 1 | 24.95 | 24.95 |
| 32 | 44323 | 9 | VB002 | 1 | 7.99 | 7.99 |
| 33 | 44323 | 9 | VK002 | 1 | 14.95 | 14.95 |
| 34 | 44337 | 8 | VB003 | 1 | 9.99 | 9.99 |
| 35 | 44337 | 8 | VK003 | 1 | 19.95 | 19.95 |
| 36 | 44337 | 8 | VK004 | 1 | 24.95 | 24.95 |
| 37 | 44352 | 3 | BK002 | 1 | 24.95 | 24.95 |
| 38 | 44352 | 3 | VB001 | 1 | 7.99 | 7.99 |
| 39 | 44352 | 3 | VB002 | 2 | 7.99 | 15.98 |
| 40 | 44352 | 3 | VK001 | 1 | 14.95 | 14.95 |
| 41 | 44352 | 3 | VK002 | 2 | 14.95 | 29.90 |
| 42 | 44352 | 11 | VB002 | 2 | 7.99 | 15.98 |
| 43 | 44352 | 11 | VK002 | 2 | 14.95 | 29.90 |
| 44 | 44352 | 12 | BK002 | 1 | 24.95 | 24.95 |
| 45 | 44352 | 12 | VB003 | 1 | 9.99 | 9.99 |
| 46 | 44352 | 12 | VK002 | 1 | 14.95 | 14.95 |
| 47 | 44352 | 12 | VK003 | 1 | 19.95 | 19.95 |
| 48 | 44352 | 12 | VK004 | 1 | 24.95 | 24.95 |

(d) PRODUCT_SALES Fact Table

**FIGURE 12-13**

The HSD_DW Table Data

BY THE WAY    The TimeID values are the sequential *serial values* used in Microsoft Excel to represent dates. Starting with 01-JAN-1900 as date value 1, the date value is increased by 1 for each calendar day. Thus, 05-JUN-2021 = 44352. For more information, search "Date formats" in the Excel help system.

A dimension table is used to record values of attributes that describe the fact measures in the fact table, and these attributes are used in queries to select and group the measures in the fact table. Thus, CUSTOMER records data about the customers referenced by CustomerID in the SALES table, TIMELINE provides data that can be used to interpret the SALES event in time (which month? which quarter?), and so on. A query to summarize product units sold by Customer (CustomerName) and Product (ProductName) would be:

```
/* *** SQL-Query-CH12-01 *** */
SELECT          C.CustomerID, C.CustomerName,
                P.ProductNumber, P.ProductName,
                SUM(PS.Quantity) AS TotalQuantity
FROM            CUSTOMER AS C, PRODUCT_SALES AS PS, PRODUCT AS P
WHERE           C.CustomerID = PS.CustomerID
AND             P.ProductNumber = PS.ProductNumber
GROUP BY        C.CustomerID, C.CustomerName,
                P.ProductNumber, P.ProductName
ORDER BY        C.CustomerID, P.ProductNumber;
```

The results of this query are shown in Figure 12-14.

In Chapter 6, we discussed how an N:M relationship is created in a database as two 1:N relationships by use of an intersection (or association) table. We also discussed how additional attributes can be added to the intersection table in an association relationship. In a star schema, the fact table is an intersection table for the relationships between the dimension tables with additional measures stored in it. And, as with all other intersection and association tables, the key of the fact table is a composite key made up of all the foreign keys to the dimension tables. Thus, a fact table will be on the "many" side of a join.

### Illustrating the Dimensional Model

When you think of the word *dimension*, you might think of "two dimensional" or "three dimensional." And the dimensional models can be illustrated by using a two-dimensional matrix and a three-dimensional cube. Figure 12-15 shows the SQL query results from Figure 12-14 displayed as a two-dimensional matrix of Product (using ProductNumber) and Customer (using CustomerID), with each cell showing the number of units of each product purchased by each customer. Note how ProductNumber and CustomerID define the two dimensions of the matrix: CustomerID labels what would be the *x*-axis, and ProductNumber labels the *y*-axis.

Figure 12-16 shows a three-dimensional cube with the same ProductNumber and CustomerID dimensions, but now with the added Time dimension on the *z*-axis. Now instead of occupying a two-dimensional box, the total quantity of products purchased by each customer on each day occupies a small three-dimensional cube, and all these small cubes combine to form a large cube.

As human beings, we can visualize two-dimensional matrices and three-dimensional cubes. Although we cannot visualize models with four, five, and more dimensions, BI systems and dimensional databases routinely handle such models.

### Multiple Fact Tables and Conformed Dimensions

Data warehouse systems build dimensional models, as needed, to analyze BI questions, and the HSD_DW star schema in Figure 12-11 would be just one schema in a set of schemas. Figure 12-17 shows an extended HSD_DW schema.

In Figure 12-17, a second fact table named SALES_FOR_RFM has been added:

**SALES_FOR_RFM (*TimeID*, *CustomerID*, InvoiceNumber, PreTaxTotalSale)**

This table shows that fact table primary keys do not need to be composed solely of foreign keys that link to dimension tables. In SALES_FOR_RFM, the primary key includes the InvoiceNumber attribute. This attribute is necessary because the composite key (TimeID, CustomerID) will not be unique and thus cannot be the primary key (a customer can place multiple orders on the same day). Note that SALES_FOR_RFM links to the same

| | CustomerID | CustomerName | ProductNumber | ProductName | TotalQuantity |
|---|---|---|---|---|---|
| 1 | 1 | Jacobs, Nancy | BK001 | Kitchen Remodeling Basics For Everyone | 1 |
| 2 | 1 | Jacobs, Nancy | VB001 | Kitchen Remodeling Basics | 1 |
| 3 | 1 | Jacobs, Nancy | VK001 | Kitchen Remodeling Basics | 1 |
| 4 | 3 | Able, Ralph | BK001 | Kitchen Remodeling Basics For Everyone | 1 |
| 5 | 3 | Able, Ralph | BK002 | Advanced Kitchen Remodeling For Everyone | 1 |
| 6 | 3 | Able, Ralph | VB001 | Kitchen Remodeling Basics | 2 |
| 7 | 3 | Able, Ralph | VB002 | Advanced Kitchen Remodeling I | 2 |
| 8 | 3 | Able, Ralph | VK001 | Kitchen Remodeling Basics | 2 |
| 9 | 3 | Able, Ralph | VK002 | Advanced Kitchen Remodeling | 2 |
| 10 | 4 | Baker, Susan | BK001 | Kitchen Remodeling Basics For Everyone | 1 |
| 11 | 4 | Baker, Susan | BK002 | Advanced Kitchen Remodeling For Everyone | 1 |
| 12 | 4 | Baker, Susan | VB001 | Kitchen Remodeling Basics | 1 |
| 13 | 4 | Baker, Susan | VK001 | Kitchen Remodeling Basics | 1 |
| 14 | 4 | Baker, Susan | VK002 | Advanced Kitchen Remodeling | 1 |
| 15 | 4 | Baker, Susan | VK004 | Heather Sweeney Seminar Live in Dallas on 25-OCT-19 | 1 |
| 16 | 5 | Eagleton, Sam | BK001 | Kitchen Remodeling Basics For Everyone | 1 |
| 17 | 5 | Eagleton, Sam | VB001 | Kitchen Remodeling Basics | 1 |
| 18 | 5 | Eagleton, Sam | VK001 | Kitchen Remodeling Basics | 1 |
| 19 | 6 | Foxtrot, Kathy | BK002 | Advanced Kitchen Remodeling For Everyone | 1 |
| 20 | 6 | Foxtrot, Kathy | VB003 | Kitchen Remodeling Dallas Style | 1 |
| 21 | 6 | Foxtrot, Kathy | VK002 | Advanced Kitchen Remodeling | 1 |
| 22 | 6 | Foxtrot, Kathy | VK003 | Kitchen Remodeling Dallas Style | 1 |
| 23 | 6 | Foxtrot, Kathy | VK004 | Heather Sweeney Seminar Live in Dallas on 25-OCT-19 | 1 |
| 24 | 7 | George, Sally | BK001 | Kitchen Remodeling Basics For Everyone | 1 |
| 25 | 7 | George, Sally | BK002 | Advanced Kitchen Remodeling For Everyone | 1 |
| 26 | 7 | George, Sally | VK003 | Kitchen Remodeling Dallas Style | 1 |
| 27 | 7 | George, Sally | VK004 | Heather Sweeney Seminar Live in Dallas on 25-OCT-19 | 2 |
| 28 | 8 | Hullett, Shawn | VB003 | Kitchen Remodeling Dallas Style | 1 |
| 29 | 8 | Hullett, Shawn | VK003 | Kitchen Remodeling Dallas Style | 1 |
| 30 | 8 | Hullett, Shawn | VK004 | Heather Sweeney Seminar Live in Dallas on 25-OCT-19 | 1 |
| 31 | 9 | Pearson, Bobbi | BK001 | Kitchen Remodeling Basics For Everyone | 1 |
| 32 | 9 | Pearson, Bobbi | VB001 | Kitchen Remodeling Basics | 1 |
| 33 | 9 | Pearson, Bobbi | VB002 | Advanced Kitchen Remodeling I | 1 |
| 34 | 9 | Pearson, Bobbi | VK001 | Kitchen Remodeling Basics | 1 |
| 35 | 9 | Pearson, Bobbi | VK002 | Advanced Kitchen Remodeling | 1 |
| 36 | 11 | Tyler, Jenny | VB002 | Advanced Kitchen Remodeling I | 2 |
| 37 | 11 | Tyler, Jenny | VB003 | Kitchen Remodeling Dallas Style | 2 |
| 38 | 11 | Tyler, Jenny | VK002 | Advanced Kitchen Remodeling | 2 |
| 39 | 11 | Tyler, Jenny | VK003 | Kitchen Remodeling Dallas Style | 2 |
| 40 | 11 | Tyler, Jenny | VK004 | Heather Sweeney Seminar Live in Dallas on 25-OCT-19 | 2 |
| 41 | 12 | Wayne, Joan | BK002 | Advanced Kitchen Remodeling For Everyone | 1 |
| 42 | 12 | Wayne, Joan | VB003 | Kitchen Remodeling Dallas Style | 1 |
| 43 | 12 | Wayne, Joan | VK002 | Advanced Kitchen Remodeling | 1 |
| 44 | 12 | Wayne, Joan | VK003 | Kitchen Remodeling Dallas Style | 1 |
| 45 | 12 | Wayne, Joan | VK004 | Heather Sweeney Seminar Live in Dallas on 25-OCT-19 | 1 |

**FIGURE 12-14**

The HSD_DW Query Results: Summarize Product Units Sold by Customer and Product

| ProductNumber | CustomerID | | | | | | | | | | | |
|---|---|---|---|---|---|---|---|---|---|---|---|---|
| | 1 | 2 | 3 | 4 | 5 | 6 | 7 | 8 | 9 | 10 | 11 | 12 |
| BK001 | 1 | | 1 | 1 | | | 1 | | 1 | | | |
| BK002 | | | 1 | 1 | | 1 | 1 | | | | | 1 |
| VB001 | 1 | | 2 | 1 | 1 | | | | 1 | | | |
| VB002 | | | 2 | | | | | | 1 | | 2 | |
| VB003 | | | | | | 1 | | 1 | | | 2 | 1 |
| VK001 | 1 | | 2 | 1 | 1 | | | | 1 | | | |
| VK002 | | | 2 | 1 | | 1 | | | 1 | | 2 | 1 |
| VK003 | | | | | | 1 | 1 | 1 | | | 2 | 1 |
| VK004 | | | | 1 | | 1 | 2 | 1 | | | 2 | 1 |

**Each cell shows the total quantity of each product that has been purchased by each customer**

**FIGURE 12-15**

**The Two-Dimensional ProductNumber–CustomerID Matrix**

CUSTOMER and TIMELINE dimension tables as PRODUCT_SALES. This is done to maintain consistency within the data warehouse. When a dimension table links to two or more fact tables, it is called a **conformed dimension**. TIMELINE and CUSTOMER are conformed dimensions in this example.

Why would we add a fact table named SALES_FOR_RFM? To explain that, we need to discuss reporting systems.

## Reporting Systems

The purpose of a reporting system is to create meaningful information from disparate data sources and to deliver that information to the proper users on a timely basis. As stated earlier, reporting systems differ from data mining because they create information using the basic operations of sorting, filtering, grouping, and making simple calculations. We begin this section with a description of a typical reporting problem: RFM analysis. The section will continue with a detailed example of an OLAP report.

### RFM Analysis

**RFM analysis** is a way of analyzing and ranking customers according to their purchasing patterns. It is a simple technique that considers how *recently* (**R score**) a customer ordered, how *frequently* (**F score**) a customer ordered, and how much *money* (**M score**) the customer spent per order. RFM is summarized in Figure 12-18.

To produce an RFM score, we need only two things: customer data and sales data for each purchase (including the date of the sale and the total amount of the sale) made by each customer. If you look at the SALES_FOR_RFM table and its associated CUSTOMER and

**Each cell will show the total quantity of each product that has been purchased by each customer on a specific date**

**FIGURE 12-16**

**The Three-Dimensional Time–ProductNumber–CustomerID Cube**

**FIGURE 12-17**

The Extended HSD_DW Star Schema

TIMELINE dimension tables in Figure 12-17, you see that we have exactly those data: the SALES_FOR_RFM table is the starting point for RFM analysis in the HSD_DW BI system.

To produce an RFM score, customer purchase records are first sorted by the date of their most recent (R) purchase. In a common form of this analysis, the customers are divided into five groups, and a score of 1 to 5 is given to customers in each group. Thus, the 20 percent of the customers with the most recent orders are given an R score of 1, the 20 percent of the customers with the next most recent orders are given an R score of 2, and so forth, down to the last 20 percent, who are given an R score of 5.

The customer records are then sorted on the basis of how frequently they order. The 20 percent of the customers who order most frequently are given an F score of 1, the next 20 percent most frequently ordering customers are given a score of 2, and so forth, down to the least frequently ordering customers, who are given an F score of 5.

**FIGURE 12-18**

RFM Analysis

| RFM Analysis |
|---|
| • Simple report-based customer classification scheme |
| • Score customers on recentness, frequency, and monetary size of orders |
| • Typically, divide each criterion into 5 groups and score from 1 to 5 |

**FIGURE 12-19**

The RFM Score
Report

Each customer is
ranked for **R** (recent),
**F** (frequent), and
**M** (money)
characteristics—1 is
highest (best) and 5 is
lowest (worst) score

| Customer | RFM Score | | |
|---|---|---|---|
| | R | F | M |
| Able, Ralph | 1 | 1 | 2 |
| Baker, Susan | 2 | 2 | 3 |
| George, Sally | 3 | 3 | 3 |
| Tyler, Jenny | 5 | 1 | 1 |
| Jacobs, Chantel | 5 | 5 | 5 |

Finally, the customers are sorted again according to the average amount of money spent on their orders. The 20 percent who have placed the most expensive orders are given an M score of 1, the next 20 percent are given an M score of 2, and so forth, down to the 20 percent who spend the least, who are given an M score of 5.

Figure 12-19 shows sample RFM data for Heather Sweeney Designs. (Note that these data have *not* been calculated from the actual HSD data and are for illustrative purposes only.) The first customer, Ralph Able, has a score of {1 1 2}, which means that he has ordered recently and orders frequently. His M score of 2 indicates, however, that he does not order the most expensive goods. From these scores, the salespeople can surmise that Ralph is a good customer who may be open to purchasing more expensive goods or larger quantities of goods.

Susan Baker (RFM score of {2 2 3}) is above average in terms of how recently she shopped and how frequently she shops, but her purchases are average in value. Sally George (RFM score of {3 3 3}) is truly in the middle. Jenny Tyler (RFM score of {5 1 1}) is a problem. Jenny has not ordered in some time, but in the past, when she did order, she ordered frequently and her orders were of the highest monetary value. These data suggest that Jenny might be going to another vendor. Someone from the sales team should contact her immediately. However, no one on the sales team should be talking to Chantel Jacobs (RFM score of {5 5 5}). She has not ordered for some time, she doesn't order frequently, and when she does order, she only buys inexpensive items and not many of them.

### Producing the RFM Report

Like most reports, an RFM report can be created using a series of SQL expressions. This section presents two SQL Server stored procedures that produce RFM scores. Figure 12-20 shows the SQL scripts to create the five tables that are used.

The CUSTOMER_SALES table contains the raw data that are used in the RFM calculations. CUSTOMER_RFM contains CustomerID and the final R, F, and M scores. The remaining three tables—CUSTOMER_R, CUSTOMER_F, and CUSTOMER_M—are used to store intermediate results. Note that all CustomerID columns are NOT NULL.

The stored procedure shown in Figure 12-21 is used to calculate and store the R, F, and M scores. It begins by deleting the results of any prior analysis from the CUSTOMER_R, CUSTOMER_F, and CUSTOMER_M tables. It then calls three procedures for computing the R, F, and M scores. Next, it displays the numbers of customers with each R, F, and M score. Finally, it stores the R, F, and M scores in the CUSTOMER_RFM table. Only this table is needed for reporting purposes.

The Calculate_R stored procedure shown in Figure 12-22 illustrates how the R score is calculated. This procedure first places the date of each customer's most recent order into the MostRecentOrderDate column. Then, it uses the **SQL TOP . . . PERCENT expression** in a series of SQL SELECT statements to set the R_Score values. The first UPDATE statement sets the value of R_Score to 1 for the top 20 percent of customers (after they have been sorted in descending order according to MostRecentOrderDate). Then it sets the R_Score to 2 for the top 25 percent of remaining customers who have a null value for R_Score in descending order of MostRecentOrderDate. The procedure continues to set the R values for all customers. The Calculate_F and Calculate_M procedures are similar and will be left to you as question 12.73.

**FIGURE 12-20**

Microsoft SQL Server 2019
Tables for the RFM Analysis

```
CREATE TABLE CUSTOMER_SALES (
        TransactionID               Int                    NOT NULL,
        CustomerID                  Int                    NOT NULL,
        TransactionDate             Date                   NOT NULL,
        OrderAmount                 Money                  NOT NULL,
        CONSTRAINT    Customer_Sales_PK    PRIMARY KEY(TransactionID)
        );

CREATE TABLE CUSTOMER_RFM (
        CustomerID                  Int                    NOT NULL,
        R                           SmallInt               NULL,
        F                           SmallInt               NULL,
        M                           SmallInt               NULL,
        CONSTRAINT    Customer_RFM_PK      PRIMARY KEY(CustomerID)
        );

CREATE TABLE CUSTOMER_R (
        CustomerID                  Int                    NOT NULL,
        MostRecentOrderDate         Date                   NULL,
        R_Score                     SmallInt               NULL,
        CONSTRAINT    Customer_R_PK        PRIMARY KEY(CustomerID)
        );

CREATE TABLE CUSTOMER_F (
        CustomerID                  Int                    NOT NULL,
        OrderCount                  Int                    NULL,
        F_Score                     SmallInt               NULL,
        CONSTRAINT    Customer_F_PK        PRIMARY KEY(CustomerID)
        );

CREATE TABLE CUSTOMER_M (
        CustomerID                  Int                    NOT NULL,
        AverageOrderAmount          Money                  NULL,
        M_Score                     SmallInt               NULL,
        CONSTRAINT    Customer_M_PK        PRIMARY KEY(CustomerID)
        );
```

Figure 12-23 shows how the CUSTOMER_RFM table is used for reporting purposes. It shows a SELECT on CUSTOMER_RFM that was prepared using a data extract of 5061 records from a database of more than 5,000 customers and over 1 million transactions. The records were imported from an Excel worksheet into a table, and that data was used to populate the CUSTOMER_SALES table, which is the basis for the data in the CUSTOMER_RFM table.

The results in Figure 12-23 are interesting, but unless this information is delivered to the correct users, it will be of no ultimate value to the organization. For example, the first row in this figure shows that 237 customers have an RFM score of {5 1 5}. These customers recently placed expensive orders, but they have not ordered frequently. The company may want to encourage them to order more often. Somehow this report and the customers who have these scores (see review question 12.34) need to be made available to the appropriate sales personnel. To understand the modern means for accomplishing this, we will consider the components of a reporting system after first presenting an example of OLAP reporting.

## OLAP

OLAP (online analytical processing) provides the ability to sum, count, average, and perform other simple arithmetic operations on groups of data. OLAP systems produce **OLAP reports**. An OLAP report is also called an **OLAP cube**. This is a reference to the dimensional data model, and some OLAP products show OLAP displays using three axes, like a geometric cube. The remarkable characteristic of an OLAP report is that it is

**FIGURE 12-21**

Microsoft SQL Server
2019 RFM_Analysis Stored
Procedure

```
CREATE PROCEDURE RFM_Analysis

AS

/* Delete any existing RFM data   ***************************/

DELETE FROM CUSTOMER_RFM;
DELETE FROM CUSTOMER_R;
DELETE FROM CUSTOMER_F;
DELETE FROM CUSTOMER_M;

/* *** Compute R, F, M Scores ******************************/
Exec Calculate_R;
Exec Calculate_F;
Exec Calculate_M;

/* *** Dipslay Results *************************************/
SELECT       R_Score, Count(*)AS R_Count
FROM         CUSTOMER_R
GROUP BY     R_Score;

SELECT       F_Score, Count(*)AS F_Count
FROM         CUSTOMER_F
GROUP BY     F_Score;

SELECT       M_Score, Count(*) AS M_Count
FROM         CUSTOMER_M
GROUP BY     M_Score;

/* *** Store Results **************************************/
INSERT INTO CUSTOMER_RFM (CustomerID)
     (SELECT       CustomerID
      FROM   CUSTOMER_SALES);

UPDATE CUSTOMER_RFM
SET   R =
      (SELECT R_Score
       FROM CUSTOMER_R
       WHERE CUSTOMER_RFM.CustomerID = CUSTOMER_R.CustomerID);

UPDATE CUSTOMER_RFM
SET   F =
      (SELECT F_Score
       FROM CUSTOMER_F
       WHERE CUSTOMER_RFM.CustomerID = CUSTOMER_F.CustomerID);

UPDATE CUSTOMER_RFM
SET   M =
      (SELECT M_Score
       FROM CUSTOMER_M
       WHERE CUSTOMER_RFM.CustomerID = CUSTOMER_M.CustomerID);

/* *** End of Procedure RFM Analysis *********************/
```

dynamic: the format of an OLAP report can be changed by the viewer, hence the term *online* in the name *online analytical processing*.

OLAP uses the dimensional database model discussed earlier in this chapter, so it is not surprising to learn that an OLAP report has measures and dimensions. A measure is a dimensional model *fact*—the data item of interest that is to be summed or averaged or otherwise processed in the OLAP report. For example, sales data may be summed to produce Total Sales or averaged to produce Average Sales. The term *measure* is used because you are dealing with quantities that have been or can be measured and recorded. A dimension, as you have already learned, is an attribute or a characteristic of a measure. Purchase date (TimeID), customer location (City), and sales region (ZIP or State) are all examples of dimensions, and in the HSD_DW database, you saw how the time dimension is important.

In this section, we will generate an OLAP report by using an SQL query from the HSD_DW database and a Microsoft Excel **PivotTable**.

**FIGURE 12-22**

Microsoft SQL Server
2019 Calculate_R Stored
Procedure

```sql
CREATE PROCEDURE Calculate_R

AS

/* *** Compute R_Score  ************************************/

INSERT INTO CUSTOMER_R (CustomerID, MostRecentOrderDate)
        (SELECT      CustomerID, MAX (TransactionDate)
         FROM  CUSTOMER_SALES
         GROUP BY CustomerID);

UPDATE          CUSTOMER_R
        SET    R_Score = 1
        WHERE CustomerID IN
                (SELECT TOP 20 PERCENT CustomerID
                 FROM CUSTOMER_R
                 ORDER BY MostRecentOrderDate DESC);

UPDATE          CUSTOMER_R
        SET    R_Score = 2
        WHERE CustomerID IN
                (SELECT TOP 25 PERCENT CustomerID
                 FROM CUSTOMER_R
                 WHERE R_Score IS NULL
                 ORDER BY MostRecentOrderDate DESC);

UPDATE          CUSTOMER_R
        SET    R_Score = 3
        WHERE CustomerID IN
                (SELECT TOP 33 PERCENT CustomerID
                 FROM CUSTOMER_R
                 WHERE R_Score IS NULL
                 ORDER BY MostRecentOrderDate DESC);

UPDATE          CUSTOMER_R
        SET    R_Score = 4
        WHERE CustomerID IN
                (SELECT TOP 50 PERCENT CustomerID
                 FROM CUSTOMER_R
                 WHERE R_Score IS NULL
                 ORDER BY MostRecentOrderDate DESC);

UPDATE          CUSTOMER_R
        SET    R_Score = 5
        WHERE CustomerID IN
                (Select CustomerID
                 FROM CUSTOMER_R
                 WHERE R_Score IS NULL);
```

> **BY THE WAY**    We use Microsoft SQL Server and Microsoft Excel to illustrate this discussion of OLAP reports and PivotTables. For other DBMS products, such as MySQL, you can use the DataPilot feature of the Calc spreadsheet application in the LibreOffice or Apache OpenOffice product suites.

There are three ways we can proceed:

- Manually copy and format an SQL query result as a formatted table in a Microsoft Excel worksheet:
  - Copy the SQL query results into an Excel worksheet.
  - Add column names to the results.
  - Format the query results as an Excel table (optional).
  - Select the Excel range containing the results with column names.
  - Create the PivotTable.

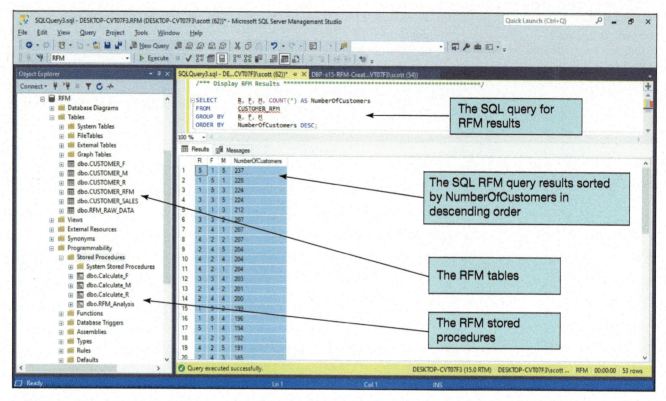

**FIGURE 12-23**

**Example RFM Results**

- *Or* connect to a DBMS data source using the Microsoft Excel Get Data Command:
  - Click the Get Data command on the DATA command tab.
  - Select a Microsoft SQL Server database as the data source.
  - Specify that the data should go into a Microsoft Excel table.
  - Create the PivotTable.
- *Or* use the Microsoft Power Pivot for Excel 2019 add-in feature to connect to a DBMS data source and then create the PivotTable.

We will present an SQL query for the first method but will focus on the third method. The purpose of our OLAP report is to analyze the sales of Heather Sweeney Designs products based on selected dimensions in the HSD_DW database. For example, we might want to see how product sales vary based on the city the customer lives in. We begin by writing an SQL query to gather the required information from the dimensional database. We can then use the results of this query if we *copy* the data into an Excel worksheet. The SQL query, as used in SQL Server 2019, is:

```
/* *** SQL-Query-CH12-02 *** */
SELECT      C.CustomerID, CustomerName, C.City,
            P.ProductNumber, P.ProductName,
            T.Year, T.QuarterText,
            SUM(PS.Quantity) AS TotalQuantity
FROM        CUSTOMER C, PRODUCT_SALES PS, PRODUCT P, TIMELINE T
WHERE       C.CustomerID = PS.CustomerID
    AND     P.ProductNumber = PS.ProductNumber
    AND     T.TimeID = PS.TimeID
GROUP BY    C.CustomerID, C.CustomerName, C.City,
            P.ProductNumber, P.ProductName,
            T.QuarterText, T.Year
ORDER BY    C.CustomerName, T.Year, T.QuarterText;
```

However, if we wish to use the second or third approaches (both of which connect Microsoft Excel to a DBMS data source), we must first create a *view* (see Chapter 7) based on this query. This is because SQL Server (and other SQL-based DBMS products, such as Oracle Database and MySQL) can store views but not queries. The SQL query to create HSDDWProductSalesView, as used in SQL Server 2019, is:

```
/* *** SQL-CREATE-VIEW-CH12-01 *** */
CREATE VIEW HSDDWProductSalesView AS
SELECT     C.CustomerID, C.CustomerName, C.City,
           P.ProductNumber, P.ProductName,
           T.Year, T.QuarterText,
           SUM(PS.Quantity) AS TotalQuantity
FROM       CUSTOMER C, PRODUCT_SALES PS, PRODUCT P, TIMELINE T
WHERE      C.CustomerID = PS.CustomerID
   AND     P.ProductNumber = PS.ProductNumber
   AND     T.TimeID = PS.TimeID
GROUP BY   C.CustomerID, C.CustomerName, C.City,
           P.ProductNumber, P.ProductName,
           T.QuarterText, T.Year;
```

> **BY THE WAY**  The Microsoft Power Pivot feature for Microsoft Excel 2019 add-in provides additional tools and the ability to work with larger datasets than can be handled by Microsoft Excel 2019 itself. It is a useful tool and well worth looking into. If the Power Pivot tab is not in your Microsoft Excel ribbon, you can add it by going to File, Options, Add-Ins, and it can be found in the COM Add-Ins section.

We can now use HSDDWProductSalesView when we connect to the database as the data source for an OLAP report. We will do this using the standard Microsoft Excel 2019 Power Pivot tools, and Figure 12-24(a) shows our starting point, a blank Microsoft Excel 2019 workbook (named DBP-e16-HSD-BI.xlsx).

To connect to the HSD_DW data, we click the **Power Pivot** command tab. As shown in Figure 12-24(a), this displays the Power Pivot commands. Here we click the **Manage** button, which gives us a new **Power Pivot for Excel** window, as shown in Figure 12-24(b).

Clicking the **From Database** button followed by the **From SQL Server** option starts the **Table Import Wizard** window shown in Figure 12-24(c). We select the SQL Server we want to use (in our case, the local computer name DESKTOP-CVT07F3) and our database name (HSD_DW) and then click the **Next** button.

> **BY THE WAY**  Figure 12-24(c) used DESKTOP-CVT-07F3 as the instance name because it is the default instance on the local machine. If you connect to a non-default instance, use the computer name then the instance name, for example DESKTOP-CVT-07F3\MSSQLSERVER.

In the next Table Import Wizard Window, titled Choose How to Import the Data, we keep the default selection as shown in Figure 12-24(d) and click Next. As shown in Figure 12-24(e), in the **Select Tables and Views** dialog box, select the **HSDDWProductSalesView** as the source of our data—note how useful the SQL-CREATE-VIEW-CH12-01 statement and

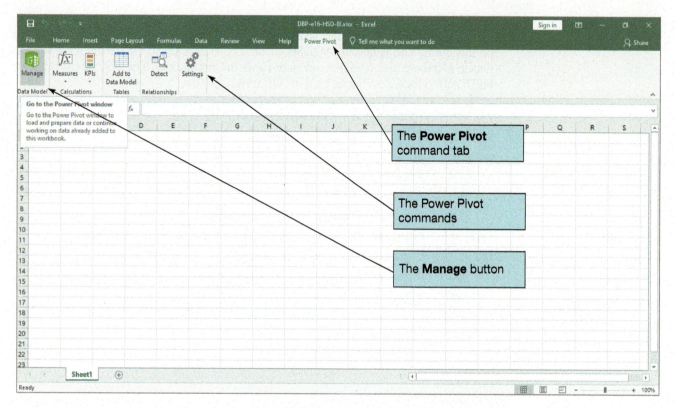

(a) The Power Pivot Tab

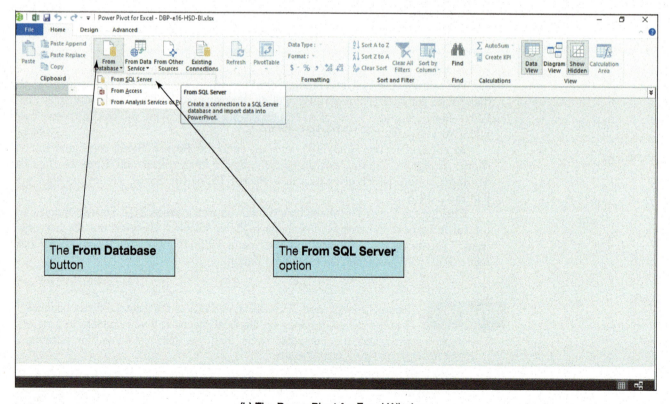

(b) The Power Pivot for Excel Window

**FIGURE 12-24**

**Creating OLAP Reports**

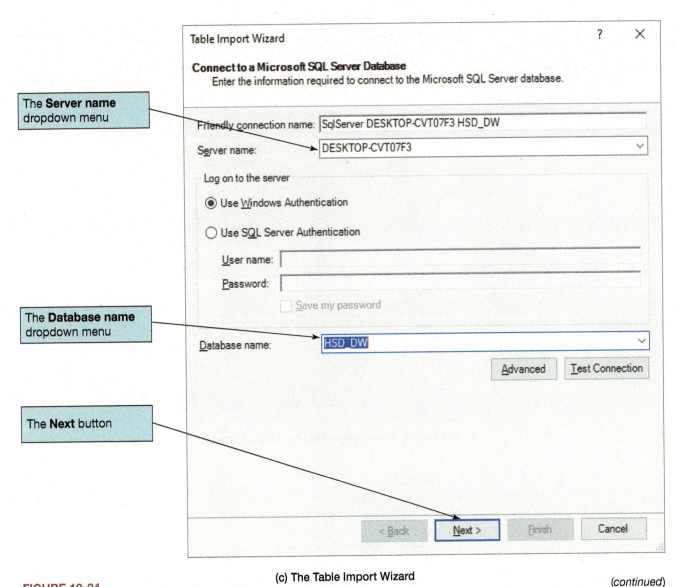

**(c) The Table Import Wizard**

The **Server name** dropdown menu

The **Database name** dropdown menu

The **Next** button

**FIGURE 12-24**
Continued

*(continued)*

the resulting HSDDWProductSalesView view are in making it easy to get exactly the data we want for the PivotTable OLAP report. After selecting the view, we click the **Finish** button and we should see the *Success* message in the **Importing** dialog box, at which point we can click **Close**.

At this point we want to store our data in a Pivot Table within the original DBP-e16-HSD-BI.xlsx workbook. To do this, as shown in Figure 12-24(f), in the **Power Pivot** window, open the drop-down menu under **PivotTable** and select the **PivotTable** option.

As shown in Figure 12-24(g), the **Create Pivot Table** dialog box is displayed. We want to store our data in an existing worksheet in our Microsoft Excel workbook *before* we create the PivotTable, so click the **Existing Worksheet** button then click the **OK** button.

The pivot table will appear as shown in Figure 12-24(h). Selecting the appropriate fields in the **PivotTable Fields** pane then creates the PivotTable itself, as seen in Figure 12-24(i): select CustomerName, City, ProductNumber, Year, and TotalQuantity as the PivotTable fields. Drag ProductNumber from the ROWS section to the COLUMNS section and ensure the ROWS section has the order City, CustomerName, and Year. The VALUES section should contain Sum of TotalQuantity. Note that we have also renamed the worksheet to better reflect its purpose.

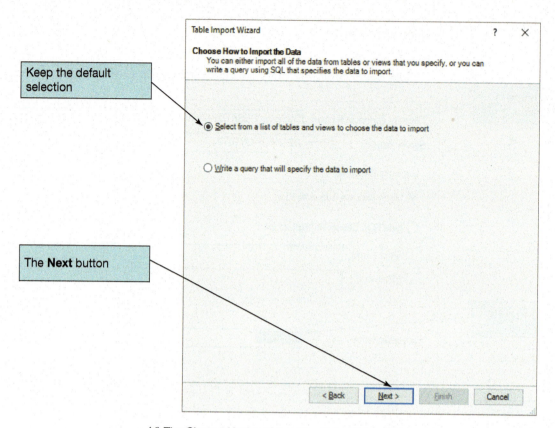

Keep the default selection

The **Next** button

(d) The Choose How to Import the Data Dialog Box

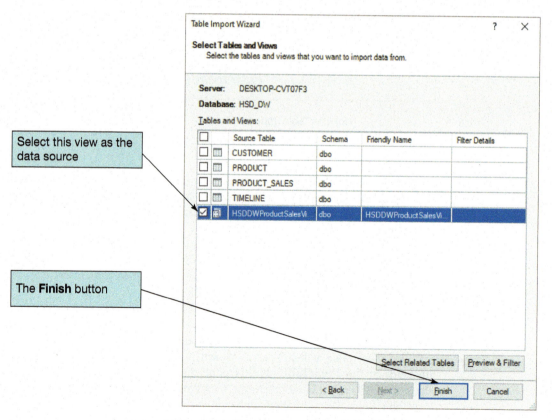

Select this view as the data source

The **Finish** button

(e) The Select Tables and Views Dialog Box

**FIGURE 12-24**
Continued

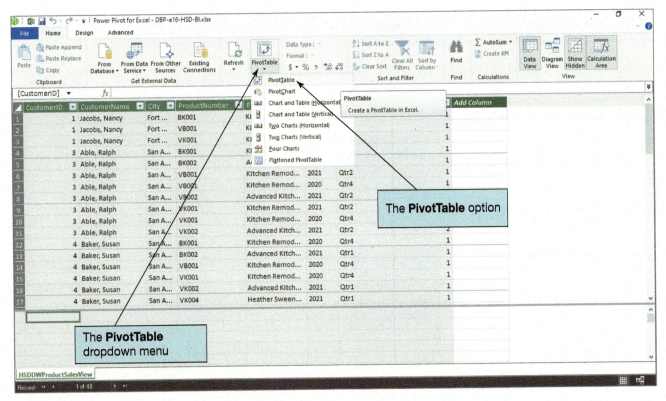

(f) Creating the Pivot Table

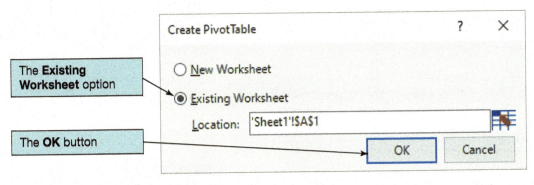

(g) The Create Pivot Table Dialog Box                                              *(continued)*

**FIGURE 12-24**

**Continued**

In Figure 12-24(i), the measure is quantity sold, and the dimensions are ProductNumber and City. This report shows how quantity varies by product and city. For example, four copies of VB003 (Kitchen Remodeling Dallas Style video companion) were sold in Dallas, but none were sold in Austin.

We generated the OLAP report in Figure 12-24(i) by using a simple SQL view and Microsoft Excel, but many DBMS and BI products include more powerful and sophisticated tools. For example, Microsoft SQL Server 2019 Developer Edition (used in this text) includes SQL Server Analysis Services.[1] It is possible to display OLAP cubes in many ways other than with Excel. Some third-party vendors provide more sophisticated graphical displays, and OLAP reports can be delivered just like any of the other reports described for report management systems.

---

[1] Although OLAP reports can be created without SQL Server Analysis Services, as we have done here, Analysis Services adds considerable functionality. It is a standard part of SQL Server 2019 Developer Edition, and it provides data mining functionality directly in the DBMS.

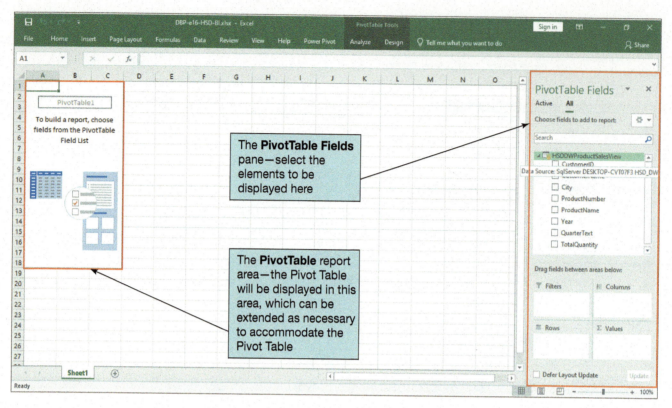

(h) The Empty Pivot Table in the New Worksheet

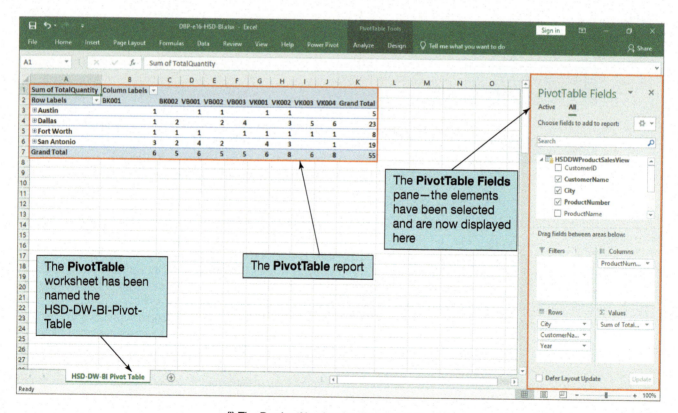

(i) The ProductNumber by City OLAP Report

FIGURE 12-24

Continued

**FIGURE 12-25**

OLAP ProductNumber by City, Customer, and Year Report

Sum of TotalQuantity — Column Labels

| Row Labels | BK001 | BK002 | VB001 | VB002 | VB003 | VK001 | VK002 | VK003 | VK004 | Grand Total |
|---|---|---|---|---|---|---|---|---|---|---|
| **Austin** | | | | | | | | | | |
| ⊞ Pearson, Bobbi | 1 | | 1 | 1 | | 1 | 1 | | | 5 |
| **Dallas** | | | | | | | | | | |
| ⊞ Foxtrot, Kathy | | 1 | | | 1 | | 1 | 1 | 1 | 5 |
| ⊞ George, Sally | 1 | 1 | | | | | | 1 | 2 | 5 |
| ⊞ Hullett, Shawn | | | | | 1 | | | 1 | 1 | 3 |
| ⊞ Tyler, Jenny | | | | 2 | 2 | | 2 | 2 | 2 | 10 |
| **Fort Worth** | | | | | | | | | | |
| ⊞ Jacobs, Nancy | 1 | | 1 | | | 1 | | | | 3 |
| ⊞ Wayne, Joan | | 1 | | | 1 | | 1 | 1 | 1 | 5 |
| **San Antonio** | | | | | | | | | | |
| ⊟ Able, Ralph | | | | | | | | | | |
|   2020 | | | 1 | | | 1 | | | | 2 |
|   2021 | 1 | 1 | 1 | 2 | | 1 | 2 | | | 8 |
| ⊞ Baker, Susan | 1 | 1 | 1 | | | 1 | 1 | | 1 | 6 |
| ⊞ Eagleton, Sam | 1 | | 1 | | | 1 | | | | 3 |
| **Grand Total** | 6 | 5 | 6 | 5 | 5 | 6 | 8 | 6 | 8 | 55 |

*The City = San Antonio data are also showing customer data*

*The Customer = Able, Ralph data are also showing year data*

The distinguishing characteristic of an OLAP report is that the user can alter the format. Figure 12-25 shows an alteration in which the user added two additional dimensions, customer and year, to the horizontal display. Quantity sold is now broken out by customer within each city and, in one case, by year within a customer. With an OLAP report, it is possible to **drill down** into the data—that is, to further divide the data into more detail. In Figure 12-25, for example, the user has drilled down into the San Antonio data to display all customer data for that city and to display yearly sales data for Ralph Able.

In an OLAP report, it is also possible to change the order of the dimensions. Figure 12-26 shows city quantities as vertical data and ProductID quantities as horizontal data. This OLAP report shows quantity sold by city, by product, by customer, and by year.

Both displays are valid and useful, depending on the user's perspective. A product manager might like to see product families first (ProductID) and then location data (City). A sales manager might like to see location data first and then product data. OLAP reports provide both perspectives, and the user can switch between them while viewing a report.

Unfortunately, all of this flexibility comes at a cost. If the database is large, doing the necessary calculating, grouping, and sorting for such dynamic displays will require substantial computing power. Although standard, commercial DBMS products do have the features and functions required to create OLAP reports, and they continue to evolve to provide more sophisticated reporting capabilities in general, they are often busy providing rapid response to transaction processing applications, such as those for order entry or manufacturing planning. Thus, even though DBMS products are getting better at providing analytical features, the data warehousing and BI features are typically still run as a separate installation.

Accordingly, special-purpose products called **OLAP servers** have been developed to perform OLAP analyses. As shown in Figure 12-27, an OLAP server reads data from an operational database, performs preliminary calculations, and stores the results of those calculations in an OLAP database. For performance and security reasons, the OLAP server and the DBMS usually run on separate computers, even if the OLAP server is part of a DBMS package, as some are. The OLAP server would normally be located in the data warehouse or a data mart.

## Reporting System Components

Whether reports come from an OLAP system or via RFM or via some other type of reporting system, they need to be made available to the proper people at the proper time. In order to understand how this can be done in a modern database system, we will describe the components of reporting systems in this section and the functions of reporting systems in the

The City variable is the column designator

The ProductID variable is the primary row designator

The ProductID = VB001 data are also showing Customer data

The Customer = Able, Ralph data are also showing year data

| Sum of TotalQuantity | Column Labels | | | | |
|---|---|---|---|---|---|
| Row Labels | Austin | Dallas | Fort Worth | San Antonio | Grand Total |
| ⊟ BK001 | | | | | |
| ⊟ Able, Ralph | | | | | |
| 2021 | | | | 1 | 1 |
| ⊞ Baker, Susan | | | | 1 | 1 |
| ⊞ Eagleton, Sam | | | | 1 | 1 |
| ⊞ George, Sally | | 1 | | | 1 |
| ⊞ Jacobs, Nancy | | | 1 | | 1 |
| ⊞ Pearson, Bobbi | 1 | | | | 1 |
| ⊟ BK002 | | | | | |
| ⊟ Able, Ralph | | | | | |
| 2021 | | | | 1 | 1 |
| ⊞ Baker, Susan | | | | 1 | 1 |
| ⊞ Foxtrot, Kathy | | 1 | | | 1 |
| ⊞ George, Sally | | 1 | | | 1 |
| ⊞ Wayne, Joan | | | 1 | | 1 |
| ⊟ VB001 | | | | | |
| ⊟ Able, Ralph | | | | | |
| 2020 | | | | 1 | 1 |
| 2021 | | | | 1 | 1 |
| ⊞ Baker, Susan | | | | 1 | 1 |
| ⊞ Eagleton, Sam | | | | 1 | 1 |
| ⊞ Jacobs, Nancy | | | 1 | | 1 |
| ⊞ Pearson, Bobbi | 1 | | | | 1 |
| ⊞ VB002 | 1 | 2 | | 2 | 5 |
| ⊞ VB003 | | 4 | 1 | | 5 |
| ⊞ VK001 | 1 | | 1 | 4 | 6 |
| ⊞ VK002 | 1 | 3 | 1 | 3 | 8 |
| ⊞ VK003 | | 5 | 1 | | 6 |
| ⊞ VK004 | | 6 | 1 | 1 | 8 |
| Grand Total | 5 | 23 | 8 | 19 | 55 |

**FIGURE 12-26**

OLAP City by ProductNumber, Customer, and Year Report

**FIGURE 12-27**

Role of the OLAP Server and OLAP Database

**FIGURE 12-28**

Components of a Reporting System

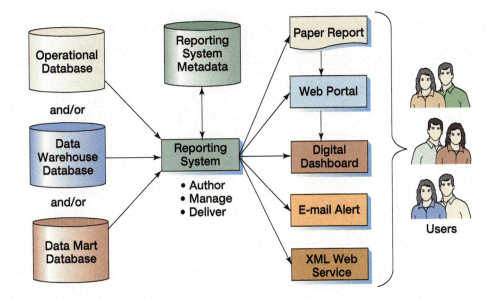

next section. Figure 12-28 shows the major components of a reporting system. Data from disparate sources are read and processed. As shown, reporting systems can obtain data from operational databases, data warehouses, and data marts.

A reporting system maintains a database of reporting metadata. The metadata describes reports, users, groups, roles, events, and other entities involved in the reporting activity. The reporting system uses the metadata to prepare and deliver appropriate reports to the proper users in the correct format on a timely basis. As shown in Figure 12-28, reports can be prepared in a variety of media or formats.

Figure 12-29 lists report characteristics, which we describe in more detail now.

### Report Types

Some reports are **static reports**. They are prepared once from the underlying data, and they do not change. A report of the past year's sales, for example, is a static report. Other reports are **dynamic reports**—at the time of their creation, the reporting system reads the latest, most current data and generates the report using those fresh data. Reports on today's sales and on current stock prices are dynamic reports.

**Query reports** are prepared in response to information entered by users. Google Web search is an example of a reporting system that uses query reports: You enter the keywords you want to search for, and Google's reporting system searches its database and generates a response that is particular to your query. Within a specific organization, such as Heather Sweeney Designs, a query report could be generated to show current inventory levels. The user would enter item numbers, and the reporting system would respond with inventory levels of those items.

In terms of the reporting system, OLAP reports enable the user to dynamically change the report grouping structures.

### Report Media

As illustrated in Figure 12-28 and summarized in Figure 12-29, reports are delivered via many different channels. Some reports are printed on paper or its electronic equivalents, such as PDF format. Other reports are delivered via **Web portals**. An organization might place a sales report on the sales department's Web portal and a report on customers serviced on the customer service department's Web portal.

A **digital dashboard** is an electronic display that is customized for a particular user. Companies such as Google, MSN, and Yahoo! offer digital dashboard services that you might have seen or used. Users can define the content they want to see—say, a local weather forecast, a list of stock prices, and a list of news sources—and the vendor constructs a customized display for each user. Such pages are called, for example, myhomemsn.com

FIGURE 12-29
Report Characteristics

| Type | Media | Mode |
|------|-------|------|
| Static | Paper | Push |
| Dynamic | Web portal | Pull |
| Query | Digital dashboard | |
| OnLine Analytical Processing (OLAP) | E-mail/alert | |
| | XML Web service and application specific | |

and My Yahoo! Other dashboards are designed specifically for organizations. Executives at a manufacturing organization, for example, might have a dashboard that shows up-to-the-minute production and sales activities. These dashboards can be provided by companies such as IBM and SAP.

Reports can also be delivered via **alerts**. Users can indicate that they want to be notified of news and events by email or cell phone. "Smart cell phones" such as the iPhone and those using the Android operating system are capable of displaying Web pages and can use digital dashboards.

Finally, reports can be delivered to other information systems. One way to do this is to publish reports via **XML Web Services**, as discussed in Chapter 11. This style of reporting is particularly useful for interorganizational information systems, such as supply chain management.

### Report Modes

The final report characteristic summarized in Figure 12-29 is the report mode. A **push report** is sent to users based on a predetermined schedule. Users receive the report without any activity on their part. In contrast, users must request a **pull report**. To obtain a pull report, a user goes to a Web portal or digital dashboard and clicks a link or button to cause the reporting system to produce and deliver the report.

### Reporting System Functions

As shown in Figure 12-28, report systems serve three functions: report authoring, report management, and report delivery.

### Report Authoring

**Report authoring** involves connecting to the required data sources, creating the report structure, and formatting the report. Reports created using a report authoring system are then assigned to groups and users. The report assignment metadata not only includes the user or group and the reports assigned but also indicates the format of the report that should be sent to the user, the channel by which the report will be delivered, and whether the report is to be pushed or pulled. If it is to be pushed, the administrator declares whether the report is to be generated on a regular schedule or as an alert based on a specific event in a database.

Figures 12-30, 12-31, and 12-32 show the use of **SQL Server Data Tools (SSDT)** to author a report that publishes the results of an RFM analysis done in SQL Server.

SQL Server Data Tools (SSDT) is a tool available in Microsoft Visual Studio 2019 that is downloadable[2] from the Microsoft Web site. SSDT is now part of Visual Studio 2019,

---

[2]See *https://docs.microsoft.com/en-us/sql/ssdt/download-sql-server-data-tools-ssdt.*

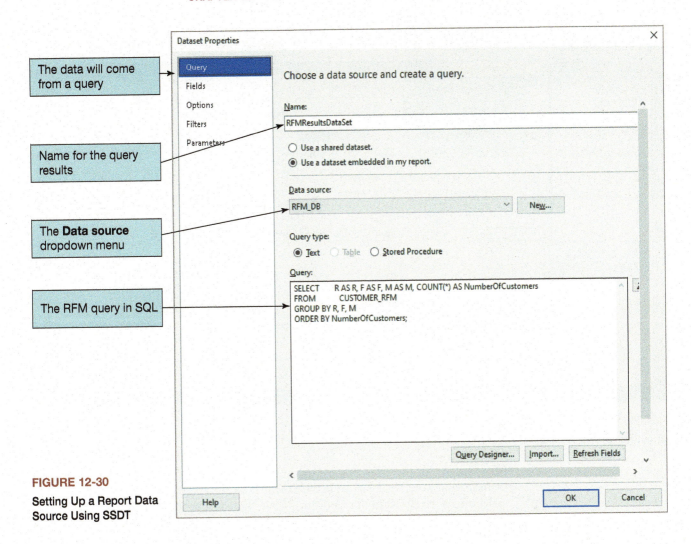

**FIGURE 12-30**

Setting Up a Report Data Source Using SSDT

including the free Community Edition, but must specifically be activated during or after Visual Studio 2019 installation by adding SQL Server Data Tools as a *Workload*. In addition, in order to take advantage of Microsoft Reporting Services, that must be installed (which is done from within Visual Studio using the *Manage Extensions* feature). In Figure 12-30, the developer has specified a *data source* (RFM_DB) that contains the CUSTOMER_RFM table and has just entered the SQL statement shown in Figure 12-23 as the *data set* from within the RFM_DB data source to be used to build the report.

In Figure 12-31, the report author creates the format of the report by specifying the headings and selecting the format for the data items as well as a sort order (which is not automatically carried over from the data set). In a more complicated report, the author would specify additional grouping of data items as well as other features. The data sources and data sets used in the report, including the fields available from the data sets, are shown in the Report Data pane on the left side of Figure 12-31. A preview of the report in SSDT is shown in Figure 12-32. The final report, materialized as a static Web page in a Web browser, is partially shown in Figure 12-33. To learn more about this application, search for "SSDT reporting services" at *www.microsoft.com*.

### Report Management

**Report management** consists of defining who receives what reports, when, and by what means. Most report management systems enable the report system administrator to define user accounts and user groups and to assign particular users to particular groups.

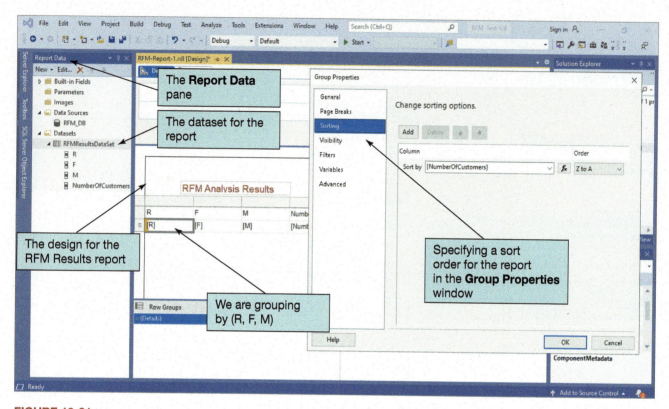

**FIGURE 12-31**

Formatting a Report Using SSDT

For example, all the salespeople would be assigned to the Sales group, all upper-level management would be assigned to the Executive group, and so forth. All these objects and assignments are stored in the reporting system metadata shown in Figure 12-28. Reports created using the report authoring system are assigned to groups and users. Assigning reports to groups saves the administrator work; when a report is created, changed, or removed, the administrator need only change the report characteristics for the group. All of the users in the group will inherit the changes. For example, Figure 12-34 shows part of the RFM report materialized (by SQL Server Reporting Services via Visual Studio Microsoft Reporting Tools and SSDT) in XML. The XML file can then be input into any program that consumes XML and can be manipulated via XSL, as described in Chapter 11 and Appendix H.

As stated earlier, the report management metadata indicates which format of the report should be sent to which user. It also indicates what channel is to be used and whether the report is to be pushed or pulled. If pushed, the administrator declares whether the report is to be generated on a regular schedule or as an alert based on some event in the database.

### Report Delivery

The **report delivery** function of a reporting system pushes reports or allows them to be pulled based on the report management metadata. Reports can be delivered by hand, via an email server, via a Web portal as indicated in Figure 12-33, via XML Web Services as indicated in Figure 12-34, or by other program-specific means. The report delivery system uses the operating system and other program security components to ensure that only authorized users receive authorized reports, and it also ensures that push reports are produced at appropriate times.

For query reports, the report delivery system serves as an intermediary between the user and the report generator. It receives a user query request, such as the item numbers in an inventory query; passes the query request to the report generator; receives the resulting report; and delivers the report to the user.

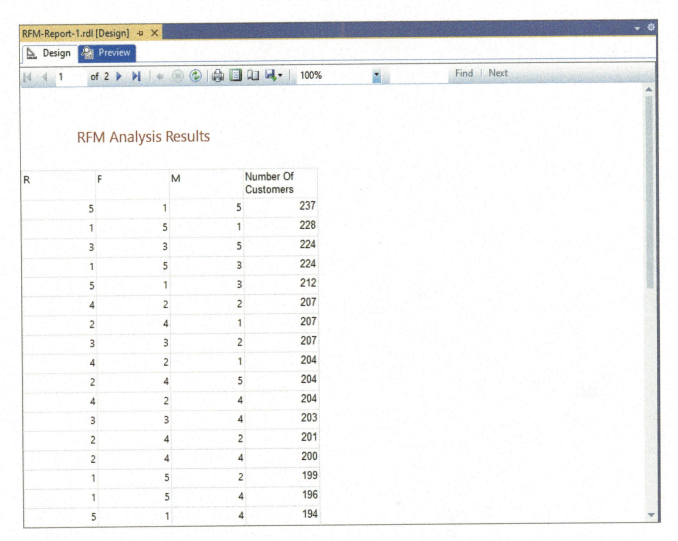

**FIGURE 12-32**

Previewing a Report Using SSDT

## Data Mining

Instead of the basic calculations, filtering, sorting, and grouping used in reporting applications, data mining involves the application of sophisticated mathematical and statistical techniques to find patterns and relationships that can be used to classify data and predict future outcomes. As shown in Figure 12-35, data mining represents the convergence of several phenomena. Data mining techniques have emerged from the statistical and mathematics disciplines and from the artificial intelligence and machine-learning communities. In fact, data mining terminology is an odd combination of terms used by these different disciplines.

Data mining techniques take advantage of developments for processing enormous databases that have emerged in the past two decades. Of course, all these data would not have been generated were it not for fast and inexpensive computers, and without such computers, results from the new techniques would be impossible to produce in a reasonable time frame.

Most data mining techniques are sophisticated and difficult to use. However, such techniques are valuable to organizations, and some business professionals, especially those in finance and marketing, have developed expertise in their use. Almost all data mining techniques require specialized software. Popular data mining products are Enterprise Miner from SAS Corporation, SPSS Modeler from IBM, and Vertica from Micro Focus.

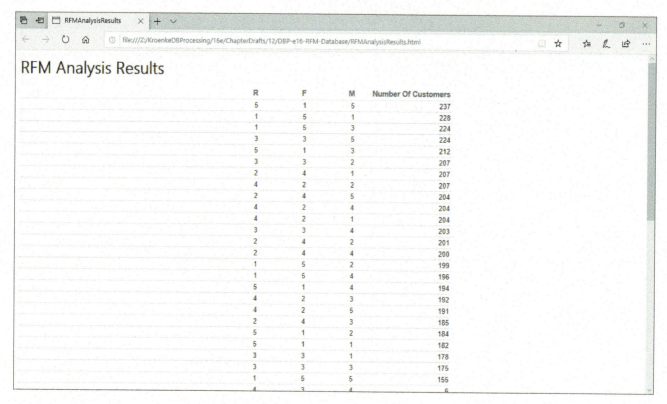

**FIGURE 12-33**

The RFM Report in a Web Browser

However, there is a movement to make data mining available to more users. For example, many data mining features are included in SQL Server Machine Learning Services, but these also require programming expertise in R or Python. Oracle also offers data mining functionality via the "Oracle Advanced Analytics" option, with a GUI as part of SQL Developer (no programming required). Figure 12-36 shows the result of clustering applied to the HSD-DWProductSalesView data using Oracle Data Miner. Creation of data mining models takes place in the Oracle Advanced Analytics package, which is part of Oracle Database Express Edition 18c. They can be processed and visualized using the Oracle Data Miner tool in SQL Developer. The clusters shown in Figure 12-36 appear to show a high correlation between the city and the quarter in which a purchase was made: purchase records in Cluster 3 all come from San Antonio; those in Cluster 2 all come only from other cities, etc. This is of course a tiny database, but even here we can come to conclusions such as "very little seems to be happening in San Antonio in the first quarter of 2021." The clusters shown in the figure were created using Oracle's own "OC" clustering algorithm, but Oracle Data Miner also provides other popular clustering algorithms such as K-Means (seen on another tab in Figure 12-36).

## Unsupervised Versus Supervised Data Mining

Data mining techniques fall into two broad categories: unsupervised and supervised.

### Unsupervised Data Mining

When using **unsupervised data mining** techniques, analysts do not create a model or hypothesis prior to beginning the analysis. Instead, the data mining technique is applied to the data, and results are observed. After the analysis, explanations and hypotheses are created to explain the patterns found.

One commonly used unsupervised technique is **cluster analysis**. With cluster analysis, statistical techniques are used to identify groups of entities that have similar characteristics. A common use for cluster analysis is to find customer groups in (1) order data and (2) customer demographic data. For example, Heather Sweeney Designs could use cluster analysis to determine which groups of customers are associated with the purchase of specific products. A cluster analysis could be created using the same HSD_DW data table developed to create the OLAP reports. In this case, the cluster analysis tool might indicate that there are

**FIGURE 12-34**

A Portion of the RFM Report in XML Format

```xml
<?xml version="1.0" encoding="utf-8"?>
<Report xsi:schemaLocation="RFM-Report-1 http://reportserver?%2FRFM-Report-
1&amp;rs%3AFormat=XML&amp;rc%3ASchema=True" Name="RFM-Report-1"
xmlns:xsi="http://www.w3.org/2001/XMLSchema-instance" xmlns="RFM-Report-1">
    <Tablix1>
        <Details_Collection>
            <Details R="5" F="1" M="5" NumberOfCustomers="237"/>
            <Details R="1" F="5" M="1" NumberOfCustomers="228"/>
            <Details R="3" F="3" M="5" NumberOfCustomers="224"/>
            <Details R="1" F="5" M="3" NumberOfCustomers="224"/>
            <Details R="5" F="1" M="3" NumberOfCustomers="212"/>
            <Details R="4" F="2" M="2" NumberOfCustomers="207"/>
            <Details R="2" F="4" M="1" NumberOfCustomers="207"/>
            <Details R="3" F="3" M="2" NumberOfCustomers="207"/>
            <Details R="4" F="2" M="1" NumberOfCustomers="204"/>
            <Details R="2" F="4" M="5" NumberOfCustomers="204"/>
            <Details R="4" F="2" M="4" NumberOfCustomers="204"/>
            <Details R="3" F="3" M="4" NumberOfCustomers="203"/>
            <Details R="2" F="4" M="2" NumberOfCustomers="201"/>
            <Details R="2" F="4" M="4" NumberOfCustomers="200"/>
            <Details R="1" F="5" M="2" NumberOfCustomers="199"/>
            <Details R="1" F="5" M="4" NumberOfCustomers="196"/>
            <Details R="5" F="1" M="4" NumberOfCustomers="194"/>
            <Details R="4" F="2" M="3" NumberOfCustomers="192"/>
            <Details R="4" F="2" M="5" NumberOfCustomers="191"/>
            <Details R="2" F="4" M="3" NumberOfCustomers="185"/>
            <Details R="5" F="1" M="2" NumberOfCustomers="184"/>
            <Details R="5" F="1" M="1" NumberOfCustomers="182"/>
            <Details R="3" F="3" M="1" NumberOfCustomers="178"/>
            <Details R="3" F="3" M="3" NumberOfCustomers="175"/>
            <Details R="1" F="5" M="5" NumberOfCustomers="155"/>
            <Details R="4" F="3" M="4" NumberOfCustomers="6"/>
            <Details R="2" F="5" M="4" NumberOfCustomers="5"/>
            <Details R="3" F="4" M="3" NumberOfCustomers="5"/>
            <Details R="1" F="4" M="4" NumberOfCustomers="5"/>
            <Details R="4" F="3" M="2" NumberOfCustomers="4"/>
            <Details R="3" F="2" M="1" NumberOfCustomers="4"/>
            <Details R="2" F="5" M="3" NumberOfCustomers="4"/>
            <Details R="5" F="2" M="2" NumberOfCustomers="4"/>
            <Details R="2" F="5" M="2" NumberOfCustomers="3"/>
            <Details R="2" F="5" M="1" NumberOfCustomers="3"/>
            <Details R="3" F="4" M="1" NumberOfCustomers="2"/>
            <Details R="1" F="4" M="5" NumberOfCustomers="2"/>
            <Details R="1" F="4" M="1" NumberOfCustomers="2"/>
            <Details R="5" F="2" M="4" NumberOfCustomers="2"/>
            <Details R="4" F="3" M="5" NumberOfCustomers="2"/>
        </Details_Collection>
    </Tablix1>
</Report>
```

**FIGURE 12-35**

Convergence of Disciplines for Data Mining

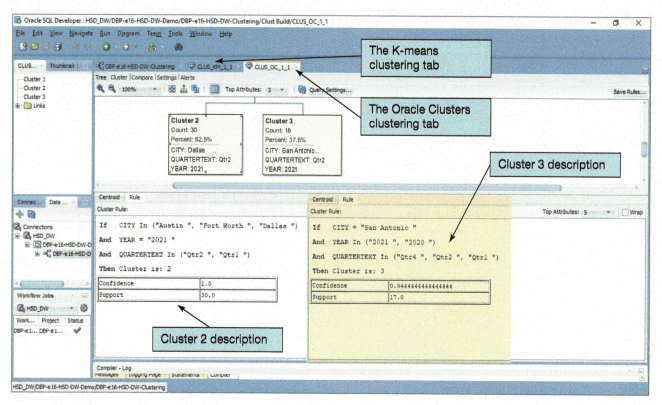

**FIGURE 12-36**

**Clustering in Oracle Database Data Miner**

different sales patterns for the Dallas area and the non-Dallas area. For example, sales of specific videos may differ markedly in between the two clusters. An example clustering created by SQL Server Analysis Services is shown in Figure 12-36.

Market basket analysis is another form of unsupervised data mining. As this is one of the most common and important forms of data mining, we will describe it in more detail later in this chapter.

### Supervised Data Mining

When using **supervised data mining** techniques, data miners develop a model prior to the analysis and then apply statistical techniques to the data to estimate parameters of the model. For example, suppose that marketing experts at a communications company believe that the use of cell phone weekend minutes is determined by the age of the customer and the number of months the customer has had the cell phone account. A data mining analyst could then run a statistical analysis technique known as **regression analysis** to determine the coefficients of the equation of that model. A possible result is:

$$\text{CellPhoneWeekendMinutes} = 12 + (17.5 * \text{CustomerAge})$$
$$+ (23.7 * \text{NumberMonthsOfAccount})$$

As you may learn in statistics classes, considerable skill is required to interpret the quality of such a model. The regression tool will create an equation; whether the equation is a good predictor of future cell phone usage depends on a variety of factors beyond the scope of this book, such as *t* values, confidence intervals, and related statistical techniques.

Some other popular supervised data mining techniques are described in the next section. One of these, decision trees, is then introduced in detail in the following section.

### Four Popular Data Mining Techniques

Four popular data mining techniques are market basket analysis, decision tree analysis, logistic regression, and neural networks. **Market basket analysis** is an unsupervised data mining technique often used to discover patterns of purchasing (e.g., what items are usually purchased together). The other three methods are supervised data mining techniques. **Decision tree analysis** classifies customers or other entities of interest into two or more groups, according to history. **Logistic regression** produces equations that offer probabilities that particular events will occur. Common applications of logistic regression are using donor characteristics to predict the likelihood of a donation in a given period and using customer characteristics to predict the likelihood that customers will switch to another vendor. **Neural networks** are complex statistical prediction techniques. The name is somewhat of a misnomer—although there is some similarity between the structure of a neural network and a network of biological neurons, the similarity is only superficial. In data mining, neural networks are just a technique for creating very complex mathematical functions for making predictions.

These four techniques, like almost all data mining techniques, require specialized software, some examples of which were listed earlier in this chapter. All of these products have facilities for importing data from relational databases, and as a database professional, you may be asked to prepare data for input to a data mining product. Typically, this work involves joining relations together into a large flat file and then filtering the data for particular data cases. Simple SQL is used to create such files. In addition, as mentioned previously, many enterprise-class DBMS products, such as Microsoft SQL Server and Oracle Database, now include this functionality within the DBMS.

## Market Basket Analysis

Data mining techniques are usually complex. However, market basket analysis is a data mining technique that can be readily implemented with pure SQL. All the major data mining products have features and functions to perform market basket analysis. Market basket analysis is also known as **association rules**.

Suppose that you run a dive shop, and one day you realize that one of your salespeople is much better than others at up-selling your customers. Any of your sales associates can fill a customer's order, but this particular salesperson is especially able to sell customers items in addition to those for which they ask. One day you ask him how he does it.

"It's simple," he says. "I just ask myself, 'What is the next product they'll want to buy?' If someone buys a dive computer, I don't try to sell her fins. If she's buying a dive computer, she's already a diver, and she already has fins. But, look, these dive computer displays are hard to read. A better mask makes it easier to read the display and get the full benefits from the dive computer." Thus, the market basket analysis might include an association rule that says, "If a customer buys a dive computer, then that customer may also buy a mask." Clearly not all customers buying a dive computer will also buy a mask, of course, so the market basket analysis will need to determine the likelihood that this will occur.

Market basket analysis is a data mining technique for determining such patterns. A market basket analysis shows the products that customers tend to purchase at the same time. Several different statistical techniques, including SQL queries, can be used to generate a market basket analysis. Here we discuss a technique that involves, as implied earlier, conditional probabilities.

Figure 12-37 shows hypothetical data from 1,000 transactions at a dive shop. The first row of numbers (shaded blue) under each column is the total number of transactions that include the product in that column. For example, the 270 near the top of the Mask column means that 270 of the 1,000 transactions include the purchase of a mask. The 120 under Dive Computer means that 120 of the 1,000 purchase transactions included a dive computer.

Note that in this example, every transaction involves one or two items among those listed in Figure 12-37; those transactions with two different items will be counted in two columns of the blue row. Also note that some of the 1,000 transactions do not contain any of the five products listed in the table (e.g., somebody purchases a wet suit and nothing else).

You can use the numbers in the blue row to estimate the probability that a customer will purchase an item. Because 270 out of 1,000 transactions included a mask, you can estimate the likelihood that a customer will buy a mask to be 270/1,000, or .27.

FIGURE 12-37

A Market Basket Analysis
Example

| 1,000 Transactions | Mask | Tank | Fins | Weights | Dive Computer |
|---|---|---|---|---|---|
| | 270 | 200 | 280 | 130 | 120 |
| Mask | 20 | 20 | 150 | 20 | 50 |
| Tank | 20 | 80 | 40 | 30 | 30 |
| Fins | 150 | 40 | 10 | 60 | 20 |
| Weights | 20 | 30 | 60 | 10 | 10 |
| Dive Computer | 50 | 30 | 20 | 10 | 5 |
| No Additional Product | 10 | – | – | – | 5 |

Support = P (A & B)       Example: P (Fins & Mask) = 150 / 1000 = .15
Confidence = P (A | B)    Example: P (Fins | Mask) = 150 / 270 = .55556
Lift = P (A | B)/ P (A)   Example: P (Fins | Mask) / P (Fins) = .55556 / .28 = 1.98
Note:                     P (Mask | Fins) / P (Mask) = 150 / 280 / .27 = 1.98

Similarly, the likelihood of a tank purchase is 200/1,000, or .2, and the likelihood of a fins purchase is 280/1,000, or .28. The next five rows in this table show the occurrences of transactions that involve two items. For example, the last column indicates that 50 transactions included both a dive computer and a mask, 30 transactions included a dive computer and a tank, 20 included a dive computer and fins, 10 included a dive computer and weights, 5 included a dive computer and another dive computer (meaning the customer bought two dive computers), and 5 transactions had a dive computer and no other product.

These data are interesting, but we can refine the analysis by computing additional factors. Marketing professionals define **support** as the probability that two items will be purchased together. From these data, the support for fins and mask is 150 out of 1,000, or .15. Similarly, the support for dive computer and mask (the combination cited earlier by a salesperson) is 50/1,000, or .05.

**Confidence** is defined as the probability of a customer buying one product, given that he or she is buying another product. The confidence of fins, given that the customer is purchasing a mask, is the number of purchases of fins and masks out of the number of purchases of masks. Thus, in this example, the confidence is 150 out of 270, or .55556. The confidence that a customer purchases a tank, given that the customer has purchased fins, is 40 out of 280, or .14286. As another example, the confidence in the rule alluded to by our star salesperson ("If a customer buys a dive computer, then that customer will also buy a mask") is 50/120 = .41667, or roughly 42%.

**Lift** is defined as the ratio of confidence divided by the base probability of an item purchase. The lift for fins, given a mask, is the probability that a customer buys fins (given that the customer is purchasing a mask) divided by the overall probability that the customer buys fins. If the lift is greater than 1, then the probability of buying fins goes up when a customer buys a mask; if the lift is less than 1, the probability of buying fins goes down when a customer buys a mask.

For the data in Figure 12-37, the lift for fins, given a mask purchase, is .55556/.28 or 1.98. This means that when someone purchases a mask, the likelihood he or she will also purchase fins almost doubles. The lift for fins, given a dive computer purchase, is 20/120 (the confidence of fins, given a dive computer) divided by .28, the probability that someone buys fins (280 of the 1,000 transactions involved fins). Therefore, 20/120 is .16667, and .16667/.28 is .59525. So the lift for fins, given purchase of a dive computer, is just under .6, meaning that when a customer buys a dive computer the likelihood that he or she will buy fins decreases. Finally, returning to our salesperson's example, the lift for a mask, given the purchase of a dive computer, is .41667 (the confidence in our "rule") divided by the overall likelihood of buying a mask, which is .27. This gives a lift of .41667/.27 = 1.5432, meaning that our salesperson's intuition was correct: purchasing a dive computer increases the odds of a mask being purchased at the same time.

Note that, as shown in the last line of Figure 12-37, lift is symmetrical. If the lift of fins, given purchase of a mask, is 1.98, then the lift of mask, given purchase of fins, is also 1.98.

## Decision Trees

The potential for straightforward graphical representation makes decision trees, once they are constructed, possible to interpret without a lot of background and training. Constructing decision trees, on the other hand, requires sophisticated algorithms and enough experience to properly parameterize those algorithms. In this section, we will focus on the intuition behind decision tree structure and usage by examining an example that is further explored in the exercises.

A decision tree, intuitively, represents a set of rules that can be easily expressed in English or in SQL. As a simple example, consider the situation of a child deciding whether to read a particular book. Based on his or her experience, the child has determined some characteristics of books that are likely to make them either good or bad choices for the child to read. For example, the child may not like books that are too long and may like short books only if they have plenty of pictures. Without realizing it, that child is using a decision tree similar to that shown in Figure 12-38.

The structure in Figure 12-38 is referred to as a tree. (In computing, we draw trees upside down, with the root of the tree at the top of the diagram and the leaves at the bottom.) Any tree, including decision trees, will have just one **root** and will have just one way to get from the root to any specific **leaf**. In this example, as with all decision trees, we begin with a single question asked at the root of the tree. We will represent questions by rectangles and decisions using ovals.

The question first asked by the child is whether the book is less than 100 pages long or at least 100 pages long. The root question of the tree contains the name of the attribute being examined, in this case the Length of the book. If the book is at least 100 pages long, then the questioning follows the arrow coming out of the right side of the root. At the end of that arrow is a leaf with the word "NO," indicating that the child is not interested in reading this book. Note that the arrow is labeled with the value(s) of the Length attribute that will lead the questioning that way.

If the answer to the question at the root is that the book is less than 100 pages long, then another question is required in order to make the final decision. In this case, we follow the arrow to the left of the root (labeled "< 100") to arrive at the second question. This question is based on how many pictures the book has. If the book has at least one picture per page, then the child wants to read the book. This corresponds to following the arrow coming from the right side of the PicturesPerPage rectangle. This arrow is labeled, as elsewhere, with the conditions under which it will be followed (PicturesPerPage >= 1). On the other hand,

**FIGURE 12-38**

**A Decision Tree Example**

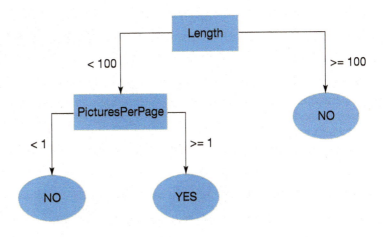

or not be the operational DBMS. Characteristics of reporting and data mining applications are listed in Figure 12-2.

Direct reading of operational databases is not feasible for any but the smallest and simplest BI applications and databases—for several reasons. Querying operational data can unacceptably slow the performance of operational systems; operational data have problems that limit their usefulness for BI applications; and BI system creation and maintenance require programs, facilities, and expertise that are normally not available for an operational database.

Problems with operational data are listed in Figure 12-3. Because of the problems with operational data, many organizations have chosen to create and staff data warehouses and data marts. Extract, Transform, and Load (ETL) systems are used to extract data from operational systems, transform the data, and load it into data warehouses. Data warehouses also maintain metadata that describe the source, format, assumptions, and constraints of the data. A data mart is a collection of data that is smaller than that held in a data warehouse and addresses a particular component or functional area of the business.

Operational databases and dimensional (data warehouse) databases have different characteristics, as shown in Figure 12-7. Dimensional databases use a star schema and must deal with slowly changing dimensions, and therefore a time dimension is important in a dimensional database. Fact tables hold measures of interest, and dimension tables hold attribute values used in queries. The star schema can be extended with additional fact tables, dimension tables, and conformed dimensions.

The purpose of a reporting system is to create meaningful information from disparate data sources and to deliver that information to the proper users on a timely basis. Reports are produced by sorting, filtering, grouping, and making simple calculations on the data. RFM analysis is a typical reporting application. It ranks customers along the three dimensions of recency, frequency, and monetary value by dividing the customers into (typically) five bins for each dimension. An RFM report can be produced using SQL statements.

Online analytical processing (OLAP) reporting applications, which often use dimensional databases, enable users to dynamically restructure reports. A measure is a data item of interest. A dimension is a characteristic of a measure. An OLAP report, or OLAP cube, is an arrangement of measures and dimensions. With OLAP, users can drill down and exchange the order of dimensions.

Data mining is the application of mathematical and statistical techniques to find patterns and relationships and to classify and predict. Data mining has arisen in recent decades because of the confluence of factors shown in Figure 12-35. The two main kinds are data mining are supervised and unsupervised. Market basket analysis (also known as association rules) is a popular form of unsupervised data mining in which the user often wants to discover rules about products or other data (e.g., someone who buys coffee will also buy eggs 76% of the time). These rules can be measured by various useful statistics including support, confidence, and lift. Decision trees are a common form of supervised data mining. A decision tree allows one to categorize new data by starting at the root of the tree and proceeding toward the leaves, answering a specific question about the new data point at each branch of the tree to determine where to go next. When a leaf of the tree has been reached, the new data point has been categorized.

# Key Terms

| | | |
|---|---|---|
| alert | confidence | data mining application |
| association rules | conformed dimension | data warehouse |
| business intelligence (BI) system | curse of dimensionality | data warehouse metadata database |
| click-stream data | data lake | date dimension |
| cluster analysis | data mart | decision tree analysis |

digital dashboard
dimension
dimension table
dimensional database
dirty data
drill down
dynamic report
enterprise data warehouse (EDW)
    architecture
Extract, Transform, and Load (ETL)
    system
F score
fact table
inconsistent data
leaf
lift
logistic regression
M score
market basket analysis

measure
missing value
neural networks
node
nonintegrated data
OLAP cube
OLAP report
OLAP server
online analytical processing (OLAP)
online transaction processing (OLTP)
    system
operational system
PivotTable
pull report
push report
query report
R score
regression analysis
report authoring

report delivery
report management
reporting system
RFM analysis
root
slowly changing dimension
SQL Server Data Tools (SSDT)
SQL TOP . . . PERCENT expression
star schema
static report
supervised data mining
support
testing phase
time dimension
training phase
transactional system
unsupervised data mining
Web portal
XML Web Services

# Review Questions

**12.1**  What are BI systems?

**12.2**  How do BI systems differ from transaction processing systems?

**12.3**  Name and describe the two main categories of BI systems.

**12.4**  What are the three sources of data for BI systems?

**12.5**  Explain the difference in processing between reporting and data mining applications.

**12.6**  Describe three reasons why direct reading of operational data is not feasible for BI applications.

**12.7**  Summarize the problems with operational databases that limit their usefulness for BI applications.

**12.8**  What are dirty data? How do dirty data arise?

**12.9**  What is an ETL system, and what functions does it perform?

**12.10**  What does it mean to transform data? Give an example other than the ones used in this book.

**12.11**  Why is server time not useful for Web-based order entry BI applications?

**12.12**  What is click-stream data? How is it used in BI applications?

**12.13**  Why are data warehouses necessary?

**12.14**  Why do the authors describe the data in Figure 12-5 as "frightening"?

**12.15**  Give examples of data warehouse metadata.

**12.16**  Explain the difference between a data warehouse and a data mart. Use the analogy of a supply chain.

**12.17**  What is the enterprise data warehouse (EDW) architecture?

**12.18**  Describe the differences between operational databases and dimensional databases.

**12.19**  What is a star schema?

**12.20**  What is a fact table? What type of data is stored in fact tables?

**12.21**  What is a measure?

**12.22**  What is a dimension table? What type of data is stored in dimension tables?

**12.23**  What is a slowly changing dimension?

**12.24**  Why is the time dimension important in a dimensional model?

**12.25**  What is a conformed dimension?

**12.26**  State the purpose of a reporting system.

**12.27**  What do the letters *RFM* stand for in RFM analysis?

**12.28**  Describe in general terms how to perform an RFM analysis.

**12.29**  Explain the characteristics of customers with the following RFM scores: {1 1 5}, {1 5 1}, {5 5 5}, {2 5 5}, {5 1 2}, {1 1 3}.

**12.30**  In the RFM analysis in Figures 12-20 through 12-23, what role does the CUSTOMER_RFM table serve? What role does the CUSTOMER_R table serve?

**12.31**  Explain the purpose of the following SQL statement from Figure 12-22:

```
INSERT INTO CUSTOMER_R (CustomerID, MostRecentOrderDate)
          (SELECT      CustomerID, MAX (TransactionDate)
           FROM        CUSTOMER_SALES
           GROUP BY    CustomerID);
```

**12.32**  Explain the purpose and operation of the following SQL statement from Figure 12-22:

```
UPDATE    CUSTOMER_R
     SET       R_Score = 1
     WHERE     CustomerID IN
                    (SELECT      TOP 20 PERCENT CustomerID
                     FROM        CUSTOMER_R
                     ORDER BY    MostRecentOrderDate DESC);
```

**12.33**  Explain the purpose and operation of the following SQL statement from Figure 12-22:

```
UPDATE    CUSTOMER_R
     SET       R_Score = 2
     WHERE     CustomerID IN
                    (SELECT      TOP 25 PERCENT CustomerID
                     FROM        CUSTOMER_R
                     WHERE       R_Score IS NULL
                     ORDER BY    MostRecentOrderDate DESC);
```

**12.34**  Write an SQL statement to query the CUSTOMER_RFM table and display the CustomerID values for all customers having an RFM score of {5 1 1} or {4 1 1}. Why are these customers important?

**12.35** What does OLAP stand for?

**12.36** What is the distinguishing characteristic of OLAP reports?

**12.37** Define *measure, dimension,* and *cube.*

**12.38** Give an example, other than one in this text, of a measure, two dimensions related to your measure, and a cube.

**12.39** What is drill down?

**12.40** Explain how the OLAP report in Figure 12-26 differs from that in Figure 12-25.

**12.41** What is the purpose of an OLAP server?

**12.42** Name and describe the purpose of the major components of a reporting system.

**12.43** What are the major functions of a reporting system?

**12.44** Summarize the types of reports described in this chapter.

**12.45** Describe the various media used to deliver reports.

**12.46** Summarize the modes of reports described in this chapter.

**12.47** Describe the major tasks in report management. Explain the role of report metadata in report management.

**12.48** Name three tasks of report authoring.

**12.49** Describe the major tasks in report delivery.

**12.50** Define *data mining.*

**12.51** Explain the difference between unsupervised and supervised data mining.

**12.52** Name five popular data mining techniques.

**12.53** What is the purpose of market basket analysis?

**12.54** Define the terms *support* and *confidence* as they relate to market basket analysis.

**12.55** Define the term *lift* as it relates to market basket analysis.

**12.56** What does it mean to say, in market basket analysis, that the support of buying items A and B together is 20%?

**12.57** What does it mean to say, in market basket analysis, that the confidence of someone buying item B if they are already buying item A is 20%?

**12.58** What does it mean to say, in market basket analysis, that the lift of someone buying item B if they are already buying item A is 1.5?

**12.59** What is the purpose of a decision tree?

**12.60** At what part of a decision tree do we begin to ask questions when trying to categorize new data?

**12.61** In constructing decision trees, what is the purpose of the training phase?

**12.62** In constructing decision trees, what is the purpose of the testing phase?

**12.63** When a decision tree is used to categorize a new data point, how many more questions remain to be asked about the data point when you reach a leaf of the tree?

**12.64** If two decision trees do an equally good job categorizing new data points but one of them is taller than the other, which one is better, and why?

# Morgan Importing Project Questions

If you have not already implemented the Morgan Importing database shown in Chapter 7 in a DBMS product, create and populate the MI database now in the DBMS of your choice (or as assigned by your instructor).

James Morgan wants to analyze shipper performance based on the difference between a shipment's scheduled departure date and the actual departure date. This value will be named DepartureDelay, with the values measured in days. The values of Days can be positive (the shipment departed later than the scheduled departure date), zero (the shipment departed on the scheduled departure date), or negative (the shipment departed before the scheduled departure date).

Because Morgan Importing purchasing agents are responsible for contacting the shippers and arranging the shipments, James also wants an analysis of purchasing agents' performance based on the same measure.

**A.** Design a data warehouse star schema for a dimensional database named MI_DW. The fact table measure will be DepartureDelay (the difference between ScheduledDepartureDate and ActualDepartureDate). Dimension tables will be TIMELINE, SHIPMENT, SHIPPER, and PURCHASING_AGENT (PURCHASING_AGENT is a subset of EMPLOYEE containing data on only the employees who are purchasing agents).

**B.** Create the MI_DW database in a DBMS product.

**C.** What transformations of data will need to be made before the MI_DW database can be loaded with data? List all the transformations, showing the original format of the MI database and how it appears in the MI_DW database.

**D.** Write the complete set of SQL statements necessary to load the transformed data into the MI_DW database.

**E.** Populate the MI_DW database using the appropriate MI database data or transformations of that data.

**F.** Write an SQL query similar to SQL-Query-CH12-02 that uses DepartureDelay as the measure.

**G.** Write the SQL view equivalent of the SQL query you wrote to answer part F.

**H.** Create the SQL view you wrote to answer part G in your MI_DW database.

**I.** Create a Microsoft Excel 2019 workbook named MI-DW-BI-Exercises.xlsx.

**J.** Using either the results of your SQL query from part F (copy the results of the query into a worksheet in the MI-DW-BI.xlsx workbook and then format this range as a worksheet table) or your SQL view from part H (create a Microsoft Excel data connection to the view), create an OLAP report similar to the OLAP report shown in Figure 12-24(i). (Hint: If you need help with the necessary Microsoft Excel actions, search in the Microsoft Excel help system for more information.)

**K.** Note that since the Morgan Importing database that we have created is intended to track purchases and shipping rather than customer purchases, RFM cannot be applied to customer data in the database since there is none. Nevertheless, describe how an RFM analysis could be useful to Morgan Importing. What part of the business would you apply RFM analysis to?

**L.** Note that since the Morgan Importing database that we have created is intended to track purchases and shipping rather than customer purchases, market basket analysis cannot be applied to customer data since there is none. Nevertheless, describe in general terms how a market basket analysis could be useful to Morgan Importing by considering item categories that are shipped together on the same shipment. Pick a pair of categories that have been shipped together more than once and, using the data in the database, compute the support and confidence for rules involving them. For example, if your categories are A and B, compute the support of A and B, the confidence of B given A, and the confidence of A given B.

**M.**  Morgan Importing would like to be able to characterize certain shipments as high-risk based on prior experience. Describe, in general terms, how a decision tree might help them to do this.

# 13

# Big Data, NoSQL, and the Cloud

## Chapter Objectives

- To learn the basic concepts of Big Data
- To understand the limitations and trade-offs of replicated, partitioned stores as indicated by the CAP theorem
- To learn the basic concepts of distributed databases and object-relational databases
- To learn the basic concepts of NoSQL, the MapReduce process, and Hadoop
- To learn the basic concepts of non-relational database management systems
- To learn the basic concepts of key-value databases

- To learn the basic concepts of document databases
- To learn the basic concepts of column family databases
- To learn the basic concepts of graph databases
- To learn the basic concepts of virtualization and virtual machines
- To learn the basic concepts of cloud computing
- To obtain a practical introduction to the Microsoft Azure cloud environment to set up an account, create SQL databases, and run a simple document query on Azure Cosmos DB

**This chapter introduces** topics that build on the fundamentals you have learned in the other chapters of this book. Now that we have designed and built a database, we are ready to put it to work. In Chapter 11, we built a Web database application for the View Ridge Gallery (VRG) Information System. In Chapter 12, we extended our concept of what we can do with databases by looking at business intelligence (specifically reporting and data mining) applications. This chapter takes us in another dimension and looks at the problems associated with the rapidly expanding amount of data that is being stored and used in enterprise information systems and some of the technology that is being used to address those problems.

These problems are generally included in the need to deal with **Big Data** (also often written as *big data*), which is the current term for the enormous datasets generated by Web applications such as search tools (for example, Google and Bing); Web 2.0 social networks (for example, Facebook, LinkedIn, and Twitter); scientific and sensor-based data (for example, the Large Hadron Collider and DNA-derived

636

genomics data); and large volumes of historical transactional data (such as that generated by banks and large retailers).[1]

Just how big is Big Data? Figure 13-1 defines some commonly used terms for data storage capacity. Note that computer storage is calculated based on binary numbers (base 2), not the usual decimal (base 10) numbers we are more familiar with. Therefore, a kilobyte is 1,024 bytes instead of the 1,000 bytes we would otherwise expect, a megabyte is 1,024 kilobytes, and so forth.

If we consider the desktop and notebook computers generally in use as this book is being written (2020), a quick check online of available computers shows laptops being sold with hard drives commonly 1 TB in capacity (5 TB drives can be purchased), whereas some desktops can be equipped with 14 TB drives. That is just for one computer with one drive. As of early 2020, Instagram reported having over 50 billion user images, with over 100 million more photos and videos being added each day. Assuming that rate continues, that is about 36 billion new images per year.[2] If a typical digital photo is about 2 MB in size, that would require over 67 PB of new storage each year!

As another measure of Big Data, Amazon.com reported that for the year ending May 31, 2020, small and medium-sized U.S.-based businesses sold over 6,500 products per minute through Amazon's website. This is an average of 108 product orders per second[3] and an increase of 63 percent over the previous year. Remember that this does not include large sellers or non-U.S. sellers, so it is just a fraction of Amazon's volume. This volume of both primary business transactions (item sales) and supporting transactions (shipping, tracking, and financial transactions) truly requires Amazon.com to handle Big Data. As another example, the Large Hadron

**FIGURE 13-1**

**Storage Capacity Terms**

| Name | Symbol | Approximate Value for Reference | Actual Value |
| --- | --- | --- | --- |
| Byte | | | 8 bits [Store one character] |
| Kilobyte | KB | About $10^3$ | $2^{10}$ = 1,024 bytes |
| Megabyte | MB | About $10^6$ | $2^{20}$ = 1,024 KB |
| Gigabyte | GB | About $10^9$ | $2^{30}$ = 1,024 MB |
| Terabyte | TB | About $10^{12}$ | $2^{40}$ = 1,024 GB |
| Petabyte | PB | About $10^{15}$ | $2^{50}$ = 1,024 TB |
| Exabyte | EB | About $10^{18}$ | $2^{60}$ = 1,024 PB |
| Zettabyte | ZB | About $10^{21}$ | $2^{70}$ = 1,024 EB |
| Yottabyte | YB | About $10^{24}$ | $2^{80}$ = 1,024 ZB |

[1]For more information, see the Wikipedia article *Big Data* at *http://en.wikipedia.org/wiki/Big_data* (accessed July 2020)

[2]*www.omnicoreagency.com/instagram-statistics/* (accessed July 2020)

[3]*www.businesswire.com/news/home/20200721005239/en/Amazon-2020-SMB-Impact-Report-Highlights-Success* (accessed July 2020)

Collider generates about 30 PB of data annually for physicists to analyze. It reached the 200 PB milestone in 2017, while generating about 1 PB per second of data from subatomic particle collisions. These data are filtered to keep the most "interesting" for future processing; otherwise their systems would be quickly overwhelmed.[4] The Internet of Things (IoT; see Chapter 1) continues to grow, with over 40 billion connected devices predicted by 2025.[5] If each such device produces one byte of data each hour (and many will do much more than this), that becomes nearly 26 TB each month of new data.

The need to deal with larger and larger datasets has grown over time. We will look at some of the components of this growth. Many of the techniques being brought to bear on Big Data (such as cloud storage and data models more complex than the relational model) have origins in earlier, more traditional avenues of database development such as distributed databases and object-relational databases. We will thus look at distributed databases (precursors of cloud databases) and object-relational systems (which include complex data types like those used in many NoSQL systems), and finally we will focus on the evolving NoSQL systems that have been developed in large part to manage Big Data. Because the development of NoSQL and the cloud are so closely related, we will also briefly describe cloud computing and the related virtualization technology that enables cloud computing. Many NoSQL systems are deployed in the cloud, and many cloud-based databases are NoSQL systems, so a typical NoSQL database existing in the cloud brings together earlier ideas from object-relational and distributed database systems while at the same time providing an affordable platform for transactional and BI activities to be performed on large datasets.

## What Is Big Data?

*Big Data* is a hot topic. *Big Data* is a "buzz word."

According to the Merriam-Webster dictionary, *Big Data* (aka *big data*) is "an accumulation of data that is too large and complex for processing by traditional database management tools."[6] And yet, as danah boyd (who prefers all lowercase letters in her name) and Kate Crawford[7] point out, U.S. Census datasets that have been gathered over many decades are larger than some datasets now considered Big Data. They note the social phenomena aspects of Big Data and write that

We define Big Data as a cultural, technological, and scholarly phenomenon that rests on the interplay of:

1. *Technology*: maximizing computation power and algorithmic accuracy to gather, analyze, link, and compare large data sets.
2. *Analysis*: drawing on large data sets to identify patterns in order to make economic, social, technical, and legal claims.

---

[4]*https://home.cern/news/news/computing/cern-data-centre-passes-200-petabyte-milestone* (accessed July 2020)

[5]*www.zdnet.com/article/what-is-the-internet-of-things-everything-you-need-to-know-about-the-iot-right-now/* (accessed July 2020)

[6]Merriam-Webster online dictionary at *www.merriam-webster.com/dictionary/big%20data* (accessed July 2020)

[7]danah boyd and Kate Crawford, "Critical Questions for Big Data," *Information, Communication and Society* 15, no. 5 (2012): 662–79. *http://doi.org/10.1080/1369118X.2012.678878* (accessed July 2020)

3. *Mythology*: the widespread belief that large data sets offer a higher form of intelligence and knowledge that can generate insights that were previously impossible, with the aura of truth, objectivity, and accuracy.[8]

Most users of Big Data would probably agree with the first two parts of this definition, while we should definitely be thinking about the third part and its implications.

### The Three Vs Plus One

In early 2001, Doug Laney, working as a member of the META Group (which is now part of Gartner), needed a way to explain Big Data to his clients. He created and popularized the **3V framework** for discussing Big Data.[9] The 3V framework discussed Big Data in terms of:

- **Volume**: the extremely large amount of data that needs to be stored.
- **Velocity**: the speed and continuous nature of data acquisition.
- **Variety**: the many different forms of data being acquired and stored.

#### Volume

In their 2012 book *Understanding Big Data*[10] (an e-book available from and sponsored by IBM), Paul Zikopoulos and his colleagues note that in 2012 Twitter needed to store more than 7 terabytes of data per day and that Facebook was generating 10 terabytes daily. They projected that 35 zettabytes of data would need to be stored by 2020. IBM, in its illustration *The FOUR V's of Big Data*,[11] projects data growth of 40 zettabytes in 2020 and claims that over 2.3 trillion gigabytes of data are created each day! In 2018, cloud computing provider DOMO estimated that humans generated just over 2 EB of data daily.[12] Figure 13-1 shows what these terms mean relative to each other, and remember that as this is being written in 2020, 1 terabyte hard drives are a typical purchase for personal computers and larger ones up to 14 terabytes of capacity are available.

#### Velocity

Saying that Twitter adds 7 terabytes (that is a one with 12 zeros!) per day is not only a measure of volume (the amount of data needing to be stored), it is also a measure of the speed that the data arrives at: 7 terabytes / *day* = over 290 gigabytes / *hour* = over 4.8 gigabytes / *minute* = over 81 megabytes / *second*. The data arrives, and it must be stored and, hopefully, processed. And it keeps coming!

#### Variety

Twitter stores tweets (IBM's illustration claims 400 million tweets per day), which are short text messages of up to 280 characters and stored in JSON format. YouTube stores and streams video content. Facebook stores text, pictures, "likes," and friend connection data. Instagram stores pictures, "likes," and comments (more text!). Pandora stores and streams music. The term *variety* reflects all the different types of content data that need to be stored.

#### Veracity

IBM added **veracity**, having to do with the uncertainty of the quality and accuracy of data, to the list of Vs. How many Vs do we need? We certainly need to understand the original three: volume, velocity, and variety. Some consideration of the correctness or usefulness of

[8]Ibid., 663.

[9]Doug Laney, *3-D Data Management: Controlling Data Volume, Velocity and Variety* (Stamford, CT: META Group Inc., 2001). See *https://ctovision.com/deja-vvvu-others-claiming-gartners-construct-for-big-data/* (accessed October 2020); the original paper is available there.

[10]Paul Zikopoulos, Chris Eaton, Dirk deRoos, Thomas Deutsch, and George Lapis, *Understanding Big Data: Analytics for Enterprise Class Hadoop and Streaming Data* (New York: McGraw Hill Bulk Sales, 2012). Available online at (accessed July 2020).

[11]Available at *www.ibmbigdatahub.com/infographic/four-vs-big-data* (accessed July 2020)

[12]*www.domo.com/solution/data-never-sleeps-6* (accessed July 2020)

**FIGURE 13-2**

**The 3 Vs Plus 1**

the data would argue, as IBM does, for the possible inclusion of veracity. Other Vs have been proposed, but that complicates rather than helps a model intended to clarify our understanding of Big Data, so we will settle for the 3 Vs plus 1, as shown in Figure 13-2.

## Big Data and NoSQL Systems

We have used the relational database model and SQL throughout this book. However, there is another school of thought that has led to what was originally known as the **NoSQL** movement but now is usually referred to as the **Not only SQL** movement.[13] It has been noted that most but not all DBMSs associated with the NoSQL movement are non-relational DBMSs. There have been several classification systems proposed for grouping and classifying NoSQL databases based on their (non-relational) data models.

For our purposes, we will adopt and use a set of four categories of NoSQL databases:[14]

- **Key-value**: Examples are DynamoDB and MemcacheDB.
- **Document**: Examples are ArangoDB, Couchbase Server, MongoDB, and Azure Cosmos DB.
- **Column family**: Examples are Apache Cassandra and HBase.
- **Graph**: Examples are Neo4j and AllegroGraph.

Many NoSQL DBMSs have features from more than once category, and some NoSQL DBMSs are **multimodel**: **ArangoDB**, for example, supports document, key-value, and graph data. In addition to the data model used, most NoSQL DBMSs differ from relational systems in how they make use of networks of computers (servers). A NoSQL DBMS is typically a distributed, replicated database and is used where this type of a DBMS is needed to support large datasets. The important features of the four basic NoSQL models are introduced later in this chapter, after we describe other data models that led to their development and the basics of distributed databases. NoSQL databases also often use cloud or virtualization technology, which is introduced at the end of this chapter.

NoSQL databases are used by widely recognized Web applications—for example, both Facebook and Twitter use the Apache Software Foundation's Cassandra database. In this chapter, we will briefly introduce all four categories. Online Chapter 10D describes document databases in much more detail, in the context of ArangoDB (which also supports the key-value and graph models). Many organizations today use both relational and one or more NoSQL databases to fit specific needs; this is known as **polyglot persistence**.

A major motivating factor for the development of NoSQL database systems, especially when applied to Big Data, was the need to rapidly process large datasets. One must either "scale up" or "scale out" to gain storage and processing capacity. Maintaining a DBMS on a

---

[13]For a good overview, see the Wikipedia article *NoSQL*, *https://en.wikipedia.org/wiki/NoSQL* (accessed July 2020)

[14]This set of categories corresponds to the four categories used in the Wikipedia article *NoSQL* as Wikipedia's taxonomy of NoSQL databases and is also used in Ian Robinson, Jim Webber, and Emil Eifrem, *Graph Databases* (Sebastopol, CA: O'Reilly Media, 2013).

single computer system makes it easier to maintain database consistency, but there is a limit to the number of processors and the amount of storage that can be attached to a single computer system. Scaling up might initially work but will usually become untenable as data storage and processing requirements grow rapidly. Many NoSQL database systems have built-in support for running on clusters of computers—scaling out—that allows capacity to be added fairly easily and cheaply.

One technique is to make one or more copies of a set of data and maintain each on a different server. Each copy is called a **replica set**. Replication, described more in the next section, increases the processing capacity of our system by allowing several servers to access the data simultaneously. It also can increase availability of our system since processing can continue if a server fails. However, this can lead to consistency problems. If a data item is updated on one server, it will take some time before the update can propagate to the other replica sets on other servers. This is known as **eventual consistency**. Some applications may end up reading stale data. This may or may not be a problem, depending on the application. What if two different updates are made to the same data item at the same time on different servers? Again, the severity of the problem depends on the application.

This availability versus consistency trade-off is one of many that must be taken in consideration when using clusters, which brings us to the CAP theorem.

### The CAP Theorem

As with relational DBMSs, there are many important trade-offs to consider when choosing a DBMS and when implementing the database in that DBMS. Many concepts and design decisions in relational systems, described in Chapters 1–9 and Appendix F of this book, have counterparts in NoSQL databases. For example, Chapter 9 briefly discusses some performance issues important in relational databases, such as indexing, query optimization, and physical placement of data on secondary storage. The details of these issues in a NoSQL setting are beyond the scope of this book, but you should be aware that such decisions made by the DBA can greatly affect the performance of both NoSQL and relational systems. Some of these issues are addressed for NoSQL document databases in online Chapter 10D.

The CAP theorem exemplifies some of these important design decisions in a NoSQL setting by describing what combinations of features are possible to achieve simultaneously in a NoSQL database. The CAP theorem originated in 2000, when Eric Brewer made a proposal in his keynote presentation at the Symposium on Principles of Distributed Computing (PODC). The proposal was formally proved as a theorem by Seth Gilbert and Nancy Lynch.[15] It is now known the **CAP theorem**. In 2012, Brewer himself reflected on the early history of the CAP theorem and some of its ramifications and uses.[16]

Basically, the CAP theorem defines three properties of distributed database systems:

1. Consistency
2. Availability
3. Partition tolerance

**Consistency** means that all the database replicas see the same data at any given point in time. **Availability** means that every request received by a server will result in a response, as long as the network is available. **Partition tolerance** means that the distributed database can continue to operate even when the cluster is partitioned by network failures into two or more disconnected sections (partitions).

The CAP theorem, illustrated in Figure 13-3, states that *all three of these properties cannot be guaranteed at the same time*—at least one of the properties will be at least somewhat compromised, as there may be several levels of these properties.

---

[15]See the Wikipedia article *CAP theorem* (*https://en.wikipedia.org/wiki/CAP_theorem* (accessed July 2020)) and Seth Gilbert and Nancy Lynch, "Brewer's Conjecture and the Feasibility of Consistent, Available, Partition-Tolerant Web Services," *ACM SIGACT News* 33, no. 2 (2002).

[16]See Eric Brewer, *CAP Twelve Years Later: How the "Rules" Have Changed* on the InfoQ Web site at *www.infoq.com/articles/cap-twelve-years-later-how-the-rules-have-changed* (accessed July 2020)

**FIGURE 13-3**

The CAP Theorem—You Can't Have All Three at the Same Time!

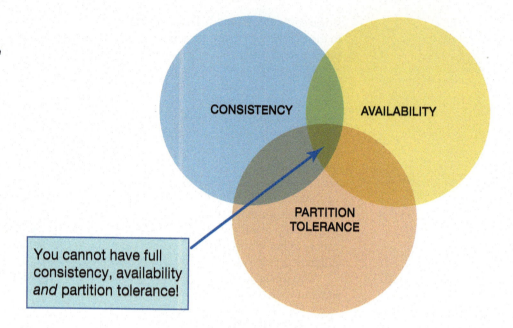

CONSISTENCY   AVAILABILITY

PARTITION TOLERANCE

You cannot have full consistency, availability *and* partition tolerance!

For example, allowing partition tolerance will degrade consistency if each partition independently allows updates, resulting in different values for the same data item in other replica sets, or we could choose to lose availability by only allowing reads or by shutting down the entire system in the event of a partition.

The CAP theorem gives us a basis for a comparison of relational DBMSs to non-relational "NoSQL" DBMSs. Relational DBMSs can be said to favor consistency and availability (since they are often running on a single, non-partitioned database system), while non-relational DBMSs must be designed according to whether they want to emphasize consistency or availability in their design (since they are by definition designed for clustered, distributed, and therefore partitioned systems). The CAP theorem also provides a framework for thinking about some of the important concepts and trade-offs in NoSQL DBMSs: each such DBMS has its own levels of support for the three properties listed in the CAP theorem, and we can use that as a guide to choosing a DBMS. In addition, some NoSQL DBMSs allow the DBA to make choices about the levels of support for these concepts, and the CAP theorem can help a DBA with these choices. Online Chapter 10D describes some of the issues in the context of ArangoDB, a multimodel NoSQL DBMS.

## Distributed Database Processing

Before proceeding with the specifics of modern NoSQL processing and models, we first examine two topics that predate and heavily influence NoSQL and Big Data solutions as well as some typical NoSQL processing scenarios. This section describes distributed database processing, and the next sections describe object-relational databases and Big Data processing models.

One of the first solutions to increase the amount of data that could be stored by a DBMS (predating NoSQL systems by decades) was to simply spread the data among several database servers instead of just one. A group of associated servers is known as a **server cluster**,[17] and the database shared between them is called a distributed database. A **distributed database** is a database that is stored and/or processed on more than one computer. Depending on the type of database and the processing that is allowed, distributed databases can present significant problems as well as significant opportunities. Let us consider the types of distributed databases.

---

[17]For more information on computer clusters, see the Wikipedia article *Computer cluster* at *https://en.wikipedia.org/wiki/Computer_cluster* (accessed September 2020)

## Types of Distributed Databases

A database can be distributed by **partitioning**, often called **sharding** in the NoSQL context, which means breaking the database into pieces and storing the pieces on multiple computers; by **replication**, which means storing copies of the database on multiple computers; or by a combination of replication and partitioning. Figure 13-4 illustrates these alternatives.

Figure 13-4(a) shows a nondistributed database with four pieces labeled W, X, Y, and Z and two applications labeled AP1 and AP2. In Figure 13-4(b), the database has been partitioned but not replicated. Portions W and X are stored and processed on Computer 1, and portions Y and Z are stored and processed on Computer 2. Figure 13-4(c) shows a database that has been replicated but not partitioned. The entire database is stored and processed on Computers 1 and 2. Finally, Figure 13-4(d) shows a database that is partitioned and replicated. Portion Y of the database is stored and processed on Computers 1 and 2.

The portions to be partitioned or replicated can be defined in many different ways. A database that has five tables (for example, CUSTOMER, SALESPERSON, INVOICE, LINE_ITEM, and PART) could be partitioned by assigning CUSTOMER to portion W, SALESPERSON to portion X, INVOICE and LINE_ITEM to portion Y, and PART to portion Z. Alternatively, different rows of each of these five tables could be assigned to different computers (this is called horizontal partitioning), or different columns of each of these tables could be assigned to different computers (this is called vertical partitioning).

Databases are distributed for two major reasons: performance and control. Having a database on multiple computers can improve throughput, either because multiple computers are sharing the workload or because communications delays can be reduced by placing the partitions closer to their users. Distributing the database can improve control by segregating different portions of the database to different computers, each of which can have its own set of authorized users and permissions.

**FIGURE 13-4**

Types of Distributed Databases

(a) Nonpartitioned, Nonreplicated Alternative

(b) Partitioned, Nonreplicated Alternative

(c) Nonpartitioned, Replicated Alternative

(d) Partitioned, Replicated Alternative

## Challenges of Distributed Databases

Significant challenges must be overcome when distributing a database, and those challenges depend on the type of distributed database and the activity that is allowed. In the case of a fully replicated database, if only one computer is allowed to make updates on one of the copies, then the challenges are not too great. All update activity occurs on that single computer, and copies of that database are periodically sent to the replication sites. The challenge is to ensure that only a logically consistent copy of the database is distributed (no partial or uncommitted transactions, for example) and to ensure that the sites understand that they are processing data that might not be current because the most recent changes at other copies may not yet have reached the local copy.

If multiple computers can make updates to a replicated database, then difficult problems arise. Specifically, if two computers are allowed to process the same row at the same time, they can cause three types of error: they can make inconsistent changes, one computer can delete a row that another computer is updating, or the two computers can make changes that violate uniqueness constraints (for example, two computers inserting data into a table with the same primary key value).

To prevent these problems, some type of record locking is required. Because multiple computers are involved, standard record locking, as discussed in Chapter 9, does not work. Instead, a far more complicated locking scheme, called **distributed two-phase locking**, must be used. The specifics of the scheme are beyond the scope of this discussion; for now, just know that implementing this algorithm is difficult and expensive. If multiple computers can process multiple replicas of a distributed database, then significant problems must be solved.

If the database is partitioned but not replicated [Figure 13-4(b)], then problems will occur if any transaction updates data that span two or more distributed partitions. For example, suppose the CUSTOMER and SALESPERSON tables are placed on a partition on one computer and that the INVOICE, LINE_ITEM, and PART tables are placed on a second computer. Further suppose that when recording a sale all five tables are updated in an atomic transaction. In this case, a transaction must be started on both computers, and it can be allowed to commit on one computer only if it can be allowed to commit on both computers. In this case, distributed two-phase locking also must be used.

If the data are partitioned in such a way that no transaction requires data from multiple partitions, then regular locking will work. However, in this case the databases are actually two separate databases, and some would argue that they should not be considered a distributed database.

If the data are partitioned in such a way that no transaction updates data from multiple partitions but one or more transactions read data from one partition and update data on a second partition, then problems might or might not result with regular locking. If dirty reads are possible, then some form of distributed locking is required in order to avoid them; otherwise, regular locking should work.

If a database is partitioned and at least one of those partitions is replicated, then locking requirements are a combination of those just described. If the replicated portion is updated, if transactions span the partitions, or if dirty reads are possible, then distributed two-phase locking is required; otherwise, regular locking might suffice. There are other ways to address this problem, using *timestamps* and *quorums*. **Quorums** are briefly described now. To increase the consistency of our database, we can request that database reads or writes be propagated to several of the replica sets before indicating to the application that the request has completed successfully. A typical scenario is to ensure that the read or write operation completes on a majority (quorum) of the servers. Increasing the number of replica sets that must respond increases consistency but makes processing slower. The quorum values for read operations can be different from those for write operations.

Distributed processing is complicated and can create substantial problems. Except in the case of replicated, read-only databases, only experienced teams with a substantial budget and significant time to invest should attempt distributed databases. Such databases also require data communications expertise. Distributed databases are not for the faint of heart, but many of their important concepts are being used in today's NoSQL systems.

## Object-Relational Databases

**Object-oriented programming (OOP)** is a methodology for designing and writing computer programs. Today, most new program development is done using OOP techniques. Java, Python, C++, C#, and Visual Basic .NET are object-oriented programming languages (or they at least provide object-oriented features).

**Objects** are data structures that have both **methods**, which are programs that perform some task with the object, and **properties**, which are data items owned and controlled by an object. Objects are organized into classes, and all objects of a given class have the same methods and properties, but each has its own set of data values within those properties. When using an OOP language, the properties of the object are created and stored in main memory. Permanently storing the values of properties of an object in secondary memory (usually disk) is called **object persistence**. Many different techniques have been used for object persistence. One of them is to use some variation of database technology.

Although relational databases can be used for object persistence, using this method requires substantial work on the part of the programmer. The problem is that, in general, object data structures are more complicated than a row of a table. Typically, several, or even many, rows of several different tables are required to store object data. This means the OOP programmer must design a mini-database just to store objects. Usually, many classes of objects are involved in an information system, so many different mini-databases need to be designed and processed. This method is so undesirable that it is seldom used.

In the early 1990s, several vendors developed special-purpose DBMS products for storing object data. These products, which are called **object-oriented DBMSs (OODBMSs)**, never achieved commercial success. The problem was that by the time they were introduced, billions of bytes of data were already stored in relational databases, and very few organizations wanted to convert their data to OODBMS format to be able to use an OODBMS. Consequently, such products failed to capture a large share of the relational data market, but some of these OODBMSs are still available and occupy a niche market for DBMSs (ObjectDB, Objectivity/DB, ObjectStore—notice the pattern).

However, the need for object persistence did not disappear. The current SQL standard defines many object-based features (classes, inheritance, methods, etc.). Some vendors, most notably Oracle, added many of these features and functions to their relational DBMS products to create **object-relational databases**. These features and functions are basically add-ons to a relational DBMS that facilitate object persistence. With these features, object data can be stored more readily than with a purely relational database. However, an object-relational database can still process relational data at the same time.[18]

Although OODBMSs have not achieved commercial success, OOP is here to stay, and modern programming languages are object based. This is important because these are the programming languages that are being used to create the latest technologies that are dealing with Big Data. This is also useful when embedding queries in a programming language: A more straightforward mapping of concepts is possible when the type systems of the programming language and the DBMS match. This reduces what is often called the **impedance mismatch** between the ways the object and relational paradigms manage data structuring and processing. A DBMS with a type system similar to that of the programming language will have an advantage. In addition, many of the complex data structuring concepts developed for object-oriented and object-relational systems are used heavily in NoSQL databases and the languages that support them, so both object-oriented and object-relational systems have played important roles in the evolution of DBMS technology. In fact, one DBMS, SAP's OrientDB, is a multimodel NoSQL DBMS that also supports the object data model.

---

[18]To learn more about object-relational databases, see the Wikipedia article *Object-relational database* at *https://en.wikipedia.org/wiki/Object-relational_database* (accessed September 2020)

# Big Data Processing Models

First, we should note that many enterprise-class relational DBMSs can and do already process large amounts of data quickly. Some are better at it than others, and at some point any of them may need to yield to a Big Data–centric NoSQL DBMS for reasons of performance, but it is important to note that not every Big Data applications requires a NoSQL DBMS.

A NoSQL DBMS is often a distributed, replicated database, as described earlier in this chapter. NoSQL databases also often use some of the post-relational data structuring concepts from object-relational systems. Many also use virtualization and cloud technology, described later in this chapter. Another thing many NoSQL DBMSs have in common is a variety of processing and storage strategies. Two of the most common are MapReduce and Hadoop. It should be noted that any of the four standard kinds of NoSQL DBMS (key-value, column, document, and graph) can use or benefit from these processing and storage strategies in different ways.

## MapReduce

Although NoSQL modeling techniques provide the means to store data in a Big Data system, the data themselves can be analyzed in many ways. One important way of doing this is using the **MapReduce** process. Because Big Data may involve extremely large datasets, it is difficult for one computer to process all of the data by itself. Thus, we deploy a set of clustered computers using a distributed processing system based on the distributed database system concepts discussed previously in this chapter.

The MapReduce process is used to break a large analytical task into smaller tasks, assign (map) each smaller task to a separate computer in the cluster, gather the results of each of those tasks, and combine (reduce) them into the final product of the original task. The term *Map* refers to the work done on each individual computer, and the term *Reduce* refers to combining the individual results into the final result.

A commonly used example of the MapReduce process is counting how many times each word is used in a document. This is illustrated in Figure 13-5, where we can see how the original document is broken into sections and then each section is passed to a separate computer in the cluster for processing by the Map process. The output from each of the Map processes is then passed to one computer, which uses the Reduce process to combine the results from each Map process into the final output, which is the list of words and how many times each appears in the document. Most NoSQL database systems support MapReduce and other, similar processes. In some systems this support is direct, in the sense that MapReduce is a function you can call. In other systems, the MapReduce functionality must be programmed by the DBA or a sophisticated user or programmer.

## Hadoop

Another Apache Software Foundation project that is becoming a fundamental Big Data development platform is the **Hadoop Distributed File System (HDFS)**, which provides standard file services to clustered servers so their file systems can function as one distributed file system that can support large-scale MapReduce or similar processing. Hadoop originated as part of Cassandra, but the Hadoop project has spun off a non-relational data store of its own called HBase and a query language named Pig. The Hadoop project also includes Hive, a data warehouse infrastructure that supports data aggregation (summarization), data analysis, and an SQL-like query language called HiveQL.

Further, all the major DBMS players are supporting Hadoop. Microsoft has deployed a Microsoft Hadoop distribution called HDInsight as part of their Azure cloud[19] service and has teamed up with HP, Dell, and others to offer the Microsoft Analytics Platform System[20]

[19]See https://azure.microsoft.com/en-us/services/hdinsight/ (accessed July 2020)
[20]See www.microsoft.com/en-us/sql-server/analytics-platform-system (accessed July 2020)

**FIGURE 13-5**

The MapReduce Process

(formerly known as SQL Server Parallel Data Warehouse). Oracle has developed the Oracle Big Data Appliance, which uses Hadoop.[21] A search of the Web on the term "MySQL Hadoop" quickly reveals ways to integrate Hadoop and MySQL as well. And, of course, many NoSQL DBMSs can work together with HDFS.

New developments in the Big Data world recognize that some forms of analysis do not easily fit the MapReduce model. Sometimes many chained MapReduce steps are needed to obtain the required result. Each MapReduce step requires reading from and writing to the file system, slowing things down. Recent Hadoop releases support **Apache Tez**, a programming framework based on HDFS that supports a more generalized processing model than MapReduce. Tez processing can be modeled by a directed acyclic graph (a process-flow model that does not have loops in it). Figure 13-6 gives an example. A graph data structure is created to direct Tez processing. The data are read from HDFS at the start of the process (at the top of the diagram) and written back to HDFS at the end of the process (at the bottom of the diagram). The intermediate steps are performed in memory. Tez is replacing MapReduce in Hadoop's Hive and Pig products.

There are also new products that use the Tez processing model, such as **Apache Spark**, a "unified analytics engine for large-scale data processing" that allows programmers to quickly write data analysis applications in several languages: SQL, Python, Scala, Java, and R—a powerful statistical language. Many machine learning functions are available in Spark's MLlib library. Spark can connect to several types of data sources including Hive, HBase, Cassandra, HDFS, and cloud provider data sources including Amazon's EMR file system and Microsoft's Azure Storage.

---

[21]See www.oracle.com/engineered-systems/big-data-appliance/index.html (accessed July 2020)

**FIGURE 13-6**

Example of Apache Tez
Directed Acyclic Graph

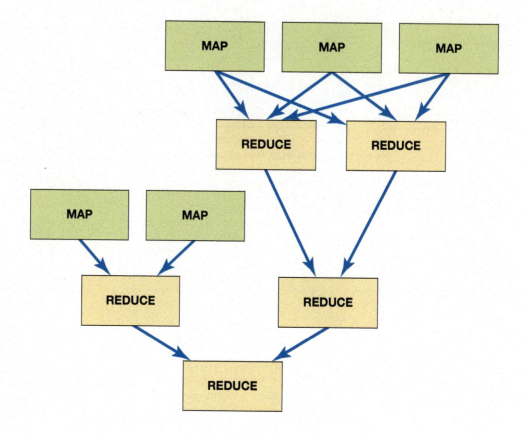

## Non-Relational Database Management Systems

These systems can be divided into four major categories, which are described in the following subsections. Most NoSQL DBMSs, no matter which of the four categories they belong to, have one thing in common: There is often no schema for the database, as there is in a relational database. We often refer to such databases as **schemaless** databases. There are also fewer restrictions on the way data can be structured. Such systems, especially the document variety of NoSQL DBMS, are often based on XML (described in Appendix H and Chapter 11) or JSON (briefly described later in this chapter and in more detail in online Chapter 10D).

These systems are also often called **semistructured databases** or **unstructured databases** (depending on the level of structuring available) as opposed to the highly structured relational data model. For example, a STUDENT relation in a relational DBMS is highly structured: All rows have the same number of columns with the same column names and column data types, and every column value is a single value (first normal form). Some column family DBMSs are highly structured, like a traditional relational database; others more resemble document databases, which are semistructured. (There is structure to the data, but the structuring requirements are much more flexible than those of relations, as we will illustrate in detail later.) At the far end of the spectrum from relations is unstructured data, which is found in key-value databases or text databases.

The first three types of NoSQL systems (key-value, document, and column family) can store "aggregates." This is also true to some extent of some graph-based NoSQL DBMSs. By **aggregates** we mean more complex data structures than a simple row in a relational table, as aggregates can represent composite data (e.g., an address consists of street, city, and country data items) as well as lists (e.g., a set of phone numbers for a customer) that would normally be represented in separate relational tables to store 1:N or 1:1 relationships. Thus, we have a collection of data items that are treated as a unit. Aggregate data can be described using the data modeling languages XML and JSON. In relational databases, which are designed for consistency, there is support for "atomic" transactions that require all updates to complete successfully before the data are committed to the database (see Chapter 9). For aggregate NoSQL databases, we often have to think of "transactions" in a different way. Although operations on a single aggregate are atomic, there is usually not built-in support for operations across more than one aggregate data object. Thus, the design of the aggregates and the application itself become important considerations when consistency is a goal.

JSON, which is used in several document databases, has some similarities to XML, but there is no notion of any schema external to the data. A document ("object" in JSON terminology) consists of a set of (field, value) pairs. Values can be simple values (strings or numbers) or other objects. Values can also be arrays of values or objects. Here is a JSON representation for two documents containing student data:

```
{

    id: "student1",
    lastName: "Smith",
    firstName: "John",
    majors: ["History", "Computer Science"]
}
{

    id: "student2",
    firstName: "Mary",
    minor: "English",
    majors: ["Math"],
    GPA: 3.2

}
```

As you can see, the number, order, types, and (in some systems) names of columns are less restricted in JSON or XML; in addition, fields can be multivalued, such as the *majors* field above. Note that the second student has some fields the first does not, and vice versa. These features, available using XML and JSON, are common among NoSQL DBMSs. The data in the preceding example can be stored, in different ways, in each of the four kinds of non-relational DBMSs described later.

## Key-Value Databases

Key-value databases use a pairing of a simple key and its associated value. Each key (similar to a relational DBMS primary key) appears only once in each database. An example key-value DBMS is **DynamoDB**, which was developed by Amazon.com. Another key-value database is **MemcacheDB**. Apache **Cassandra** is typically classified as a column family database, though it is built on Amazon's DynamoDB and Google's Bigtable, so it has some features of key-value databases as well.[22]

A key-value database is extremely simple and allows for easy distribution of the key-value pairs in a networked cluster. Note that the value can be anything: a string, a large binary object, a list of things, a JSON object, and so on. Key-value databases are ideal for large amounts of data that need fast storage and retrieval of simple (small or large) objects but do not need the full complexity of SQL queries, since the DBMS is unaware of the internal structures within the value object. Thus, queries cannot be based on internal fields. The basic operations available to query a key value database are:

- **get (key):** Retrieves the value associated with a key
- **set (key, value):** Creates or updates a key-value pair
- **delete (key):** Removes a key-value pair

[22]See the Wikipedia article *Apache_Cassandra* (*https://en.wikipedia.org/wiki/Apache_Cassandra* (accessed July 2020)) and the Apache Cassandra Web site.

These commands are typically issued from within a program in some programming language or from a command-line interface in some systems. Here are some sample data that might appear in a typical key-value database that stores information about email accounts and the last computer IP address from which those accounts were accessed:

```
("joe@somewhere.com", "172.13.233.1")
("mary@nowhere.com", "177.10.254.1")
```

The email addresses are the *keys* and the IP addresses are the *values*. Remember that the values can be much more complex or larger, but in a key-value database, any structure within the values must be managed by the application after the key value database retrieves the value.

## Document Databases

Document databases store data according to a document-oriented format, the two most popular of which are **XML (eXtensible Markup Language)**, which we introduced in Chapter 11 and discuss in detail in Appendix H, and **JSON (Java Script Object Notation)**. Two document DBMS examples are Couchbase Server and ArangoDB, which use JSON storage. Document databases, using ArangoDB as a case study, are described in more detail in online Chapter 10D. MongoDB is another popular document database; it uses BSON (Binary JSON) storage, which is a binary-encoded version of JSON documents, with a few additional data types available.

There is a trend for non-relational database systems to support more than one NoSQL category: Amazon's DynamoDB supports both key-value and document data storage; ArangoDB and Microsoft's Azure Cosmos DB support key-value, document, and graph data models. Even some relational DBMSs like MySQL support JSON as a data type and have some document storage and query capabilities.

In a document database, documents (e.g. JSON objects) are usually stored within a set. (In ArangoDB and MongoDB, this is called a **collection**.) This is roughly equivalent to the idea of a relational database as a set of relations, each of which is a set of rows. A collection of documents is similar to a relational table. In a document database, of course, there is usually no notion of a schema, so the documents within a collection can be completely heterogeneous. More typically, though, the documents in a collection will be similar in structure to facilitate storage and querying.

A document database is designed to provide fast processing of queries over a single large collection of similar documents. The data construction and querying facilities of most document DBMSs exist to facilitate the processing of such queries. Queries linking documents from multiple collections (analogous to joins in the relational model) are not directly supported in many document database query languages. (ArangoDB is an exception.) Some would argue that if you have a database that will require a lot of join queries, you should keep it in a relational DBMS instead of a document DBMS. Nevertheless, there will be times in a document database when querying multiple collections is required, so there is always some way to do this, either through the query language (as in ArangoDB) or via a programming language.

As with key-value databases, interaction with the database can be done either from within a program written in a programming language like Java or Python or via a command-line environment (and, in some systems, a graphical environment). In addition, most document-based NoSQL DBMSs provide SQL-like query languages. (ArangoDB's AQL is described in detail in online Chapter 10D). Typical commands available either via the command-line or via embedding in a programming language (using a generic syntax) include:

- **insert (doc, collection):** put document "doc" into the collection called "collection"
- **update (collection, doc_specifier, update_action):** within "collection," update all documents matching the "doc_specifier" (e.g., all students with last name 'Smith'). The "update_action" can alter the values of multiple fields within each document.

- **delete (collection, doc_specifier):** removes all documents from "collection" that match the "doc_specifier"
- **find (collection, doc_specifier):** retrieves all documents in "collection" matching the "doc_specifier"

In addition, most document databases provide some level of built-in support for MapReduce and other aggregation tasks. The preceding four basic document database commands are often referred to as the **CRUD (Create, Read, Update, Delete)** commands. (*Create* and *insert* are synonymous in this context, as are *read* and *find*.) Most document databases provide some version of these commands.

Here is some sample data, more complicated than that presented earlier, that might appear in a document database regarding student and advisor information. The first document would be stored in a collection of similar "Advisor" documents, and the second would be stored in a collection of similar "Student" documents. The curly braces indicate a document (a set of (field, value) pairs), and the square brackets indicate an array. The syntax is standard JSON syntax:

```
{

    id: "Advisor1",
    name: "Shire, Robert",
    dept: "History",
    yearHired: 1993

}

{

    id: 555667777,
    name: "Tierney, Doris",
    majors: ["Music", "Spanish"],
    addresses: [
        {
        street: "14510 NE 4th Street",
        city: "Bellevue",
        state: "WA",
        zip: "98005"
        },
        {
        street: "335 Aloha Street",
        city: "Seattle",
        state: "WA",
        zip: "98109"
        }
        ],
    favoritePet:
        {
            name: "Tiger",
            species: "cat"
        },
    advisorID: "Advisor1"

}
```

The "id" field is the globally unique key identifying the document within the database. (Different systems use the field slightly differently, of course, so always read the documentation carefully.) The advisor document is straightforward. The student has two majors (each of which is simple string) and two addresses (each of which is itself a document embedded within the student's "addresses" field.) The student's "advisorID" field contains the identifier for the student's advisor, analogous to a foreign key in a relational database. The "favoritePet" field introduces the ability of JSON to store a single document within another document (versus an array of documents within another document). Note that many of these features (document references, embedded documents, arrays, lack of a required schema) are unavailable in a simple key-value database. As you can see, document databases may be a good choice when your data have some structure, but that structure may be complex or inconsistent among the various documents. And, unlike key-value databases, document databases support queries based on the internal structure of the document.

The definition of JSON's structuring abilities is very concise and can be found at the JSON.org web site (http://json.org). In JSON, there are two data structuring concepts: the object (which we will typically refer to as a document) and the array.

An object, as in the examples shown earlier, is delimited by { and }, and it consists of a comma-separated list of fieldName:value pairs. An array is delimited by [ and ], and it consists of a comma-separated list of values (no field names). The real power of JSON, however, lies in the definition of "value." A value can be:

- A simple, single data point (string, number, Boolean, or null)
- An object (document)
- An array of values

This is a recursive definition, since values are defined partially in terms of other values. This means that the structure of data can be arbitrarily complex, nested to as many levels of structuring as is natural for the application, as determined by the DBA. JSON itself simply describes the structure of documents. Recall, however, that a typical JSON-based document database consists of a set of collections, and each of those collections contains documents that follow the JSON standard just described.

Increasingly, support for queries in an SQL-like query language is being provided at a larger scale in document databases. Some of these languages have many similarities to SQL (for example, ArangoDB's **AQL (ArangoDB Query Language)**), while others may look entirely different (such as MongoDB's query language, whose queries are actually written in a JSON-like format). These document database query languages support queries based on the internal structure of the documents. There is no standard ad-hoc query language yet for document databases, but see online Chapter 10D for an introduction to AQL, which contains most of the common features in some form.

## Column Family Databases

The basis for much of the development of column family (also known as "column-oriented" or simply "column") databases was a structured storage mechanism developed by Google named **Bigtable**, and column family databases are now widely available, with a good example being the Apache Software Foundation's Cassandra project. Facebook did the original development work on Cassandra and then turned it over to the open source development community in 2008.

A column family database example is shown in Figure 13-7. The column family database storage equivalent of a relational DBMS (RDBMS) table has a very different construction. Although similar terms are used, they do *not* mean the same thing that they mean in a relational DBMS.

The smallest unit of storage is called a **column**, but it is really the equivalent of an RDBMS table cell (the intersection of an RDMBS row and column). A column consists of three elements: the *column name*, the *column value* or datum, and a *timestamp* to record when the value was stored in the column. This is shown in Figure 13-7(a) by the LastName column, which stores the LastName value Able.

Columns can be grouped into sets referred to as **super columns**. This is shown in Figure 13-7(b) by the CustomerName super column, which consists of a FirstName column and a LastName column and which stores the CustomerName value Ralph Able.

Columns and super columns are grouped to create column families, which are the column family database storage equivalent of RDBMS tables, as they are typically stored together. In a column family, we have rows of grouped columns, and each row has a **RowKey**, which is similar to the primary key used in an RDBMS table. However, unlike an RDBMS table, a row in a column family does not have to have the same number of columns as another row in the same column family (i.e., in some column family DBMSs the data may be semistructured). This is illustrated in Figure 13-7(c) by the Customer column family, which consists of three rows of data on customers.

Figure 13-7(c) clearly illustrates the difference between structured storage column families and RDBMS tables: Column families can have variable columns and data stored in each row in a way that is impossible in an RDBMS table. This storage column structure is definitely *not* in 1NF as defined in Chapter 3, let alone BCNF! For example, note that the first row has no Phone or City columns, while the third row not only has no FirstName, Phone, or City columns but also contains an EmailAddress column that does not exist in the other rows.

**FIGURE 13-7**

A Column Family Database Storage System

| Name: LastName |
| Value: Able |
| Timestamp: 40324081235 |

**(a) A Column**

| Super Column Name: | CustomerName | |
| --- | --- | --- |
| Super Column Values: | Name: FirstName | Name: LastName |
| | Value: Ralph | Value: Able |
| | Timestamp: 40324081235 | Timestamp: 40324081235 |

**(b) A Super Column**

| Column Family Name: | Customer | | | |
| --- | --- | --- | --- | --- |
| RowKey001 | Name: FirstName | Name: LastName | | |
| | Value: Ralph | Value: Able | | |
| | Timestamp: 40324081235 | Timestamp: 40324081235 | | |
| RowKey002 | Name: FirstName | Name: LastName | Name: Phone | Name: City |
| | Value: Nancy | Value: Jacobs | Value: 817-871-8123 | Value: Fort Worth |
| | Timestamp: 40335091055 | Timestamp: 40335091055 | Timestamp: 40335091055 | Timestamp: 40335091055 |
| RowKey003 | Name: LastName | Name: EmailAddress | | |
| | Value: Baker | Value: Susan.Baker@elsewhere.com | | |
| | Timestamp: 40340103518 | Timestamp: 40340103518 | | |

**(c) A Column Family**

(continued)

| Super Column Family Name: | Customer | | | |
|---|---|---|---|---|
| **Rowkey001** | Customer Name | | CustomerPhone | |
| | Name: FirstName | Name: LastName | Name: Areacode | Name: PhoneNumber |
| | Value: Ralph | Value: Able | Value: 210 | Value: 281–7987 |
| | Timestamp: 40324081235 | Timestamp: 40324081235 | Timestamp: 40335091055 | Timestamp: 40335091055 |
| **Rowkey002** | Customer Name | | Customer Phone | |
| | Name: FirstName | Name: LastName | Name: Areacode | Name: PhoneNumber |
| | Value: Nancy | Value: Jacobs | Value: 817 | Value: 871–8123 |
| | Timestamp: 40335091055 | Timestamp: 40335091055 | Timestamp: 40335091055 | Timestamp: 40335091055 |
| **Rowkey003** | Customer Name | | Customer Phone | |
| | Name: FirstName | Name: LastName | Name: Areacode | Name: PhoneNumber |
| | Value: Susan | Value: Baker | Value: 210 | Value: 281–7876 |
| | Timestamp: 40340103518 | Timestamp: 40340103518 | Timestamp: 40340103518 | Timestamp: 40340103518 |

**(d) A Super Column Family**

**FIGURE 13-7**

Continued

All the column families are contained in a **keyspace**, which provides the set of unique RowKey values that can be used in the data store. RowKey values from the keyspace are shown being used in Figure 13-7 to identify each row in a column family. While this structure may seem odd at first, in practice it allows for great flexibility because columns to contain new data may be introduced at any time without modifying an existing table structure or schema. It is up to the application, however, to handle the possibly different row structures.

As shown in Figure 13-7(d), a **super column family** is similar to a column family but uses super columns (or a combination of columns and super columns) instead of columns. A super column is a named collection of related columns. The Cassandra DBMS supports super columns.

One of the main purposes of column family databases is to improve the performance of some queries. In particular, queries that are based on retrieving just a small number of columns of data from a table (or column family) may in some cases be more efficient. This is explored more in the exercises. Querying column family databases is very similar, on the surface, to querying relational tables in SQL. Apache Cassandra, for example, has an SQL-like language called CQL to manipulate column families, and many queries in CQL have exact counterparts in SQL. Of course, there are some important differences, but the basic structure of the languages is very similar to SQL (much more so than with document query languages). Other column family DBMSs support SQL directly as their main query language.

Of course, there is more to column family database storage than discussed here, but now you should have an understanding of the basic principles of column family databases.

### Graph Databases

Based on mathematical graph theory, graph databases are composed of three elements:

1. Nodes
2. Properties
3. Edges

An example graph DBMS is **Neo4j**. ArangoDB, used as the basis of online Chapter 10D as an example of a NoSQL document database, is also a graph DBMS. (It is multimodel.)

**Nodes** are equivalent to entities in E-R data modeling and tables (or relations) in database design. They represent the things that we want to keep track of or about which we want to store data.

Properties are equivalent to attributes in E-R data modeling and columns (or fields) in database design. They represent the data items that we want to store for each node.

**Edges** are similar to but not identical to the relationships in E-R data models and database designs. They are similar because they connect nodes as relationships connect entities, but they are different because they also store data. Edges can also have a "direction."

Figure 13-8 shows an abstract representation of a graph database based on part of the HSD database used in Chapters 7 and 12. Note that the some of the data in the HSD SEMINAR, CUSTOMER, and SEMINAR_CUSTOMER tables is replicated in this database. CUSTOMER data are here, SEMINAR data are here, and the data about what customer attended which seminar are also here. However, the graph database adds some additional data. First, the edges labeled *Attendees* form a group named Attendees: While this grouping could be obtained by an SQL query in a relational database, it is a built-in component of the graph database. Similarly, the edge with ID 3001 and labeled *knows* adds entirely new data to the dataset—additional data about the relationships between customers that does not exist in the original HSD database design.

Clearly, the graph database model can easily extend our original data model and provide additional pathways between nodes.

**FIGURE 13-8**

A Partial HSD Graph Database

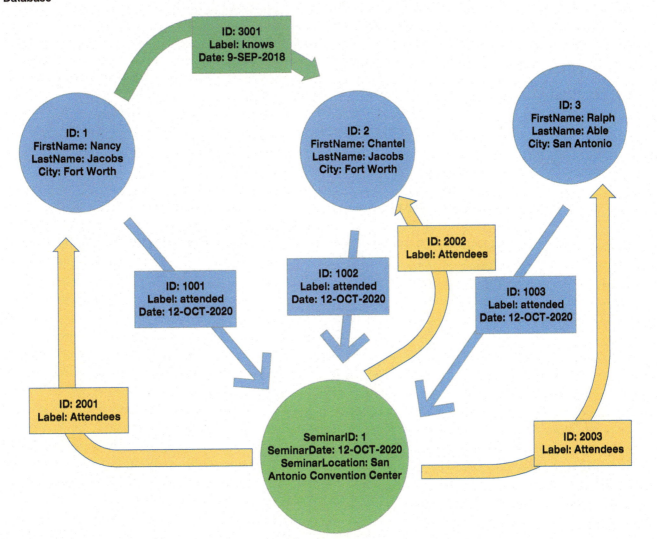

As a more concrete example, consider adding more data about which HSD customers know which other HSD customers. Figure 13-8 has one example of this, but now we will add more, show its representation in ArangoDB (using that system's graph database features), and demonstrate a simple graph-based query on the data. Figure 13-9 shows some of the HSD customers and some data about who knows whom, in an ArangoDB screenshot. Note that for this example we are assuming the "know" relationship is not necessarily symmetric: I can know who someone is without them knowing who I am. In Figure 13-9, we see that Ralph Able knows who Susan Baker and Nancy Jacobs are, Nancy Jacobs knows who Chantel Jacobs is, and so on. The edges are labeled with the date the customer began to know the other customer.

Of course, we can run queries on graph databases. Since the standard operations vary widely among graph DBMSs (even more so than in key-value and document databases), we will consider an example. The following AQL query (AQL, the ArangoDB Query Language, is covered in more detail in online Chapter 10D) will give us the emails of all people who are known to Ralph Able or known to someone who is known to him:

```
FOR Cust IN 1..2 OUTBOUND

    "CUSTOMERS/RalphAble" GRAPH "KnowsGraph"

    RETURN DISTINCT Cust.EmailAddress
```

This query can be interpreted as follows: Starting with customer Ralph Able and following the "Knows" edges either 1 or 2 steps, return the email addresses of every customer encountered. The DISTINCT ensures that we do not return Chantel Jacobs twice, as she is known (indirectly) to Ralph Able in two different ways, as can be seen in Figure 13-9. The result of this query in JSON format is:

```
[ "Nancy.Jacobs@somewhere.com",

"Chantel.Jacobs@somewhere.com",

"Susan.Baker@elsewhere.com" ]
```

**FIGURE 13-9**

Some HSD Graph Data in
ArangoDB

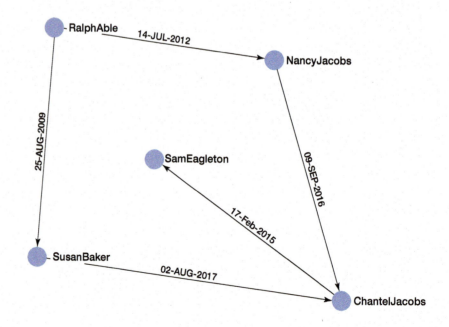

# Virtualization

**Virtualization** is using hardware and software to simulate another hardware resource. For example, we can provide the illusion of additional virtual memory by storing small chunks of memory called pages on disk drives and moving them back and forth between the real (physical) memory and disk. The CPU and the operating system assist in providing this resource to application programs that run as if they had their own copy of the full set of memory that the CPU architecture provides.

A major development in computing occurred when systems administrators realized that the hardware resources (CPU, memory, input/output from/to disk storage) were often underutilized on most servers in a data center. For example, as shown in Figure 13-10, the CPU is not very busy most of the time and there may be a lot of unused memory. This realization led to the idea of combining several servers into one larger server. It is cheaper and easier to manage multiple server environments (including the operating system, libraries, and applications) if they are consolidated into a larger server with a higher utilization. This can also conserve data center space, electricity, air conditioning, hardware maintenance, and software licensing costs.

But how can this be done? The answer is to have one physical computer host one or more virtual computers, more commonly known as **virtual machines**. To do this, the actual computer hardware, now called the **host machine**, runs a special program known as a **virtual machine manager** or **hypervisor**. The hypervisor creates and manages the virtual machines and controls the interaction between each virtual machine and the physical hardware. For example, if a virtual machine is allocated 2 GB of main memory for its use, the hypervisor is responsible for making sure the actual physical memory is allocated and available to the virtual machine. The virtual machines are unaware that they are sharing a physical computer with other virtual machines. The systems administrator can interact with the hypervisor to start new virtual machine instances, shut them down, or adjust virtual

**FIGURE 13-10**

The Underutilization of Computer Resources

machine configurations. Most of the screenshot and other database work for this book was done on a collection of virtual machines.

There are two basic ways to implement hypervisors. The first is the "bare metal," or type 1 hypervisor shown in Figure 13-11(a). These are loaded into memory, or "booted," before any other programs. Thus, the hypervisor has direct control over the hardware and provides the illusion to virtual machines that they are running on the physical hardware. Type 1 hypervisors are typically used in large data centers. Type 2, or "hosted," hypervisors, as shown in Figure 13-11(b), are typically used by students and other computer users to run multiple operating systems as regular applications on their desktop or laptop computer. If you own a Mac, you know that Microsoft Access is not available on Apple's Mac OS. However, you can use a type 2 hypervisor to load Windows as another application on your Mac and use the Windows version of Office on your Mac by using it within the Windows virtual machine. Another common scenario is to be able to boot Linux as an application on a Windows machine. Figure 13-11 illustrates the basic differences between type 1 and type 2 hypervisors. Both type 1 and type 2 hypervisors can run different operating systems as "guest" operating systems in virtual machines.

Type 1 hypervisor products include VMware's vSphere/ESXi, the open source KVM and Xen hypervisors, Red Hat's Enterprise Virtualization, and Microsoft's Hyper-V. Type 2 hypervisors include VMware's Player, Fusion, and Workstation products; Oracle's Virtual Box; and Parallels' Desktop for Mac. Some type 2 products are designed to run on a PC; others run on Macs.

Another form of virtualization, known as **containerization**, shown in Figure 13-11(c), is becoming more popular and is used to support the rapid and seamless deployment of new software releases. Rather than simulating an entire machine, containerization simulates separate operating system environments—the program libraries, filesystems, and configuration files—needed to run applications. This approach to virtualization is sometimes called "operating system-level virtualization."

A "Container Engine" manages the execution of several container instances. Note that the Container Engine itself runs on a single copy of an operating system. Container instances managed by the same engine share some of the resources of the underlying operating system. Thus, all container instances must use the same underlying operating system. Containers were originally developed for Unix systems but are now available on Windows as well.

**FIGURE 13-11**

Type 1 and Type 2 Hypervisors Versus Containers

(a) Type 1 Hypervisor

**(b)** Type 2 Hypervisor

**(c)** Container Architecture

**FIGURE 13-11**
Continued

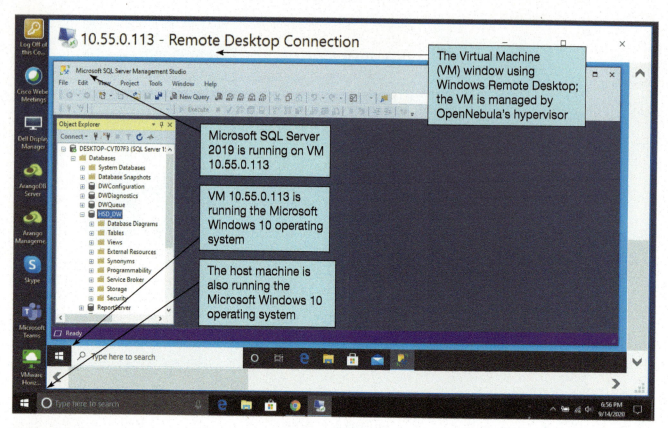

**FIGURE 13-12**

Microsoft SQL Server 2019
Running In a Microsoft
Windows 10 Virtual Machine

Applications are isolated from each other by separate file systems and library versions that the application depends on. Thus, applications that use different versions of software libraries can run on the same host.

A major advantage of container instances is that they are smaller than virtual machine instances, allowing them to be moved from place to place and started up very quickly. Perhaps containers are not quite as reliable as virtual machines in providing execution independence for separate applications, but operating systems are very stable nowadays, and the ease of deploying new containers makes up for this disadvantage in many cases. Although not shown here, running containers in a virtual machine is possible. This is known as "hybrid containerization," where the Container Engine runs on top of an operating system that in turn runs on a hypervisor.

Containerization vendors include Docker, Rancher Labs, Iron, Cloud66, OpenShift, and Kubernetes.

Figure 13-12 shows a desktop computer running Windows 10, within which is a virtual machine accessed using Windows Remote Desktop. This VM, which is managed by OpenNebula's hypervisor, also runs Windows 10. This virtual machine is in turn running Microsoft SQL Server 2019 and has been used to obtain some of the SQL Server 2019 screenshots that appear in this book.

## Cloud Computing

For many years, systems administrators and database administrators knew exactly where their servers (physical or virtual) were located—in a dedicated, secure machine room on the company premises. With the advent of the Internet, companies started offering hosting services on servers (physical or virtual) that were located away from their customers' premises. The term **cloud computing** is somewhat of a misnomer. Although networks are sometimes diagrammed using cloud icons, the important thing to remember is that cloud services are ultimately provided by large data centers. It is possible to reconfigure cloud-based data center resources (servers, storage, and network capacity) dynamically–using software or commands from administrators. This allows customers to expand or contract the data center capacity they lease to meet their current needs. That is why Amazon's cloud service is called EC2–Elastic Compute Cloud.

Advanced virtualization technologies are key to providing cloud services. For example, disk storage is external to servers for maximum flexibility, reliability, and speed. **Storage area networks (SANs)** have dedicated network paths from servers to disk arrays, where several physical disks may be combined together to act as a single larger disk. These **redundant arrays of independent disks (RAID)** can be configured for maximum access speed or for reliability to keep operating even if some disks fail. Other sophisticated virtualization features include server and storage migration. Server migration allows running virtual machines to move from one physical server host to another. Storage migration allows active files to be moved from one set of disks to another, and even to other file servers, all without noticeable delays or downtime, and all invisibly to the end users. One way to visualize the cloud is shown in Figure 13-13. Our Internet customers see us by our presentation at our company's Web site and related services on the Internet at *www.ourcompany.com*. They don't care whether the servers providing the services (e.g., being able to view and buy our products) are located physically at our company or elsewhere "in the cloud" as long as the services work reliably.

There are three basic ways to lease cloud services. The simplest is **software as a service (SaaS)**, where access to specific software applications is provided. An example of this type of service is Salesforce.com. Their customer relationship management (CRM) application is hosted on Salesforce's servers and accessed by customers remotely. The software and user data are also maintained by Salesforce.com. Companies wishing to develop their own software and deploy it over the Web can choose **platform as a service (PaaS)**, where operating systems, software development tools, and system program libraries are provided for customers to add their applications to. Lastly, some companies may wish to lease only the physical hardware servers, disk storage, and network devices and manage their own software environment completely using **infrastructure as a service (IaaS)**.

**FIGURE 13-13**

**The Cloud Computing Environment**

Hosting services in the cloud has become an established and lucrative business, and it continues to grow. Hosting companies range from Web site hosting companies such as eNom, HostMonster, and Yahoo! Small Business to companies that offer complete business support packages such as Microsoft Office 365 and Google Business Solutions, to companies that provide various components such as complete virtual servers, file storage, DBMS services, and much more. Oracle has been encouraging cloud-based use of its software by releasing new versions of Oracle Database for cloud use several months before downloads of the software become available.

In this last category, significant players include Microsoft with **Microsoft Azure** (*http://azure.microsoft.com/en-us/*) and Amazon.com with **Amazon Web Services (AWS)** (*http://aws.amazon.com/*). Of course there are others, such as Oracle and Google, but these two provide a good starting point. Windows Azure, like any Microsoft product, is Microsoft centric and not currently as expansive in its product offerings as AWS, but it is becoming more flexible. Azure has both relational and non-relational DBMS services, along with Hadoop cluster processing capabilities, as described earlier in this chapter. The next section includes several examples of using Microsoft Azure to work with databases. Of particular interest in AWS are the **EC2 service**, which provides complete virtual servers; the **DynamoDB database service,** which provides a key-value NoSQL data store; and the **Relational DBMS Service (RDS)**, which provides online instances of Microsoft SQL Server, Oracle Database, and MySQL database services, among others. AWS can also provide Hadoop servers for Big Data analysis. Free trial accounts are available on both Azure and AWS, providing an excellent way to continue learning about cloud computing. The AWS Free Tier has limited free services available for 12 months. It is fairly easy to set up an account on AWS, select an operating system such as Linux, and use Web components such as PHP and MySQL to provide hosted Web applications.

At this point we will use RDS to illustrate how we can use online database services to do the things we have been doing in this book. We have created one RDS instance of SQL Server 2019 Express (the latest version available at AWS as of this writing) named *sv-aws-db*. Although hosted by AWS, if we connect to this database instance using SQL Server Management Studio, it will appear to us just like any other SQL Server instance. Figure 13-14 illustrates

**FIGURE 13-14**

The SV-AWS-DB SQL Server 2019 DB Instance in Locally Run SQL Server Management Studio

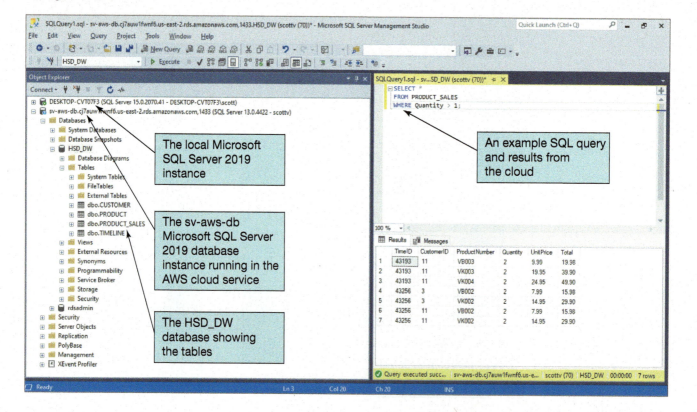

this by showing the *sv-aws-db* database instance in Microsoft SQL Server Management Studio. We have created and populated the HSD_DW database as described in Chapter 12 and have run an example query. Everything we see here is exactly the same as if the database was located on our desktop or local server. This shows how easy it is to use computing resources hosted "in the cloud."

Finally, note that cloud and virtualization technology can be (but need not be) used together. For example, the VM running in Figure 13-12 was created and hosted by a Nebula hypervisor operating in the cloud, but it is certainly possible to use virtualization technology in a local setting. There is no doubt that we will see more and more use of cloud computing.

## Using a Cloud Database Management System

Now it is time to put your cloud knowledge to work. In this section, you will learn how to create an account on the Microsoft Azure cloud service (which we will, like Microsoft, sometimes refer to simply as Azure) and then migrate an existing relational database from your local computer to the Azure cloud. We will then create an SQL database on Azure SQL Database using scripts. Lastly, we will create a simple document database using Azure Cosmos DB and run a MongoDB-style query on it. As you perform the steps, keep in mind the functions that the various components are performing. These components include: the local SQL Server database server, the SQL Server Management Studio that runs on your local computer and can connect to local and remote database servers, the remote database SQL Server, and the Azure Portal accessed using a browser that we use to set up and configure our cloud services.

This section is not a detailed how-to guide but rather a conceptual overview (a mini-tour) of how all the components on a local computer interact with the Azure cloud portal and services on Azure to create and query a database. The author installed on one of his virtual machines both SQL Server and the SSMS (Microsoft SQL Server Management Studio) client software. SSMS functions as the graphical frontend to SQL Server and to the SQL Database functionality on Azure. Microsoft offers a free account on Azure. The SQL Database server on Azure is very similar to but not exactly the same as SQL Server. Some of the advanced features of SQL Server are not supported on Azure's SQL Database, but for our purposes they are the same.

The following sections assume you have performed the actions in Chapter 10A, "Getting Started with Microsoft SQL Server 2019," to install SQL Server 2019 and SSMS. We further assume you have created the Heather Sweeney Designs (HSD) database in SQL Server.

### Connecting to Microsoft Azure

In this section we briefly describe how to obtain an account on Azure and set up an empty database to get an idea of what information is typically required by cloud providers to set up an account. Using a Web browser, we connect to the Azure home page at *http://azure.microsoft.com/en-us/free*. As shown in Figure 13-15, we selected the **Start Free** button. In the future, after we create our account, we will use the **MY ACCOUNT** button on the top right to log in to manage our Azure services or to check our billing status.

The sign-up process is outlined here, but it may change at Microsoft's discretion.

1.  A **Sign in** dialog box requesting your account information is displayed. Select "No account? Create one!" In the **Create account** dialog box, enter your email account and then click the **Next** button to begin the account setup process. In the **Create a Password** dialog box, create a password and click **Next**.
2.  After gathering some more personal information, Microsoft will then send a verification code to your email address to confirm that you own the email account. In the **Verify Email** dialog box, enter the numeric code that was sent to you, then click **Next**.

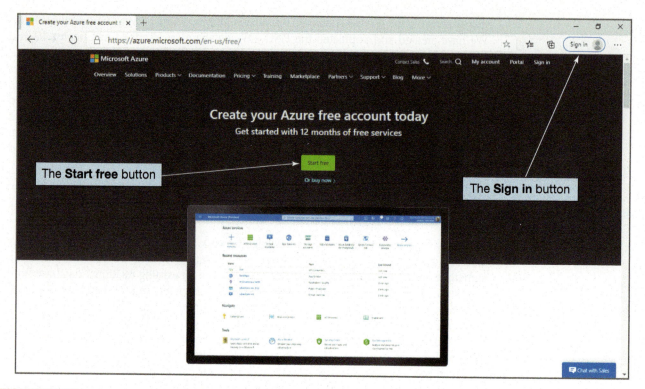

**FIGURE 13-15**

Create Your Free Azure
Account

3. To ensure that a real person is creating the account (and not a programmed "bot"), enter the characters displayed in the image on the **Create account** dialog box and click **Next**.

4. The **Try Azure for free** screen, where you enter some information such as your name and phone number, appears. Enter the information then click **Next**. After clicking **Text me**, you will receive a text message with a verification number that you then enter in an identity verification by phone dialog box. Click the **Verify code** button.

5. The **identity verification by card** dialog box asks for your credit card information as another way to confirm your identity. Note that you will not be charged unless you explicitly request to be charged later. The card is used for identification and verification only at this stage. Fill in the information then click the **Next** button. Finish the sign-up process by checking the first **Agreement** box at the bottom of the screen and clicking **Sign up**. Your account will be set up, and you will get the Welcome to Microsoft Azure screen, where you can start the demonstration tour or get started. After your trial period is up, you may elect to continue your Azure account under a "pay as you go" plan.

### Creating a New SQL Database

Now that you have an account, you can always go directly to the main azure portal (access) page, portal.azure.com. Sign in, then you will see the main Azure services screen as shown in Figure 13-16. As you can see, Azure has a rich selection of services, including virtual machines, data storage, SQL databases, and NoSQL database servers (**Azure Cosmos DB**, which we will use later in this chapter). We can now create and configure a new relational database in Azure by clicking the **SQL databases** button and then selecting the **Create SQL Database** button in the next screen (not shown) to bring us to the screen shown in Figure 13-17.

We need to set up a resource group, create a new database server, and create our administrator login and password. In the **Resource group** section, click **Create new** to create a new resource group (a "resource group" contains memory, disk space, and CPU cycles that will be used to store and process this, and possibly other, databases). Choose any name you

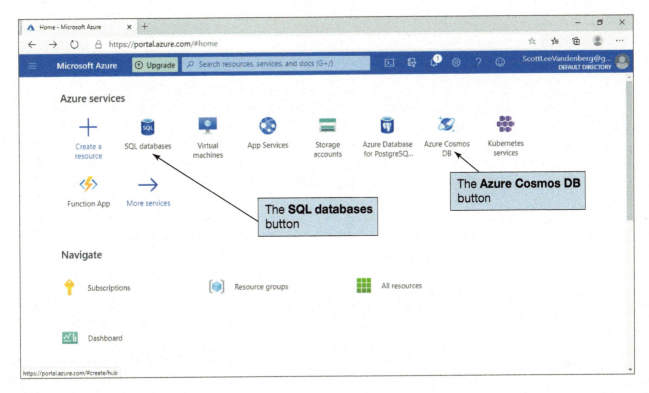

**FIGURE 13-16**

**The Microsoft Azure Services Screen**

like for the resource group (we chose scott-rg). Scroll down to see the rest of the **Create SQL Database** window, as seen in Figure 13-18. Enter the name "test" for the database name then click **Create new** to create a new server within the resource group. We enter our new Server name, administrator login information, and the server location in the **New server** pane, as shown on the right side of Figure 13-18. It is a good idea to record your login and password somewhere! When using cloud services, it is also a good idea to pick the geographic location of the cloud server nearest you to minimize network transmission time.

**FIGURE 13-17**

**The Create SQL Database Screen, Part I**

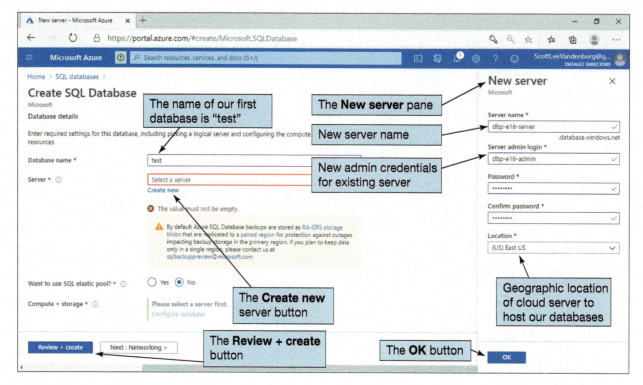

**FIGURE 13-18**

**The Create SQL Database Screen, Part II**

To complete the process, we click the **OK** button in the bottom right to configure the new server and to bring us back to the **SQL database** screen. Click the **Review + create** button to continue the process, then click the **Create** button in the next window.

The "Your deployment is complete" message briefly appears, as shown in Figure 13-19. Click the **Go to resource** button and you will see all the relevant information for the "test"

**FIGURE 13-19**

**The Deployment Complete Screen**

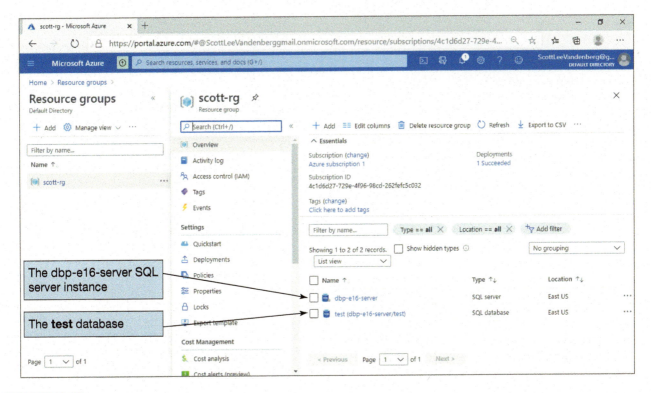

**FIGURE 13-20**

The New Resource Group in Azure

database you have just created. The next step is to set up a "Firewall rule" that will allow our computer's Internet IP address to connect to the remote database server on Azure.

### Setting Up Our Database Server Firewall Rules

After we establish our administrator account and a blank database, we need to configure our Azure firewall to allow only certain computers (IP addresses) to access our databases. Security is very important in cloud computing. From the Portal Menu (see Figure 13-19), select the **Resource groups** button and then our **resource group name** (in this example, it is scott-rg). Our server instance and test database are listed as members of our resource group, as shown in Figure 13-20. We select the SQL server instance (in this example, dbp-e16-server) to see the SQL database server details screen in Figure 13-21 and then select the **Show firewall settings** command near the top right of the pane.

In the **Firewalls and virtual networks** screen as shown in Figure 13-22, our IP address will appear as a computer that is allowed access to all the databases in the server (the author's own IP address is hidden in the figure for security reasons). If you wish to add the IP addresses of other computers that are allowed to access this SQL server, you would add them using the **Add client IP** button. We will not do that now. Note that IP addresses may change if using a wireless Internet connection in public or organizational networks.

Our free Azure account is set up, along with the physical resources needed and a server to contain the database. In the next section, we will mostly be interacting with Azure SQL Server through our local SQL Server Management Studio (SSMS) to migrate the existing Heather Sweeney Designs (HSD) data warehouse database (created in Chapter 12) from our local PC to Azure and to run a query against it. The following sections will use Azure directly to create relational and NoSQL databases.

### Migrating Our Existing Local HSD_DW Database to Azure

We use SSMS as our graphical interface to connect to our local SQL Server database and to our remote SQL databases in the Azure cloud. We start SSMS and connect to our local SQL Server installation first using local windows authentication as shown in Figure 13-23 and then connect to our database server on Azure using the **Connect | Database Engine** command from the Object Explorer window to get the dialog box shown in Figure 13-24.

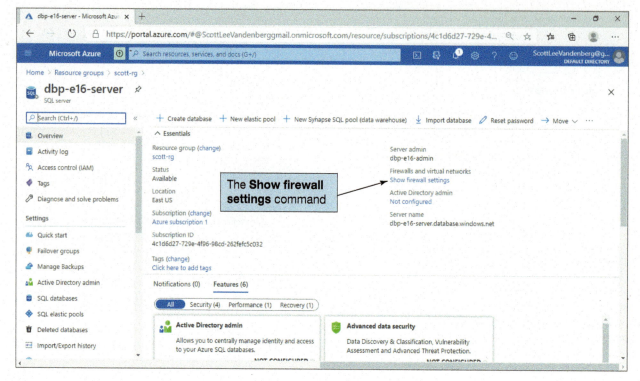

**FIGURE 13-21**

**The SQL Server Details Screen**

We enter the name of our Microsoft Azure server and its administrator login and password and then click on the **Connect** button. The local HSD tables are shown in the Object Explorer pane on the left.

Note that SSMS is now connected to two servers: our local server listed at the top of the Object Explorer pane in Figure 13-24 and the remote dbp-e16-server.database.windows.net server in the Azure data center as shown in Figure 13-25.

**FIGURE 13-22**

**The Server Firewalls and Virtual Networks Screen**

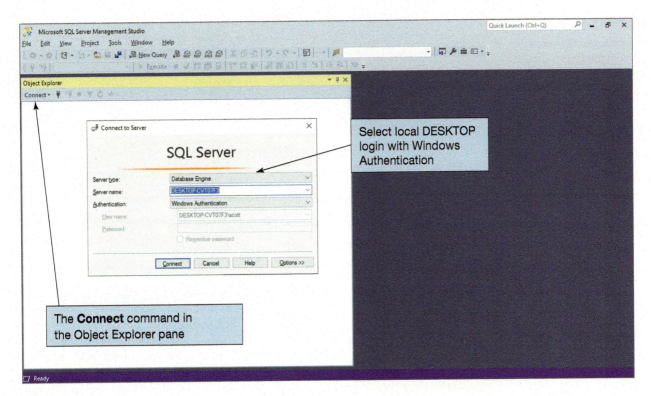

**FIGURE 13-23**

Connect to Local SQL
Database Server Using
SSMS

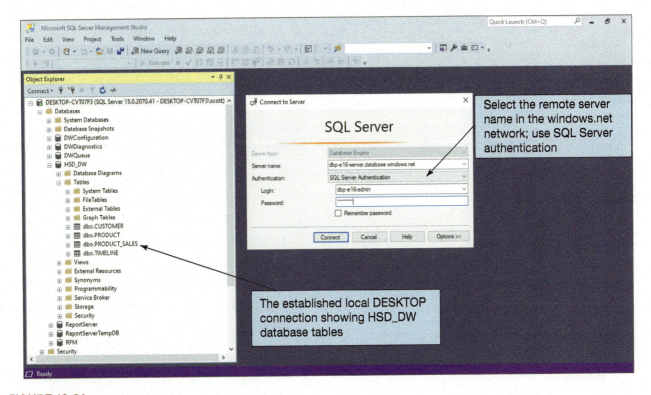

**FIGURE 13-24**

Connect to Remote Azure
Database Server Using
SSMS

**FIGURE 13-25**

Remote Azure Database
Server in the Object Explorer
Pane of SSMS

We are still connected to the local
SQL Server instance also

The remote server connection

Now, in the Object Explorer pane of SSMS, we right-click the local HSD_DW
database to show the submenu and then select **Tasks | Deploy Database to Microsoft
Azure SQL Database** command, as shown in Figure 13-26. The **Deploy Database
Introduction** screen appears, as shown in Figure 13-27, and we click the **Next** button to
start the process.

In the **Deployment Settings** page as shown in Figure 13-28, the **Connect...** button
brings up the **SQL Server Connect to Server** dialog box again to enter the remote connection credentials to Azure.

**FIGURE 13-26**

Preparing to Deploy
Database to Microsoft Azure
SQL Database

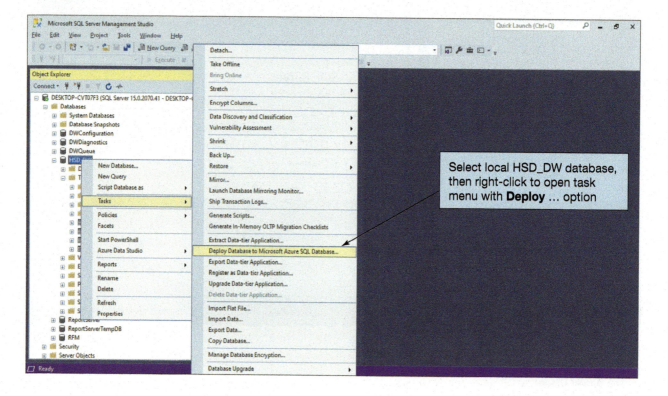

Select local HSD_DW database,
then right-click to open task
menu with **Deploy ...** option

**FIGURE 13-27**

Deploy Database to
Microsoft Azure SQL
Database

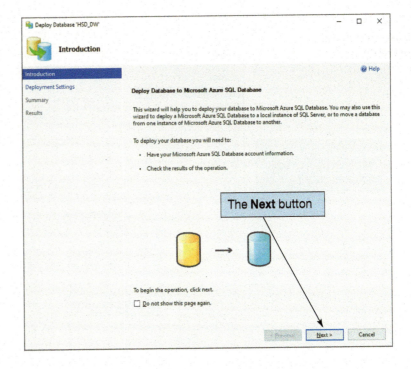

Once the login and password are provided, the deployment settings for the server connection are filled in, as shown in Figure 13-29, and we use the **Next** button to set up the actual migration process. The local SSMS program cooperates with the local SQL Server DBMS and the remote Azure DBMS server to transfer the table definitions and data to the remote end. The **Summary** page will appear after several seconds, as shown in Figure 13-30.

**FIGURE 13-28**

The Deployment Settings
Screen

**FIGURE 13-29**

The Filled-In Deployment
Settings Screen

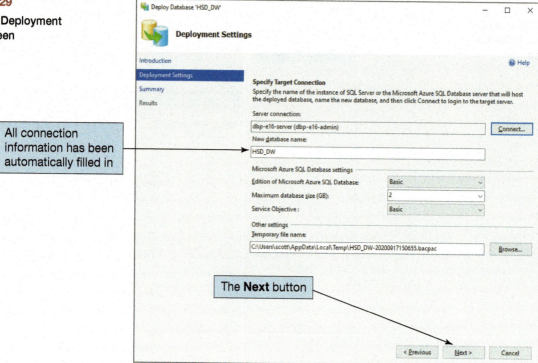

All connection
information has been
automatically filled in

The **Next** button

**FIGURE 13-30**

The Deployment Summary
Screen

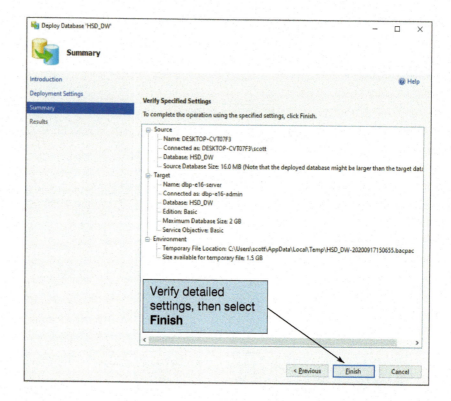

Verify detailed
settings, then select
**Finish**

The **Finish** button begins the migration process. The **Progress** screen appears, but we must be patient, as it may take a minute or so to import the database to the remote Microsoft Azure server. Eventually the **Results: Operation Complete** screen appears, as shown in Figure 13-31. The **Close** button allows us to see the new database HSD_DW appear in SSMS under the remote server name, as shown in Figure 13-32.

**FIGURE 13-31**

Results: Deployment
Operation Complete

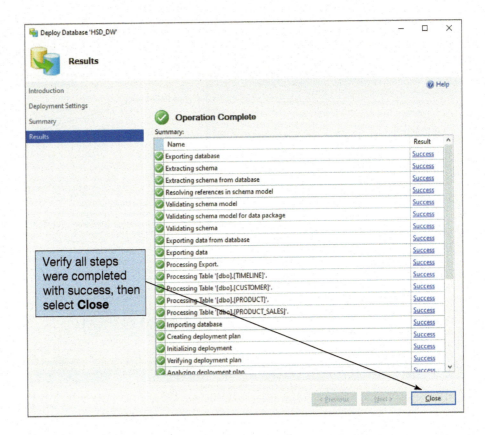

Verify all steps
were completed
with success, then
select **Close**

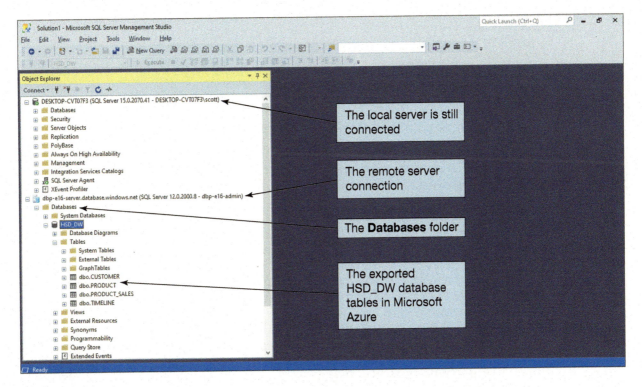

The local server is still
connected

The remote server
connection

The **Databases** folder

The exported
HSD_DW database
tables in Microsoft
Azure

**FIGURE 13-32**

SSMS Object Explorer
Showing New Azure
HSD_DW Database

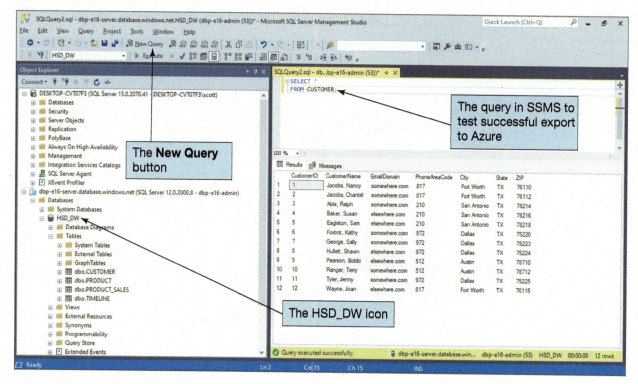

**FIGURE 13-33**

Query Results of HSD_DW
Database Migrated to Azure

To test the HSD_DW database on Azure, we select the HSD_DW icon, then the **New Query** button, as shown in figure 13-33. A new SQL query blank window opens. We enter the simple SQL query:

```
SELECT *
FROM CUSTOMER;
```

We then execute it; the query and results are also shown in Figure 13-33.

## Creating a New Relational Database on Microsoft Azure

In this section, rather than copying a local database to Azure, we will be running SQL scripts to create tables and insert data into a remote database directly on Azure. We have already migrated the Heather Sweeney Designs Data Warehouse database to Azure so we can manage and use it from our local SSMS. Now we will use the HSD scripts to create a new HSD (transactional, not warehouse) database directly on Azure. This will enable Heather Sweeney Designs to have all of their data (transactional and warehouse) in the cloud, with some of it managed via SSMS and some via the Azure Portal.

Start SSMS. We will again be connecting to both our local Microsoft SQL Server and remote Microsoft Azure SQL databases. If you are not already connected, use the **File | Connect Object Explorer** command to connect to your local SQL Server 2019 database engine, as shown in Figure 13-23. Connect to the remote Azure Database engine and enter the password, as shown in Figure 13-24. Note that for Microsoft Azure we use SQL Server authentication and for our local instance we use Windows Authentication. If you have previously created the HSD database, then you already have the DBP-e16-MSSQL-HSD-Create-Tables.sql script file in the Projects | HSD Database folder on your computer. If not, refer to the Appendix 10A section "Creating an SQL Script in Microsoft SQL Server 2019" that creates the tables and the following section "How Do I Use SQL Statements to Insert Database Data?" that describes how to create a script to insert the data into the newly created tables. Hopefully you named it something like DBP-e16-MSSQL-HSD-Insert-Data.sql.

**FIGURE 13-34**

**SSMS New Database Screen**

Don't run the scripts yet! We first need to create the empty HSD database on Microsoft Azure. In SSMS, under your remote Microsoft Azure server section of Object Explorer, select the **Databases** folder, as shown in Figure 13-32. Right-click it and select the **New Database...** command. After a few seconds a **New Database** window appears, as shown in Figure 13-34. Enter the new database name HSD and then click the **OK** button at the bottom of the screen (not shown).

The new database name HSD should appear in the Object Explorer window in SSMS under the remote server object name. You may need to use the refresh button, as shown in Figure 13-35. Select the remote server in SSMS object explorer. Next select the **File | Open | File . . .** command, browse to DBP-e16-MSSQL-HSD-Create-Tables.sql and then open it. There is an important difference with using Azure here. What database will the script run against? We have been using the SQL commands "USE HSD" and "GO" inside the files to select the database that our commands apply to. However, in this case we need to delete those commands from the script and then enter the database name HSD using the "Available Databases" box at the top left of the SSMS command ribbon, as shown in Figure 13-36, to make it the active database. Click the **Execute** command

**FIGURE 13-35**

**SSMS Object Explorer Showing Remote HSD Database**

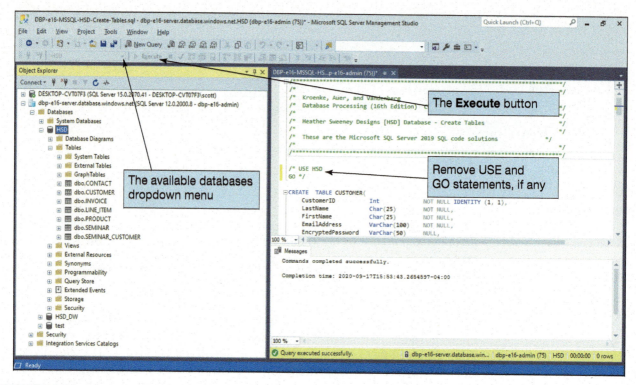

**FIGURE 13-36**

Successful Execution
of Create Table Script in
Remote HSD Database

button in the SSMS command ribbon on top. If the create tables script runs correctly, open (remove USE and GO statements) and then execute DBC-e16-MSSQL-HSD-Insert-Data, again making sure that HSD is the active database.

Test your new cloud-based relational database by using the **New Query** button on the Menu bar. Enter a simple query like:

```
SELECT * FROM CUSTOMER;
```

and run it. If it worked, congratulations! If not, recheck your previous steps, making sure that the database names are correct and that HSD is the active database.

## Creating and Using a NoSQL Document Database in Azure

The purpose of this section is to get you started with creating a simple NoSQL document database in Azure. Unfortunately, using Azure Cosmos DB now requires a separate Cosmos DB account that needs to be added to the Azure account (subscription). First we will create the new Cosmos DB account, and then we will create a Microsoft Azure Cosmos DB blank database. Then we will create a collection of Students, insert two JSON documents into the Students collection (each representing a student), and run a simple query. This will get you started so that you can learn more about Cosmos DB at your leisure and perhaps try some queries on a more sophisticated database.

To begin, login to Microsoft Azure (portal.azure.com) and enter the Azure Portal. Figure 13-37 shows our Azure Portal home page. As shown in the figure, select Azure Cosmos DB.

You will see the Cosmos DB directory, with no databases yet created, as shown in Figure 13-38.

There are several options at this point. We could explicitly create a new Cosmos DB account using the **Create Azure Cosmos DB account** button. We could create a temporary account using the **Try now** button. Or we could create a new database using the **Add** button, which will also force us to create an account. That will be our choice here. Click the **Add** button to create a new database; this will also force you to create a new Cosmos DB account. As shown in Figure 13-39, we will use the same account name (dbp-e16-admin) and password we used for the general Azure account as well as the same resource group

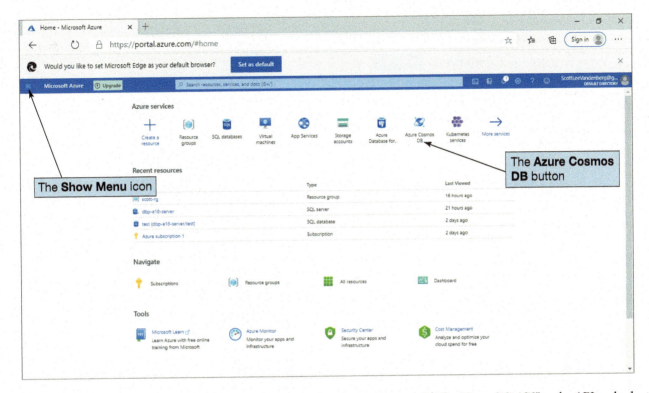

**FIGURE 13-37**

Microsoft Azure Portal Home Page

("scott-rg"). Make sure you select "Azure Cosmos DB for MongoDB API" as the API and select "Apply" to ensure it remains free. Application Program Interfaces (APIs) are used by application programs to connect to and use services provided by other systems. In this case, Cosmos DB has libraries that duplicate the functionality of other NoSQL DBMSs. Cosmos supports an API for Cassandra (key-value) and Gremlin (graph) systems as well. Click the **Review + create** button. In the next window, verify your settings then click **Create**.

Be patient: It may take some time to create and deploy your new account (Azure will give you an estimate before you create the account). When the deployment is complete, click

**FIGURE 13-38**

Microsoft Azure Cosmos DB Directory

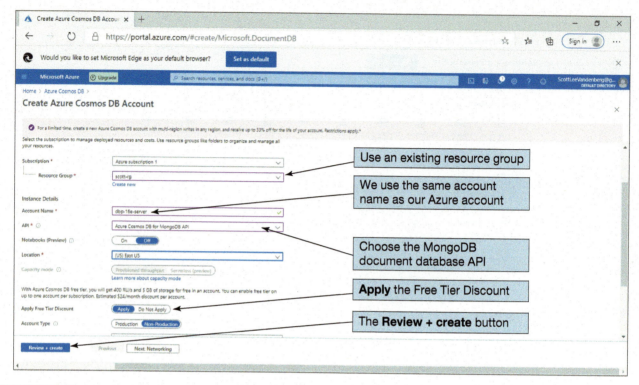

**FIGURE 13-39**

Create New Azure Cosmos
DB Account

**FIGURE 13-40**

New Cosmos DB Document
Account Created

the **Home** button to return to the Azure Portal home page. You will see your Azure Cosmos DB account as one of the resources, as shown in Figure 13-40.

Select your new Cosmos DB account. You will see the *dbp-16e-server* pane, showing its information and options, as in Figure 13-41. Note: The first time this screen is entered, you may see information about .NET and other programming interfaces. We will not be using them, as we are just getting started, but advanced applications will use programs written in a programming language such as Java to interact directly with Cosmos databases.

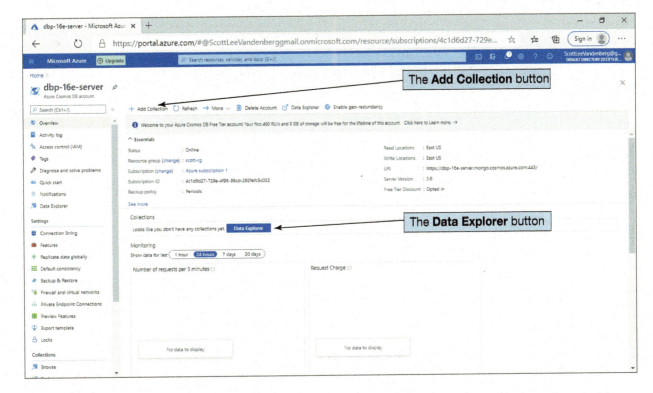

**FIGURE 13-41**

**The Azure Cosmos DB Account Overview Pane**

Click the **Add Collection** button at the top of the pane, as shown in Figure 13-41. This will be the first collection for the account, which means we also need to create a new database within the account to hold this collection. Enter the Collection Id "students" and enter the new database name and other information as shown in Figure 13-42. Click the **OK** button at the bottom of the pane to create the collection.

**FIGURE 13-42**

**Creating a New Collection and Database**

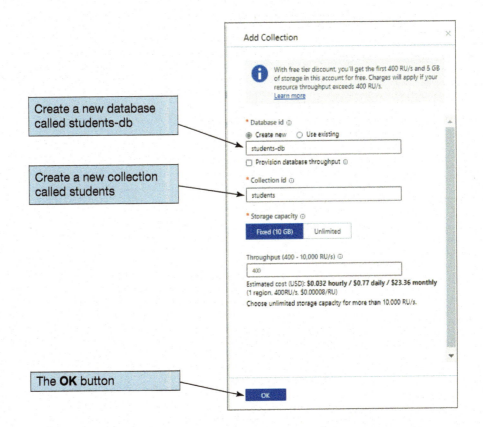

You will then see the *dbp-16e-server* Data Explorer screen showing the list of MongoDB NoSQL databases, collections, and documents as shown in Figure 13-43.

Click the New Document button, as shown in Figure 13-43, and enter the following in place of the text that automatically appears there (see Figure 13-44):

```
{
    "id": "555667777",
    "name": "Tierney, Doris",
    "majors": ["Music", "Spanish"],
    "addresses": [
        {
        "street": "14510 NE 4th Street",
        "city": "Bellevue",
        "state": "WA",
        "zip": "98005"
        },
        {
        "street": "335 Aloha Street",
        "city": "Seattle",
        "state": "WA",
        "zip": "98109"
        }
        ],
    "advisorID": "Advisor1"
}
```

**FIGURE 13-43**

**The Document Database Collections List**

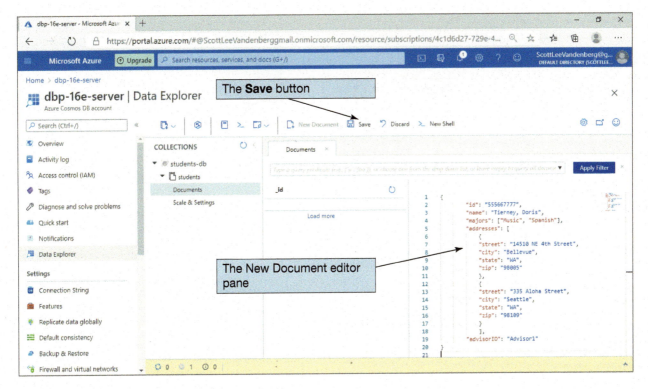

**FIGURE 13-44**

**The New Document Editor Pane**

Click the **Save** button, as shown in Figure 13-44, to save the document into the Students collection. The **Save** button text changes to **Update** after the first save.

Create another student document with the following data:

```
{
    "id": "901667777",
    "name": "Orsini, Meg",
    "majors": ["Math"],
    "addresses": [
        {
        "street": "21 Knob Ave",
        "city": "Valley View",
        "state": "NY",
        "zip": "12943"
        }
        ],
    "advisorID": "Advisor3"
}
```

There should be two entries in the **_id** header in the middle pane when you are done, as seen in Figure 13-45.

We are almost done. Let's test our database by running a simple query. Click the **New Shell** button at the top of the Data Explorer screen (see Figure 13-45). This creates an interactive command prompt to your cloud-based MongoDB database. MongoDB queries are

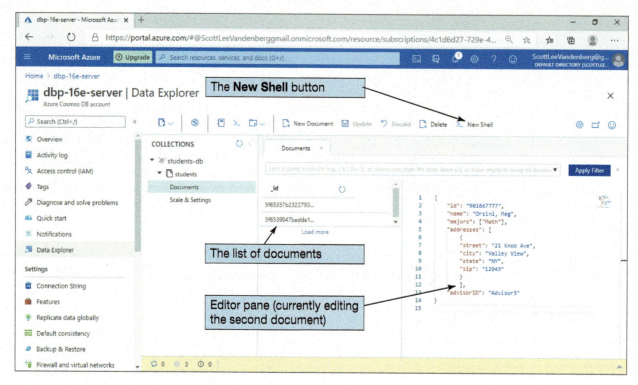

**FIGURE 13-45**

**The New Documents Saved in the Collection**

specified as parameters to the "db.<collection>.find()" command. As shown in Figure 13-46, type the following command in the Mongo Shell

**FIGURE 13-46**

**Create and Run a Simple MongoDB Query**

```
db.students.find ({"name": "Orsini, Meg"})
```

followed by the Enter key. The data for Meg will appear in the results section at the lower part of the screen. Even the queries are JSON-like in MongoDB.

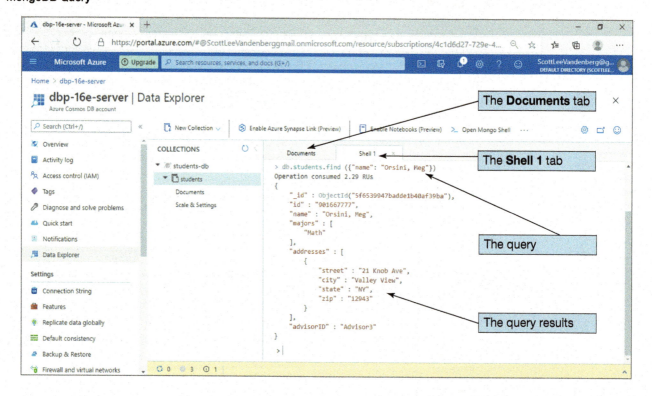

The previous query is similar to the following SQL query:

```
SELECT *
FROM STUDENTS
WHERE name = 'Orsini, Meg';
```

At this point, we have created a new Cosmos DB document database, created a new collection (similar to a RDBMS table), and uploaded two students (similar to rows in a table). We then ran a simple MongoDB query. You may log off from Azure by clicking on the account information at the upper-right corner of the screen then selecting **Sign out**.

Congratulations, you are finished and ready to continue exploring on your own! Online Chapter 10D has more information about NoSQL databases, focusing on the ArangoDB document DBMS.

## Cloud Reflections

We have just touched the surface of all the capabilities of the cloud in our little tour. We could have gone on to show how to manage our databases and connect applications to use relational and non-relational databases on Azure.

Think of the cloud as a set of data centers containing servers, software, disk storage, and network equipment that one can rent and configure as needed to meet one's computing needs. Understanding how the Web, cloud portals, and local applications interoperate will become increasingly important to information professionals.

The economic case for cloud computing is compelling. Computing equipment has a high capital cost, yet it depreciates rapidly. The support infrastructure costs for a data center are prohibitive for small companies and include the computer room, power, air-conditioning, and electric power backup systems. Hardware support and software licensing costs along with salaries for systems administrators, security, and operations personnel are driving the popularity of large cloud-based data centers where economies of scale can be taken advantage of.

## Big Data, NoSQL Systems, and the Future

The usefulness and importance of these Big Data products to organizations such as Facebook demonstrate that we can look forward not only to the development of improvements to relational DBMSs but also to a very different approach to data storage and information processing that may combine several technologies. Big Data and products associated with Big Data are rapidly changing and evolving, and you should expect many developments in this area in the near future.

> **BY THE WAY** The Not only SQL world is an exciting one, but you should be aware that if you want to participate in it, you will need to sharpen your OOP programming skills. Whereas we can develop and manage databases in Microsoft Access, Microsoft SQL Server, Oracle Database, and MySQL using management and applications development tools that are very user friendly (Microsoft Access itself, Microsoft SQL Server Management Studio, Oracle SQL Developer, and MySQL Workbench), application development in the NoSQL world is currently done primarily in programming languages.
>
> This, of course, may change, and we look forward to seeing the future developments in the Not only SQL realm. For now, you'll need to sign up for that programming course!

# Summary

This chapter introduced a number of concepts that go beyond the "standard" setting of a relational database housed on a single computer. The sheer volume and complexity of modern data management have led to a resurrection and expansion of ideas from distributed computing and object databases, now used in DBMS processing in the form of cloud/virtualization and NoSQL databases.

A distributed database is a database that is stored and processed on more than one computer. A replicated database is one in which multiple copies of some or all of the database are stored on different computers. A partitioned (or sharded) database is one in which different pieces of the database are stored on different computers. A distributed database can include both replication and partitioning.

Distributed databases pose processing challenges. If a database is updated on a single computer, then the challenge is simply to ensure that the copies of the database are logically consistent when they are distributed. However, if updates are to be made on more than one computer, the challenges become significant. If the database is partitioned and not replicated, then challenges occur if transactions span data on more than one computer. If the database is replicated and if updates occur to the replicated portions, then a special locking algorithm called distributed two-phase locking is required. Implementing this algorithm can be difficult and expensive. Many Big Data and NoSQL databases are distributed.

Objects consist of methods and properties (data attributes). All objects of a given class have the same methods, but they have different property values. Object persistence is the process of storing object property values on disk. Relational databases are difficult to use for object persistence. Some specialized products called object-oriented DBMSs were developed in the 1990s but never received large-scale commercial acceptance. Oracle and others, following the SQL standard, have extended the capabilities of their relational DBMS products to provide support for object persistence. Such databases are referred to as object-relational databases. Some of these data structuring techniques are found in NoSQL databases.

Data processing of the very large datasets found in Big Data is often done by the Map-Reduce process, which breaks a data processing task into many parallel tasks performed by many computers in the cluster and then combines these partial results to produce a final result. One common platform supported by Microsoft and Oracle Corporation (and many others) is the Hadoop Distributed File System (HDFS), with its spinoffs HBase, a non-relational storage component, and Pig, a query language. Newer versions of Hadoop use Apache Tez, an improvement over the original MapReduce that allows processing to be defined in a more general manner and avoids writing to files by using in-memory processing wherever possible.

The NoSQL movement (now often read as "Not only SQL") is built upon the need to meet the Big Data storage needs of many modern applications, including those of companies such as Amazon.com, Google, and Facebook. These systems typically make use of cloud technology (derived in part from earlier work on distributed databases) and complex structuring techniques (derived in part from earlier work on object databases). The tools used to do this are non-relational DBMSs, sometimes referred to as semi-structured storage or NoSQL DBMSs. Such systems have their own design decisions that a DBA needs to make, much as in a relational DBMS. Some of these important choices are captured in the CAP theorem, which states that no DBMS can provide partition tolerance, availability, and consistency at the same time.

An early NoSQL DBMS is Cassandra, a column family DBMS, and more recent popular examples are MongoDB and ArangoDB, each supporting the document model. Document DBMS products most often use JSON (or sometimes XML) to structure the data, which allows documents (analogous to records) to contain simple values, other documents, or arrays of values or documents. Queries about the internal structure of documents are possible in document DBMSs. Column family products such as Vertica use a non-normalized table structure built on columns, super columns, column families, and super column families tied together by RowKey values from a keyspace. Graph databases such as Neo4j connect nodes with edges; both nodes and edges can have properties and queries can be asked based on the connections formed by these edges. Key-value databases are the simplest NoSQL database variety, with data values being uninterpreted chunks of bytes and only very simple (but efficient) operations available. Oracle's NoSQL DBMS is one example.

The physical setting for much NoSQL and Big Data work is often in the cloud and/or on virtual machines, which allows us to consolidate several logical servers into one larger physical one and to provide tremendous flexibility in dynamically provisioning servers, storage, and network resources. A special program called a hypervisor provides the virtual environment and manages the virtual machines. Containers are another form of virtualization that allows applications to share the same operating system but also have different software libraries and file systems. Cloud computing allows remote computers to host data, software, or both, taking advantage of the Internet to provide availability and scalability. Thus, portions of data centers can be leased by customers who are charged only for the resources they use.

Microsoft Azure is a cloud-based platform allowing deployment of both relational (using local SSMS installations if we prefer) and NoSQL databases (using Azure Cosmos DB). These databases can be created directly in Azure or by importing from local databases.

# Key Terms

3V framework
aggregate
Amazon Web Services (AWS)
Apache Spark
Apache Tez
AQL (ArangoDB Query Language)
ArangoDB
availability
Azure Cosmos DB
Big Data
Bigtable
CAP theorem
Cassandra
cloud computing
collection
column
column family [NoSQL database category]
consistency
containerization
CRUD (Create, Read, Update, Delete)
distributed database
distributed two-phase locking
document [NoSQL database category]
DynamoDB
DynamoDB database service
EC2 service
edge

eventual consistency
graph [NoSQL database category]
Hadoop Distributed File System (HDFS)
host machine
hypervisor
impedance mismatch
infrastructure as a service (IaaS)
JSON (Java Script Object Notation)
keyspace
key-value [NoSQL database category]
MapReduce
MemcacheDB
method
Microsoft Azure
multimodel
Neo4j
node
NoSQL
Not only SQL
object
object-oriented DBMS (OODBMS)
object-oriented programming (OOP)
object persistence
object-relational database
partition tolerance
partitioning

platform as a service (PaaS)
polyglot persistence
property
quorums
redundant array of independent disks (RAID)
Relational DBMS Service (RDS)
replica set
replication
RowKey
schemaless
semistructured database
server cluster
sharding
software as a service (SaaS)
storage area network (SAN)
super column
super column family
unstructured database
variety [Big Data]
velocity [Big Data]
veracity [Big Data]
virtual machine
virtual machine manager
virtualization
volume [Big Data]
XML (eXtensible Markup Language)

# Review Questions

**13.1**  What is Big Data?

**13.2**  Based on Figure 13-1, what is the relationship between 1 MB of storage and 1 EB of storage?

**13.3**  What are the original three Vs? Define each term.

**13.4**  Define consistency and give an example other than ones used in this book.

**13.5**  Define availability and give an example other than ones used in this book.

**13.6**  Define partition tolerance and give an example other than ones used in this book.

**13.7**  What is the CAP theorem? How has it stood up over time?

**13.8**  What is the NoSQL movement? What are the four categories of NoSQL databases used in this book?

**13.9**  Define *distributed database*.

**13.10**  Explain one way to partition a database that has three tables: T1, T2, and T3.

**13.11**  Explain one way to replicate a database that has three tables: T1, T2, and T3.

**13.12**  Explain what must be done when fully replicating a database but allowing only one computer to process updates.

**13.13**  If more than one computer can update a replicated database, what three problems can occur?

**13.14**  What solution is used to prevent the problems in Review Question 13.13?

**13.15**  Explain what problems can occur in a distributed database that is partitioned but not replicated.

**13.16**  What organizations should consider using a distributed database?

**13.17**  Explain the meaning of the term *object persistence*.

**13.18**  In general terms, explain why relational databases are difficult to use for object persistence.

**13.19**  What does OODBMS stand for, and what is its purpose?

**13.20**  According to this chapter, why were OODBMSs not successful?

**13.21**  What is an object-relational database?

**13.22**  Explain MapReduce processing.

**13.23**  What is Hadoop, and what is the history of the development of Hadoop to its current state? What are HBase and Pig?

**13.24**  Why is the new Apache Tez processing model an improvement over MapReduce?

**13.25**  What were the first two non-relational data stores to be developed, and who developed them?

**13.26**  Define the term aggregate as it relates to NoSQL data structuring.

**13.27**  What NoSQL categories does Cassandra support?

**13.28**  As illustrated in Figure 13-7, what is column family database storage, and how are column family database storage systems organized? How does this compare to RDBMS systems?

**13.29**  Give a small example of column family data other than the ones used in this book.

**13.30**  What is a graph database? What are nodes, properties, and edges?

**13.31**  Give a small example of graph data other than the ones used in this book.

**13.32**  What is a key-value database?

**13.33**  Give a small example of key value data other than the ones used in this book.

**13.34**  Under what circumstances is a key-value database most useful?

**13.35**  In a key-value database, where does processing relating to the structure of data values take place?

**13.36**  What are the main features of data in a document database?

**13.37**  Give a small example of document data other than the ones used in this book.

**13.38**  What are the basic operations and utilities provided by a document DBMS?

**13.39**  Name at least two document NoSQL database systems that have query languages.

**13.40**  What is virtualization?

**13.41**  What is a hypervisor, and what is the difference between a type 1 hypervisor and a type 2 hypervisor?

**13.42**  What is containerization? How is it different from hypervisor-based virtualization?

**13.43**  What is cloud computing?

**13.44**  What major technology enables cloud computing?

**13.45**  What are the differences between SaaS, PaaS, and IaaS?

**13.46**  What data models are supported by database services in Microsoft Azure?

**13.47**  Describe two ways of creating relational databases in Microsoft Azure.

**13.48**  What is the purpose of the Microsoft Azure firewall?

**13.49**  In Microsoft Azure (and cloud computing in general), why is it important to consider your choice of servers in geographic terms?

**13.50**  How does Microsoft Azure charge users for their services?

# Exercises

**13.51**  Describe the process used to migrate an SQL database from a local computer to Azure. What components (SSMS, Azure Portal, local and remote database servers) are involved in each step of the process?

**13.52**  Develop a graph database based on a portion of the WP EMPLOYEE and PROJECT tables that will look similar to Figure 13-8. Use WP data to model only Project 1300 and the employees assigned to it. The Project and the Employees will be nodes; the Assignment relationship is bidirectional (AssignedTo and ProjectWorkers) and becomes the edges and labels; properties will be from the data fields.

**13.53  A.**  Develop a JSON file describing the first customer from the HSD CUSTOMER table. Be sure to represent CustomerID (value will be 1). Use the expressive power of JSON to extend the data to allow multiple phone numbers and also to express Address as a composite containing StreetAddress, City, State, and ZIP. Make up a second phone number for Nancy Jacobs and enter it.

    **B.**  Create a database and collection in Microsoft Azure Cosmos DB and enter into it the data you created in Part A.

**13.54**  Describe in general the steps used to set up and to configure an Azure account. What important decisions needs to be made during this process?

**13.55**  Describe the process used to create an SQL database on Azure. What components (SSMS, Azure Portal, local and remote database servers) are involved in each step of the process?

**13.56**  Give an example of a query on the column store database in Figure 13-7 that you would expect to run more efficiently than the same query in a relational system. Explain your answer.

**13.57**  Migrate the Cape Codd database from your local computer to the cloud using Microsoft Azure.

**13.58**  Create the Cape Codd database directly in Microsoft Azure.

# Case Questions

## Marcia's Dry Cleaning

Marcia has been successfully using a relational database, as described in online Chapters 10A, 10B, and 10C, for a while now, but her business is expanding rapidly; it's time for some Big Data solutions! In particular, she now has 10 different locations (not just one) and a large and growing number of customers. She is ready to embrace polyglot persistence.

    **A.**  Design and justify one possible scheme for sharding and replicating all or part of Marcia's data.

    **B.**  Give an example of how part of the MDC database might benefit from being stored in a key-value DBMS. Justify your choice.

    **C.**  As part of her expansion, Marcia now does deliveries and thus includes latitude and longitude coordinates for each of her customers. In order to plan deliveries, it is helpful to know which customers are near each other and how far apart they are. Show, in a way similar to Figure 13-8 or Figure 13-9, how some of Marcia's customer data might be stored in a graph DBMS. Make up suitable latitude, longitude, and distance values.

    **D.**  Marcia has decided to use a document DBMS to store the INVOICE and INVOICE_ITEM data in a single collection. Create a JSON file with this data.

    **E.**  Marcia has also heard about the cloud and wants to put at least some of her data there. Using Microsoft Azure (or some other cloud-based NoSQL document database), put the data you created in Part D in a cloud database.

    **F.**  Marcia is hedging her bets on this new-fangled NoSQL technology, so she also wants her entire old relational database (as described in online Chapters 10A, 10B, and 10C) to be placed in the cloud. Do this by either migrating the data from a local machine or creating it directly in a cloud-based relational platform such as Microsoft Azure. Maintaining both the relational and NoSQL versions of her data for a time will allow her to compare the two.

    **G.**  Marcia also wants to check out some column family database storage. Help her think of a query on her relational database that would run better in a column family database, and explain why it would.

## The Queen Anne Curiosity Shop Project Questions

The Queen Anne Curiosity Shop has been successfully using a relational database, as described in Chapter 7, for a while now, but its business is expanding rapidly; it's time for some Big Data solutions! In particular, the company now has 12 different locations (not just one) and a large and growing number of customers and curiosities. It is ready to embrace polyglot persistence.

**A.** Design and justify one possible scheme for sharding and replicating all or part of the QACS data.

**B.** Give an example of how part of the QACS database might benefit from being stored in a key-value DBMS. Justify your choice.

**C.** As part of its expansion, the Queen Anne Curiosity Shop now does deliveries to its customers and pickups from its vendors and thus includes latitude and longitude coordinates for each of its customers and vendors. In order to plan deliveries and pickups, it is helpful to know which customers and vendors are near each other and how far apart they are. Show, in a way similar to Figure 13-8 or Figure 13-9, how some of the QACS customer and vendor data might be stored in a graph DBMS. Make up suitable latitude, longitude, and distance values.

**D.** The Queen Anne Curiosity Shop has decided to use a document DBMS to store the SALE, SALE_ITEM, and ITEM data in two collections. Propose two different approaches to doing this. Create a JSON file with this data for one of the approaches, and explain why you chose it.

**E.** The Queen Anne Curiosity Shop has also heard about the cloud and wants to put at least some of its data there. Using Microsoft Azure (or some other cloud-based NoSQL document database), put the data you created in Part D in a cloud database.

**F.** The Queen Anne Curiosity Shop is hedging its bets on this new-fangled NoSQL technology, so it also wants its entire old relational database (as described in Chapter 7) to be placed in the cloud. Do this by either migrating the data from a local machine or creating it directly in a cloud-based relational platform such as Microsoft Azure. Maintaining both the relational and NoSQL versions of its data for a time will allow the company to compare the two.

**G.** The Queen Anne Curiosity Shop also wants to check out some column family database storage. Help it think of a query on its relational database that would run better in a column family database, and explain why it would.

## Morgan Importing Project Questions

Morgan Importing has been successfully using a relational database, as described in Chapter 7, for a while now, but its business is expanding rapidly; it's time for some Big Data solutions! In particular, the company now has 23 different locations (not just one) and a large and growing number of customers and imported products. It is ready to embrace polyglot persistence.

**A.** Design and justify one possible scheme for sharding and replicating all or part of the Morgan Importing (MI) data.

**B.** Give an example of how part of the MI database might benefit from being stored in a key-value DBMS. Justify your choice.

**C.** As part of its expansion, Morgan Importing now picks up items from its shippers and thus includes latitude and longitude coordinates for each of these shippers as well as for its stores. In order to plan pickups, it is helpful to know which shippers and stores are near each other and how far apart they are. Show, in a way similar to Figure 13-8 or Figure 13-9, how some of the MI shipper and store data might be stored in a graph DBMS. Make up suitable latitude, longitude, and distance values.

**D.** Morgan Importing has decided to use a document DBMS to store the SHIPMENT, SHIPMENT_ITEM, and SHIPMENT_RECEIPT data in one collection. Create a JSON file with this data.

**E.** Morgan Importing has also heard about the cloud and wants to put at least some of its data there. Using Microsoft Azure (or some other cloud-based NoSQL document database), put the data you created in Part D in a cloud database.

**F.** Morgan Importing is hedging its bets on this new-fangled NoSQL technology, so it also wants its entire old relational database (as described in Chapter 7) to be placed in the cloud. Do this by either migrating the data from a local machine or creating it directly in a cloud-based relational platform such as Microsoft Azure. Maintaining both the relational and NoSQL versions of its data for a time will allow the company to compare the two.

**G.** Morgan Importing also wants to check out some column family database storage. Help it think of a query on its relational database that would run better in a column family database, and explain why it would.

# Online Appendices

Complete versions of these appendices are available on this textbook's website.

Go to *www.pearsonhighered.com/kroenke* and scroll down to the *Database Processing, 16/e* links in the Database Management section.

# Bibliography

## Web Links

### News

CNET News.com: *www.news.com*
Wired: *www.wired.com*
ZDNet: *www.zdnet.com*

### Data Mining

IBM SPSS Software: *www.ibm.com/analytics/spss-statistics-software*
KDnuggets: *www.kdnuggets.com/*
SAS Enterprise Miner: *www.sas.com/technologies/analytics/datamining/miner*

### DBMS and Other Vendors

Oracle Database 19c: *www.oracle.com/database/technologies/*
Oracle Database 18c Express Edition (Oracle Database XE):
   *www.oracle.com/database/technologies/appdev/xe.html*
SQL Server 2019: *www.microsoft.com/en-us/sql-server/sql-server-2019*
SQL Server 2019 Developer Edition:
   *www.microsoft.com/en-us/sql-server/sql-server-downloads*
SQL Server 2019 Express Edition:
   *www.microsoft.com/en-us/sql-server/sql-server-downloads*
MySQL: *www.mysql.com*
MySQL Community Server 8.0: *https://dev.mysql.com/*
MySQL Workbench: *https://dev.mysql.com/*
ArangoDB: *arangodb.com*
Eclipse IDE: *www.eclipse.org/*
PHP: *www.php.net/*
NetBeans: *https://netbeans.apache.org/*
Microsoft Visual Studio Community Edition:
   *https://visualstudio.microsoft.com/vs/community/*
Altova XMLSpy: *www.altova.com/xmlspy-xml-editor*

### Standards

JDBC: *www.oracle.com/java/technologies/javase/javase-tech-database.html* and
   *https://en.wikipedia.org/wiki/JDBC*
JSON: *https://tools.ietf.org/html/rfc7159* and
   *https://www.json.org/json-en.html*
ODBC: *https://en.wikipedia.org/wiki/Open_Database_Connectivity*
World Wide Web Consortium (W3C): *www.w3.org*
XML: *www.w3.org/XML/, www.xml.org,* and
   *https://en.wikipedia.org/wiki/XML*

### Online Publications

Database Journal: *www.databasejournal.com/*

## Classic Articles and References

ANSI X3. *American National Standard for Information Systems–Database Language SQL.* ANSI, 1992.
Bruce, T. *Designing Quality Databases with IDEF1X Information Models.* New York: Dorset House, 1992.
Chamberlin, D. D., et al. "SEQUEL 2: A Unified Approach to Data Definition, Manipulation, and Control." *IBM Journal of Research and Development* 20 (November 1976).
Chen, P. *Entity-Relationship Approach to Information Modeling.* E-R Institute, 1981.
Chen, P. "The Entity-Relationship Model: Toward a Unified Model of Data." *ACM Transactions on Database Systems* 1 (March 1976).
Coar, K. A. L. *Apache Server for Dummies.* Foster City, CA: IDG Books, 1997.
Codd, E. F. "A Relational Model of Data for Large Shared Data Banks." *Communications of the ACM* 13 (June 1970).
Codd, E. F. "Extending the Relational Model to Capture More Meaning." *Transactions on Database Systems* 4 (December 1979).
Date, C. J. *An Introduction to Database Systems,* 8th ed. Upper Saddle River, NJ: Pearson Education, 2003.
Embley, D. W. "NFQL: The Natural Forms Query Language." *ACM Transactions on Database Systems* 14 (June 1989).
Eswaran, K. P., J. N. Gray, R. A. Lorie, and I. L. Traiger. "The Notion of Consistency and Predicate Locks in a Database System." *Communications of the ACM* 19 (November 1976).
Fagin, R. "A Normal Form for Relational Databases That Is Based on Domains and Keys." *Transactions on Database Systems* 6 (September 1981).
Fagin, R. "Multivalued Dependencies and a New Normal Form for Relational Databases." *Transactions on Database Systems* 2 (September 1977).
Hammer, M., and D. McLeod. "Database Description with SDM: A Semantic Database Model." *Transactions on Database Systems* 6 (September 1981).
Keuffel, W. "Battle of the Modeling Techniques." *DBMS Magazine* (August 1996).
Kroenke, D. "Waxing Semantic: An Interview." *DBMS Magazine* (September 1994).
Moriarty, T. "Business Rule Analysis." *Database Programming and Design* (April 1993).
Muller, R. J. *Database Design for Smarties: Using UML for Data Modeling.* San Francisco: Morgan Kaufmann, 1999.
Nijssen, G., and T. Halpin. *Conceptual Schema and Relational Database Design: A Fact-Oriented Approach.* Upper Saddle River, NJ: Prentice Hall, 1989.
Nolan, R. *Managing the Data Resource Function.* St. Paul: West Publishing, 1974.
Ratliff, C. Wayne, "dStory: How I Really Developed dBASE." *Data Based Advisor* (March 1991).
Rogers, D. "Manage Data with Modeling Tools." *VB Tech Journal* (December 1996).
Ross, R. *Principles of the Business Rule Approach.* Boston: Addison-Wesley, 2003.
Zloof, M. M. "Query by Example." *Proceedings of the National Computer Conference, AFIPS* 44 (May 1975).

## Useful Books

Atkinson, Paul, and Robert Vieira. *Beginning Microsoft SQL Server 2012 Programming.* Indianapolis, IN: John Wiley & Sons, Inc., 2012.
Ben-Gan, Itzik, Dejan Sarka, and Ron Talmage. *Querying Microsoft SQL Server 2012: Exam 70-461 Training Kit.* Sebastopol, CA: O'Reilly Media, Inc., 2012.

Bordoloi, Bijoy, and Douglas Bock. *Oracle SQL*. Upper Saddle River, NJ: Prentice Hall, 2003.

Bordoloi, Bijoy, and Douglas Bock. *SQL for SQL Server*. Upper Saddle River, NJ: Prentice Hall, 2003.

Bryla, B., and Kevin Loney. *Oracle Database 12c: The Complete Reference*. Columbus, OH: McGraw-Hill Education, 2013.

Celko, J. *SQL for Smarties*, 5th ed. San Francisco: Morgan Kaufmann, 2014.

Celko, J. *SQL Puzzles and Answers*, 2nd ed. San Francisco: Morgan Kaufmann, 2006.

Conger, Steve. *Hands-On Database: An Introduction to Database Design and Development*, 2nd ed. Upper Saddle River, NJ: Pearson, 2013.

Date, C. J. *An Introduction to Database Systems*, 8th ed. Upper Saddle River, NJ: Pearson, 2003.

Fields, D. K., and M. A. Kolb. *Web Development with Java Server Pages*. Greenwich, CT: Manning Press, 2000.

Garcia-Molina, Hector, Jeffrey D. Ullman, and Jennifer Widom. *Database Systems: The Complete Book*, 2nd ed. Upper Saddle River, NJ: Prentice Hall, 2009.

Harold, E. R. *XML: Extensible Markup Language*. New York: IDG Books Worldwide, 1998.

Hoffer, Jeffrey A., V. Ramesh, and Heikki Topi. *Modern Database Management*, 12th ed. Upper Saddle River, NJ: Prentice Hall, 2015.

Jorgensen, Adam, Bradley Ball, Steven Wort, Ross LoFortre, and Brian Knight. *Professional Microsoft SQL Server 2014 Administration*. Indianapolis, IN: Wrox, 2014.

Jukić, Nenad, Susan Vrbsky, and Svetlozar Nestrorov. *Database Systems: Introduction to Databases and Data Warehouses*. Burlington, VT: Prospect Press, 2016.

Kay, M. *XSLT 2.0 and XPath 2.0 Programmer's Reference*, 4th ed. Indianapolis, IN: Wrox Press, 2008.

Kendall, Kenneth E., and Julie E. Kendall. *Systems Analysis and Design*, 9th ed. Upper Saddle River, NJ: Prentice Hall, 2014.

Linoff, G., and M. Berry. *Data Mining Techniques for Marketing, Sales, and Customer Relationship Management*, 3rd ed. New York: Wiley, 2011.

Muench, S. *Building Oracle XML Applications*. Sebastopol, CA: O'Reilly, 2000.

Muller, R. J. *Database Design for Smarties: Using UML for Data Modeling*. San Francisco: Morgan Kaufmann, 1999.

Mundy, J., W. Thornthwaite, and R. Kimball. *The Microsoft Data Warehouse Toolkit*, 2nd ed. Indianapolis, IN: Wiley, 2011.

Nixon, Robin. *Learning PHP, MySQL, JavaScript, CSS & HTML5*, 3rd ed. Sebastopol, CA: O'Reilly Media, Inc., 2014.

Petkovic, D. *Microsoft SQL Server 2016: A Beginner's Guide*, 6th ed. Columbus, OH: McGraw-Hill Education, 2016.

Pyle, D. *Data Preparation for Data Mining*. San Francisco: Morgan Kaufmann, 1999.

Ruel, C. and M. Wessler. *Oracle 12c for Dummies*. Indianapolis, IN: For Dummies, 2013.

Sadalage, Pramod, and Martin Fowler. *NoSQL Distilled: A Brief Guide to the Emerging World of Polyglot Persistence*. Upper Saddle River, NU: Addison-Wesley, 2013.

Sarka, Dejan, Matija Lah, and Grega Jerkic. *Implementing a Data Warehouse with Microsoft SQL Server 2012: Exam 70-463 Training Kit*. Redmond, WA: Microsoft Press, 2012.

Thomas, Orin, Peter Ward, and Bob Taylor. *Administering Microsoft SQL Server 2012 Databases: Exam 70-462 Training Kit*. Redmond, WA: Microsoft Press, 2012.

**Identifier.** An attribute that names, or identifies, an entity.

**Identifying relationship.** A relationship that is used when the child entity is ID-dependent upon the parent entity.

**IDENTITY ({StartValue}, {Increment}) property.** For Microsoft SQL Server 2019, the attribute that is used to create a surrogate key.

**IE Crow's Foot model.** James Martin's version of the Information Engineering (IE) model for diagramming data models, which uses a crow's foot symbol to indicate the many side of a relationship. *See also* Information Engineering (IE) model.

**iisstart.htm.** The default Web page used by the Microsoft Internet Information Server Web server. *See also* Internet Information Server (IIS).

**Impedance mismatch.** The disconnect between the data modeling facilities of a DBMS and the data structures provided by a programming language that can interact with that DBMS.

**Implementation.** In object-oriented programming, a set of objects that instantiates a particular object-oriented interface.

**Implicit COMMIT.** A commit generated by the DBMS itself to provide concurrency control. *Contrast with* explicit COMMIT.

**Implicit join.** In SQL statements, a join that does not use the SQL JOIN ON syntax. *See also* SQL JOIN ON syntax.

**Implicit lock.** A lock that is automatically placed by the DBMS.

**Inclusive subtype.** In data modeling and database design, a subtype that allows a supertype entity to be associated with more than one subtype.

**Inconsistent backup.** A backup file that contains uncommitted changes.

**Inconsistent data.** Slightly different formats for values of the same data. For example, one user might enter *Corn, Large Can* while another enters *Large Can Corn*.

**Inconsistent read problem.** In a transaction, a series of reads of a set of rows in which some of the rows have been updated by a second transaction and some of the rows have not been updated by that second transaction. Can be prevented by two-phase locking and other strategies.

**Inconsistent values.** When the same data values has more than one form, due to encoding the same data value in different ways or data entry errors.

**Index.** Data created by the DBMS to improve access and sorting performance. Indexes can be constructed for a single column or groups of columns. They are especially useful for columns used by WHERE clauses, for conditions in joins, and for sorting.

**index.html.** A default Web page name provided by most Web servers.

**Inetpub folder.** In Windows operating systems, the root folder for the IIS Web server.

**Information.** (1) Knowledge derived from data, (2) data presented in a meaningful context, or (3) data processed by summing, ordering, averaging, grouping, comparing, or other similar operations.

**Information Engineering (IE) model.** An E-R model developed by James Martin.

**Infrastructure as a service (IaaS).** A way for cloud providers to lease physical computing and network resources to customers that want to manage their own operating system and application software on it.

**INNER.** An SQL keyword indicating an inner join. *See* join, inner join.

**Inner join.** Synonym for join. *Contrast with* outer join. *See also* outer join.

**InsertCommand object.** The ADO.NET DataAdapter object used to insert new data from a DataSet back to the actual DBMS data.

**Insertion anomaly.** In a relation, the condition that exists when, to add a complete row to a table, one must add facts about two or more logically different themes.

**Instance.** A specific occurrence of an object of interest.

**Instance failure.** A failure in the operating system or hardware that causes the DBMS to fail.

**Integrated Definition 1, Extended (IDEF1X).** *See* IDEF1X (Integrated Definition 1, Extended). *See also* entity-relationship (E-R) model.

**Integrated development environment (IDE).** An application that provides a programmer or application developer with a complete set of development tools in one package.

**Integrated tables.** Database tables that store both data and the relationships among the data.

**Integrity constraint.** A statement (or business rule) about the data that must be enforced in the database (e.g. primary key, foreign key, functional dependency, domain, specific values, etc.).

**Interface.** (1) The means by which two or more programs call each other; the definition of the procedural calls between two or more programs. (2) In object-oriented programming, the design of a set of objects that includes the objects' names, methods, and attributes.

**International Organization for Standardization (ISO).** The international standards organization that works on SQL standards, among others.

**Internet.** The network that connects the entire earth, and the basis for much of modern computing.

**Internet Information Services (IIS).** A Microsoft product that operates as an HTTP server.

**Internet Information Services Manager.** The application used to manage Microsoft's IIS Web server.

**Interrelation constraint.** A data constraint between two tables. *See also* data constraint, domain integrity constraint, intrarelation constraint, range constraint.

**Intersection.** A set theory operation similar to a logical AND operation. *See also* set theory.

**Intersection table.** A table (relation) used to represent a many-to-many relationship. It contains the keys of the tables (relations) in the relationship. The relationships from the parent tables to the intersection tables must have a minimum cardinality of either mandatory-optional or mandatory-mandatory.

**Intrarelation constraint.** A data constraint within one table. *See also* data constraint, domain integrity constraint, interrelation constraint, range constraint.

**iPhone.** A smartphone built by Apple, Inc.

**IS-A relationship.** A relationship between a supertype and a subtype. For example, EMPLOYEE and ENGINEER have an IS-A relationship.

**Isolated.** One of the four qualities needed for an ACID transaction: The four qualities are atomic, consistent, isolated, and durable. *See also* ACID transaction, transaction isolation level.

**Isolation level.** *See* transaction isolation level.

**Java.** An object-oriented programming language that has better memory management and bounds checking than C++. It is used primarily for Internet applications, but it also can be used as a general-purpose programming language. Java compilers generate Java bytecode that is interpreted on client computers. Many believe that Microsoft C# is a near-copy of Java.

**Java Data Objects (JDO).** Part of the Oracle Corporation's Java Platform. *See also* Java, Java platform.

**Java Database Connectivity (JDBC).** A standard interface by which application programs written in Java can access and process SQL databases (or table structures such as spreadsheets and text tables) in a DBMS-independent manner. Although originally it did not stand for Java Database Connectivity, it does now and is an acronym. *See also* Java, Java platform.

**Java platform.** The complete set of Java tools provided by Oracle Corporation. *See also* Java.

**Java programming language.** *See* Java, Java platform.

**Java Runtime Environment (JRE).** Part of the Oracle Corporation's Java Platform that must be installed on individual computers to enable the use of Java applications. *See also* Java, Java platform.

**Java servlet.** *See* servlet.

**Java virtual machine.** A Java bytecode interpreter that runs on a particular machine environment; for example, Intel or AMD. Such interpreters are usually embedded in browsers, included with the operating system, or included as part of a Java development environment.

**JavaScript.** A proprietary scripting language originally created by Netscape but now owned by Oracle Corporation. The Microsoft version is called JScript; the standard version is called ECMA-262. These are easily learned interpreted languages that are used for both Web server and Web client application processing. Sometimes written as *Java Script.*

**JavaScript Object Notation (JSON).** A standard for describing structured data. JSON is often used to represent data in NoSQL Document databases and to exchange data between JavaScript and PHP programs.

**JavaServer Pages (JSP).** A combination of HTML and Java that is compiled into a Java servlet that is a subclass of the HttpServlet class. Java code embedded in a JSP has access to HTTP objects and methods. JSPs are used similarly to ASPs, but they are compiled rather than interpreted, as ASP pages are.

**JDBC.** *See* Java Database Connectivity (JDBC).

**JDBC Connection object.** One of a set of objects created by a Java application to connect to a database using JDBC. *See also* Java, Java Database Connectivity (JDBC).

**JDBC DriverManager.** The JDBC application that routes program calls for JDBC objects to the proper JDBC driver to connect to the database. *See also* Java, Java Database Connectivity (JDBC).

**JDBC ResultSet object.** One of a set of objects created by a Java application to connect to a database using JDBC. *See also* Java, Java Database Connectivity (JDBC).

**JDBC ResultSetMetaData Object.** One of a set of objects created by a Java application to connect to a database using JDBC. *See also* Java, Java Database Connectivity (JDBC).

**JDBC Statement object.** One of a set of objects created by a Java application to query or update a database using JDBC. *See also* Java, Java Database Connectivity (JDBC).

**Join.** In a relational database, the process of combining data rows from two tables. A row from one table is concatenated with a row from the other table based on a specified join condition, which typically involves comparing column values from the two rows. The result of a join is all concatenated rows matching the condition. *See also* SQL join operation, equijoin.

**Joining two tables.** In SQL, the process of combining data rows from two tables. *See also* Join, SQL join operation.

**JScript.** A proprietary scripting language owned by Microsoft. The Netscape/Oracle version is called JavaScript; the standard version is called ECMAScript-262. These are easily learned interpreted languages used for both Web server and Web client application processing.

**JSP.** *See* JavaServer Pages (JSP).

**Key.** (1) A group of one or more attributes identifying a unique row in a relation. Because relations may not have duplicate rows, every relation must have at least one key, which is the composite of all of the attributes in the relation. A key is sometimes called a logical key. (2) With some relational DBMS products, an index on a column used to improve access and sorting speed. It is sometimes called a physical key.

**Keyset cursor.** An SQL cursor that combines some of the features of static cursors with some of the features of dynamic cursors. *See also* cursor, cursor type.

**Keyspace.** In a column family database, the domain of possible key values in a database (collection of column families, supercolumns, etc.). The keyspace may also contain information about distribution of data in a distributed column family database.

**Key-value [NoSQL database category].** A non-relational database structure based on data values identified by key values.

**Knowledge worker.** An information system user who prepares reports, mines data, and does other types of data analysis.

**Labeled namespace.** In an XML Schema document, a namespace that is given a name (label) within the document. All elements preceded by the name of the labeled namespace are assumed to be defined in that labeled namespace.

**LAMP.** A version of AMP that runs on Linux. *See also* AMP.

**Language Integrated Query (LINQ).** A Microsoft .NET Framework component that allows SQL queries to be run directly from application programs.

**LEFT OUTER join.** A join that includes all the rows of the first table listed in the SQL statement (the "left" table) regardless of whether they have a matching row in the other table. *See also* join, outer join.

**Lift.** In market basket analysis, confidence divided by the base probability of an item purchase.

**Linux.** An open source personal computer operating system (OS) associated with one of its main creators, Linus Torvalds.

**Local area network (LAN).** A computer network that operates with computers in a definable small area, such as a business or university.

**Lock.** The process of allocating a database resource to a particular transaction in a concurrent-processing system. The size of the resource locked is known as the lock granularity. With an exclusive lock, no other transaction may read or write the resource. With a shared lock, other transactions may read the resource, but no other transaction may write it.

**Lock granularity.** The size of a locked data element. The lock of a column value of a particular row is a small granularity lock, and the lock of an entire table is a large granularity lock.

**Locking behavior.** How a DBMS controls locks on database elements such as tables during SQL operations.

**Log.** A file containing a record of database changes. The log contains before images and after images.

**Logical unit of work (LUW).** An equivalent term for transaction. *See also* transaction.

**Login name.** The character string that a user uses to log into a computer.

**Logistic regression.** A form of supervised data mining that estimates the parameters of an equation to calculate the odds that a given event will occur.

**Lost update problem.** Same as concurrent update problem.

**M score.** In RFM analysis, the "how much money" score, which reflects how much a customer spends per purchase. *See also* RFM analysis.

**Managed Extensibility Framework (MEF).** An extension to the Microsoft .NET Framework added in version 4.5 to provide support for Windows 8 apps.

**Mandatory.** In a relationship, when the minimum number of entity instances that *must* participate in a relationship is one, then participation in the relationship is said to be *mandatory*. *See also* minimum cardinality, optional.

**Mandatory-to-mandatory (M-M) relationship.** A relationship in which entity instances are required on both sides of the relationship.

**Mandatory-to-optional (M-O) relationship.** A relationship in which an entity instance is required on the left-hand side of the relationship but not on the right-hand side.

**Many-to-many (N:M) relationship.** A relationship in which one parent entity instance (or row in the parent table) can be associated with many child entity instances (or rows in the child table). At the same time, one child entity instance (or row in the child table) can be associated with many parent entity instances (or rows in the parent table). In an actual database, these relationships are transformed into two one-to-many relationships between the original entities (tables) and an intersection table.

**Market basket analysis.** A type of data mining that estimates the correlations of items that are purchased together. *See also* confidence, lift.

**MapReduce.** A Big Data processing technique that breaks a data analysis into many parallel processes (the Map function) and then combines the results of these processes into one final result (the Reduce function).

**MAX.** In SQL, a function that determines the largest value in a set of numbers. *See also* SQL built-in functions.

**Maximum cardinality.** (1) In a binary relationship in the entity-relationship data model, the maximum number of entities on each side of the relationship. Common values are 1:1, 1:N, and N:M. (2) In a relationship in the relational model database design, the maximum number of rows on each side of the relationship. Common values are 1:1 and 1:N. An N:M relationship is not possible in the relational model database design, where an additional intersection relation (table) must be used to link the two relations (tables) via two 1:N relationships.

**Measure.** In OLAP, the source data for the cube—data that are displayed in the cells. They may be raw data, or they may be functions of raw data, such as SUM, AVG, or other computations.

**Media failure.** A failure that occurs when the DBMS is unable to write to or read from a disk. Usually caused by a disk head crash or other disk failure.

**Metadata.** Data concerning the structure of data that are used to describe tables, columns, constraints, indexes, and so forth. Metadata is data about data.

**Method.** A program attached to an object-oriented programming (OOP) object. A method can be inherited by lower-level OOP objects.

**Microsoft Access 2019.** Microsoft's personal database product.

**Microsoft Azure.** Microsoft's general-purpose cloud platform. Cloud-based document database. Now incorporated into Azure Cosmos DB, which has support for document, key-value, and graph data models. Azure also includes many other non-database products.

**Microsoft Edge.** Microsoft's new Web browser, introduced in Windows 10. *See also* Microsoft Internet Explorer.

**Microsoft Internet Explorer.** Microsoft's older Web browser, still in use but being replaced with Microsoft Edge as of Windows 10. *See also* Microsoft Edge.

**Microsoft SQL Server Management Studio.** The GUI utility that is used with Microsoft SQL Server 2019 and earlier versions of Microsoft SQL Server.

**Microsoft Transaction Server (MTS).** Part of Microsoft's OLE DB. *See also* OLE DB.

**Microsoft Windows.** A Microsoft operating system (OS) for personal computers.

**Microsoft Windows PowerShell.** A Microsoft command-line utility.

**Microsoft Windows Server.** A Microsoft operating system (OS) for server computers.

**MIN.** In SQL, a function that determines the smallest value in a set of numbers. *See also* SQL built-in functions.

**Minimum cardinality.** (1) In a binary relationship in the entity-relationship model, the minimum number of entities required on each side of a relationship. (2) In a binary relationship in the relational model, the minimum number of rows required on each side of a relationship. Common values of minimum cardinality for both definitions are optional to optional (O-O), mandatory to optional (M-O), optional to mandatory (O-M), and mandatory to mandatory (M-M).

**Minimum cardinality enforcement actions.** Activities that must be taken to preserve minimum cardinality restrictions.

**Missing value.** A value that is not provided, leaving the attribute as NULL. Not the same as a blank, a NULL value is ambiguous and could mean several things. *See also* null value.

**Modification anomaly.** In a relation, the situation that exists when the storage of one row records facts about two or more entities or when the deletion of one row removes facts about two or more entities.

**Mozilla Firefox.** Mozilla's open source Web browser.

**Multimodel.** A NoSQL DBMS that provides more than one of the four standard NoSQL data models for data storage and processing.

**Multivalue, multicolumn problem.** A poorly designed table may attempt to store several attributes representing the same data item. For example, storing multiple phone contact numbers as Phone1, Phone2, Phone3, etc. This leads to wasted space, awkward queries, or a need to redesign the table to add a fourth phone. The best solution is to use two 1:N relations.

**Multivalued dependency.** A condition in a relation with three or more attributes in which independent attributes appear to have relationships they do not have. Formally, in a relation R (A, B, C), with key (A, B, C) where A is matched with multiple values of B (or of C or both), B does not determine C, and C does not determine B. An example is the relation EMPLOYEE (EmpNumber, EmpSkill, DependentName), where an employee can have multiple values of EmpSkill and DependentName. EmpSkill and DependentName do not have any relationship, but they do appear to in the relation.

**MUST constraint.** A constraint that requires one entity to be combined with another entity.

**MUST COVER constraint.** The binary relationship indicates all combinations that must appear in the ternary relationship.

**MUST NOT constraint.** The binary relationship indicates combinations that are not allowed to occur in the ternary relationship.

**MySQL AUTO_INCREMENT property.** In MySQL, the method used to generate surrogate primary key values of sequenced numbers.

**MySQL Workbench.** The GUI utility used with MySQL 8.0 and some earlier versions.

**Natural join.** A join of a relation A having attribute A1 with relation B having attribute B1, where A1 equals B1. The joined relation, C, contains either column A1 or B1 but not both. *Contrast with* equijoin.

**NetBeans IDE.** An open source GUI integrated development environment (IDE) from Oracle Corporation.

**Neural networks.** A form of supervised data mining that estimates complex mathematical functions for making predictions. The name is a misnomer. Although there is some loose similarity between the structure of a neural network and a network of biological neurons, the similarity is only superficial.

**N:M.** The abbreviation for a many-to-many relationship between two entities or relations.

**Node.** In a graph database, a node stores information about an entity and typically has attributes. It is related to other nodes, potentially, via edges.

**Nonidentifying relationship.** In data modeling, a relationship between two entities such that one is *not* ID-dependent on the other. *See also* identifying relationship.

**Nonintegrated data.** Data of the same type, such as customer orders, that is broken up and stored on more than one business system. In order for the entire dataset to be analyzed, the separate subsets of data must be combined into one integrated dataset.

**Non-prime attribute.** In normalization, an attribute that is not contained in any candidate key.

**Nonrepeatable read.** The situation that occurs when a transaction reads data it has previously read and finds modifications or deletions caused by a committed transaction.

**Normal form.** A rule or set of rules governing the allowed structure of relations. The rules apply to attributes, functional dependencies, multivalue dependencies, domains, and constraints. The most important normal forms are first normal form, second normal form, third normal form, Boyce-Codd normal form, fourth normal form, fifth normal form, and domain/key normal form.

**Normalization.** (1) The process of constructing one or more relations such that in every relation the determinant of every functional dependency is a candidate key (BCNF). (2) The process of removing multivalued dependencies (4NF). (3) In general, the process of evaluating a relation to determine whether it is in a specified normal form and of converting it to relations in that specified normal form, if necessary.

**NoSQL.** *See* Not only SQL.

**NOT NULL constraint.** In SQL, a constraint that specifies that a column must contain a value in every row.

**Not only SQL.** Actually referring to the creation and use of non-relational DBMS products instead of just not using the SQL language, this movement was originally mislabeled as the NoSQL movement. Such systems may or may not use SQL-like query languages for data retrieval. It is now recognized that both relational and non-relational DBMS products are needed in management information systems and that they must interact with each other. Thus, the term *not only SQL*.

**Not-type-valid document.** An XML document that either does not conform to its document type declaration (DTD) or does not have a DTD. *See also* schema-valid document, type-valid document.

**NULL.** A NULL is stored in a table when no data is provided for that attribute.

**NULL constraint.** In SQL, a constraint that specifies that a column may have empty cells in some or all rows.

**Null status.** Whether the column has a NULL constraint or a NOT NULL constraint. *See also* NOT NULL constraint, NULL constraint.

**Null value.** An attribute value that has never been supplied. Such values are ambiguous and can mean that (a) the value is unknown, (b) the value is not appropriate, or (c) the value is known to be blank.

**Object.** In object-oriented programming, as well as both object-oriented and object-relational databases, an abstraction that is defined by its properties and methods. *See also* object-oriented programming (OOP).

**Object class.** In object-oriented programming, as well as both object-oriented and object-relational databases, a set of objects with a common structure. *See also* object-oriented programming (OOP).

**Object Linking and Embedding (OLE).** Microsoft's object standard. OLE objects are Component Object Model (COM) objects and support all required interfaces for such objects.

**Object-oriented DBMS (OODBMS or ODBMS).** A DBMS that can store the objects similar to those used in OOP. *See also* object-oriented programming (OOP).

**Object-oriented programming (OOP).** A programming methodology that defines objects and the interactions between them to create application programs.

**Object persistence.** Permanently storing the property values of an object in a database.

**Object-relational databases.** DBMS products that support both relational and object-oriented programming data structures, such as Oracle Database and PostgreSQL.

**ODBC.** *See* Open Database Connectivity (ODBC) standard.

**ODBC conformance level.** In ODBC, definitions of the features and functions that are made available through the driver's application programming interface (API). A driver API is a set of functions that the application can call to receive services. There are three conformance levels: Core API, Level 1 API, and Level 2 API.

**ODBC data source.** In the ODBC standard, a database and its associated DBMS, operating system, and network platform.

**ODBC Data Source Administrator.** The application used to create ODBC data sources.

**ODBC driver.** In ODBC, a program that serves as an interface between the ODBC driver manager and a particular DBMS product. Runs on the client machines in a client/server architecture.

**ODBC driver manager.** In ODBC, a program that serves as an interface between an application program and an ODBC driver. It determines the required driver, loads it into memory, and coordinates activity between the application and the driver. On Windows systems, it is provided by Microsoft.

**ODBC multiple-tier driver.** In ODBC, a two-part driver, usually for a client/server database system. One part of the driver resides on the client and interfaces with the application; the second part resides on the server and interfaces with the DBMS.

**ODBC single-tier driver.** In ODBC, a database driver that accepts SQL statements from the driver manager and processes them without invoking another program or DBMS. A single-tier driver is both an ODBC driver and a DBMS. It is used in file-processing systems.

**ODBC SQL conformance levels.** ODBC SQL conformance levels specify which SQL statements, expressions, and data types an ODBC driver can process. Three SQL conformance levels are defined: Minimum SQL Grammar, Core SQL Grammar, Extended SQL Grammar.

**OLAP.** *See* online analytical processing (OLAP).

**OLAP cube.** In OLAP, a presentation structure with axes upon which data dimensions are placed. Measures of the data are shown in the cells of the cube. Also called a hypercube.

**OLAP report.** The output of an OLAP analysis in tabular format. For example, this can be an Excel Pivot Table. *See also* OLAP cube.

**OLAP server.** A server specifically developed to perform OLAP analyses.

**OLE DB.** The COM-based foundation of data access in the Microsoft world. OLE DB objects support the OLE object standard. ADO is based on OLE DB.

**1:N.** The abbreviation for a one-to-many relationship between two entities or relations.

**One-to-many (1:N) relationship.** A relationship in which one parent entity instance (or row in the parent table) can be associated with many child entity instances (or rows in the child table). At the same time, one child entity instance (or row in the child table) can be associated with only one parent entity instance (or row in the parent table).

**One-to-one (1:1) relationship.** A relationship in which one parent entity instance (or row in the parent table) can be associated with only one child entity instance (or row in the child table). At the same time, one child entity instance (or row in the child table) can be associated with only one parent entity instance (or row in the parent table).

**Online analytical processing (OLAP).** A form of dynamic data presentation in which data are summarized, aggregated, disaggregated, and viewed in the frame of a table or a cube.

**Online transaction processing (OLTP).** Routine business interactions conducted over a network.

**Online transaction processing (OLTP) system.** An operational database system available for, and dedicated to, transaction processing.

**Open Database Connectivity (ODBC).** A standard interface by which application programs can access and process relational databases, spreadsheets, text files, and other table-like structures in a DBMS or in a program-independent manner. The driver manager portion of ODBC is incorporated into Windows. ODBC drivers are supplied by DBMS vendors and by third-party software developers.

**Operating system.** A complex program that manages the physical hardware resources of a computer to provide users with security, file systems, and to run programs without interfering with other users' programs.

**Operational system.** A database system in use for the routine operations of the enterprise, typically an OLTP system. *See also* online transaction processing (OLTP) system.

**Optimistic locking.** A locking strategy that assumes no conflict will occur, processes a transaction, and then checks to determine whether conflict did occur. If conflict did occur, no changes are made to the database and the transaction is repeated. *See also* pessimistic locking.

**Optional.** In a relationship, when the minimum number of entity instances that *must* participate in a relationship is zero, then participation in the relationship is said to be *optional*. *See also* mandatory, minimum cardinality.

**Optional-to-mandatory (O-M) relationship.** A relationship in which an entity instance is required on the right-hand side of the relationship but not on the left-hand side.

**Optional-to-optional (O-O) relationship.** A relationship in which an entity instance is not required on either side of the relationship.

**Oracle SQL Developer.** The GUI utility for Oracle Database.

**Outer join.** A join in which all of the rows of a table appear in the join result, regardless of whether they have a match in the join condition. In a left outer join, all of the rows in the left-hand relation appear; in a right outer join, all of the rows in the right-hand relation appear.

**Overlapping candidate keys.** Two candidate keys are said to be overlapping candidate keys if they have one or more attributes in common.

**Parameter.** A data value that is passed as input to a stored procedure or other application.

**Parent.** An entity or row on the one side of a one-to-many relationship.

**Parent mandatory and child mandatory (M-M).** A relationship where the minimum cardinality of the parent is 1 and the minimum cardinality of the child is 1.

**Parent mandatory and child optional (M-O).** A relationship where the minimum cardinality of the parent is 1 and the minimum cardinality of the child is 0.

**Parent optional and child mandatory (O-M).** A relationship where the minimum cardinality of the parent is 0 and the minimum cardinality of the child is 1.

**Parent optional and child optional (O-O).** A relationship where the minimum cardinality of the parent is 0 and the minimum cardinality of the child is 0.

**Partially dependent.** In normalization, a condition where an attribute is dependent on only part of a composite primary key instead of on the whole key.

**Partition tolerance.** In distributed databases, a DBMS that can continue operating even when the network containing the database servers has been separated by failures into two or more completely separate, but still functioning, sections (partitions).

**Partitioning.** For databases, separating a database into parts, which will normally be stored on separate DBMS servers.

**Passive repository.** Repositories that are filled only when someone takes the time to generate the needed metadata and place it in the repository. *See also* data repository.

**Persistent object.** In object-oriented programming, an object that has been written to persistent storage.

**Personal computer (PC).** Also known as a *micro-computer*, a small computer intended for use by one person as his or her own computer.

**Personal database system.** A DBMS product intended for use by an individual or small workgroup. Such products typically include application development tools such as form and report generators in addition to the DBMS. For example, Microsoft Access 2019.

**Pessimistic locking.** A locking strategy that prevents conflict by locking data resources, processing the transaction, and then unlocking the data resources. *See also* deadlock, optimistic locking.

**Phantom read.** The situation that occurs when a transaction reads data it has previously read and finds new rows that were inserted by a committed transaction.

**PHP.** A Web page programming language that runs routines on the Web server rather than on the user's client device. *See also* PHP: Hypertext Processor (PHP).

**PHP concatenation operator.** This operator (.-) is used to append strings together in the PHP language.

**PHP Data Objects (PDO).** A consistent data-access specification for PHP that allows a programmer to use the same functions independent of which DBMS is being used.

**PHP: Hypertext Processor (PHP).** A Web page scripting language used to create dynamic Web pages. It now includes an object-oriented programming component and PHP Data Objects (PDO). *See also* PHP Data Objects (PDO).

**PHP plugin.** Provides a PHP development environment for the NetBeans IDE.

**PivotTable.** Microsoft's name for its OLAP client, as used in Microsoft Excel 2019. *See also* OLAP.

**Platform as a service (PaaS).** A way for cloud providers to lease physical computing, network, and operating systems software to customers that want to develop and manage their own applications software on it.

**PL/SQL.** *See* Procedural Language/SQL (PL/SQL).

**PL/SQL SEQUENCE object.** An Oracle Database object used to implement surrogate primary keys by providing sequences of numbers.

**Point of sale (POS) system.** A collection of hardware and software allowing an organization to record sales data, track inventories, and manage customer data when and where the sales take place.

**Polyglot persistence.** The use of multiple data storage models or technologies, e.g. multiple DBMSs, differing data models, DBMS and file system, and so on.

**Portable Class Libraries.** An extension to the Microsoft .NET Framework added in version 4.5 to provide support for Windows 8 apps.

**POST method.** In PHP, a method of passing data values from one Web page to another for processing.

**PowerShell sqlps utility [MSSQL].** In Microsoft SQL Server 2019, an add-in to the Microsoft PowerShell command-line utility that allows it to work with Microsoft SQL Server.

**Prepared Statement object.** A JDBC object used to invoke database compiled queries and stored procedures.

**Primary key.** A candidate key selected to be the key of a relation; the primary key is used as a foreign key for representing relationships.

**PRIMARY KEY constraint.** In SQL, a constraint statement used to create a primary key for a table.

**PrimaryKey property.** The ADO.NET DataSet object used to enforce row uniqueness in a DataTable object.

**Procedural programming language.** A programming language where each step necessary to obtain a result must be specified. The language may have the ability to contain sets of steps in structures called procedures or subprocedures.

**Procedural Language/SQL (PL/SQL).** An Oracle-supplied language that augments SQL with programming language structures such as while loops, if-then-else blocks, and other such constructs. PL/SQL is used to create functions, stored procedures, and triggers.

**Processing rights and responsibilities.** Organizational policies regarding which groups can take which actions on specified data items or other collections of data.

**Program/data independence.** The condition existing when the structure of the data is not defined in application programs. Rather, it is defined in the database and then the application programs obtain it from the DBMS. In this way, changes can be made in the data structures that may not necessarily be made in the application programs.

**Programmer.** A person who creates application programs in a programming language.

**Project-Join Normal Form (PJ/NF).** Another name for 5NF. *See also* fifth normal form (5NF).

**Property.** Same as attribute.

**Proposed values.** One type of ADO.NET DataSet object data values stored in a DataRow collection in a DataTable object.

**Prototype.** A quickly developed demonstration of an application or portion of an application.

**Pseudofile.** The term used to describe the results of an SQL statement, used in conjunction with a cursor. *See also* cursor.

**Pull report.** In reporting systems, a report that must be requested by users.

**Push report.** In reporting systems, a report that is sent to users according to a schedule.

**QBE.** *See* query by example (QBE).

**Query.** A request for database data that meets specific criteria. This can be thought of as asking the database a question and getting an answer in the form of the data returned.

**Query by example (QBE).** A style of query interface, first developed by IBM but now used by Microsoft Access 2019 and other DBMS products, that enables users to express queries by providing examples of the results they seek.

**Query optimizer.** A component of a DBMS that evaluates alternative strategies for executing a query and chooses an efficient strategy.

**Query report.** A report generated by a DBMS in response to information entered by users.

**Question mark (?) wildcard character.** A character used in Access 2019 queries to represent a single unspecified character. *See also* SQL underscore (_) wildcard character.

**Quorum.** In a distributed database using certain consistency models, the number of servers need to commit a change to the data or confirm a read of the data.

**R score.** In RFM analysis, the "how recently" score, which reflects how recently a customer made a purchase. *See also* RFM analysis.

**Range constraint.** A data constraint that specifies that data values must be within a specific range of values. *See also* data constraint, domain integrity constraint, interrelation constraint, intrarelation constraint.

**Read-committed isolation level.** A level of transaction isolation that prohibits dirty reads but allows nonrepeatable reads and phantom reads.

**Read-uncommitted isolation level.** A level of transaction isolation that allows dirty reads, nonrepeatable reads, and phantom reads.

**Record.** (1) In a relational model, a synonym for row and tuple. (2) A group of fields pertaining to the same entity; used in file-processing systems.

**Recordset.** An ADO.NET object that encapsulates a relation; created as the result of the execution of an SQL statement or a stored procedure.

**Recovery via reprocessing.** Recovering a database by restoring the last full backup and then re-creating each transaction since the backup.

**Recovery via rollback/rollforward.** Recovering a database by restoring the last full backup and then using data stored in a transaction log to modify the database as needed by either adding transactions (rollforward) or removing incomplete transactions (rollback).

**Recursive procedure.** A procedure that calls itself.

**Recursive relationship.** A relationship among entities or rows of the same type. For example, if CUSTOMERs refer to other CUSTOMERs, the relationship is recursive.

**ReDo files.** In Oracle Database, backups of rollback segments used for backup and recovery. ReDo files may be online or offline.

**Redundant array of independent disks (RAID).** A set of disks that operate as a single disk to increase capacity or fault-tolerance. Used in most data centers.

**Referential integrity (RI) action.** In general, a rule that specifies the activities that must take place when insert, update, or delete actions occur on either the parent or child entities in a relationship. In this text, we use referential integrity actions only to document activities needed to preserve required parents. Other actions can be defined as part of the database design. *See also* minimum cardinality enforcement actions and Chapter 6.

**Referential integrity constraint.** A relationship constraint on foreign key values. A referential integrity constraint specifies that the values of a foreign key must be a subset of the values of the primary key to which it refers.

**Regression analysis.** A form of supervised data mining in which the parameters of equations are estimated by data analysis.

**Relation.** A two-dimensional array containing single-value entries and no duplicate rows. Values for a given entity are shown in rows; values of attributes of that entity are shown in columns. The meaning of the columns is the same in every row. The order of the rows and columns is immaterial.

**Relational database.** A database consisting of relations. In practice, relational databases contain relations with duplicate rows. Most DBMS products include a feature that removes duplicate rows when necessary and appropriate. Such a removal is not done as a matter of course because it can be time-consuming to enforce.

**Relational DBMS Service (RDS).** A part of Amazon's AWS that provides a relational database service in the cloud.

**Relational model.** A data model in which data are stored in relations and relationships between rows are represented by data values.

**Relational schema.** A set of relations with constraints.

**Relationship.** An association between two entities or rows.

**Relationship cardinality constraint.** A constraint on the number of rows that can participate in a relationship. Minimum cardinality constraints determine the minimum number of times an entity must participate; maximum cardinality constraints specify the largest number of times an entity can participate. *See also* maximum cardinality, minimum cardinality.

**Relationship class.** An association between entity classes.

**Relationship instance.** (1) An association between entity instances; (2) a specific relationship between two tables in a database.

**Repeatable-read isolation level.** A level of transaction isolation that disallows both dirty reads and nonrepeatable reads. Phantom reads can occur.

**Replication.** In distributed databases, the act of maintaining multiple copies of the same data (relation or partition) on more than one computer.

**Report.** A formatted set of information created to meet a user's need.

**Reporting system.** A business intelligence system that processes data by filtering, sorting, and making simple calculations. OLAP is a type of reporting system. *Contrast with* data mining systems.

**Repository.** A collection of metadata about database structure, applications, Web pages, users, and other application components. Active repositories are maintained automatically by tools in the application-development environment. Passive repositories must be maintained manually.

**Requirements analysis.** The second step in the systems development life cycle (SDLC) model. User requirements are gathered and analyzed, and a set of user approved project requirements is created. The data model is created in this step.

**Reserved word.** A word that has a special meaning in the DBMS or ODBC and should not be used as a table, column, or other name in a database. *See also* DBMS reserved word.

**Resource locking.** *See* lock.

**Reverse engineered (RE) data model.** The structure that results from reverse engineering. It is not really a data model because it includes physical structures such as intersection tables. It is, instead, a thing unto itself; midway between a data model and a relational database design.

**Reverse engineering.** The process of reading the structure of an existing database and creating a reverse-engineered data model from that schema.

**RFM analysis.** A type of reporting system in which customers are classified according to how recently (R), how frequently (F), and how much money (M) they spend on their orders.

**RIGHT OUTER join.** A join that includes all the rows of the second table listed in the SQL statement (the "right" table) regardless of whether they have a matching row in the other table. *See also* join, outer join.

**Role.** In database administration, a defined set of permissions that can be assigned to users or groups.

**Rollback.** The process of recovering a database in which before images are applied to the database to return to an earlier checkpoint or other point at which the database is logically consistent.

**Rollforward.** The process of recovering a database by applying after images to a saved copy of the database to bring it to a checkpoint or other point at which the database is logically consistent.

**Root.** (1) In MySQL, the name of the DBMS administrator account. (2) The top record, row, or node in a tree. A root does not have a parent.

**Routers.** Networking devices used to move messages across the Internet and other connected networks.

**Row.** A group of columns in a table. All the columns in a row pertain to the same entity. A row is the same as a tuple and a record.

**Rowset.** In OLE DB, an abstraction of data collections such as recordsets, email addresses, and non-relational and other data.

**SAX.** Simple API (Application Programming Interface) for XML. An event-based parser that notifies a program when the elements of an XML document have been encountered during document parsing.

**Scalar-valued function.** A user-defined function that operates on a single row of data and returns a single value.

**Schema.** (1) In MySQL, a synonym for *database*. (2) A complete logical view of the database.

**Schemaless.** Unstructured data stores, such as NoSQL databases, often support flexible records that can vary in the number of fields and data types.

**Schema-valid document.** An XML document that conforms to its XML Schema definition.

**SCN.** *See* system change number.

**Scrollable cursor.** A cursor type that enables forward and backward movement through a recordset. Three scrollable cursor types discussed in this text are snapshot, keyset, and dynamic.

**Second normal form (2NF).** A relation in first normal form in which all nonkey attributes are dependent on all of the key attributes.

**Secure Sockets Layer (SSL).** A protocol and technology for establishing an encrypted line of communication between a website and a browser.

**SelectCommand object.** The ADO.NET DataAdapter object used to query data in a DataSet.

**Self-describing.** In a database, the characteristic of including data about the database in the database itself. Thus, the data that define a table are included in a database along with the data that are contained in that table. These descriptive data are called *metadata*. *See also* metadata, relation, table.

**Semantic object model.** A method of building a data model created by David Kroenke. The constructs and conventions used to create a model of the users' data. The things in the users' world are represented by semantic objects (sometimes called objects). Relationships are modeled in the objects, and the results are usually documented in object diagrams. Not in general use, as users prefer the extended entity-relationship data modeling techniques.

**Semistructured database.** A database using a schemaless data model such as a document database or some graph databases. Applies to many NoSQL DBMS products, and indicates that any

structure within the data, even though it might be complex, is optional. *See also* unstructured database.

**Sequence.** The Oracle Database SQL statement used to create surrogate key values.

**Serializable.** A collection of concurrent transactions in which the end result in the database is the same as if the transactions had been executed serially in some order.

**Serializable isolation level.** A level of transaction isolation that disallows dirty reads, nonrepeatable reads, and phantom reads.

**Server.** A robust computer operated by information systems staff and used to run the server portion of client/server application such as Web pages and email. Servers are thus said to provide services to users. *See also* service, client/server architecture.

**Server cluster.** A group of servers that communicate and coordinate with each other.

**Service.** The provision of some utility to users. For example, a Web server provides the Web service, which is providing Web pages to users. *See also* server.

**Service provider.** An OLE DB data provider that transforms data. A service provider is both a data consumer and a data provider.

**Servlet.** A compiled, machine-independent Java bytecode program that is run by a Java virtual machine located on a Web server.

**Set.** In mathematical set theory, a collection of unique things (often referred to as *objects*). *See also* set theory.

**Set operators.** In mathematical set theory, the symbols for the operations that may be done with sets. In SQL, the SQL set operators that mimic set operations are specifically UNION, INTERSECT, and EXCEPT. The SQL logical operators AND, OR, and NOT also implement some set theory functionality. *See also* set theory.

**Set theory.** The area of mathematics that works with sets. *See also* set.

**SGML.** *See* Standard Generalized Markup Language (SGML).

**Sharding.** Distribution of data replicas and/or partitions in a server cluster. *See also* partitioning, replication.

**Shared lock.** A lock against a data resource in which only one transaction may update the data but many transactions can concurrently read that data.

**Shrinking phase.** In two-phase locking, the stage at which locks are released but no lock is acquired.

**Sibling.** A record or node that has the same parent as another record or node.

**Simple Object Access Protocol.** A standard used for remote procedure calls. It uses XML for definition of the data and HTTP for transport. *Contrast with* SOAP.

**Slowly changing dimension.** In a dimensional database, a data column with values that change occasionally but irregularly over time; for example, a customer's address or phone number.

**Smartphone.** A cell phone that is capable of running user client applications (apps) in a client/server environment. *See also* cell phone, client/server architecture.

**Snowflake schema.** In a dimensional database or an OLAP database, the structure of tables such that dimension tables may be several levels away from the table storing the measure values. Such dimension tables are usually normalized. *Contrast with* star schema.

**SOAP.** Originally, Simple Object Access Protocol. Today, it is a protocol for remote procedure calls that differs from the Simple Object Access Protocol because it involves transport protocols in addition to HTTP. It is no longer an acronym.

**Software as a service (SaaS).** A way for cloud providers to lease only applications software to their customers. The development, maintenance, and hosting of the software are the responsibility of the provider.

**Software development kit (SDK).** A group of development tools provided to programmers to help them create applications.

**SQL.** *See* Structured Query Language (SQL).

**SQL ALTER TABLE statement.** The SQL command used to change the structure of a database table.

**SQL AND operator.** The SQL operator used to combine conditions in an SQL WHERE clause.

**SQL asterisk (*) wildcard character.** A shorthand for listing all columns of a table in the SELECT clause

**SQL built-in aggregate functions.** In SQL, the functions COUNT, SUM, AVG, MAX, or MIN.

**SQL CMD utility.** A command-line utility used with SQL Server 2019.

**SQL COUNT(*) function.** The SQL built-in function used to count the number of rows in a table that meet a specific criteria. If no criteria is specified, it simply counts how many rows are in the table.

**SQL CREATE FUNCTION statement.** The SQL command used to create a SQL/PSM user-define function. *See also* SQL/Persistent Stored Modules (SQL/PSM).

**SQL CREATE INDEX statement.** The SQL command used to create an index on a table. *See also* index.

**SQL CREATE TABLE statement.** The SQL command used to create a database table.

**SQL CREATE VIEW statement.** The SQL command used to create a database view.

**SQL Data Control Language (DCL).** The SQL statements to grant and/or revoke user permissions to perform operations on tables and other database components.

**SQL DELETE statement.** The SQL command used to remove data from a table. It can be associated with a trigger, and fire that trigger when the DELETE statement is executed. Unlike the SQL TRUNCATE statement, it does not reset surrogate key values. *See also* SQL TRUNCATE TABLE statement.

**SQL DISTINCT keyword.** Indicates that duplicates are to be removed from the result of an SQL query.

**SQL DROP TABLE statement.** The SQL command used to remove a table from a database.

**SQL EXCEPT operator.** A binary set operation whose result is all rows in the first table that are not also in the second table.

**SQL EXISTS comparison operator.** Used in an SQL query with a subquery, the EXISTS operator returns a non-empty set of values if any row in the subquery meets a specified condition. *See also* subquery.

**SQL expression.** A formula or set of values that determines the exact results of an SQL query. We can think of an SQL expression as anything that follows an actual or implied equal to (=) character (or any other relational operator, such as greater than [>], less than [<], and so on) or that follows certain SQL keywords, such as LIKE and BETWEEN.

**SQL FROM clause.** The part of an SQL SELECT statement that specifies conditions used to determine which tables are used in a query.

**SQL GRANT statement.** Used to give permissions (e.g. SELECT, INSERT, UPDATE, DELETE) on database objects to users or groups of users. *See* SQL REVOKE statement.

**SQL GROUP BY clause.** The part of an SQL SELECT statement that specifies conditions for grouping rows when determining the query results.

**SQL HAVING clause.** The part of an SQL SELECT statement that specifies conditions used to determine which rows are in the groupings in a GROUP BY clause.

**SQL IN operator.** Returns true if a column value is an element of a list of specific values.

**SQL injection attack.** The use of hacker-modified SQL statements, usually by manipulating input data in Web forms, to attack and infect an SQL database attached to a website. Preventable by careful application coding. The Lizamoon SQL injection attack in March 2011 affected more than 1.5 million URLs.

**SQL INSERT statement.** The SQL command used to initially populate a table with rows of data.

**SQL INTERSECT operator.** A binary set operation in which the result is a relation containing every row that appears in both relations, but no rows that appear in just one of the relations.

**SQL join operation.** In SQL, the process of combining data rows from two tables by using a relational algebra operation on two relations, A and B, which produces a third relation, C. A row of A is concatenated with a row of B to form a new row in C if the rows in A and B meet a restriction concerning their values. Normally, the restriction is that one or more columns of A equal one or more columns of B. For example, suppose that A1 is an attribute in A and B1 is an attribute in B. The join of A with B in which A1 = B1 will result in a relation, C, with the concatenation of rows in A and B in which the value of A1 equals the value of B1. In theory, restrictions other than equality are allowed; a join could be made in which A1 > B1. Such nonequal joins are rarely used in practice, however.

**SQL IS NOT NULL operator.** The SQL operator used to find data with actual values rather than NULL values.

**SQL IS NULL operator.** The SQL operator used to find data with NULL values.

**SQL JOIN keyword.** The SQL keyword used to specify tables in an SQL query using JOIN ON syntax. *See also* SQL JOIN ON syntax.

**SQL JOIN ON syntax.** The SQL syntax used to create an explicit join. Tables are specified using the SQL JOIN keyword, and conditions of the join are specified using the SQL ON clause.

**SQL like operator.** Used, often with wildcard characters, to find string column values that match a certain pattern. *See also* SQL percent sign (%) wildcard character, SQL underscore (_) wildcard character.

**SQL logical operators.** The operators AND, OR, and NOT.

**SQL MERGE statement.** This SQL command is essentially a combination of the SQL INSERT and SQL UPDATE statements, where an INSERT or UPDATE is performed depending upon existing data.

**SQL NOT EXISTS comparison operator.** Used in an SQL query with a subquery, the NOT EXISTS operator returns an empty set of values if *all* row in the subquery *fail to meet* a specified condition. *See also* subquery.

**SQL OR operator.** The SQL operator used to specify alternate conditions in an SQL WHERE clause.

**SQL ORDER BY clause.** The part of an SQL SELECT statement that specifies how the query results should be sorted when they are displayed.

**SQL outer join.** An SQL join operation that include all rows from one of the tables in the join regardless of whether they match associated rows in the other table.

**SQL percent sign (%) wildcard character.** The standard SQL wildcard character used to specify multiple characters. Microsoft Access 2019 uses an asterisk (*) character instead of the percent character.

**SQL/Persistent Stored Modules (SQL/PSM).** SQL statements that extend SQL by adding procedural programming capabilities, such as variables and flow-of-control statements, and thus provide some programmability within the SQL framework. SQL/PSM is used to create user-defined functions, stored procedures, and triggers. *See also* trigger, stored procedure, user-defined function.

**SQL/PSM.** *See* SQL/Persistent Stored Modules (SQL/PSM).

**SQL query.** An SQL statement that uses the SQL SELECT/FROM/WHERE framework to "ask" a question that can be "answered" using database data. *See also* SQL SELECT/FROM/WHERE framework.

**SQL REVOKE statement.** Used to remove permissions on database objects from users or groups of users. *See* SQL GRANT statement.

**SQL script.** A set of SQL statements that are intended to be executed as a group.

**SQL script comment.** A comment in an SQL script. *See also* SQL script.

**SQL script file.** A file that holds an SQL script for repeated use. *See also* SQL script.

**SQL SELECT clause.** The part of an SQL SELECT statement that specifies which columns are in the query results.

**SQL SELECT \* statement.** A variant of an SQL SELECT query that returns all columns for all tables in the query.

**SQL SELECT . . . for XML statement.** A variant of an SQL SELECT query that returns the query results in XML format.

**SQL SELECT/FROM/WHERE framework.** The basic structure of an SQL query. *See also* SQL SELECT clause, SQL FROM clause, SQL WHERE clause, SQL ORDER BY clause, SQL GROUP BY clause, SQL HAVING clause, SQL AND operator, SQL OR operator.

**SQL Server IDENTITY ({StartValue}, {Increment}) expression.** The Microsoft SQL Server syntax used to provide surrogate key values of sequential numbers.

**SQL set operators.** The operators UNION, INTERSECT, and EXCEPT.

**SQL Transaction Control Language (TCL).** The SQL statements used to create and control SQL managed transactions and thus protect database data.

**SQL TRUNCATE TABLE statement.** The SQL TRUNCATE TABLE command removes all data from a database table while leaving the table structure in place.

**SQL underscore (\_) wildcard character.** The standard SQL wildcard character used to match a single character. Microsoft Access 2019 uses a question mark (?) character instead of the underscore character.

**SQL UNION operator.** A binary set operation in which the result is a relation containing every row that appears in either the first relation or the second relation or both.

**SQL UPDATE statement.** The SQL command used to change values of existing data.

**SQL WHERE clause.** The part of an SQL SELECT statement that specifies conditions used to determine which rows are in the query results.

**SQL view.** A named relation that is constructed from a single SQL SELECT statement. The term *view* in most DBMS products, including MySQL, Oracle Database, and Microsoft SQL Server, means SQL view.

**SQL\*Plus.** A command-line utility in Oracle Database.

**Standard Generalized Markup Language (SGML).** A standard means for tagging and marking the format, structure, and content of documents. HTML is an application of SGML. XML is a subset of SGML.

**Star schema.** In a dimensional database or an OLAP database, the structure of tables such that every dimension table is adjacent to the table storing the measure values. In the star schema, the dimension tables are often not normalized. *Contrast with* snowflake schema.

**Statement-level consistency.** All rows affected by a single SQL statement are protected from changes made by other users during the execution of the statement. *Contrast with* transaction-level consistency.

**Static cursor.** A cursor that takes a snapshot of a relation and processes that snapshot.

**Static report.** In reporting systems, a report that is prepared once from underlying data and does not change when the underlying data change. *Contrast with* dynamic report.

**Stock-keeping unit (SKU).** A unique identifier for each product available from a vendor.

**Storage area network (SAN).** A dedicated communications network connecting servers to disk storage.

**Stored procedure.** A collection of SQL statements stored as a file that can be invoked by a single command. Usually, DBMS products provide a language for creating stored procedures that augments SQL with programming language constructs. Oracle Database provides PL/SQL for this purpose; Microsoft SQL Server provides T-SQL; MySQL also adds procedural capabilities but does not use a separate name for these additions. With some products, stored procedures can be written in a standard language such as Java. Usually, stored procedures are stored within the database itself.

**Strong entity.** In an entity-relationship model, any entity whose existence in the database does not depend on the existence of any other entity. *See also* ID-dependent entity, weak entity.

**Strong password.** A password that meets requirements intended to make it difficult to guess or unencrypt.

**Structured Query Language (SQL).** A language for defining the structure and processing of a relational database. It can be used as a stand-alone language, or it may be embedded in application programs. SQL has been adopted as a national standard by the American National Standards Institute (ANSI). The most common version used today is SQL-92, the version adopted by ANSI in 1992. SQL was originally developed by IBM.

**Stylesheet.** A document used by XSLT to indicate how to transform the elements of an XML document into another format.

**Subquery.** In SQL, a SELECT statement within another SELECT statement.

**Subset.** In mathematical set theory, a portion of a set. *See also* set.

**Subtype.** In generalization hierarchies, an entity or object that is a subspecies or subcategory of a higher-level type, called a supertype. For example, ENGINEER is a subtype of EMPLOYEE.

**SUM.** In SQL, a function that adds up a set of numbers. *See also* SQL built-in functions.

**Super column.** In Column Family databases, a collection of columns combined together under a separate name.

**Super column family.** In column family non-relational DBMSs, a set of rows, each of which consists of a key and a set of supercolumns.

**Supertype.** In generalization hierarchies, an entity or object that logically contains subtypes. For example, EMPLOYEE is a supertype of ENGINEER, ACCOUNTANT, and MANAGER.

**Supervised data mining.** A form of data mining in which an analyst creates a prior model or hypothesis and then uses the data to test that model or hypothesis.

**Support.** In market basket analysis, the probability that two items will be purchased together.

**Surrogate key.** A unique, system-supplied identifier used as the primary key of a relation. It is created when a row is created, it never changes, and it is destroyed when the row is deleted. The values of a surrogate key have no meaning to the users and are usually hidden within forms and reports.

**System change number (SCN).** In Oracle Database, a database-wide value that is used to order changes made to database data. The SCN is incremented whenever database changes are committed.

**System data source.** An ODBC data source that is local to a single computer and can be accessed by that computer's operating system and select users of that operating system.

**System maintenance.** The fifth step in the systems development life cycle (SDLC) model. The implemented system is modified to correct errors and to implement new changes, and user responses and requests are gathered for the next iteration of the SDLC. *See also* systems development life cycle (SDLC).

**Systems analysis and design.** The process of studying business processes, and designing management information systems to support those processes. *See also* systems development life cycle (SDLC).

**Systems development life cycle (SDLC).** The five-stage cycle used to develop management information systems.

**Table.** A database structure of rows and columns to create cells that hold data values. Also known as a *relation* in a relational database, although strictly only tables that meet specific conditions can be called relations. *See also* relation.

**Table alias.** An alternate name for a relation within an SQL query; sometimes called a range variable.

**TableName.ColumnName syntax.** A syntax used to indicate which table a column is associated with. For example, CUSTOMER.LastName indicates the LastName column in the CUSTOMER table.

**Tablet.** A handheld user device that can run user client applications. Similar to a cell phone, but generally larger and without the telephone capability.

**Table-valued function.** In SQL/PSM, a user-defined function that returns a table of values.

**Tabular data provider.** An OLE DB data provider that presents data in the form of rowsets.

**Ternary relationship.** A relationship between three entities.

**Third normal form (3NF).** A relation in second normal form that has no transitive dependencies.

**Three-tier architecture.** A system of computers with a database server, a Web server, and one or more client computers. The database server hosts a DBMS, the Web server hosts an HTTP server, and the client computer hosts a browser. Each tier can run a different operating system.

**Time dimension.** A required dimension table in a dimensional database. The time dimension allows the data to be analyzed over time.

**Top level query.** The first SELECT statement in an SQL query using a subquery.

**Transaction.** (1) A group of actions that is performed on the database automatically; either all actions are committed to the database or none of them is. (2) In general, the record of an event in the business world.

**Transaction control language (TCL).** Statements that are used to mark transaction boundaries and control transaction behavior.

**Transaction isolation level.** The degree to which a database transaction is protected from actions by other transactions. The 1992 SQL standard specified four isolation levels: Read Uncommitted, Read Committed, Repeatable Reads, and Serializable.

**Transaction-level consistency.** All rows affected by any of the SQL statements in a transaction are protected from changes during the entire transaction. This level of consistency is expensive to enforce and reduces throughput. It may also mean that a transaction cannot see its own changes. *Contrast with* statement-level consistency.

**Transact-SQL (T-SQL).** A Microsoft-supplied language that is part of Microsoft SQL Server. It augments SQL with programming language structures such as while loops, if-then-else blocks, and other such constructs. Transact-SQL is used to create stored procedures and triggers.

**Transactional system.** A database dedicated to processing transactions such as product sales and orders. It is designed to make sure that only complete transactions are recorded in the database. *See also* OLTP.

**Transitive dependency.** In a relation with at least three attributes, for example, R (A, B, C), the situation in which A determines B, B determines C, but B does not determine A.

**Tree.** A collection of records, entities, or other data structures in which each element has one parent, except for the top element, which has no parent.

**Trigger.** A special type of stored procedure that is invoked by the DBMS when a specified condition occurs. BEFORE triggers are executed before a specified database action, AFTER triggers are executed after a specified database action, and INSTEAD OF triggers are executed in place of a specified database action. INSTEAD OF triggers are normally used to update data in SQL views.

**T-SQL.** *See* Transact-SQL (T-SQL).

**Tuple.** Same as row.

**Two dashes (--).** Symbols used to indicate a single-line comment in a stored procedure or a trigger in SQL Server 2019, Oracle Database, and MySQL 8.0.

**Two-phase locking.** The procedure by which locks are obtained and released in two phases. During the growing phase, the locks are obtained; during the shrinking phase, the locks are released. After a lock is released, no other lock will be granted for that transaction. Such a procedure ensures consistency in database updates in a concurrent-processing environment.

**Two-tier architecture.** In a Web-based database processing environment, the Web server and the DBMS are running on the same computer. One tier is for the Web browsers, and one is for the Web server/DBMS computer.

**Type-valid XML document.** An XML document that conforms to its document type declaration (DTD). *Contrast with* not-type-valid document.

**UML.** *See* Unified Modeling Language (UML).

**Unary relationship.** A relationship between a table and itself. Also called a recursive relationship.

**Unified Modeling Language (UML).** A set of diagrams, structures, and techniques for modeling and designing object-oriented programs and applications. It is a set of tools for object-oriented development that has led to a development methodology. UML incorporates the entity-relationship model for data modeling.

**Union.** A set operation similar to a logical OR operation. *See also* set theory.

**Union rule.** When a determinant determines two or more attributes, we can combine the functional dependencies into a single dependency. For example, $A \rightarrow B$ and $A \rightarrow C$ can be combined into $A \rightarrow B, C$. *See also* decomposition rule.

**UNIQUE Constraint.** In SQL, a constraint that specifies that the values in a column must be unique.

**Unstructured database.** A database in which the data have no internal format or structure that can specified (e.g. a database of text). *See also* semistructured database.

**Unsupervised data mining.** A form of data mining in which analysts do not create a prior model or hypothesis but rather let the data analysis reveal a model.

**Updatable view.** An SQL view that can be updated. Such views are usually very simple, and the rules that allow updating are normally quite restrictive. Nonupdatable views can be made updatable by writing application-specific INSTEAD OF triggers.

**Update anomaly.** A data error created in a non-normalized table when an update action modifies one data value without modifying another occurrence of the same data value in the table.

**UpdateCommand object.** The ADO.NET DataAdapter object used to update existing data from a DataSet back to the actual DBMS data.

**User.** A person using an application.

**User-defined function (stored function).** A stored set of SQL statements that is *called by name* from an SQL statement, that may have *input parameters* passed to it by the calling SQL statement, and that *returns an output value* to the SQL statement that called the function.

**User data source.** An ODBC data source that is available only to the user who created it.

**User group.** A group of users. *See also* user.

**Username.** The set of characters that a user identifies himself/herself with for authentication purposes to log onto a computer.

**Variable.** A value that may be assigned or calculated by a stored procedure or a trigger in SQL Server 2019 T-SQL, Oracle Database PL/SQL, and MySQL 8.0 SQL.

**Venn diagram.** In mathematical set theory, the visual diagrams used to represent sets and their interactions.

**Virtual machine.** A simulated computer hardware environment provided by a hypervisor that allows several operating systems to run on a physical server. Each operating system runs in its own virtual machine and is usually unaware that it is running in a virtual environment.

**Virtual machine manager.** *See* hypervisor.

**Virtualization.** A technique for sharing the hardware resources of one computer by having that one physical computer host one or more virtual computers, more commonly known as virtual machines. To do this, the actual computer hardware, now called the host machine, runs an application program known as a virtual machine manager or hypervisor. The hypervisor creates and manages the virtual machines and controls the interaction between the virtual machine and the physical hardware. For example, if a virtual machine has been allocated two gigabytes of main memory for its use, the hypervisor is responsible for making sure the actual physical memory is allocated and available to the virtual machine.

**WAMP.** AMP running on a Windows operating system. *See also* AMP.

**Weak entity.** In an entity-relationship model, an entity whose logical existence in the database depends on the existence of another entity. All ID-dependent entities are weak, but not all weak entities are ID-dependent.

**Web (the).** A synonym for the World Wide Web. *See also* World Wide Web.

**Web 2.0.** Websites that allow users to contribute content.

**Web browser.** The client application used to view and interact with websites. *See also* client/server architecture, Website.

**Web portal.** A Web page designed to be an entrance point for a website. It may display information from several sources and may require authentication to access.

**Website.** A location on the World Wide Web. *See also* World Wide Web.

**World Wide Web.** The set of interconnected hypertext objects accessible on the Internet, organized into websites.

**World Wide Web Consortium (W3C).** The group that creates, maintains, revises, and publishes standards for the World Wide Web including HTML, XML, and XHTML.

**WWW.** A synonym for the World Wide Web. *See also* World Wide Web.

**wwwroot folder.** The root folder or base directory of a website on a Microsoft IIS Web server.

**XML (Extensible Markup Language).** A standard markup language that provides a clear separation between structure, content, and materialization. It can represent arbitrary hierarchies and hence can be used to transmit any database view.

**XML namespaces.** A standard for assigning names to defined collections. X:Name is interpreted as the element Name as defined in namespace X. Y:Name is interpreted as the element Name as defined in namespace Y. Useful for disambiguating terms.

**XML schema.** An XML document that defines the structure of other XML documents. Extends and replaces document type declarations (DTDs).

**XPath.** A sublanguage within XSLT that is used to identify parts of an XML document to be transformed. Can also be used for calculations and string manipulation. Commingled with XSLT.

**XPointer.** A standard for linking one document to another. XPath has many elements from XPointer.

**XQuery.** A standard for expressing database queries as XML documents. The structure of the query uses XPath facilities, and the result of the query is represented in an XML format.

**XSL (XSLT Stylesheet).** The document that provides the {match, action} pairs and other data for XSLT to use when transforming an XML document.

**XSLT (Extensible Style Language: Transformations).** A program (or process) that applies XSLT Stylesheets to an XML document to produce a transformed XML document.